Contents

New to This Edition ix

Introduction xi

Preface xv

Acknowledgments xvii

About the Authors xxi

Chapter 1   History and Scope of Epidemiology 1
             Introduction 2
             Epidemiology Defined 6
             Foundations of Epidemiology 13
             Historical Antecedents of Epidemiology 20
             Recent Applications of Epidemiology 37
             Conclusion 43

Chapter 2   Practical Applications of Epidemiology 49
             Introduction 50
             Applications for the Assessment of the Health Status
                of Populations and Delivery of Health Services 52
             Applications Relevant to Disease Etiology 71
             Conclusion 87
             Appendix 2—Leading Causes of Death and Rates
                for Those Causes in 1900 and 2003 92

Chapter 3   Measures of Morbidity and Mortality
                Used in Epidemiology 93
             Introduction 94
             Definitions of Count, Ratio, Proportion, and Rate 94

Risk Versus Rate 104
Interrelationship Between Prevalence and Incidence 106
Applications of Incidence Data 108
Crude Rates 108
Specific Rates 118
Adjusted Rates 123
Conclusion 133
Appendix 3—Data for Study Questions 2 Through 4 138

Chapter 4   **Descriptive Epidemiology: Person, Place, Time 141**
Introduction 142
Characteristics of Persons 146
Characteristics of Place 175
Characteristics of Time 187
Conclusion 193
Appendix 4—Project: Descriptive Epidemiology of a
      Selected Health Problem 201

Chapter 5   **Sources of Data for Use in Epidemiology 203**
Introduction 204
Criteria for the Quality and Utility of
      Epidemiologic Data 205
Computerized Bibliographic Databases 206
Confidentiality, Sharing of Data, and Record Linkage 207
Statistics Derived from the Vital Registration
      System 215
Reportable Disease Statistics 216
Screening Surveys 223
Disease Registries 223
Morbidity Surveys of the General Population 225
Insurance Data 229
Hospital Data 230
Diseases Treated in Special Clinics and Hospitals 231
Data from Physicians' Practices 232
Absenteeism Data 233
School Health Programs 233
Morbidity in the Armed Forces: Data on Active
      Personnel and Veterans 234
Other Sources of Data Relevant to
      Epidemiologic Studies 235
Conclusion 236

Epidemiology for Public Health Practice

Fourth Edition

Robert H. Friis, PhD
Professor and Chair
Health Science Department
California State University
Long Beach, California

Thomas A. Sellers, PhD, MPH
Director
Moffitt Research Institute
Tampa, Florida

JONES AND BARTLETT PUBLISHERS
*husetts
DON   SINGAPORE

World Headquarters
Jones and Bartlett Publishers
40 Tall Pine Drive
Sudbury, MA 01776
978-443-5000
info@jbpub.com
www.jbpub.com

Jones and Bartlett Publishers Canada
6339 Ormindale Way
Mississauga, Ontario L5V 1J2
Canada

Jones and Bartlett Publishers International
Barb House, Barb Mews
London W6 7PA
United Kingdom

Jones and Bartlett's books and products are available through most bookstores and online booksellers. To contact Jones and Bartlett Publishers directly, call 800-832-0034, fax 978-443-8000, or visit our website www.jbpub.com.

Substantial discounts on bulk quantities of Jones and Bartlett's publications are available to corporations, professional associations, and other qualified organizations. For details and specific discount information, contact the special sales department at Jones and Bartlett via the above contact information or send an email to specialsales@jbpub.com.

This publication is designed to provide accurate and authoritative information in regard to the subject matter covered. It is sold with the understanding that the publisher is not engaged in rendering legal, accounting, or other professional service. If legal advice or other expert assistance is required, the service of a competent professional person should be sought.

Library of Congress Cataloging-in-Publication Data
Friis, Robert H.
Epidemiology for public health practice / by Robert H. Friis and Thomas Sellers. — 4th ed.
    p. ; cm.
Includes bibliographical references and index.
ISBN-13: 978-0-7637-5161-6 (pbk.)
ISBN-10: 0-7637-5161-8 (pbk.)
    1. Epidemiology.   2. Public health personnel.   I. Sellers, Thomas A.   II. Title.
[DNLM: 1. Epidemiology.   2. Public Health.   WA 105 F912e 2008]
RA651.F686 2008
614.4—dc22   2007051846
6048

Production Credits
Publisher: Michael Brown
Associate Editor: Katey Birtcher
Production Director: Amy Rose
Production Editor: Renée Sekerak
Production Assistant: Julia Waugaman
Marketing Manager: Sophie Fleck

Manufacturing and Inventory Supervisor: Amy Bacus
Composition: ATLIS Graphics
Cover Design: Kristin E. Ohlin
Text Printing and Binding: Malloy Incorporated
Cover Printing: Malloy Incorporated

Printed in the United States of America
12 11 10 09 08   10 9 8 7 6 5 4 3 2 1

Chapter 6   **Study Designs: Ecologic, Cross-Sectional, Case-Control** **241**

Introduction 242

Observational Versus Experimental Approaches
in Epidemiology 243

Overview of Study Designs Used in Epidemiology 244

Ecologic Studies 249

Cross-Sectional Studies 256

Case-Control Studies 262

Conclusion 276

Chapter 7   **Study Designs: Cohort Studies** **283**

Introduction 284

Cohort Studies Defined 284

Sampling and Cohort Formation Options 295

Temporal Differences in Cohort Designs 301

Practical Considerations 303

Measures of Interpretation and Examples 307

Summary of Cohort Studies 318

Comparisons of Observational Designs 319

Conclusion 319

Chapter 8   **Experimental Study Designs** **327**

Introduction 328

Hierarchy of Study Designs 328

Intervention Studies 330

Clinical Trials 331

Community Trials 344

Conclusion 356

Chapter 9   **Measures of Effect** **361**

Introduction 362

Absolute Effects 362

Relative Effects 365

Statistical Measures of Effect 371

Evaluating Epidemiologic Associations 374

Models of Causal Relationships 376

Conclusion 381

Appendix 9—Cohort Study Data for Coffee Use
and Anxiety 384

Chapter 10   **Data Interpretation Issues** **385**
Introduction.. 386
Validity of Study Designs 386
Sources of Error in Epidemiologic Research 390
Techniques to Reduce Bias 396
Methods to Control Confounding 399
Bias in Analysis and Publication 403
Conclusion.. 404

Chapter 11   **Screening for Disease in the Community** **409**
Introduction.. 410
Screening for Disease 410
Appropriate Situations for Screening Tests
    and Programs.. 414
Characteristics of a Good Screening Test 417
Evaluation of Screening Tests 418
Sources of Unreliability and Invalidity............................ 421
Measures of the Validity of Screening Tests..................... 422
Effects of Prevalence of Disease on Screening
    Test Results... 424
Relationship Between Sensitivity and Specificity 426
Evaluation of Screening Programs 428
Issues in the Classification of Morbidity
    and Mortality 429
Conclusion.. 432
Appendix 11—Data for Problem 6 436

Chapter 12   **Epidemiology of Infectious Diseases** **437**
Introduction.. 438
Agents of Infectious Disease 439
Characteristics of Infectious Disease Agents 441
Host.. 442
The Environment... 445
Means of Transmission: Directly or Indirectly
    from Reservoir... 446
Measures of Disease Outbreaks 451
Procedures Used in the Investigation of Infectious
    Disease Outbreaks 456
Epidemiologically Significant Infectious Diseases
    in the Community... 457
Conclusion.. 482

Appendix 12—Data from a Foodborne Illness
Outbreak in a College Cafeteria................................... 488

Chapter 13   **Epidemiologic Aspects of Work and the
Environment**.. **489**
Introduction... 490
Health Effects Associated with Environmental
Hazards 491
Study Designs Used in Environmental
Epidemiology 491
Toxicologic Concepts Related to Environmental
Epidemiology 495
Types of Agents.. 497
Environmental Hazards Found in the Work Setting........ 506
Noteworthy Community Environmental
Health Hazards... 509
Conclusion.. 519

Chapter 14   **Molecular and Genetic Epidemiology** **529**
Introduction... 530
Definitions and Distinctions: Molecular Versus
Genetic Epidemiology 531
Epidemiologic Evidence for Genetic Factors................... 539
Causes of Familial Aggregation...................................... 540
Shared Family Environment and
Familial Aggregation... 542
Gene Mapping: Segregation and Linkage Analysis.......... 545
Genome-Wide Association Studies (GWAS) 553
Linkage Disequilibrium Revisited: Haplotypes............... 556
Application of Genes in Epidemiologic Designs.............. 558
Genetics and Public Health.. 565
Conclusion.. 568

Chapter 15   **Psychologic, Behavioral, and Social
Epidemiology**... **575**
Introduction... 576
Research Designs Used in Psychologic, Behavioral,
and Social Epidemiology 580
The Social Context of Health.. 581
Independent Variables... 582
Moderating Factors in the Stress-Illness Relationship 588

Outcome Variables: Physical Health, Mental Health,
        Affective States... 600
    Conclusion.. 605

Chapter 16   **Epidemiology as a Profession** **613**
    Introduction... 614
    Specializations Within Epidemiology 615
    Career Roles for Epidemiologists 617
    Epidemiology Associations and Journals......................... 620
    Competencies Required of Epidemiologists..................... 624
    Resources for Education and Employment..................... 625
    Professional Ethics in Epidemiology 627
    Conclusion.. 632

    **Appendix A—Guide to the Critical Appraisal of an
        Epidemiologic/Public Health Research Article 635**

    Appendix B—Answers to Selected Study Questions.... 641

    Glossary **651**

    Index **668**

New to This Edition

- Information on new disease outbreaks:
  - *E. coli* in spinach
  - Avian influenza
  - Extensively drug resistant tuberculosis (XDR TB)
- Expanded coverage of history of epidemiology
- New coverage of the natural history of disease
- Updated coverage of morbidity and mortality data throughout the text
- Method for rate adjustment updated to the 2000 standard population
- New information on health disparities, including the Hispanic mortality paradox
- Updated information on data sources including notifiable diseases
- Additional statistical measures provided, e.g., measures of life expectancy
- New coverage of models of causality
- New chapter on professional issues in epidemiology
- Exciting new figures, tables, and exhibits provided throughout
- Additional exercises and study questions

Introduction

Epidemiology is an exciting and rewarding field! Evidence of the importance of epidemiology to society comes from the incessant flow of media reports on flare-ups of new diseases, outbreaks of illness on cruise ships, and, even more ominous, the intentional spread of pathogenic microorganisms through acts of bioterrorism. One of the difficult tasks for the authors has been to incorporate with sufficient breadth and depth all of the fascinating components of this discipline.

Since the publication of the earlier editions of this book, epidemiologic researchers have continued to develop an even greater wealth of findings that have won the attention of the popular media as well as space in professional journals. It has indeed been a challenge to select information from all the excellent research that has been published within the past few years balanced with those during the entire history of the field. For example, some of these recent discoveries relate to continuing advances in genetics and molecular biology, recognition of emerging infections, and the growing use of the Internet. As a result, the *Second Edition* introduced several enhancements: a new chapter on molecular and genetic epidemiology, a new chapter on experimental epidemiology, material on epidemiology Internet sites, and updated charts and tables throughout the text. The *Third Edition* incorporated a new chapter on cohort designs, a glossary, and expanded coverage of ecologic and case-control study designs. The *Third Edition* also included new material on the role of epidemiology in policy-making, epidemiology and geographic information systems, and the definition of race used in Census 2000. A new Appendix A provided an extended guide to critiquing published research studies in public health and epidemiology. Several new tables summarized unadjusted measures of morbidity and mortality, contrasted different types of observational study designs, and compared observational versus intervention study designs.

This *Fourth Edition* presents new information on infectious disease threats associated with *E. coli* foodborne illness and avian influenza. We have expanded the historical background of epidemiology as well. Chapter 3, "Measures of Morbidity and Mortality Used in Epidemiology," has been updated to reflect the use of the 2000 standard population in age standardization. In this chapter as well as Chapter 12, we have updated tables and figures in order to provide the most recent information. A new Chapter, 16, is titled "Epidemiology as a Profession." Numerous changes have been made elsewhere in the text.

We intend the audience for the textbook to be beginning public health master's degree students, undergraduate and graduate health education and social ecology students, undergraduate medical students, nursing students, residents in primary care medicine, and applicants who are preparing for medical board examinations. These students are similar to those with whom both authors have worked over the years. Students from the social and behavioral sciences also have found epidemiology to be a useful tool in medical sociology and behavioral medicine. We have included study questions and exercises at the end of each chapter; this material would be helpful to review for board examinations. Appendix B contains an expanded answer set to selected problems.

Each chapter begins with a list of learning objectives and an outline to help focus the reader's attention to key points. Some of the major issues and examples are highlighted in text boxes and tables. Chapter 1, which defines epidemiology and provides a historical background for the discipline, is complemented by Chapter 2, which provides examples of practical applications of epidemiology as well as a discussion of causal inference. While examples of epidemiologic statistical techniques are interspersed throughout the book, Chapter 3 focuses on the "nuts and bolts" of measures of morbidity and mortality. Chapters 4 through 11 deal with the important topics of descriptive epidemiology: data sources, study designs, measures of effect, data interpretation, and screening. Chapters 12 through 15 focus on four content areas in epidemiology: infectious diseases, occupational and environmental health, molecular and genetic epidemiology, and psychosocial epidemiology. Finally, Chapter 16 covers professional issues in epidemiology. This text provides a thorough grounding in the key areas of methodology, causality, and the complex issues that surround chronic and infectious disease investigations. The authors assume that the reader will have had some familiarity with introductory biostatistics, although the text is intelligible to those who do not have such familiarity.

A coordinated web page is available for the text. This web page provides extensive resources for students and instructors. We recommend that instructors navigate through the web page during class time. For example, flashcards available on the web page may be used as part of an in-class activity to drill students for the class examinations. Robert Friis uses in-class Internet access in order to show students how to locate resources for the project shown in Appendix 4 (end of Chapter 4). Completion of the project, "Descriptive epidemiology of a selected health problem," can be one of the major assignments in an epidemiology class. In addition to completing a written version of the assignment, students enjoy delivering a brief PowerPoint presentation of their research to the entire class. Students' motivation and success in an epidemiology course are enhanced by reviewing the flashcards, giving an in-class report, and accessing other links shown in the web page.

Preface

My interest in epidemiology began during the 1960s when, as an undergraduate student at the University of California at Berkeley and a graduate student at Columbia University, I observed the student revolts and activism that occurred during that era. Student unrest was, I believed, a phenomenon that occurred in large groups and could be explained by a theoretical framework, perhaps one that would include such concepts as alienation or anomie. I became interested in studying the distribution of these psychologic states in student populations. Unknowingly, I had embarked upon epidemiologic research. I find epidemiology to be a field that has great personal appeal, because it is capable of impacting the health of large groups of people through improvements in social conditions and environmental modifications.

My formal training in epidemiology began at the Institute for Social Research of the University of Michigan, where I spent two years as a postdoctoral fellow. My first professional position in epidemiology was as an assistant professor in the Division of Epidemiology at the School of Public Health, Columbia University. As a fledging professor, I found epidemiology to be a fascinating discipline, and began to develop this textbook from my early teaching experiences. I concluded that there was a need for a textbook that would be oriented toward the beginning practitioner in the field, would provide coverage of a wide range of topics, and would emphasize the social and behavioral foundations of epidemiology as well as the medical model. This textbook has evolved from my early teaching experience at Columbia as well as later teaching and research positions at Albert Einstein College of Medicine, Brooklyn College, the University of California at Irvine, and the California State University system. Practical experience in epidemiology, as an epidemiologist in a local health department in Orange County, California, is also reflected in the book.

—*Robert H. Friis*

Like many others now reading this book, I had absolutely no idea what epidemiology was before I took my first required class in it at Tulane University School of Public Health and Tropical Medicine. What I discovered was a method to combine my training in nutrition and interest in health with an aptitude for math and analytical reasoning. This led to a change in majors and ultimately a PhD in epidemiology.

My first faculty appointment was at the University of Minnesota School of Public Health. Before I knew it, I was assigned to teach the introduction to epidemiology course during the winter quarter. This was the time of year when only nonmajors enrolled. I quickly learned, as had my predecessors, that my teaching and learning style was quite different from those of my students. Moreover, most of the textbooks available at that time were geared toward epidemiology majors. For nine years I studied learning styles (and even codeveloped and cotaught a graduate course on teaching) and experimented to find new ways to present the fundamentals of epidemiology in a nontechnical, nontheoretical, intuitive manner. This text reflects these learning experiences.

—*Thomas A. Sellers*

Acknowledgments

First, I express my gratitude to my teachers and colleagues at the settings where I have worked during the past three decades. Their insights and suggestions have helped me clarify my thinking about epidemiology. Among these individuals are the late Dr. Sidney Cobb and the late Dr. John R. P. French, Jr., who were my postdoctoral supervisors at the University of Michigan's Institute for Social Research. Dr. Mervyn Susser was responsible for offering me my first professional employment in epidemiology at the School of Public Health, Columbia University. He and Dr. Zena Stein helped me to increase greatly my fund of knowledge about research and teaching in the field. The late Professor Anna Gelman provided me with many practical ideas regarding how to teach epidemiology. Dr. Stephen A. Richardson also contributed to my knowledge about epidemiologic research. Finally, Dr. Jeremiah Tilles, Associate Dean, California College of Medicine, University of California at Irvine, provided extremely valuable instruction regarding the epidemiology of infectious diseases.

I also thank students in my epidemiology classes who contributed their suggestions and read early drafts of the *First Edition*. The comments of anonymous reviewers were particularly helpful in revising the manuscript. Jonathan Horowitz, former instructor in Health Science at California State University, Long Beach, spent a great deal of time reviewing several chapters of a very early version of the text, and I acknowledge his contributions. Sherry Stock, a former student in medical sociology at Long Beach, typed the first draft and provided much additional valuable assistance in securing bibliographic research materials. Dr. Yee-Lean Lee, Associate Professor, Infectious Disease Division in the Department of Medicine at the University of California at Irvine, reviewed and commented on the chapter dealing with the epidemiology of infectious diseases. Also, Dr. Harold Hunter, Professor of Health Care Administration, California State University, Long Beach, reviewed several chapters of the manuscript.

Finally, my wife, Carol Friis, typed the final version of the manuscript and made helpful comments. Without her support and assistance, completion of the text would not have been possible.

For the *Second Edition* of the text, I again thank my epidemiology students, who continued to provide much useful feedback. Graduate students Janelle Yamashita, Cindy Bayliss, and Jocelin Sabado were extremely helpful in conducting literature searches and preparing the text. Sharon Jean assisted with typing the manuscript.

With respect to the *Third Edition,* I would like to thank students at my home university and at other universities who provided many worthwhile suggestions for enhancement of the text. I am also grateful for the informal feedback I received from faculty members (across the United States and in several foreign countries) who adopted this text in their courses. California State University graduate student Ibtisam Khoury conducted background research, provided ideas for clarification of complex concepts, and helped to develop several new tables. Faculty members Dr. Javier Lopez-Zetina and Dr. Dennis Fisher, housed at the same university, reviewed several of the chapters. Critiques from anonymous reviewers also were instrumental in development of the *Third Edition.* Once again, I am deeply indebted to my wife, Carol Friis, who assisted with editing and typing the manuscript. Without her keen eye, writing this book would have been a much more difficult task.

Regarding the *Fourth Edition,* I once again acknowledge my students' suggestions for continued improvement of this book. Although many students are worthy of recognition, I would especially like to thank graduate student Lesley Shen. Claire Garrido-Ortega, a former student and now a lecturer in the Department of Health Science, contributed her ideas to the new edition. I have received many suggestions from the readers of the previous edition of this text; I would like to thank them also—particularly Dr. Lee Caplan at Morehouse University. Once more, I recognize the support of my wife, Carol Friis, who helped with preparation of the text.

R.H.F.

I have been most fortunate to have received training and guidance from a significant number of individuals. First and foremost I thank Dr. Dorothy Clemmer, who taught me my first course in epidemiology at Tulane University School of

Public Health and Tropical Medicine. Her enthusiasm and support helped me to "see the light." The early years of my education included mentorship with Dr. Gerald Berenson and Dr. Robert C. Elston. Both have been extremely influential in my practical and theoretical understanding of this discipline. Dr. J. Michael Sprafka was a great supporter and colleague for those first precarious episodes of teaching. I owe many thanks to the numerous bright and challenging public health students at the University of Minnesota for their support, encouragement, and patience while I experimented with methods of presentation to find out what worked best for "nonmajors." Finally, I acknowledge my father, Gene R. Sellers, who has published many fine textbooks and gave me the courage to attempt this project; my loving wife, Barbara, for her understanding and enduring belief in me; and my two sons, Jamison Thomas and Ryan Austin, who are my inspiration and loves of my life.

For the *Second Edition,* I acknowledge the encouragement of the students and colleagues who had used the *First Edition* of this text. I also thank our publisher and their staff for their professionalism. Finally, I acknowledge the drive and creativity of Bob Friis, whose energies made this book a reality and a success.

For the *Fourth Edition,* I would like to particularly thank my wonderful friends and colleagues at the Moffitt Cancer Center (especially Yifan Huang, Cathy Phelan, Jong Park, and Anna Giuliano) and the Mayo Cancer Center (especially Ellen Goode, Jim Cerhan, Celine Vachon, and Shane Pankratz) for their brilliance and dedication. I've learned that the application of the epidemiologic method can be fun if you work with the right team. I have certainly benefited from being around such a wonderful cast of bright and stimulating people. This has translated into exciting research projects, new knowledge, and practical insights added to this edition. Moreover, they share my hope and dream for an end to cancer and the terrible impact of this disease.

T.A.S.

About the Authors

Robert H. Friis, PhD, is a Professor of Health Science and Chair of the Department of Health Science at California State University, Long Beach, and Director of the CSULB-VAMC, Long Beach, Joint Studies Institute. He is also Clinical Professor of Community and Environmental Medicine at the University of California at Irvine. Previously, he was an Associate Clinical Professor in the Department of Medicine, Department of Neurology, and School of Social Ecology, University of California at Irvine. His entire professional career has been devoted to the field of epidemiology. He has conducted research and taught epidemiology and related subjects for more than three decades at universities in New York City and Southern California. In addition to previous employment in a local health department as an epidemiologist, he has conducted research and has published and presented numerous papers related to mental health, chronic disease, disability, minority health, and psychosocial epidemiology. His new text-book, *Essentials of Environmental Health,* is also published by Jones and Bartlett. Dr. Friis has been principal investigator or co-investigator on grants and con-tracts from University of California's Tobacco-Related Disease Research Program, from the National Institutes of Health, and from other agencies for re-search on geriatric health, depression in Hispanic populations, nursing home in-fections, and environmental health issues. His research interests have led him to conduct research in Mexico City and European countries. He has been a visiting professor at the Center for Nutrition and Toxicology, Karolinska Institute, Stockholm, Sweden; the Max Planck Institute, Munich, Germany; and Dresden Technical University, also in Germany. He reviews articles for scientific journals, including *International Migration Review* and *Social Science and Medicine.* Dr. Friis is a member of the Society for Epidemiologic Research, the American Public Health Association (epidemiology section), is a past president of the Southern California Public Health Association, and is a fellow of the Royal

Academy of Public Health. Among his awards were a postdoctoral fellowship for study at the Institute for Social Research, University of Michigan, and the Achievement Award for Scholarly and Creative Activity from California State University, Long Beach. His biography is listed in *Who's Who in America.*

Thomas A. Sellers, PhD, MPH, is Director of the Moffitt Research Institute, Associate Center Director for Cancer Prevention and Control, and Executive Vice President of the H. Lee Moffitt Cancer Center and Research Institute. Prior to this position in sunny, warm Tampa, Florida, he was Professor of Epidemiology in the Department of Health Sciences Research at the Mayo Clinic and the Deputy Director of the Mayo Clinic Cancer Center. He began his career at the University of Minnesota School of Public Health, where he taught the Introduction to Epidemiology course to nonmajors for nine years. His primary research interests include understanding the etiology of common adult cancers, particularly breast and ovarian cancer. He has published more than 200 peer-reviewed scientific articles, reviews, and book chapters, and now serves as a Senior Editor of *Cancer Epidemiology, Biomarkers and Prevention* and as Associate Editor of the *American Journal of Epidemiology*. Dr. Sellers is a long-standing member of the Society for Epidemiologic Research, the American Association for Cancer Research, and the American Society for Preventive Oncology, and is a founding member of the International Genetic Epidemiology Society. He is an elected member of the American Epidemiological Society. Dr. Sellers has been an invited member of Advisory Committees to the National Cancer Institute, has provided invited lectures worldwide, and has served on numerous grant review panels.

CHAPTER 1

History and Scope
of Epidemiology

LEARNING OBJECTIVES

By the end of this chapter the reader will be able to:

- define the term *epidemiology*
- define the components of epidemiology (determinants, distribution, morbidity, and mortality)
- name and describe characteristics of the epidemiologic approach
- discuss the importance of Hippocrates' hypothesis and how it differed from the common beliefs of the time
- discuss Graunt's contributions to biostatistics and how they affected modern epidemiology
- explain what is meant by the term *natural experiments,* and give at least one example

CHAPTER OUTLINE

   I. Introduction
  II. Epidemiology Defined
 III. Foundations of Epidemiology
 IV. Historical Antecedents of Epidemiology
  V. Recent Applications of Epidemiology
 VI. Conclusion
VII. Study Questions and Exercises

Introduction

Controversies and speculations regarding the findings of epidemiologic research are frequent topics of media reports; these findings sometimes arouse public hysteria. Examples of the questions raised by media reports include: "Is it more dangerous to vaccinate an entire population against smallpox (with resulting complications from the vaccine) or to risk infection with the disease itself through a terrorist attack?" "Is Ebola virus a danger to the general public?" "Should I give up eating fatty foods?" "Is it safe to drink coffee or alcoholic beverages?" "Will chemicals in the environment cause cancer?" "Should one purchase bottled water instead of consuming tap water from public drinking supplies?" Will medications for chronic diseases such as diabetes cause harmful side effects?" "Will the foods that I purchase in the supermarket make me sick?"

Consider a major outbreak of *Escherichia coli (E. coli)* infections that affected multiple states in the United States and captured media headlines for several months. The 2006 outbreak became a mystery that gradually unfolded over time (Exhibit 1–1). Initially, the outbreak was linked to prepackaged spinach as the most likely vehicle. The spinach was traced back to its source, Natural Selection Foods near Salinas, California. The mechanism for contamination of the spinach with *E. coli* bacteria was never established definitively.

Epidemiologic research methods are a powerful tool for studying health in the population. In many instances, epidemiology resembles detective work, because the causes of disease occurrence are often unknown. Exhibit 1–1 raises several issues that are typical of many epidemiologic research studies:

- When there is a linkage or association between a factor (i.e., as contaminants in food and water) and a health outcome, does this observation mean that the factor is a cause of disease?
- If there is an association, does the amount of disease vary according to the amount of exposure to the factor?
- Based on the observation of such an association, what practical steps should individuals and public health departments take? What should the individual consumer do?
- Do the findings from an epidemiologic study merit panic or a measured response?
- How applicable are the findings to settings other than the one in which the research was conducted? What are the policy implications of the findings?

In this chapter as well as in later chapters of this book, we answer the foregoing questions. We discuss the stages that are necessary to unravel mysteries about

EXHIBIT 1–1

E. coli O157:H7 Associated with Prepackaged Spinach: A Mysterious and Unsolved Problem

E. coli O157:H7 is a bacterial agent that can be ingested in contaminated food. *E. coli* refers to *Escherichia coli*, a bacterium that includes some strains that are normal inhabitants of the intestines of human beings as well as animals. The form of this bacterium known as *E. coli* O157:H7 can act as an enteric pathogen, which can produce bloody diarrhea and, in some instances, the hemolytic-uremic syndrome (HUS), a type of kidney failure. Severe cases of *E. coli* O157:H7 can be fatal.

An outbreak of *E. coli* O157:H7 in the late summer and early fall of 2006 sickened 199 persons across the United States and caused three deaths (as of October 6, 2006, when the outbreak appeared to have subsided). The 2006 outbreak caused 102 (51%) of the ill persons to be hospitalized; 31 patients (16%) were afflicted with HUS. The majority of cases (141, 71%) were female. A total of 22 children under 5 years of age were affected.[1] Data reported before October 6 indicated that the frequency of cases peaked from August 30 to September 1 (Refer to Figure 1-1a).[2] Two of the

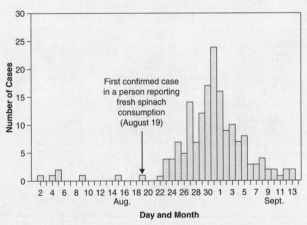

*Confirmed cases with known dates of illness onset reported as of 1:00 p.m. EDT on September 26, 2006.

FIGURE 1–1   (a) Number of confirmed cases (*n* = 171) of *Escherichia coli* serotype O157:H7 infection, by date of illness onset in the United States from August to September 2006.

continues

EXHIBIT 1–1 *continued*

deaths occurred among elderly persons and one among a 2-year-old child. The outbreak spread across 26 U.S. states; Ohio, Utah, and Wisconsin reported the greatest number of cases (Figure 1–1b).

Tracking down the origins of the outbreak required extensive detective work. First, attention turned to the possible source of the infection. On September 13, 2006, epidemiologists in Wisconsin and Oregon reported to the Centers for Disease Control and Prevention (CDC) that fresh spinach was suspected as the source. Similarly, epidemiologists in New Mexico reported that raw spinach was associated with a cluster of *E. coli* O157:H7 cases. By using a method of genetic fingerprinting known as pulsed-field gel electrophoresis, CDC officials confirmed that some strains of *E. coli* O157:H7 were present in materials isolated from the patients. As of September 26, 2006, 123 of 130 patients reported that they had consumed raw fresh spinach during the 10-day interval before becoming ill. Investigators obtained three open bags of spinach consumed by the patients and confirmed the presence of *E. coli* O157:H7. The U.S. Food and

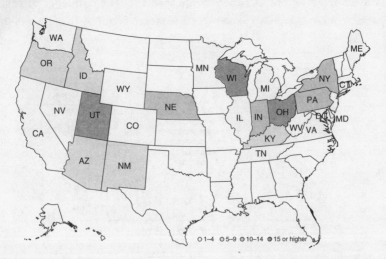

FIGURE 1–1   (b) Distribution of cases across the United States. *Source:* From Centers for Disease Control and Prevention. Ongoing multistate outbreak of *Escherichia coli* serotype O157:H7 infections associated with consumption of fresh spinach—United States, September 2006. *MMWR.* 2006;55:1045–1046.

continues

EXHIBIT 1–1 *continued*

Drug Administration (FDA) issued a warning to consumers not to eat bagged fresh spinach.

Next, the investigation turned to identifying the growers of the spinach and any environmental factors that could have caused the fresh spinach to become contaminated with *E. coli* O157:H7. The FDA linked the raw spinach involved in the outbreak to Natural Selection Foods LLC of San Juan Bautista, California.[3] The producer announced a recall of spinach on September 15, 2006. The FDA and State of California conducted a trace back investigation, which implicated four ranches in Monterey and San Benito Counties.[4] Cattle feces from one of the four ranches contained a strain of *E. coli* O157:H7 that matched the strain that had contaminated the spinach as well as the strain found in the 199 cases.

Noteworthy is the fact that subsequent to this major outbreak, *E. coli* O157:H7 continues to threaten the food supply of the United States, not only from spinach but also from other foods. During November through December 2006, Taco Bell restaurants in the northeastern United States experienced a major outbreak that caused at least 71 persons to fall ill. The source of the outbreak was not established clearly.[5] Contamination of Topp's brand frozen ground beef patties and Totino's or Jeno's brand pizzas with *E. coli* O157:H7 is believed to have sickened more than 60 residents of the eastern half of the United States during summer and early fall 2007. ■

diseases, such as those due to environmental exposures or those for which the cause is entirely unknown.

Epidemiology is a discipline that describes, quantifies, and postulates causal mechanisms for health phenomena in populations. Using the results of epidemiologic studies, public health practitioners are aided in their quest to control health problems such as disease outbreaks. The investigation into the *E. coli* outbreak illustrates some of the classic methods of epidemiology: first, describing all of the cases, enumerating them, and then following up with additional studies. Exhibit 1–1 illustrates the extensive detective work involved in identifying the cause of a disease outbreak. The hypothesized causal mechanism that was ultimately linked to contaminated spinach was the bacterium *E. coli*. All of the features described in the investigation are hallmarks of the epidemiologic approach. In this example, the means by which *E. coli* contaminated the spinach remains an unresolved issue.

Epidemiology Defined

The word *epidemiology* derives from *epidemic*, a term that provides an immediate clue to its subject matter. Epidemiology originates from the Greek words *epi* (upon) + *demos* (people) + *logy* (study of). Although some conceptions of epidemiology are quite narrow, we suggest a broadened scope and propose the following definition:

> Epidemiology is concerned with the distribution and determinants of health and diseases, morbidity, injuries, disability, and mortality in populations. Epidemiologic studies are applied to the control of health problems in populations. The key aspects of this definition are determinants, distribution, population, and health phenomena (e.g., morbidity and mortality).

Determinants

Determinants are factors or events that are capable of bringing about a change in health. Some examples are specific biologic agents (e.g., bacteria) that are associated with infectious diseases or chemical agents that may act as carcinogens. Other potential determinants for changes in health may include less specific factors, such as stress or adverse lifestyle patterns (lack of exercise or a diet high in saturated fats). The following four vignettes illustrate the concern of epidemiology with disease determinants. For example, consider the steps taken to track down the source of the bacteria that caused anthrax and were sent through the mail; contemplate the position of an epidemiologist once again. Imagine a possible scenario for describing, quantifying, and identifying the determinants for each of the vignettes.

Case 1: Intentional Dissemination of Bacteria That Cause Anthrax

After the United States experienced its worst terrorist attack on September 11, 2001, reports appeared in the media about cases of anthrax in Florida beginning in early October. In the United States, anthrax usually affects herbivores (livestock and some wild animals); human cases are unusual. Anthrax is an acute bacterial disease caused by exposure to *Bacillus anthracis*. Cutaneous anthrax affects the skin, pro-

continues

CASE 1 *continued*

ducing lesions that develop into a black scab. Untreated cutaneous anthrax has a case-fatality rate of 5% to 20%. The much more severe inhalational form, which affects the lungs and later becomes disseminated by the bloodstream, has a high case fatality rate.[6] Observations of an alert infectious disease specialist along with the support of laboratory staff led to the suspicion that anthrax had been deliberately sent through the postal system.[7] The CDC, in collaboration with officials at the state and local levels, identified a total of 21 anthrax cases (16 confirmed and five suspected) as of October 31, 2001. The majority of the cases occurred among employees located in four areas: Florida, New York City, New Jersey, and the District of Columbia.[8-11] Figure 1-2 portrays the distribution of the 21 cases in four geographic areas of the United States. ■

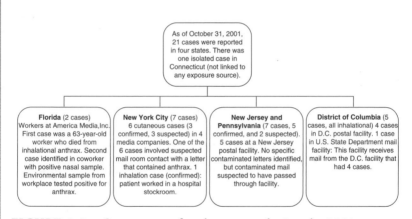

FIGURE 1–2   Occurrence of anthrax cases during the 2001 terrorist incident according to the investigation by the Centers for Disease Control and Prevention.

Case 2: Outbreak of Fear

When a 36-year-old lab technician known as Kinfumu checked into the general hospital in Kikwit, Zaire, . . . complaining of diarrhea and a fever, anyone could have mistaken his illness for the dysentery that was plaguing the city. Nurses, doctors, and nuns did what they could to help

continues

CASE 2 *continued*

the young man. They soon saw that his disease wasn't just dysentery. Blood began oozing from every orifice in his body. Within four days he was dead. By then the illness had all but liquefied his internal organs.

That was just the beginning. The day Kinfumu died, a nurse and a nun who had cared for him fell ill. The nun was evacuated to another town 70 miles to the west where she died—but not until the contagion had spread to at least three of her fellow nuns. Two subsequently died. In Kikwit, the disease raged through the ranks of the hospital's staff. Inhabitants of the city began fleeing to neighboring villages. Some of the fugitives carried the deadly illness with them. Terrified health officials in Kikwit sent an urgent message to the World Health Organization. The Geneva-based group summoned expert help from around the globe: a team of experienced virus hunters composed of tropical-medicine specialists, microbiologists, and other researchers. They grabbed their lab equipment and their bubble suits and clambered aboard transport planes headed for Kikwit.[12] ■

Case 3: Fear on Seventh Avenue

On normal workdays, the streets of New York City's garment district are lively canyons bustling with honking trucks, scurrying buyers, and sweating rack boys pushing carts loaded with suits, coats, and dresses. But during September 1978 a tense new atmosphere was evident. Sanitation trucks cruised the side streets off Seventh Avenue flushing pools of stagnant water from the gutters and spraying out disinfectant. Teams of health officers drained water towers on building roofs. Air conditioners fell silent for inspection, and several chilling signs appeared on 35th Street: "The New York City Department of Health has been advised of possible causes of Legionnaires' disease in this building." By the weekend, there were six cases of the mysterious disease, 73 more suspected and two deaths. In the New York City outbreak, three brothers were the

continues

CASE 3 *continued*

first victims. Carlisle, Gilbert, and Joseph Leggette developed the fever, muscle aches, and chest congestion that make the disease resemble pneumonia. Joseph and Gilbert recovered; Carlisle did not. "He just got sick and about a week later he was dead," said John Leggette, a fourth brother who warily returned to his own job in the garment district the next week. "I'm scared," he said. "But what can you do?"[13] ■

Case 4: Red Spots on Airline Flight Attendants

From January 1 to March 10, 1980, Eastern Airlines received 190 reports of episodes of red spots appearing on the skin of flight attendants (FAs) during various flights. Complaints of symptoms accompanying the spots were rare, but some FAs expressed concern that the spots were caused by bleeding through the skin and might indicate a serious health hazard. On March 12, investigators from the CDC traveled to Miami to assist in the investigation. No evidence of damage to underlying skin was noted on these examinations, nor was any noted by consultant dermatologists who examined affected FAs after the spots had disappeared. Chemical tests on clinical specimens for the presence of blood were negative. Airline personnel had investigated the ventilation systems, cleaning materials and procedures, and other environmental factors on affected aircraft. Airflow patterns and cabin temperatures, pressures, and relative humidity were found to be normal. Cleaning materials and routines had been changed, but cases continued to occur. Written reports by FAs of 132 cases occurring in January and February showed that 91 different FAs had been affected, 68 once and 23 several times. Of these cases, 119 (90%) had occurred on a single type of aircraft. Of the 119 cases from implicated aircraft, 96% occurred on north- or south-bound flights between the New York City and Miami metropolitan areas, flights that are partially over water. Only rarely was a case reported from the same airplane when flying transcontinental or other east-west routes.[14] ■

Health departments, the CDC in Atlanta, and epidemiologic researchers frequently confront a problem that has no clear determinants or etiologic basis. The methods and findings of epidemiologic studies may direct one to, or suggest, particular causal mechanisms underlying health-related events or conditions, such as the four examples cited in the vignettes: anthrax, the suspected outbreak of Ebola virus, Legionnaires' disease, and red spots on airline FAs. Read the following solution to clear up the mystery of Case 4.

Solution to Case 4: Red Spots

The investigation then concentrated on defining the clinical picture more clearly. An Eastern Airlines (EAL) physician, a consultant dermatologist, and a physician from the National Institute for Occupational Safety and Health (NIOSH) rode on implicated flights on March 14 and examined three new cases considered by the EAL physician and other flight attendants (FAs) to be typical cases. Although the spots observed consisted of red liquid, they did not resemble blood. To identify potential environmental sources of red-colored material, investigators observed the standard activities of FAs on board implicated flights. At the beginning of each flight FAs routinely demonstrated the use of life vests, required in emergency landings over water. Because the vests used for demonstration were not actually functional, they were marked in bright red ink with the words "Demo Only." When the vests were demonstrated, the red ink areas came into close contact with the face, neck, and hands of the demonstrator. Noting that on some vests the red ink rubbed or flaked off easily, investigators used red material from the vests to elicit the typical clinical picture on themselves. On preliminary chemical analyses, material in clinical specimens of red spots obtained from cases was found to match red-ink specimens from demonstration vests. On March 15 and 16, EAL removed all demonstration model life vests from all its aircraft and instructed FAs to use the standard, functional, passenger-model vests for demonstration purposes. The airline . . . continue[d] to request reports of cases to verify the effectiveness of this action. Although all demonstration vests were obtained from the same manufacturer, the vests removed from specific aircraft were noted to vary somewhat in the color of fabric and in the color and texture of red ink, suggesting that many different production lots may have been in use simultaneously on any given aircraft.[14] ■

Distribution

Frequency of disease occurrence may vary from one population group to another. For example, hypertension may be more common among young African-American men than among young white men. Mortality from coronary heart disease may vary between Hispanics and non-Hispanics.[15] Such variations in disease frequency illustrate how disease may have different distributions depending upon the underlying characteristics of the populations being studied.

Population

Epidemiology examines disease occurrence among population groups rather than among individuals. Lilienfeld[16] noted that this focus is a widely accepted feature of epidemiology. For this reason, epidemiology is often referred to as "population medicine." The epidemiologic and clinical descriptions of a disease are quite different as a result. Note the different descriptions of toxic shock syndrome (TSS), a condition that showed sharp increases during 1980 in comparison to the immediately previous years. TSS is a severe illness that in the 1980 outbreak was found to be associated with vaginal tampon use. The clinical description of TSS would include specific signs and symptoms, such as high fever, headache, malaise, and other more dramatic symptoms, such as vomiting and profuse watery diarrhea. The epidemiologic description would indicate which age groups would be most likely to be affected, time trends, geographic trends, and other variables that affect the distribution of TSS. A second example is myocardial infarction (MI; heart attack). A clinical description of MI would list specific signs and symptoms, such as chest pain, heart rate, nausea, and other individual characteristics of the patient. The epidemiologic description of the same condition would indicate which age groups would be most likely to be affected, seasonal trends in heart attack rates, geographic variations in frequency, and other characteristics of persons associated with the frequency of heart attack in populations.

Referring again to the vignettes, one may note that the problem that plagued Kinfumu in Case 2 was recognized as a particularly acute problem for epidemiology when similar complaints from other patients were discovered and the disease began to spread. If more than one person complains about a health problem, the health provider may develop the suspicion that some widespread exposure rather than something unique to an individual is occurring. The clinical observation might suggest further epidemiologic investigation of the problem.

Health Phenomena

As indicated in the definition, epidemiology is used to investigate many different kinds of health outcomes. These range from infectious diseases to chronic disease, and various states of health, such as disability, injury, limitation of activity, and mortality.[17] Other health outcomes have included positive functioning of the individual and active life expectancy as well as health-related events, including mental disorders, suicide, substance abuse, and injury. Epidemiology's concern with positive states of health is illustrated by research into active life expectancy among geriatric populations. This research seeks to determine the factors associated with optimal mental and physical functioning as well as enhanced quality of life and ultimately aims to limit disability in later life.

Morbidity and Mortality

Two other terms central to epidemiology are *morbidity* and *mortality*. The former, morbidity, designates illness, whereas the latter, mortality, refers to death. Note that most measures of morbidity and mortality are defined for specific types of morbidity or causes of death.

Aims and Levels

The preceding sections hinted at the complete scope of epidemiology. As the basic method of public health, epidemiology is concerned with efforts to describe, explain, predict, and control.

- To *describe* the health status of populations means to enumerate the cases of disease, to obtain relative frequencies of the disease within subgroups, and to discover important trends in the occurrence of disease.
- To *explain* the etiology of disease means to discover causal factors as well as to determine modes of transmission.
- To *predict* the occurrence of disease is to estimate the actual number of cases that will develop as well as to identify the distribution within populations. Such information is crucial to planning interventions and allocation of healthcare resources.
- To *control* the distribution of disease, the epidemiologic approach is used to prevent the occurrence of new cases of disease, to eradicate existing cases, and to prolong the lives of those with the disease.

The implication of these aims is that epidemiology has two different goals. One is improved understanding of the natural history of disease and the factors that influence its distribution. With the knowledge that is obtained from such efforts, one can then proceed to accomplish the second goal: intervention.

Foundations of Epidemiology

Epidemiology Is Interdisciplinary

Epidemiology is an interdisciplinary field that draws from biostatistics and the social and behavioral sciences as well as from the medically related fields of toxicology, pathology, virology, genetics, microbiology, and clinical medicine. Terris[18] pointed out that epidemiology is an extraordinarily rich and complex science that derives techniques and methodologies from many disciplines. He wrote that epidemiology "must draw upon and synthesize knowledge from the biological sciences of man and of his parasites, from the numerous sciences of the physical environment, and from the sciences concerned with human society."[18(p. 203)]

To elaborate, some of the contributions of microbiology include information about specific disease agents, including their morphology and modes of transmission. The investigations of anthrax, Legionnaires' disease, TSS, and infant botulism (a condition linked to ingestion of spores, often found in honey, that cause botulism) utilized microbiologic techniques to identify possible infectious agents. When the infectious agent is a virus, the expertise of a virologist may be required. Clinical medicine is involved in the diagnosis of the patient's state of health, particularly when defining whether the patient has a specific disease or condition. A pathologist's expertise may help differentiate between normal and diseased tissue. From our previous examples, clinical medicine diagnosed the individuals' symptoms or signs of ill health. Astute physicians and nurses may suggest epidemiologic research on the basis of clinical observations. Toxicology is concerned with the presence and health effects of chemical agents, particularly those found in the environment and the workplace. Regarding hazardous waste sites, toxicologic knowledge helps determine the presence of noxious chemical agents and whether the health effects observed are consistent with the known effects of exposure to toxic agents. When responses to exogenous agents vary from person to person, geneticists may become part of the team. Social and behavioral sciences elucidate the role of race, social class, education, cultural group membership, and behavioral practices in health-related phenomena. Social and behavioral science disciplines, that is, sociology and psychology, are devoted respectively to the development of social theory and the study of behavior. The special concern of social epidemiologic approaches is the study of social conditions and disease processes.[19] Furthermore, much of the methodology on sampling, measurement, questionnaire development, design, and delivery, and methods of group comparison are borrowed from the social sciences. Finally, the field of biostatistics is critical to the evaluation of epidemiologic data, especially when one is trying to separate chance from meaningful observations. Epidemiology profits from the interdisciplinary approach because the causality of a particular disease in a population may involve the interaction of multiple factors. The contributions of many disciplines help unravel the factors associated with a particular disease.

Methods and Procedures

Population research is empirical and requires quantification of relevant factors. Quantification refers to the translation of qualitative impressions into numbers. Qualitative sources of information about disease may be, in illustration, a physician's observations derived through medical practice about the types of people among whom a disease seems to be common. Epidemiologists enumerate cases of disease to objectify subjective impressions. Quantification is a central activity of epidemiology; the standard epidemiologic measures often require counting the number of cases of disease and examining their distribution according to demographic variables, such as age, sex, race, and other variables, such as exposure category and clinical features. The following quotation illustrates a summary of the characteristics of 51 suspected cases of severe acute respiratory syndrome (SARS) that were reported to the CDC as of early 2003:

The Language of Quantification
Severe Acute Respiratory Syndrome (SARS) in the United States

As of March 26, [2003] CDC has received 51 reports of suspected SARS cases from 21 states . . . identified using the CDC updated interim case definition [refer to Table 1-1] . . . The first suspected case was identified on March 15, in a man aged 53 years who traveled to Singapore and became ill on March 10. Four clusters of suspected cases have been identified, three of which involved a traveler who had visited Southeast Asia (including Guangdong province, Hong Kong, or Vietnam) and a single family contact. One of these clusters involved suspected cases in

continues

Table 1–1 Exposure Category, Clinical Features, and Demographics of Reported Severe Acute Respiratory Syndrome (SARS) Cases* in Selected Locations, 2003

Category	Hong Kong N	(%)	Vietnam N	(%)	Thailand N	(%)	Taiwan N	(%)	United States N	(%)
Total cases† (As of date)	290§ (3/25/03-S/P)	(100)	59 (3/24/03-P)	(100)	4 (3/23/03-S/P)	(100)	6 (3/25/03-S)	(100)	51§ (3/25/03-P)	(100)
Exposure										
Healthcare worker	134	(46)	37	(63)	1	(25)	0		2	(4)
Close contact¶	156	**	NA††		0		2	(33)	5	(10)
Clinical features										
Ever hospitalized	290	(100)§	59	(100)	4	(100)	6	(100)	20§	(39)
Pneumonia	286	(99)	NA		3	(75)	6	(100)	14	(27)
Ever ventilated	NA		5	(9)	1	(25)	2	(33)	1	(2)
Dead	10	(4)§	2	(3)	0		0		0§	(2)
Demographics										
Age, median	NA		38 yrs		38 yrs		53 yrs		42 yrs	
Age, range	NA		18–66 yrs		1–49 yrs		25–64 yrs		8 mos–78 yrs	
Sex §§										
Female	~50%		37	(63)	1	(25)	3	(50)	26	(51)
Male	~50%		22	(37)	3	(75)	3	(50)	25	(49)

Abbreviation: N, number.

* Locations used different SARS case definitions. †S, suspected case; P, probable case; U, unknown.

§ One U.S. resident (Patient B) was hospitalized in Vietnam and died in Hong Kong before he could return to the United States. He is counted as a Hong Kong case.

¶ Person having cared for, lived with, or had direct contact with respiratory secretions and body fluids of a person with SARS.

** Of the 290 SARS patients in Hong Kong, most of the remaining 156 patients are believed to be close contacts.

†† Not available. §§ Only percentages were reported for sex data.

Source: Modified from Centers for Disease Control and Prevention. Update: Outbreak of severe acute respiratory syndrome—worldwide, 2003. *MMWR.* 2003;52:244.

patients L and M . . . who had stayed together at hotel M during March 1–6, when other hotel guests were symptomatic. Patient L became sick on March 13 after returning to the United States. His wife, patient M, became ill several days after the onset of her husband's symptoms, suggesting secondary transmission. Three patients in the United States with suspected SARS (patients I, L, and M) reported staying at hotel M when other persons staying in the hotel were symptomatic. The fourth cluster began with a suspected case in a person who traveled in Guangdong province and Hong Kong. Two [health care workers] subsequently became ill at the U.S. hospital where this patient was admitted.[20(p. 244)] Since 2005, no additional SARS cases have been reported. ■

Epidemiologists sometimes present quantified information as graphs and tables that illustrate pictorially the frequency of disease. Quantification enables the epidemiologist to investigate the sources of variation of a disease by time, place, and person: When did the case occur? Where was it located? Who was affected?

We offer many examples of quantification throughout this text. Table 1–1 reports the characteristics of SARS cases in selected locations in 2003.

Other key methods for the graphic presentation of data are the use of pie charts, bar charts, and line graphs. Figure 1–3 shows an example of each type: a pie chart (A, fatal occupational injuries in the United States); a bar chart (B, firearm injury death rates); and a line graph (C, motor vehicle traffic death rates). Epidemiologists use these types of graphs to describe characteristics of data, such as subgroup differences and time trends.[21]

Use of Special Vocabulary

Epidemiology employs a unique vocabulary of terms to describe the frequency of occurrence of disease. These terms are presented in Chapters 3 and 4. A different collection of terms is used in reference to the array of study designs available to epidemiologists. Chapters 6, 7, and 8 define and characterize these study approaches. Finally, special terms have been developed to convey the results and to aid in the interpretation of epidemiologic investigations. These are defined and illustrated in Chapter 10.

Dorland's Illustrated Medical Dictionary defines the word *epidemic* as "attacking many people at the same time, widely diffused and rapidly spreading." More

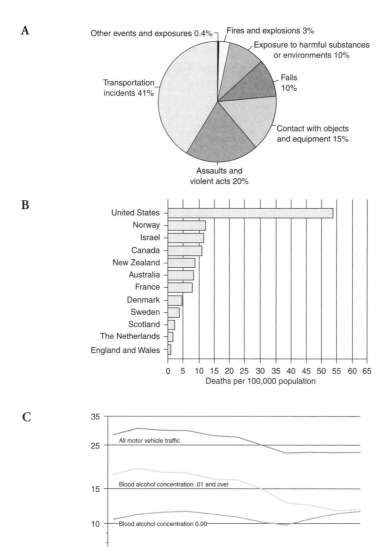

FIGURE 1-3   Examples of three different presentations of epidemiologic data. (A) Pie chart. Percentage distribution of fatal occupational injuries, according to the event: United States, 1994–1995. (B) Bar graph. Firearm injury death rates among males 15 to 24 years of age for selected countries and selected years (1992–1995). (C) Line graph. Motor vehicle traffic death rates by alcohol involvement among persons 1 to 34 years of age in the United States during 1985–1995. *Source:* Reprinted from Fingerhut LA, Warner M. *Injury Chartbook. Health, United States, 1996–97.* National Center for Health Statistics; 1997.

precisely, an epidemic refers to an excessive occurrence of a disease: "Most current definitions [of epidemic] stress the concept of excessive prevalence as its basic implication in both lay and professional usage."[22(p. 2)] The following passage illustrates this notion by defining an epidemic as:

> The occurrence in a community or region of cases of an illness (or an outbreak) clearly in excess of expectancy. The number of cases indicating presence of an epidemic will vary according to the infectious agent, size and type of population exposed, previous experience or lack of exposure to the disease, and time and place of occurrence; epidemicity is thus relative to usual frequency of the disease in the same area, among the specified population, at the same season of the year. A single case of a communicable disease long absent from a population or the first invasion by a disease not previously recognized in that area requires immediate reporting and epidemiologic investigation; two cases of such a disease associated in time and place are sufficient evidence of transmission to be considered an epidemic.[23(pp. 569–570)]

In current thinking, an epidemic is not confined to infectious diseases. Take, for example, the Love Canal incident that generated spirited public debate and media attention during the late 1970s. Love Canal was a toxic waste disposal site located in Niagara Falls, New York. It was the location for burial of thousands of chemical-filled drums deposited by the Hooker Chemicals & Plastics Corporation. Eventually, the waste disposal site was covered and converted into a housing tract. Subsequently, residents of the area reported several different types of health effects, including miscarriages, birth defects, and mental retardation. The Love Canal site was the focus of extensive health effects studies and epidemiologic research.

By referring to the case studies reported in this text, you have seen additional examples—red spots among airline FAs and TSS—that illustrate two instances in which epidemiologic methodology was employed to study noninfectious conditions. TSS and red spots among airline FAs both represented apparent epidemics because the usual or expected rate was nil. Epidemiologic methods also are used to investigate occupationally associated illness (e.g., brown lung disease among textile workers and asbestosis among shipyard workers), environmental health hazards (e.g., toxic chemicals and air pollution), and conditions associated with lifestyle (e.g., accidents, ischemic heart disease, and certain forms of cancer).

Related to the term epidemic is the term *pandemic,* which refers to an epidemic on a worldwide scale; during a pandemic, large numbers of persons may be affected and a disease may cross international borders. Examples are flu pandemics, such as the pandemic of 1918 and more recent flu pandemics that occur periodically. The term *endemic* is used to characterize a disease that is habitually present in a particular geographical region. To illustrate, malaria is endemic in some tropical areas of Asia, and cholera is endemic to less developed countries where sanitation is lacking. Previously, during the 19th century, cholera was endemic to Western countries, such as England and the United States. However, cholera is no longer endemic to these two countries because of the introduction of sanitation and other public health measures.

Methods for Ascertainment of Epidemic Frequency of Disease

The CDC and vital statistics departments of state and local governments collect surveillance data on a continuing basis to determine whether an epidemic is taking place. The word *surveillance* denotes the systematic collection of data pertaining to the occurrence of specific diseases, the analysis and interpretation of these data, and the dissemination of consolidated and processed information to contributors to the surveillance program and other interested persons. For example, if 500 heart attack deaths are reported in an upstate New York community during a particular year, this information by itself would be insufficient to justify the assertion that an epidemic of heart attacks has occurred. The usual frequency of heart attacks would need to be determined in the same community at some prior time, and the size, age, and sex distribution of the population would need to be known. A second example is shown in Figure 1–4 for influenza and pneumonia deaths.

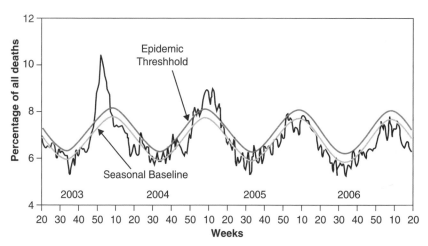

FIGURE 1–4   Pneumonia and influenza mortality for 122 U.S. cities, week ending May 19, 2007. *Source:* From Centers for Disease Control and Prevention. Influenza (Flu) Weekly Report: Influenza Summary Update Week ending May 19, 2007–Week 20. Available at: http://www.cdc.gov/ flu/weekly/weeklyarchives2006–2007/weekly20.htm. Accessed October 11, 2007.

Figure 1–4 exhibits weekly pneumonia and influenza deaths in the United States from winter 2003 to spring 2007. It demonstrates that influenza has an underlying seasonal baseline, reflected in its cyclic seasonal increases and declines in mortality. The lower line denotes the usual number of total deaths to be expected from pneumonia and influenza during each week of the year. An upper parallel line indicates the frequency of disease at the epidemic threshold, that is, the minimum number of deaths that would support the conclusion that an epidemic was underway. Figure 1–4 demonstrates that the combined pneumonia and influenza deaths exceeded the epidemic threshold during the 2003–2004 and 2004–2005 flu seasons.

Historical Antecedents of Epidemiology

To put the discipline in proper perspective, we now outline some of the historical trends that led to the development of epidemiology or were historically significant for the field. It may be said that epidemiology began with the Greeks, who in their concern for the ancient epidemics and deadly toll of diseases, attributed disease causality to environmental factors. Early causal explanations for epidemics included the wrath of the gods, the breakdown of religious beliefs and morality, the influence of weather, and "bad air." During the medieval period, the Black Death caused by plague killed more than 25% of the European population. Another terrible scourge was smallpox: Edward Jenner's work led to the development of an effective vaccination against smallpox. During the late Renaissance, pioneering biostatisticians quantified morbidity and mortality trends. Often cited as another major development is John Snow's investigations of London cholera outbreaks, reported in *Snow on Cholera*.[24] A contemporary of Snow, William Farr, promoted innovative uses of vital statistics data. During the 19th century, early microbiologists formalized the germ theory of disease, which attributed diseases to specific organisms. At the beginning of the 20th century, a flu pandemic killed more than 50 million people worldwide. Each of these historical developments that contributed to the genesis of epidemiology is discussed in turn below.

Environment as a Factor in Disease Causation

The following account of a deadly disease by Thucydides records, in detail, the ravages produced by "Thucydides' plague"[25]; such graphic descriptions of major epidemics in history indicate this early author's concern with the causality of these remarkable phenomena:

Many who were in perfect health, all in a moment, and without apparent reason, were seized with violent heats in the head and with redness and inflammation of the eyes. Internally the throat and the tongue were quickly suffused with blood, and the breath became unnatural and fetid. There followed sneezing and a hoarseness; in a short time the disorder, accompanied by a violent cough, reached the chest; then fastening lower down, it would move the stomach and bring on all the vomits of bile to which physicians have ever given names; and they were very distressing. An ineffectual retching producing violent convulsions attacked most of the sufferers; some as soon as the previous symptoms had abated, others not until long afterwards. The body externally was not so very hot to the touch, nor yet pale; it was of a livid color inclining to red, and breaking out in pustules and ulcers. But the internal fever was intense; the sufferers could not bear to have on them even the finest linen garment; they insisted on being naked, and there was nothing which they longed for more eagerly than to throw themselves into cold water . . . While the disease was at its height, the body, instead of wasting away, held out amid these sufferings in a marvelous manner, and either they died on the seventh or ninth day, not of weakness, for their strength was not exhausted, but of internal fever, which was the end of most; or, if they survived, then the disease descended into the bowels and there produced violent ulceration; severe diarrhea at the same time set in, and at a later stage caused exhaustion, which finally with a few exceptions carried them off.[25(p. 21)]

Hippocrates, in *On Airs, Waters, and Places*,[26] gave birth in about 400 BC to the idea that disease might be associated with the physical environment; his thinking represented a movement away from supernatural explanations of disease causation to a rational account of the origin of humankind's illnesses. Note in the following passage his reference to climate and physical environment:

Whoever wishes to investigate medicine properly should proceed thus: in the first place to consider the seasons of the year, and what effects each of them produces (for they are not at all alike, but differ much from themselves in regard to their changes). Then the winds, the hot and the cold, especially such as are common to all countries, and then such as are peculiar to each locality. We must also consider the qualities of the waters, for as they differ from one another in taste and weight, so also do they differ much in their qualities. In the same manner, when one comes into a city to which he is a stranger, he ought to consider its situation, how it lies as to the winds and the rising of the sun; for its influence is not the same whether it lies to the north or the south, to the rising or to the setting sun. These things one ought to consider most attentively, and concerning the waters which the inhabitants use, whether they be marshy and soft, or hard, and running from elevated and rocky situations, and then if saltish and unfit for cooking; and the ground, whether it be naked and deficient in water, or wooded and well watered, and whether it lies in a hollow, confined situation, or is elevated and cold; and the mode in which the inhabitants live, and what are their pursuits, whether they are fond of drinking and eating to excess, and given to indolence, or are fond of exercise and labor, and not given to excess in eating and drinking.[26(pp. 156–157)]

The Black Death

Occurring between 1346 and 1352, the Black Death is a dramatic example of a pandemic of great historical significance to epidemiology.[27] The Black Death is noteworthy because of the scope of human mortality that it produced as well as for its impact upon medieval civilization. Estimates suggest that the Black Death claimed about one-quarter to one-third of the population of Europe. Northern Africa and the near Middle East also were affected severely; at the inception of the outbreak, the population of this region including Europe numbered about 100 million people; 20 to 30 million people are believed to have died in Europe.

Historians attribute the Black Death to bubonic plague, which is the most common of the three forms of plague.[28] The bacterium *Yersinia pestis* produces swelling of the lymph nodes in the groin and other sites of the body. These painful swellings, called buboes, are followed in several days by high fever and the appearance of black splotches on the skin. The reservoir for *Y. pestis* is various types of rodents, including rats. Plague can be transmitted when fleas that feed on rodents bite a human host. At the time of the Black Death, no method for treatment of plague existed. Most victims died within a few days after the occurrence of buboes. Currently, plague is treatable with antibiotics. In addition, improvement in sanitary conditions has led to the decline in plague cases; 2,118 cases were reported worldwide in 2003.

Use of Mortality Count

In 1662, John Graunt published *Natural and Political Observations Mentioned in a Following Index, and Made Upon the Bills of Mortality*.[29] This work recorded descriptive characteristics of birth and death data, including seasonal variations, infant mortality, and excess male over female differences in mortality. Graunt's work made a fundamental contribution by discovering regularities in medical and social phenomena. He is said to be the first to employ quantitative methods in describing population vital statistics by organizing mortality data in a mortality table and has been referred to as the Columbus of statistics. Graunt's procedures allowed the discovery of trends in births and deaths due to specific causes. Although his conclusions were sometimes erroneous, his development of statistical methods was highly important.[30]

Concerning sex differences in death rates, Graunt wrote:

> *Of the difference between the numbers of Males and Females.* The next Observation is, That there be more Males than Females . . . There have been Buried from the

year 1628, to the year 1662, *exclusive,* 209436 *Males,* and but 190474 *Females:* but it will be objected, That in *London* it may be indeed so, though otherwise elsewhere; because *London* is the great Stage and Shop of business, wherein the *Masculine Sex* bears the greatest part. But we Answer, That there have been also *Christened* within the same time 139782 *Males,* and but 130866 *Females,* and that the Country-Accounts are consonant enough to those of *London* upon this matter.[29(p. 44)]

Figure 1–5 shows the 10 leading causes of mortality from the Yearly Mortality Bill for 1632.

Edward Jenner and Smallpox Vaccination

The term *vaccination* derives from the Latin word for cow (vacca), the source of the cowpox virus that was used to create a vaccine against smallpox. A precursor of smallpox vaccination was variolation, which referred to an early Asian method of conferring immunity to smallpox by introducing dried scabs from smallpox patients into the noses of potential victims who wished to be protected from this disease.[31] Variolation often produced a milder case of disease with a much lower fatality rate than that caused by community-acquired smallpox. The method

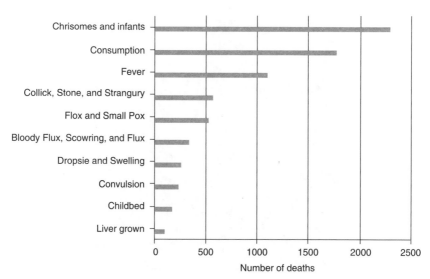

FIGURE 1–5   Yearly Mortality Bill for 1632: The 10 leading causes of mortality in Graunt's Time. *Source:* Data from Graunt J. *Natural and Political Observations, Mentioned in a Following Index, and Made upon the Bills of Mortality,* 2nd ed. London: Tho. Roycroft; 1662: p. 8.

gained popularity in Europe during the early 1700s, when the procedure was modified by injecting infectious material under the skin; variolation was first tested among abandoned children and prisoners. When it was declared safe, members of the English royal family were inoculated.

Edward Jenner (Figure 1–6) is credited with the development of the smallpox vaccination, a lower-risk method for conferring immunity against smallpox than variolation.[32] He was fascinated by folk wisdom, which suggested that dairy-maids who had contracted cowpox seemed to be immune to smallpox. Infection with the cowpox virus produced a much less severe form of disease than small-pox. Jenner conducted an experiment in which he used scabs from the cowpox lesions on the arm of a dairy maid, Sarah Nelmes (Figure 1–7), to create a small-pox vaccine. He then used the material to vaccinate an eight-year-old boy, James

FIGURE 1–6   Edward Jenner. *Source:* From the National Library of Medicine. Smallpox: A great and terrible scourge: Vaccination. Available at: http://www.nlm.nih.gov/exhibition/smallpox/sp_vaccination.html. Accessed October 11, 2007.

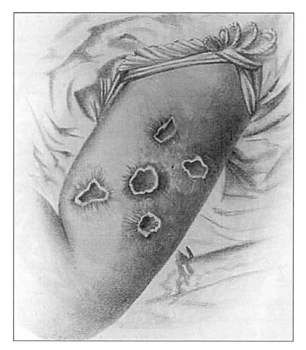

FIGURE 1–7   Arm of Sarah Nelmes with lesions of cowpox. *Source:* From the National Library of Medicine. Smallpox: A great and terrible scourge: Vaccination. Available at: http://www.nlm.nih.gov/exhibition/smallpox/sp_vaccination.html. Accessed October 11, 2007.

Phipps. Following the vaccination, Phipps appeared to develop immunity to the smallpox virus to which he was re-exposed several times subsequently. Later, Jenner vaccinated his own son and several other children, obtaining similar positive findings, which were published in 1798. (In 1978, smallpox was finally eliminated worldwide; as of 1972, routine vaccination of the nonmilitary population of the United States was discontinued.)[33]

Use of Natural Experiments

Snow investigated a cholera epidemic that occurred during the mid-19th century in Broad Street, Golden Square, London. Snow's work, a classic study that linked the cholera epidemic to contaminated water supplies, is noteworthy because it utilized many of the features of epidemiologic inquiry: a spot map of cases and tabulation of fatal attacks and deaths. Through the application of his keen powers of observation and inference, he developed the hypothesis that contaminated water might be associated with outbreaks of cholera. He made several observations that others had not previously made. One observation was that cholera was associated with water from one of two water supplies that served the Golden Square district of London.[34] Broad Street was served by two separate water companies, the Lambeth Company and the Southwark and Vauxhall Company. Lilienfeld and Lilienfeld[35] wrote:

> In London, several water companies were responsible for supplying water to different parts of the city. In 1849, Snow noted that the cholera rates were particularly high in those areas of London that were supplied by the Lambeth Company and the Southwark and Vauxhall Company, both of whom obtained their water from the Thames River at a point heavily polluted with sewage.[35(p. 36)]

Snow's account of the outbreak of 1849 is found in Exhibit 1–2.

Between 1849 and 1854 the Lambeth Company had its source of water relocated to a less contaminated part of the Thames. In 1854, another epidemic of cholera occurred. This epidemic was in an area that consisted of two-thirds of London's resident population south of the Thames and was being served by both companies. In this area, the two companies had their water mains laid out in an interpenetrating manner, so that houses on the same street were receiving their water from different sources.[35]

This was a naturally occurring situation, a "natural experiment," if you will, because in 1849 all residents received contaminated water from the two water companies. After 1849, the Lambeth Company used less contaminated water by relocating its water supply. Snow demonstrated that a disproportionate number of residents who contracted cholera in the 1854 outbreak used water from one water company, which received polluted water, in comparison with the other company, which used relatively unpolluted water.

Snow's methodology maintains contemporary relevance. His methods utilized logical organization of observations, a natural experiment, and a quantitative approach.[35] All these methods are hallmarks of present-day epidemiologic inquiry. Note that it is possible to visit the site of the pump that figured so prominently in Snow's investigation of cholera; a London public house on the original site of the pump has been named in Snow's honor. A replica of the pump is located nearby. Refer to Exhibit 1–3 for pictures and a reproduction of the text on the base of the replica.

Another study, occurring during the mid-19th century, also used nascent epidemiologic methods. Ignaz Semmelweis,[36] in his position as a clinical assistant in obstetrics and gynecology at a Vienna hospital, observed that women in the maternity wards were dying at high rates from puerperal fever. In 1840, when the medical education system changed, he found a much higher mortality rate among the women on the teaching wards for medical students and physicians than on the teaching wards for midwives. He postulated that medical students and physicians had contaminated their hands during autopsies. As a result, they transmitted infections while attending women in the maternity wards.[37] When the practice of hand washing with chlorinated solutions was introduced, the death rate for puerperal fever in the wards for medical students and physicians dropped to a rate equal to that in the wards for midwives.

EXHIBIT 1-2

Snow on Cholera

The most terrible outbreak of cholera which ever occurred in this kingdom, is probably that which took place in Broad Street, Golden Square, and the adjoining streets, a few weeks ago. Within two hundred and fifty yards of the spot where Cambridge Street joins Broad Street, there were upwards of five hundred fatal attacks of cholera in ten days. The mortality in this limited area probably equals any that was ever caused in this country, even by the plague; and it was much more sudden, as the greater number of cases terminated in a few hours. The mortality would undoubtedly have been much greater had it not been for the flight of the population. Persons in furnished lodgings left first, then other lodgers went away, leaving their furniture to be sent for when they could meet with a place to put it in. Many houses were closed altogether, owing to the death of the proprietors; and, in a great number of instances, the tradesmen who remained had sent away their families: so that in less than six days from the commencement of the outbreak, the most afflicted streets were deserted by more than three-quarters of their inhabitants.

There were a few cases of cholera in the neighbourhood of Broad Street, Golden Square, in the latter part of August; and the so-called outbreak, which commenced in the night between the 31st August and the 1st September, was, as in all similar instances, only a violent increase of the malady. As soon as I became acquainted with the situation and extent of this irruption of cholera, I suspected some contamination of the water of the much-frequented street-pump in Broad Street, near the end of

continues

EXHIBIT 1–2 *continued*

Cambridge Street; but on examining the water, on the evening of the 3rd September, I found so little impurity in it of an organic nature, that I hesitated to come to a conclusion. Further inquiry, however, showed me that there was no other circumstance or agent common to the circumscribed locality in which this sudden increase of cholera occurred, and not extending beyond it, except the water of the above mentioned pump. I found, moreover, that the water varied, during the next two days, in the amount of organic impurity, visible to the naked eye, on close inspection, in the form of small white, flocculent particles; and I concluded that, at the commencement of the outbreak, it might possibly have been still more impure.

The deaths which occurred during this fatal outbreak of cholera are indicated in the accompanying map [Figure 1–8, see a copy of the complete map at the end of the book], as far as I could ascertain them . . . The dotted line on the map surrounds the sub-districts of Golden Square, St. James's, and Berwick Street, St. James's, together with the adjoining portion of the sub-district of St. Anne, Soho, extending from Wardour Street to Dean Street, and a small part of the sub-district of St. James's Square enclosed by Marylebone Street, Titchfield Street, Great Windmill Street, and Brewer Street. All the deaths from cholera which were registered in the six weeks from 19th August to 30th September within this locality, as well as those of persons removed into Middlesex Hospital, are shown in the map by a black line in the situation of the house in which it occurred, or in which the fatal attack was contracted . . . The pump in Broad Street is indicated on the map, as well as all the surrounding pumps to which the public had access at the time. It requires to be stated that the water of the pump in Marlborough Street, at the end of Carnaby Street, was so impure that many people avoided using it. And I found that the persons who died near this pump in the beginning of September, had water from the Broad Street pump. With regard to the pump in Rupert Street, it will be noticed that some streets which are near to it on the map, are in fact a good way removed, on account of the circuitous road to it. These circumstances being taken into account, it will be observed that the deaths either very much diminished, or ceased altogether at every point where it becomes decidedly nearer to send to another pump than to the one in Broad Street.

continues

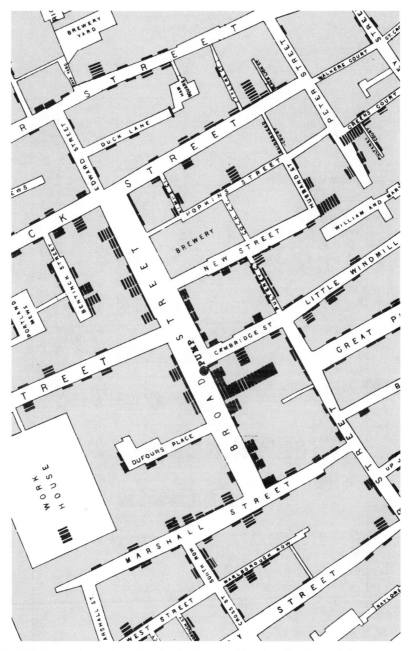

FIGURE 1–8   Cholera deaths in the neighborhood of Broad Street, August 19 to September 30, 1849. *Source*: Reprinted from Snow J. *Snow on Cholera,* pp. 38–51, Harvard University Press © 1965.

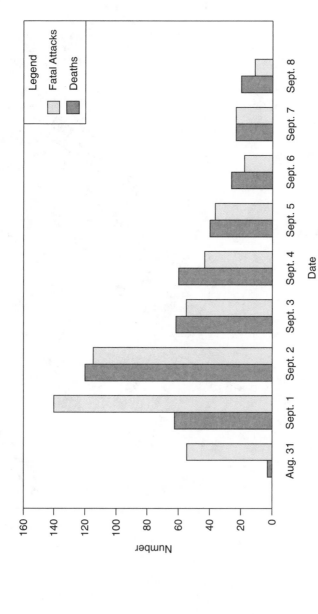

FIGURE 1–9   The 1849 cholera outbreak in Golden Square district, London. Fatal attacks and deaths, August 31–September 8. *Source:* Reprinted from Snow J. *Snow on Cholera,* p. 49, Harvard University Press, © 1965.

EXHIBIT 1–2 *continued*

It may also be noticed that the deaths are most numerous near to the pump where the water could be more readily obtained . . . The greatest number of attacks in any one day occurred on the 1st of September, immediately after the outbreak commenced. The following day the attacks fell from one hundred and forty-three to one hundred and sixteen, and the day afterwards to fifty-four . . . The fresh attacks continued to become less numerous every day. On September the 8th—the day when the handle of the pump was removed—there were twelve attacks; on the 9th, eleven; on the 10th, five; on the 11th, five; on the 12th, only one; and after this time, there were never more than four attacks on one day. During the decline of the epidemic the deaths were more numerous than the attacks, owing to the decrease of many persons who had lingered for several days in consecutive fever [Figure 1–9]. ■

Source: Reprinted from Snow J. *Snow on Cholera*, p. 38–51, Harvard University Press, © 1965.

William Farr

A contemporary of John Snow, William Farr assumed the post of "Compiler of Abstracts" at the General Register Office (located in England) in 1839 and held this position for 40 years. Among Farr's contributions to public health and epidemiology was the development of a more sophisticated system for codifying medical conditions than was previously in use. Farr's classification scheme, which departed from a narrow medical view, provided the foundation for the International Classification of Diseases in use today. Also noteworthy is the fact that Farr used data such as census reports to study occupational mortality in England. In addition, he explored the possible linkage between mortality rates and population density, showing that both the average number of deaths and births per 1,000 living persons increased with population density (defined as number of persons per square mile). Because of the excess of births over deaths in all except the most crowded areas, the population tended to increase in the less crowded areas. With respect to deaths in high mortality districts, such as Liverpool, which had a mortality rate more than 22 per 1,000 greater than that experienced in healthier districts, he attributed mortality to factors such as ". . . impurities of water, pernicious dirts, floating dusts, zynotic contagions, [and] crowdings in lodgings, . . ."[38(p. 90)] The healthier districts had ". . . a salubrious soil, and supply the inhabitants with water generally free from organic impurities."[38(pp. 90–91)]

Identification of Specific Agents of Disease

In the late 1800s, Robert Koch verified that a human disease was caused by a specific living organism. His epoch-making study, *Die Aetiologie der Tuberkulose,* was published in 1882. This breakthrough made possible greater refinement of the classification of disease by specific causal organisms.[39] Previously, the grouping together of diseases according to grosser classifications had hampered their epidemiologic study.

King[40] noted that Koch's postulates are usually formatted as follows:

1. The microorganism must be observed in every case of the disease.
2. It must be isolated and grown in pure culture.
3. The pure culture must, when inoculated into a susceptible animal, reproduce the disease.
4. The microorganism must be observed in, and recovered from, the experimentally diseased animal.[40]

King noted, "What Koch accomplished, in brief, was to demonstrate for the first time in any human disease a strict relation between a micro-organism and a disease."[40(p. 351)] This specification of the causal disease organism provided a definite criterion for the identification of a disease, rather than the vague standards Koch's predecessors and contemporaries had employed.

Increasing awareness of the role of microbial agents in the causation of human illness—the germ theory of disease—eventually reached the public health community. One method to limit the spread of infectious disease was through the use of cartoons published in the popular media. Figure 1–10 suggested that skirts that trail on the ground (in fashion around the turn of the 20th century) could bring deadly germs into the household.[41]

The 1918 Influenza Pandemic

So great was its impact, this outbreak has been referred to as "the Mother of All Pandemics."[42] Also known as the Spanish Flu, the pandemic that occurred during the period of 1918 to 1919 killed from 50 to 100 million persons worldwide. Estimates suggest that one-third of the world's population of 1.5 billion at the time was infected and developed clinically observable illness. This very severe form of influenza had case-fatality rates of approximately 2.5% compared with the 0.1% or lower rates observed in other influenza pandemics. Differentiating this form of influenza from other outbreaks was its impact on healthy young

FIGURE 1-10 Samuel D. Erhart, "The Trailing Skirt: Death Loves a Shining Mark," *Puck,* August 8, 1900 (original in color). *Source:* Reprinted with permission from Hansen B. The Image and Advocacy of Public Health in American Caricature and Cartoons from 1860 to 1900, *American Journal of Public Health,* Vol 87, No 11, p. 1805, ©1997, American Public Health Association.

EXHIBIT 1–3

A Visit to the Broad Street Pump and the Sir John Snow Public House, Located at 39 Broadwick Street, London, England W1F9QJ

FIGURE 1–11
Photograph of John Snow.

Figure 1–11 shows John Snow. Figure 1–12 displays a replica of the Broad Street pump, and Figure 1–13 presents a picture of the John Snow Pub. Broad Street has been renamed Broadwick Street. The following section is reprinted from a plaque at the base of the replica. The plaque describes "The Soho Cholera Epidemic":

"Dr. John Snow (1813–1858), a noted anaesthesiologist, lived near the focus of the 1854 Soho cholera epidemic, which centered on Broad Street, as Broadwick Street was then called. In September of that year alone, over 500 people died in Soho from the disease. Snow had studied cholera in the 1848–49 epidemic in Southwark and Wandsworth. His theory that polluted drinking water was the [source] of transmission of the disease [was] confirmed when he mapped cholera deaths in Soho with the source of the victims' drinking water. He found that they were concentrated on the Broad Street public water pump. His theory initially met with some disbelief but such was his conviction that he had the pump handle removed to prevent

continues

EXHIBIT 1–3 *continued*

its further use. Soon afterwards the outbreak ended. The original pump is believed to have been situated outside the nearby 'Sir John Snow Public House.'" ■

FIGURE 1–12   Replica of Broad Street pump near its approximate original location.

FIGURE 1–13   The John Snow Pub named in honor of the British Anesthesiologist.

adults; persons aged 20 to 40 accounted for nearly half of the mortality toll in this pandemic, whereas influenza deaths normally are more frequent among the very young and the very old.[43,44] The pandemic spread in three distinct waves during a one-year period throughout Europe, Asia, and North America; the first wave began in spring, 1918, with two subsequent waves occurring during the fall and winter of 1918 to 1919. In the United States, the flu's impact was so great that healthcare facilities were taxed to the limit. As a result of large numbers of deaths, the bodies of victims accumulated in morgues awaiting burial, which was delayed because of a shortage of coffins and morticians.

A repeat of the 1918 pandemic is within the realm of possibility, raising questions about how modern society would cope with such an event. Will healthcare facilities have adequate "surge" capacity to deal with a sudden and large increase in the number of flu patients? Will it be necessary to enforce "social distancing" to reduce the spread of epidemic flu? How will essential services be maintained? These are examples of issues for which the public health community will need to be prepared.

Other Significant Historical Developments

Alexander Fleming, Alexander Langmuir, Wade Hampton Frost, and Joseph Goldberger made several other historically significant contributions. Scottish researcher Fleming is credited with discovering the antimicrobial properties of the mold *Pencillium notatum* in 1928. This discovery led to development of the antibiotic penicillin, which became available toward the end of World War II. Langmuir, regarded as the father of infectious disease epidemiology, in 1949 established the epidemiology section of the federal agency presently called the Centers for Disease Control and Prevention. This section later came to be known as the Epidemiologic Intelligence Service (EIS), which celebrated its 50th anniversary in 2001 and is discussed later in this chapter. Frost, who held the first professorship of epidemiology in the United States beginning in 1930 at Johns Hopkins University, advocated the use of quantitative methods to illuminate public health problems, although his concept of epidemiology tended to be restricted narrowly to the study of infectious diseases. (Frost's seminal work on cohort analysis is covered in Chapter 7.) Finally, Goldberger's discovery of the cure for pellagra, a nutritional deficiency disease characterized by the so-called three Ds (dermatitis, diarrhea, and dementia), led to reductions in the occurrence of the disease, which had gained attention in the early 1900s.

Recent Applications of Epidemiology

Epidemiologic activity has exploded during the past several decades.[45] For example, the ongoing Framingham Heart Study, begun in 1948, is one of the pioneering research investigations of risk factors for coronary heart disease.[46] Another development, occurring after World War II, was research on the association between smoking and lung cancer.[47] An example is the work of Doll and Peto,[48] based on a fascinating study of British physicians.

The computer and powerful statistical software have aided the proliferation of epidemiologic research studies. Popular interest in epidemiologic findings is also intense. Almost every day now, one encounters media reports of epidemiologic research into such diverse health concerns as acquired immune deficiency syndrome, chemical spills, breast cancer screening, and the health effects of secondhand cigarette smoke. Table 1–2 reports triumphs in epidemiology; these are

Table 1–2   Triumphs in Epidemiology

Risk Factor Categories	Disease	Risk Factors	Direction
Alcohol	Esophageal cancer	alcohol (interaction with smoking)	IR
Viruses	Liver cancer	hepatitis B virus	IR
	Burkitt lymphoma	Epstein Barr virus	IR
	Kaposi sarcoma	Herpes simplex virus type B	IR
	Cervical cancer	something transmitted sexually (human papilloma virus)	IR
	Nasopharyngeal carcinoma	Epstein Barr virus	IR
	Yellow fever	"something transmitted by mosquitos" (*Flavivirus*)	IR
	New variant (nv) Creutzfeldt-Jacob disease	prions (interaction with genotype)	IR
Bacteria	Cholera	"something in water" (*Vibrio cholera*)	IR
	Peptic ulcer	*Helicobactor pylori*	IR
	Puerperal fever	"something on doctor's hands" (group B *Streptococcus*)	IR
Nutrition	Pellagra	"something in bread" (niacin)	P
	Neural tube defects	folic acid, folate	P
	Oral clefts	folic acid	P
Occupation	Lung cancer	asbestos (interaction with smoking)	IR
	Bladder cancer	aniline dye	IR
	Mesothelioma	asbestos	IR
	Lung cancer	asbestos (interaction with smoking)	IR
	Angiosarcoma	vinyl chloride	IR
	Infertility (male)	DBCP	IR
	Nasal cancer	nickel smelting	IR
	Lung cancer	"something in uranium mines" (interaction with smoking)	IR

continues

Table 1–2 *continued*

Risk Factor Categories	Disease	Risk Factors	Direction
Environment	Dental caries	fluoride [deficiency]	P
	Cancer	arsenic	IR
Drugs/ Devices	Myocardial infarction	aspirin	P
	Micoagthnia	iso-retinene during pregnancy	IR
	Pelvic inflammatory disease	Dalkon Shield IUD	IR
	Septic abortion	Dalkon Shield IUD	IR
Hormones	Clear cell adenocarcinoma of the vagina	diethylstilbestrol prenatally	IR
	Venous thromboembolism	combined estrogen/progestin (oral contraceptives)	IR
	Venous thromboembolism	postmenopausal estrogen	IR
	Ovarian cancer	oral contraceptives	P
	Endometrial cancer	combined estrogen/progestin	P
	Endometrial cancer	oral contraceptives: postmenopausal estrogen	IR
	Iron deficiency anemia	oral contraceptives	P
	Benign breast disease	oral contraceptives	P
	Myocardial infarction	oral contraceptives (interaction with smoking)	IR
	Ischemic stroke	oral contraceptives (interaction with hypertension; modified by dose)	IR
Genetics	Breast cancer	"something genetic" (*BRCA1, BRCA2* mutations)	IR
	Ovarian cancer	"something genetic" (*BRCA2* mutations)	IR
	Colon cancer	"something genetic" (*APC1* mutations)	IR
Miscellaneous	Toxic shock syndrome	super absorbent tampons	IR
	SIDS	prone sleep position	IR
	Reyes syndrome	aspirin (interaction with infection)	IR
Smoking	Lung cancer	smoking	IR
	Coronary disease	smoking	IR
	Hemorrhagic stroke	smoking	IR
	Ischemic stroke	smoking	IR
	Abdominal aortic aneurism	smoking	IR
	Peripheral vascular disease	smoking	IR
	Parkinson's disease	smoking	P
	Ulcerative colitis	smoking	P
	Laryngeal cancer	smoking	IR
	Intrauterine growth retardation	smoking during pregnancy	IR
	Toxemia/pre-eclampsia	smoking during pregnancy	P

Abbreviations: IR, increased risk; P, protective (see Chapters 3, 6, and 7).

Source: Compiled by Diane Petitti. Adapted with permission from *The Epidemiology Monitor,* October 2001, p. 6.

examples in which epidemiologists have identified risk factors for cancer, heart disease, infectious diseases, and many other conditions. One triumph in Table 1–2 is how epidemiology helped to uncover the association between the human papilloma virus and cervical cancer. On June 8, 2006, the FDA announced the licensing of the first vaccine (Gardisil®) to prevent cervical cancer caused by four types of human papillomavirus and approved its use in females aged 9 to 26 years. Returning to Table 1–2, the reader should note that although many of the terms used in the table have not yet been discussed in this book, later sections of the text will cover some of them. Additional examples of applications of epidemiology are provided below.

Infectious Diseases in the Community

Infectious disease epidemiology, one of the most familiar types of epidemiology, investigates the occurrence of epidemics of infectious and communicable diseases. Examples are studying diseases caused by bacteria, viruses, and microbiologic agents; tracking down the cause of foodborne illness; and investigating new diseases such as SARS and avian influenza (Exhibit 1–4). An illustration is the use of epidemiologic methods to attempt to eradicate, when possible, polio, measles, smallpox, and other communicable diseases. Another example is outbreaks of infectious diseases in hospitals (nosocomial infections). More information about this topic is presented in Chapter 12. The role of the Epidemic Intelligence Service in investigating disease outbreaks is defined as follows:

> The Epidemic Intelligence Service (EIS) is a corps of disease detectives who work for the Centers for Disease Control (CDC) in Atlanta, Georgia. The EIS consists of approximately 65 physicians, nurses, and other public health experts who are on call 24 hours a day for two years. Up to 3,000 disease outbreaks occur each year in the United States. EIS officers may be responsible for tracking down unusual disease outbreaks in the United States as well as in foreign countries. For example, an outbreak of cholera in Guinea-Bissau, Africa, was linked to the body of a dockworker smuggled home for burial. About half of the participants at a funeral feast for the deceased later developed cholera. Other investigative work has included: measles outbreaks, hepatitis in a day care center, tuberculosis in New York City, and Lyme disease in Connecticut. The CDC monitors a wide range of health conditions that include influenza epidemics, chronic diseases, such as heart disease, and AIDS.[49]

Health and the Environment

Occupational exposure, air pollution, contaminated drinking water, accidental injuries, and other environmental agents may affect human health. Occupational

EXHIBIT 1-4

Avian Influenza (H5N1)

Investigations into an outbreak of highly pathogenic avian influenza demonstrate the role of epidemiology in containing outbreaks of infectious diseases that threaten the health of the population. The arrival of avian influenza (caused by the H5N1 virus) that began in the late 1990s is an example of the occurrence of an infectious disease with potential to impact a specific community as well as the entire world. This highly fatal condition worried public health authorities who were concerned that avian influenza could create a worldwide pandemic, mirroring the 1918 pandemic and lesser influenza epidemics that occurred later in the 20th century. The emergence of a pandemic might be the consequence of mutation of the virus into a version that could be communicated rapidly on a person-to-person basis.

Beginning in 1997, avian influenza appeared in Hong Kong, with an initial 18 human cases, of which 6 were fatal.[50] These human cases coincided with outbreaks among poultry on farms and in markets that sold live poultry. Authorities destroyed the entire chicken population in Hong Kong; subsequently, no additional human cases linked to the source in Hong Kong were reported. Two additional human cases were reported in Hong Kong in 2003 and were associated with travel to mainland China.

The epidemic did not end in Hong Kong: additional cases began appearing in Southeast Asia during late 2003. Virus outbreaks involving animals and humans were limited primarily to Vietnam and some other areas of Southeast Asia (e.g., Thailand). One case of probable person-to-person spread of H5N1 virus is believed to have occurred in Thailand. Then, in 2005, the virus manifested itself in central Asia, spreading to Europe, Africa, and the Middle East. From December 1, 2003, to April 30, 2006, nine countries reported a total of 205 laboratory-verified cases to the World Health Organization with 113 of these illnesses being fatal. At about the same time, infection with the virus was reported among flocks of domestic and wild birds in 50 countries.

Officials remain concerned that migrating flocks of wild birds that cover a vast geographical area could spread H5N1 to domestic poultry in many parts of the world (Figure 1–14).[51] Humans who come into contact

continues

EXHIBIT 1–4 *continued*

FIGURE 1–14   Pathogenic avian influenza (H5N1) can appear in wild and domestic avian flocks.

with these domestic birds would be at risk of contracting the highly pathogenic virus. The theoretical possibility remains that the virus could mutate into a form that is transmissible from person to person. Worldwide, epidemiologists have been involved with tracking and surveillance of the H5N1 virus. By November 2007, a total of 335 cases and 206 deaths had occurred worldwide. In 2007, Indonesia and Egypt accounted for more than 80% of the 72 cases of avian influenza that were reported during that year. ■

and environmental epidemiology address the occurrence and distribution of conditions such as dust diseases, occupational dermatoses, or diseases linked to harmful physical energy, such as ionizing radiation from x-ray machines or other sources. Many of the diseases studied by environmental epidemiologists have agent factors and manifestations similar to those in occupational epidemiology, for example, the role of pesticides in causing environmentally associated illness.

Injury control epidemiology studies risk factors associated with motor vehicle accidents, bicycle injuries, falls, and occupational injuries. Study results may suggest preventive measures by modifying the environment. Reproductive and perinatal epidemiology investigates environmental and occupational exposures and birth outcomes. Related topics are sudden infant death syndrome, epidemiology of neonatal brain hemorrhage, early pregnancy, and methodological issues in drug epidemiology. Chapter 13 covers environmental and occupational epidemiology.

Chronic Disease, Lifestyle, and Health Promotion

An example of this category is the role of lifestyle (e.g., exercise, diet, smoking, and alcohol consumption) in physical health outcomes such as obesity, coronary heart disease, arthritis, diabetes, and cancer. Hypothesized risk factors studied include antecedent variables within the person's physical and psychosocial environment that may be associated with health and disease. To illustrate, there have been studies of the relationship between obesity and the tendency of the built environment to dissuade people from walking. Also, poor dietary choices, smoking, substance abuse, and excessive alcohol consumption are linked to many chronic illnesses. Regarding the psychosocial environment, cultural practices affect behaviors that are linked to health and disease. More information about this topic is presented in Chapters 4 and 15.

Psychological and Social Factors in Health

Stress, social support, and socioeconomic status may affect mental health and physical illnesses such as arthritis, some gastrointestinal conditions, and essential hypertension. A related area involves epidemiologic studies of personality factors and disease, exemplified by the type A personality and its potential link to heart disease. Psychiatric epidemiology is concerned with the distribution and determinants of mental illness. Examples are the definition and measurement of mental illness, social factors related to mental illness, and urban and rural differences in frequency of mental disorders. Major research studies have investigated the epidemiology of depressive symptomatology. Also studied are factors that affect the distribution of mental retardation, including certain genetic syndromes. Social, cultural, and demographic factors (socioeconomic status, gender, employment, marital status, and race) are considered correlates of mental health status. Chapter 15 considers this area in more detail.

Molecular and Genetic Epidemiology

Genetic epidemiology studies the distribution of genetically associated diseases among the population. For example, research on the genetic bases for disease hypothesized possible inherited susceptibility to severe alcoholism[52] and to breast and ovarian cancer.[53] Molecular epidemiology applies the techniques of molecular biology to epidemiologic studies. An illustration is the use of genetic and molecular markers, including deoxyribonucleic acid typing, to examine their influence upon behavioral outcomes and host susceptibility to disease. An overview of molecular and genetic epidemiology is provided in Chapter 14.

Conclusion

Epidemiology is the study of the distribution and determinants of diseases, states of health, disability, morbidity, and mortality in the population. Epidemiology, which examines disease occurrence in the population rather than in the individual, is sometimes called population medicine. Several examples demonstrated that the etiologic bases of disease and health conditions in the population are often unknown. Epidemiology is used as a tool to suggest factors associated with occurrence of disease and to introduce methods to control disease in the population.

Three aspects characterize the epidemiologic approach. The first is quantification, that is, counting of cases of disease and construction of tables that show variation of disease by time, place, and person. The second is use of special vocabulary, for example, epidemic and epidemic frequency of disease. The third is its interdisciplinary composition, which draws from microbiology, biostatistics, social and behavioral sciences, and clinical medicine.

The historical antecedents of epidemiology began with Hippocrates, who implicated the environment as a factor in disease causation. Second, Graunt, one of the biostatistics pioneers, compiled vital statistics in the mid-1600s. Third, Snow used natural experiments to track a cholera outbreak in Golden Square, London. Finally, Koch's postulates advanced the theory of specific disease agents. At present, epidemiology is relevant to many kinds of health problems found in the community.

Study Questions and Exercises

1. Using your own words, give a definition of epidemiology. Before you read Chapter 1, what were your impressions regarding the scope of

epidemiology? Based on the material presented in this chapter, what topics are covered by epidemiology? That is, to what extent does epidemiology focus exclusively upon the study of infectious diseases or upon other types of diseases and conditions?

2. How would the clinical and epidemiologic descriptions of a disease differ, and how would they be similar?

3. To what extent does epidemiology rely on medical disciplines for its content, and to what extent does it draw upon other disciplines? Explain the statement that epidemiology is interdisciplinary.

4. Describe the significance for epidemiology of the following historical developments:
   a. associating the environment with disease causality
   b. use of vital statistics
   c. use of natural experiments
   d. identification of specific agents of disease

5. Explain what is meant by the following components of the definition of epidemiology:
   a. determinants
   b. distribution
   c. morbidity and mortality

6. The following questions pertain to the term epidemic.
   a. What is meant by an epidemic? Give a definition in your own words.
   b. Describe a scenario in which only one or two cases of disease may represent an epidemic.
   c. What is the purpose of surveillance?
   d. Give an example of a disease that has cyclic patterns.
   e. What is the epidemic threshold for a disease? In what sense is it possible to conceive of the epidemic threshold as a statistical concept?

7. Epidemiologic research and findings often receive dramatic media coverage. Find an article in a media source (e.g., *The New York Times*) on a topic related to epidemiology. In a one-page essay, summarize the findings and discuss how the article illustrates the approach of epidemiology to the study of diseases (health conditions) in populations.

8. During the next week, read your local or national newspaper carefully. Try to find the following terms used in newspaper articles; keep a record of them and describe how they are used:
   a. epidemiology
   b. epidemiologist

    c. infectious disease

    d. chronic disease

    e. clinical trial

    f. increased risk of mortality associated with a new medication

9. What is the definition of a natural experiment? Identify any recent examples of natural experiments. To what extent might changes in legislation to limit smoking in public places or to increase the speed limit on highways be considered natural experiments?

10. Review Exhibit 1–2, Snow on Cholera. What do you believe was the purpose of each of the following observations by Snow?

    a. "small white, flocculent particles" in the water from the Broad Street pump

    b. the location of cholera deaths as shown in Figure 1–8

    c. people who died avoided the pump in Marlborough Street and instead had the water from the Broad Street pump

    d. "the greatest number of attacks in any one day occurred on the 1st of September, . . ."

    e. "On September 8th—the day when the handle of the pump was removed . . ." To what extent do you think removing the pump handle was effective in stopping the disease outbreak?

11. How does quantification support the accomplishment of the four aims of epidemiology?

12. How did Koch's postulates contribute to the advancement of epidemiology? To what extent is identification of specific agent factors a prerequisite for tracking down the causes of disease outbreaks?

13. What are the characteristics that distinguish pandemic disease from epidemic disease? Name some examples of notorious pandemics that occurred in history. Why did the "Spanish Flu" of 1918 qualify as a pandemic? In giving your answer, be sure to distinguish among the terms epidemic, pandemic, and endemic.

14. Identify some infectious diseases that could reach pandemic occurrence during the 21st century. What conditions do you believe exist at present that could incite the occurrence of pandemics? Why have public health officials been concerned about the emergence of new diseases such as "bird flu"? Speculate about what might happen to organized society and the health care system should an outbreak of pandemic influenza occur.

15. The Black Death that occurred during the Middle Ages eradicated a large proportion of the world population at that time. Estimate how likely it

would be for a similar epidemic of plague to develop during the current decade.

16. In developed countries, many safeguards exist for the prevention of food-borne illness. Discuss how it would be possible for a foodborne illness outbreak such as the one caused by *E. coli* to erupt in a developed country.

References

1. Centers for Disease Control and Prevention. *Update on Multi-State Outbreak of* E. coli *O157:H7 Infections From Fresh Spinach*, October 6, 2006. Available at: http://www.cdc.gov/foodborne/ecolispinach/100606.htm. Accessed October 10, 2007.

2. Centers for Disease Control and Prevention. Ongoing multistate outbreak of *Escherichia coli* serotype O157:H7 infections associated with consumption of fresh spinach—United States, September 2006. *MMWR.* 2006;55:1045–1046.

3. State of California, Department of Health Services. *CDHS* E-Coli *Update for Oct. 18, 2006.* Available at: http://www.dhs.ca.gov/opa/ecoli. Accessed October 10, 2007.

4. U.S. Food and Drug Administration. *FDA News: FDA Statement on Foodborne* E. coli *O157:H7 Outbreak in Spinach.* Available at: http://www.fda.gov/bbs/topics/NEWS/2006/NEW01489.html. Accessed October 10, 2007.

5. Centers for Disease Control and Prevention, Foodborne and Diarrheal Diseases Branch. *Multistate outbreak of* E. coli *O157 infections, November–December 2006.* Available at: http://www.cdc.gov/ecoli/2006/december/121406.htm. Accessed October 10, 2007.

6. Karin M. Anthrax invades and evades the immune system to cause widespread infection. *Environmental Health News, Highlights in Environmental Health Sciences Research, 2002 Highlights.* Division of Extramural Research and Training, National Institute of Environmental Health Sciences. 2002:1–2. Available at: http://www.niehs.nih.gov/research/supported/sep/2002/anthrax.cfm. Accessed October 10, 2007.

7. Hughes JM, Gerberding JL. Anthrax bioterrorism: Lessons learned and future directions. *Emerg Infect Dis* [serial online]. 2002;8:1–4. Available at: http://www.cdc.gov/ncidod/EID/vol8no10/02-0466.htm. Accessed January 2, 2008.

8. Centers for Disease Control and Prevention. Update: Investigation of bioterrorism-related anthrax and interim guidelines for clinical evaluation of persons with possible anthrax. *MMWR.* 2001;50:941–948.

9. Maillard J-M, Fischer M, McKee KT Jr, et al. First case of bioterrorism-related inhalational anthrax, Florida, 2001: North Carolina investigation. *Emerg Infect Dis* [serial online]. 2002;8(10). Available at: http://www.cdc.gov/ncidod/EID/vol8no10/02-0389.htm. Accessed October 10, 2007.

10. Centers for Disease Control and Prevention. Ongoing investigation of anthrax—Florida, October 2001. *MMWR.* 2001;50:877.

11. Centers for Disease Control and Prevention. Update: investigation of bioterrorism-related anthrax—Connecticut, 2001. *MMWR.* 2001;50:1077–1079.

12. Mathews T, Lee ED. Outbreak of fear. *Newsweek.* 1995; May 22:48, 50.

13. Fear on Seventh Ave. *Newsweek.* 1978; September 18:30.

14. Centers for Disease Control and Prevention. Red spots on airline flight attendants. *MMWR.* 1980;29:141.

15. Friis RH, Nanjundappa G, Prendergast T, et al. Hispanic coronary heart disease mortality and risk in Orange County, California. *Public Health Rep.* 1981;96:418–422.

16. Lilienfeld DE. Definitions of epidemiology. *Am J Epidemiol.* 1978;107:87–90.

17. Mausner JS, Kramer S. *Epidemiology: An Introductory Text,* 2nd ed. Philadelphia: Saunders; 1985.

18. Terris M. The epidemiologic tradition. *Public Health Rep.* 1979;94:203–209.

19. Syme SL. Behavioral factors associated with the etiology of physical disease: a social epidemiological approach. *Am J Public Health.* 1974;64:1043–1045.

20. Centers for Disease Control and Prevention. Update: Outbreak of severe acute respiratory syndrome—worldwide, 2003. *MMWR.* 2003;52:244.

21. Fingerhut LA, Warner M. *Injury Chartbook. Health, United States, 1996–97.* Hyattsville, MD: National Center for Health Statistics; 1997.

22. MacMahon B, Pugh TF. *Epidemiology Principles and Methods.* Boston: Little, Brown; 1970.

23. Heymann DL, ed. *Control of Communicable Diseases Manual,* 18th ed. Washington, DC: American Public Health Association; 2004.

24. Snow J. *Snow on Cholera.* Cambridge, MA: Harvard University Press; 1965.

25. Marks G, Beatty WK. *Epidemics.* New York: Scribner's; 1976.

26. Hippocrates. *On Airs, Waters, and Places.* In: Adams F, ed. *The Genuine Works of Hippocrates.* New York: Wood; 1886.

27. McEvedy C. The Bubonic Plague. *Scientific American.* 1988;258(Feb):118–123.

28. National Institutes of Health, National Institute of Allergy and Infectious Diseases. Plague. Available at: http://www.niaid.nih.gov/factsheets/plague.htm. Accessed October 10, 2007.

29. Graunt J. *Natural and Political Observations, Mentioned in a Following Index, and Made Upon the Bills of Mortality,* 2nd ed. London: Tho. Roycroft; 1662.

30. Kargon R. John Graunt, Francis Bacon, and the Royal Society: the reception of statistics. *J Hist Med Allied Sci.* 1963;October:337–348.

31. National Library of Medicine. *Smallpox: A Great and Terrible Scourge: Variolation.* Available at: http://www.nlm.nih.gov/exhibition/smallpox/sp_variolation.html. Accessed October 10, 2007.

32. National Library of Medicine. *Smallpox: A Great and Terrible Scourge: Vaccination.* Available at: http://www.nlm.nih.gov/exhibition/smallpox/sp_vaccination.html. Accessed October 10, 2007.

33. Centers for Disease Control and Prevention. Smallpox. Available at: http://www.bt.cdc.gov/training/smallpoxvaccine/reactions/smallpox.html. Accessed October 10, 2007.

34. Enterline PE. Epidemiology: "nothing more than common sense?" *Occup Health Saf.* 1979;January/February:45–47.

35. Lilienfeld AM, Lilienfeld DE. *Foundations of Epidemiology,* 2nd ed. New York: Oxford University Press; 1980.

36. Semmelweis IP, Murphy FB, trans. *The Etiology, the Concept and Prophylaxis of Childbed Fever* (1861). In: *Med Classics.* 1941;5:350–773.

37. Iffy L, Kaminetzky HA, Maidman JE, et al. Control of perinatal infection by traditional preventive measures. *Obstet Gynecol.* 1979;54:403–411.

38. Whitehead M. William Farr's legacy to the study of inequalities in health. *Bull World Health Organ.* 2000;78:86–96.

39. Susser M. *Causal Thinking in the Health Sciences.* New York: Oxford University Press; 1973.

40. King LS. Dr Koch's postulates. *J Hist Med.* Autumn 1952:350–361.

41. Hansen B. The image and advocacy of public health in American caricature and cartoons from 1860 to 1900. *Am J Public Health.* 1997;87:1798–1807.

42. Taubenberger JK, Morens DM. 1918 influenza: the mother of all pandemics. *Emerg Infect Dis.* 2006;12:15–22.

43. PandemicFlu.gov. Pandemics and pandemic threats since 1900. Available at: http://pandemicflu.gov/general/historicaloverview.html. Accessed October 10, 2007.

44. Billings M. The influenza pandemic of 1918. Available at: http://www.stanford.edu/group/virus/uda/. Accessed October 10, 2007.

45. Rothman KJ. *Modern Epidemiology.* Boston: Little, Brown; 1986.

46. Kannell WB, Abbott RD. Incidence and prognosis of unrecognized myocardial infarction: an update on the Framingham study. *N Engl J Med.* 1984;311:1144–1147.

47. Monson RR. *Occupational Epidemiology.* Boca Raton, FL: CRC Press; 1990.

48. Doll R, Peto R. Mortality in relation to smoking: 20 years' observation on male British doctors. *Br Med J.* 1976;2:1525–1536.

49. Jaret P. The disease detectives. *National Geogr Mag.* 1991;January:116–140.

50. World Health Organization. Epidemiology of WHO-confirmed human cases of avian influenza A (H5N1) infection. *Weekly Epidemiological Record.* 2006;81:249–260.

51. Centers for Disease Control and Prevention. Avian influenza (bird flu). Spread of avian influenza viruses among birds. Available at: http://www.cdc.gov/flu/avian/gen-info/spread.htm. Accessed October 10, 2007.

52. Blum K, Noble EP, Sheridan PJ, et al. Association of the A1 allele of the D2 dopamine receptor gene with severe alcoholism. *Alcohol.* 1991;8:409–416.

53. Biesecker BB, Boehnke M, Calzone K, et al. Genetic counseling for families with inherited susceptibility to breast cancer and ovarian cancer. *JAMA.* 1993;269:1970–1974.

CHAPTER 2

Practical Applications of Epidemiology

LEARNING OBJECTIVES

By the end of this chapter the reader will be able to:

- discuss uses and applications of epidemiology
- define the influence of population dynamics on community health
- state how epidemiology may be used for operations research
- discuss the clinical applications of epidemiology
- cite causal mechanisms from the epidemiologic perspective

CHAPTER OUTLINE

I. Introduction
II. Applications for the Assessment of the Health Status of Populations and Delivery of Health Services
III. Applications Relevant to Disease Etiology
IV. Conclusion
V. Study Questions and Exercises

Introduction

This chapter provides a broad overview of the range of applications of the epidemiologic approach. As the basic method of public health, epidemiology touches many aspects of the health sciences (see Exhibit 2–1 for a statement of seven uses of epidemiology[1]). Among its applications, epidemiology is used to help define the full clinical picture of a disease. By describing the occurrence of disease in the community, epidemiology helps public health practioners and administrators plan for allocation of resources. Once needed services are implemented, the epidemiologic approach can help evaluate their function and utility. The first part of this chapter considers these types of applications.

The second part of the chapter focuses on applications of epidemiology that are relevant to disease etiology. The causes of many diseases remain unknown; epidemiologists in research universities and federal and private agencies continue to search for clues as to the nature of disease. Knowledge that is acquired through such research may be helpful in efforts to prevent the occurrence of disease. Results of these types of epidemiologic studies are often quite newsworthy. A 1990 editorial in the *New England Journal of Medicine* was devoted to the issue of the growing number of epidemiologic studies being reported.[2] Among the key reasons for the proliferation of these studies were, first, that they concentrate on associations between diseases and possible lifestyle factors, such as a habit, type of behavior, or some element of the diet, that presumably can be changed. Consequently, "The reports are . . . often of great interest to the popular media and the public, as well as to physicians interested in preventive medicine."[2(p. 823)] A second reason is that the major diseases that are predominant in American society are "chronic, degenerative diseases that probably have several contributing causes, some of which have to do with life style, operating over long periods."[2(p. 823)] The editorial pointed out:

> It is usually very difficult to investigate such risk factors through experimental (or interventional) studies. In some cases it is impractical and in some it is unethical. For example, researchers cannot expose half of a group of children to lead for 10 years to compare their IQs 20 years later with those of the unexposed children. We must therefore rely on epidemiologic (or observational) studies.[2(p. 823)]

Because of the increasingly important function that epidemiology performs in clinical decision-making, this chapter also touches on some of the valuable considerations of this application. Finally, a few words of caution are presented on limitations of epidemiology in determining the cause of disease. To permit a fuller understanding of these issues, there is coverage of the general concept of causality.

EXHIBIT 2–1

Seven Uses of Epidemiology

The epidemiological method is the only way of asking some questions in medicine, one way of asking others, and no way at all to ask many. Several uses of epidemiology have been described:

1. To study the *history of the health of populations,* and of the rise and fall of diseases and changes in their character. Useful projections into the future may be possible.

2. To *diagnose the health of the community* and the condition of the people, to measure the true dimensions and distribution of ill-health in terms of incidence, prevalence, disability and mortality; to set health problems in perspective and define their relative importance; to identify groups needing special attention. Ways of life change, and with them the community's health; new measurements for monitoring them must therefore constantly be sought.

3. To study the *working of health services* with a view to their improvement. Operational research translates knowledge of (changing) community health and expectations in terms of needs for services and measure [sic] how these are met. The success of services delivered in reaching stated norms, and the effects on community health—and its needs—have to be appraised, in relation to resources. Such knowledge may be applied in action research pioneering better services, and in drawing up plans for the future. Timely information on health and health services is itself a key service requiring much study and experiment. Today, information is required at many levels, from the local district to the international.

4. To estimate from the group experience what are the *individual* risks on average of disease, accident and defect, and the *chances* of avoiding them.

5. To *identify syndromes* by describing the distribution and association of clinical phenomena in the population.

continues

EXHIBIT 2–1 *continued*

6. To *complete the clinical picture* of chronic diseases and describe their natural history: by including in due proportion all kinds of patients, wherever they present, together with the undemanding and the symptomless cases who do not present and whose needs may be as great; by following the course of remission and relapse, adjustment and disability in defined populations. Follow-up of cohorts is necessary to detect early sub-clinical and perhaps reversible disease and to discover precursor abnormalities during the pathogenesis which may offer opportunities for prevention.

7. To *search for causes* of health and disease by computing the experience of groups defined by their composition, inheritance and experience, their behaviour [sic] and environments. To confirm particular causes of the chronic diseases and the patterns of multiple causes, describing their mode of operation singly and together, and to assess their importance in terms of the relative risks of those exposed. Postulated causes will often be tested in naturally occurring *experiments of opportunity* and sometimes by *planned experiments*. ■

Source: Reprinted from Morris JN. *Uses of Epidemiology*, 3rd ed., pp. 262–263, © 1975, with permission of Elsevier.

Applications for the Assessment of the Health Status of Populations and Delivery of Health Services

As noted by Morris,[1] principal uses of epidemiology under this category include the history of the health of populations, diagnosis of the health of the community, and the working of health services.

Historical Use of Epidemiology: Study of Past and Future Trends in Health and Illness

An example of the historical use of epidemiology is the study of changes in disease frequency over time (secular trends). Illnesses that afflict humanity, with certain exceptions, have shown dramatic changes in industrialized nations from the beginning of modern medicine to the present day. In general, chronic conditions have replaced acute infectious diseases as the major causes of morbidity and mortality in contemporary industrialized societies.

Figure 2–1 identifies the top 10 causes of death for two contrasting years: 1900 and 2003. The data show that influenza moved from top position in 1900 to seventh in 2003; diseases of the heart became the leading cause of death, and

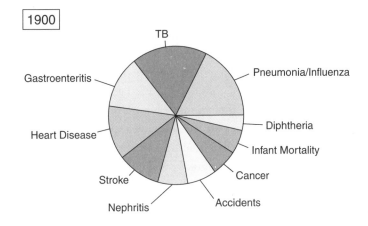

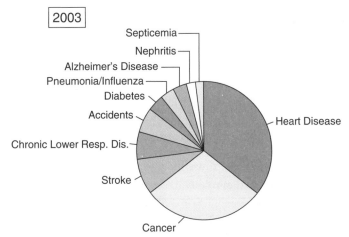

FIGURE 2–1 Leading causes of mortality, 1900 and 2003. *Source:* Data from Ventura SJ et al., Statistical Abstract of the United States: 1957, p. 69, U.S. Bureau of the Census; and from Hoyert DL, Heron MP, Murphy SL, Kung H. Deaths: Final Data for 2003, *National Vital Statistics Reports.* Vol 46, No 13, p. 5. Hyattsville, MD: National Center for Health Statistics, 2006.

the overall death rate from all causes declined drastically during this period of about one century.

The leading causes of death over decades of time have shown marked changes (Figure 2–2). In determining the reasons for these trends, one must take into account certain conditions that may affect the reliability of observed changes. According to MacMahon and Pugh, these are "variation in diagnosis, reporting, case fatality, or some other circumstance other than a true change of incidence."[3(p. 159)] Specific examples are as follows:

- Lack of comparability over time due to altered diagnostic criteria. The diagnostic criteria used in a later time period reflect new knowledge about disease; some categories of disease used in earlier eras may be omitted altogether. The diagnostic criteria may be more precise at a later time; for instance, considerable information has been obtained over three-quarters of a century about the chronic diseases. In some cases, when changes in diagnostic procedures are due to known alterations in diagnostic coding systems, the changes will be abrupt and readily identifiable.
- Aging of the general population. As the population ages as a result of reduced impact of infectious diseases, improved medical care, and a decline in the death rate, there may be greater uncertainty about the precise cause of death. Also, there may be inaccurate assignment of the underlying cause of death when older individuals are affected by chronic disease because multiple organ systems may fail simultaneously.
- Changes in the fatal course of the condition. Such changes would be reflected over the long run in decreases in the number of people with disease who actually die of it.

Despite the factors that reduce the reliability of observed changes in morbidity and mortality, four trends in disorders may be identified[4]: disappearing, residual, persisting, and new epidemic disorders. These are defined as follows:

- Disappearing disorders are those disorders that were formerly common sources of morbidity and mortality in developed countries but that at present have nearly disappeared in their epidemic form. Under this category are smallpox (currently eradicated), poliomyelitis, and other diseases that have been brought under control by means of immunizations, improvement in sanitary conditions, and the use of antibiotics and other medications.
- Residual disorders are diseases for which the key contributing factors are largely known but specific methods of control have not been effectively implemented. The sexually transmitted diseases, perinatal and infant mor-

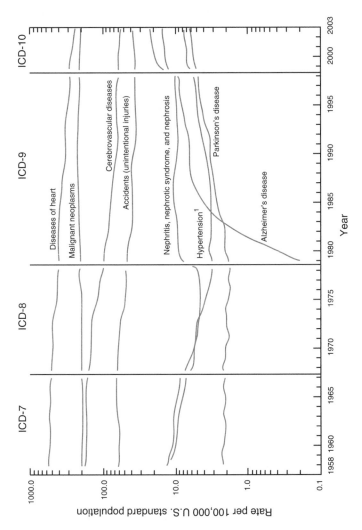

FIGURE 2–2 Age-adjusted death rates for selected causes of death in the United States from 1958 to 2003. *Source:* From Hoyert DL, Heron MP, Murphy SL, Kung H. Deaths: Final Data for 2003, *National Vital Statistics Reports.* Vol 46, No 13, p. 8. Hyattsville, MD: National Center for Health Statistics; 2006.

tality among the economically disadvantaged, and health problems associated with use of tobacco and alcohol are examples.

- Persisting disorders are diseases that remain common because an effective method of prevention or cure evades discovery. Some forms of cancer and mental disorders are representative of this category.

- New epidemic disorders are diseases that are increasing markedly in frequency in comparison with previous time periods. The reader may surmise that examples of these are lung cancer, and, most recently, acquired immune deficiency syndrome (AIDS). The emergence of new epidemics of diseases may be a result of the increased life expectancy of the population, new environmental exposures, or changes in lifestyle, diet, and other practices associated with contemporary life. Increases in the levels of obesity and type 2 diabetes in many parts of the world, notably in developed countries and also in developing areas, are examples of this category of disorders.

Predictions about the Future

The study of population dynamics in relation to sources of morbidity and mortality reveals much about possible future trends in the health of a population. A population pyramid represents the age and sex composition of the population of an area or country at a point in time.[5] By examining the distribution of a population by age and sex, one may view the impact of acute conditions as well as the quality of medical care available to a population.

Figure 2–3 shows the age and sex distribution of the population of a more developed and a less developed region. The less developed region has a triangular population distribution with fewer older people in comparison with younger people. Infections take a heavy toll during the childhood years as a result of a constellation of factors associated with poverty and deprivation: poor nutrition, lack of education and potable water, and unavailability of basic immunizations, antibiotics, and sewage disposal and treatment.

Developed (industrialized) societies manifest a more rectangular distribution of the population. Characteristically, there are more older individuals in comparison with a less developed area, approximately equal numbers of individuals at each age grouping except the very oldest age groups, and more older women than men. Because of reduced mortality due to infectious diseases and improved medical care in comparison with a less developed region, residents of developed countries enjoy greater life expectancy. With continuing advances in medical care, one may predict that there will be an increasingly aging population in developed countries. The U.S. Bureau of the Census estimates that about one-

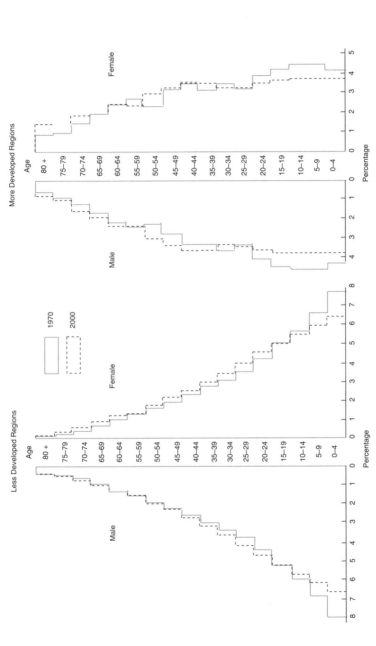

FIGURE 2–3   Sex-age structure of the population in less developed and more developed regions, 1970 and 2000.
Source: Reprinted from *The Population Debate: Dimensions and Perspectives*, by the United Nations, p. 195, © 1974. The United Nations is the author of the original material.

fifth of the U.S. population in 2030 will be 65 years of age and older. There will be a need for health services that affect aging and all its associated dimensions. Specifically, to give one illustration, programs for the major chronic diseases, both preventive care in the early years and direct care in the older years, will need to be expanded.

Population Dynamics and Epidemiology

As the population pyramid portends, population characteristics are related to the pattern of health problems found in the community. Three factors affect the size of populations: births, deaths (see Chapter 3), and migration.[5] When these factors do not contribute to net increases or decreases in the number of persons, the population is in equilibrium. A fixed population adds no new members and, consequently, decreases in size as a result of deaths only; a dynamic population is one that adds new members through migration and births or loses members through emigration and deaths.[6] A population is in steady state when the number of members exiting equals the number entering. The term *demographic transition* refers to the historical shift from high birth and death rates found in agrarian societies to much lower birth and death rates found in developed countries.[5] Decline in the death rate has been attributed in part to improvement in general hygienic and social conditions. Industrialization and urbanization contribute to a decline in the birth rate. The term *epidemiologic transition* is used to describe a shift in the pattern of morbidity and mortality from causes related primarily to infectious and communicable diseases to causes associated with chronic, degenerative diseases. The epidemiologic transition accompanies the demographic transition. The demographic transition, however, is not without its own set of consequences: Both industrialization and urbanization have led to environmental contamination, concentration of social and health problems in the urban core areas of the United States, and out-migration of inner city residents to the suburbs.

Health of the Community

This section describes two applications of epidemiology that pertain to the health of the community. First, we will highlight epidemiology as a descriptive tool, and second we will cover the potential role of epidemiology in policy evaluation. Epidemiology is a tool that may be used to describe the overall health of a particular community. The resulting description may then provide a key to the types of problems that require attention and also to the need for specific health services. A complete epidemiologic description would include indices of health

Loan Receipt
Liverpool John Moores University
Library Services

Borrower Name: K C,Anjana
Borrower ID: *********7112

Violence against women :
31111014652828
Due Date: 08/04/2016 23:59

Total Items: 1
16/03/2016 12:13

Please keep your receipt in case of
dispute.

as well as indicators of the psychosocial milieu of the community. A representative list of variables that might be covered in a description of the health of the community is given in Exhibit 2–2.

A more thorough review of how the set of variables shown in Exhibit 2–2 would affect the health of the community is given in Chapter 4. One example is the relationship between age and sex composition and typical health problems. In a community that consists primarily of senior citizens (as in a retirement community), health problems related to aging would tend to predominate. Because of the longer life expectancy of women, an older population would tend to have a majority of elderly women, who might have unique health needs. In contrast, a younger community might be more concerned with immunizations against infectious diseases and sexually transmitted diseases or prevention of accidental death and injury.

Exhibit 2–2 lists socioeconomic status (a variable comprising income level, educational attainment, and type of occupation) as a descriptive variable for the health of the community. The socioeconomic characteristics of the community relate in part to the availability of health and social services and ability to pay for health care services (refer to Chapter 4 for an additional discussion of socioeconomic status). The wealthier communities, because of their greater tax resources, may provide a greater range of social and health-related services, which may be more conveniently located than in less affluent areas. Low-income residents may utilize, as their primary source of medical care, public health services, which may be less up to date and more difficult to reach by public transportation. Socioeconomic status also relates to community environmental aspects, such as the quality of housing stock and the presence of toxic lead and dangerous asbestos in older housing. Some low socioeconomic status communities tend to be overcrowded and are more likely to have associated unsanitary conditions, which obviously are linked to ill health and transmission of infectious diseases. By definition, low socioeconomic status is associated also with low education levels. Individuals who have low education levels may be less aware of dietary and exercise habits that promote good health than more highly educated persons. The less affluent urban communities of some parts of the United States also are experiencing an out-migration of the younger residents, leaving a majority of older and indigent individuals. It should be pointed out, however, that some of the newer communities, such as those in the Sunbelt of the southern United States, are characterized also by a high degree of residential mobility and lack of social stability. The constant shifting of residents may contribute to a sense of alienation and lack of social connectedness in the community, which in turn may

EXHIBIT 2–2

Descriptive Variables for the Health of the Community

Demographic and social variables:

1. Age and sex distribution
2. Socioeconomic status
3. Family structure, including marital status and number of single-parent families
4. Racial, ethnic, and religious composition

Variables related to community infrastructure:

1. Availability of social and health services including hospitals and emergency rooms
2. Quality of housing stock including presence of lead-based paint and asbestos
3. Social stability (residential mobility)
   - Community policing
   - Employment opportunities

Health-related outcome variables*:

1. Homicide and suicide rates
2. Infant mortality rate
3. Mortality from selected conditions (cause specific)
4. Scope of chronic and infectious diseases
5. Alcoholism and substance abuse rates
6. Teenage pregnancy rates
7. Occurrence of sexually transmitted diseases
8. Birth rate

Environmental variables:

1. Air pollution from stationary and mobile sources
2. Access to parks/recreational facilities
3. Availability of clean water
4. Availability of markets that supply healthful groceries
5. Number of liquor stores and fast-food outlets
6. Nutritional quality of foods and beverages vended to school-children
7. Soil levels of radon

*Definitions of some of these terms are given in Chapter 3.

be associated with an increased incidence of mental health problems as well as social pathology.

The racial, ethnic, and religious composition of the community affects the health status of its members because certain health problems may be more common in one racial or ethnic group than in another, for example sickle cell anemia among African Americans or Tay-Sachs disease among persons of Eastern European Jewish extraction. Also, adherents to some religious denominations may adopt lifestyle and dietary practices that may affect the community health profile, especially when a particular group is concentrated in a given community. For example, members of some religious groups may abstain from alcohol consumption and smoking or avoid certain food products. Communities that have large concentrations of members of such groups would be expected to have lower frequencies of adverse health outcomes related to alcohol consumption and tobacco use. Thus, the health of the community may be determined to some extent by racial, ethnic, and religious factors.

Measures of disease frequency are a barometer of community health needs. An elevated infant mortality rate may reflect inadequate prenatal care, inadequate maternal diet, or a deficit of relevant social and health services. Alienation within the community may produce increased suicide rates and also elevated rates of alcoholism and substance abuse. A resurgence of infectious diseases, such as measles and tuberculosis, may reflect the failure of immunization and community infectious disease surveillance programs. Increases in the occurrence of pregnancies, births, and sexually transmitted diseases among teenagers within specific communities suggest the need for appropriate education and counseling services targeted to this age group. Finally, homicide rates and firearm death rates are indicators of the health of the community. Figure 2–4 portrays motor vehicle, homicide, and firearm death rates for the South Atlantic states (plus Washington, D.C.) in the United States during 2003. According to data reported for 2003, Washington, D.C., led all the other areas in mortality caused by assault and firearms, with age-adjusted death rates of 31.5 and 26.9, respectively, per 100,000 population.

Numerous adverse environmental factors are implicated in the health of the community. Members of some economically disadvantaged communities have high levels of exposure to air pollution that emanate from diesel trucks and other vehicles on freeways that traverse the community. Other sources of air pollution include nearby industrial and power plants as well as port facilities where ships are off-loaded. Access to playgrounds and public parks may be limited as is access to nutritious and healthful foods, particularly meals supplied to schoolchildren.

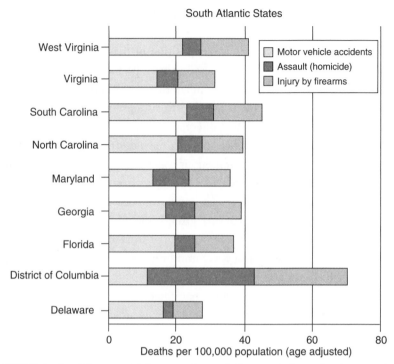

FIGURE 2–4   Motor vehicle, assault, and firearm injury death rates (age adjusted), South Atlantic States, United States, 2003. *Source:* Data from Hoyert DL, Heron MP, Murphy SL, Kung H. Deaths: Final Data for 2003, *National Vital Statistics Reports.* Vol 46, No 13, p. 5. Hyattsville, MD: National Center for Health Statistics, 2006.

In some communities, the dominant food source may be snacks from liquor stores, the fare sold by fast-food outlets, and sugar-laden beverages sold in vending machines.

Using epidemiology to describe the health of the community relates to Goal 2, "Eliminate Health Disparities" of Healthy People 2010. Goal 2 strives ". . . to eliminate health disparities among segments of the population, including differences that occur by gender, race or ethnicity, education or income, disability, geographic location, or sexual orientation."[7(p. 5 of 16)] Health disparities have been defined as, ". . . differences in the incidence, prevalence, mortality, and burden of diseases and other adverse health conditions that exist among specific population groups in the United States."[8(p. 4)] Six areas are the focus of the U.S.

Department of Health and Human Services: infant mortality, cancer screening and management, cardiovascular disease, diabetes, human immunodeficiency virus infection/AIDS, and immunizations.

For example, consider infant mortality, which as noted previously is an indicator of the health of the community. While the infant mortality rate in the United States has trended downward, it is 27th (based on 2006 data; see Chapter 3 for more information) in comparison with other developed nations. Within the United States, African-American infants have approximately 2.45 times the mortality rate of white infants (14.01 per 1,000 vs. 6.85 per 1,000 in 2003).[9] When epidemiology is used to study the health of the community, this discipline can identify geographic areas that have elevated rates of infant mortality (as well as other adverse health conditions) and assist in identifying risk factors for these elevated rates.

Regarding the health of the community, epidemiology is not only a descriptive tool, but also plays a role in policy evaluation. As Ibrahim has pointed out, "Health planning and policy formulation in the ideal sense should apply to total communities and employ a centralized process, which facilitates an overview of the whole rather than selected health problems."[10(p. 4)] Samet and Lee wrote: "The findings of epidemiologic research figure prominently in nearly all aspects of developing policies to safeguard the public's health. Epidemiologic evidence receives consideration at the national and even global levels, while also directly and indirectly influencing individual decisions concerning lifestyle, work, and family."[11(p. S1)]

Legislators and government officials are charged with the responsibility of enacting laws, enforcing them, and creating policies, many of which have substantial impacts on public health. Numerous examples that have occurred in distant and recent history come to mind, including fluoridation of water, helmet protection for motorcycle riders, mandatory seat belt use in motor vehicles, and requiring automobile manufacturers to install air bags in vehicles. Other examples of laws that impact health are shown in Table 2–1. The remainder of this section will advocate for an increasing role for epidemiologists in informing the policy-making process.

The question arises as to whether such policies merely satisfy public whim, appease well-meaning interest groups, or in fact do have an established scientific rationale and documented efficacy. The term *evidence-based decisions,* as applied to public health policies, implies the enactment of laws that have empirical support for their need as well as for their effectiveness.

Table 2-1   Examples of Laws and Ordinances That Affect Public Health

Tobacco control policies
   Smokefree bar, restaurant, and worksite laws in the United States (As of 2007, 18 U.S. states
     ban smoking in restaurants and bars and 11 states ban smoking in worksites.)
   Prohibition of smoking in commercial aircraft
   Prohibition of smoking in airports (United States, Germany, England, Spain, and other
     countries)
Drug treatment systems for nonprescription drugs, such as cocaine and heroin
Needle distribution programs for prevention of needle sharing among intravenous drug users
Laws to regulate amount of particulate matter emitted from automobiles
Ban on plastic bags in some communities (or local ordinances that provide for recycling of plastic
   bags)
Removal of high fat and high sugar content foods from vending machines in schools

Support for the involvement of epidemiologists in public health policy-making has been advocated strongly.[12] Epidemiologists have an important role to play in the development of evidence-based decisions because of their expertise in studying about risks associated with certain exposures and their familiarity with findings based on human subjects.[13] A clear illustration of epidemiologists' involvement in risk assessment arises in the determination of dose-response relationships in environmental health studies. (This issue is discussed in more detail in Chapter 13.)

Further, in their traditional activities, epidemiologists participate in policy-making related to education, research, and publication of manuscripts.[12] Expertise in these areas can be applied readily to other policy arenas. Matanoski pointed out that ". . . epidemiologists can predict future risks based on current trends and knowledge of changing risk factors in the population. Planning for future needs and setting goals to meet these needs will require population-based thinking, for which epidemiologists are well trained."[13(p. 541)]

The issue of policy development, which is extremely complex, encompasses several phases known as the policy cycle. These phases include examination of population health, assessment of potential interventions, alternative policy choices, policy implementation, and policy evaluation[14] (see Figure 2-5 for a diagram of factors that influence policy decision-making). As you can see from Figure 2-5, an epidemiologist might be able to provide input into a number of phases of decision-making, for example, those phases that pertain to scientific fact (human health), interpretation of science, cost/benefit analysis, and risk assessment. Refer to the case study (Exhibit 2-3) in which we describe an applied epidemiologic study (conducted by Robert Friis and Julia Lee) to evaluate responses to the Smokefree Bars Law in California.

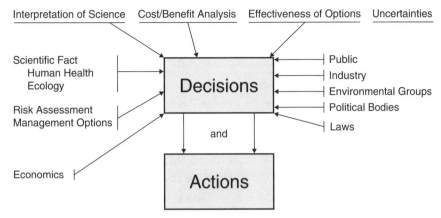

FIGURE 2–5   Factors influencing policy decision-making. *Source:* Reprinted from Matanoski GM. Conflicts between two cultures: implications for epidemiologic researchers in communicating with policy-makers. *Am J Epidemiol.* 2001:154(Suppl 12):S37. Reprinted by permission of Oxford University Press.

EXHIBIT 2–3

Case Study: Using Epidemiologic Methods to Conduct a Policy Evaluation of the Smokefree Bars Law

This research project investigated a community's response to the California Smokefree Bars (SFB) Law, a change in tobacco control policy that was implemented as Assembly Bill (AB) 3037 on January 1, 1998. The SFB Law removed the exemption for bars, taverns, and lounges that had been included in AB 13, the 1995 Workplace Safety Law. AB13/3037 banned smoking in all bars throughout the state (with some exemptions for bars with no employees). For our epidemiologic research, the SFB Law was viewed as a natural experiment, with its scope and timing under the control of the California State Legislature.

Tobacco control policy in the form of laws and local ordinances is occurring with increasing frequency as part of the anti-tobacco efforts to reduce the deleterious first- and secondhand health effects of cigarette smoke. Evidence suggests that secondhand smoke has harmful health

continues

EXHIBIT 2–3 *continued*

consequences from which customers and workers in alcohol-serving establishments need protection. These adverse effects include cancer, emphysema and other lung disorders, and heart disease. Policies to reduce exposure to secondhand smoke need to be investigated to understand their potential to effect health-related changes in population groups and to suggest recommendations regarding their efficacy.

Our policy analysis of the response to the SFB Law was conducted within Long Beach, which is the fifth-largest city (population, 460,000) in the state of California and the second largest in Los Angeles County, the county in which Long Beach is located. Noteworthy is the fact that Long Beach has a distinguished record of local tobacco control. In September 1994, Long Beach was one of 22 cities in the state recognized for protecting the health of its residents through strong tobacco control policies. The Long Beach Smoking Ordinance, enacted in 1991, prohibited smoking in all enclosed workplaces and public places. In 1993, the Long Beach City Council strengthened the ordinance by prohibiting smoking in all restaurants and restaurant/bar combinations. Additionally, Long Beach is one of the few cities in the state with its own health department, a key factor for the positive community response to both local and statewide tobacco control. Over the years, a very active Tobacco Education Program within the city's health department has worked closely with the city to educate the citizens regarding anti-tobacco concerns and also to implement various tobacco control policies.

In order to determine the response to the California SFB Law, we directed our efforts to gathering data from five different perspectives: bar personnel; residents; economic data from the restaurant business; compliance at the bars; and print media. The study was conducted over a four-year period (July 1998–June 2002). Trained interviewers were sent to a sample of alcohol-serving establishments, such as restaurant bars and stand-alone bars.

Observations of compliance at Long Beach bars showed a continuing decrease in the proportion of bars with inside ashtrays; no restaurant bars in the sample had ashtrays during fall 2000 or spring 2001. Inside smoking increased only for stand-alone bars during fall 2000, and then decreased in spring 2001. No inside smoking was observed in any restaurant bars in

continues

EXHIBIT 2–3 *continued*

either fall 2000 or spring 2001. Outside smoking continued to increase during the third year. The extent of the smell of smoke was significantly higher in stand-alone bars than in restaurant-bars, whether measured during daytime or early evening hours during fall 2000 and spring 2001. Based upon the odor of smoke, we concluded that compliance with the law was higher within restaurant-bars than stand-alone bars, although smoking continued in some restaurant-bars.

In year 1 (with a follow-up in year 3), a telephone survey of a cross-sectional sample of Long Beach residents was conducted with over 1500 respondents. A key result was that approval for the SFB Law increased from 66% in year 1 to 73% in year 3. Other results demonstrated that 68% approved a ban on smoking on a nearby, wooden ocean pier; 75% approved of a cigarette tax to fund early childhood development programs, and 83% approved of smokefree zones in parks frequented by children. In conclusion, this case study demonstrated how epidemiologic methods (e.g., cross-sectional surveys and other analyses of population-based data) could be used in public health policy evaluation. ■

Supported by Grant 7RT-0185, University of California Tobacco-Related Disease Research Program.

Working of Health Services: Operations Research and Program Evaluation

Epidemiology applied to operations research involves the study of the placement of health services in a community and the optimum utilization of such services. "The usual epidemiologic approaches—descriptive, analytic, and experimental—are all used in health services research and, in addition, methods of evaluation have been expanded through their application to problems in health services."[15(p. 140)] A major contribution of epidemiology to operations research is the development of research designs, analytic techniques, and measurement procedures. Operations research strives to answer the following kinds of questions, among others:

Using Epidemiology for Operations Research: Examples of Questions Asked

- What health services are not being supplied by an agency in the community?
- Is a particular health service unnecessarily duplicated in the community?
- What segments of the community are the primary utilizers of a service, and which segments are being underserved?
- What is the most efficient organizational and staff power configuration?
- What characteristics of the community, providers, and patients affect service delivery and outcome?
- What procedures could be used to assess, match, and refer patients to service facilities? ■

From the community perspective, there may be a wide variety of uncoordinated programs operated by providers who are not in adequate communication with one another. The results may be low efficiency, duplication, service gaps, delays in securing services, fragmented services, and a lack of service continuity. It is often impossible for one agency or program to provide all the needed services to individuals who are afflicted with severe health problems, such as multiple sclerosis or mental disorders. One agency may specialize in diagnosis, evaluation, and treatment of the client's physical problems, whereas another may emphasize mental health issues. Because the mental and physical dimensions of the person may be intertwined, the holistic medical concept argues that there should be greater coordination among various health care agencies that specialize in a sub-aspect of health. Furthermore, coordination and integration of services probably would yield the fringe benefit of better utilization of available funds or services.

During the 1970s, Robert Friis directed a project to improve the coordination of health services to severely developmentally disabled children in the Bronx, New York. Some of the goals of the project were to identify unmet needs for services, to identify overlapping services, and to assist the referral of clients from one agency to another. In brief, for every severely developmentally disabled youngster in the Bronx (individuals with an IQ lower than 50) who was under the age of 21, the following representative items of information were collected:

- the facility from which medical treatment or follow-up was received
- drugs or medications that the person received
- diagnostic tests received in the past
- enrollment in educational, recreational, and other specified programs
- specific conditions and disabilities presented

Through statistical analyses, the project aimed to provide information about characteristics of service utilization. For example, it would be possible to tabulate the number of separate agencies that each client visited, to develop a profile of the types of services provided by each agency by cross-tabulating the medical conditions and functional disabilities prevalent in the population with services being received, and to determine quantitatively how many kinds of services would be needed in the community to make projections for sufficient funding of health services. Although this description is a simplification of the goals of the project, it illustrates how the epidemiologic approach may be utilized for operations research purposes.

Another example of the use of epidemiologic methods for operations research comes from the National Ambulatory Medical Care Survey, which is a "survey of the private office-based, non-Federal physicians practicing in the United States."[16(p. 1)] Figure 2–6 presents data from this source for the percent distribution of office visits by primary expected source of payment according to patient's age. Figure 2–6 shows the relative importance of various methods of payment, such as Medicare, Medicaid, private medical insurance, and self-pay. Such information contributes to improvement of access to health care in the United States.

The foregoing examples illustrate the role of epidemiology in evaluation of healthcare utilization and needs assessment. A related application is for program evaluation. Specifically, how well does a health program meet certain stated goals? To illustrate, if the goal of a national health insurance program is to provide equal access to health services, an evaluation of the program should include utilization by socioeconomic status variables. The program would be on target if the analysis revealed little discrepancy in service utilization by social class. Epidemiologic methods may be employed to answer this question by providing the following methodologic input:

- methods for selecting target populations to be included in the evaluation
- design of instruments for data collection
- delimitation of types of health-related data to collect
- methods for assessment of healthcare needs

Evaluation of a clinic program or other health service can make use of epidemiologic tools. An example of an issue to include in the evaluation is the

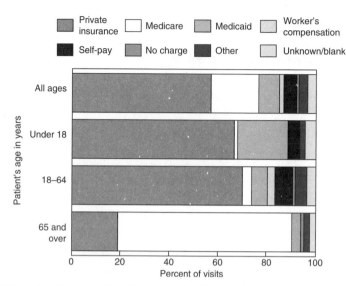

FIGURE 2–6   Percent distribution of office visits by primary expected source of payment according to patient's age: United States, 2000. *Source:* Data from Cherry DK, Woodwell DA. National Ambulatory Medical Care Survey: 2000 Summary. Advance data from *Vital and Health Statistics:* No. 328. Hyattsville, Maryland: National Center for Health Statistics, 2002.

extent to which a program reaches minority individuals or socially and economically disadvantaged persons, the aged, or other targeted groups. An evaluation also might address the issue of changes or improvements in the overall health status of a target population. Other epidemiologic evaluations have studied patient satisfaction with medical care.

Socioeconomic indices may be employed in the epidemiologic evaluation of utilization of surgical operations. Data from the National Health Interview Survey suggest that differentials in surgical utilization between advantaged and disadvantaged socioeconomic groups decreased between 1963 and 1970, although some difference in utilization by race and place of residence remained in 1970.[17] Surgical utilization increased among the aged, lower educated, and nonwhites in urban areas. Income was positively associated with surgical utilization, standardizing for age and sex, although the relationship was weaker in 1970 than in 1963.

Another example of this use of epidemiology is in the evaluation of minority populations' access to health insurance coverage. In an analysis of epidemiologic data from the Hispanic Health and Nutrition Examination Survey, 1982–1984, researchers examined the percentages of health insurance coverage among three major subpopulations (Mexican, Puerto Rican, and Cuban) of adult Latinas. The findings demonstrated that Mexican-origin women had the lowest level of any health insurance coverage, about 64% in comparison to the two other groups (about 74% and 81%, respectively). The disparity was even more pronounced for older women, particularly those between 50 and 64 years of age.[18]

Applications Relevant to Disease Etiology

The second group of applications encompasses uses of epidemiology that are closely connected with disease etiology. Under this general area, Morris[1] noted the search for causes, individual risks, and specific clinical concerns.

Causality in Epidemiologic Research

As an observational science, epidemiology is frequently subject to criticism. The prestigious journal *Science* ran a special news report entitled, "Epidemiology Faces Its Limits."[19] The subtitle read: "The Search for Subtle Links between Diet, Life Style, or Environmental Factors and Disease Is an Unending Source of Fear—but Often Yields Little Certainty." A portion of the report follows:

> The news about health risks comes thick and fast these days, and it seems almost constitutionally contradictory. In January of last year, for instance, a Swedish study found a significant association between residential radon exposure and lung cancer. A Canadian study did not. Three months later, it was pesticide residues. The *Journal of the National Cancer Institute* published a study in April reporting—contrary to previous, less powerful studies—that the presence of DDT metabolites in the bloodstream seemed to have no effect on the risk of breast cancer. In October, it was abortions and breast cancer. Maybe yes. Maybe no. In January of this year it was electromagnetic fields (EMF) from power lines . . .

These are not isolated examples of the conflicting nature of epidemiologic studies; they are just a few to hit the newspapers.

Over the years, such studies have come up with a mind-numbing array of potential disease-causing agents, from hair dyes (lymphomas, myelomas, and leukemia) to coffee (pancreatic cancer and heart disease), to oral contraceptives and other hormone treatments (virtually every disorder known to woman). The pendulum swings back and forth, subjecting the public to an "epidemic of anxiety," as Lewis Thomas put it over a decade ago. Indeed, the *New England Journal of Medicine* published an editorial by editors Marcia Angell and Jerome Kassirer asking the pithy question, "What Should the Public Believe?" "Health-conscious Americans," they wrote, "increasingly find themselves beset by contradictory advice. No sooner do they learn the results of one research study than they hear of one with the opposite message."[19]

Part of the reason for the skepticism about epidemiologic research is the inability of the discipline to "prove" anything. Recall from Chapter 1 the contributions of Koch. His postulates, first developed by Henle, adapted in 1877, and further elaborated in 1882, also are referred to as the Henle-Koch postulates. They were instrumental in efforts to prove (or disprove) the causative involvement of a microorganism in the pathogenesis of an infectious disease. The postulates specified that the agent must be present in every case of the disease, must be isolated and grown in pure culture, must reproduce the disease when reintroduced into a healthy susceptible animal, and must be recovered and grown again in a pure culture. In addition, the agent should occur in no other disease: the one agent–one disease criterion. This classical Henle-Koch concept of causality, sometimes referred to as pure determinism, becomes problematic when one attempts to apply it to the chronic diseases prevalent in modern eras. Let us examine separately three of the four criteria that form part of Koch's concept of causality:

1. Agent present in every case of the disease. How would this criterion apply to CVD? Decades of research have established that individuals who develop CVD tend to be overweight, physically inactive, cigarette smokers, and have high blood pressure and high total cholesterol. If we were to apply Koch's postulates strictly, then every case of CVD would have all these characteristics. Clearly not true.

2. One agent–one disease. How would this criterion hold up against cigarette smoking? We just pointed out that smokers are more likely to develop CVD than nonsmokers. Is CVD the only disease associated with smoking? No. In fact, smoking is associated with lung cancer, pancreatic cancer, oral cancer, nasopharyngeal cancer, cervical cancer, emphysema, chronic obstructive pulmonary disease, and stroke, to name just a few. Therefore, the one agent–one disease criterion is not particularly helpful, especially for diseases of noninfectious origin.

3. Exposure of healthy subjects to suspected agents. The ethical conduct of research on humans forbids exposure of subjects to risks that exceed potential benefits. Would it be reasonable to suspect the smoking-lung

cancer association even if such an experiment was never conducted? As pointed out in the introduction to this chapter, there are simply some exposures that cannot be evaluated in the context of controlled experimental studies. Epidemiology must be relied upon to provide such information.

In addition to the three issues just discussed that are direct tests of Koch's postulates, there are others that must be considered. It is relatively straightforward to categorize individuals with respect to the presence or absence of an exposure when the exposure is an infectious agent; one is either exposed or not exposed. However, even this simplification ignores the complicating issue of biologically effective dose. What about something such as blood pressure? Individuals with "elevated" blood pressure are more likely to develop a stroke than individuals with "low" blood pressure. Where does one draw the line between elevated and normal (or low)? At what level should an individual be considered obese?

A more subtle concept to consider is the fact that, for diseases of unknown etiology, we are dealing with imperfect knowledge. For example, although we may know that smokers are 20 times more likely to develop lung cancer than nonsmokers, why is it that not all smokers develop the disease? There must be other factors (diet, alcohol intake, host susceptibility, etc.) that are part of the total picture of causality. When not all the contributing factors are known, it is problematic indeed to know truly and accurately the complete cause of a given disease. The issue of causality and epidemiology has been the focus of debate for decades. Some of the early writings are still fascinating and relevant today. An excellent text in this regard is the collection of readings assembled by Greenland[20] as well as *Causal Thinking in the Health Sciences*, by Susser.[21]

To summarize, it is now widely accepted that there is no single causal agent but rather multiple factors that produce chronic diseases such as CVD. Cassel, in the fourth Wade Hampton Frost Lecture, noted that early theories stated "disease occurred as a result of new exposure to a pathogenic agent." The single agent causal model was extended to "the well-known triad of host, agent and environment in epidemiologic thinking."[22(pp. 107–108)] (covered in Chapter 12). The formulation was satisfactory to explain diseases of importance during the late 19th and early 20th centuries, when agents of overwhelming pathogenicity and virulence produced conditions such as typhoid and smallpox. Cassel suggested that the triad of agent, host, and environment is no longer satisfactory because, "In a modern society the majority of citizens are protected from these overwhelming agents and most of the agents associated with current diseases are ubiquitous in our environment . . . [There may be] categories or classes of environmental factors that are capable of changing human resistance in important ways." Cassel argued that the social environment ("presence of other members of the same species") might be capable of profoundly influencing host susceptibility to environmental disease agents, whether they are microbiologic or physiochemical.[22]

Risk Factors Defined

Because of the uncertainty of "causal" factors in epidemiologic research, it is customary to refer to an exposure that is associated with a disease as a risk factor. There are three requisite criteria for risk factors:

1. The frequency of the disease varies by category or value of the factor. Consider cigarette smoking and lung cancer. Light smokers are more likely to develop lung cancer than nonsmokers, and heavy smokers are more likely still to develop the disease.
2. The risk factor must precede the onset of disease. Continuing with the smoking-lung cancer example, if individuals with lung cancer began to smoke after the onset of disease, it would be incorrect to assign smoking as the cause of the disease. This issue is particularly relevant to chronic diseases of long duration.
3. The observed association must not be due to any source of error. There are several points during the conduct of an epidemiologic investigation where error may be introduced: in the selection of the study groups, in the measurement of exposure and disease, and in the analysis. (These topics are covered in Chapter 10.)

Modern Concepts of Causality

Causal inferences derived from epidemiologic research (especially in the realm of noninfectious diseases) gained increasing popularity as a topic of formal discussion as a result of findings (in the early 1950s) regarding the association between smoking and lung cancer.[23] The publication of *Smoking and Health, Report of the Advisory Committee to the Surgeon General of the Public Health Service* listed five criteria for the judgment of the causal significance of an association[24] (Exhibit 2–4). These criteria were addressed subsequently in other writings by Susser,[25] Rothman,[6] and Hill.[26] One of the seminal articles that elaborated on the five criteria for causality in epidemiologic research was published in 1965 by Sir Austin Bradford Hill, then Professor Emeritus of Medical Statistics at the University of London.[26] The article, which was his President's Address to the Section of

EXHIBIT 2-4

Case Study: Does Smoking Cause Lung Cancer?

The first Surgeon General's report on smoking and health was published in 1964.[24] This report generated global reaction by stating that cigarette smoking is a cause of lung cancer in men and is linked to other disabling or fatal diseases. Five criteria were identified as necessary for the establishment of a causal relationship between smoking and lung cancer. The report's authors concluded that, to judge the causal significance of the association between cigarette smoking and lung cancer, several of these criteria would have to be taken into account in combination and no single criterion would, in itself, be "pathognomonic" (pathognomonic means characteristic or diagnostic). The criteria of judgment were strength of association, time sequence, consistency of relationship upon repetition, specificity of association, and coherence of explanation.

1. Strength of association: The report stated that the relative risk ratio* is the most direct measure of the strength of association between smoking and lung cancer; several retrospective* and prospective* studies completed up to the time of the report demonstrated high relative risks for lung cancer among smokers and nonsmokers. Thus, it was concluded that the criterion of strength of association was supported.

2. Time sequence: The report argued that early exposure to tobacco smoke and late manifestation seems to meet the criterion of time sequence, at least superficially.

3. Consistency upon repetition: With regard to the causal relationship between smoking and health, the report asserted that this criterion was strongly confirmed for the relationship between smoking and lung cancer. Numerous retrospective and prospective studies demonstrated highly significant associations between smoking and lung cancer; it is unlikely that these findings would be obtained unless the associations were causal or else due to unknown factors.

continues

EXHIBIT 2–4 *continued*

4. Specificity: The hypothesis that smoking causes lung cancer has been attacked because of the lack of specificity of the relationship; smoking has been linked to a wide range of conditions, including cardiovascular disease (CVD), low birth weight, and bladder cancer. The report claimed, however, that rarely in the biologic realm does an agent always predict the occurrence of a disease; in addition, accumulating evidence about chronic diseases suggests that a given disease may have multiple causes.

5. Coherence of explanation: The report contended that the association between cigarette smoking and lung cancer was supported for this criterion. Evidence noted included the rise in lung cancer mortality with increases in per capita consumption of cigarettes and increases in lung cancer mortality as a function of age cohort* patterns of smoking among men and women; the sex differential in mortality was consistent with sex differences in tobacco use. General smoking rates were higher among men than among women; the report noted that young women were increasing their rates of smoking, however. ▪

*The terms *relative risk ratio, retrospective, prospective,* and *cohort* are defined in Chapters 6 and 7.

Occupational Medicine of the Royal Society of Medicine, lists nine aspects of an empirical association to consider when one is trying to decide whether the association is consistent with cause and effect. These were not intended to be interpreted as criteria of causality, but nonetheless they have been presented as such in several textbooks. The following is a quotation from his article:

> I have no wish, nor the skill, to embark upon a philosophical discussion of the meaning of "causation." The "cause" of illness may be immediate and direct, it may be remote and indirect, underlying the observed association. But with the aims of occupational, and almost synonymously preventive, medicine in mind the decisive question is whether the frequency of the undesirable event B will be influenced by a change in the environmental feature A. How such a change exerts that influence may call for a great deal of research. However, before deducing "causation" and taking action we shall not invariably have to sit around awaiting the results of that research. The whole chain may have to be unraveled or a few links may suffice. It will depend upon circumstances.[26(p. 295)]

This landmark article identified nine issues that are relevant to causality and epidemiologic research.

1. Strength of association. One example cited by Hill was the observation of Percival Pott that chimney sweeps in comparison to other workers had an enormous increase in scrotal cancer; the mortality was more than 200 times that of workers not exposed to tar and mineral oils. A strong association is less likely to be the result of errors.

2. Consistency upon repetition. This term refers to whether the association between agent and putative health effects has been observed by different persons in different places, circumstances, and times. The Surgeon General's report of 1964 cited a total of 36 different studies that found an association between smoking and lung cancer.[24] Hill felt that consistency was especially important when the exposure was rare.

3. Specificity. With respect to occupational exposures, Hill noted that if "the association is limited to specific workers and to particular sites and types of disease and there is no association between the work and other modes of dying, then clearly that is a strong argument in favor of causation."[26(p. 297)] He later went on to acknowledge that specificity should be used as evidence in favor of causality, not as refutation against it.

4. Time sequence. In Hill's words, "Which is the cart and which is the horse?" For example, if one is trying to identify the role of diet in the pathogenesis of colon cancer, one has to be careful to sort out dietary preferences that lead to colon cancer versus dietary changes that result from early stages of the disease. There is some evidence that low intakes of calcium are associated with increased risk of colon cancer. If early stages of disease create problems with digestion of milk products (which are good sources of calcium), individuals may lower their intake of milk (and calcium) as a consequence of the disease. The shorter the duration between exposure to an agent and development of the disease (i.e., the *latency* period), the more certain one is regarding the hypothesized cause of the disease. For this reason, many of the acute infectious diseases or chemical poisonings are relatively easy to pinpoint as to cause. Diseases having longer latency periods (many forms of cancer, for example) are more difficult to relate to a causal agent; it is said that the onset of chronic diseases is insidious and that one is ignorant of the precise induction periods for chronic diseases. Many different causal factors could intervene during the latency period. This is why a great deal of detective

work was needed to link early exposure to asbestos in shipyards to subsequent development of mesothelioma, a form of cancer of the lining of the abdominal cavity.

5. Biologic gradient. Evidence of a dose-response curve is another important criterion. Hill notes, "the fact that the death rate from lung cancer increases linearly with the number of cigarettes smoked daily adds a great deal to the simpler evidence that cigarette smokers have a higher death rate than non-smokers."[26(p. 298)] MacMahon and Pugh state, "the existence of a dose-response relationship—that is, an increase in disease risk with increase in the amount of exposure—supports the view that an association is a causal one."[3(p. 235)] Figure 2–7 illustrates a dose-response relationship between number of cigarettes smoked per day and lung cancer mortality among male British physicians.

6. Plausibility. If an association is biologically plausible, it will be helpful. The weakness of this line of evidence is that it is necessarily dependent upon the biologic knowledge of the day.

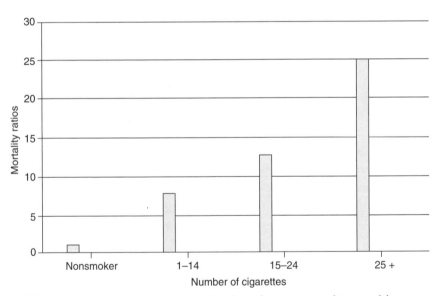

FIGURE 2–7   Dose-response relationships between smoking and lung cancer mortality among British physicians. *Source:* Data from Doll R, Peto R. Mortality in Relation to Smoking: 20 Years' Observation on Male British Doctors. *British Medical Journal,* Vol 2 (6051), pp. 1525–1536, BMJ Publishing Group, © 1976.

7. Coherence of explanation. The association must not seriously conflict with what is already known about the natural history and biology of the disease. Data from laboratory experiments on animals may be most helpful. For example, the ability of tobacco extracts to cause skin cancer in mice is coherent with the theory that consumption of tobacco products in humans causes lung cancer.

8. Experiment. In some instances there may be "natural experiments" that shed important light on a topic. The observation that communities with naturally fluoridated water had fewer dental caries among their citizens than communities without fluoridated water is one example.

9. Analogy. The examples Hill cites are thalidomide and rubella. Thalidomide, administered in the early 1960s as an anti-nausea drug for use during pregnancy, was associated subsequently with severe birth defects. Rubella (German measles), if contracted during pregnancy, has been linked to birth defects, stillbirths, and miscarriages. Given that such associations have already been demonstrated, "we would surely be ready to accept slighter but similar evidence with another drug or another viral disease in pregnancy."[26(p. 299)]

Although it is not critical that all these lines of evidence be presented to uphold the concept of causality, the more that are supported, the more the case of causality is strengthened. More important, careful consideration of these concepts is helpful in trying to decide at what point one needs to take action. One of Hill's concluding remarks was particularly poignant: "All scientific work is incomplete, whether it be observational or experimental. All scientific work is liable to be upset or modified by advancing knowledge. That does not confer upon us a freedom to ignore the knowledge we already have, or to postpone the action that it appears to demand at a given time."[26(p. 300)] It also should be noted that the processes of causal inference and statistical inference (refer to Chapter 9) frequently overlap yet represent different principles. According to Susser, "Formal statistical tests are framed to give mathematical answers to structured questions leading to judgments, whereas in any field practitioners must give answers to unstructured questions leading from judgment to decision and implementation."[25(p. 1)]

Evans,[27] in a compelling discussion of causality, drew an analogy between ascertainment of causality and establishment of guilt in a criminal trial. Evans' detailed arguments are found in Exhibit 2–5.

EXHIBIT 2-5

Rules of Evidence: Criminality and Causality

Mayhem or murder and criminal law	Morbidity, mortality, and causality
1. Criminal present at scene of crime.	1. Agent present in lesion of the disease.
2. Premeditation.	2. Causal events precede onset of disease.
3. Accessories involved in the crime.	3. Cofactors and/or multiple causalities involved.
4. Severity or death related to state of victim.	4. Susceptibility and host response determine severity.
5. Motivation: The crime must make sense in terms of gain to the criminal.	5. The role of the agent in the disease must make biologic and common sense.
6. No other suspect could have committed the crime.	6. No other agent could have caused the disease under the circumstances given.
7. The proof of the guilt must be established beyond a reasonable doubt.	7. The proof of causation must be established beyond reasonable doubt or role of chance.

"In criminal law, the presence of the criminal at the scene of the crime would be equivalent to the presence of the agent in a lesion of the disease. Premeditation would be similar to the requirement that the causal exposure should precede the onset of the disease. The presence of accessories at the scene of the crime might be compared to the presence of cofactors and/or multiple causes for human diseases. The severity of the crime or the consequence of death might be loosely equivalent to susceptibility and the host responses which determine the severity of the illness. The motivation involved in a crime should make sense in terms of reward to the criminal, just as the role of the causal agent should make biologic sense. The absence of other suspects and their elimination in a criminal trial would be similar to that of the exclusion of other putative causes in human illness. Finally, need that the proof of guilt must be established beyond a reasonable doubt would be true for both criminal justice and for disease causation." ▪

Source: Adapted from Evans AS. Causation and Disease: A Chronological Journey, *American Journal of Epidemiology*, Vol 108, No 4, pp. 254–255, with permission of the Johns Hopkins University, School of Hygiene and Public Health. © 1978.

Study of Risks to Individuals

Epidemiologic research on disease etiology typically involves collection of data on a number of individual members of different study groups or study populations. Two main types of observational studies are employed. These are discussed in greater detail in Chapters 6 and 7, but at this time suffice it to say that the case-control design compares a group of individuals who have a disease of interest (the cases) with a group who does not have the disease (the controls). The two groups are compared with respect to a variety of exposures (e.g., diet, exercise habits, or use of sunscreens). Differences in exposure that are observed between the two groups may suggest why one group has the disease and the other does not. Another research method is the cohort study. In this approach, a study group free of disease is assembled and measured with respect to a variety of exposures that are hypothesized to increase (or decrease) the chance of getting the disease. One then follows the group over time for the development of disease, comparing the frequency with which disease develops in the group exposed to the factor and the group not exposed to the factor. Either type of study may demonstrate that a disease or other outcome is more likely to occur in those with a particular exposure.

The issue of whether the results of an epidemiologic study influence clinical decision-making is in part determined by the criteria of causality covered in the previous section. How large is the effect? How consistent is the finding with previous research? Is there biologic plausibility? All these issues are important, but a major issue for the clinician is the relevance to each particular patient. Epidemiologic studies employ groups of individuals; the studies provide evidence that groups with particular exposures or lifestyle characteristics are more or less likely to develop disease than groups of individuals without the exposures. Extrapolation to the individual from findings based on observations of groups should be made with caution. The observation that cigarette smokers are 20 times more likely to develop lung cancer than nonsmokers does not necessarily entitle someone to tell a smoker, "You are 20 times more likely to get lung cancer than a nonsmoker." The problem is that there are a number of other factors that may be important contributors to the cause of lung cancer. A more accurate statement would be "Collectively, groups of individuals who smoke are 20 times more likely to develop lung cancer than nonsmokers." The difference is subtle, yet important.

Another issue for the clinician is the size of the risk; an example is the slight risk of mortality from CVD associated with a high serum cholesterol level. If the risk is small, a person may reasonably not wish to change his or her lifestyle.[28]

The 1990 editorial in the *New England Journal of Medicine* is particularly illustrative.[2] Suppose that the 10-year risk of death is 1.7% in middle-aged men with cholesterol levels below 200 mg/dL but 4.9% if the cholesterol level is above 240 mg/dL.[29] This difference in risk of approximately 3.0% may not be sufficient to induce an otherwise healthy man to try to lower his cholesterol level. Conversely, even if the risk factor is strong, it may still be unimportant to individual patients if the disease is rare.

The extrapolation of epidemiologic research to individuals thus is complicated. Another aspect of risk concerns public health implications. A risk factor that may be relatively unimportant for individuals indeed may be important when the effect is multiplied over the population as a whole, especially if the disease is common. Refer to Chapter 9 for more detail.

This application of epidemiology also makes possible the prediction of the individual's prognosis and likelihood of survival if afflicted by a serious disease. Such information can be used to inform the patient about his or her chances for survival and ultimate recovery. It also demonstrates the efficacy of medical intervention by showing whether the practice yields an increase in long-term survival for a population of cases. Some illustrations of the use of epidemiology to study risks to the individual are predictions of mortality from cancer and other serious chronic diseases and studies of the relationship between longevity and coronary bypass surgery.

Epidemiologic research indicates that there is a low, but nevertheless important, contribution to mortality from common infectious diseases, such as influenza and colds. Mortality results from complications that occur in the neonatal and elderly groups or in debilitated individuals. Without population-based data, mortality from these "minor" diseases might not be obvious. In 2003, influenza was responsible for slightly less than 1 death per 100,000 individuals in the United States.[9]

Epidemiologic data may be used to predict cancer prognosis and mortality. Both vary by site of the tumor, type, and a number of social variables, such as socioeconomic status, race, and sex. Figure 2–8 presents the five-year relative survival rate for selected forms of cancer by race from 1996 to 2002. Differences in survival are evident by both cancer type and race. Among African Americans in comparison to whites, the five-year survival rates for all cancer sites were 57% and 68%, respectively.

Another illustration of the study of risks to the individual draws upon investigations of prognosis of survival from coronary bypass surgery. The Veterans

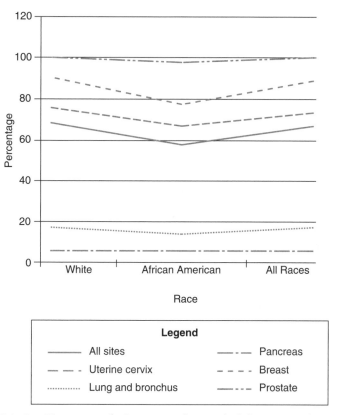

FIGURE 2–8   Five-year relative survival rates (%) by race and year of diagnosis in the United States, 1996–2002. *Source:* Data from American Cancer Society, *Cancer Facts & Figures 2007.* Atlanta: American Cancer Society, Inc.; 2007, p. 18.

Administration Cooperative Study[30] traced the survival of 596 patients treated by medication or by surgery for chronic stable angina in a large-scale prospective, randomized study. Findings indicated no differences in survival at 21 and 36 months between surgery patients and medically treated patients. Thus, the factors of mortality from surgery itself and expense of the operation need to be weighed against increases in life expectancy and improvement in the quality of life due to improved arterial circulation. This is an epidemiologic question that may be raised about risks associated with other types of surgical procedures as well.

Enlargement of the Clinical Picture of Disease

When a new disease first gains the attention of health authorities, usually the most dramatic cases are the ones observed initially. One may conclude incorrectly that the new disease is an extremely acute or fatal condition; later epidemiologic studies may reveal that the most common form of the new disease is a mild, subclinical illness that occurs widely in the population. To develop a complete clinical picture of the disease, thorough studies are necessary to find out about the subacute cases; an adequate study may require a survey of a complete population.

An instance in which epidemiology has added to clinical knowledge about a disease that appeared to be new and highly virulent was the Legionnaires' disease situation. During July of 1976, public attention and concern were evoked by the outbreak of a mysterious illness that ravaged participants at a convention of the American Legion in Philadelphia. Local and federal epidemiologists were called in to investigate the outbreak. It was found subsequently that Legionnaires' disease is associated with a previously unidentified bacterium, that about 15% of the people who developed the disease died of it, and that the disease had probably occurred sporadically in other areas of the country before 1976.

Prevention of Disease

One of the potential applications of research on disease etiology is to identify where, in the disease's natural history, effective intervention might be implemented. The natural history of disease refers to the course of disease from its beginning to its final clinical end points. Figure 2–9 illustrates the natural history of any disease in humans. As the figure demonstrates, the natural history signifies the progression of disease over time.

The period of prepathogenesis occurs before the precursors of disease (e.g., the bacterium that causes Legionnaires' disease) have interacted with the host (the person who gets the disease). The period of pathogenesis occurs after the precursors have interacted with the host, an event that is marked by initial appearance of disease (the presymptomatic stage) and is characterized by tissue and physiologic changes. Later stages of the natural history include development of active signs and symptoms, and eventually recovery, disability, or death (all examples of clinical end points).

According to the model that Leavell and Clark[31] have advanced, three strategies for disease prevention—primary, secondary, and tertiary—coincide with the

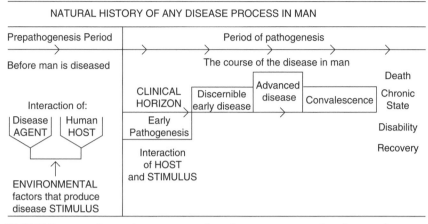

FIGURE 2–9   Prepathogenesis and pathogenesis periods of natural history. *Source:* Modified with permission from Leavell HR, Clark EG. *Preventive Medicine for the Doctor in His Community: An Epidemiologic Approach,* 3rd ed. New York: McGraw-Hill Book Company; 1965, p. 18.

periods of prepathogenesis and pathogenesis. Figure 2–10 demonstrates these three levels of prevention, which are described in more detail in the following sections.

Primary Prevention

Primary prevention occurs during the period of prepathogenesis. As shown in Figure 2–10, primary prevention includes health promotion and specific protection against diseases. The former is analogous to a type of prevention known as primordial prevention. The term *primordial prevention* denotes ". . . actions and measures that inhibit the emergence and establishment of environmental, economic, social and behavioral conditions, cultural patterns of living, etc., known to increase the risk of disease."[32(p. 141)] Primordial prevention is concerned with minimizing health hazards in general, whereas primary prevention seeks to lower the occurrence of disease. Primordial prevention is achieved in part through health promotion, which includes health education programs in general, marriage counseling, sex education, and provision of adequate housing.

Examples of primary prevention that involve specific protection against disease-causing hazards are wearing protective devices to prevent occupational injuries, utilization of specific dietary supplements to prevent nutritional

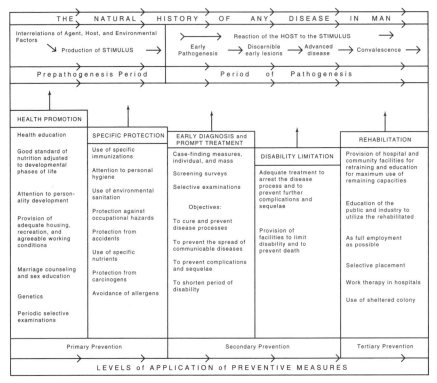

FIGURE 2–10   Levels of application of preventive measures in the natural history of disease. *Source:* Modified with permission from Leavell HR, Clark EG. *Preventive Medicine for the Doctor in His Community: An Epidemiologic Approach*, 3rd ed. New York: McGraw-Hill Book Company; 1965, p. 21.

deficiency diseases, immunizations against specific infectious diseases, and education about the hazards of starting smoking. Interventions to reduce the number of alcohol-related traffic accidents similarly may focus on education, media campaigns, and warning labels on alcohol-containing beverages.

Primary prevention may be either active or passive. Active prevention necessitates behavior change on the part of the subject. Wearing protective devices and obtaining vaccinations require involvement of the individual to receive the benefit. Passive interventions, on the other hand, do not require any behavior change. Fluoridation of public water supplies and vitamin fortification of milk and bread products achieve their desired effects without any voluntary effort of the recipients.

Secondary Prevention

Secondary prevention, which takes place during the pathogenesis phase of the natural history of disease, encompasses early diagnosis and prompt treatment as well as disability limitation. One example of secondary prevention is early diagnosis and prompt treatment linked to cancer screening programs, which are efforts to detect cancer in its early stages (when it is treated more successfully) among apparently healthy individuals. One should note that in the instance of a positive screening result confirmed by a diagnostic workup, cancer is already present; however, detection of the tumor before the onset of clinical symptoms reduces the likelihood of progression to death. Most cancer screening programs are forms of secondary prevention. However, screening for colorectal cancer can be considered also as primary prevention: Because most colorectal cancers arise through a precancerous lesion (adenomatous polyp), screening that detects and removes polyps can prevent cancer, rather than merely detect cancer early.

Later in the natural history of disease (when discernible lesions or advanced disease have appeared), there occurs a type of secondary prevention called disability limitation, which is designed to limit and shorten the period of disability and prevent death from a disease. Another goal of disability limitation is to prevent the side effects and complications that may be associated with a disease.

Tertiary Prevention

Tertiary prevention takes place during late pathogenesis (advanced disease and convalescence stages). Thus, disease already has occurred and has been treated clinically, but rehabilitation is needed to restore the patient to an optimal functional level. Examples include physical therapy for stroke victims, halfway houses for persons recovering from alcohol abuse, sheltered homes for the developmentally disabled, and fitness programs for heart attack patients. This category of prevention seeks to achieve maximum use of the capacities of persons who have disabilities and help them regain full employment.

Conclusion

This chapter identified seven uses of epidemiology. The historical use of epidemiology traced changes in rates of disease from early in this century to the present. Dramatic changes in morbidity and mortality rates were noted. Predictions of future trends in health status employ population dynamics or shifts in the demographic composition of populations. Operations research and program evaluation are examples of using epidemiologic methods to improve healthcare services. Epidemiology also is used to describe the health of the community, to identify causes of disease, and to study risks to individuals. One of the most important applications is the study of the causality of disease; a detailed account of causality was provided. The chapter concluded with a review of primary, secondary, and tertiary prevention of diseases.

Study Questions and Exercises

1. Define in your own words the following terms:
   a. secular changes
   b. operations research
   c. risk factor
   d. the natural history of disease
   e. demographic transition
   f. epidemiologic transition
   g. disorders: disappearing, residual, persisting, epidemic
   h. population pyramid
2. Name three approaches for prevention (primary, secondary, and tertiary) of each of the following health problems/conditions:
   a. motor vehicle accidents
   b. obesity
   c. hepatitis A
   d. hepatitis B and C
   e. foodborne illness on cruise ships
   f. mortality due to gang violence
3. State the seven uses of epidemiology according to Morris.[1] Are the uses of epidemiology defined in the chapter distinct or overlapping? Can you think of other uses of epidemiology not identified in the chapter? Do all of the uses belong exclusively to the domain of epidemiology?
4. Describe a role for epidemiology in the field of policy evaluation. Consider how the field of epidemiology might inform policy evaluation of laws that regulate tobacco consumption in public places.
5. How are the rules of evidence for criminality similar or different from the rules of evidence for disease causality? (Refer to Exhibit 2–5 to help with your answer.)

6. Clinicians and epidemiologists differ in their assessment of the importance of risks. State how the clinical and epidemiologic approaches differ. Give an example by using a disease or condition that is important for society.

7. Describe how it is possible for an infectious disease, when it first comes to the attention of public health authorities, to be considered an extremely acute or fatal condition—and then later is found to be mild or benign in its most common form. Give an example of such a disease.

8. This chapter stated how epidemiology may be applied to the study of the causality of disease. Suggest other examples of how epidemiology might be applied to study the causality of disease.

9. The following questions refer to Table 2A–1 in Appendix 2 at the end of this chapter.
    a. Calculate the percentage decline in the death rate for all causes. What generalizations can be made about changes in disease rates that have occurred between 1900 and the present?
    b. Contrast the changes in death rates due to cancer, heart disease, and cerebrovascular diseases. What additional information would be useful to specify better the changes in these conditions?
    c. Note the decline in mortality for the four communicable diseases (1, 2, 3, and 10). With the exception of pneumonia and influenza, these are no longer among the 10 leading causes of death. Can you speculate regarding how much of each is due to environmental improvements and how much to specific preventive and curative practices?
    d. Among the 10 leading causes of death in 2003 were chronic lower respiratory diseases (43.5 per 100,000—rank 4), diabetes (25.5 per 100,000—rank 6), Alzheimer's disease (21.8 per 100,000—rank 8), and septicemia (11.7 per 100,000—rank 10). (Note: Data are not shown in Table 2A–1.) In 1900, these were not among the 10 leading causes of death. How do you account for these changes?

10. The following questions refer to Figure 2–1.
    a. List and describe the trends in death rates by the five leading causes of death.
    b. Describe the trend for hypertension and Parkinson's disease. Can you suggest an explanation for the trends in hypertension and Parkinson's disease deaths?
    c. Does the curve for accidental deaths correspond to our expectations from various publicity reports?
    d. What is the trend for Alzheimer's disease? Can you offer an explanation?

References

1. Morris JN. *Uses of Epidemiology*, 3rd ed. Edinburgh, UK: Churchill Livingstone; 1975.
2. Angell M. The interpretation of epidemiologic studies. Editorial. *N Engl J Med.* 1990;323:823–825.
3. MacMahon B, Pugh TF. *Epidemiology Principles and Methods.* Boston, MA: Little, Brown; 1970.
4. Susser MW, Watson W, Hopper K. *Sociology in Medicine*, 3rd ed. New York, NY: Oxford University Press; 1985.
5. Mausner JS, Kramer S. *Epidemiology: An Introductory Text*, 2nd ed. Philadelphia: Saunders; 1985.
6. Rothman KJ. *Modern Epidemiology.* Boston, MA: Little, Brown; 1986.
7. U.S. Department of Health and Human Services. *Healthy People 2010: Understanding and Improving Health*, 2nd ed. Washington, DC: U.S. Government Printing Office, November 2000.
8. National Institutes of Health. Strategic Research Plan to Reduce and Ultimately Eliminate Health Disparities: Fiscal Years 2002–2006. Draft: October 6, 2000. Available at: http://www.nih.gov/about/hd/strategicplan.pdf. Accessed November 24, 2007.
9. Hoyert, DL, Heron MP, Murphy SL, et al. Deaths: Final Data for 2003. *National Vital Statistics Reports;* Vol. 54, No. 13. Hyattsville, MD: National Center for Health Statistics. 2006.
10. Ibrahim MA. *Epidemiology and Health Policy.* Gaithersburg, MD: Aspen Publishers; 1985.
11. Samet JM, Lee NL. Bridging the gap: perspectives on translating epidemiologic evidence into policy. *Am J Epidemiol.* 2001;154(12 Suppl):S1–S3.
12. Weed DL, Mink PJ. Roles and responsibilities of epidemiologists. *Ann Epidemiol.* 2002;12:67–72.
13. Matanoski GM. Conflicts between two cultures: implications for epidemiologic researchers in communicating with policy-makers. *Am J Epidemiol.* 2001;154(12 Suppl):S36–S42.
14. Spasoff RA. *Epidemiologic Methods for Health Policy.* New York, NY: Oxford University Press; 1999.
15. Hulka BS. Epidemiological applications to health services research. *J Community Health.* 1978;4:140–149.
16. Woodwell DA. *Office Visits to General Surgeons 1989–90, National Ambulatory Medical Care Survey. Advance Data from Vital and Health Statistics.* Report 228. Hyattsville, MD: National Center for Health Statistics; December 22, 1993.
17. Bombardier C, Fuchs VR, Lillard LA, et al. Social economic factors affecting the utilization of surgical operations. *N Engl J Med.* 1977;297:699–705.
18. de la Torre A, Friis R, Hunter HR, Garcia L. The health insurance of U.S. Latino women: a profile from the 1982-1984 HHANES. *Am J Public Health.* 1996; 86:533–537.
19. Epidemiology faces its limits. *Science.* 1995;269:164–169.
20. Greenland S. *Evolution of Epidemiologic Ideas: Annotated Readings on Concepts and Methods.* Chestnut Hill, MA: Epidemiology Resources; 1987.

21. Susser M. *Causal Thinking in the Health Sciences*. New York, NY: Oxford University Press; 1973.

22. Cassel J. The contribution of the social environment to host resistance. *Am J Epidemiol*. 1976;104:107–123.

23. Winkelstein W Jr. Invited commentary on "Judgment and causal inference: criteria in epidemiologic studies." *Am J Epidemiol*. 1995;141:699–700.

24. U.S. Department of Health, Education and Welfare, Public Health Service. *Smoking and Health, Report of the Advisory Committee to the Surgeon General of the Public Health Service*. Public Health Service publication 1103. Washington, DC: Government Printing Office; 1964.

25. Susser M. Judgment and causal inference: criteria in epidemiologic studies. *Am J Epidemiol*. 1977;105:1–15.

26. Hill AB. The environment and disease: association or causation? *Proc R Soc Med*. 1965;58:295–300.

27. Evans AS. Causation and disease: a chronological journey. *Am J Epidemiol*. 1978;108:254–255.

28. Brett AS. Treating hypercholesterolemia: how should practicing physicians interpret the published data for patients? *N Engl J Med*. 1989;321:676–680.

29. Pekkanen J, Linn S, Heiss G, et al. Ten-year mortality from cardiovascular disease in relation to cholesterol level among men with and without preexisting cardiovascular disease. *N Engl J Med*. 1990;322:1700–1707.

30. Murphy M, Hultgren HN, Detre K, et al. Treatment of chronic stable angina: a preliminary report of survival data of the randomized Veterans Administration Cooperative Study. *N Engl J Med*. 1977;297:621–627.

31. Leavell HR, Clark EG. *Preventive Medicine for the Doctor in His Community: An Epidemiologic Approach*, 3rd ed. New York: McGraw-Hill Book Company; 1965.

32. Last JM. *A Dictionary of Epidemiology*, 4th ed. New York, NY: Oxford University Press; 2001.

APPENDIX
2

Table 2A-1 Leading Causes of Death and Rates for Those Causes in 1900 and 2003, United States

Rank 1900	Cause of Death*	Rate per 100,000 Population	
		1900	2003[1]
	All causes	1,719.1	841.9
1	Influenza and pneumonia, except pneumonia of newborn	202.2	22.4
2	Tuberculosis, all forms	194.4	NA†
3	Gastroenteritis	142.7	NA
4	Disease of heart	137.4	235.6
5	Cerebrovascular diseases	106.9	54.2
6	Chronic nephritis	81.0	14.6
7	Accidents and adverse effects	72.3	37.6[2]
8	Malignant neoplasms	64.0	191.5
9	Certain diseases of early infancy	62.6	NA
10	Diphtheria	40.3	NA

* Some categories may not be strictly comparable because of change in classification.

† NA: These are no longer listed among the top 10 causes of death.

[1] Crude death rate

[2] Accidents (unintentional injuries)

Source: Data from Ventura SJ et al, U.S. Bureau of the Census, *Statistical Abstract of the United States: 1957,* p. 69, and from Hoyert DL, Heron MP, Murphy SL, Kung H. Deaths: Final Data for 2003. *National Vital Statistics Reports,* Vol 46, No 13, p. 5. Hyattsville, MD: National Center for Health Statistics; 2006.

CHAPTER 3

Measures of Morbidity and Mortality Used in Epidemiology

CHAPTER OUTLINE

    I. Introduction
   II. Definitions of Count, Ratio, Proportion, and Rate
  III. Risk versus Rate
  IV. Interrelationship Between Prevalence and Incidence
   V. Applications of Incidence Data
  VI. Crude Rates
 VII. Specific Rates
VIII. Adjusted Rates
  IX. Conclusion
   X. Study Questions and Exercises

Introduction

Chapter 1 stated that, because the work of the epidemiologist involves the enumeration of cases of diseases and health-related phenomena, epidemiology tends to be a quantitative discipline. This chapter defines several of the more common measures of disease frequency that are employed in epidemiology. The ability to measure carefully and accurately the occurrence of morbidity and mortality forms the foundation of studies designed to identify etiology, monitor trends, and evaluate public health interventions designed to reduce disease frequency.

Definitions of Count, Ratio, Proportion, and Rate

Count

The simplest and most frequently performed quantitative measure in epidemiology is a count. As the term implies, a *count* merely refers to the number of cases of a disease or other health phenomenon being studied. Several examples of counts include the number of:

- cases of influenza reported in Westchester County, New York, during January of a particular year
- traffic fatalities in the borough of Manhattan during a 24-hour period
- participants screened positive in a hypertension screening program organized by an industrial plant in northern California
- college dorm residents who had hepatitis
- stomach cancer patients who were foreign born

Ratio

A *ratio* is defined as "the value obtained by dividing one quantity by another: a general term of which rate, proportion, percentage, etc., are subsets."[1] A ratio therefore consists of a numerator and a denominator. The most general form of a ratio does not necessarily have any specified relationship between the numerator and denominator. A ratio may be expressed as follows: ratio = X/Y. For example, of 1,000 motorcycle fatalities, 950 victims are men and 50 are women. The sex ratio for motorcycle fatalities is:

$$\frac{\text{Number of male cases}}{\text{Number of female cases}} = \frac{950}{50} = 19{:}1 \text{ male to female}$$

Proportion

A *proportion* is a type of ratio in which the numerator is part of the denominator; proportions may be expressed as percentages. Let us consider how a proportion can be helpful in describing health issues by reexamining a count. For a count to be descriptive of a group, it usually should be seen relative to the size of the group. Referring to the foregoing examples, suppose there were 10 college dorm residents who had hepatitis. How large a problem did these 10 cases represent? To answer this question, one would need to know whether the dormitory housed 20 students or 500 students. If there were only 20 students, then 50% (or 0.50) were ill. Conversely, if there were 500 students in the dormitory, then only 2% (or 0.02) were ill. Clearly, these two scenarios paint a completely different picture of the magnitude of the problem. In this situation, expressing the count as a proportion is indeed helpful.

Table 3–1 illustrates the calculation of the proportion of African-American male deaths among African-American and white boys aged 5 to 14 years.

In most situations, it will be informative to have some idea about the size of the denominator. Although the construction of a proportion is straightforward, one of the central concerns of epidemiology is to find and enumerate appropriate denominators to describe and compare groups in a meaningful and useful way.

The previous discussion may leave the reader with the impression that counts, in and of themselves, are of little value in epidemiology; this is not true, however. In fact, case reports of patients with particularly unusual presentations or combinations of symptoms often spur epidemiologic investigations. In addition, for some diseases even a single case is sufficient to be of public health importance. For example, if a case of smallpox or Ebola virus were reported, the size of the denominator would be irrelevant. That is, in these instances a single case, regardless of the size of the population at risk, would stimulate an investigation.

Rate

Also a type of ratio, a *rate* differs from a proportion because the denominator involves a measure of time. The numerator consists of the frequency of a disease

Table 3–1 Calculation of the Proportion of African-American Male Deaths Among African-American and White Boys Aged 5 to 14 Years

A	B	Total (A + B)
Number of deaths among African-American boys	Number of deaths among white boys	Total
1,150	3,810	4,960

Proportion = A/(A + B) × 100 = (1,150/4,960) × 100 = 23.2%

over a specified period of time, and the denominator is a unit size of population (Exhibit 3–1). It is critical to remember that, to calculate a rate, two periods of time are involved: the beginning of the period and the end of the period.

Medical publications may use the terms ratio, proportion, and rate without strict adherence to the mathematical definitions for these terms. Hence, one must be alert to how a measure is defined and calculated.[2] In the formula shown in Exhibit 3–1, the denominator also is termed the *reference population* and by definition is the population from which cases of a disease have been taken. For example, in calculating the annual death rate (crude mortality rate) in the United States, one would count all the deaths that occurred in the country during a certain year and assign this value to the numerator. The value for the denominator would be the size of the population of the country during a particular year. The best estimate of the population would probably be the population around the

---

EXHIBIT 3–1

Rate Calculation

Rate: A ratio that consists of a numerator and a denominator and in which time forms part of the denominator.
  Epidemiologic rates contain the following elements:

- disease frequency
- unit size of population
- time period during which an event occurs

Example:

$$\text{Crude death rate} = \frac{\text{Number of deaths in a given year}}{\substack{\text{Reference population} \\ \text{(during midpoint of the year)}}} \times 100,000$$

(Either rate per 1,000 or 100,000 is used as the multiplier)

Calculation problem (crude death rate in the United States):

Number of deaths in the United States during 2003 = 2,448,288
Population of the United States as of July 1, 2003 = 290,810,789

$$\text{Crude death rate} = \frac{2,448,288}{290,810,789} = 841.9 \text{ per } 100,000$$

midpoint of the year, if such information could be obtained. Referring to Exhibit 3–1, one calculates the U.S. crude mortality rate as 841.9 per 100,000 persons for 2003.

Rates improve one's ability to make comparisons, although they also have limitations. Rates of mortality or morbidity for a specific disease (see the section on cause-specific mortality rates later in this chapter) reduce that standard of comparison to a common denominator, the unit size of population. To illustrate, the U.S. crude death rate for diseases of the heart in 2003 was 235.6 per 100,000. One also might calculate the heart disease death rate for geographic subdivisions of the country (also expressed as frequency per 100,000 individuals). These rates could then be compared with one another and with the rate for the United States to judge whether the rates found in each geographic area are higher or lower. For example, the crude death rates for diseases of the heart in New York and Texas were 288.0 and 188.9 per 100,000, respectively. It would appear that the death rate is higher in New York than in Texas based on the crude death rates. This may be a specious conclusion, however, because there may be important differences in population composition (e.g., age differences between populations) that would affect mortality experience. Later in this chapter, the procedure to adjust for age differences or other factors is discussed.

Rates can be expressed in any form that is convenient (e.g., per 1,000, per 100,000, or per 1,000,000). Many of the rates that are published and routinely used as an indicator of public health are expressed in a particular convention. For example, cancer rates are typically expressed per 100,000 population, and infant mortality is expressed per 1,000 live births. One of the determinants of the size of the denominator is whether the numerator is large enough to permit the rate to be expressed as an integer or an integer plus a trailing decimal (e.g., 4 or 4.2). For example, it would be preferable to describe the occurrence of disease as 4 per 100,000 rather than 0.04 per 1,000, even though both are perfectly correct. Throughout this chapter, the multiplier for a given morbidity or mortality statistic is provided.

Exhibit 3–2 describes the Iowa Women's Health Study (IWHS). ˉ   data collected illustrate the various measures of disease frequency defined ˙   ˉr.

Prevalence

The term *prevalence* refers to the number of existing cases condition in a population at some designated time.[1] A prevalence is analogous to water that has collected in a fall. Prevalence data provide an indication of the exte

EXHIBIT 3–2

The Iowa Women's Health Study

The IWHS is a longitudinal study of mortality and cancer occurrence in older women.[3,4] The state of Iowa was chosen as the site of this study because of the availability of cancer incidence and mortality data from the State Health Registry of Iowa. This registry is a participant in the National Cancer Institute's Surveillance, Epidemiology, and End Results Program. The sample was selected from a January 1985 current drivers list obtained from the Iowa Department of Transportation. The list contained the names of 195,294 women aged 55 to 69 and represented approximately 94% of the women in the state of Iowa in this age range.

In December 1985, a 50% random sample of the eligible women was selected, yielding 99,826 women with an Iowa mailing address. A 16-page health history questionnaire was mailed on January 16, 1986, followed by a reminder postcard one week later and a follow-up letter four weeks later; a total of 41,837 women responded. Information was collected about basic demographics, medical history, reproductive history, personal and family history of cancer, usual dietary intake, smoking and exercise habits, and medication use. A paper tape measure also was provided along with detailed instructions for the subject to record selected body measurements: height, weight, and circumferences of the waist and hips.

The primary focus of the study was to determine whether distribution of body fat centrally (i.e., around the waist) rather than peripherally (i.e., on the hips) is associated with increased risk of cancer. The occurrence of cancer was determined by record linkage with the State Health Registry. A computer program was used to match new cancer cases in the registry with study participants on name, ZIP code, birth date, and Social Security number. ■

thus may have implications for the scope of health services needed in the community. Consider three examples: The prevalence of diarrhea in a children's camp on July 13 was 33%, the prevalence of phenylketonuria-associated mental retardation in institutions for the developmentally disabled was 15%, and the prevalence of obesity among women aged 55 to 69 years was 367 per 1,000. These examples ___te that the designated time can be specified (e.g., one day) or unspecified. ___e period is unspecified, prevalence usually implies a particular point ___ifically, these examples refer to *point prevalence.*

FIGURE 3–1   Analogy of prevalence and incidence. The water flowing down the waterfall symbolizes incidence and the water collecting in the pool at the base symbolizes prevalence.

$$\text{Point prevalence} = \frac{\text{Number of persons ill}}{\text{Total number in the group}} \text{ at a time point}$$

Example: In the IWHS, respondents were asked: "Do yo[...]
rettes now?" The total number in the group was 41,837[...]
ber who responded yes to the smoking question was[...]
the prevalence of current smokers in the IWHS on Ja[...]
6,234/41,837. This result could be expressed as a[...]
as a frequency per 1,000 (149.0).

A second type of prevalence measure is *period prevalence,* which denotes the total number of cases of a disease that exist during a specified period of time, for instance a week, month, or longer time interval. To determine the period prevalence, one must combine the number of cases at the beginning of the time interval (the point prevalence) with the new cases that occur during the interval. Because the denominator may have changed somewhat (the result of people entering or leaving during the period of observation), one typically refers to the average population. Note that for period prevalence, cases are counted even if they die, migrate, or recur as episodes during the period.

$$\text{Period prevalence} = \frac{\text{Number of persons ill}}{\text{Average population}} \text{ during a time period}$$

Example: In the IWHS, women were asked: "Have you ever been diagnosed by a physician as having any form of cancer, other than skin cancer?" Note that the question did not ask about current disease but rather about the lifetime history. Thus, it refers to period prevalence, the period being the entire life span. To calculate the period prevalence, one needs to know the average population (still 41,837) and the number who responded yes to the question (2,293). Therefore, the period prevalence of cancer in the study population was 2,293/41,837, or 5.5%.

Technically speaking, both measures of prevalence are proportions. As such, they are dimensionless and should not be described as rates, a mistake that is commonly made.

To illustrate the distinction between point and period prevalence, consider as an example the issue of homelessness in the United States. The conditions surrounding homelessness present a serious public health problem, particularly in the control of infectious diseases and the effect on homeless persons' physical and mental health. Consequently, there is a legitimate need to estimate the magnitude of the problem, an issue that has produced intense debate. Surveys of currently homeless people pose extremely challenging ethodologic difficulties that have led some authorities to believe that point nce may lead to serious underreporting. According to Link and col- first problem is finding people who are currently homeless.

Surveys may miss the so-called hidden homeless, who sleep in box cars, on the roofs of tenements, in campgrounds, or in other places that researchers cannot effectively search. [Even if located] . . . respondents may refuse to be interviewed or deliberately hide the fact that they are homeless."[5(p. 1907)] People who experience relatively short or intermittent episodes of literal homelessness are likely to be missed in brief surveys. To address these problems, Link et al.[5] conducted a national household telephone survey to provide lifetime and five-year period prevalence estimates. They found that 14% of the sample had ever been homeless, 4.6% in the last five years. Compared with previous estimates based on point prevalence, the investigators concluded that the magnitude of the problem was much greater than previous estimates had indicated.

Prevalence data are useful in describing the health burden of a population, to estimate the frequency of an exposure, and in allocation of health resources, such as facilities and personnel. Typically, prevalence data are not as helpful for studies of etiology. There are several reasons for this, but the main concern has to do with the possible influences of differential survival. That is, for a case to be included in a prevalence study, he or she would have had to survive the disease long enough to participate. Cases who died before participation would obviously be missed, resulting in a truncated sample of eligible cases. Risk factors for rapidly fatal cases may be quite different from risk factors for less severe manifestations. One situation in which the use of prevalent cases may be justified for studies of disease etiology arises when a condition has an indefinite time of onset, such as occurs in mental illness.[2]

Incidence Rate (Cumulative Incidence)

The term *incidence* describes the rate of development of a disease in a group over a certain time period; this period of time is included in the denominator. In Figure 3–1, incidence is analogous to water flowing in the waterfall (new cases). An incidence rate (Exhibit 3–3) includes three important elements:

1. a numerator: the number of new cases
2. a denominator: the population at risk
3. time: the period during which the cases accrue

Number of New Cases

The incidence rate uses the frequency of new cases in the numerator. This means that individuals who have a history of the disease are not included.

EXHIBIT 3-3

Incidence Rate

$$\text{Incidence rate} = \frac{\begin{array}{c}\text{Number of new cases}\\\text{over a time period}\end{array}}{\begin{array}{c}\text{Total population at risk}\\\text{during the same time period}\end{array}} \times \begin{array}{c}\text{multiplier}\\\text{(e.g., 100,000)}\end{array}$$

The denominator consists of the population at risk (i.e., those who are at risk for contracting the disease).

Example: Calculate the incidence rate of postmenopausal breast cancer in the IWHS. The population at risk in this example would not include women who were still premenopausal ($n = 569$), women who had had their breasts surgically removed ($n = 1,870$), and women with a previous diagnosis of cancer ($n = 2,293$). Thus, the denominator is 37,105 women. After eight years of follow-up, 1,085 cases were identified through the State Health Registry. The incidence rate is therefore 1,085/37,105 per eight years. To express this rate per 100,000 population: divide 1,085 by 37,105 (answer: 0.02924). This is the rate over an eight-year period. For the annual rate, divide this number by eight years (answer: 0.003655) and multiply by 100,000. ■

Answer: 365.5 cases of postmenopausal breast cancer per 100,000 women per year.

Population at Risk

The denominator for incidence rates is the population at risk. One therefore should exclude individuals who have already developed the disease of interest (e.g., those who have had heart attacks) or are not capable of developing the disease. For example, if one wanted to calculate the rate of ovarian cancer in the IWHS, women who had had their ovaries removed (oophorectomized women) should be excluded from the cohort at risk. It is not uncommon, however, to see some incidence rates based on the average population as the denominator rather than the population at risk. This distinction really must be made for those infectious diseases that confer lifetime immunity against recurrence. Regarding chronic diseases to which most people appear to be susceptible, the distinction is less critical. The population at risk may include those exposed to a disease agent or unimmunized or debilitated people, or it may consist of an entire population (e.g., a county, a city, or a nation). The population at risk may represent special risk categories; occupational injury and illness incidence rates are calculated for full-time workers in various occupations, for example, because these are the populations at risk.

Specification of a Time Period

The definition of incidence entails the designation of a time period, such as a week, a month, a year, or a multiyear time period. To determine an incidence rate, one must be able to specify the date of onset for the condition during the time period. Some acute conditions (e.g., a severe stroke or an acute myocardial infarction) may have a readily identifiable time of onset. Other conditions (e.g., cancer) may have an indefinite time of onset, which is defined by the initial definitive diagnosis date for the disease.[6]

Attack Rate

The *attack rate (AR)* is an alternative form of the incidence rate that is used when the nature of the disease or condition is such that a population is observed for a short time period, often as a result of specific exposure.[2] In reporting outbreaks of *Salmonella* infection or other foodborne types of gastroenteritis, epidemiologists employ the AR. The formula for the AR is:

$$AR = Ill/(Ill + well) \times 100 \text{ (during a time period)}$$

As shown in this formula, the numerator consists of people who are ill as a result of exposure to the suspected agent, and the denominator consists of all people, whether well or ill, who were exposed to the agent during a time period. Strictly speaking, the AR is not a true rate because the time dimension is often uncertain or specified arbitrarily.

Although the AR often is used to measure the incidence of disease during acute infectious disease epidemics, it also may be used for the incidence of other conditions where the risk is limited to a short time period or the etiologic factors operate only within certain age groups. An example is hypertrophic pyloric stenosis, which occurs predominantly in the first three months of life and is practically unknown after the age of six months. Illustrations of the methods to calculate an AR and secondary AR are given in Chapter 12.

Risk Versus Rate

Epidemiologists have been known to use the terms risk and rate interchangeably. However, if pressed to explain the difference, they would be able (one hopes) to identify several key distinctions. First, risk is a statement of the probability or chance that an individual will develop a disease over a specified period, conditioned on that individual's not dying from any other disease during the period.[7] As such, risk ranges from 0 to 1 and is dimensionless. Statements of risk also require a specific reference period, for example, the five-year risk of developing asthma. Risk can be estimated as the cumulative incidence of a particular disease. The *cumulative incidence* is the proportion of a fixed population that becomes diseased during a stated period of time. The illustration regarding the incidence of postmenopausal breast cancer in the IWHS is an example of a cumulative incidence.

Because the population is fixed, no individuals are allowed to enter the denominator after the start of the observation period, and the numerator can include only individuals who were members of that fixed population. Calculation of cumulative incidence also requires that disease status be determined for everyone in the denominator. That is, once a group of individuals is selected for follow-up for disease occurrence, subsequent information about the occurrence of disease is obtained for everyone selected, which is difficult to achieve even in the best of circumstances. Most of the regions where we live and work contain dynamic populations; people move into and out of the area. Some individuals who were not in the study population at the baseline period may move into the region and become ill. Thus, the numerator has increased but the denominator has not. Conversely, if an individual moves away and then develops the disease, he or she would be counted in the denominator but not in the numerator. One solution to the problem of geographic mobility and loss to follow-up is to use rates as an indicator of risk. A simple perspective is that groups with high rates of disease are at greater risk than are groups with low rates of disease. The issue is a bit more complicated than that perspective (and beyond the scope of this book). The main caveat is that rates can be used to estimate risk only when the period of follow-up is short and the rate of disease over that interval is relatively constant. Thus, to estimate small risks, one simply multiplies the average rate times the duration of follow-up.[8]

A special problem occurs when a population or study group is under observation for different lengths of time. This may occur for a variety of reasons, including attrition or dropout, mortality, or development of the disease under study. Consider the calculation of the incidence of postmenopausal breast cancer in the

IWHS. Although the study was able to identify all cancers diagnosed within the state, some women may have moved out of state after the initial questionnaire administration. Any cancers diagnosed among these women would be unknown to the investigators. Other women died before the end of the follow-up period. In the previous calculation, we merely counted the number of cases over the eight-year period of follow-up ($n = 1,042$) and divided by the number of women at risk ($n = 37,105$). The implicit assumption of this calculation is that each of the 37,105 women was "observed" for the full eight-year period. Clearly, this could not be the case. To allow for varying periods of observation of the subjects, one uses a modification of the formula for the incidence in which the denominator becomes person-time of observation. Incidence density is defined in Exhibit 3–4.[2] An example of how to calculate person-years is shown in Table 3–2.

In Table 3–2, person-years were derived simply by summing the product of each category of length of observation and the number of subjects in the category. A more difficult issue is how one actually determines the length of observation for each individual. Visiting again the IWHS example, a computer program was used to tabulate, for each individual, the amount of time that elapsed from receipt of the mailed questionnaire until the occurrence of one of the following

EXHIBIT 3-4

Incidence Density

$$\text{Incidence density} = \frac{\text{Number of new cases during the time period}}{\text{Total person-time of observation}}$$

When the period of observation is measured in years, the formula becomes:

$$\text{Incidence density} = \frac{\text{Number of new cases during the time period}}{\text{Total person-years of observation}}$$

Example: In the IWHS, the 37,105 women at risk for postmenopausal breast cancer contributed 276,453 person-years of follow-up. Because there were 1,085 incident cases, the rate of breast cancer using the incidence density method is $1,085/276,453 = 392.5$ per 100,000 per year. Note that, had each woman been followed for the entire eight-year period of follow-up, the total person-years would have been 296,840. Because the actual amount of follow-up was 20,000 person-years less than this, the estimated rate of breast cancer was higher (and more accurate) using the incidence density method. ■

Table 3–2   Person-Years of Observation for Hypothetical Study Subjects in a 10-Year Heart Disease Research Project

A Number of Subjects	B Length of Observation (Years)	A × B Person-Years
30	10	300
10	9	90
7	8	56
2	7	14
1	1	1
Totals 50		461

Number of health events (heart attacks) observed during the 10-year period: 5.

Incidence density = (5/461) × 100 = 1.08 per 100 person-years of observation.

events (listed in order of priority): breast cancer diagnosis, death (if in Iowa), a move out of Iowa (if known through the National Change of Address Service), midpoint of interval between date of last contact and December 30, 1993, or midpoint of interval between date of last contact and date of death (for deaths that occurred out of Iowa, identified through the National Death Index). Women who did not experience any of these events were assumed to be alive in Iowa and contributed follow-up until December 30, 1993. This real-life example illustrates that actual computation of person-years, although conceptually straightforward, can be a fairly complicated procedure.

Interrelationship Between Prevalence and Incidence

Interrelationship: $P \cong ID$

The prevalence (P) of a disease is proportional to the incidence rate (I) times the duration (D) of a disease.

For conditions of short duration and high incidence, one may infer from this formula that, when the duration of a disease becomes short and the incidence is high, the prevalence becomes similar to incidence. For diseases of short duration, cases recover rapidly or are fatal, eliminating the build-up of prevalent cases. Some of the infectious diseases of short duration, such as the common cold, are examples. Many chronic diseases generally have a low incidence and long duration; as the duration of the disease increases, even though incidence is low the prevalence of the disease increases relative to incidence.

Figure 3–2 illustrates the relationship between incidence and prevalence. Suppose that there is an outbreak of meningococcal disease in a summer school class of 10 students. The frequency of the disease is recorded for two weeks. Individual cases plotted by the duration of each case for the period July 1 through July 14 are shown in Figure 3–2. For the 10-day period (July 5 through July 14), the period prevalence of meningococcal disease was 8/10; the point prevalence of disease on July 5 was 5/10. Because the disease in this example is one that can affect individuals more than once (no lifetime immunity after initial infection), the incidence rate of disease was 3/10. Note that on July 5 cases A, B, C, D, and F were existing cases of disease and were not included in the count for incidence; subsequently, case A was a recurrent case and should be counted once for incidence and twice for period prevalence. The measure of incidence would be more accurate if the cumulative duration of observation (person-days) were used in the denominator. If one was interested only in the first occurrence of

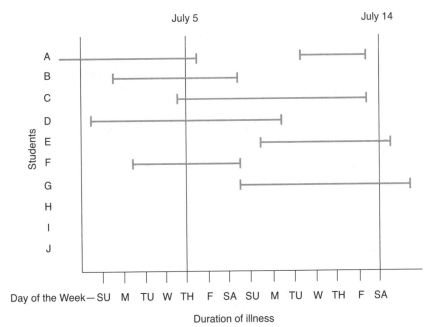

FIGURE 3–2 Outbreak of meningococcal infections in a summer school class of 10 students. *Note:* Students H, I, and J were not ill.

meningococcal disease, then students A, B, C, D, and F would not have been included in the estimation of incidence, because they were prevalent cases on July 5. In that situation, the incidence would have been 2/5.

Applications of Incidence Data

It was noted earlier that prevalence data are useful for determining the extent of a disease (particularly chronic diseases) or health problem in the community. Prevalence data are not as helpful as incidence data for studies of etiology because of the possible influence of differential survival. Incidence data (e.g., cumulative incidence rates) help in research on the etiology of disease because they provide estimates of risk of developing the disease. Thus, incidence rates are considered to be fundamental tools in research that pursues the causality of diseases. Note how the incidence rate of postmenopausal breast cancer was calculated in the IWHS. As we shall see in Chapter 7, comparison of incidence rates in population groups that differ in exposures permits one to estimate the effects of exposure to a hypothesized factor of interest. This topic is discussed also in Chapter 9.

Crude Rates

The basic concept of a rate can be broken down into three general categories: crude rates, specific rates, and adjusted rates. *Crude rates* are summary rates based on the actual number of events in a population over a given time period. An example is the crude death rate, which approximates the proportion of a population that dies during a time period of interest.[1] Refer to the study questions and exercises at the end of this chapter for calculation problems. Some of the more commonly used crude rates are presented in Exhibit 3–5. The definitions for measures of natality (statistics associated with births) come from *Health, United States, 2006.*[9]

Birth Rate

The *crude birth rate* refers to the number of live births during a specified period of time (e.g., one calendar year) per the resident population during the midpoint of the time period (expressed as rate per 1,000). The crude birth rate is a useful measure of population growth and is an index for comparison of developed and developing countries; as noted in Chapter 2, the crude birth rate is generally higher in less developed areas than in more developed areas of the world. As an illustration of this measure, Figure 3–3 presents birth rates categorized by age of mother for the United States for the years 1990 to 2004.

$$\text{Crude birth rate} = \frac{\text{Number of live births within a given period}}{\text{Population size at the middle of that period}} \times 1,000 \text{ population}$$

Sample calculation: 4,112,052 babies were born in the United States during 2004, when the U.S. population was 293,655,404. The birth rate was 4,112,052/293,655,404 = 14.0 per 1,000.

EXHIBIT 3-5

Examples of Crude Rates: Overview of Measures That Pertain to Birth, Fertility, Infant Mortality, and Related Phenomena

- *Crude birth rate:* used to project population changes; it is affected by the number and age composition of women of childbearing age.
- *Fertility rate:* used for comparisons of fertility among age, racial, and socioeconomic groups.
- *Infant mortality rate:* used for international comparisons; a high rate indicates unmet health needs and poor environmental conditions.
- *Fetal death rate* (and late fetal death rate): used to estimate the risk of death of the fetus associated with the stages of gestation.
- *Fetal death ratio:* provides a measure of fetal wastage (loss) relative to the number of live births.
- *Neonatal mortality rate:* reflects events happening after birth, primarily:
  1. Congenital malformations
  2. Prematurity (birth before gestation week 28)
  3. Low birth weight (birth weight less than 2,500 g)
- *Postneonatal mortality rate:* reflects environmental events, control of infectious diseases and improvement in nutrition. Since 1950, neonatal mortality in the United States has declined; postneonatal mortality has not declined greatly.
- *Perinatal mortality rate:* reflects events that occur during pregnancy and after birth; it combines mortality during the prenatal and postnatal periods.
- *Maternal mortality rate:* reflects health care access and socioeconomic factors; it includes maternal deaths resulting from causes associated with pregnancy and puerperium (during and after childbirth). ■

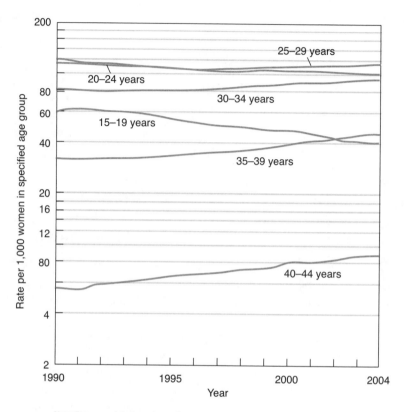

Note: Rates are plotted on a log scale.

FIGURE 3–3   Birth rates by age of mother: United States, 1990–2004. *Source:* Reprinted from JA Martin, BE Hamilton, PD Sutton, et al. Births: Final data for 2004, *National Vital Statistics Reports,* Vol 55, No 1, p. 7. Hyattsville, MD: National Center for Health Statistics; 2006.

Fertility Rate

There are several types of fertility rates, but one of the most noteworthy is the *general fertility rate.* This rate consists of the number of live births reported in an area during a given time interval (for example, during 1 year), divided by the number of women aged 15 to 44 years in that area. The population size for the number of women aged 15 to 44 years is assessed at the midpoint of the year. Sometimes the age range of 15 to 49 years is used. Figure 3–4 illustrates fertility rates for the United States from 1950 to 1992. (The general fertility rate is often referred to more generically as the fertility rate.)

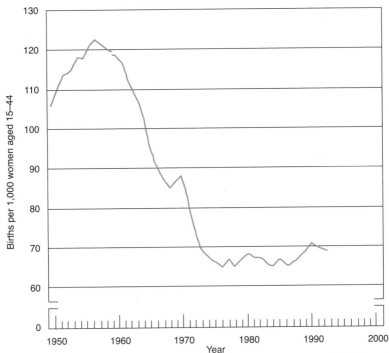

NOTE: Beginning with 1959, trend line is based on registered live births; trend line for 1950–1959 is based on live births adjusted for underregistration.

FIGURE 3–4   Fertility rates: United States, 1950–1992. *Source:* Reprinted from National Center for Health Statistics, Annual Summary of Births, Marriages, Divorces and Deaths, United States, 1992, *Monthly Vital Statistics Report*, Vol 41, No 13, p. 3. Hyattsville, MD: National Center for Health Statistics; 1993.

$$\text{General fertility rate} = \frac{\text{Number of live births within a year}}{\text{Number of women aged 15–44 years during the midpoint of the year}} \times 1{,}000 \text{ women aged 15–44}$$

Sample calculation: During 2004, there were 62,033,402 women aged 15 to 44 in the United States. There were 4,112,052 live births. The general fertility rate was 4,112,052/62,033,402 = 66.3 per 1,000 women aged 15 to 44.

Infant Mortality Rate

The infant mortality rate measures the risk of dying during the first year of life among infants born alive. Note that not all infants who die in a calendar year are born in that year, which represents a source of error. Typically, however, the number of infant deaths from previous years' births is balanced by an equal number of deaths during the following year among the current year's births. The following is the definition of the infant mortality rate:

$$\text{Infant mortality} = \frac{\text{Number of infant deaths among infants aged 0–365 days during the year}}{\text{Number of live births during the year}} \times 1{,}000 \text{ live births}$$

Sample calculation: In the United States during 2003, there were 28,025 deaths among infants under 1 year of age and 4,089,950 live births. The infant mortality rate was (28,025/4,089,950) × 1,000 = 6.85 per 1,000 live births.

Infant mortality rates are highest among the least developed countries of the world (e.g., Sierra Leone with 165 per 1,000 births in 2005) in comparison with some developing countries (e.g., India with 56 per 1,000), less developed countries of Eastern Europe (e.g., Romania with 16 per 1,000), and developed market economies (e.g., Sweden with 3 per 1,000).[10] Figure 3–5 shows trends in U.S. infant mortality by race from 1940 to 1995 (Part A) and from 1995 to 2004 (Part B). Note how total infant mortality rates declined steadily until 2000 and have declined very little since then. The disparity between whites and African Americans continues. Figure 3–6 presents a comparison of the infant mortality rate of the U.S. with that reported by other industrialized nations. In year 2000, the U.S. infant mortality rate ranked 27th.

Fetal Mortality

Fetal mortality indices depend on estimation of fetal death after a certain number of weeks of gestation. In the following three definitions, the gestation time is stated or presumed. The fetal death rate is defined as the number of fetal deaths after 20 weeks or more gestation divided by the number of live births plus fetal deaths (after 20 weeks or more gestation). It is expressed as rate per 1,000 live

A

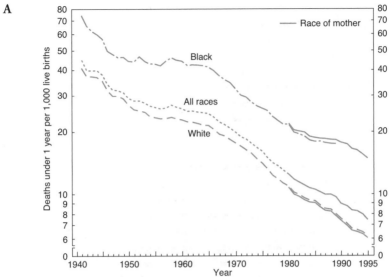

NOTE: Infant deaths are classified by race of decedent. 1940–1990, live births are classified by race of child and for 1980–1994, by race of mother.

B

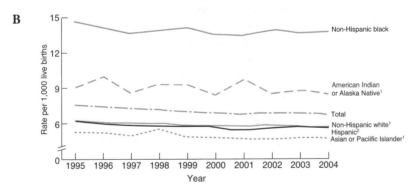

[1]Includes persons of Hispanic and Non-Hispanic origin.
[2]Persons of Hispanic origin may be of any race.

FIGURE 3–5   Part A: Infant mortality rates by race: United States, 1950–1995. *Source:* Modified from Anderson RN, Kochanek KD, and Murphy SL. Report of Final Monthly Statistics, 1995, *Monthly Vital Statistics Report*, Vol 45, No 11, Suppl 2, p. 12. Hyattsville, MD: National Center for Health Statistics; 1997. Part B: Infant mortality rates by race and ethnicity, 1995–2004. *Source:* From Mathews TJ, MacDorman MF. Infant mortality statistics from the 2004 period linked birth/infant death data set, *National Vital Statistics Reports*; Vol 55, No 15, p. 1. Hyattsville, MD: National Center for Health Statistics; 2007.

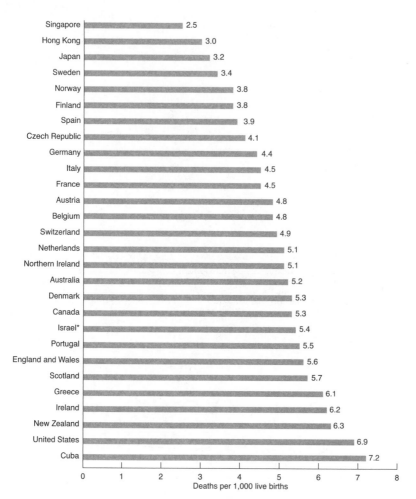

FIGURE 3–6 Comparison of international infant mortality rates, 2000. *Includes data for East Jerusalem and Israeli residents in certain other territories under occupation by Israeli military since June 1967. *Source:* From Child Health USA 2004, International Infant Mortality Rates. Available at: http://mchb.hrsa.gov/mchirc/chusa_04/pages/ 0405iimr.htm. Accessed October 12, 2007.

births and fetal deaths. The late fetal death rate refers to fetal deaths after 28 weeks or more gestation. Both measures pertain to a calendar year.

The fetal death ratio refers to the number of fetal deaths after gestation of 20 weeks or more divided by the number of live births during a year. It is expressed as rate per 1,000 live births.

Fetal death rate (per 1,000 live births plus fetal deaths)

$$= \frac{\text{Number of fetal deaths after 20 weeks or more gestation}}{\text{Number of live births + number of fetal deaths after 20 weeks or more gestation}} \times 1,000$$

Late fetal death rate (per 1,000 live births plus late fetal deaths)

$$= \frac{\text{Number of fetal deaths after 28 weeks or more gestation}}{\text{Number of live births + number of fetal deaths after 28 weeks or more gestation}} \times 1,000$$

Fetal death ratio

$$= \frac{\text{Number of fetal deaths after 20 weeks or more gestation}}{\text{Number of live births}} \times 1,000 \text{ (during a year)}$$

Sample calculation: During 1 year there were 134 fetal deaths with 20 weeks or more gestation and 10,000 live births. The fetal death ratio is (134/10,000) = 13.4 per 1,000. Note that the fetal death rate is (134/10,134) = 13.2 per 1,000, which is slightly lower than the fetal death ratio.

Neonatal Mortality Rate

The neonatal mortality rate measures risk of dying among newborn infants who are under the age of 28 days (0–27 days) for a given year. The formula is as follows:

Neonatal mortality rate

$$= \frac{\text{Number of infant deaths under 28 days of age}}{\text{Number of live births}} \times 1,000 \text{ live births (during a year)}$$

Postneonatal Mortality Rate

A statistic that is related to the neonatal mortality rate is the postneonatal mortality rate. The postneonatal mortality rate measures risk of dying among older infants during a given year.

Postneonatal mortality rate

$$= \frac{\begin{array}{c}\text{Number of infant deaths from}\\ \text{28 days to 365 days after birth}\end{array}}{\text{Number of live births} - \text{neonatal deaths}} \times 1{,}000 \text{ live births}$$

Figure 3–7 illustrates trends in infant mortality rates, neonatal mortality rates, and postneonatal mortality rates in the United States. According to the National Center for Health Statistics, with the exception of 2002 (not apparent in the figure), the infant mortality rate decreased or remained constant from 1958 to 2003.[11] The postneonatal mortality rate also declined during this time period, but

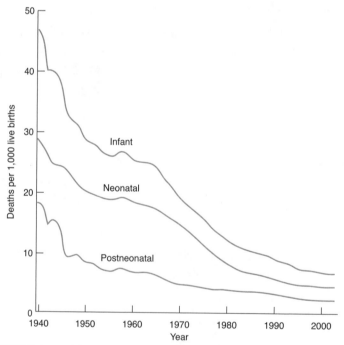

NOTE: Rates are infant (under 1 year), neonatal (under 28 days), and postneonatal (28 days–11 months) deaths per 1,000 live births in specified group.

FIGURE 3–7   Infant, neonatal, and postneonatal mortality rates: United States, 1940–2003. *Source:* From Hoyert DL, Heron MP, Murphy SL, Kung H. Deaths: Final Data for 2003. *National Vital Statistics Reports,* Vol 54, No 13, p. 12. Hyattsville, MD: National Center for Health Statistics; 2006.

not as steeply. The infant mortality rate is higher than neonatal and postneonatal mortality rates; in addition, both infant and neonatal mortality rates are higher than the postneonatal mortality rate. Between 2002 and 2003, the decline in neonatal mortality (4.66 vs. 4.62) was not statistically significant. The postneonatal mortality rate decreased by 3.5% (from 2.31 to 2.23 per 1,000 live births).

Perinatal Mortality

Two measures of perinatal mortality are the perinatal mortality rate and the perinatal mortality ratio. The perinatal period used in these measures captures late fetal deaths plus infant deaths within seven days of birth.

Perinatal mortality rate

$$= \frac{\text{Number of late fetal deaths after 28 weeks or more gestation + infant deaths within 7 days of birth}}{\text{Number of live births + number of late fetal deaths}} \times 1{,}000 \text{ live births and fetal deaths}$$

Perinatal mortality ratio

$$= \frac{\text{Number of late fetal deaths after 28 weeks or more gestation + infant deaths within 7 days of birth}}{\text{Number of live births}} \times 1{,}000 \text{ live births}$$

Maternal Mortality Rate

The maternal mortality rate is the number of maternal deaths ascribed to childbirth (i.e., pregnancy and puerperal causes) per 10,000 or 100,000 live births. Factors that affect maternal mortality include maternal age, socioeconomic status, nutritional status, and healthcare access.

Maternal mortality rate
(per 100,000 live births, including multiple births)

$$= \frac{\text{Number of deaths assigned to causes related to childbirth}}{\text{Number of live births}} \times 100{,}000 \text{ live births (during a year)}$$

Specific Rates

Although the crude rates described so far are important and useful summary measures of the occurrence of disease, they are not without limitations. A crude rate should be used with caution in making comparative statements about disease frequencies in populations. Observed differences between populations in crude rates of disease may be the result of systematic factors within the populations rather than true variations in rates. Systematic differences in sex or age distributions would affect observed rates. To correct for factors that may influence the make-up of populations and in turn influence crude rates, one may construct specific and adjusted rates. Specific rates refer to a particular subgroup of the population defined, for example, in terms of race, age, or sex, or they may refer to the entire population but be specific for some single cause of death or illness. Two other measures that have been defined previously also can be considered specific measures: incidence and prevalence. That is, both are typically specific to a particular end point.

Cause-Specific Rate

An example of a cause-specific rate is the cause-specific mortality rate. As the name implies, it is the rate associated with a specific cause of death. A sample calculation is shown in Table 3–3. The number of deaths among the 25- to 34-year-old age group (population 39,872,598) due to human immunodeficiency virus (HIV) infection was 1,588 during 2003. The cause-specific mortality rate due to HIV was (1,588/39,872,598), or 4.0 per 100,000.

Cause-specific rate

$$= \frac{\text{Mortality (or frequency of a given disease)}}{\text{Population size at midpoint of time period}} \times 100,000$$

Proportional Mortality Ratio

The *proportional mortality ratio (PMR)* is the number of deaths within a population due to a specific disease or cause divided by the total number of deaths in the population.

Table 3-3 The 10 Leading Causes of Death, 25-34 Years, All Races, Both Sexes, United States, 2003 (Number in population aged 25-34 years = 39,872,598)

Rank Order	Cause of Death	Number	Proportional Mortality Ratio (%)	Cause-Specific Death Rate per 100,000
1	Accidents (unintentional injuries)	12,541	30.4	31.5
2	Intentional self-harm (suicide)	5,065	12.3	12.7
3	Assault (homicide)	4,516	10.9	11.3
4	Malignant neoplasms	3,741	9.1	9.4
5	Diseases of the heart	3,250	7.9	8.2
6	Human immunodeficiency virus (HIV) disease	1,588	3.8	4.0
7	Diabetes mellitus	657	1.6	1.6
8	Cerebrovascular diseases	583	1.4	1.5
9	Congenital malformations, deformations and chromosomal abnormalities	426	1.0	1.1
10	Influenza and pneumonia	373	0.9	0.9
	All causes	41,300		

Source: Adapted from Heron MP, Smith BL. Deaths: Leading Causes for 2003. *National Vital Statistics Reports,* Vol 55, No 10, p. 18. Hyattsville, MD: National Center for Health Statistics; 2007.

PMR (%)

$$= \frac{\text{Mortality due to a specific cause during a time period}}{\text{Mortality due to all causes during the same time period}} \times 100$$

Sample calculation: In a certain community, there were 66 deaths due to coronary heart disease during a year and 200 deaths due to all causes in that year. The PMR is $(66/200) \times 100 = 33\%$.

Refer to Table 3-3 for a more detailed example of a PMR. In Table 3-3, the PMR is calculated according to the formula given above. For example, the proportional mortality ratio for HIV among the 25- to 34-year-old group was 3.8% (1,588/41,300). This PMR should be used with caution when comparisons are made across populations, especially those that have different rates of total mortality. To illustrate, consider that two countries have identical death rates from cardiovascular disease (perhaps 5 per 100,000 per year) and that each country has exactly 1 million inhabitants. Therefore, one would expect 50 deaths from cardiovascular disease to occur in each country (5 per 100,000 per year × 1,000,000). Suppose further, however, that in country A the total death rate per 100,000 per year is 30 and that it is only 10 in country B. Therefore, the expected total number of deaths would be 300 in country A and only 100 in country B. When these data are used to construct a PMR, one sees that the proportion of deaths from cardiovascular disease is higher in country B (0.50) than in country A (0.17). The PMR is not a measure of the risk of dying of a particular cause. It merely indicates, within a population, the relative importance of a specific cause of death. For a health administrator, such information may be useful to determine priorities and planning. To an epidemiologist, such differences may indicate an area for further study. For example, why does country A have such higher total mortality rates than country B? Is it merely because of differences in age structure? Is the difference a result of access to health care or certain behavioral or lifestyle patterns associated with elevated mortality? The PMR is not to be confused with a case fatality rate (see Chapter 12). The case fatality rate expresses the proportion of fatal cases among all cases of disease during a specific time period.

Age-Specific Rates

To calculate age-specific rates, one subdivides (or stratifies) a population into age groups, such as those defined by 5- or 10-year intervals. Then, one divides the frequency of a disease in a particular age stratum by the total number of persons within that age stratum to find the age-specific rate. A similar procedure may be employed to calculate sex-specific rates. An example of an age-specific cancer mortality rate is shown in Exhibit 3–6. A second example of the calculation of age-specific mortality rates for the U.S. population is shown in Table 3–4 (some age-specific death rates shown in Table 3–4 differ from published rates because of differences in estimation of population size and use of different intervals for age groups).

Table 3–5 presents a summary of unadjusted measures of morbidity and mortality discussed in this chapter. We provide this table to assist you with future review and reference to these measures.

EXHIBIT 3-6

Age-Specific Rate (R_i)

Age-specific rate: The number of cases per age group of population (during a specified time period).

Example:

$$R_i = \frac{\text{Number of deaths among those aged 5–14 years}}{\text{Number of persons who are aged 5–14 years}} \times 100{,}000$$
$$\text{(during time period)}$$

Sample calculation: In the United States during 2003, there were 1,651 deaths due to malignant neoplasms among the age group 5 to 14 years, and there were 40,968,637 persons in the same age group. The age-specific malignant neoplasm death rate in this age group is (1,651/40,968,637) = 4.0 per 100,000. ■

Table 3–4 Method of Calculation of Age-Specific Death Rates

Age Group (Years)	Number of Deaths (D_i) in 2003	Number in Population (P_i) as of July 1, 2003*	Age-Specific Rate (R_i) per 100,000
Under 1	28,025	4,003,606	700.0
1–4	4,965	15,765,673	31.5
5–14	6,954	40,968,637	17.0
15–24	33,568	41,206,163	81.5
25–34	41,300	39,872,598	103.6
35–44	89,461	44,370,594	201.6
45–54	176,781	40,804,599	433.2
55–64	262,519	27,899,736	940.9
65–74	413,497	18,337,044	2,255.0
75–84	703,024	12,868,672	5,463.1
85+	687,852	4,713,467	14,593.3
Not stated	342	NA	NA
Totals	2,448,288	290,810,789	841.9**

* Estimated

** The crude mortality rate for the United States

Source: Data from Hoyert DL, Heron MP, Murphy SL, Kung H. Deaths: Final Data for 2003. *National Vital Statistics Reports,* Vol 54, No 13, pp. 23 and 112. Hyattsville, MD: National Center for Health Statistics; 2006.

Table 3–5 Summary of Unadjusted Measures of Morbidity and Mortality Discussed in this Chapter*

Measure	Numerator (x)	Denominator (y)	Expressed per Number at Risk (10^n)
Age-specific rate (e.g., mortality rate)	Number of deaths among a specific age group of the population during a specified time period	Number of persons who comprise that age group during the same time period	100,000
Attack rate	Number ill during a time period	Number ill + well during the same time period	100 (or percent)
Case fatality rate (discussed in Chapter 12)	Number of deaths due to disease "X" during a given time interval	Number of new cases of that disease reported during the same time interval	100 (or percent)
Cause-specific rate, (e.g., cause-specific death or mortality rate)	Number of deaths (mortality) assigned to a specific cause during a year	Estimated population size during the midpoint of that same year	100,000
Crude birth rate	Number of live births within a given period	Population size at the midpoint of that time period	1,000
Crude death rate	Number of deaths during a given year	Reference population during the midpoint of the year	100,000
Fetal death rate	Number of fetal deaths after 20 weeks or more gestation during a year	Number of live births + number of fetal deaths after 20 weeks or more gestation during the same year	1,000
Fetal death ratio	Number of fetal deaths after 20 weeks or more gestation during a year	Number of live births during the same year	1,000
General fertility rate	Number of live births within a year	Number of women aged 15–44 years during the midpoint of the year	1,000
Incidence density	Number of new cases during a time period	Total person-years of observation during the same time period	Varies (e.g., 100,000)
Incidence rate	Number of new cases during a time period	Total population at risk during the same time period	Varies (e.g., 100,000)

continues

Table 3–5 *continued*

Measure	Numerator (x)	Denominator (y)	Expressed per Number at Risk (10^n)
Infant mortality rate	Number of infant deaths under 1 year of age (0–365 days) during a year	Number of live births reported during that same year	1,000
Late fetal death rate	Number of fetal deaths after 28 weeks or more gestation during a year	Number of live births + number of fetal deaths after 28 weeks or more gestation during the same year	1,000
Maternal mortality rate	Number of deaths assigned to causes related to childbirth during a year	Number of live births during the same year	100,000
Neonatal mortality rate	Number of infant deaths under 28 days of age during a year	Number of live births during the same year	1,000
Perinatal mortality rate	Number of late fetal deaths after 28 weeks or more gestation + infant deaths within 7 days of birth during a year	Number of live births + number of late fetal deaths during the same year	1,000
Perinatal mortality ratio	Number of late fetal deaths after 28 weeks or more gestation + infant deaths within 7 days of birth during a year	Number of live births during the same year	1,000
Postneonatal mortality rate	Number of infant deaths from 28 days to 365 days after birth during a year	Number of live births − neonatal deaths during the same year	1,000
Proportional mortality ratio	Mortality due to a specific cause during a year	Mortality due to all causes during that same year	100 or 1,000

*Note: The foregoing measures are expressed in the general form $\frac{x}{y} \times 10^n$.

Adjusted Rates

Specific rates are a much better indicator of risk than crude rates, especially if it is possible to construct rates specific to refined subsets of the population (e.g., age, race, and sex specific). However, in some instances, the stratum-specific data to derive such rates may not be available. In situations where this occurs, the use of adjusted rates can be an extremely valuable alternative for evaluation of the magnitude of a health problem. In addition, specific rates can make it difficult to see the "big picture" in those situations where data are stratified on several factors. For example, Table 3–6 shows the age-specific cancer incidence rates by sex, age group, and year of diagnosis. Most people would find it difficult to synthesize the data from a 30 × 15 array and see any specific trends. Some readers may find it helpful to consider summary-adjusted rates for each individual year as a function of time (i.e., a 1 × 15 array of rates adjusted for age and sex). Adjusted rates are summary measures of the rate of morbidity or mortality in a population in which statistical procedures have been applied to remove the effect of differences in composition of the various populations. Note that each rate in Table 3–6 is age adjusted.

A common factor for rate adjustment is age, which is probably the most important variable in risk of morbidity and mortality, although rates can be adjusted for other variables. Crude rates mask differences between populations that differ in age and thus are not satisfactory for comparing health outcomes in such populations.[12] For example, members of older populations have a much greater risk of mortality than those in younger populations. When a population is older, the crude mortality rate will be higher than when the population is younger. Refer to Table 3–7.

The crude death rates (all ages) in Group A and Group B are 50 per 1,000 and 40 per 1,000, respectively; these rates suggest that Group A has a higher mortality rate than Group B. Next, we will examine the age-adjusted death rates for the same populations: these rates are 42 per 1,000 and 52 per 1,000. (For the time being, ignore the procedures for age adjustment; these will be described later.) Group A has a lower age-adjusted mortality rate than Group B because the population of Group A is older.

Now let's examine methods for adjusting rates: Two methods for the adjustment of rates are the direct method and the indirect method. An easy way to remember how they differ is that direct and indirect refer to the source of the rates. The direct method may be used if age-specific death rates in a population to be standardized are known and a suitable standard population is available.

The direct method is presented in Table 3–8. Note that each age-specific rate found in Table 3–4 is multiplied by the number of persons in the age group in the standard population. Before the year 2000, the U.S. population in 1940 was used as the standard; now the standard shown in Table 3–8 is the estimated number in the standard population in the year 2000 (see Exhibit 3–7 for information on the development of the year 2000 standard for age

Table 3-6 15-Year Trends: Age-Specific Cancer Incidence Rates* (By Sex, Age Group, and Year of Diagnosis, SEER Program, 1973–1987; All Sites Combined, All Races)

Sex/Age	Year of Diagnosis														
	1973	1974	1975	1976	1977	1978	1979	1980	1981	1982	1983	1984	1985	1986	1987
Males & Females	319.9	332.3	331.8	337.2	336.6	336.7	340.2	344.0	349.7	350.2	355.4	362.4	368.9	369.9	377.2
0-54:	97.2	101.7	98.7	100.7	99.9	98.9	98.0	97.5	98.3	97.3	97.8	100.9	103.7	105.4	106.6
0-14	12.6	13.0	11.3	12.7	12.7	13.0	12.9	12.7	12.1	12.8	12.7	13.6	14.0	13.7	13.4
15-34	35.8	37.8	38.1	37.5	39.0	38.2	37.9	37.9	38.2	38.5	39.1	39.4	40.7	41.7	40.0
35-44	160.3	159.4	159.2	151.8	156.5	159.3	152.1	154.3	155.5	156.6	160.8	169.3	172.2	176.1	178.0
45-54	405.0	431.8	413.9	433.3	419.3	410.9	412.7	407.6	412.5	402.1	399.9	410.5	422.7	429.6	441.2
55-64	844.4	896.7	900.6	899.6	887.9	896.9	893.4	897.5	925.3	929.7	943.0	955.1	982.5	953.4	961.7
65+:	1660	1700	1717	1756	1767	1768	1814	1853	1878	1887	1924	1958	1976	1998	2055
65-74	1457	1483	1496	1520	1532	1529	1583	1614	1632	1650	1686	1720	1741	1773	1806
75+	1992	2054	2076	2139	2151	2158	2192	2242	2280	2274	2312	2345	2359	2364	2461
Males	365.2	372.1	377.8	388.9	392.7	394.8	400.5	407.5	411.5	411.7	419.2	423.0	426.8	430.7	441.9
0-54:	77.5	79.4	77.9	80.4	83.0	81.6	81.4	83.2	82.0	81.5	83.3	84.9	87.7	90.9	91.1
0-14	14.1	14.3	12.3	13.6	12.7	13.9	13.3	12.7	12.9	13.6	13.8	13.9	14.9	15.0	14.1
15-34	30.8	31.4	32.3	30.9	32.7	31.9	33.0	33.8	33.8	33.4	36.1	36.3	38.0	40.0	38.0
35-44	106.0	99.8	104.7	102.2	115.5	107.9	104.4	107.6	106.4	111.6	117.0	121.1	128.9	132.3	136.4
45-54	328.5	346.3	333.3	353.9	356.4	353.7	354.0	363.3	355.2	346.2	345.9	352.1	356.9	371.4	375.6
55-64	882.6	910.0	924.4	948.2	936.6	960.2	963.2	979.1	1010	1007	1024	1032	1059	1019	1025
65+:	2245	2274	2331	2401	2429	2439	2496	2538	2560	2568	2613	2632	2623	2672	2779
65-74	1854	1884	1914	1948	1991	1997	2040	2071	2102	2100	2142	2164	2165	2213	2283
75+	2883	2911	3012	3139	3143	3160	3239	3298	3305	3331	3381	3394	3370	3419	3588

continues

Table 3-6 *continued*

Sex/Age	1973	1974	1975	1976	1977	1978	1979	1980	1981	1982	1983	1984	1985	1986	1987
Females	293.2	311.0	306.7	307.7	303.5	302.3	304.3	305.4	312.3	313.4	316.5	326.3	334.5	333.4	338.4
0–54:	116.1	123.1	118.6	120.2	116.2	115.5	114.0	111.4	114.0	112.6	111.8	116.6	119.1	119.5	121.7
0–14	11.0	11.6	10.3	11.9	12.6	12.0	12.5	12.7	11.3	12.0	11.5	13.4	13.0	12.3	12.7
15–34	40.8	44.1	43.8	44.1	45.3	44.4	42.6	41.9	42.5	43.5	42.1	42.6	43.4	43.3	42.0
35–44	212.7	217.2	212.2	200.1	196.3	209.4	198.8	200.1	203.7	200.8	203.7	216.7	214.8	219.1	218.9
45–54	477.4	513.1	490.4	508.8	479.2	465.3	468.5	449.7	467.1	455.6	451.5	466.4	485.7	485.5	504.3
55–64	809.5	885.1	879.3	856.0	844.1	839.8	830.6	824.2	849.6	860.4	870.4	885.8	914.3	894.6	905.0
65+:	1268	1320	1318	1337	1339	1336	1377	1416	1441	1453	1483	1528	1563	1568	1591
65–74	1148	1173	1176	1192	1181	1170	1231	1262	1267	1300	1330	1375	1410	1429	1432
75+	1463	1559	1550	1574	1597	1607	1617	1668	1724	1702	1732	1777	1813	1793	1849

Column header spanning the years: **Year of Diagnosis**

* Rates are per 100,000 and are age adjusted to the 1970 US standard population. Each rate has been age-adjusted by 5-year age group.

Source: Reprinted from Kosary CL et al., *SEER Cancer Statistics Review, 1973–1992: Tables and Graphs,* p. II.23, 1995, NIH Pub No 96-2789, National Cancer Institute.

Table 3–7 Group Comparison of Crude and Age-Adjusted Death Rates

Age	Group A				Group B				Standard Population (9)	Standard Weight[3] (10)
	Deaths (1)	Population (2)	Rate[1] (3)	Weighted Rate[2] (4)	Deaths (5)	Population (6)	Rate[1] (7)	Weighted Rate[2] (8)		
All ages	500	10,000	50	...	400	10,000	40	...	10,000	1.0
0–24 years	20	1,000	20	6	180	6,000	30	9	3,000	0.3
25–64 years	120	3,000	40	12	150	3,000	50	15	3,000	0.3
65 years and over	360	6,000	60	24	70	1,000	70	28	4,000	0.4
Age-adjusted death rate[1]	...	...	...	42	...	...	...	52	...	...

· · · Category not applicable.

[1] Rate per 1,000 population.

[2] The weighted rate is calculated by multiplying the age-specific rate by the standard weight.

[3] The standard weight for each age group is calculated by dividing the standard population at each age by the total standard population.

Source: From Anderson RN, Rosenberg HM. Age Standardization of Death Rates: Implementation of the Year 2000 Standard, *National Vital Statistics Reports*, Vol 47, No 3, p. 2. National Center for Health Statistics; 1998.

Table 3–8   Direct Method for Adjustment of Death Rates

Age Group (Years)	2003 Age-Specific Death Rate per 100,000†	Number in Standard Population, 2000*	Expected Number of Deaths
Under 1	700.0	3,794,901	26,564.08
1–4	31.5	15,191,619	4,784.22
5–14	17.0	39,976,619	6,785.62
15–24	81.5	38,076,743	31,018.66
25–34	103.6	37,233,437	38,566.36
35–44	201.6	44,659,185	90,042.86
45–54	433.2	37,030,152	160,428.66
55–64	940.9	23,961,506	225,462.73
65–74	2,255.0	18,135,514	408,952.54
75–84	5,463.1	12,314,793	672,765.23
85+	14,593.3	4,259,173	621,555.36
Totals		274,633,642	2,286,926.31

† Age-specific death rates are from Table 3–4.

* Estimated

Age-adjusted rate per 100,000 = 832.7

(total expected number of deaths/estimated 2000 population) × 100,000

(2,286,926.31/274,633,642) × 100,000

Source: Data from Hoyert DL, Heron MP, Murphy SL, Kung H. Deaths: Final Data for 2003. *National Vital Statistics Reports,* Vol 54, No 13, p. 114. Hyattsville, MD: National Center for Health Statistics; 2006.

adjustment). As indicated in the fourth column of Table 3–8, the result is the expected number of deaths in each age group, which is then summed across all age groups to determine the total number of expected deaths. The age-adjusted rate is the total expected number of deaths divided by the total estimated 2000 population times 100,000: [(2,286,926.31/274,633,642) × 100,000] = 832.7 per 100,000.

To summarize, direct adjustment requires the application of the observed rates of disease in a population to some standard population to derive an expected number (rate) of mortality. The same procedure would be followed for other populations that one might wish to compare. By standardizing the observed rates of disease in the populations being compared to the same reference population, one is thereby assured that any observed differences that remain are not simply a reflection of differences in population structure with respect to factors such as age, race, and sex.

EXHIBIT 3–7

The National Center for Health Statistics Adopts a New Standard Population for Age Standardization of Death Rates

The crude death rate is a widely used measure of mortality. However, crude rates are influenced by the age composition of the population. As such, comparisons of crude death rates over time or between groups may be misleading if the populations being compared differ in age composition. This is relevant, for example, in trend comparisons of U.S. mortality, given the aging of the U.S. population . . . The crude death rate for the United States rose from 852.2 per 100,000 population to 880.0 during 1979 to 1995. This increase in the crude death rate was due to the increasing proportion of the U.S. population in older age groups that have higher death rates. Age standardization, often called age adjustment, is one of the key tools used to control for the changing age distribution of the population, and thereby to make meaningful death comparisons of vital rates over time and between groups. In contrast to the rising crude death rate, the age-adjusted death rate for the United States dropped from 577.0 per 100,000 U.S. standard population to 503.9 during 1979 to 1995. This age-adjusted comparison is free from the confounding effect of changing age distribution and therefore better reflects the trend in U.S. mortality. To use age adjustment requires a standard population, which is a set of arbitrary population weights.

The new standard is based on the year 2000 population and beginning with data year 1999 will replace the existing standard based on the 1940 population . . . Currently, at least three different standards are used among Department of Health and Human Services agencies. Implementation of the year 2000 standard will reduce confusion among data users and the burden on state and local agencies. Use of the year 2000 standard also will result in age-adjusted death rates that are substantially larger than those based on the 1940 standard. Further, the new standard will affect trends in age-adjusted rates for certain causes of death and will narrow race differentials in age-adjusted death rates. ■

Source: Adapted from Anderson RN, Rosenberg HM. Age Standardization of Death Rates: Implementation of the Year 2000 Standard, *National Vital Statistics Reports,* Vol 47, No 3, p. 1. National Center for Health Statistics; 1998.

A method of direct adjustment that achieves the same results as those reported in Table 3–8 uses year 2000 standard weights (refer to Table 3–9). From the previous discussion, you may have inferred the following relationship:

$$R_i = \frac{D_i}{P_i}$$

where R_i = the age-specific death rate for the ith row (interval) in Table 3–4 and:

D_i = number of deaths in age interval i

P_i = number of persons in age interval i at midyear

We may assign standard weights (W_{si}) to each interval according to the following formula:

$$W_{si} = \frac{P_{si}}{\sum_i P_{si}}$$

where W_{si} is the standard weight associated with the ith interval of the year 2000 standard U.S. population and:

P_{si} = the population in the ith age interval in the standard population

$\sum_i P_{si}$ = total number in the standard population

Table 3–9 Weighted Method for Direct Rate Adjustment

Age Group (Years)	Number in Standard Population, 2000* (P_{si})	Standard Weight (W_{si}) for 2000	Age-Specific Death Rate (R_i), 2003†	$W_{si} \cdot R_i$
Under 1	3,794,901	0.013818	700.0	9.6726
1–4	15,191,619	0.055316	31.5	1.7420
5–14	39,976,619	0.145563	17.0	2.4708
15–24	38,076,743	0.138646	81.5	11.2946
25–34	37,233,437	0.135575	103.6	14.0428
35–44	44,659,185	0.162164	201.6	13.7865
45–54	37,030,152	0.134835	433.2	15.4155
55–64	23,961,506	0.087249	940.9	18.0958
65–74	18,135,514	0.066035	2,255.0	148.9084
75–84	12,314,793	0.044841	5,463.1	244.9682
85+	4,259,173	0.015509	14,593.3	266.3216
Totals	$\sum_i P_{si} = 274,633,642$	1.0	N/A	$\sum_i W_{si} \cdot R_i = 832.7$

* Estimated

† From Table 3–4.

Source: Data from Hoyert DL, Heron MP, Murphy SL, Kung H. Deaths: Final Data for 2003. *National Vital Statistics Reports,* Vol 54, No 13, p. 114. Hyattsville, MD: National Center for Health Statistics; 2006.

Example (see Table 3–9): For age interval 1–4 years,

$$W = \frac{15,191,619}{274,633,642} = 0.055316$$

Then the age-adjusted death rate (AADR) is:

$$AADR = \sum_i W_{si} \cdot \frac{D_i}{P_i} = \sum_i W_{si} \cdot R_i = 832.7$$

The formula for AADR indicates that the year 2000 standard weights for each age group are multiplied by the age-specific death rates in that same row. These products are then summed to obtain the AADR (see Table 3–9). Note that the results for this method of standardization are the same as those reported in Table 3–8.

A second method of age adjustment is the indirect method, which may be used if age-specific death rates of the population for standardization are unknown or unstable (e.g., because the rates to be standardized are based on a small population). The stratum-specific rates of a larger population, such as that of the United States, are applied to the number of persons within each stratum of the population of interest to obtain the expected numbers of deaths. Thus, the indirect method of standardization does not require knowledge of the actual age-specific incidence or mortality rates among each age group for the population to be standardized. By applying the rates of disease from a standard population (in this example, the 2003 population) to the observed structure of the population of interest, one is left with an expected number of cases (or deaths) in the study population if the rates of disease were the same as in the standard population. One way to evaluate the result is to construct a standardized morbidity ratio or a standardized mortality ratio (SMR).

$$SMR = \frac{Observed\ deaths}{Expected\ deaths} \times 100$$

Sample calculation: The number of observed deaths due to heart disease is 600 in a certain county during year 2003. The expected number of deaths is 1,000. The SMR = (600/1,000) × 100 = 60% (0.6).

If the observed and expected numbers are the same, the SMR would be 100% (1.0), indicating that the observed morbidity or mortality in the study population is not unusual. An SMR of 200% (2.0) is interpreted to mean that the death (or disease) rate in the study population is two times greater than expected.

A second example of the indirect method of adjustment is shown in Table 3–10. Note that the standard age-specific death rates for the year 2003 (which we will designate as the year for obtaining the standard population) from Table 3–4 were multiplied by the number in each age group of the population of interest to obtain the expected number of deaths. To calculate the SMR, the observed number of deaths was divided by the expected number. The crude mortality rate is 502/230,109 = 218.2 per 100,000. The SMR is (502/987.9) × 100 = 50.8%. From the SMR, one may conclude that the observed mortality in this population falls below expectations, because the SMR is less than 1.0 or 100%.

Note that construction of an SMR is not the only way to interpret the net effect of the indirect adjustment procedure. An alternative is to compute a mortality rate per 100,000 by using the expected number of deaths as the numerator, rather than the observed number of deaths in the study population. If we wanted to focus on an outcome other than mortality, we could use the expected number of morbid events as the numerator. In either case, the calculation would be based on the expected numbers derived from the standard population. Referring to the example in Table 3–10, the total population size was 230,109 and the total expected number of deaths was 987.9. The adjusted death rate would be 987.9/230,109 × 100,000 = 429.3 per 100,000 per year. In comparison, the unadjusted death rate was 502/230,109 or 218.2 per 100,000 per year.

Table 3–10 Illustration of Indirect Age Adjustment: Mortality Rate Calculation for a Fictitious Population of 230,109 Persons

Age (Years)	Number in Population of Interest	Death Rates (per 100,000) in Standard Population*	Expected Number of Deaths in Population of Interest
15–24	7,989	81.5	6.5
25–34	37,030	103.6	38.4
35–44	60,838	201.6	122.6
45–54	68,687	433.2	297.6
55–64	55,565	940.9	522.8
Totals	230,109		987.9

Total expected number of deaths = 987.9
Observed number of deaths in this population = 502

* Standard death rates are from Table 3–4.

It is important to be aware that the numeric magnitude of an SMR in this situation is a reflection of the standard population. That is, if one were to use the age distribution of the 1970 U.S. population instead of the 2003 U.S. population for age adjustment, the adjusted rates that one would find would be quite different. Accordingly, SMRs for different populations typically cannot be compared with one another unless the same standard population has been applied to them. In addition, SMRs sometimes can be misleading: As a summary index, the overall SMR can be equal to 1.0 across different populations being compared, yet there might still be important differences in mortality in various subgroups. Finally, the longer a population is followed, the less information the SMR provides. Because it is expected that everyone in the population will die eventually, the SMR will tend to be equal to 1.0 over time.

Conclusion

This chapter defined several measures of disease frequency that are commonly employed in epidemiology. Counts or frequency data refer to the number of cases of a disease or other health phenomenon being studied. A ratio consists of a numerator and a denominator that express one number relative to another (e.g., the sex ratio). Prevalence is a measure of the existing number of cases of disease in a population at a point in time or over a specified period of time. A rate is defined as a proportion in which the numerator consists of the frequency of a disease during a period of time and the denominator is a unit size of population. Rates improve one's ability to make comparisons of health indices across contrasting populations. Examples of rates include the crude mortality rate, incidence rates, and infant mortality rates. Other examples of rates discussed were the birth rate, fertility rate, and perinatal mortality rate. Specific rates are more precise indicators of risk than crude rates. It was noted that, to make comparisons across populations, adjusted rates also may be used. Two techniques were presented on how to adjust rates. Finally, the chapter gave illustrations of how the SMR (an example of indirect adjustment) is used.

Study Questions and Exercises

1. Define the following terms:
    a. crude death rate
    b. age-specific rate
    c. cause-specific rate

     d. proportional mortality ratio (PMR)

     e. maternal mortality rate

     f. infant mortality rate

     g. neonatal mortality rate

     h. fetal death rate and late fetal death rate

     i. fetal death ratio

     j. perinatal mortality rate

     k. postneonatal mortality rate

     l. crude birth rate

     m. general fertility rate

     n. age-adjusted (standardized) rate

     o. direct method of adjustment

     p. indirect method of adjustment

     q. standardized mortality ratio (SMR)

2. Using Table 3A–1 in the Appendix at the end of this chapter, calculate age-specific death rates for the category of malignant neoplasms of trachea, bronchus, and lung. What inferences can be made from the age-specific death rates for malignant neoplasms of trachea, bronchus, and lung?

3. Using Table 3A–2 in the Appendix at the end of this chapter, calculate the following for the United States: The age-specific death rates and age- and sex-specific death rates per 100,000 (for age groups 20–24, 25–34, and 35–44 years). Note that there are nine calculations and answers. For example, the age- and sex-specific death rate for females aged 15 to 19 years is [(3,889/9,959,789) × 100,000].

4. Refer to both Table 3A–2 and Table 3A–3 in the Appendix at the end of this chapter. The total population in 2003 was 290,810,789 (males = 143,037,290; females = 147,773,499). For 2003, the total number of live births was 4,089,950.

     a. Calculate the crude death rate (per 100,000) and the cause-specific death rates (per 100,000) for accidents, malignant neoplasms, and Alzheimer's disease. Repeat these calculations for males and females separately.

     b. What is the PMR (percent) for accidents, malignant neoplasms, and Alzheimer's disease? Repeat these calculations for males and females separately.

     c. Calculate the maternal mortality rate (per 100,000 live births).

     d. Calculate the infant mortality rate (per 1,000 live births).

     e. Calculate the crude birth rate (per 1,000 population).

f. Calculate the general fertility rate (per 1,000 women aged 15 to 44 years).

5. The population of Metroville was 3,187,463 on June 30, 2008. During the period January 1 through December 31, 2008, a total of 4,367 city residents were infected with HIV. During the same year, 768 new cases of HIV were reported. Calculate the prevalence per 100,000 population and incidence per 100,000 population.

6. Give definitions of the terms prevalence and incidence. What are appropriate uses of prevalence and incidence data? State the relationships among prevalence, incidence, and duration of a disease.

7. Suppose that "X" represents the name of a disease. An epidemiologist conducts a survey of disease "X" in a population. The prevalence of disease "X" among women is 40/1,000 and among men is 20/1,000. Assuming that the data have been age adjusted, is it correct to conclude that women have twice the risk of disease "X" as men? Explain.

8. The following data regarding alcohol drinking status among persons in the United States were reported for 2005:

	Number in thousands	
	All persons 18 years of age and older	Current regular alcoholic beverage drinkers
Male	104,919	59,300
Female	112,855	44,373

a. What is the sex ratio of male to female regular alcoholic beverage drinkers?

b. What proportion (percent) of regular alcoholic beverage drinkers are women?

c. What is the prevalence per 1,000 of regular alcoholic beverage drinking among men only, women only, and the total population aged 18 and older?

9. During 2005, the following statistics were reported regarding the frequency of diabetes, ulcers, kidney disease, and liver disease:

Diabetes	7% of adults had ever been told by their doctor that they had diabetes
Ulcers	7% had ever been told by their doctor that they had an ulcer
Kidney	2% had been told in the past 12 months that they had kidney disease
Liver	1% had been told in the past 12 months that they had liver disease

Which of the foregoing statistics were stated as incidence data and which as prevalence data?

a. Diabetes

b. Ulcers

c. Kidney disease

d. Liver disease

10. The National Health Interview Survey reported the percent of respondents with a hearing problem by age group during 2005:

Age (years)	Reporting a hearing problem, %
18–44	8.2
45–64	19.2
65–74	30.4
75+	48.1

Would it be correct to state that the risk of hearing loss increases with age? Be sure to explain and defend your answer.

11. During January 1 through December 31, 2008, epidemiologists conducted a prevalence survey of type 2 diabetes; 500,000 cases were detected in a population of 10,000,000 persons. It was known that the incidence of diabetes in this population was 10 per 1,000. Estimate the percentage of the prevalent cases that were newly identified during the year.

References

1. Last JM, ed. *A Dictionary of Epidemiology*, 4th ed. New York, NY: Oxford University Press; 2001.

2. Hennekens CH, Buring JE. *Epidemiology in Medicine*. Boston, MA: Little, Brown; 1987.

3. Folsom AR, Kaye SA, Sellers TA, et al. Body fat distribution and 5-year risk of death in older women. *JAMA*. 1993;269:331–339.

4. Sellers TA, Kushi LH, Potter JD, et al. Effect of family history, body-fat distribution, and reproductive factors on the risk of postmenopausal breast cancer. *N Engl J Med*. 1992;326:1323–1329.

5. Link BG, Susser E, Stueve A, Phelan J, Moore RE, Struening E. Lifetime and five-year prevalence of homelessness in the United States. *Am J Public Health*. 1994;84:1907–1912.

6. Mausner JS, Kramer S. *Epidemiology: An Introductory Text*, 2nd ed. Philadelphia, PA: Saunders; 1985.

7. Kleinbaum DG, Kupper LL, Morgenstern H. *Epidemiologic Research: Principles and Quantitative Methods*. Belmont, CA: Lifetime Learning; 1982.

8. Rothman KJ. *Modern Epidemiology*. Boston, MA: Little, Brown; 1986.

9. National Center for Health Statistics. *Health, United States, 2006*. With Chartbook on Trends in the Health of Americans. Hyattsville, MD: 2006.

10. World Health Organization (WHO). World Health Statistics 2007. Health status: mortality, 2007. Available at: http://www.who.int/whosis/whostat2007_1mortality.pdf. Accessed November 21, 2007.

11. Hoyert DL, Heron MP, Murphy SL, Kung H. Deaths: Final Data for 2003. *National Vital Statistics Reports*. Vol 54, No 13. Hyattsville, MD: National Center for Health Statistics; 2006.

12. Anderson RN, Rosenberg HM. Age Standardization of Death Rates: Implementation of the Year 2000 Standard. *National Vital Statistics Reports*. Vol 47, No 3. Hyattsville, MD: National Center for Health Statistics; 1998.

APPENDIX
3

Data for Study Questions 2 Through 4

Table 3A-1 Malignant Neoplasms of Trachea, Bronchus, and Lung Deaths by Age Group, United States, 2003

Age (Years)	Population	Malignant Neoplasms of Trachea, Bronchus, and Lung* Deaths
25–34	39,872,598	154
35–44	44,370,594	2,478
45–54	40,804,599	12,374
55–64	27,899,736	30,956
65–74	18,337,044	49,386

* Includes ICD-10, 1992 codes C33–C34.

Source: Data are from Hoyert DL, Heron MP, Murphy SL, Kung H. Deaths: Final Data for 2003, *National Vital Statistics Reports,* Vol 54, No 13, p. 30. Hyattsville, MD: National Center for Health Statistics; 2006; and from Heron MP, Smith BL. Deaths: Leading Causes for 2003, *National Vital Statistics Reports,* Vol 55, No 10, p. 92. Hyattsville, MD: National Center for Health Statistics; 2007.

Table 3A-2 Mortality by Selected Age Groups, Males and Females, United States, 2003

Age (Years)	Males		Females		Total	
	Population	Number of Deaths	Population	Number of Deaths	Population	Number of Deaths
15–19	10,518,680	9,706	9,959,789	3,889	20,478,469	13,595
20–24	10,663,922	14,964	10,063,772	5,009	20,727,694	19,973
25–34	20,222,486	28,602	19,650,112	12,698	39,872,598	41,300
35–44	22,133,659	56,435	22,236,935	33,026	44,370,594	89,461
45–54	20,043,656	110,682	20,760,943	66,099	40,804,599	176,781

Source: Data are from Heron MP, Smith BL. Deaths: Leading Causes for 2003, *National Vital Statistics Reports,* Vol 55, No 10, p. 92. Hyattsville, MD: National Center for Health Statistics; 2007; and from Hoyert DL, Heron MP, Murphy SL, Kung H. Deaths: Final Data for 2003, *National Vital Statistics Reports,* Vol 54, No 13, p. 21. Hyattsville, MD: National Center for Health Statistics; 2006.

Table 3A–3   Total Mortality from Selected Causes, Males and Females, United States, 2003

Cause of Death	Males	Females	Total
All Causes	1,201,964	1,246,324	2,448,288
Accidents	70,532	38,745	109,277
Malignant Neoplasms	287,990	268,912	556,902
Alzheimer's Disease	18,335	45,122	63,457
Infant Deaths	15,902	12,123	28,025
Maternal Deaths	NA	495	495

Source: Data are from Heron MP, Smith BL. Deaths: Leading Causes for 2003, *National Vital Statistics Reports,* Vol 55, No 10, p. 7–8. Hyattsville, MD: National Center for Health Statistics; 2007; and Hoyert DL, Heron MP, Murphy SL, Kung H. Deaths: Final Data for 2003, *National Vital Statistics Reports,* Vol 54, No 13, p. 101–102. Hyattsville, MD: National Center for Health Statistics; 2006.

CHAPTER 4

Descriptive Epidemiology: Person, Place, Time

LEARNING OBJECTIVES

By the end of this chapter the reader will be able to:

- state the three primary objectives of descriptive epidemiology
- provide examples of the main subtypes of descriptive studies
- list at least two characteristics of each person, place, and time, and provide a rationale for why they are associated with variations in health and disease
- characterize the differences between descriptive and analytic epidemiology
- describe the difference between secular trends and cohort effects

CHAPTER OUTLINE

I. Introduction
II. Characteristics of Persons
III. Characteristics of Place
IV. Characteristics of Time
V. Conclusion
VI. Study Questions and Exercises

Introduction

The basic premise of epidemiology is that disease does not occur randomly, but rather in patterns that reflect the operation of underlying factors. Therefore, it is critical to the ultimate elucidation of etiology that these patterns be carefully and accurately described. The purpose of this chapter is to provide a brief survey of some of the ways that one can describe the pattern of disease. Each of the characteristics falls into one of three categories: person, place, or time. By using the tools in Chapter 3 regarding how to measure the frequency of disease, one can now extend the process to consider more intimately the details of the occurrence of disease. Person characteristics speak to the question of who is being affected: young versus old? males versus females? rich versus poor? overnourished versus undernourished? more educated versus less educated? Throughout the remainder of the chapter, the authors identify a variety of personal characteristics that may help to describe the pattern of disease and generate hypotheses regarding the underlying causes.

Place speaks to the question of where the problem is occurring: urban versus rural? some states more than others? only in particular cities? national versus international variation? in regions of high altitude or low altitude? where there is plentiful rainfall or little rainfall? in polluted areas more than unpolluted areas? Time refers to the issue of when the problem is occurring: Was there a sudden increase over a short period of time? Is the problem greater in winter than in summer? Is the problem gradually increasing over long periods of time or increasing greatly over just a few years? The occurrence of disease with respect to the characteristics of person, place, and time is central to the field of epidemiology.

Person, place, and time may directly or indirectly relate to the occurrence of illness because they affect a wide range of exposures associated with lifestyle, behavior patterns, access to medical care, and exposure to environmental hazards, to name a few examples. In illustration, being male is more likely to be associated with accidental death or injury than being female; behavior patterns characteristic of a particular ethnic group may affect subcultural levels of stress and methods for coping with social stresses. Suchman[1] referred to these variables as social group membership factors that affect perceptions, interpretations, and reactions to the social and physical environment. Membership in specific groups influences "exposure to and patterns of perceiving, interpreting, and reacting to health hazards."[1(p. 109)] We shall observe also that combinations of variables, for example, age and sex, are noteworthy.

Descriptive Versus Analytic Epidemiology

It is important at this point to make a distinction between two broad categories of epidemiologic studies. Descriptive studies are concerned with characterizing the amount and distribution of disease within a population. Analytic studies, on the other hand, are concerned with the determinants of disease, the reasons for relatively high or low frequency of disease in specific population subgroups. Descriptive studies generally precede analytic studies: The former are used to identify any health problems that may exist, and the latter proceed to identify the cause(s) of the problem.

Objectives of Descriptive Epidemiology

It is possible to identify three broad objectives of descriptive epidemiology:

1. to permit evaluation of trends in health and disease and comparisons among countries and subgroups within countries; this objective includes monitoring of known diseases as well as the identification of emerging problems
2. to provide a basis for planning, provision, and evaluation of health services; data needed for efficient allocation of resources often come from descriptive epidemiologic studies
3. to identify problems to be studied by analytic methods and to suggest areas that may be fruitful for investigation

The acquired immune deficiency syndrome (AIDS) epidemic illustrates how these objectives are implemented. Descriptive data on the epidemiology of AIDS provided an indication of the emergence of the epidemic (objective 1), were useful for allocation of hospital beds and treatment centers (objective 2), and spurred etiologic studies into why intravenous drug users and gay and bisexual men were more likely than other groups to develop the disease (objective 3).

Descriptive Studies and Epidemiologic Hypotheses

The third objective relates to the use of descriptive epidemiology to aid in the creation of hypotheses. "For any public health problem, the first step in the search for possible solutions is to formulate a reasonable and testable hypothesis."[2(p. 112)] "Hypotheses are suppositions that are tested by collecting facts that lead to their acceptance or rejection. They are not assumptions to be taken for granted, neither are they beliefs that the investigator sets out to prove. They are 'refutable predictions.'"[3(p. 40)] Three common ways of stating hypotheses are as follows[3]:

1. *Positive declaration (research hypothesis):* The infant mortality rate is higher in one region than another.
2. *Negative declaration (null hypothesis):* There is no difference between the infant mortality rates of two regions.
3. *Implicit question:* To study the association between infant mortality and geographic region of residence.

Hypotheses should be made as explicit as possible and not left as implicit.

Mill's Canons

What is the source of hypotheses that guide epidemiologic research? The logical processes for deriving hypotheses are patterned after John Stuart Mill's canons of inductive reasoning.[4] The following are four of his canons:

1. the method of difference
2. the method of agreement
3. the method of concomitant variation
4. the method of residues

The Method of Difference

All of the factors in two or more domains are the same except for a single factor. The frequency of a disease that varies across the two settings is hypothesized to result from variation in the single causative factor. The method of difference has been employed widely in epidemiologic research. It is similar to classic experimental design. A hypothetical example of its use would be the study of the role of physical activity in reducing morbidity from coronary heart disease (CHD). Suppose groups of workers in the same factory were compared when the factors of age, diet, socioeconomic status, and other variables were constant. It is plausible that workers in a particular factory might have similar sociodemographic and lifestyle characteristics but differ greatly in physical activity levels on the job. The hypothesis would be that differences in morbidity from CHD are due to level of physical activity, that is, sedentary workers are at greater risk of developing heart attacks than physically active workers.

The Method of Agreement

A single factor is common to a variety of different settings. It is hypothesized that the common factor is a cause of the disease. Wherever air pollution is present, for example, there is an increased prevalence of chronic respiratory diseases, such as emphysema. This finding leads to the hypothesis that air pollution, if present, is a contributing factor to lung diseases.

The Method of Concomitant Variation

The frequency of a disease varies according to the potency of a factor, and this linked association suggests that the factor is the causative agent for the disease. An example confirmed by a large body of research is that the incidence of bronchitis, emphysema, and lung cancer is directly related to the number of cigarettes smoked by an individual. That is, the greater the number of cigarettes smoked, the greater the risk of incurring these conditions.

The Method of Residues

The method of residues involves subtracting potential causal factors to determine which individual factor or set of factors makes the greatest impact upon a dependent variable. In research on heart disease, statistical methods similar to the method of residues (e.g., multiple regression analysis) have been used to determine which of a number of risk factors may be associated with coronary attack or death from CHD. The individual contribution to CHD of one's heredity, diet, stress level, amount of exercise, and blood lipid level can be quantified. One then can determine which factor has the greatest impact.

The Method of Analogy

The fifth method for developing hypotheses is taken from MacMahon and Pugh.[5] The mode of transmission and symptoms of a disease of unknown etiology bear a pattern similar to that of a known disease. It is suggested by this information that the unknown disease is caused by an agent similar to that of the known disease. There are many examples of this method in the field of infectious diseases. The symptoms of Legionnaires' disease are similar to those produced by an infectious respiratory disease agent of either viral or bacterial origin.

Three Approaches to Descriptive Epidemiology

The three approaches to descriptive epidemiology are case reports (counts), case series, and cross-sectional studies. In Chapter 3, we covered the role of counts in epidemiology. It was argued that, although counts are sometimes useful, they are usually more informative when expressed relative to a denominator (as a proportion). One could view case reports (counts) as the simplest form of descriptive epidemiology. Astute clinical observations on unusual cases may spur additional investigation to determine whether there are a large number of cases with similar presentations and to explore underlying mechanisms.

The second approach is a case series. Because it can be difficult to draw firm conclusions from a single case report, one may wish to extend the observations to include a case series. Typically this series involves a summary of the characteristics of a consecutive listing of patients from one or more major clinical settings. Having a large number of observations permits the generation of summary measures to help derive typical features.

The third major approach to descriptive epidemiology comprises cross-sectional studies. These are surveys of the population to estimate the prevalence of a disease or exposures. One can sometimes use data from repeated cross-sectional surveys at different points in time to examine time trends in prevalence of disease or risk factors. Cross-sectional studies are covered in greater detail in Chapter 6.

Characteristics of Persons

Age

Age is perhaps the most important factor to consider when one is describing the occurrence of virtually any disease or illness, because age-specific disease rates usually show greater variation than rates defined by almost any other personal attribute. For this reason, public health professionals often use age-specific rates when comparing the disease burden among populations.

Here is some information regarding overall age trends in mortality from the leading causes of death; these trends fluctuate markedly according to age group. During 2003, unintentional injury (accidents) was the leading cause of death among persons aged 1 to 44 years of age. Other important causes of death among persons younger than 45 years of age were assault (homicide) and intentional self-harm (suicide). At the same time, younger persons within this broad age group also were affected by cancer and heart disease, congenital malformations, deformations, and chromosomal abnormalities. The importance of three causes of mortality—accidents, homicide, and suicide—differed according to age group, with this trio accounting for 75% of deaths among the 15 to 19 age group. In comparison with individuals younger than age 45, persons aged 45 and older experienced chronic diseases such as heart disease and cancer as the leading killers.[6]

Childhood: For infants, developmental problems such as congenital birth defects and immaturity are among the major causes of death. Incidence of some infectious and communicable diseases, e.g., otitis media (ear infections), measles, mumps, chickenpox, and meningococcal disease, tend to occur most commonly in childhood. For example, Figure 4–1 illustrates the decreasing incidence of meningococcal disease with increasing age.

Teenage years: Aside from acne, other health issues that impact teenagers are accidents, violence, and suicide. Additional problems that remain important for teenagers are unplanned pregnancy and substance abuse. Because many teenagers enjoy playing with the latest electronic gadgets, excessive "screen time" may lead to obesity, a risk factor for subsequent development of chronic diseases.

Adults: In the age group 20 to 34 years, accidental injury is the leading cause of death. The remaining six major causes are homicide, suicide, cancer, diseases of the heart, and human immunodeficiency virus (HIV) disease. Among the group aged 35 to 44 years, accidents remain the leading cause of death, but homicide drops to sixth place. Malignant neoplasms, diseases of the heart, suicide, and HIV disease are in the second through fifth place, respectively, in importance.

Older adults: Chronic diseases such as heart disease and cancer become the dominant sources of morbidity and mortality after age 45. Although these conditions also impact younger persons, they are the leading causes of death among older adults. For example, cancer incidence tends to increase with age, as demonstrated by the generally log-linear increase in age-specific incidence rates. Note in Figure 4–2 how the cancer incidence rates by sex and race increase with increasing age groups. The apparent decline around age group 80 to 84 is somewhat deceptive because the rates are presented on a log scale and because the sizes of the numerators and denominators for the very elderly categories are smaller than for other age groups, resulting in unstable estimates.

MacMahon and Pugh[5] suggested four reasons for age associations. These are:

- the validity of diagnoses across the life span
- multimodality (e.g., bimodality) of trends
- latency effects
- action of the "human biologic clock"

The validity of diagnoses across the life span may be affected by classification errors. Age-specific incidence rates may be inaccurate among older age groups, causing distortions in the shape of an age-incidence graph. Inaccuracies may result from the difficulty in fixing the exact cause of death among older individuals, who may be afflicted concurrently with a number of sources of morbidity.

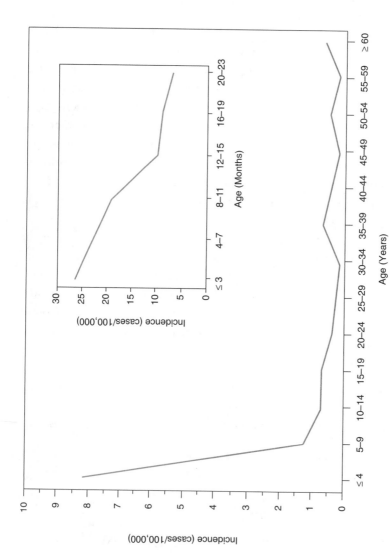

FIGURE 4–1 Incidence of meningococcal disease, by age group, in selected U.S. areas during 1989–1991. *Source:* Reprinted from Centers for Disease Control and Prevention. Laboratory-based surveillance for meningococcal disease in selected areas–United States, 1989–1991, *MMWR*, Vol 42, No SS-2, p. 25, June 4, 1993.

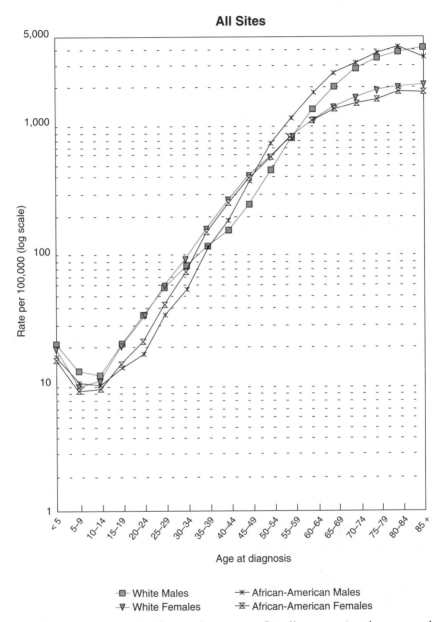

FIGURE 4–2 Age-specific incidence rates for all cancer sites by race and sex during 1986–1990 in the United States. *Source:* Reprinted from Miller BA et al. *SEER Cancer Statistics Review: 1973–1990,* p II.33, National Cancer Institute, National Institutes of Health, Publication No. 93-2789, 1993.

Some health conditions may show multimodal age-specific incidence curves, meaning that there are several peaks and declines in the frequency of the diseases at various ages. One example is tuberculosis (TB), which has two peaks, one between age 0 and 4 years and another around age 20 to 29 years. Another example is Hodgkin's disease, which shows a peak in the mid-20s and another in the early 70s.[5] Bimodal (two-peak) distributions for these conditions may suggest two different causal mechanisms. For example, in the case of TB, the increase in prevalence of the disease in the early years of life may be due to the increased susceptibility of children to infectious diseases, and the other peak during young adulthood may reflect the increased social interaction of individuals at this age or change in immune status due to puberty.

Another explanation for age effects on mortality is that they reflect the long latency period between environmental exposures and the development of disease. An example of a long latency period is the passage of many years between initial exposure to a potential carcinogen and the subsequent appearance of cancer later in life. Furthermore, older individuals in comparison with younger persons have had a greater opportunity to be exposed to multiple potential carcinogens. The additive effects of such exposures would be more likely to affect older persons than younger individuals.

The "human biologic clock" phenomenon refers to an endogenous process associated with increased vulnerability to disease. For example, as a component of the aging process the immune system may wane, producing increased tissue susceptibility to disease. Another manifestation of the biologic clock is the triggering of conditions that are believed to have a genetic basis (e.g., Alzheimer's disease, which usually occurs among older persons).

Other causes (not specified by MacMahon and Pugh) of age-related changes in rates of morbidity and mortality are related to life cycle and behavioral phenomena. As noted previously, accidents, homicide, and suicide as causes of mortality differ greatly in importance according to age group; variations in these three causes of death are influenced by factors such as personal behavior and risk taking, especially among the young. Lifestyle influences the occurrence of diabetes and other chronic diseases, many of which are believed to have significant behavioral components. Some aging-associated problems, which impact the far end of the age distribution, illustrate life cycle phenomena. As the elderly population continues to increase, more epidemiologic studies will be needed on the topics of the "retirement syndrome," the bereavement process, and other behaviorally related health issues among the aged.

Sex

Numerous epidemiologic studies have shown sex differences in a wide scope of health phenomena, including mortality. The following discussion presents data on sex differences in mortality. With the exception of some calendar years, the population age-adjusted death rate has declined in the United States since 1980.[6] Males generally have higher all-cause age-specific mortality rates than females from birth to age 85 and older[7]; the ratio of male to female age-specific death rates in 2003 was 1.4 to 1.[7]

A classic study noted that male versus female morbidity differences were the reverse of the differences for mortality—females were reported to have higher age-standardized morbidity rates for acute conditions, chronic conditions, and disability due to acute conditions.[8] This phenomenon is known as the female paradox. Women suffer from higher rates of pain, some respiratory ailments such as asthma and lung difficulties not induced by cancer, and depression. Problems that are more common among men are hearing impairment, smoking-associated conditions, and cardiovascular diseases.[9] Men who are affected by the same chronic diseases (e.g., lung cancer, cardiovascular disease, and diabetes) as women are more likely to develop severe forms of these conditions and die from them. Other research has suggested that sex differences in morbidity have narrowed and some conditions, such as hypertension and cancer, produce increased morbidity rates among men in comparison with women.[10]

Speculations regarding the sources of sex differences in morbidity and mortality are fascinating and capable of inspiring heated debate. An interesting question concerns the extent to which sex differences in mortality will narrow as the lifestyle, employment, and health-related behaviors of women become more similar to those of men. Specific research studies have investigated genetic and environmental factors, differentials in exposure to stress, reporting of illness, and the effects of women's changing role in society upon mortality. Waldron's[11] venerable research attributed higher male mortality to greater frequency of smoking, a greater prevalence of the coronary-prone behavior pattern, higher suicide and motor vehicle accident rates, as well as risky behavioral patterns that are expected of and condoned among men. Consider the example of lung cancer mortality. Data for this cause of mortality, especially between 1975 and 1990, show that it increased among women much faster than among men, supporting the view that certain behavioral and lifestyle variables (i.e., smoking behavior) may relate to male/female lung cancer mortality differences (Figures 4–3 and 4–4). A study conducted in Denmark isolated smoking as the major factor that explained sex differences in mortality in that country.[12]

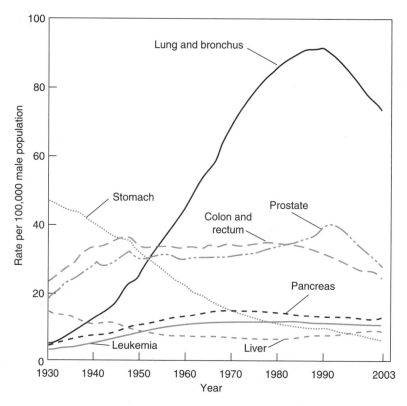

* Per 100,000, age-adjusted to the 2000 U.S. standard population.

FIGURE 4–3   Age-adjusted cancer death rates: * males by site, United States, 1930–2003. *Source:* American Cancer Society, *Cancer Facts & Figures 2007.* Atlanta: American Cancer Society, Inc.; 2007, p. 2.

Coronary Heart Disease (CHD) is the leading cause of death for both men and women. However, sex differences in mortality from CHD persist between men and women, even when both have high-risk factor status for serum cholesterol, blood pressure, and smoking. This finding implicates important biologic parameters as the basis for the observed differences (e.g., differences in hormonal profiles). Production of estrogen changes during menopause; the result is that heart disease typically does not leave its mark on women until after age 60. Among women, endogenous estradiol is strongly implicated in cardiovascular changes that are similar to the effects of exercise. These effects cause the "jogging female heart" that may account for the lower incidence of cardiovascular disease before menopause and postmenopausal increases in rates of cardiac disease.[13]

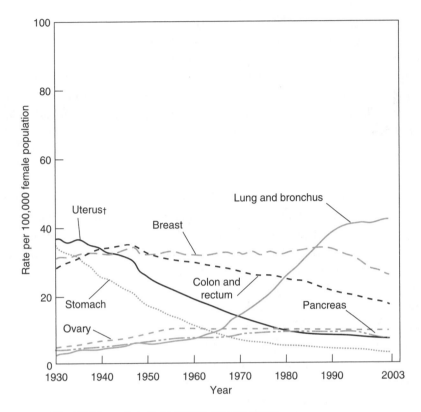

* Per 100,000, age-adjusted to the 2000 U.S. standard population.
†Uterus cancer death rates are for uterine cervix and uterine corpus combined.

FIGURE 4–4   Age-adjusted cancer death rates:* females by site, United States, 1930–2003. *Source:* American Cancer Society, *Cancer Facts & Figures 2007.* Atlanta: American Cancer Society, Inc.; 2007, p. 3.

Many women are unaware of the fact that they may be at high risk of cardiac disease.[14] Consequently, women may not be alert for symptoms of CHD, causing delay in seeking treatment when symptoms occur. Women also may resist lifestyle changes such as increased activity level and consumption of low-fat food. Concern also has been raised about poorer care for women who present with cardiac disease. Although women who have myocardial infarctions may receive slightly different treatment from men in some respects (e.g., lower use of aspirin and greater use of angiotensin-converting enzyme inhibitors), multivariate analyses of data from the Cooperative Cardiovascular Project and the National Heart Failure Project as well as other databases did not disclose major gender biases among patients 65 years of age and older.[15]

In some regions of the United States, particularly the economically disadvantaged areas, minority women face a higher burden of morbidity from chronic diseases than men. For example, minority women who live in Los Angeles County confront higher rates of diabetes, hypertension, and elevated cholesterol. During 2005, almost one-half of all women in the county reported little physical activity. The frequency of obesity was high, particularly among Latinas (more than 25%) and African Americans (about 33%).[16]

Marital Status

Marital status includes the following categories: single or non-married (never married, divorced, separated, and widowed); married, and living with a partner. In general, epidemiologic research has shown that married individuals, especially men, have lower rates of morbidity and mortality than those who are single, divorced, or widowed. Also, data suggest that among older women, divorce and separation are associated with adverse health outcomes such as physical impairments.[17] Schoenborn reported that "Regardless of population subgroup (age, sex, race, Hispanic origin, education, income, or nativity) or health indicator (fair or poor health, limitations in activities, low back pain, headaches, serious psychological distress, smoking, or leisure-time physical inactivity), married adults were generally found to be healthier than adults in other marital status categories."[18(p. 1)] The exception was that among the various categories of marital status, never married adults were least likely to be overweight or obese; being married was associated with obesity, especially among men.[18]

An influential analysis of U.S. nationwide trends showed lower rates of mortality from chronic diseases among married individuals for coronary diseases and many forms of cancer as well as suicide, motor vehicle accidents, and some infectious diseases.[19] Swedish data indicated that being unmarried or divorced was linked with higher rates of mortality than those observed among married persons.[20] Among Danish younger males, marital breakups, divorce, and widowhood were reported to be independent predictors of mortality.[21] A 2007 Japanese study reported similar mortality trends: In the Japan Collaborative Cohort Study (a prospective study of 94,062 Japanese men and women aged 40–79), single individuals experienced a higher mortality risk than married persons. Furthermore, divorce and widowhood affected men and women differently; men had higher mortality risks than women if divorced or widowed.[22]

Another dimension of marital status is its relationship with suicide rates, which appear to be elevated among widowed persons, especially young men. In a national study of suicide in the United States, investigators reported a 17-fold elevation in suicide rates among widowed white men who were aged 20 to 34 years and a 9-fold elevation among young African-American men in comparison with married men in the same age group; widows did not have similarly elevated suicide rates.[23]

Schottenfeld[24] presented data on the risk of developing breast cancer among single women compared with ever-married women and for ever-married nulliparous women compared with parous married women. Married women had a reduced risk of breast cancer mortality in comparison with single women, and among all married women childbirth slightly reduced the risk. Following Schottenfeld's groundbreaking research, other investigators reported that even controlling for stage of cancer diagnosis, married women had lower breast cancer mortality rates than non-married women.[25]

A theoretical account of the action of marital status upon health posits that marriage may operate as either a protective or a selective factor.[26] The protective hypothesis suggests that marriage makes a positive contribution to health by influencing lifestyle factors, providing mutual psychological and social support, and increasing available financial resources. According to the marital selection model, physically attractive individuals are more likely to compete for a partner successfully and are healthier than those persons who never marry, resulting in the lower morbidity and mortality rates observed among married persons. Furthermore, the model proposes that less healthy individuals, if married, are more predisposed than healthy persons to gravitate to non-married status. In summary, the marital environment and factors associated with marriage apparently reduce the risk of death and, therefore, should be considered possible sources of differences in disease rates.[26] Currently, perceptions of marital status have changed within the American society, lessening the stigma that was once associated with divorce and living together without being officially married. These changing perceptions may impact associations between marital status and health.

Race and Ethnicity

Increasingly, with respect to race and ethnicity, the United States is becoming more diverse than at any time in history (Figure 4–5). Race and ethnicity are, to some extent, ambiguous characteristics that tend to overlap with nativity and religion. Scientists have proposed that race is a social and cultural construct, rather than a biological construct.[27] In Census 2000, the U.S. Bureau of the Census classified race into five major categories: white; black or African American; American Indian and Alaska Native; Asian; and Native Hawaiian and

FIGURE 4–5 Racial and ethnic diversity. *Source:* Reprinted with permission from Nebraska Department of Health and Human Services, Office of Minority Health. Equalizing health outcomes and eliminating health disparities. Available at: http://www.hhs.state.ne.us/minorityhealth/. Accessed November 25, 2007.

other Pacific Islander. To a degree, race tends to be synonymous with ethnicity because people who come from a particular racial stock also may have a common ethnic and cultural identification. Also, assignment of some individuals to a particular racial classification on the basis of observed characteristics may be difficult. Often, one must ask the respondent to elect the racial group with which he or she identifies. The responses one elicits from such a question may not be consistent: Individuals may change ethnic or racial self-identity or respond differently on different occasions, depending on their perception of the intent of the race question. Classification of persons of mixed racial parentage also may be problematic.[28] The 2000 census allowed respondents to check a multiracial category, which was used for the first time. Changes in the definitions of racial categories affect the denominators (i.e., the numbers in a particular racial subgroup) of rates used to track various health outcomes and the consequent assessments of unmet needs and social inequalities in health.[29]

Assuming that race can be measured with some degree of validity, it does have implications for differences in incidence and prevalence of disease, as numerous epidemiologic studies have determined. Noteworthy variations in the rates of disease and risk factors for disease have been identified by using race as a variable in epidemiologic and public health research.[30] Further definitions and explanations of the race questions used in Census 2000 are in Exhibit 4–1.

EXHIBIT 4–1

Overview of Race and Hispanic Origin, Census 2000

Understanding Race and Hispanic Origin Data From Census 2000

The 1990 census questions on race and Hispanic origin were changed for Census 2000

The federal government considers race and Hispanic origin to be two separate and distinct concepts. For Census 2000, the questions on race and Hispanic origin were asked of every individual living in the United States. The question on Hispanic origin asked respondents if they were Spanish, Hispanic, or Latino. The question on race asked respondents to report the race or races they considered themselves to be. Both questions are based on self-identification. The question on Hispanic origin for Census 2000 was similar to the 1990 census question, except for its placement on the questionnaire. For Census 2000, the question on Hispanic origin was asked directly before the question on race. For the 1990 census, the order was reversed: the question on race preceded questions on age and marital status, which were followed by the question on Hispanic origin. The question on race for Census 2000 was different from the one for the 1990 census in several ways. Most significantly, respondents were given the option of selecting one or more race categories to indicate their racial identities. Because of these changes, the Census 2000 data on race are not directly comparable with data from the 1990 census or earlier censuses. Caution

continues

EXHIBIT 4–1 *continued*

must be used when interpreting changes in the racial composition of the U.S. population over time.

[Refer to Figure 1 for the questions on race and Hispanic origin used in Census 2000.]

NOTE: Please answer BOTH Questions 5 and 6.

5. Is this person Spanish/Hispanic/Latino? Mark ☒ the **"No"** box if **not** *Spanish/Hispanic/Latino.*
   - ❏ No, not Spanish/Hispanic/Latino   ❏ Yes, Puerto Rican
   - ❏ Yes, Mexican, Mexican Am., Chicano ❏ Yes, Cuban
   - ❏ Yes, other Spanish/Hispanic/Latino—*Print group.*

6. What is this person's race? Mark ☒ **one or more races** to indicate what this person considers himself/herself to be.
   - ❏ White
   - ❏ Black, African Am., or Negro
   - ❏ American Indian or Alaska Native—Print name of enrolled or principal tribe.
   - ❏ Asian Indian   ❏ Japanese   ❏ Native Hawaiian
   - ❏ Chinese   ❏ Korean   ❏ Guamanian or Chamorro
   - ❏ Filipino   ❏ Vietnamese   ❏ Samoan
   - ❏ Other Asian—*Print race.*   ❏ Other Pacific Islander—*Print race.*
   - ❏ Some other race—*Print race.*

EXHIBIT 4–1, FIGURE 1   Reproduction of questions on race and Hispanic origin from Census 2000. *Source:* U.S. Census Bureau, Census 2000 questionnaire.

How are the race categories used in Census 2000 defined?

"White" refers to people having origins in any of the original peoples of Europe, the Middle East, or North Africa. It includes people who indicated their race or races as "White" or wrote in entries such as Irish, German, Italian, Lebanese, Near Easterner, Arab, or Polish.

"Black or African American" refers to people having origins in any of the black racial groups of Africa. It includes people who indicated their race or races as "Black, African Am., or Negro," or wrote in entries such as African American, Afro American, Nigerian, or Haitian.

continues

EXHIBIT 4–1 *continued*

"American Indian and Alaska Native" refers to people having origins in any of the original peoples of North and South America (including Central America), and who maintain tribal affiliation or community attachment. It includes people who indicated their race or races by marking this category or writing in their principal or enrolled tribe, such as Rosebud Sioux, Chippewa, or Navajo.

"Asian" refers to people having origins in any of the original peoples of the Far East, Southeast Asia, or the Indian subcontinent. It includes people who indicated their race or races as "Asian Indian," "Chinese," "Filipino," "Korean," "Japanese," "Vietnamese," or "Other Asian," or wrote in entries such as Burmese, Hmong, Pakistani, or Thai.

"Native Hawaiian and Other Pacific Islander" refers to people having origins in any of the original peoples of Hawaii, Guam, Samoa, or other Pacific Islands. It includes people who indicated their race or races as "Native Hawaiian," "Guamanian or Chamorro," "Samoan," or "Other Pacific Islander," or wrote in entries such as Tahitian, Mariana Islander, or Chuukese.

[Refer to Table 1 for a distribution of the U.S. population according to race.]

Exhibit 4–1, Table 1   Population by race and Hispanic origin for the United States, 2000

Race and Hispanic or Latino	Number	% of Total Population
RACE		
Total population	281,421,906	100.0
One race	274,595,678	97.6
White	211,460,626	75.1
Black or African American	34,658,190	12.3
American Indian and Alaska Native	2,475,956	0.9
Asian	10,242,998	3.6
Native Hawaiian and Other Pacific Islander	398,835	0.1
Some other race	15,359,073	5.5
Two or more races	6,826,228	2.4
HISPANIC OR LATINO		
Total population	281,421,906	100.0
Hispanic or Latino	35,305,818	12.5
Not Hispanic or Latino	246,116,088	87.5

Source: U.S. Census Bureau, Census 2000 Redistricting (Public Law 94-171) Summary File, Tables PL1 and PL2.

Source for Exhibit 4–1: Adapted from Grieco EM, Cassidy RC. *Overview of Race and Hispanic Origin: Census 2000 Brief.* Available at: http://www.census.gov/prod/2001pubs/c2kbr01-1.pdf. Accessed November 25, 2007.

Infant mortality rates illustrate variation by race. The National Center for Health Statistics reported the following infant mortality rates due to birth defects (congenital malformation, deformations, and chromosomal abnormalities) among U.S. infants born in 2003: African Americans (173.2 per 100,000 live births); American Indians (167.2 per 100,000); whites (133.1 per 100,000); and Asian or Pacific Islanders (98.6 per 100,000).[31] A second illustration, AIDS cases among five racial/ethnic groups, shows that AIDS was most common among African Americans and lowest among American Indians/Alaska Natives.[32] (See Figure 4–6.) Other illustrations follow.

African Americans

According to a study of differential mortality in the United States, African Americans had the highest mortality of any of several racial groups examined.[19] In 2003, the African-American population experienced an age-adjusted death rate that was 1.3 times that of the white population.[6] African Americans in the United States are one of the groups that are afflicted by disparities with respect to

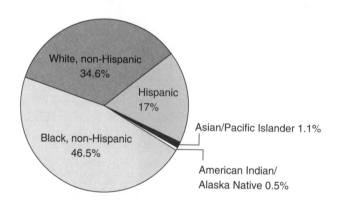

* For 0.3% of respondents, race/ethnicity was unknown.

Of persons reported with AIDS during 2005, the greatest percentage were non-Hispanic blacks, followed by non-Hispanic whites, Hispanics, Asians/Pacific Islanders, and American Indians/Alaska Natives.

FIGURE 4–6   Acquired immunodeficiency syndrome (AIDS). Percentage of reported cases, by race/ethnicity* in the United States in 2005. *Source:* From Centers for Disease Control and Prevention, Summary of notifiable diseases–United States, 2005, *MMWR*, Vol 54, No 53, p. 40, 2007.

many health conditions. Persons who self-identify as non-Hispanic black carry a greater burden from mortality and morbidity as well as injury and disability in comparison with non-Hispanic whites.[33] Included in the 10 leading causes of death among non-Hispanic blacks are homicide, HIV disease, and septicemia, whereas these conditions are not among the 10 leading causes of death among non-Hispanic whites. The age-adjusted incidence of certain forms of cancer is much higher among African Americans than whites. In comparison with four other racial/ethnic groups (whites, American Indians/Alaska Natives, Asians/Pacific Islanders, and Hispanics), African Americans have the highest age-adjusted female breast cancer death rate.[34] Possible explanations for this disparity include differences in access to and quality of mammography services as well as access to treatment for breast cancer.[35] African-American males have twice the death rate for prostate cancer as white males, a finding that points to a need for improvement in early detection and treatment of prostate cancer among the former group. Figure 4–7 presents life expectancy by race and sex in the United States between 1970 and 2003. African-American males had the lowest life expectancy rates of the four groups shown; nevertheless, differences in life expectancy between the African-American and white populations narrowed between 2002 and 2003.

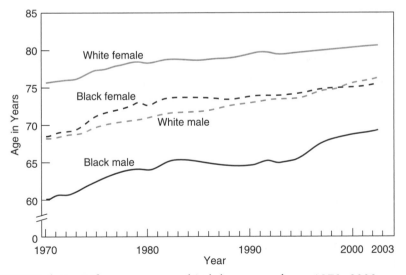

FIGURE 4–7   Life expectancy at birth by race and sex: 1970–2003. *Source:* From Arias E. *National Vital Statistics Reports*, Vol 54, No 14, p. 4. Washington, D.C.: National Center for Health Statistics; 2006.

The prevalence of hypertension is substantially higher among African Americans than among whites. The National Health and Nutrition Examination Surveys for 1992 to 2002 obtained rates of hypertension among African-American and white adults 20 years of age and older of 40.5% and 27.4%, respectively.[36] African Americans develop hypertension at younger ages and suffer from more severe health consequences than whites.[37] Mortality from hypertension-related conditions is higher among African Americans than among whites. For example, the 2003 deaths rates from hypertensive heart disease among African Americans and whites were 17.9 versus 8.8 deaths per 100,000. The death rates from hypertension, including hypertensive renal disease, were 11.8 and 7.2 deaths per 100,000, respectively.[6] A number of factors could account for increased rates of hypertension among African Americans, including dietary factors (e.g., low consumption of fruits and vegetables), exposure to stress, reduced social support, higher rates of obesity, and lack of participation in cardiovascular risk reduction programs.

American Indians/Alaska Natives

American Indian/Alaska Native (AI/AN) adults have high rates of chronic diseases, adverse birth outcomes, and infectious diseases such as TB and hepatitis A in comparison with the general U.S. population. AI/ANs also have decreased life expectancy.[38] During the late 20th century, hospitalizations for infectious diseases represented nearly one-quarter of all hospitalizations among elderly AI/AN adults. Although the rates of such hospitalizations increased slightly in the United States between 1990 and 2002, those rates increased even more (by about one-fifth) in Alaska and the Southwest.[39] In comparison with AI/AN females, AI/AN males bear a heavier burden from many illnesses and tend to underutilize health care services.[40]

Knowler et al.[41] published a seminal study of the incidence and prevalence of diabetes mellitus in nearly 4,000 members of the Pima Tribe (a group of North American Indians native to Arizona) aged 5 years and older over a 10-year period. The investigators reported a diabetes prevalence of about 21%, adjusting for age and sex; the incidence rate was about 26 cases per 1,000. Diabetes incidence was about 19 times greater than that of a predominantly white comparison population in Rochester, Minnesota.

During 1975 through 1984, the Pima Indians who resided in the Gila River Indian community had a death rate of 1.9 times that for all races in the United States. Among men aged 25 to 34 years, the Pima death rate was 6.6 times that for all races in the United States. Diseases of the heart and malignant neoplasms accounted for 59% of the U.S. deaths in 1980, but only 19% for the American Indian community. The age- and sex-adjusted mortality rate was 5.9 times the rate for all races in the United States for accidents, 6.5 times for cirrhosis of the liver, 7.4 times for homicide, 4.3 times for suicide, and 11.9 times for diabetes. TB and coccidioidomycosis also were important causes of death in the Pima, for whom infectious disease was the tenth leading cause of death among all causes of death.[42] As a group, the general AI/AN population in 2002 had an age-adjusted TB case rate that was twice that of the U.S. population and seven times that of the non-Hispanic white population.[43]

The number of AI/ANs who live in cities is increasing. Urban AI/ANs experience disparities in health and socioeconomic characteristics when contrasted with the general U.S. population.[44] Among women, these disparities include poorer birth outcomes due to inadequate prenatal care and sudden infant death syndrome associated with alcohol consumption. As a group, AI/ANs tend to be poorer, have lower rates of college graduation, and have higher levels of unemployment than other urban residents.

Asians/Pacific Islanders

The Japanese, in comparison with other racial groups in the United States, have low mortality rates: one-third the rates for whites of both genders.[16] Japanese culture seems to afford a protective influence that results in lower mortality, especially from chronic diseases such as CHD and cancer. The orientation of the Japanese culture even in our age of industrialization is toward conformity and group consensus rather than toward the "rugged individualism" and competitiveness that pervade the American culture.[45] Degree of acculturation to Japan was related to low rates of CHD mortality.[45] Acculturation is defined as modifications that individuals or groups undergo when they come into contact with another culture.[46]

According to Marmot,[47] "Among industrialised countries, Japan is remarkable for its low rate of ischaemic heart disease. It is unlikely to be the result of some genetically-determined protection, as Japanese migrants to the USA lose this apparent protection."[47(p. 378)] The Honolulu Heart Study prospectively followed a large population of men of Japanese ancestry who resided on the island of Oahu at the beginning of the study.[48,49] Various measures of the degree of early exposure to Japanese culture were collected, including: birthplace in Japan; total number of years of residence in that country; ability to read, write, and speak Japanese; and a preference for the Japanese diet. After adjusting for the influence of well-established risk factors for CHD (age, serum cholesterol, systolic blood pressure, and cigarette smoking), there was a gradient in incidence of CHD across variables related to identification with the Japanese culture. For example, men who could read and write Japanese well had an incidence rate about half that reported for those who could neither read nor write Japanese. Other studies of Japanese men living in Japan, Hawaii, and California have shown an increasing gradient in mortality, prevalence, and incidence of CHD from Japan to Hawaii to California. Observed lower rates of CHD in Japan in comparison with the United States have been attributed to a low-fat diet among the Japanese and to institutionalized stress-reducing strategies (e.g., community bonds and group cohesion) within Japanese society.[50]

Studies of acculturation among the Japanese provide evidence that environmental and behavioral factors influence chronic disease rates and provide a rationale for intervention and prevention of chronic disease.[51] The Japanese who migrated shared a common ethnic background. After migrating to diverse geographic and cultural locales, they experienced a shift in rates of chronic disease to rates more similar to those found in the host countries. This finding among the Japanese is consonant with the *acculturation hypothesis,* which proposes that as immigrants become acculturated to a host country, their health profiles tend to converge with that of the native-born population.

In the case of the United States, the originating culture of migrants sometimes affords protection against morbidity and mortality. This protective effect may be a function of health-related behaviors associated with a culture. During the late 20th century, foreign-born persons lived about two to four years longer than the native-born U.S. population; however, the risk of disability and chronic conditions grew as immigrants lived in the United States for longer periods of time.[52]

Some Asian groups have high rates of smoking when compared with the general U.S. population. Among all Asians, rates of cigarette smoking tend to be higher among men than among women. One Asian group that is thought to have high smoking rates is Cambodian Americans, who have rates as high as 70%; in addition, the frequency of smoking among Cambodian American men is reported to be three to four times the frequency among women.[53]

Asians/Pacific Islanders (APIs) have the highest TB rates of five racial and ethnic groups, although the incidence declined among APIs by 18 per 100,000

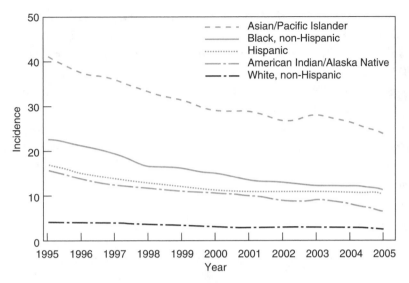

* Per 100,000 population.

Asians/Pacific Islanders had the highest tuberculosis rates, which declined from 43.5 per 100,000 population in 1995 to 25.5 in 2005. During 2004–2005, rates per 100,000 population declined by ≥ 50% in other racial/ethnic populations: among non-Hispanic blacks, from 23.2 to 10.9; among Hispanics, from 17.2 to 9.5; among American Indians/Alaska Natives, from 15.7 to 6.9; and among non-Hispanic whites, from 3.1 to 1.3.

FIGURE 4–8   Tuberculosis. Incidence,* by race/ethnicity: United States, 1995–2005. *Source:* From Centers for Disease Control and Prevention, Summary of notifiable diseases–United States, 2005, *MMWR.* Vol 54, No 53, p. 70, 2007.

between 1995 and 2005. In 2005, the incidence rate among APIs was almost 20 times that of non-Hispanic whites (Figure 4–8).

Hispanics/Latinos

In the United States, Hispanic/Latino populations include the major groups—Mexican Americans, Puerto Ricans, and Cubans—as well as other groups that have migrated to the United States from Latin America. In comparison with other whites, Latinos have unique morbidity and mortality profiles. Although Mexican Americans represent one of the dominant ethnic minorities in the southwestern United States, this group has been relatively under-researched for prevalence of hypertension, CHD, diabetes, and other chronic diseases. The first special population survey of Hispanics in the United States was the Hispanic Health and Nutrition Examination Survey (HHANES). Conducted by the National Center for Health Statistics, HHANES assessed the health and nutritional status of Mexican Americans, mainland Puerto Ricans, and Cuban Americans.[54] An entire supplement issue of the *American Journal of Public Health* covered findings from HHANES.[55] As more research is conducted among Latinos, it is becoming apparent that they are highly diverse and should be studied as distinct subpopulations (e.g., Cuban Americans or Salvadoran Americans). Low rates of CHD among Mexican Americans may be due to cultural factors, such as dietary preferences and the availability of social support mechanisms found in large and extended family systems. A study of CHD among Puerto Ricans reported a low prevalence of this condition.[56]

A major epidemiologic investigation of diabetes and other cardiovascular risk factors in Mexican Americans and non-Hispanic whites is the San Antonio Heart Study.[57] Among the findings were the high prevalence of obesity and non–insulin-dependent diabetes mellitus among the Mexican-American population. Despite a higher prevalence of diabetes mellitus and other risk factors for chronic disease, Hispanics/Latinos in the United States have a lower mortality rate than non-Latino whites. The mortality differential is sometimes referred to as the Hispanic mortality paradox (refer to the textbox).

Hispanic (Latino) Mortality Paradox

In the United States, Hispanics have a lower mortality rate than non-Hispanic whites and African Americans: 24.8% lower than the rate for the non-Hispanic white population and 42.7% lower than that of the non-Hispanic black population.[31] This differential in mortality is surprising, because Hispanics as a group tend to have a less-advantaged socioeconomic profile than non-Hispanic whites.

The cause-specific mortality of Hispanics differs from that of non-Hispanic whites, who experience more years of potential life lost due to

continues

lung cancer. In contrast, Latinos have more years of life lost to HIV and diabetes among both men and women and to homicide and liver disease among men.[58]

How is it possible for Hispanics to have lower overall mortality rates than non-Hispanic whites? One of the proposed explanations for the Hispanic mortality paradox is the "salmon bias effect," where persons of Hispanic heritage who have immigrated to the United States may return to their original countries, where they die. Thus, they become "statistically immortal."[59]

Research has examined mortality differences among Hispanic subgroups that are able to migrate, those that are restricted from migrating, and those from territories of the United States. For example, Mexican Americans are able to return to their homeland, whereas Cuban Americans are limited in their ability to return to their country of birth. Mortality statistics for Puerto Ricans are included with U.S. national mortality statistics. Thus, it is most feasible to test the salmon bias hypothesis among Mexican Americans. Support for the "salmon bias effect" is suggested for Mexican Americans, although the effect is by no means clear-cut and requires further research.[59,60] Nevertheless, Cuban Americans and Puerto Ricans also maintain lower mortality rates than non-Hispanic whites, a difference that has not yet been fully explained.[59,61]

At present, the reasons for the Hispanic mortality paradox have not been elucidated fully. Two other possible explanations are the healthy migrant effect (discussed further in the next section) and the acculturation hypothesis, which suggests that the cultural orientation of Hispanics is associated with protective health behaviors. Later, these protective behaviors wane as Hispanics become increasingly acculturated to the United States.[62] ■

Nativity and Migration

Nativity refers to the place of origin of the individual or his or her relatives. A common subdivision used in epidemiology is foreign-born or native-born. Thus, nativity is inextricably tied to migration because foreign-born persons have immigrated to their host country. As a result, nativity and migration frequently overlap the epidemiologic categories of race, ethnicity, and religion, because streams of immigrants may bring their cultural and religious practices to the new land, or may comprise a common racial background.

The phenomenon of migration meets the criteria for a natural experiment in which the effects of change from one environment can be studied. For example, migration research has examined various health dimensions, including stress, acculturation, chronic disease, and infectious disease. Classic epidemiologic research conducted in the late 1930s examined rates of admission to mental hospitals in New York State. Admission rates were higher among foreign-born than native-born persons, suggesting that foreign-born individuals may experience stresses associated with migration to a new environment.[5]

Another impact of migration has been to modify the profile of infectious diseases seen in public health departments throughout the developed world. Some immigrants from Southeast Asia and Mexico may import "Third World" diseases to the United States. For example, local health departments in Southern California have found that intestinal parasites, malaria, and certain other tropical diseases may occur among newly arrived immigrants from endemic areas in developing countries; the same conditions are rare in the resident U.S. population. Likewise, the number of cases of Hansen's disease (leprosy) rose dramatically along with increased immigration from Southeast Asia between 1978 and 1988 (Figure 4–9).

Another impact of migration of people from developing countries has been the need to establish specialized TB and nutritional screening programs for refugees and the need to reeducate physicians with respect to formerly uncommon (in the United States) tropical diseases. The inadequate immunization status of some migrants and refugees with respect to measles and other vaccine-preventable diseases has hampered the efforts of health officials to eradicate these conditions in the United States.

Researchers who strive to examine the health of migrants are confronted with significant methodologic challenges. One is the difficulty in separating environmental influences in the host country from selective factors operative among those who choose to migrate. The term *healthy migrant effect* acknowledges the observation that healthier, younger persons usually form the majority of migrants. Nevertheless, despite methodologic difficulties, such as the healthy migrant effect, migration research is a fascinating area that has already yielded many intriguing findings. For a review, refer to Friis, Yngve, and Persson.[63]

Religion

Religious beliefs also may be salient for rates of morbidity and mortality that are observed in the population. For example, adherents to some religious denomina-

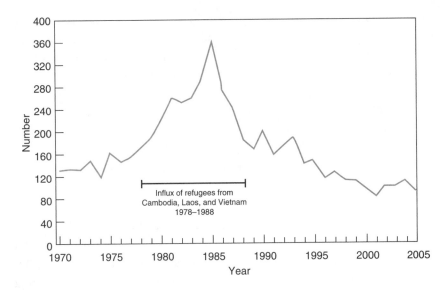

NOTE: The number of reported cases of Hansen's disease has remained stable for the last six years.

FIGURE 4–9   Hansen's disease (leprosy). Number of reported cases, by year: United States, 1970–2005. *Source:* From Centers for Disease Control and Prevention, Summary of notifiable diseases–United States, 2005, *MMWR.* Vol 54, No 53, p. 55, 2007.

tions that prescribe particular lifestyles may demonstrate characteristic morbidity or mortality profiles. In addition, religiosity itself is believed to have health impacts. A thoughtful review of the subject of religion and health pointed out that the epidemiologic literature on this topic is extensive, with several hundred epidemiologic studies reporting statistically significant associations between religious indicators and morbidity and mortality.[64] While there is definitive evidence of an association among these dimensions, the question remains unanswered as to whether the association is causal. For some patients who are confronting a chronic disease, religion and spirituality may improve the quality of their lives. Healthcare providers can reinforce the coping skills of cancer patients by recognizing their religious needs.[65,66] We provide several examples of work in this area that examine the occurrence of morbidity and mortality among population subgroups classified by religious membership.

The Seventh-Day Adventist church endorses a lacto-ovovegetarian diet, which consists of meat, poultry, or fish less than once per week with no restriction on egg or dairy consumption. Members are encouraged to abstain from alcohol, tobacco, and pork products.[67] The low rates of CHD observed among this religious group suggest that the corresponding lifestyle has health benefits. Seventh-Day Adventists also have been reported to have low mortality rates from other chronic diseases. Armstrong et al.[68] studied Seventh-Day Adventists in western Australia and found that mean systolic and diastolic blood pressures were significantly lower than those of the comparison population. Phillips[69] reported findings of reduced risk of cancer and other chronic diseases among the Seventh-Day Adventist population in the United States. The latter research was conducted as part of the Adventist Mortality Study and the Adventist Health Study 1 (1974–1988).

The Adventist Health Study 2 was initiated in 2002 for the purpose of obtaining information on the association of dietary and other lifestyle practices with cancer risk.[70] A preliminary analysis using these data compared black and white Adventist respondents with regard to disease and lifestyle characteristics. Although the study found similarities and discrepancies (sometimes favoring whites and other times favoring blacks) between the two racial groups with respect to health characteristics, the health profile of black Adventists tended to be superior to that of blacks nationally.[71]

Jarvis[72] summarized findings on Mormons and other groups and presented data on Mormon mortality rates in Canada. He noted that, compared with the general U.S. population, Canadian Mormons have lower incidence and mortality rates due to cancer and other diseases. The study of mortality rates among Mormons in Alberta, Canada, generally confirmed mortality findings for the United States. Jarvis speculated that mortality differences may be due to restrictions on the intake of coffee, tea, and meats and lifestyle variables related to physical fitness, social support, and a stress-reducing religious ideology. Data on Mormons in Alameda County, California, corroborate findings from previous descriptive studies of an unusually low risk for cancer.[73]

Socioeconomic Status

Social class variations in health have been observed, formally and informally, since the beginning of organized society. The relationship between socioeconomic status (SES) and health is remarkably consistent, having been demonstrated for a wide range of health outcomes and confirmed by a massive body of evidence.[74] Particularly noteworthy are social class differences in mortality, with persons lower in the social hierarchy having higher mortality rates than do persons in upper levels.[75] Link et al. wrote, "This dynamic connection between SES and risk factors has led to the observation of a persistent association between SES and mortality. We refer to social conditions whose association with mortality persists in this manner as 'fundamental social causes' of inequalities in health."[76(p. 377)] Enduring low income is especially consequential for mortality.[77] Berkman and Syme[78] concluded that low social class standing is related to excess mortality, morbidity, and disability rates. Some of the more obvious explanations for the negative health effects of low social class membership are poor housing, crowding, racial disadvantages, low income, poor education, and unemployment. A complex web of factors includes exposure to environmental and work-related hazards, both material and social deprivation, lack of access to health care, and negative lifestyle. Socioeconomic factors also may play a role in the association of race and ethnicity with health.[79]

> There is a striking consistency in the distribution of mortality and morbidity between social groups. The more advantaged groups, whether expressed in terms of income, education, social class or ethnicity, tend to have better health than the other members of their societies. The distribution is not bipolar (advantaged vs. the rest) but graded, so that each change in the level of advantage or disadvantage is in general associated with a change in health.[80(p. 903)]

Measurement

Much of the terminology of social class that is used in epidemiologic research has been derived from sociology, in particular the branch of sociology dealing with social class and social stratification. Social class also is related to ethnicity, race, religion, and nativity. This is because some ethnic and other minority groups often occupy the lowest social class rankings in the United States. There are several different measures of social class that draw upon the individual's economic position in society. Such measures include the prestige of the individual's occupational or social position, educational attainment, income, or combined indices of two or more of these variables. Occupational prestige is often employed as a measure of social class. For example, learned professionals (e.g., physicians, college professors, lawyers, and similar occupational groups) are accorded the highest occupational prestige, and other occupations are ranked below them. A mea-sure of occupational prestige derived by the British Registrar General has five levels of occupational prestige. The U.S. Bureau of the Census has derived a ranked measure of occupational status that has more levels with finer categories within each of the major levels. Some measures of social class represent a composite of variables, including occupation, education, and income.[81] Two approaches are illustrative of the work in this field. Hollingshead and Redlich[82] derived a two-factor measure of social class that combines level of education with occupational prestige (see Exhibit 4–2). Duncan[83] developed a three-factor SES index that has been used in epidemiologic research.

Problems arise in the assignment of social class to unemployed or retired persons and to students, who may ultimately occupy a high social class position in society upon graduation but who temporarily have low income and occupational prestige. It is difficult to assign social class ranking to a family when both mother and father work and have occupations that are disparate in occupational prestige. People who occupy the same category of occupational prestige may be quite diverse in income and other characteristics.

Measurement of income also is fraught with difficulty. The individual may not want to reveal income information or may not actually know the precise income of the family, as in the case of children, when it is necessary for the researcher to measure their social class. Also, two workers who have low-status occupations may have a combined family income that is higher than the total family income of one professional worker. The correct method for assigning social class in these situations may not be readily discernible.

EXHIBIT 4–2

Socioeconomic Status and Mental Illness Survey of New Haven, Connecticut

Hollingshead and Redlich[82] classified New Haven, Connecticut, into five social class levels according to prestige of occupation, education, and address. These were some of the findings of the study:

- There was a strong inverse association between social class and the likelihood of being a mental patient under treatment.
- With respect to severity of mental illness, upper socioeconomic individuals were more likely to be neurotics, whereas lower socioeconomic individuals were more likely to be psychotics (i.e., less severe forms of mental illness occurred in the upper social class strata, and the highest incidence of schizophrenia was found in the lowest social classes).
- The type of treatment varied by SES ranking. It was more common for upper socioeconomic individuals to receive treatment from a psychiatrist, whereas lower SES individuals were treated in state and public hospitals, where they received organic modes of treatment, such as shock therapy. ■

Education (measured by number of years of formal schooling completed) is another component of SES. Higher levels of education, in contrast to income or occupation, appear to be the strongest and most important predictor of positive health status.[81]

Findings

Despite the unreliability of measures of social class, studies of the association between social class and health have yielded noteworthy findings; thus, social class usually should be considered when one is evaluating the occurrence of disease. Among the major illustrations of the association between social class and health are the findings on the frequency of mental illness. Exhibit 4–2 concerns one of the most noteworthy studies in this field, carried out by Hollingshead and Redlich,[82] who surveyed New Haven, Connecticut, half a century ago, and reported that as SES increased, the severity of mental illness decreased.

Dunham[84] and others proposed two alternative hypotheses for the finding of highest incidence of severe mental illness among the lowest social classes. One, the social causation explanation (known as the "breeder hypothesis") suggested that conditions arising from membership in the low social class groups produced schizophrenia and other mental illnesses.[85] However, an equally plausible explanation was the "downward drift hypothesis," which stated that the clustering of psychosis was an artifact of drift of schizophrenics to impoverished areas of a city. Murphy et al.[86] indicated that during the 1950s and 1960s, the prevalence of depression was significantly and persistently higher in the low SES population than at other socioeconomic levels. Stresses associated with poverty may be linked to depression, which in turn may be associated with subsequent downward social mobility. Downward drift is consonant with the view that the concentration of depressed people at the lower end of the social hierarchy may result from handicapping aspects of the illness. Although epidemiologic research that shows variation in mental disorders by position in social structures has generated much excitement, additional work is needed to develop adequate theories to explain these findings.[84]

Low social class standing correlates with increased rates of infectious disease, including TB, rheumatic fever, influenza, pneumonia, and other respiratory diseases.[78] It is reasonable to attribute increased rates of these conditions to overcrowding, increased exposure to infection, lack of medical care, nutritional deficiencies, and poor sanitary conditions.

In comparison with upper socioeconomic groups, lower socioeconomic groups have higher infant mortality rates and overall mortality rates and lower life expectancy.[87] The influence of psychosocial and behavioral factors on differential health outcomes associated with varying SES levels is not fully understood.[88] Social class differences in mortality and morbidity have persisted over time, even with overall reductions in infant mortality and infectious diseases.[78] Life expectancies, based on data from the National Longitudinal Mortality Study for 1979 to 1985, were estimated for white men and white women by education, family income, and employment status. Life expectancy varied directly with amount of schooling and family income.[89] Similarly, more recent data from the National Occupational Mortality Surveillance Program for 1984 through 1997 demonstrated an inverse gradient between SES and mortality among employed persons in the United States.[90] Comparative international studies found socioeconomic inequalities in cardiovascular disease mortality, with higher levels among persons who were less educated or had lower occupational classifications.[91] Although inadequate medical care and exposure to environmental hazards may account for some of the social differences in morbidity and mortality, other factors also may be relevant, such as exposure to stressful life events, stresses associated with social and cultural mobility, poverty, and health behaviors including smoking.

When the effects of poverty and limited access to health care are removed, infant mortality rates among African Americans improve. In illustration, researchers examined infant mortality rates among the dependents of African-American military personnel. These personnel had guaranteed access to health care and tended to have levels of family income and education that were higher than those of the U.S. African-American population. The infant mortality rates in this study group were somewhat lower than those for the general U.S. population.[92] For persons who were younger than 65 years of age, mortality rates were lower among those with higher family incomes for both African Americans and whites and for both men and women. However, at each level of income, African Americans had higher mortality rates than whites. Higher levels of family income also were associated with lower death rates from cardiovascular diseases and cancer.[93]

Wide differentials in cancer survival were observed among socioeconomic groups in England and Wales.[94] Lower socioeconomic groups tended to have a larger proportion of cancers with poor prognoses in comparison with upper socioeconomic groups. Poor survival rates among the lower socioeconomic groups might have been due to delay in seeking health care. Health system barriers, such as lack of access to care and the financial burden of diabetes care in the United States, may affect the health of insulin-dependent diabetes mellitus patients, which increases mortality rates among people 25 to 37 years of age.[95]

Among the other conditions that vary by social class is a specific form of mental retardation: mild mental retardation (IQ 60 through 75). Research reported a gradation of the frequency of mild mental retardation by social class; low social class groups had the highest prevalence of mild retardation. More severe forms of mental retardation tended to be more uniformly distributed across social classes.[96] Because few recent investigations have been reported on SES as a correlate of mental retardation, this topic merits additional research.

Characteristics of Place

Types of Place Comparisons

International
Geographic (within-country) variations
Urban/rural differences
Localized occurrence of disease

International Comparisons of Disease Frequency

The World Health Organization (WHO), which sponsors and conducts ongoing surveillance research, is a major source of information about international variations in rates of disease. WHO statistical studies portray international variations in infectious and communicable diseases, malnutrition, infant mortality, suicide, and other conditions. As might be expected, both infectious and chronic diseases show great variation from one country to another. Some of these differences may be attributed to climate, cultural factors, national dietary habits, and access to health care. Such variations are reflected in great international differences in life expectancy. Among the 37 countries shown in Figure 4–10, the United States ranked 26th for males (life expectancy = 74.4 years) and 25th for females (life expectancy = 79.8 years) in 2001. Japan reported the highest life expectancy (78.1 and 84.9 years, respectively. Russia had the lowest life expectancy (59.1 and 72.3 years, respectively).

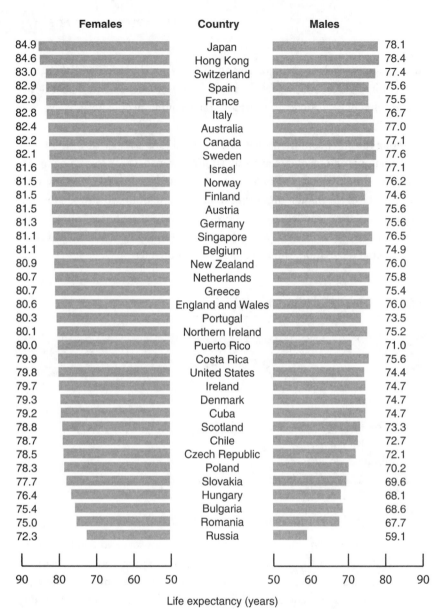

Females	Country	Males
84.9	Japan	78.1
84.6	Hong Kong	78.4
83.0	Switzerland	77.4
82.9	Spain	75.6
82.9	France	75.5
82.8	Italy	76.7
82.4	Australia	77.0
82.2	Canada	77.1
82.1	Sweden	77.6
81.6	Israel	77.1
81.5	Norway	76.2
81.5	Finland	74.6
81.5	Austria	75.6
81.3	Germany	75.6
81.1	Singapore	76.5
81.1	Belgium	74.9
80.9	New Zealand	76.0
80.7	Netherlands	75.8
80.7	Greece	75.4
80.6	England and Wales	76.0
80.3	Portugal	73.5
80.1	Northern Ireland	75.2
80.0	Puerto Rico	71.0
79.9	Costa Rica	75.6
79.8	United States	74.4
79.7	Ireland	74.7
79.3	Denmark	74.7
79.2	Cuba	74.7
78.8	Scotland	73.3
78.7	Chile	72.7
78.5	Czech Republic	72.1
78.3	Poland	70.2
77.7	Slovakia	69.6
76.4	Hungary	68.1
75.4	Bulgaria	68.6
75.0	Romania	67.7
72.3	Russia	59.1

Life expectancy (years)

FIGURE 4–10   Life expectancy at birth, by sex in selected countries in 2001. Rankings are from the highest to lowest female life expectancy at birth, as published in *Health, United States 2005* (HUS, 2005). Life expectancy at birth represents the average number of years that a group of infants would live if the infants were to experience throughout life the age-specific death rates present at birth. Data are reported by countries. Because calculation of life-expectancy estimates varies by country, comparisons should be made with caution. Certain life-expectancy estimates were revised and differ from those published in HUS 2005. *Source:* From Centers for Disease Control and Prevention, *MMWR.* Vol 55, No 22, p. 631, 2006.

CHD, hypertension, stroke, and diabetes are among the "diseases of affluence," conditions formerly confined primarily to the developed world, but now occurring more frequently in developing regions as living standards improve. Nevertheless, mortality due to CHD is the leading cause of death in the United States and tends to be increasingly common in other areas as well. Countries that have high economic standards tend to foster behavioral and lifestyle factors implicated in CHD and other chronic diseases: lack of exercise, rich diets, and use of tobacco products. Fortunately, CHD mortality in the United States is on the decline, possibly due to preventive efforts that aim to modify these behavioral and lifestyle factors.

Cancer rates are increasing worldwide, especially as the population ages.[97] Lung cancer is the most common form of cancer in the world, showing declines in nations where it was formerly on the rise: Britain and the United States. The eastern European countries have the highest rates of lung cancer in the world. High rates occur in parts of the developing world where smoking is common, although exposure to environmental pollution may play a small role.

According to WHO statistics reported in 1977, stomach cancer was the second most common form of cancer worldwide.[97] Japan as well as parts of Central and South Asia formed a high-risk area. Risk factors for stomach cancer include consumption of preserved, cured, or salted foods. Decline in stomach cancer rates in some areas is related to improved diet (e.g., greater consumption of fresh vegetables). Stomach cancer death rates in Japan declined from 70.3 per 100,000 and 37.0 per 100,000 in 1958–1962 to 34.5 per 100,000 and 15.2 per 100,000 in 1988–1992 for males and females, respectively.[98] Nevertheless, despite a declining trend, stomach cancer death rates remained higher in Japan than rates observed in many other countries.

There are numerous examples of international variations in infectious diseases and related conditions. Schistosomiasis (see Chapter 12) is endemic to the Nile River area of Africa and to sections of Latin America, but it rarely occurs in the United States unless it is imported into the country from an endemic area. Yaws tends to be localized in tropical climates and does not ordinarily occur in the temperate climate of the United States. Countries in tropical Africa account for more than 80% of all clinical cases of parasitic infections and more than 90% of all parasite carriers.[99] Approximately 800,000 children died from malaria in 2000 in malaria-affected regions of Africa.[100] Exacerbations of malaria outbreaks follow major ecologic or social changes, such as agricultural or other economic exploitation of jungle areas or sociopolitical unrest.

Infectious diseases account for fewer than 5% of all deaths in developed countries but—alarmingly—about 50% of deaths in less developed nations. Deaths from infections hamper the efforts of developing nations to advance economically. As noted in Chapter 12, HIV/AIDS takes a major toll in these countries. Some types of communicable diseases that show international variation are cutaneous leishmaniasis, Chagas disease, dengue fever, malaria, and cholera. Zoonotic diseases (transmitted from animal hosts to humans) vary greatly from one country to another. One example is vampire bat rabies, which increased during the 1980s as a cause of human death in Peru and Brazil.[101] Another example is bovine spongiform encephalopathy (BSE; also known as mad cow disease), which at first was confined largely to the United Kingdom, then spread to Europe and later to Japan, Canada, and the United States. BSE has been linked to variant Creutzfeldt-Jakob disease in humans (refer to case study on BSE).

Suicide rates for selected countries show marked differences between the lowest and highest ranked countries. Low rates are reported in Mexico, Greece, and Italy; the United States and Canada fall in the middle range; and Belgium, Switzerland, Finland, and Hungary have the highest rates.[102]

There also are widely varying international differences in infant mortality rates: Central African nations have the highest rates of infant mortality followed by North Africa, the Middle East, and India. As noted in Chapter 3, the lowest rates exist in Japan, the Scandinavian countries, and France. The United States, Great Britain, Canada, and Australia all have higher rates of infant mortality than the foregoing countries. Social factors, education, and availability of medical care may account, in part, for the international variation in infant mortality. (See Figure 3–6, page 114.)

Many countries, especially those in Africa, have had to reduce drastically their budgets for health services in the past decade, creating a wide discrepancy in health status between those countries and the developed world. For example, the life expectancy in Swaziland is estimated at 32.2 years, in contrast with the European country Andorra (83.5 years).[103] In developing countries, high population growth also reduces the available resources for healthcare and prevention programs and at the same time increases the potential for spread of infection through crowding. Korte et al.[104] argue that environmentally related health problems and adverse impacts of industrialization, urbanization, and slum growth will challenge the healthcare resources of developing countries in the future.

Within-Country Geographic Variation in Rates of Disease

Many of the countries of Europe and North America have substantial variations in climate, geology, latitude, environmental pollution, and concentrations of ethnic and racial stock, all of which may be related to differences in frequency of disease. Examples of within-country comparisons made in the United States include case rates by region (e.g., Pacific, Mountain, Central, Atlantic). Sometimes, comparisons in rates are made by states, or, if fine comparisons are to be made across the United States, rates may be calculated by counties. In the United States, infectious diseases (e.g., intestinal parasites, influenza, AIDS, and many others) and chronic diseases (e.g., some forms of cancer and multiple sclerosis) show variation in frequency across the country. For example, high death rates due to leukemia are concentrated in the upper Midwest, whereas malignant melanoma of the skin appears to be related to latitude, the lowest rates occurring in the northern tier of the country and the highest rates being concentrated along the Sunbelt.[105] Multiple sclerosis varies according to latitude in the United States.[106] There is a gradient in rates from 15 per 100,000 in the South (Charleston, New Orleans, and Houston) to intermediate rates in Denver to high rates in Rochester, Minnesota (more than 40 per 100,000).[107]

The frequency of intestinal parasites varies from state to state in the United States, according to the findings of intestinal parasite surveillance programs conducted by the Centers for Disease Control and Prevention (CDC). During 1987, the states surrounding the Great Lakes and states in the Northwest had the highest percentage of stool samples positive for *Giardia lamblia* protozoan. Stool samples positive for hookworm tended to be found most frequently in nine states (ranging from California to Wisconsin), although no consistency emerged from the distribution of positive specimens. Several factors may account for the variations in the prevalence and geographic distribution of intestinal parasites, including the arrival in the United States of large numbers of immigrants from endemic areas, increases in parasitic infections among patients with AIDS, and the recognition of *Giardia lamblia* species as frequently occurring pathogens in daycare centers.[108]

Variations in morbidity and mortality rates due to pneumonia and influenza may be seen for different geographic sections of the United States, but the pattern changes from year to year and is also related to the variant of the influenza virus. Influenza epidemics remain an important cause of hospitalization and also are a cause of mortality as well as a factor that exacerbates health problems among the elderly and persons with a chronic disease. During the 2002–2003 influenza season in the United States (for the dates September 29, 2002 through March 8, 2003), the CDC reported that influenza activity was mild. Nevertheless, occurrence of influenza varied by region and according to virus strain (i.e., influenza A or influenza B). "For the season, influenza type A viruses have predominated in the New England, East North Central, Mountain, Pacific, and Mid-Atlantic regions, and influenza B viruses have predominated in the

West South Central, South Atlantic, West North Central, and East South Central regions."[109] Approximately 14 years earlier, during the 1988–1989 season, influenza appeared with essentially equal frequency regionally, although the predominance of two strains (variants)—influenza A and B—alternated.[110]

AIDS incidence varies considerably within the United States. The highest reported rates (greater than 30.0 per 100,000 population, data for 1996 and 1997) tended to be concentrated in the northeastern, southeastern, and western states. Approximately 4/5 of reported cases could be attributed to the residents of large metropolitan areas (500,000 or more population).[111] The distribution during 2005 (about 10 years later) was similar, with concentrations in the Northeast, Southwest, U.S. Virgin Islands, and Puerto Rico. Figure 4–11 depicts variations in AIDS cases in the United States during 2005.

Early in the present century, the frequency of AIDS cases remained approximately constant in most regions of the United States. At the same time, an epidemic of AIDS occurred in the Deep South, where cases were more common among African Americans, women, and rural inhabitants than among similar groups in other regions.[112] Adding to the burden of AIDS in the Deep South are high poverty rates and low health insurance levels, which limit the availability of treatment and prevention programs.

Case Study: Mad Cow Disease (BSE)

Bovine spongiform encephalopathy (BSE) refers to a group of diseases that are caused by an unusual transmissible agent named a prion. The mechanism by which the infectious agent replicates is not entirely known. As the name implies, BSE affects cattle (but is also capable of infecting sheep, goats, and some other animals) by causing degenerative diseases of the brain.[a] Strong evidence suggests that there is ". . . a causal relationship between ongoing outbreaks in Europe of a disease in cattle called bovine spongiform encephalopathy (BSE, or 'mad cow disease') and a disease in humans called variant Creutzfeldt-Jakob disease (vCJD)."[b]

"From 1995 through mid August 2006, a total of 195 human cases of vCJD were reported worldwide, 162 in the United Kingdom (UK), 20 in France, 4 in Ireland, 2 in the United States, and 1 each in Canada, Italy,

continues

CASE STUDY *continued*

Japan, Netherlands, Portugal, Saudi Arabia and Spain. Seven of the non-UK case-patients were most likely exposed to the BSE agent in the UK because of their having resided there during a key exposure period of the UK population to the BSE agent. These latter case-patients were those from Canada, Japan, the United States, 1 of the 20 from France, and 2 of the 4 from Ireland. The median age at death from vCJD in the United Kingdom has been 28 years and almost all cases have been in persons under age 55 years. The reasons for this age distribution are not well understood but it suggests that through the oral route of exposure, older adults are much less susceptible to vCJD than children and young adults. By year of onset, the incidence of vCJD in the UK appears to have peaked in 1999 and to have been declining thereafter. In contrast, the number of reported cases in France has been increasing since the beginning of 2005. However, the future pattern of these ongoing epidemics remains uncertain. The identification in 2003 of a BSE case in Canada, and the subsequent identification later that year of a BSE case in the United States that had been imported from Canada led to the concern that indigenous transmission of BSE may be occurring in North America. In 2004, both countries had implemented new safeguards to reduce the risk for human exposure to BSE. . . ."[c]

"To reduce any risk of acquiring vCJD from food, concerned travelers to Europe or other areas with indigenous cases of BSE may consider either avoiding beef and beef products altogether or selecting beef or beef products, such as solid pieces of muscle meat (rather than brains or beef products like burgers and sausages), that might have a reduced opportunity for contamination with tissues that may harbor the BSE agent. These measures, however, should be taken with the knowledge of the very low risk of disease transmission, particularly to older persons, as discussed above. Milk and milk products from cows are not believed to pose any risk for transmitting the BSE agent."[c]

[a] Heymann DL, ed. *Control of Communicable Diseases Manual.* 18th ed. Washington, DC: American Public Health Association; 2004.

[b] Centers for Disease Control and Prevention. vCJD (Variant Creutzfeldt-Jakob Disease). Epidemiology of vCJD and BSE. Available at: http://www.cdc.gov/ncidod/dvrd/vcjd/epidemiology.htm. Accessed December 6, 2007.

[c] Centers for Disease Control and Prevention. vCJD (Variant Creutzfeldt-Jakob Disease). Risk for Travelers. Available at: http://www.cdc.gov/ncidod/dvrd/vcjd/risk_travelers.htm. Accessed December 6, 2007.

○ 0–4.9   ○ 5.0–9.9   ◐ 100–14.9   ● 15 or higher

* Per 100,000 population.
† Included 209 persons with unknown state of residence.

The highest AIDS rates were observed in the northeastern part of the country. High incidence (i.e.,
≥ 15 cases per 100,000 population) also was reported in the southeastern states, the U.S. Virgin
Islands, and Puerto Rico.

FIGURE 4–11   Acquired immune deficiency syndrome (AIDS).
Incidence*United States† and U.S. territories, 2005. *Source:* From Centers
for Disease Control and Prevention, Summary of notifiable
diseases–United States, 2005, *MMWR.* Vol 54, No 53, p. 40, 2007.

Urban/Rural Differences in Disease Rates

Urban and rural sections of the United States both have characteristic risks for
morbidity and mortality. Urban diseases and causes of mortality are those that
are more likely to be spread by person-to-person contact, crowding, and poverty
or to be associated with urban pollution. Lead poisoning has been associated
with inadequate housing and is found in inner city areas, where increased exposure of children occurs through ingestion of lead-based paints. Although such
paints are now outlawed for interior residential use, exposure may still be high in
low-income urban areas. Mortality rates due to atherosclerotic heart disease, TB,
and cirrhosis of the liver are higher in urban areas than in rural areas. Urban areas
also show higher rates of bladder, lung, larynx, liver, and oral cancer and cancer

of the pharynx and cervix, whereas rural areas show excesses in cancer of the lip in both sexes and cancer of the eye among men.[113] Among African Americans, data for the prevalence, incidence, and mortality of CHD reflect higher rates for urban residents than for rural residents.[114]

Among all racial and ethnic groups, the residents of rural areas could be affected by environmental and cultural factors that reinforce unhealthful behaviors.[115] Health and economic status of rural residents vary according to the region of the country in which they live: Southern rural inhabitants are poorer, smoke more frequently, and are more physically inactive; consequently, their rate of ischemic heart disease mortality is higher. Western rural inhabitants are afflicted more frequently by alcohol abuse and suicide. Northeastern rural dwellers endure a greater frequency of tooth loss.

A number of studies have examined the health status of minority populations found in rural areas of the United States. Racial/ethnic minority populations in rural areas are reported to experience more disadvantages caused by health disparities and lack of access to health care than similar minority groups in urban areas.[116]

For urban/rural comparisons, data from the standard metropolitan statistical areas (SMSAs) are often employed. SMSAs are standard areas of the United States established by the U.S. Bureau of the Census to make regional comparisons in disease rates and also to make urban/rural comparisons.

Localized Place Comparisons

A local outbreak of a disease or localized elevated morbidity rate may be due to the unique environmental or social conditions found in a particular area of interest. Fluorosis, a disease resulting in mottled teeth, is most common in those areas of the world and the United States where there are naturally-elevated fluoride levels in the water. Goiter, associated with iodine deficiency in the diet, was historically more common in land-locked areas of the United States, where seafood was not consumed, although this problem has been greatly alleviated by the introduction of iodized salt.

Localized concentrations of ionizing radiation have been studied in relation to cancer incidence. Ohio communities with high risk of exposure to radon had higher rates than the rest of Ohio of all cancers in general and cancer of the respiratory system in particular.[117] Ontario, Canada, gold miners had excess mortality from carcinoma of the lung. This excess mortality was linked to exposure to radon decay products, arsenic, and high dust concentrations.[118] Local geologic formations may affect water hardness, which, some studies suggest, is a protective factor against heart disease deaths. For 1969 to 1983, one study reported an east–west regional gradient in cardiovascular mortality within seven counties in central Sweden, supporting other reports that have suggested water hardness to be inversely related to cardiovascular mortality.[119] Variation in water hardness accounted for 41% of the variation in the ischemic heart disease mortality rate and 14% of the variation in the stroke mortality rate. A second Swedish study attributed variation in mortality rates for coronary disease to exposure to cold weather, which was positively associated with heart disease and negatively associated with water hardness.[120] However, the evidence for this hypothesis has been both positive and negative.

Geographic Information Systems

Increasingly, public health practitioners are using Geographic Information Systems (GIS) as a method to provide a spatial perspective on the geographic distribution of health conditions. Although GIS has existed for some time, newer software has increased the ease of application of GIS methods by nonexperts.[121] As a result, GIS has generated much excitement in the epidemiology community with respect to fresh applications. It is an advance that has enormous possibilities for defining new methods of comprehending data.[122]

A GIS is defined as ". . . a constellation of computer hardware and software that integrates maps and graphics with a database related to a defined geographical space . . . The geographical data may be spatial or descriptive in nature. A GIS can be defined as an integrated set of tools within an automated system capable of collecting, storing, handling, analyzing, and displaying geographically referenced information."[123(p. 1)] A GIS contains a database, maps, and a method to link these elements.[121] "GIS is, at its heart, a simple extension of statistical analyses that join epidemiological, sociological, clinical, and economic data with references to space. A GIS system does not create data but merely relates data using a system of references that describe spatial relationships."[122(p. 18.3)]

Although many uses exist, an important application of GIS is to map locations that have higher disease occurrence or mortality risk than do other areas. Planners then are able to target these high-risk areas with appropriate social and health interventions. Subsequently, GIS facilitates the assessment of the impact of these interventions, which presumably would result in reductions of disease occurrence that could be visualized on a map. Thus, it is apparent that the use of GIS in epidemiology follows from the heritage of John Snow who, as noted in Chapter 1, produced a map of the cholera outbreak in Broad Street, Golden

Square, London. At present, epidemiologists use GIS for many purposes, including research and planning in environmental health, infectious disease outbreaks, and policy evaluation.[121] Table 4–1 provides examples of applications of GIS.

To obtain more information about GIS, navigate the CDC Web site, "Resources for creating public health maps" (http://www.cdc.gov/epiinfo/maps.htm; accessed October 19, 2007). The CDC Web site lists more than one dozen software packages that are available for purchase or free download. An example is Epi Info™, freeware developed at the CDC. In conclusion, Figure 4–12 presents an example of a GIS map of infant mortality rates in the U.S. state of Idaho. This map is called a choropleth map, defined as a map that represents disease rates (or other numerical data) for a group of regions by different degrees of shading.

Reasons for Place Variation in Disease

Concentration or clustering of racial, ethnic, or religious groups within a specific geographic area may result in higher or lower rates of diseases, depending upon the lifestyle and behaviors of the particular religious or ethnic group. The Seventh-Day Adventists, who espouse vegetarianism, are concentrated, among other places, in parts of the Los Angeles basin, and the rates for CHD tend to be low in these corresponding geographic areas. Similarly, low rates of cancer tend to be found in areas where a large proportion of the residents are Mormons, possibly because their religious beliefs advocate avoidance of stimulants, tobacco, and alcohol.

Table 4–1 Representative Applications of
Geographic Information Systems (GIS)

Mapping of environmental health risks
   Pesticide pollution of groundwater
   Drifting of crop pesticides
   Average air pollution concentrations
   Exposure to elevated levels of magnetic fields
   Lead hazards
Portraying the geographic distribution of infectious diseases
   Bovine spongiform encephalopathy (BSE) in Europe
   Surveillance of disease outbreaks (e.g., Lyme disease, hepatitis C)
   Mapping of water-borne, vector-borne, and tropical diseases
Health policy/planning
   Risk assessment
   Intervention evaluation
   Health services needs assessment
   Hospital accessibility

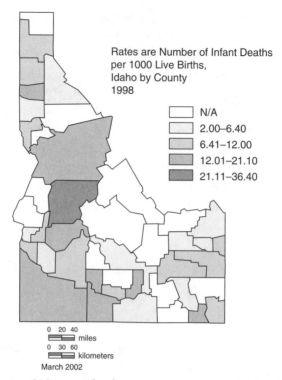

FIGURE 4–12   GIS map of infant mortality rates in Idaho, United States. *Source:* Idaho Department of Health and Welfare, Bureau of Vital Statistics. Available at: http://inside.uidaho.edu/data/statewide/esri/idtm/ atlas/infamr98_id_esri.gif. Accessed: October 22, 2007.

The genetic characteristics of the population may interact with the environment, suggesting a dynamic interplay between noxious environmental factors and genetic make-up. An example of gene/environment interaction is the increased prevalence of the sickle-cell gene among people who live in sections of Africa that have high malaria rates.[5] The sickle-cell trait is a genetic mutation that confers a selection advantage in areas where malaria is endemic. Tay-Sachs disease is especially common among persons of Jewish extraction and Eastern European origin. It is now more widely distributed around the world as a result of the migration of the descendants of the original carriers.

Place variations in rates of disease may reflect the influence of climate (e.g., temperature and humidity) or environmental factors (e.g., the presence of environmental carcinogens). Certain geographic areas that have mild or tropical climates permit the survival of pathogenic organisms. Trypanosomiasis (African sleeping sickness) survives only in an environment that has the tsetse fly. Yaws and Hansen's disease are found primarily in the tropics. As a consequence of global warming, disease vectors that survive only in mild climates may be able to move northward. Ectoparasites are more common in temperate climates because people wear many layers of clothing, which may harbor these organisms. Naturally occurring or human-made chemical agents in particular geographic areas may be associated with the development of cancers or other diseases. For example, the concentration of fallout from U.S. nuclear testing has elicited concerns about the health effects of exposure to ionizing radiation (discussed in more detail in Chapter 13).

In summary, Hutt and Burkitt stated:

> The disease pattern in any country or geographical region is dependent on the constellation of environmental factors that affect each member of the population from birth to the grave. Within a particular geographical situation the response of individuals to any noxious influences may be modified by their genetic make-up. In general terms exogenous factors which play a role in the causation of disease can be categorized into one of four groups; physical agents, chemical substances, biological agents (which include all infective organisms), and nutritional factors. These are determined by the geographical features of the region, the cultural life of population groups living in the area, the socio-economic status of these groups, and, in certain situations, by specific occupational hazards. Often, the individual's or group's experience of specific factors is determined by a combination of geographical, cultural, and socio-economic influences; this particularly applies to the type and quantity of food eaten.[107(p. 3)]

Characteristics of Time

Temporal aspects of disease occurrence also must be critically examined. Variations in the pattern of disease associated with time may permit important insights into the pathogenesis of disease or the recognition of emerging epidemics. Just as important, when one compares measures of disease frequency between two populations or within a population over time, the timing of data collection may need to be considered if there are seasonal or cyclic variations in the rate of disease.

Cyclic Fluctuations

Cyclic fluctuations are increases and decreases in the frequency of diseases and health conditions over a period of years or within each year. For example, birth rates show a seasonal trend, increasing in the early summer, as do depressive symptoms.[124,125] Influenza, drownings, accidents, and mortality from heart attacks manifest seasonal variations within each year. Analysis of data from a community registry of heart disease found that fatal and nonfatal coronary events in an Australian population were 20% to 40% more likely to occur in winter and spring than at other times of the year.[126] Seasonal variations may be caused by seasonal changes in the behavior of persons that place them at greater risk for certain diseases, changes in exposure to infectious or environmental agents, or endogenous biologic factors.

Pneumonia-influenza deaths in the United States demonstrate cyclic fluctuations, showing both annual peaks and periodic epidemics every few years. Seasonal increases in flu begin during the cold winter months of the year, peak in February, decrease in March and April, and then reach a minimum in June. Meningococcal disease (Figure 4–13) is another condition that varies by season, apparently peaking in the winter and declining in the late summer.

Many diseases demonstrate cyclic increases and decreases related to changes in lifestyle of the host, seasonal climatic changes, and virulence of the infectious agent for a communicable disease. Heart disease mortality peaks during the winter months, when sedentary men are suddenly required to free their automobiles from the aftermath of a snowstorm. Colds increase in frequency when people spend more time indoors and are in close contact with one another, whereas accidents tend to peak during the summer, and Rocky Mountain spotted fever increases in the spring, when the ticks that carry the *rickettsia* bacteria become more active. Reported malaria cases in the Americas and some Asian countries show marked seasonality related to cyclic occurrence of heavy rains, leading to occasional epidemics or serious exacerbations of endemicity.[127]

Other examples of health phenomena that may show cyclic variation are responses of persons to temporary stressors. There may be an association between plasma lipid and lipoprotein levels among tax accountants during the tax season and among students at examination time. However, research has not shown such variation consistently.[128]

Point Epidemics

A *point epidemic* may indicate the response of a group of people circumscribed in place to a common source of infection, contamination, or other etiologic factor to which they were exposed almost simultaneously.[5] Acute infectious diseases and enteric infections sometimes manifest this type of relationship with time, as does mass illness due to exposure to chemical agents and noxious gases. Figure

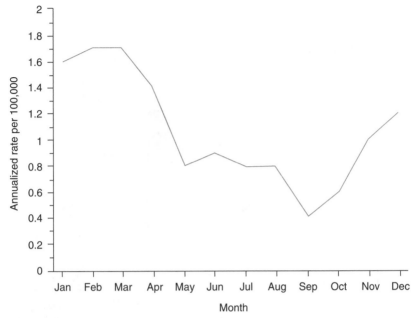

FIGURE 4–13   Seasonal variance in incidence of meningococcal disease in selected U.S. areas during 1989–1991. *Source:* Reprinted from Centers for Disease Control and Prevention, Laboratory-Based Surveillance for Meningococcal Disease in Selected Areas–United States, 1989–1991. *MMWR.* Vol 42, No SS-2, p. 24, June 4, 1993.

4–14 illustrates time clustering of cases of *Mycoplasma pneumoniae* during an outbreak reported by the CDC. Note that the most frequent day of onset was August 7, 1993, and that there was variation in the time of onset. Figure 4–14 is typical of the distribution (marked by a rapid increase and subsequent decline) of outbreaks of acute infectious disease, foodborne illness, and acute responses to toxic substances.

Secular Time Trends

Secular trends refer to gradual changes in the frequency of a disease over long time periods, as illustrated by changes in the rates of chronic diseases. For example, although heart disease was the leading cause of death in the United States from 1970 to 1988, the age-adjusted death rate for this cause declined by 34%; the decrease was 37% for white men and 24% for African-American men.[7] These

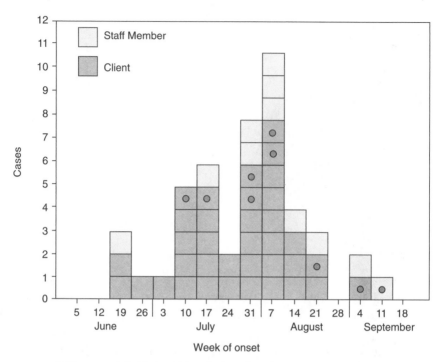

● Case suspected but not laboratory confirmed.

FIGURE 4-14   Cases of *Mycoplasma pneumoniae* among clients and staff members of a sheltered workshop, by week of onset: Ohio, June 15–September 5, 1993. *Source:* Reprinted from Centers for Disease Control and Prevention, Outbreaks of *Mycoplasma Pneumoniae* Respiratory Infection: Ohio, Texas, and New York, 1993. *MMWR.* Vol 42, p. 931, December 10, 1993.

trends may reflect the long-term impact of public health programs, diet improvements, and better treatment as well as unknown factors. With more women starting to smoke, especially teenagers and minority women, there has been a secular increase in lung cancer (see Figure 4–4). Breast cancer mortality rates showed secular decreases from 1995 to 2004, among African Americans and whites (Figure 4–15).

Cohort Effects

One of the consequences of long-term secular trends in exposure is a phenomenon known as cohort effects. Refer to Chapter 7 for more information on this topic.

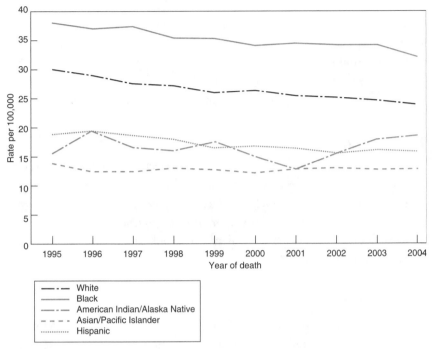

FIGURE 4–15   Age-adjusted total U.S. mortality rates for breast cancer, all ages, females for 1995–2004 by 'Expanded' race age-adjusted to the 2000 U.S. std population. *Source:* Data from Surveillance, Epidemiology, and End Results (SEER) Program (www.seer.cancer.gov) SEER*Stat Database: Mortality – All COD, Public-Use with State, Total U.S. (1990–2004), National Cancer Institute, DCCPS, Surveillance Research Program, Cancer Statistics Branch, released April 2007. Underlying mortality data provided by NCHS (www.cdc.gov/nchs).

Clustering

Case clustering refers to an unusual aggregation of health events grouped together in space or time. Examples of infectious disease clustering are the cholera epidemic in London in the 1850s (reported by John Snow) and the outbreak of Legionnaires's disease in the late 1970s. Examples of noninfectious disease clustering include the development of angiosarcoma among workers exposed to vinyl chloride and adenocarcinoma of the vagina among daughters whose mothers were prescribed diethylstilbestrol.[129] Other conditions that have been investigated for clustering include asthma, asbestos-related lung diseases, suicides, and leukemia and other cancers. Space and time clustering is one type of epidemiologic evidence that might suggest an association between common exposure to an etiologic agent and development of morbidity and mortality. Among the problems surrounding the study of clusters are the fact that health events that show clustering are usually rare (e.g., certain types of cancer), producing a small number of cases, and that some clusters may occur by chance alone.

Temporal Clustering

Postvaccination reactions (adverse reactions to vaccines), such as the development of jaundice among military personnel vaccinated for yellow fever,[5] and the development of puerperal psychoses illustrate *temporal clustering*. Postpartum depression, ranging from the "blues" to more severe psychotic episodes, occurs in up to 80% of women within a few days after childbirth and may continue for several months or longer.[130]

Spatial Clustering

Concentration of cases of disease in a particular geographic area is the definition of *spatial clustering*. Hodgkin's disease, a condition of unknown etiology, is thought to have an infectious component. This possibility could be evaluated by a formal assessment of geographic and temporal variation in the incidence of Hodgkin's disease. One investigation found that, among cases of Hodgkin's disease diagnosed in those older than age 40 in Washington State, there was evidence that cases lived closer together than expected as young children and teenagers.[131]

As another example, six childhood leukemia cases were diagnosed in a small community in northern Germany.[132] Using age-specific population and incidence data, this occurrence translated to a 460-fold standardized incidence ratio within a 5 km radius. Reports such as these can be quite alarming to the general public. Although they can be of significance, it is extremely important that they be put in perspective using appropriate epidemiologic methods. In particular, definition of the geographic area under study is critical.

Drs. Julie Ross and Leslie Robison, colleagues from the University of Minnesota, liken the situation to drawing a bull's-eye around arrows that have already been shot. For example, suppose you are standing over a large enclosed circle with a jar full of 100 marbles. You dump the jar into the circle and note where the marbles land. Invariably, there will be some areas within the circle that will be dense with marbles and some areas that will be sparse. If you picked up all the marbles and repeated the process over and over again, you would note that the marble pattern would always be random and unlikely ever to appear evenly spaced. This description is analogous, perhaps, to clusters of disease, such as the childhood cancer examples. That is, marbles (cases) may fall within a small defined area (city) within a large geographic area (county, state, or country), and one could easily identify a cluster just by drawing a bull's-eye around these cases. In order to evaluate such clusters properly, one must consider the phenomena in the context of a larger geographic area and the temporal occurrence of disease.

Conclusion

This chapter covered descriptive epidemiology: person, place, and time. We have seen, for example, that age and sex are among the most fundamental attributes associated with the distribution of health and illness in populations. Secular trends are among the more important time variables. Although it is the leading cause of U.S. mortality, heart disease mortality has declined. Among women, lung cancer mortality showed a disturbing increase and became the leading cause of female cancer mortality in the latter third of the 20th century; currently, lung cancer mortality retains its same rank, although the increasing trend has leveled off. The data for these and other descriptive variables suggest hypotheses that can be tested in analytic epidemiologic studies. For example, particularly low or high disease rates in a circumscribed geographic area may suggest interaction between ethnicity and place variables, a hypothesis that could be followed up in etiologic research.

Study Questions and Exercises

1. Define the term *descriptive epidemiology*.
2. Describe the relevance of descriptive epidemiology to the study of disease. How do descriptive studies promote hypothesis formation? What is the relevance of Mill's canons to descriptive epidemiology?
3. Give definitions and examples of categories of descriptive epidemiology.
4. What are some examples of age associations found in epidemiologic research? What explanations have been proposed to account for them? When comparing mortality rates by age, discuss the possibility of interactions between age effects and gender effects.

5. How do mortality and morbidity differ by sex? How would you account for interactions between marital status and sex in health outcomes?

6. How do protective and selective factors increase or decrease the risk for disease based on marital status?

7. How do cultural practices and religious beliefs account for mortality and morbidity differences?

8. Describe procedures for measurement of race, ethnicity, and social class. What methodologic pitfalls are inherent in the ascertainment of these characteristics?

9. What health effects do variations in race, ethnicity, and social class have?

10. Select a health problem or disease with which you are familiar. Describe the occurrence in terms of person, place, and time.

11. To what extent are rates of common health problems similar or different across different geographic areas of the United States? How might demographic variables be linked to geographic variations in disease?

12. What are examples of the differences among international, regional (within-country), urban-rural, and localized patterns in disease? What factors may be linked to these differences?

13. Explain what is meant by a Geographic Information System (GIS). Describe the applications of GIS in epidemiology.

14. What time trends would characterize the occurrence of an influenza epidemic? How do epidemiologists account for seasonal variations in meningococcal disease and other communicable diseases, as well as for other health conditions?

15. What is meant by case clustering? Give some noteworthy examples; distinguish between temporal and spatial clustering. What considerations bear upon the interpretation of spatial clustering?

16. Complete the project found in Appendix 4 at the end of this chapter.

References

1. Suchman EA. Health attitudes and behavior. *Arch Environ Health*. 1970;20:105–110.

2. Hennekins CH, Buring JE. *Epidemiology in Medicine*. Boston, MA: Little, Brown; 1987.

3. Abramson JH. *Survey Methods in Community Medicine*, 4th ed. New York: Churchill Livingstone; 1990.

4. Mill JS. *A System of Logic*. London, UK: Parker, Son & Bowin; 1856.

5. MacMahon B, Pugh TF. *Epidemiology Principles and Methods*. Boston, MA: Little, Brown; 1970.

6. Hoyert DL, Heron MP, Murphy SL, Kung H-C. Deaths: final data for 2003. *National Vital Statistics Reports.* 2006;54(13). Hyattsville, MD: National Center for Health Statistics.

7. National Center for Health Statistics. *Health, United States, 2006.* With Chartbook on Trends in the Health of Americans. Hyattsville, MD: 2006.

8. Verbrugge LM. Females and illness: recent trends in sex differences in the United States. *J Health Soc Behav.* 1976;17:387–403.

9. Yin S. Gender Disparities in Health and Mortality. Population Reference Bureau; November 2007. Available at: www.prb.org/Articles/2007/genderdisparities.aspx?p=1. Accessed November 27, 2007.

10. Williams DR. The health of men: structured inequalities and opportunities. *Am J Public Health.* 2003;93:724–731.

11. Waldron I. Why do women live longer than men? *Soc Sci Med.* 1976;10:349–362.

12. Helwig-Larsen K, Juel K. Sex differences in mortality in Denmark during half a century, 1943–92. *Scand J Public Health.* 2000;28:214–221.

13. Eskes T, Haanen C. Why do women live longer than men? *Eur J Obstet Gynecol Reprod Biol.* 2007;133:126–133.

14. Hammond J, Salamonson Y, Davidson P, et al. Why do women underestimate the risk of cardiac disease? A literature review. *Aust Crit Care.* 2007;20:53–59.

15. Gold LD, Krumholz HM. Gender differences in treatment of heart failure and acute myocardial infarction: A question of quality or epidemiology? *Cardiol Rev.* 2006;14:180–186.

16. Rosenblatt S. Minority women in L.A. County found to have higher rates of chronic disease. *Los Angeles Times.* Section B3, May 24, 2007. Search archives at: http://www.latimes.com/news. Accessed October 19, 2007.

17. Waldron I, Weiss CC, Hughes ME. Marital status effects on health: are there differences between never married women and divorced and separated women? *Soc Sci Med.* 1997;45:1387–1397.

18. Schoenborn CA. Marital status and health: United States, 1999–2002. Advance Data from Vital and Health Statistics. December 15, 2004; Number 351. Centers for Disease Control and Prevention.

19. Kitagawa EM, Hauser PM. *Differential Mortality in the United States.* Cambridge, MA: Harvard University Press; 1973.

20. Nilsson PM, Nilsson J-Å, Östergren P-O, Berglund G. Social mobility, marital status, and mortality risk in an adult life course perspective: The Malmö Preventive Project. *Scand J Public Health.* 2005;33:412–423.

21. Lund R, Holstein BE, Osler M. Marital history from age 15 to 40 years and subsequent 10-year mortality: a longitudinal study of Danish males born in 1953. *Int J Epidemiol.* 2004;33:389–397.

22. Ikeda A, Hiroyasu I, Hideaki T, et al. Marital status and mortality among Japanese men and women: the Japan Collaborative Cohort Study. *BMC Public Health.* 2007;7:73.

23. Luoma JB, Pearson JL. Suicide and marital status in the United States, 1991–1996: Is widowhood a risk factor? *Am J Public Health.* 2002;92:1518–1522.

24. Schottenfeld D. Patient risk factors and the detection of early cancer. *Prev Med.* 1972;1:335–351.

25. Osborne C, Ostir GV, Du X, et al. The influence of marital status on the stage at diagnosis, treatment, and survival of older women with breast cancer. *Breast Cancer Res Treat.* 2005;93:41–47.

26. Syme SL. Behavioral factors associated with the etiology of physical disease: a social epidemiological approach. *Am J Public Health*. 1974;64:1043–1045.

27. Fine MJ, Ibrahim SA, Thomas SB. The role of race and genetics in health disparities research (editorial). *Am J Public Health*. 2005;95:2125–2128.

28. McKenney NR, Bennett CE. Issues regarding data on race and ethnicity: the Census Bureau experience. *Public Health Rep*. 1994;109:16–25.

29. Krieger N. Editorial: counting accountably: implications of the new approaches to classifying race/ethnicity in the 2000 census. *Am J Public Health*. 2000;90: 1687–1689.

30. Kaufman JS, Cooper RS. Commentary: considerations for use of racial/ethnic classification in etiologic research. *Am J Epidemiol*. 2001;154:291–298.

31. Heron MP, Smith BL. Deaths: Leading causes for 2003. *National Vital Statistics Reports*. 2007;55(10). Hyattsville, MD: National Center for Health Statistics.

32. Centers for Disease Control and Prevention. Summary of notifiable diseases—United States, 2005. *MMWR*. 54(53):1–96.

33. Centers for Disease Control and Prevention. Health disparities experienced by black or African Americans—United States. *MMWR*. 2005;54:1–3.

34. Centers for Disease Control and Prevention. Recent trends in mortality rates for four major cancers, by sex and race/ethnicity—United States, 1990-1998. *MMWR*. 2002;51:49–53.

35. Hirschman J, Whitman S, Ansell D. The black:white disparity in breast cancer mortality: the example of Chicago. *Cancer Causes Control*. 2007;18:323–333.

36. Centers for Disease Control and Prevention. Racial/ethnic disparities in prevalence, treatment, and control of hypertension—United States, 1999-2002. *MMWR*. 2005;54:7–9.

37. Flack JM, Ferdinand KC, Nasser SA. Epidemiology of hypertension and cardiovascular disease in African Americans. *J Clin Hypertens*. 2003;5(1 Suppl 1):5–11.

38. Baldwin L-M, Grossman DC, Casey S, et al. Perinatal and infant health among rural and urban American Indians/Alaska Natives. *Am J Public Health*. 2002;92: 1491–1497.

39. Holman RC, Curns AT, Singleton RJ, et al. Infectious disease hospitalizations among older American Indian and Alaska Native adults. *Public Health Rep*. 2006;121:674–683.

40. Rhoades ER. The health status of American Indian and Alaska Native males. *Am J Public Health*. 2003;93:774–778.

41. Knowler WC, Bennett PH, Hamman RF, et al. Diabetes incidence and prevalence in Pima Indians: a 19-fold greater incidence than in Rochester, Minnesota. *Am J Epidemiol*. 1978;108:497–505.

42. Sievers ML, Nielson RG, Bennett PH. Adverse mortality experience of a southwestern American Indian community: overall death rates and underlying causes of death in Pima Indians. *J Clin Epidemiol*. 1990;43:1231–1242.

43. Schneider E. Tuberculosis among American Indians and Alaska Natives in the United States, 1993–2002. *Am J Public Health*. 2005;95:873–880.

44. Castor ML, Smyser MS, Taualii MM, et al. A nationwide population-based study identifying health disparities between American Indians/Alaska Natives and the general populations living in select urban counties. *Am J Public Health*. 2006;96: 1478–1484.

45. Yano K, Blackwelder WC, Kagan A, et al. Childhood cultural experience and the incidence of coronary heart disease in Hawaii Japanese men. *Am J Epidemiol.* 1979;109:440–450.

46. Williams CL, Berry JW. Primary prevention of acculturative stress among refugees. *Am Psychol.* 1991;46:632–641.

47. Marmot MG. Stress, social and cultural variations in heart disease. *J Psychosom Res.* 1983;27:377–384.

48. Syme SL, Marmot MG, Kagan A, Kato H, Rhoads G. Epidemiologic studies of coronary heart disease and stroke in Japanese men living in Japan, Hawaii and California: introduction. *Am J Epidemiol.* 1975;102:477–480.

49. Marmot MG, Syme SL. Acculturation and coronary heart disease in Japanese-Americans. *Am J Epidemiol.* 1976;104:225–247.

50. Matsumoto YS. Social stress and coronary heart disease in Japan: a hypothesis. *Milbank Mem Fund Q Health Soc.* 1970;48:9–36.

51. Benfante R. Studies of cardiovascular disease and cause-specific mortality trends in Japanese-American men living in Hawaii and risk factor comparisons with other Japanese populations in the Pacific region: a review. *Hum Biol.* 1992;64:791–805.

52. Singh GK, Miller BA. Health, life expectancy, and mortality patterns among immigrant populations in the United States. *Can J Public Health.* 2004;95:114–121.

53. Friis RH, Forouzesh M, Chhim HS, et al. Sociocultural determinants of tobacco use among Cambodian Americans. *Health Educ Res.* 2006;21:355–365.

54. Delgado JL, Johnson CL, Roy I, Trevino FM. Hispanic Health and Nutrition Examination Survey: methodological considerations. *Am J Public Health.* 1990;80(suppl):6–10.

55. Trevino FM, ed. Hispanic Health and Nutrition Examination Survey, 1982–84. *Am J Public Health.* 1990;80(suppl).

56. Garcia-Palmieri MR, Costas R Jr, Cruz-Vidal M, et al. Urban-rural differences in coronary heart disease in a low incidence area: the Puerto Rico Heart Study. *Am J Epidemiol.* 1978;107:206–215.

57. Hazuda HP, Haffner SM, Stern MP, Eifler CW. Effects of acculturation and socioeconomic status on obesity and diabetes in Mexican Americans. *Am J Epidemiol.* 1988;128:1289–1301.

58. Wong MD, Tagawa T, Hsieh HJ, et al. Differences in cause-specific mortality between Latino and white adults. *Med Care.* 2005;43:1058–1062.

59. Abraido-Lanza AF, Dohrenwend BP, Ng-Mak DS, Turner JB. The Latino mortality paradox: a test of the "salmon bias" and healthy migrant hypotheses. *Am J Public Health.* 1999;89:1543–1548.

60. Markides KS, Eschbach K. Aging, migration, and mortality: current status of research on the Hispanic paradox. *J Gerontol B Psychol Sci Soc Sci.* 2005;60(Spec No 2):68–75.

61. Palloni A, Arias E. Paradox lost: Explaining the Hispanic adult mortality advantage. *Demography.* 2004;41:385–415.

62. Morales LS, Kingston RS, Valdez RO, et al. Socioeconomic, cultural, and behavioral factors affecting Hispanic health outcomes. *J Health Care Poor Underserved.* 2002;13:477–503.

63. Friis R, Yngve A, Persson V. Review of social epidemiologic research on migrants' health: findings, methodological cautions, and theoretical perspectives. *Scand J Soc Med.* 1998;26:173–180.

64. Levin JS. Religion and health: is there an association, is it valid, and is it causal? *Soc Sci Med.* 1994;38:1475–1482.

65. Büssing A, Ostermann T, Matthiessen PF. Search for meaningful support and the meaning of illness in German cancer patients. *Anticancer Res.* 2005;25:1449–1455.

66. Balboni TA, Vanderwerker LC, Block SD, et al. Religiousness and spiritual support among advanced cancer patients and associations with end-of-life treatment preferences and quality of life. *J Clin Oncol.* 2007;25:555–560.

67. Fraser GE, Strahan TM, Sabate J, et al. Effects of traditional coronary risk factors on rates of incident coronary events in a low-risk population: the Adventist Health Study. *Circulation.* 1992;86:406–413.

68. Armstrong B, van Merwyk AJ, Coates H. Blood pressure in Seventh-Day Adventist vegetarians. *Am J Epidemiol.* 1977;105:444–449.

69. Phillips RL. Role of life-style and dietary habits in risk of cancer among Seventh-Day Adventists. *Cancer Res.* 1975;35:3515–3522.

70. Butler TL, Fraser GE, Beeson WL, et al. Cohort profile: The Adventist Health Study-2 (AHS-2). *Int J Epidemiol.* Aug. 27, 2007;1–6 [Epub ahead of print].

71. Montgomery S, Herring P, Yancey A, et al. Comparing self-reported disease outcomes, diet, and lifestyles in a national cohort of black and white Seventh-day Adventists. *Prev Chronic Dis.* [serial online] 2007;4(3). Available at: http://www.cdc.gov/pcd/issues/2007/jul/06_0103.htm. Accessed November 29, 2007.

72. Jarvis GK. Mormon mortality rates in Canada. *Soc Biol.* 1977;24:294–302.

73. Enstrom JE. Health practices and cancer mortality among active California Mormons. *J Natl Cancer Inst.* 1989;81:1807–1814.

74. Guralnik JM, Leveille SG. Annotation: race, ethnicity, and health outcomes—unraveling the mediating role of socioeconomic status. *Am J Public Health.* 1997;87:728–729.

75. Gregorio DI, Walsh SJ, Paturzo D. The effects of occupational-based social position on mortality in a large American cohort. *Am J Public Health.* 1997;87:1472–1475.

76. Link BG, Northridge ME, Phelan JC, et al. Social epidemiology and the fundamental cause concept: on the structuring of effective cancer screens by socioeconomic status. *Milbank Q.* 1998;76:375–402.

77. McDonough P, Duncan GJ, Williams D, House J. Income dynamics and adult mortality in the United States, 1972 through 1989. *Am J Public Health.* 1997;87:1476–1482.

78. Berkman LF, Syme SL. Social networks, host resistance, and mortality: a nine-year follow-up study of Alameda County residents. *Am J Epidemiol.* 1979;109:186–204.

79. Kington RS, Smith JP. Socioeconomic status and racial and ethnic differences in functional status associated with chronic diseases. *Am J Public Health.* 1997;87:805–810.

80. Blane D. Social determinants of health—socioeconomic status, social class, and ethnicity (editorial). *Am J Public Health.* 1995;85:903–904.

81. Winkelby MA, Jatulis DE, Frank E, Fortmann SP. Socioeconomic status and health: how education, income, and occupation contribute to risk factors for cardiovascular disease. *Am J Public Health.* 1992;82:816–820.

82. Hollingshead A, Redlich F. *Social Class and Mental Illness.* New Haven, CT: Yale University Press; 1958.

83. Duncan OD. A socioeconomic index for all occupations. In: Reiss AJ Jr, Duncan OD, Hatt PK, North CC, eds. *Occupations and Social Status.* New York: Free Press; 1961:109–138.

84. Dunham HW. Society, culture, and mental disorder. *Arch Gen Psychiatry.* 1976;33:147–156.

85. Mausner JS, Kramer S. *Epidemiology: An Introductory Text*, 2nd ed. Philadelphia, PA: Saunders; 1985.

86. Murphy JM, Olivier DC, Monson RR, et al. Depression and anxiety in relation to social status: a prospective epidemiologic study. *Arch Gen Psychiatry*. 1991;48: 223–229.

87. Antonovsky A. Social class, life expectancy and overall mortality. *Milbank Mem Fund Q Health Soc.* 1967;45:31–73.

88. Adler NE, Boyce T, Chesney MA, et al. Socioeconomic status and health: the challenge of the gradient. *Am Psychol.* 1994;49:15–24.

89. Rogot E, Sorlie PD, Johnson NJ. Life expectancy by employment status, income, and education in the National Longitudinal Mortality Study. *Public Health Rep.* 1992;107:457–461.

90. Steenland K, Hu S, Walker J. All-cause and cause-specific mortality by socioeconomic status among employed persons in 27 US states, 1984–1997. *Am J Public Health.* 2004;94:1037–1042.

91. Mackenbach JP, Bos V, Andersen O, et al. Widening socioeconomic inequalities in mortality in six Western European countries. *Int J Epidemiol.* 2003;32:830–837.

92. Rawlings JS, Weir MR. Race- and rank-specific infant mortality in a U.S. military population. *Am J Dis Child.* 1992;146:313–316.

93. Sorlie P, Rogot E, Anderson R, et al. Black-white mortality differences by family income. *Lancet.* 1992;340:346–350.

94. Kogevinas M, Marmot MG, Fox AJ, Goldblatt PO. Socioeconomic differences in cancer survival. *J Epidemiol Community Health.* 1991;45:216–219.

95. Songer TJ, DeBerry J, La Porte RE, Tuomilehto J. International comparisons of IDDM mortality. *Diabetes Care.* 1992;15(suppl 1):15–21.

96. Birch HG, Richardson SA, Baird D, et al. *Mental Subnormality in the Community: A Clinical and Epidemiologic Study.* Baltimore, MD: Williams & Wilkins; 1970.

97. World Health Organization (WHO). *The World Health Report.* Geneva, Switzerland: WHO; 1977.

98. Tominaga S, Kuroishi T, Aoki K. Cancer Mortality Statistics in 33 Countries 1953–1992. Geneva, Switzerland: International Union Against Cancer; 1998.

99. Division of Control of Tropical Diseases, World Health Organization. World malaria situation 1990. *World Health Stat Q.* 1992;45:257–266.

100. Rowe AK, Rowe SY, Snow RW, et al. The burden of malaria mortality among African children in the year 2000. *Int J Epidemiol.* 2006;35:691–704.

101. Meslin F-X. Surveillance and control of emerging zoonoses. *World Health Stat Q.* 1992;45:200–207.

102. Diekstra RFW, Gulbinat W. The epidemiology of suicidal behaviour: a review of three continents. *World Health Stat Q.* 1993;46:56–57.

103. Central Intelligence Agency. The World Factbook. Rank Order - Life expectancy at birth. Available at: https://www.cia.gov/library/publications/the-world-factbook/rankorder/2102rank.html. Accessed October 20, 2007.

104. Korte R, Rehle T, Merkle A. Strategies to maintain health in the Third World. *Trop Med Parasitol.* 1991;42:428–432.

105. Mason TJ, McKay FW, Hoover R, et al. *Atlas of Cancer Mortality in U.S. Counties: 1950–1969.* Department of Health, Education and Welfare publication (NIH) 75–780. Washington, DC: Government Printing Office; 1975.

106. Lauer K. The risk of multiple sclerosis in the USA in relation to sociogeographic features: a factor-analytic study. *J Clin Epidemiol.* 1994;47:43–48.

107. Hutt MSR, Burkitt DP. *The Geography of Non-Infectious Disease.* Oxford, UK: Oxford University Press; 1986.

108. Kappus KK, Juranek DD, Roberts JM.Results of testing for intestinal parasites by state diagnostic laboratories, United States, 1987. *MMWR CDC Surveill Summ.* 1991;40:25–30.

109. Centers for Disease Control and Prevention. Update: influenza activity–United States, 2002–03 season. *MMWR.* 2003;52:224–225.

110. Chapman LE, Tipple MA, Folger SG, et al. Influenza—United States, 1988–89. *MMWR CDC Surveill Summ.*1993;42(SS-1):9–21.

111. Centers for Disease Control and Prevention. Summary of notifiable diseases, United States, 1996. *MMWR.* 1996;45(53):18.

112. Reif S, Geonnotti KL, Whetten K. HIV infection and AIDS in the Deep South. *Am J Public Health.* 2006;96:970–973.

113. Doll R. Urban and rural factors in the aetiology of cancer. *Int J Cancer.* 1991;47:803–810.

114. Keil JE, Saunders DE Jr. Urban and rural differences in cardiovascular disease in blacks. In: Saunders E, ed. *Cardiovascular Diseases in Blacks.* Philadelphia, PA: Davis; 1991:17–28.

115. Hartley D. Rural health disparities, population health, and rural culture. *Am J Public Health.* 2004;94:1675–1678.

116. Probst JC, Moore CG, Glover SH, et al. Person and place: The compounding effects of race/ethnicity and rurality on health. *Am J Public Health.* 2004;94:1695–1703.

117. Dzik AJ. Differences in cancer mortality rates in Ohio communities with respect to uraniferous geology. *Ohio Med.* 1989;85:566–568.

118. Kusiak RA, Springer J, Ritchie AC, Muller J. Carcinoma of the lung in Ontario gold miners: possible aetiological factors. *Br J Ind Med.* 1991;48:808–817.

119. Nerbrand C, Svardsudd K, Ek J, Tibblin G. Cardiovascular mortality and morbidity in seven counties in Sweden in relation to water hardness and geological settings. The project: myocardial infarction in mid-Sweden. *Eur Heart J.* 1992;13:721–727.

120. Gyllerup S, Lanke J, Lindholm LH, Scherstén B. Water hardness does not contribute substantially to the high coronary mortality in cold regions of Sweden. *J Intern Med.* 1991;230:487–492.

121. Clarke KC, McLafferty SL, Tempalski BJ. On epidemiology and geographic information systems: A review and discussion of future directions. *Emerging Infectious Diseases.* 1996;2(2):1–11.

122. Ricketts TC. Geographic information systems and public health. *Annu Rev Public Health.* 2003;24:18.1–18.6.

123. Pan American Health Organization. Use of Geographic Information Systems in Epidemiology (GIS-Epi). *Epidemiol Bull.* 1996;17:1–6. Available at: http://www.paho.org/english/dd/ais/EB_v17n1.pdf. Accessed November 25, 2007.

124. Russell D, Douglas AS, Allan TM. Changing seasonality of birth—a possible environmental effect. *J Epidemiol Community Health.* 1993;47:362–367.

125. Maes M, Meltzer HY, Suy E, De Meyer F. Seasonality in severity of depression: relationships to suicide and homicide occurrence. *Acta Psychiatr Scand.* 1993;88:156–161.

126. Enquselassie F, Dobson AJ, Alexander HM, Steele PL. Seasons, temperature and coronary disease. *Int J Epidemiol.* 1993;22:632–636.

127. Division of Control of Tropical Diseases, World Health Organization. World malaria situation, 1988. *World Health Stat Q.* 1990;43:68–79.

128. Niaura R, Herbert PN, Saritelli AL, et al. Lipid and lipoprotein responses to episodic occupational and academic stress. *Arch Intern Med.* 1991;151:2172–2179.

129. Centers for Disease Control and Prevention. Guidelines for investigating clusters of health events. *MMWR.* 1990;39(Recomm Rep-11):1–23.

130. Romito P. Postpartum depression and the experience of motherhood. *Acta Obstet Gynecol Scand.* 1990;69(suppl 154):7–19.

131. Ross A, Davis S. Point pattern analysis of the spatial proximity of residences prior to diagnosis of persons with Hodgkin's disease. *Am J Epidemiol.* 1990;132(suppl 1):53–62.

132. Hoffman W, Diekmann H, Schmitz-Feuerhake I. A cluster of childhood leukemia near a nuclear reactor in north Germany. *Arch Environ Health.* 1997;52:275–280.

APPENDIX
4

Project: Descriptive Epidemiology of a Selected Health Problem

Select a health problem to explore in detail by using a descriptive epidemiologic approach; for examples of health problems or diseases that might be studied, refer to Exhibit 5–4. You can also access the Internet addresses shown in Exhibit 5–1 in order to develop a reference list.

The objectives of this exercise are as follows:

- to gain experience in describing and analyzing the distribution of a health disorder in a population
- to become familiar with various sources of data for the epidemiologic description of a health disorder
- to enhance the ability to make sound epidemiologic judgments related to public health problems

Examples of sources of data:

- morbidity and mortality reports (vital statistics): ˇ Organization and international reports; U.S., feᵈ annual and periodic reports
- current literature on the selected health problem
- reports of special surveys

Model for organization of paper:

1. Define the problem (nature, extent, significance, etc.).
2. Describe the agent.
3. Describe the condition (briefly).
4. Examine the above sources for data on morbidity and mortality in the selected health problem.
5. Summarize these data on the distribution of the selected health problem according to the following factors, using tables, graphs, or other illustrations whenever possible.
   A. Host characteristics
      1. Age
      2. Sex
      3. Nativity
      4. Marital status
      5. Ethnic group

   B. Environmental attributes
      1. Geographic areas
      2. Social and economic factors
         a. Income
         b. Housing
      3. Occupation
      4. Education

   C. Temporal variation
      1. Secular
      2. Cyclic
      3. Seasonal
      4. Epidemic

   D. Any additional characteristic that contributes to an epidemiologic description of the disease
6. Summarize any current hypotheses that have been proposed to explain the observed distribution.
7. List the principal gaps in knowledge about the distribution of the health problem.
8. Suggest areas for further epidemiologic research.
9. Critically appraise the data as a whole; consult primary sources and important original papers.

e: Data are from an exercise distributed at the Columbia University School of Public Health during 'y 1970s.

Sources of Data for Use in Epidemiology

CHAPTER OUTLINE

    I. Introduction
   II. Criteria for the Quality and Utility of Epidemiologic Data
  III. Computerized Bibliographic Databases
  IV. Confidentiality, Sharing of Data, and Record Linkage
   V. Statistics Derived from the Vital Registration System
  VI. Reportable Disease Statistics

VII. Screening Surveys
VIII. Disease Registries
IX. Morbidity Surveys of the General Population
X. Insurance Data
XI. Hospital Data
XII. Diseases Treated in Special Clinics and Hospitals
XIII. Data from Physicians' Practices
XIV. Absenteeism Data
XV. School Health Programs
XVI. Morbidity in the Armed Forces: Data on Active Personnel and Veterans
XVII. Other Sources of Data Relevant to Epidemiologic Studies
XVIII. Conclusion
XIX. Study Questions and Exercises

Introduction

In Chapter 3, we learned about several measures of disease frequency that epidemiologists employ to present data on health indices. Chapter 4 covered means to describe the occurrence of disease with respect to person, place, and time. The purpose of the present chapter is to provide in greater detail where and how to obtain the data to compute such measures. Whether one is talking about incidence, prevalence, secular trends, descriptive epidemiology, or analytic studies of disease etiology, the findings are only as good as the data upon which they are based.

As the basic methodology of public health, epidemiology necessarily deals with populations. The reasons are essentially twofold. First, because of the interest in the health of populations, data collected on entire populations (or representative samples thereof) improve the ability to generalize observations or findings beyond the group studied. Second, data on populations are needed for statistical inference, that is, for estimating parameters (incidence, prevalence, and similar measures) of health, morbidity, and mortality. For diseases that occur at low frequencies, data must be accumulated on large numbers of at-risk individuals to obtain reliable estimates. For these reasons, epidemiologic research usually requires or involves large data sets.

It would be an overwhelming task for any one person to amass the data needed for any particular measure of public health. To aid researchers, U.S. federal epidemiologic agencies compile a great deal of relevant information.[1] This chapter informs the reader about some of the varied data sources that are available to the general public for generating indices of morbidity and mortality. These data can be a valuable source of descriptive epidemiologic studies. However, there are a number of data sets that can be used for studies that seek to understand the etiology of disease; some of these are described also. Finally, because data collected by others may not always be perfectly suitable for all situations, this chapter covers some general issues related to primary data collection. Throughout, an attempt is made to discuss the nature of the data, their strengths versus limitations, and the population coverage.

Criteria for the Quality and Utility of Epidemiologic Data

A number of criteria relate to the quality and utility of data:

- nature of the data
- availability of the data
- completeness of population coverage
  1. representativeness (also called external validity)
  2. thoroughness (e.g., inclusion of subclinical cases)
- strengths versus limitations

The criterion *nature of the data* includes whether the data are from vital statistics, case registries, physicians' records, surveys of the general population, or hospital and clinic cases. The nature of the data affects the types of statistical analyses and inferences that are possible.

The criterion *availability of the data* relates to the investigator's access. Medical records and any associated data with personal identifiers usually are not available without a release from the individual patient. Some data from population surveys, stripped of individually identifying characteristics, are available from government and research organizations on data tapes, compact disks, and the Internet. Some organizations perturb data before they are released. Data perturbation refers to the process of modifying identifying characteristics of data in order to protect the privacy of individual respondents.

The criterion *representativeness* or *external validity* refers to generalizability of findings to the population from which the data have been taken. For a given data set, one should assess the degree to which data are representative of the target population under study. Is there evidence for omission of major subdivisions of the population, such as low socioeconomic status individuals or minority groups? Is the population base from which the data have been taken clearly defined, or do the data encompass an unspecified mixture of different populations?

Related to the extent of population coverage is the criterion *thoroughness* with which all cases of a health phenomenon, including subclinical cases, have been identified. Do the data represent only the severe cases that have come to the attention of health authorities? Are there likely to be substantial numbers of unreported cases? The criterion *strengths versus limitations* denotes the utility of the data for various types of epidemiologic research, such as investigations of mortality, detection of outbreaks of infectious disease, and studies of the incidence of chronic diseases. This criterion also includes whether there are limiting factors inherent in the data, for example, incomplete diagnostic information and case duplication. Thus, the criterion of strengths versus limitations tends to overlap with the criterion of completeness of population coverage. Because the criteria are general principles, one may apply them to data sources not specifically mentioned here, and for the evaluation of published epidemiologic research.

Computerized Bibliographic Databases

A helpful starting point for both descriptive and analytic epidemiologic studies is a systematic retrieval of information from computerized bibliographic sources. Some of the basic facts relating to the distribution of diseases may be obtained by a review of the existing literature. The Index Medicus, Psychological Abstracts, Sociological Abstracts, Education Index, and similar volumes are a valuable starting point for gathering bibliographic citations on a health problem. Nowadays, researchers use computers to retrieve literature citations. Online databases include MEDLINE, TOXLINE, and DIALOG.[1] For example, the National Library of Medicine and National Institutes of Health offer a free bibliographic search service on the Internet (National Center for Biotechnology Information, PubMed. Available at: http://www.ncbi.nlm.nih.gov/entrez/. Accessed October 22, 2007). One enters a combination of topics or authors and receives a listing of relevant article titles, authors, complete reference citations, and, depending on the specific journal and the year it was published, an abstract. In addition, each article is followed by a prompt to request more publications similar to the one highlighted. An individual user may conduct a computerized search of this storehouse of material to compile a bibliography on a given topic. Searches may be accomplished through online services from a library, office, or other location. The Internet and World Wide Web, particularly their commercial search engines such as Google, are resources for bibliographic citations and retrieval of entire articles. For example, the Health Sciences Library System at the University of Pittsburgh offers an excellent homepage to link browsers to hundreds of sources of health statistics that are available on the World Wide Web (available at: http://www.hsls.pitt.edu/. Accessed October 22, 2007. See Exhibit 5–1 for a partial list of Web sites that are relevant to epidemiology).

Confidentiality, Sharing of Data, and Record Linkage

The investigator who conducts primary or secondary analyses of epidemiologic data must maintain adequate safeguards for privacy and confidentiality of this information; such privacy is legally mandated. Information that must be kept confidential is that which pertains to any personally identifiable features about a living individual; this includes information for which the research subject has not given permission for public release. Release of information regarding whether the subject participated in a study also is proscribed.[2] Information that would permit identification of a deceased person also should be kept confidential, although the guidelines for release of information about the deceased are not well established. The Privacy Act of 1974 introduced certain necessary reforms for the protection of confidential records of individuals that are maintained by federal agencies in the United States. Specifically, one of the major provisions of the Privacy Act proscribes the release of confidential data by a federal government agency or its contractors, under most circumstances, without the permission of the client whose records are to be released. On the other hand, the Freedom of Information Act is directed toward the disclosure of government information to the public. It exempts personal and medical files, however, because release of such information would constitute an invasion of privacy. The Public Health Service Act protects the confidentiality of information collected by some federal agencies, such as the National Center for Health Statistics

EXHIBIT 5–1

Selected Internet Addresses of Interest to Epidemiologists

Administration on Aging, Department of Health and Human Services (DHHS)

    http://www.aoa.dhhs.gov/prof/Statistics/statistics.asp

Agency for Healthcare Research and Quality

    http://www.ahcpr.gov/data

American Cancer Society

  http://www.cancer.org

American Heart Association

  http://www.americanheart.org/

American Lung Association

  http://www.lungusa.org

American Public Health Association

  http://www.apha.org

British Medical Journal

  http://bmj.com/

Centers for Disease Control and Prevention

  http://www.cdc.gov

Directory of Health and Human Services Data Resources

  http://www.aspe.hhs.gov/datacncl/datadir

Emory University Woodruff Health Sciences Center Library

  http://www.healthlibrary.emory.edu

Ethics in Science

  http://www.chem.vt.edu/ethics/ethics.html

The Federal Web Locator (Auburn University)

  http://www.lib.auburn.edu/madd/docs/fedloc.html

The Food and Drug Administration

  http://www.fda.gov

Hardin Meta Directory of Internet Health Sources, University of Iowa

  http://infotree.library.ohiou.edu/single-records/1256.html

IPRC Indiana Prevention Resource Center, Indiana University Bloomington

  http://www.drugs.indiana.edu

continues

EXHIBIT 5–1 *continued*

JAMA & Archives, American Medical Association
http://pubs.ama-assn.org
MEDLINE, National Library of Medicine (NLM), National Institutes of Health (NIH)
http://www.nlm.nih.gov/
Pub Med®, National Center for Biotechnology Information (NCBI), National Institutes of Health (NIH)
http://www.ncbi.nlm.nih.gov/sites/entrez
National Center for Health Statistics (NCHS)
http://www.cdc.gov/nchs/
National Heart, Lung, and Blood Institute
http://www.nhlbi.nih.gov/
New England Journal of Medicine
http://www.nejm.org
Pan American Health Organization
http://www.paho.org
U.S. Census Bureau
http://www.census.gov
MMWR Morbidity and Mortality Weekly Report, Centers for Disease Control and Prevention data based on weekly reports from U.S. state health departments
http://www.cdc.gov/mmwr/
University of Michigan's Monitoring the Future Study
http://monitoringthefuture.org/index.html
The WWW Virtual Library: Epidemiology (Biosciences and Medicine), University of California, San Francisco
http://www.epibiostat.ucsf.edu/epidem/epidem.html
The White House Social Statistics Briefing Room
http://www.whitehouse.gov/fsbr/ssbr.html
World Health Organization Statistical Information System (WHOSIS)
http://www3.who.int/whosis/menu.cfm

All sites accessed October 22, 2007.

(NCHS). On August 21, 1996, the federal government enacted the Health Insurance Portability and Accountability Act (HIPAA). This law protects individually identifiable health information. For more information regarding the provision of the act, refer to Exhibit 5–2.

Data sharing may enhance the quality of epidemiologic data and increase the knowledge gained by research. Data sharing refers to the voluntary release of information by one investigator or institution to another for purposes of scientific

EXHIBIT 5–2

The HIPAA Privacy Rule

The Health Insurance Portability and Accountability Act of 1996 (HIPAA), Public Law 104-191, was enacted on August 21, 1996. Sections 261 through 264 of HIPAA require the Secretary of HHS to publicize standards for the electronic exchange, privacy and security of health information . . . [The date for most covered entities to comply with the Privacy Rule was April 14, 2003.]

Protected Health Information. The Privacy Rule protects all "individually identifiable health information" held or transmitted by a covered entity or its business associate, in any form or media, whether electronic, paper, or oral. The Privacy Rule calls this information *"protected health information (PHI)."* . . . *"Individually identifiable health information"* is information, including demographic data, that relates to:

- the individual's past, present or future physical or mental health or condition,
- the provision of health care to the individual, or
- the past, present, or future payment for the provision of health care to the individual,

and that identifies the individual or for which there is a reasonable basis to believe can be used to identify the individual . . . Individually identifiable health information includes many common identifiers (e.g., name, address, birth date, Social Security Number).

The Privacy Rule excludes from protected health information employment records that a covered entity maintains in its capacity as an employer and education and certain other records subject to, or defined in, the Family Educational Rights and Privacy Act, 20 U.S.C. §1232g.

continues

EXHIBIT 5–2 *continued*

De-Identified Health Information. There are no restrictions on the use or disclosure of de-identified health information . . . De-identified health information neither identifies nor provides a reasonable basis to identify an individual. There are two ways to de-identify information; either: 1) a formal determination by a qualified statistician; or 2) the removal of specified identifiers of the individual and of the individual's relatives, household members, and employers is required, and is adequate only if the covered entity has no actual knowledge that the remaining information could be used to identify the individual . . . ∎

Source: Adapted from USDHHS. OCR Privacy Brief: Summary of the HIPAA Privacy Rule. Available at: http://www.hhs.gov/ocr/hipaa/privacy.html. Accessed October 22, 2007.

research.[3] Illustrations of data sharing include linkage of large data sets and the pooling of multiple studies in meta-analyses. One of the key scientific issues in data sharing is the primary investigator's potential loss of control over intellectual property. However, because of the value of research data to society, many investigators are willing to make their non-confidential data available to the research community.

The term *record linkage* refers to joining data from two or more sources, for example, employment records and mortality data. Record linkage has been facilitated by the advent of modern computers, which are capable of rapidly processing large amounts of data that contain common identifying features (e.g., Social Security numbers) to connect data records on a single individual. Many of the European countries, particularly those in Scandinavia, which have developed extensive, nearly complete social and health records on the resident population, have used linked data in major epidemiologic research projects. Other applications of linked records include the study of clinical outcomes associated with the use of anti-inflammatory medications, genetic research, and planning of healthcare services.[4] Record linkage systems offer a potentially rich source of information. This information may facilitate research on maternal and child concerns, chronic disease tracking, and the natural history of specific diseases.[5]

Table 5–1 demonstrates that epidemiologic data are derived from numerous sources, ranging from vital statistics to reports of absenteeism from work or school. It summarizes the nature of each type of data, their availability and completeness, population coverage, and strengths versus limitations. The following sections discuss some of the data sources in more detail.

Table 5-1   Overview of Epidemiologic Data Sources

Data Source	Nature of Data	Availability	Population Coverage	Strengths versus Limitations
Mortality statistics	Data from registration of vital events	Annually, from vital registration systems and political subdivisions	Complete	Useful for studying mortality overall and by specific cause
Medical data from birth records	Data on congenital anomalies, complications of pregnancy and childbirth, birth weight, etc.	Annually, from vital registration systems and political subdivisions	Complete	Routinely available; some aspects of morbidity may be incompletely reported (e.g., etiologic factors)
Reportable disease statistics	Statistics based on physician reports, new cases of notifiable communicable diseases	Weekly reports for the United States	Complete	Useful for detection of outbreaks of infectious diseases; some conditions not completely reported
Mass diagnostic and screening surveys	Data that result from diagnostic and screening tests for specified diseases	On an ad hoc basis	Variable	Unknown completeness
Disease registries	Statistics based on existing case registries of cancer, stroke, etc.	Continuous, from national, state, and local jurisdictions	Presumably complete for selected diagnosed diseases	Useful for studying incidence of diseases such as cancer; used to select cases in a case-control study
Morbidity surveys of general population	From the U.S. Health Examination Survey (HES) and the Household Interview Survey (HIS)	Continuous, data released on computer tapes	Complete for probability sample	Useful for epidemiologic research; some HIS data may not be accurate for self-reports; HES data contain more precise diagnoses
Health insurance statistics	Cases given medical care under prepaid insurance coverage	Not generally available, although some agencies conduct research on their own insured	Covered population	Useful for healthcare utilization studies; research on morbidity and mortality in selected populations

Life insurance statistics	Mortality data and results of physical examinations of those applying for coverage	Not generally available	Insurance policyholders	Data for selected population
Hospital inpatient statistics	Cases treated in hospital; dependent on type of hospital	Generally not available without special approval	Not determinable	Diagnostic information may be of higher quality than that from other sources; difficult to relate cases to a population denominator
Hospital outpatient statistics	Patients in clinics and outpatient divisions (OPD) of hospitals	Generally not available without special approval	Not determinable	OPDs provide a large volume of care; OPD hospital records are sometimes not well developed; diagnostic data may be incomplete
Data on diseases treated in special clinics and hospitals	Dependent on nature of clinic or hospital; essentially medical care data	Generally not available without special approval	Not determinable	Counts of patients treated; difficult to determine prevalence rates; population denominator unknown
Data from public health clinics	Data from physical examinations of clients	Generally not available without special approval	Not determinable	Possible use for identification of cases of disease and for study of health services; population denominator unknown
Data from records of physicians' practices	Medical care provided in physicians' offices	Generally not available without special approval	Not determinable	May be useful for identification of cases; records may vary in completeness and quality; duplication of cases for patients who see multiple providers

continues

Table 5-1 *continued*

Data Source	Nature of Data	Availability	Population Coverage	Strengths versus Limitations
Absenteeism data	Frequency of absenteeism from work or school	By special arrangement with school system or industry	Probably complete for selected population groups	Nonspecific indicator of disability in selected population; useful for assessing acute disease outbreaks
Data from school health programs	Findings of physical examinations of schoolchildren	Generally not available	Elementary and secondary school population	Uneven quality and completeness of data
Statistics on morbidity in armed forces	Armed forces morbidity and hospitalization experience; results of selective service examinations	Generally available	Draftees and career military personnel	Comprehensive morbidity data on a selected population; important source for follow-up studies
Statistics on veterans	Veterans' hospitalization experience and deaths	Generally available	Hospitalization of those using Veterans Affairs hospitals; may be incomplete for veterans who use other facilities	Useful for studying case mix, demography, and hospitalization experience
Social Security statistics	Disability benefit data and Medicare statistics	Data are released on computer-readable media	Nationwide	Useful for studying disability
Labor statistics	Injuries and illnesses in industry	Routinely reported by the U.S. Bureau of Labor Statistics	Workers in various occupations and industries in the United States	Useful data for studying accidents, injuries, and occupational diseases
Census data	Counts, enumerations, and characteristics of populations by geographic location in the United States, including age, sex, race	Decennial census and annual estimates	Complete	Extremely useful for enumerating the population; some segments of the population may be undercounted (e.g., the homeless)

Statistics Derived from the Vital Registration System

Mortality Statistics

Data are collected routinely on all deaths that occur in the United States. Mortality data have the advantage of being almost totally complete because deaths are unlikely to go unrecorded in the United States and other developed countries. Death certificate data in the United States include demographic information about the decedent and information about the cause of death, including the immediate cause and contributing factors. The death certificate is partially completed by the funeral director. The attending physician then completes the section on date and cause of death. If the death occurred as the result of accident, suicide, or homicide, or if the attending physician is unavailable, then the medical examiner or coroner completes and signs the death certificate. Once this is done, the local registrar checks the certificate for completeness and accuracy and sends a copy to the state registrar. The state registrar also checks for completeness and accuracy and sends a copy to the NCHS, which compiles and publishes national mortality rates (e.g., in *Vital Statistics of the United States*).

Although mortality data are readily available and commonly used for indices of public health, they are hampered also by some limitations with which one should be familiar. The first is certification of the cause of death. When an older person with a chronic illness dies, the primary cause of death may be unclear. Death certificates list multiple causes of mortality as well as the underlying cause. However, assignment of the cause of death sometimes may be arbitrary. In illustration, diabetes may not be given as the immediate cause of death; rather, the certificate may list the cause of death as heart failure or pneumonia, which could be complications of diabetes. Another factor that detracts from the value of death certificates is lack of standardization of diagnostic criteria employed by various physicians in different hospitals and settings. Yet another problem is the stigma associated with certain diseases. For example, if the decedent died as a result of acquired immune deficiency syndrome (AIDS) or alcoholism and was a long-time friend of the attending physician, the physician may be reluctant to specify this information on a document that is available to the general public.

Regardless of what the true cause of death might be, a nosologist must review the death certificate and code the information for compilation; errors in coding are possible. Furthermore, the codes that are used for the causes of death change over time. Since 1900, there has been an international classification for coding mortality. When the United Nations was formed after World War II, the World Health Organization took charge of this classification. In 1948, the sixth revision of the *International Classification of Diseases* (ICD) was published.[6] The tenth revision is now entitled *International Statistical Classification of Diseases and Related Health Problems* (ICD-10).[7] If the mortality data with which one desires to work span more than one version of the ICD, one must be especially careful, because the codes and groupings of disease have changed. Therefore, sudden increases or decreases in a particular cause of death may not be real, but rather a reflection of a change in coding systems. An example of a death certificate and the type of data collected are shown in Exhibit 5–3.

Birth Statistics: Certificates of Birth and of Fetal Death

Presumably, birth and fetal death statistics are nearly complete in their coverage of the general population. Although birth certificate data are needed to calculate birth rates, information also is collected about a range of conditions that may affect the neonate, including conditions present during pregnancy, congenital malformations, obstetric procedures, birth weight, length of gestation, and demographic background of the mother. Some of the data may be unreliable, reflecting possible inconsistencies and gaps in the mother's recall of events during pregnancy. It is also possible that certain malformations and illnesses that affect the neonate may not be detected at the time of birth. Many of the foregoing deficiencies of birth certificates also apply to the data contained in certificates of fetal death. In addition, variations from state to state in requirements for fetal death certificates further reduce their utility for epidemiologic studies. Birth and fetal death certificate data have been employed in studies of environmental influences upon congenital malformations. For example, these data have been used in studies that search for clusters of birth defects in geographic areas where mothers may have been exposed to teratogens, such as pesticides or industrial pollution.

Reportable Disease Statistics

By legal statute, physicians and other healthcare providers must report cases of certain diseases, known as reportable and notifiable diseases, to health authorities. The diseases are usually infectious and communicable ones that might endanger a population; examples are the sexually transmitted diseases, rubella, tetanus, measles, plague, and food-borne disease. Individual states may elect to

EXHIBIT 5-3

Sample Death Certificate

CERTIFICATE OF DEATH
STATE OF CALIFORNIA
USE BLACK INK ONLY (NO ERASURES, WHITEOUTS OR ALTERATIONS)
VS-11 (REV.1/03)

STATE FILE NUMBER | LOCAL REGISTRATION NUMBER

DECEDENT'S PERSONAL DATA

1. NAME OF DECEDENT • • • FIRST (Given) | 2. MIDDLE | 3. LAST (FAMILY)

AKA ALSO KNOWN AS • • • Include full AKA (FIRST, MIDDLE, LAST) | 4. DATE OF BIRTH mm/dd/ccyy | 5. AGE/Yrs | IF UNDER ONE YEAR — Months, Days | IF UNDER 24 HOURS — Hours, Minutes | 6. SEX

9. BIRTH STATE/FOREIGN COUNTRY | 10. SOCIAL SECURITY NUMBER | 11. EVER IN U.S. ARMED FORCES? YES NO UNK | 12. MARITAL STATUS (at Time of Death) | 7. DATE OF DEATH mm/dd/ccyy | 8. HOUR (24 Hours)

13. EDUCATION • • • Highest Level/Degree (see worksheet on back) | 14./15. WAS DECEDENT SPANISH/HISPANIC/LATINO? (If yes, see worksheet on back) YES NO | 16. DECEDENT'S RACE • • • Up to 3 races my be listed (see worksheet on back)

17. USUAL OCCUPATION • • • Type of work for most of life. DO NOT USE RETIRED. | 18. KIND OF BUSINESS OR INDUSTRY (e.g. grocery store, road construction, employment agency, etc.) | 19. YEARS IN OCCUPATION

USUAL RESIDENCE

20. DECEDENT'S RESIDENCE (Street and number or location)

21. CITY | 22. COUNTY/PROVINCE | 23. ZIP CODE | 24. YEARS IN COUNTY | 25. STATE/FOREIGN COUNTRY

INFOR-MANT

26. INFORMANT'S NAME, RELATIONSHIP | 27. INFORMANT'S MAILING ADDRESS (Street and number or rural route number, city or town, state, ZIP)

SPOUSE AND PARENT INFORMATION

28. NAME OF SURVIVING SPOUSE • • • FIRST | 29. MIDDLE | 30. LAST (Maiden Name)

31. NAME OF FATHER • • • FIRST | 32. MIDDLE | 33. LAST | 34. BIRTH STATE

35. NAME OF MOTHER • • • FIRST | 36. MIDDLE | 37. LAST (Maiden) | 38. BIRTH STATE

FUNERAL DIRECTOR/ LOCAL REGISTRAR

39. DISPOSITION DATE mm/dd/ccyy | 40. PLACE OF FINAL DISPOSITION

41. TYPE OF DISPOSITION(S) | 42. SIGNATURE OF EMBALMER | 43. LICENSE NUMBER

44. NAME OF FUNERAL ESTABLISHMENT | 45. LICENSE NUMBER | 46. SIGNATURE OF LOCAL REGISTRAR | 47. DATE mm/dd/ccyy

SAMPLE

EXHIBIT 5–3 *continued*

SAMPLE

PLACE OF DEATH

101. PLACE OF DEATH

102. IF HOSPITAL, SPECIFY ONE: IP ☐ ER/OP ☐ DOA ☐

103. IF OTHER THAN HOSPITAL, SPECIFY ONE: Hospice ☐ Nursing Home/LTC ☐ Decedent's Home ☐ Other ☐

104. COUNTY

105. FACILITY ADDRESS OR LOCATION WHERE FOUND (Street and number or location)

108. CITY

106. DEATH REPORTED TO CORONER? YES ☐ NO ☐ REFERRAL NUMBER

CAUSE OF DEATH

107. CAUSE OF DEATH

Enter the chain of events · · · diseases, injuries, or complications · · · that directly caused death. DO NOT enter terminal events such as cardiac arrest, respiratory arrest, or ventricular fibrilation without showing the etiology. DO NOT ABBREVIATE.

Time Interval Between Onset and Death

IMMEDIATE CAUSE (A) (Final disease or condition resulting in death) (AT)

Sequentially list conditions, if any, leading to cause on Line A. Enter UNDERLYING CAUSE/(disease or injury that initiated the events resulting in death) LAST
(B) (BT)
(C) (CT)
(D) (DT)

109. BIOPSY PERFORMED? YES ☐ NO ☐

110. AUTOPSY PERFORMED? YES ☐ NO ☐

111. USED IN DETERMINING CAUSE? YES ☐ NO ☐

112. OTHER SIGNIFICANT CONDITIONS CONTRIBUTING TO DEATH BUT NOT RESULTING IN THE UNDERLYING CAUSE GIVEN

113. WAS OPERATION PERFORMED FOR ANY CONDITION IN ITEM 107 OR 112? (If yes, list type of operation)

113A. IF FEMALE, PREGNANT IN LAST YEAR? YES ☐ NO ☐ UNK ☐

PHYSICIAN'S CERTIFICATION

114. I CERTIFY THAT TO THE BEST OF MY KNOWLEDGE DEATH OCCURRED AT THE HOUR, DATE, AND PLACE STATED FROM THE CAUSES STATED.
Decedent Attended Since (A) mm/dd/ccyy   Decedent Last Seen Alive (B) mm/dd/ccyy

115. SIGNATURE   TITLE OF CERTIFIER ▲

116. LICENSE NUMBER

117. DATE mm/dd/ccyy

118. TYPE ATTENDING PHYSICIAN'S NAME, MAILING ADDRESS, ZIP CODE

CORONER'S USE ONLY

119. I CERTIFY THAT IN MY OPINION DEATH OCCURRED AT THE HOUR, DATE, AND PLACE STATED FROM THE CAUSES STATED.   Pending Investigation ☐   Could not be determined ☐

MANNER OF DEATH: Natural ☐ Accident ☐ Homicide ☐ Suicide ☐

120. INJURED AT WORK? YES ☐ NO ☐ UNK ☐

121. INJURY DATE mm/dd/ccyy

122. HOUR (24 Hours)

123. PLACE OF INJURY (e.g. name, construction site, wooded area, etc.)

124. DESCRIBE HOW INJURY OCCURRED (Events which resulted in injury)

125. LOCATION OF INJURY (Street and number, or location and city, and ZIP)

126. SIGNATURE OF CORONER / DEPUTY CORONER ▲

127. DATE mm/dd/ccyy

128. TYPE NAME, TITLE OF CORONER / DEPUTY CORONER

FAX AUTH. #

CENSUS TRACT

STATE REGISTRAR   A   B   C   D   E

maintain reports of communicable and noncommunicable diseases of local concern also.

The process of reporting diseases is known as public health surveillance, which denotes ". . . the ongoing systematic collection, analysis, interpretation, and dissemination of health data."[8(p. 290)] Healthcare providers and related workers send reports of diseases to local health departments, which in turn forward them to state health departments and then to the Centers for Disease Control and Prevention (CDC). The CDC reports the occurrence of internationally quarantinable diseases (e.g., plague, cholera, and yellow fever) to the World Health Organization. The method of reporting diseases in the United States (the information cycle) is illustrated in Figure 5–1.

Supplementing the notifiable disease surveillance system, the CDC operates a surveillance system for a few diseases of interest, such as salmonellosis, shigellosis, and influenza. For example, reports of influenza are tracked from October through May. The CDC collects information from four sources (as shown in Figure 5–2): laboratories across the United States, influenza mortality reports from 121 U.S. cities, sentinel physicians (a network of 150 family practice physicians), and state epidemiologists. For more information about surveillance systems for reporting notifiable disease statistics, refer to Centers for Disease Control and Prevention, *Principles of Epidemiology*.[8] The present text provides more information on surveillance of environmental health problems in Chapter 13.

A detailed list of reportable infectious diseases is shown in Exhibit 5–4. Some of the diseases and conditions are reportable in some states only; others are reportable in all states. For information regarding U.S. and state requirements,

FIGURE 5–1 The information cycle. *Source:* Centers for Disease Control and Prevention. *Principles of Epidemiology*, 2nd ed. Atlanta, GA: CDC; 1998, p. 305.

FIGURE 5–2 Four different surveillance systems for influenza. *Source:* Centers for Disease Control and Prevention. *Principles of Epidemiology,* 2nd ed. Atlanta, GA: CDC; 1998, p. 309.

refer to "Mandatory Reporting of Infectious Diseases by Clinicians, and Mandatory Reporting of Occupational Diseases by Clinicians," a publication of the Centers for Disease Control and Prevention.[9]

The major deficiency of this category of data for epidemiologic research purposes is the possible incompleteness of population coverage. First, not every person who develops a disease that is on this list of notifiable conditions may seek medical attention; in particular, persons who are afflicted with asymptomatic and subclinical illnesses are unlikely to go to a physician. For example, an active case of typhoid fever will go unreported if the affected individual is unaware that he or she has the disease. Another factor associated with lack of complete population coverage is the occasional failure of physicians and other providers to fill

EXHIBIT 5–4

Infectious Diseases Designated as Notifiable at the National Level During 2005

Acquired immune deficiency
syndrome (AIDS)
Anthrax
Botulism
foodborne
infant
other (wound and
unspecified)
Brucellosis
Chancroid
Chlamydia trachomatis, genital
infection
Cholera
Coccidioidomycosis
Cryptosporidiosis
Cyclosporiasis
Diphtheria
Domestic arboviral diseases,
neuroinvasive, and
non-neuroinvasive†
California serogroup virus
disease
Eastern equine encephalitis
virus disease
Powassan virus disease
St. Louis encephalitis virus
disease
West Nile virus disease
Western equine encephalitis
virus disease
Ehrlichiosis
human granulocytic
human monocytic
human, other or
unspecified agent

Enterohemorrhagic Escherichia coli
(EHEC) infection
EHEC O157:H7
EHEC Shiga toxin-positive,
serogroup non-O157
EHEC Shiga toxin-positive,
not serogrouped
Giardiasis
Gonorrhea
Haemophilus influenzae, invasive
disease
Hansen's disease (leprosy)
Hantavirus pulmonary syndrome
Hemolytic uremic syndrome,
postdiarrheal
Hepatitis A, viral, acute
Hepatitis B, viral, acute
Hepatitis B, chronic
Hepatitis B virus infection,
perinatal
Hepatitis C, viral, acute
Hepatitis C virus infection (past
or present)
Human immunodeficiency virus
(HIV) infection
adult (age ≥ 13 yrs)
pediatric (age < 13 yrs)
Influenza-associated pediatric
mortality
Legionellosis
Listeriosis
Lyme disease
Malaria
Measles
Meningococcal disease, invasive

continues

EXHIBIT 5–4 *continued*

Mumps	*Streptococcus pneumoniae*, invasive
Pertussis	disease
Plague	drug-resistant, all ages
Poliomyelitis, paralytic	age < 5 years
Psittacosis	Syphilis
Q fever	Syphilis, congenital
Rabies	Tetanus
animal	Toxic-shock syndrome (other than
human	streptococcal)
Rocky Mountain spotted fever	Trichinellosis
Rubella	Tuberculosis
Rubella, congenital syndrome	Tularemia
Salmonellosis	Typhoid fever
Severe acute respiratory syndrome–	Vancomycin-intermediate
associated coronavirus	*Staphylococcus aureus* infection
(SARS-CoV) disease	(VISA)
Shigellosis	Vancomycin-resistant *Staphylococcus*
Smallpox	*aureus* infection (VRSA)
Streptococcal disease, invasive,	Varicella infection (morbidity)
Group A	Varicella deaths
Streptococcal toxic-shock	Yellow fever
syndrome	

†The national surveillance case definition for the arboviral diseases was revised in 2005, and nonneuroinvasive arboviral diseases were added to the list of nationally notifiable infectious diseases.

Source: From Centers for Disease Control and Prevention, Summary of notifiable diseases–United States, 2005, *MMWR.* Vol 54, No 53, p. 4, 2007.

out the required reporting forms. This shortcoming can occur if responsible individuals do not keep current with respect to the frequently changing requirements for disease reporting in a local area. Also, as discussed earlier, a physician may be unwilling to risk compromising the confidentiality of the physician-patient relationship, especially as a result of concern and controversy about reporting cases of diseases that carry social stigma. For example, incompleteness of AIDS reporting may stem from the potential sensitivity of the diagnosis.[2] Robert Friis, who was previously associated with a local health department, observed that widespread and less dramatic conditions such as streptococcal pharyngitis (sore throat) sometimes are unreported. More severe and unusual diseases, such as diphtheria, are usually reported.

Screening Surveys

Screening surveys are often conducted on an ad hoc basis to identify individuals who may have infectious or chronic diseases. Often community health agencies organize neighborhood screening clinics for hypertension or breast cancer. Another example is the health fair that may be organized by civic groups. The clientele for the screening programs are highly selected because they consist primarily of individuals who are sufficiently concerned about the disease to participate in screening. Epidemiologic studies might utilize the data yielded from screening programs of this type for research purposes; nevertheless, it would be difficult to generalize the results obtained to any other setting because of the nonrepresentative nature of the sample.

Many large corporations and other employers have set up multiphasic screening programs for their employees. Multiphasic screening is the administration of two or more screening tests during a single program. In this type of screening, the employees of an entire large plant may be surveyed. Through the possible early detection of health problems, complications from chronic diseases may be reduced and the life of the employee extended. Because of the ongoing nature of multiphasic screening programs for employees as well as the possible coverage of a total working population, it may be fruitful to utilize data that have been collected for epidemiologic research. These data could be utilized in incidence studies and for research on occupational health problems. One negative feature of the data would be biases resulting from worker attrition and turnover. High loss to follow-up would compromise the validity of the study. A second difficulty is that such data may not contain etiologic information required for a specific analysis. Chapter 11 presents additional information on screening.

Disease Registries

A registry is a centralized database for collection of information about a disease. Registries are widely used for the compilation of statistical data on cancer, prominent examples being the Connecticut Tumor Registry, the California Tumor Registry, and a New York State Cancer Registry. There are many other types of registries devoted to conditions as divergent as mental retardation, strokes, accidents, and enteric diseases. The completeness of population coverage depends upon the ability of the registry staff to secure the cooperation of agencies and medical facilities that would submit data about diseases. If agencies that come into contact with new cases of disease do not report them to the registry, population coverage will be incomplete. The success of a registry is often dependent upon the conscientiousness of the staff and adequate funding. Nonreporting biases also are likely to occur as public concern grows about the confidentiality of medical data; patients may not want their personal records to be released to an outside agency by the service provider. Personal identifiers need to be attached to a medical record when it is released to a registry to permit record linkage or follow-up investigations. Coding algorithms that create a unique identifier for each medical record aid in maintaining the confidentiality of the data.

Several noteworthy applications of registries include patient tracking, development of information about trends in rates of disease, and the conduct of case-control studies. For example, registries have been used to facilitate regular follow-up of patients with cancer and to study the natural history of infectious and chronic diseases. Population-based cancer registries, such as those incorporated in the Surveillance, Epidemiology, and End Results (SEER) program, have provided unique and valuable data on cancer survival, incidence, and treatment[10] (Exhibit 5–5).

EXHIBIT 5–5

The SEER Program

The National Cancer Act of 1971 mandated the collection, analysis, and dissemination of all data useful in the prevention, diagnosis, and treatment of cancer. The act resulted in the establishment of the National Cancer Program under which the Surveillance, Epidemiology, and End Results (SEER) Program was developed. A continuing project of the National Cancer Institute (NCI), the SEER Program collects cancer data on a routine basis from designated population-based cancer registries in various areas of the country. Trends in cancer incidence, mortality and patient survival in the United States, as well as many other studies, are derived from this data bank.

"The geographic areas comprising the SEER Program's data base represent an estimated 13.9% of the United States population. The data base contained information on 1.7 million in situ and invasive cancers diagnosed between 1973 and 1991; approximately 120,000 new cases are accessioned yearly in 9 areas including the states of Connecticut, Iowa, New Mexico, Utah, Hawaii and the metropolitan areas of Detroit, San Francisco, Seattle-Puget Sound, and Atlanta. ■

Source: Reprinted from SEER Program: Surveillance, Epidemiology, and End Results, National Cancer Institute, National Institutes of Health, Publication No. 94-3074, October 1993.

Morbidity Surveys of the General Population

Morbidity surveys collect data on the health status of a population group. Typically, these surveys use a scientifically designed representative sample of a population. The purposes of morbidity surveys are to determine the frequency of chronic and acute diseases and disability, collect measurements of bodily characteristics, conduct physical examinations and laboratory tests, and probe other health-related characteristics of specific concern to those who sponsor the survey. Morbidity surveys strive to gather more comprehensive information than would be available from routinely collected data.[10]

The U.S. National Health Survey (NHS) is a notable example of a morbidity survey.[11] The survey was authorized under the National Health Survey Act of 1956 to obtain information about the health status of the U.S. population. The National Health Survey Act authorized three separate and distinct programs that are conducted by the NCHS: the National Health Interview Survey (NHIS, a household health interview survey), the Health Examination Survey (HES), and a family of surveys of health resources. The various components of the survey probe the amount, distribution, and effects of illness and disability in the United States and the services received for or because of such conditions. The NHS also is used for the development and improvement of survey and other methods for obtaining health-related data.

National Health Interview Survey

According to the NCHS, the NHIS is a:

> General household health survey of the U.S. civilian noninstitutionalized population using a multistage probability design that permits continuous sampling throughout the year. The sample is designed in such a way that the sample of households interviewed each week is representative of the target population and that weekly samples are additive over time. Independent samples are selected each year. Interviews have been conducted annually since 1957 with approximately 111,000 persons living in about 42,000 households. The sample has ranged in magnitude from a high of about 134,000 persons in some 44,000 households in 1972 to a low of about 62,000 people in approximately 35,000 households in 1986. The 1986 sample represented only one-half of the new sample, which was redesigned in 1985. About 123,000 persons in 1987 and about 122,000 persons in 1988 and 1989 were interviewed in approximately 47,000 households each year.[12(p. 26)]

The range of conditions studied is comprehensive and includes diseases, injuries, disability, and impairments. Because the survey relies on reports of medical conditions by a principal respondent reporting for everyone in the household, the results should be interpreted with caution. These responses may be even less accurate than self-reports, which are known to reflect inadequately certain chronic illnesses.[10]

Health Examination Survey

The HES is the second of the three different programs operated by NCHS as part of the National Health Survey.[11] Data are collected from a sample of the civilian, noninstitutionalized population of the United States. Although the Household Interview Survey provides data on self-reports of morbidity, the HES provides more direct information about morbidity through examinations, measurements, and clinical tests to yield data on unrecognized and untreated diseases. Many health researchers believe that direct assessment of the respondent yields optimal, standardized information about clinical, physiologic, and physical characteristics. The HES is conducted in a series of cycles that are limited to a specific segment of the U.S. population. Through the various tests and measurements that are taken, information is obtained about known conditions that the person might fail to disclose in an interview only or about previously undiagnosed conditions. One of the uses of HES data is to provide baseline measurements on physical, physiologic, and psychological characteristics not previously available for a defined population.

The HES has been amalgamated with the National Nutrition Surveillance Survey and renamed as the Health and Nutrition Examination Survey (HANES). HANES surveys include the first National Health and Nutrition Examination Survey (NHANES I). The purpose of NHANES I was to conduct a:

> survey of the U.S. civilian noninstitutionalized population ages 1–74 years, using a multistage, clustered probability sample stratified by geographic region and population size. Interviews and examinations with about 21,000 persons were conducted from 1971 through 1974. This sample was augmented with approximately 3,000 persons ages 25–74 in 1974 and 1975 . . . Data on all examined persons include household and demographic information; nutrition information; medical, dental, dermatological, and ophthalmological examinations; anthropometric measurements; hand-wrist X-rays (ages 1–17 only); and a variety of laboratory tests.[12(p. 13)]

Related surveys and data collected by the NCHS include NHANES II and the Hispanic Health and Nutrition Examination Survey (HHANES) (Exhibit 5–6). Figure 5–3 shows portable survey laboratories that are moved to field locations for data collection as part of the NHANES.

EXHIBIT 5-6

Hispanic Health and Nutrition Examination Survey (HHANES), 1982–1984

From 1982 to 1984, the HHANES was conducted by NCHS to obtain data on the health and nutritional status of three Hispanic groups:

1. Mexican Americans from Texas, Colorado, New Mexico, and California
2. Cuban Americans from Dade County, Florida
3. Puerto Ricans from the New York City area

In the Mexican-American portion, 9,894 persons were sampled, of whom 8,554 were interviewed and 7,462 were examined. In the Cuban-American portion, 2,244 persons were sampled, of whom 1,766 were interviewed and 1,357 were examined. In the Puerto Rican portion, 3,786 persons were sampled, of whom 3,369 were interviewed and 2,834 were examined. Respondents, whose ages ranged from 6 months to 74 years, were selected by using a multistage, clustered probability sample. Approximately 76% of the Hispanic origin population of the United States resides in the sampled areas. Interviews, conducted in the household or in a mobile examination clinic, included basic demographic, health history, and health practices information. A variety of tests and medical examinations were performed in the mobile clinics. The survey focused on two major aspects of health: certain important chronic conditions (e.g., heart disease, diabetes, hypertension, and depression) and nutrition status. An extensive database ($n > 12{,}000$) was collected from English or Spanish interviews. The data are available for analysis from a public use data tape. ■

Several healthcare surveys also are conducted as part of the NHS:

- National Hospital Discharge Survey
- National Ambulatory Medical Care Survey
- National Nursing Home Survey

In addition, there are several vital statistics surveys:

- National Natality Survey
- National Fetal Mortality Survey
- National Mortality Followback Survey

FIGURE 5–3   Portable units used by the National Health and Nutrition Examination Survey for data collection.

For more information regarding the data from these sources, refer to the articles by Rice[13] and Gable.[1] The NCHS releases data via its Web site http://www.cdc.gov/nchs/products/elec_prods/sitemap.htm. Users may download public use data sets or obtain data on CD ROMs and other media (refer to Figure 5–4).

FIGURE 5–4   Examples of data products available from the NCHS.

California Health Interview Survey

The California Health Interview Survey (CHIS) provides information on health and demographic characteristics of California residents. The CHIS uses telephone survey methods to study the population corresponding to age groups for adults, adolescents, and children. The CHIS collects information on physical and mental health conditions, health behaviors, health insurance coverage, and access to and use of healthcare services, including primary care and preventive services. Conducted biannually, the CHIS has surveyed from 42,000 to 56,000 households during each wave of data collection beginning in 2001. Public use data files that exclude sensitive and personally identifiable information are available for free download from the CHIS Web site. A unique feature of the Web site is /_Ask_/CHIS, a user-friendly online query program that produces data tables and charts within a few minutes. The CHIS is housed within the UCLA Center for Health Policy Research at the University of California, Los Angeles. The Web address is http://www.chis.ucla.edu/about.html.

Insurance Data

Social Security, health insurance, and life insurance statistics are all examples of insurance data that have been used widely in epidemiologic studies. One of the major problems inherent in the data is that they lack information about people who are not insured and thus may not accurately represent all segments of society.

Some of the types of information provided by insurance statistics are as follows. Social Security statistics yield data on recipients of disability benefits and participants in Medicare programs. Both types of data may be used in studies of the frequency and severity of disabling conditions. Health insurance statistics contain information about individuals who receive medical care through a prepaid medical program. Some notable examples of these programs are the Health Insurance Plan of New York and the Kaiser Medical Plan. These plans as well as health maintenance organizations are proliferating as the emphasis on cost containment and primary prevention of disease grows. A number of investigators have employed data from these programs for epidemiologic studies. Data from prepaid plans may be valuable for long-term studies of chronic disease, especially incidence studies, because data collection is often continued over a number of years for each patient; special questionnaires may be added as needed. In contrast to health insurance statistics, life insurance statistics provide data on causes of mortality among insured groups and also on the results of physical examinations for those applying for insurance policies. Health and life insurance statistics may contain an overrepresentation of healthier individuals because unhealthy individuals may not be allowed to hold life insurance policies and because an ongoing health insurance program may result in a healthier population among insured individuals than among the noninsured. Findings derived from those populations may not necessarily be representative of the overall population of the United States.

Hospital Data

Hospital statistics consist of both inpatient and outpatient data that are routinely collected when a patient enrolls in a hospital or an outpatient treatment program. These categories of data may be deficient for purposes of epidemiologic research because the individuals included do not represent any specific population but rather are collected on an ad hoc basis. Patients who are treated in the hospital setting, especially those in large metropolitan hospitals, may be drawn from all over the metropolitan area or even from other countries. Furthermore, there is often a lack of standardization in the types of information collected on each patient and the diagnostic procedures that are used by the attending physicians. There also may be variation from one physician to another in the completeness with which information is collected. Hospital data, those derived from inpatient and outpatient divisions and specialized clinics, are limited with respect to the socioeconomic composition of patients who may be treated. The majority of patients at certain specialized clinics and the renowned hospitals in urban areas may represent the upper socioeconomic strata of our society. Hospital emergency departments and outpatient clinics may contain large proportions of lower socioeconomic individuals in some urban areas because some indigent patients use the hospital emergency department and related clinics of public hospitals as their primary source of medical care.

Increasingly in the United States and other countries, hospitals are implementing electronic health records that subsequently can be incorporated into electronic databases. An electronic health record is defined as ". . . an electronic repository of patient-centric data that are identifiable, longitudinal and preferably life-long, cross-provider, cross-provider site, and cross the spectrum of healthcare, including primary care, acute hospital care, long-term care, and home care."[14(p. 3)] Electronic health records permit the sharing of information among providers and contribute to population health research.

Diseases Treated in Special Clinics and Hospitals

As is true of data from hospitals in general, these data cannot be generalized readily to a reference population because the patients of a special clinic by definition are a highly selected group. Case-control studies might be conducted with patients who present with rare and unusual diseases, but it would not be possible to determine incidence rates and prevalence of disease without making assumptions about the size of the denominator.

An exception to the general rule about special clinics and hospitals is work done by investigators at the Mayo Clinic in Rochester, Minnesota. The Rochester Epidemiology Project provides a capability for population-based studies of disease causes and outcomes that is unique in the United States, if not the world.[15] This ability is due to a medical records linkage system that has afforded access to details of the medical care provided to residents of Rochester and Olmsted County, Minnesota, since the early 1900s. This project exists, in part, because the Mayo Clinic is geographically isolated from other urban centers. Although best known as a tertiary referral center, the Mayo Clinic has always provided primary and secondary care as well as tertiary care to local residents. Because Mayo offers care in every medical and surgical specialty and subspecialty, local residents are not obliged to seek providers throughout a large region, but are able to obtain most of their medical care within the community. Indeed, in a comprehensive survey of community residents, 90% of those who sought medical assessment received care at the Mayo Clinic, the Olmsted Medical Group, or one of their affiliated hospitals, and 96% selected one of these providers when they had a major medical problem. This unusually close correspondence between a circumscribed geographic population and its healthcare providers comprises a natural laboratory for population-based studies.

The Rochester Epidemiology Project studies are facilitated by the Mayo unified medical record system, wherein all data about a specific patient are contained in a single file linked to a unique Mayo identification number. Today, the dossiers for each of the more than 5 million patients who have ever been seen at the Mayo Clinic in Rochester are maintained in a central repository and tracked by computerized bar codes. Fewer than 500 histories have been lost since the records were initiated about one century ago. In 1966, indexes were created for the records of the other providers of medical care to Rochester and Olmsted County residents. The result is linkage of medical data from almost all sources of medical care available to, and used by, the local population in and near Rochester. These sources include the Mayo Clinic and its affiliated hospitals (Saint Mary's and Rochester Methodist), the Olmsted Medical Group and its affiliated Olmsted Community Hospital, the University of Minnesota hospitals and the Department of Veterans Affairs Medical Center, located in Minneapolis, as well as other medical institutions in the region. During the past several decades, the Rochester Epidemiology Project has successfully provided the data and facilities to complete over 1,000 reports on the epidemiology of acute and chronic diseases. Several of these investigations have been descriptive studies of disease incidence or prevalence, especially long-term trends. Each year, more than half of the Olmsted County population is examined at one of the Mayo facilities, and most local residents have at least one Mayo contact during any specific three-year period. Thus, the Rochester Epidemiology Project records-linkage system provides what is essentially an enumeration of the population. Therefore, samples from this system should approximate samples of the general population. This assertion was validated in a survey in which every subject contacted through a random-digit dialing telephone sample or by residence in a local nursing home or senior citizens complex was found to have a medical record in the community.

Data from Physicians' Practices

The records from private physicians' medical practices would seem to be a logical source of information about health and illness. In reality, however, this source of information may have limited application in epidemiologic research. Because of professional codes of confidentiality and privacy, physicians may be either reluctant or forbidden to release any information about their patients without written informed consent. Also, patients of private physicians are also a highly select group that can afford the higher cost of private medical care, making them unrepresentative of the total population. Finally, little effort has been made to standardize the kinds of information collected about each individual patient, making it difficult to carry out a prevalence study or an incidence study without a considerable degree of missing or incomplete data. The records of physicians in private practice are likely to be highly idiosyncratic documents that cannot be linked readily to other data sources.

Although data exclusively from physicians' records may be insufficient to generate reliable measures of disease frequency, they nonetheless represent a valuable supplement to analytic epidemiologic studies. For example, suppose you are interested in assembling a population of women at risk for breast cancer. The plan is to measure usual dietary intake, follow the women for the development of disease, and determine whether dietary exposures measured at baseline were associated with incidence. In this situation, it would be important to exclude women who had developed cancer previously because cancers that developed among this subset would not be first cancers. Although such cancer history data could be collected by self-report, a more precise characterization of the cohort at risk could be obtained by verifying self-reported cancers with medical records. It also would be reasonable to take a sample of women who reported themselves free from cancer and verify self-reports against medical records.

Physicians' records may be an important source of exposure data also. Let us continue with the hypothetical breast cancer study and suppose one decided to collect detailed information about oral contraceptive use. Again, although this information could be obtained by self-report from the subjects themselves, because the use of oral contraceptives requires a physician's prescription, more detailed information about age at first use, duration of use, and formulation might be obtained from the medical record.

Absenteeism Data

Another kind of data that may be used for epidemiologic research are the records of absenteeism from work or school. This type of data, unfortunately, is subject to a host of possible deficiencies. First of all, these data omit populations that neither work nor attend school. Second, not all people who are absent have an illness. Third, not all people who are ill take time off from work or school. Despite these deficiencies, the data are probably useful for the study of respiratory disease outbreaks and other rapidly spreading conditions, such as epidemics of influenza, which may be reflected in massive school absenteeism.

School Health Programs

The administration office and school nurse maintain records on the immunization history of pupils in school, findings of required physical examinations, and self-reports of previous illness. Detailed information may be retained about cognitive and other tests. Health-related data from this source are probably sporadic and incomplete, although there are exceptions to this general caveat. School health data have been used in studies of intelligence and mental retardation. For studies of disease etiology, there are some well-known examples where data routinely collected on students have proven to be extremely valuable. Paffenbarger et al.[16] used historical records on college students to identify causes of common chronic diseases. They studied nearly 45,000 men and women who attended the University of Pennsylvania from 1931 through 1940 or Harvard University from 1921 through 1950. Standardized case taking by physicians in student health services provided data on medical, social, and psychological histories and an extensive physical examination. Although the methods of data collection varied slightly between universities and complete data were not obtained on all students, valuable measures were taken on such factors as vital capacity, pulse rise after exercise, urinalysis, and electrocardiogram. Information was obtained about mortality through the college alumni office, and causes of death were determined from official state or federal sources. The detailed medical, physiological, and lifestyle information plus the data on mortality afford an efficient analysis of precursive and causative factors. We will revisit this example in Chapter 7.

Morbidity in the Armed Forces: Data on Active Personnel and Veterans

The types of information collected under this heading include reported morbidity among active armed forces personnel and veterans, results of routine physical examinations, military hospitalization records, and results of selective service examinations. The last of these were, at one time, universally required of all qualified men upon reaching 18 years of age. With the abolition of the draft, physical examinations are given selectively to volunteers for military service. Thus, this source of epidemiologic data, which tends to be representative primarily of volunteer groups, is not particularly useful for estimates of disease frequency for the general population.

Nonetheless, records on military personnel may be quite useful for studies of disease etiology. For example, the National Academy of Sciences-National Research Council assembled a large panel of twins to help sort out the influences of "nature and nurture" on the pathogenesis of disease.[17] The twin panel comprised approximately 16,000 white male twin pairs born between 1917 and 1927. Both members of each twin pair served in the U.S. military during the Korean War or World War II. Zygosity was determined by blood typing for 806 pairs, by fingerprinting for 1,947 pairs, and by questionnaire for 10,732 pairs. Several investigators have used these data to examine the role of genetic factors in human obesity.[18,19] Weight and height, measured during the induction physical examination, were available for 5,884 monozygotic (identical) and 7,492 dizygotic (fraternal) pairs. A comparison of the degree of similarity in various mea-sures of obesity suggested that the identical twins were more alike than the nonidentical twins, an expectation consistent with genetic influences.[18]

Other Sources of Data Relevant to Epidemiologic Studies

The U.S. Bureau of the Census provides much information of value to epidemiologic research, for example, general, social, and economic characteristics of the U.S. population. The U.S. Census is administered every 10 years to the entire population of the nation. The decennial census attempts to account for every person and his or her residence and to characterize the population according to sex, age, family relationships, and other demographic variables.[20] Beginning with the 1940 census, a more detailed questionnaire also has been administered to representative samples of the population. The Census Bureau also makes annual estimates of the number of persons in the population. Some of the publications developed by the Bureau of the Census include the following:

- *Statistical Abstract of the United States*
- *County and City Data Book*
- *Decennial Censuses of Population and Housing*
- *Historical Statistics of the United States, Colonial Time to 1970*

Two examples of important terminology utilized by the U.S. Bureau of the Census have particular relevance to epidemiology: metropolitan statistical areas (MSAs) and census tracts. MSAs (formerly known as standard metropolitan statistical areas) are geographic areas of the United States established by the Bureau of the Census to provide a distinction between metropolitan and nonmetropolitan areas by type of residence, industrial concentration, and population concentration. According to the NCHS, "The general concept of a metropolitan area is one of a large population nucleus together with adjacent communities that have a high degree of economic and social integration with that nucleus."[21(p. 3)] To be defined as an MSA, an area must include one of the following:

- one city with a population of 50,000 or more
- an area that is defined by the U.S. Bureau of the Census, using various criteria, as urbanized; such an area would have a total MSA population of at least 100,000 (75,000 in New England)

Census tracts are small geographic subdivisions of cities, counties, and adjacent areas. The average tract has about 4,000 residents and is designed to provide a degree of uniformity of population economic status and living conditions within each tract.

Conclusion

This chapter covered a variety of types and sources of data used in epidemiologic research. Epidemiologists need to find the best quality of data in order to describe the distribution of morbidity and mortality in a population or to conduct studies of disease etiology. To assess the potential utility of data, one needs to consider the nature, availability, representativeness, and completeness of the data. The criterion *nature of the data* includes whether the data are from vital statistics, case registries, physicians' records, surveys of the general population, or hospital and clinic cases. The criterion *availability of the data* relates to the investigator's ability to gain access to the data. The criterion *representativeness or external validity* refers to generalizability of findings to populations other than the one from which the data have been obtained. Related to the extent of population coverage is the criterion *completeness of the data,* which refers to the thoroughness of identification of all cases with a particular health phenomenon, including subclinical cases. The criterion *strengths versus limitations* denotes the utility of the data for various types of epidemiologic research.

Some of the diverse sources of epidemiologic data include statistics compiled by government, industry, or organizations such as the United Nations. Much progress has been made in the development of computerized databases and the Internet; a helpful starting point for epidemiologic research studies is a systematic retrieval of information from computerized bibliographic sources. Examples of epidemiologic data are those derived from the vital registration system, reports of absenteeism from work or school, disease registries, morbidity surveys of the general population, hospital statistics, and census tracts. Epidemiologic data from these sources have many useful applications, including development of descriptive studies of trends in disease and analytic studies of disease etiology.

Study Questions and Exercises

1. Are you able to define the following?
   a. disease registry

    b. National Health Survey

    c. NHANES I and HHANES

2. What is likely to be the best routinely available data source for each of the following kinds of studies?

    a. incidence of influenza in the United States

    b. cancer morbidity

    c. congenital malformations

    d. prevalence of selected disabling conditions

    e. work-related accidents

    f. precursive factors for heart disease among college graduates

    g. ethnic differences in mortality

3. Death certificates are an important source of information for epidemiologic studies. In the United States, death certificates have which of the following advantages (circle all that apply):

    a. There is a uniform national system of collection and coding.

    b. The cause of death is usually confirmed by autopsy.

    c. The international coding system for cause of death has remained constant since 1900.

    d. Data collection is comprehensive; virtually no deaths go unrecorded.

    e. The decedent's personal physician always completes the form and can add his or her own knowledge of past illnesses.

4. Which of the following data sources are best able to provide numerator data for the calculation of incidence of death by gunshot?

    a. hospital discharge survey

    b. autopsy or coroners' records

    c. National Health Survey

    d. disease registries

    e. prepaid group practice insurance programs

5. An abrupt drop in mortality due to a specific cause is observed from one year to the next. Identify at least three possible reasons for such a change.

6. Pick up the local newspaper and search for an article on a recent medical finding or public health issue. Conduct a Medline search to find relevant published articles on the same topic.

7. Access the University of Pittsburgh's "Guide to Locating Health Statistics" on the Internet. Determine five vital statistics on your city or county: income, education, health care, land, and mortality rates.

8. State funding for a childhood injury prevention program has just become available. To gather baseline data on childhood injuries, the staff is

discussing whether to conduct a survey or establish a surveillance system. Discuss the advantages and disadvantages of these two approaches.

9. During the previous six years, one to three cases per year of Kawasaki syndrome had been reported by a state health department. During the past 3 months, 17 cases have been reported. All but two of these cases have been reported from one county. The local newspaper carried an article about one of the first reported cases, a young girl. Describe the possible causes of the increase in reported cases.

10. You have recently been hired by a state health department to run surveillance activities, among other tasks. All surveillance data are entered into a personal computer and transmitted to the Centers for Disease Control and Prevention each week. The state, however, has never generated its own set of tables for analysis. What three tables might you want to generate by computer each week?

11. [Suppose that] Last week, the state public health laboratory diagnosed rabies in four raccoons that had been captured in a wooded residential neighborhood. This information will be duly reported in the tables of the monthly state health department newsletter. Is this sufficient? Who needs to know this information?

Source (Questions 8–11): Centers for Disease Control and Prevention. *Principles of Epidemiology*, 2nd ed. Atlanta, GA: CDC; 1998:332–334.

References

1. Gable CB. A compendium of public health data sources. *Am J Epidemiol.* 1990;131:381–394.

2. Feinleib M. The epidemiologist's responsibilities to study participants. *J Clin Epidemiol.* 1991;44(suppl I):73S–79S.

3. Hogue CJR. Ethical issues in sharing epidemiologic data. *J Clin Epidemiol.* 1991;44(suppl I):103S–107S.

4. Lilienfeld DE, Stolley PD. *Foundations of Epidemiology*, 3rd ed. New York: Oxford University Press; 1994.

5. Merrill RM. Timmreck TC. *Introduction to Epidemiology.* Sudbury, MA: Jones and Bartlett; 2006.

6. World Health Organization (WHO). *International Classification of Diseases*, 6th rev. Geneva, Switzerland: WHO; 1948.

7. World Health Organization (WHO). *International Statistical Classification of Diseases and Related Health Problems.* 2nd ed. 10th revision. Geneva, Switzerland: WHO; 2004.

8. Centers for Disease Control and Prevention. *Principles of Epidemiology*, 2nd ed. Atlanta, GA: 1998.

9. Chorba TL, Berkelman RL, Safford SK, Gibbs NP, Hull HF. Mandatory reporting of infectious diseases by clinicians, and mandatory reporting of occupational diseases by clinicians. *MMWR Recomm Rep.* 1990;39(RR-9):1–17.

10. Mausner JS, Kramer S. *Epidemiology: An Introductory Text,* 2nd ed. Philadelphia, PA: Saunders; 1985.

11. Miller HW. *Plan and Operation of the Health and Nutrition Examination Survey: United States—1971–1973* (Vital and Health Statistics ser 1, no 10a). Department of Health, Education and Welfare publication (PHS)79–1310. Hyattsville, MD: National Center for Health Statistics; 1978.

12. Turczyn KM, Drury TF. *An Inventory of Pain Data from the National Center for Health Statistics.* Department of Health and Human Services publication (PHS)92–1308. Hyattsville, MD: National Center for Health Statistics; 1992.

13. Rice DP. Data needs for health policy in an aging population (including a survey of data available in the United States of America). *World Health Stat Q.* 1992;45:61–67.

14. Friedman DJ. Assessing the potential of national strategies for electronic health records for population health monitoring and research. National Center for Health Statistics. *Vital Health Stat.* 2006;2(143).

15. Melton LJ III. History of the Rochester Epidemiology Project. *Mayo Clin Proc.* 1996;71:266–274.

16. Paffenbarger RS Jr, Notkin J, Kreuger DE, et al. Chronic disease in former college students, II. methods of study and observations on mortality from coronary heart disease. *Am J Public Health.* 1966;56:962–971.

17. Jablon S, Neel JV, Gershowitz H, et al. The NAS-NRC twin panel: methods of construction of the panel, zygosity diagnosis, and proposed use. *Am J Hum Genet.* 1967;19:133–161.

18. Stunkard AJ, Foch TT, Hrubec Z. A twin study of human obesity. *JAMA.* 1986;256:51–54.

19. Selby JV, Newman B, Quesenberry CP Jr, et al. Evidence of genetic influence on central body fat in middle-aged twins. *Hum Biol.* 1989;61:179–193.

20. U.S. Bureau of the Census. *Statistical Abstract of the United States: 2008,* 127th ed. Washington, DC: U.S. Bureau of the Census; 2007.

21. Collins JG, Hendershot GE. Health Characteristics of Large Metropolitan Statistical Areas: United States, 1988–89. Department of Health and Human Services publication (PHS)93–1515. Hyattsville, MD: National Center for Health Statistics; 1993.

CHAPTER 6

Study Designs: Ecologic, Cross-Sectional, Case-Control

LEARNING OBJECTIVES

By the end of this chapter the reader will be able to:

- define the basic differences between observational and experimental epidemiology
- identify an epidemiologic study design by its description
- list the main characteristics, advantages, and disadvantages of ecologic, cross-sectional, and case-control studies
- calculate and interpret an odds ratio

CHAPTER OUTLINE

    I. Introduction
   II. Observational Versus Experimental Approaches in Epidemiology
  III. Overview of Study Designs Used in Epidemiology
  IV. Ecologic Studies
   V. Cross-Sectional Studies
  VI. Case-Control Studies
 VII. Conclusion
VIII. Study Questions and Exercises

Introduction

An arsenal of study design options is available to the epidemiologist. The selection of a particular technique from this arsenal and its application to the study of health issues is a central theme of this chapter. The discussion demonstrates that the choice of a study design is, to a certain extent, dependent on the amount of information that is already known about a particular health issue proposed for investigation. When relatively little is known, the investigator should not commence a costly and lengthy study. Rather, a more prudent approach would be to employ, if possible, a study design that uses existing data, is quick and easy to conduct, and is economical. As knowledge increases, and the complexity of the research questions increases, then more rigorous study designs may be merited.

The preceding paragraph, although an oversimplification, previews some of the factors involved in the full decision process of selecting a particular study design. This chapter is the first of three that will provide a more complete picture of the factors involved by presenting the various study designs in sequence from simpler, faster, and less expensive to more complex, time consuming, and expensive. While this chapter explores three varieties of observational studies (ecologic, cross-sectional, case-control), Chapter 7 completes the topic of observational studies by covering cohort studies, and Chapter 8 focuses on quasi-experimental and experimental designs. An attempt will be made to justify the added expense (in time, resources, and money) of each new design over its predecessors.

This chapter demonstrates that the major study designs differ from one another in several respects:

- *Number of observations made:* In some cases, observations on subjects may be made only once, whereas in others two or more examinations may be made.
- *Directionality of exposure:* This measurement relative to disease varies. The investigator may elect to start with subjects who already have a disease and ask them retrospectively about previous exposures that may have led to the outcome under study, or he or she may start with a disease-free group for which exposures are determined first. The latter group would then be followed prospectively for development of disease.
- *Data collection methods:* Some methods require almost exclusive use of existing, previously collected data, whereas others require collection of new data.
- *Timing of data collection:* If long periods of time have elapsed between measurement of exposure and disease, questions might be raised about the quality and applicability of the data.

- *Unit of observation:* For some studies the unit of observation is an entire group, whereas for others the unit of observation is the individual.
- *Availability of subjects:* Certain classes of subjects may not be available for epidemiologic research as a result of a number of considerations, including ethical issues.

In defining and characterizing the more common study designs used in epidemiology, this chapter places particular emphasis on the following key points: how study subjects are selected, how each design fits into the spectrum of design options, and how each design has inherent strengths and weaknesses. The discussion will not belabor the points about each type of design but rather will provide a sense of how they differ from one another and how they are applied.

Observational Versus Experimental Approaches in Epidemiology

A basic typology of epidemiologic research will help put the various study designs in proper perspective.[1] Consider two basic facets of research designs:

1. Manipulation of the study factor (M) means that the exposure of interest is controlled by the investigator, a government agency, or even nature, and not by the study subjects. For example, local water treatment plant personnel may have chlorinated the water supply. Water consumers are exposed to chlorine and byproducts of the chlorination process because of the water treatment regulations, and not necessarily because of their own free choice.

2. Randomization of study subjects (R) refers to a process in which chance determines the likelihood of subjects' assignment to exposure conditions. Thus, by the flip of a coin, for example, an individual may be designated to receive either an intensive, experimental smoking cessation program or the current standard of care.

The various permutations of these two factors, M and R, produce three different study types: experimental, quasi-experimental, and observational (Table 6–1). We shall learn in Chapter 8 that an experimental study involves both M and R, and that a quasi-experimental study involves M but not R. An observational study involves neither M nor R.

Table 6-1 Typology of Epidemiologic Research

M	R	Study Type
Yes	Yes	Experimental
Yes	No	Quasi-experimental
No	No	Observational

Overview of Study Designs Used in Epidemiology

To compare and contrast the main types of study designs used in epidemiology, we provide a brief summary of each of the three types.

Experimental Studies

In comparison to quasi-experimental and observational studies, *experimental studies* maintain the greatest control over the research setting; the investigator both manipulates the study factor and randomly assigns subjects to the exposed and nonexposed groups. From the perspective of epidemiology, one common experimental design is a *clinical trial,* used primarily in research and teaching hospitals for several purposes: to test the efficacy of new therapies, surgical procedures, or chemopreventive agents; to test etiologic hypotheses and estimate long-term effects; and to study the effects of interventions to modify health status. For example, dietary modification of fat intake may be tested within the context of a controlled clinical trial to determine acceptability, potential problems, and sources of dissatisfaction or confusion. Clinical trials thus may help demonstrate the feasibility of a large-scale population intervention. The number of subjects who are included in a clinical trial may limit its conclusions and generalizability. Large trials are indeed conducted, but their considerable expense, resource, and time constraints limit their use.

Community interventions are types of experimental designs that greatly enhance the potential to make a widespread impact on a population's health. Typical community interventions are oriented toward education and behavior change at the population level. Examples of issues addressed are smoking cessation, control of alcohol use, weight loss, establishment of healthy eating behaviors, and encouragement of increased physical activity. Community interventions also focus upon persons at high risk of disease within a particular population. Finally, successful community interventions may suggest public health

policies, such as mandatory seat belt use or proscription of alcohol consumption by pregnant women.

Quasi-Experimental Studies

Table 6–1 shows that *quasi-experimental studies* involve manipulation of the study factor but not randomization of study subjects; thus, in some respects they may be thought of as natural experiments. Before federal law mandated seat belt use in the United States, individual states varied in seat belt legislation; some states had seat belt laws, and others did not. Residents in the various states did not determine their own "exposure" to seat belts; rather, state politicians who enacted the seat belt laws were responsible for assignment of the "exposure." A comparison of traffic fatalities in states with and without seat belt laws represents a quasi-experimental design.

By contrasting appropriate indices before and after public health programs are implemented, the quasi-experimental design can be used to evaluate the extent to which the programs meet public health goals. For example, to evaluate the effectiveness of safety devices intended to prevent percutaneous injuries in a hospital setting, a quasi-experimental design was used. Results indicated that a 3-hour course on occupationally acquired bloodborne infections and a 2-hour hands-on training session with the devices decreased percutaneous injuries by 93%.[2] Other applications for the quasi-experimental approach are to compare programs to determine reasons for success or failure of an intervention, to compare costs and benefits, and to suggest changes in current health policies or programs. For example, the 1987 Omnibus Budget Reconciliation Act included regulation of antipsychotic drug use in nursing homes. An analysis of drug use in all Medicare- and Medicaid-certified nursing homes in Minnesota revealed that the rates of antipsychotic drug use declined by more than a third in apparent anticipation of, and as a result of, the legislation.[3] Thus, the legislation appeared to achieve its intended effect.

Observational Studies

In some instances an experiment would be impractical and in others, unethical. Accordingly, much of epidemiologic research is relegated to *observational studies*, which, as shown in Table 6–1, entail neither manipulation of the study factor nor randomization of study subjects. Rather, observational studies make use of careful measurement of patterns of exposure and disease in populations to draw inferences about etiology. There are two main subtypes of observational studies:

1. Descriptive studies, covered in Chapter 4, include case reports, case series, and cross-sectional surveys. They are used to depict individuals' health characteristics (e.g., morbidity from specific diseases or mortality) with respect to person, place, and time and to estimate disease frequency and time trends. Although descriptive studies may be used for health planning purposes and allocation of resources, they are used also to generate etiologic hypotheses.

2. Analytic studies include ecologic studies, case-control studies, and cohort studies. These designs are employed to test specific etiologic hypotheses, to generate new etiologic hypotheses, and to suggest mechanisms of causation. As a body of knowledge builds regarding likely etiologic factors for a disease, it becomes possible to generate preventive hypotheses and to suggest and identify potential methods for disease prevention.

The 2 by 2 Table

The foregoing concludes the brief overview of three types of epidemiologic research designs: experimental, quasi-experimental, and observational. The remainder of this chapter defines and illustrates one group of observational studies more fully. When thinking about study designs, it is helpful for the reader to visualize how the study groups are assembled in the context of the 2 by 2 table. The reader should bear in mind an important caveat, however: The model tends to underestimate the complexity of the potential linkage between exposure and disease. It was previously mentioned (see Chapter 2) that exposures do not always fall neatly into the categories of exposed and nonexposed. Hence, the notion of one exposure–one disease is admittedly naive. Nevertheless, a comprehension of this rather simplistic model leads one to an understanding of more complex issues, such as a single exposure with multiple levels or more than one exposure.

Table 6–2 depicts the 2 by 2 table, an important tool in evaluating the association between exposure and disease. Note that the columns represent disease status or outcome (yes or no) and that the rows represent exposure status (yes or no). To avoid confusion, remember that the first column always should refer to those with the disease and the first row should refer to those with the exposure of interest. Although this recommended standard is not critical to the representation of data, consistency in usage will establish a common frame of reference for comparison of study designs and will reduce the likelihood of errors when one is calculating measures of effect.

Table 6–2 The 2 by 2 Table Represents the Association Between Exposure and Disease Status

		Disease Status		
		Yes (People with Disease)	**No** (People without Disease)	**Total**
Exposure Status	**Yes** (exposure present)	**A** (exposure & disease present)	**B** (exposure present, but no disease)	**A + B** (total number exposed)
	No (no exposure)	**C** (no exposure, disease present)	**D** (no disease, no exposure)	**C + D** (total number with no exposure)
		A + C (total number with disease)	**B + D** (total number without disease)	**N** (sample total)

The table cross-classifies exposure status and disease status. Thus, the total number of individuals with disease is A + C, and the total number free from disease is B + D. The total number exposed is A + B, and the total number not exposed is C + D. These four totals are referred to as the marginal totals. The entries (or cells) within the table represent the cross-classification of exposure and disease. Thus, the entry labeled A reflects the number of subjects who had both exposure and disease, B reflects the number of subjects with exposure but no disease, C represents subjects with disease but without exposure, and D is the number of individuals who have neither disease nor exposure. For most study design options, the researcher is aware of the joint classification (or distribution) of exposure and disease for each subject.

One means for keeping track of the different observational study designs is to think of each in terms of the point of reference for selection of the study groups. Inspection of Figure 6–1, a simplified version of Table 6–2, reveals several options. For example, one could start by selecting a sample number (N) and then determining each subject's exposure and disease status. The results would be tabulated and entered into the four cells of the table (A, B, C, and D). The marginal totals would be determined afterward. This approach is a cross-sectional study. Alternatively, one could start with the marginal totals of exposed (A + B) and nonexposed (C + D) subjects and follow them for the development of the disease. The interior cells of the table would be filled at the conclusion of the period of follow-up. This approach represents a cohort study design. The third option would be to start with the column totals A + C (disease) and B + D (no disease) and determine exposures to complete the interior cell totals. This approach is called a case-control study. Note that for each of these study designs

	Disease Status		
	Yes	No	Total
Exposure Status Yes	A	B	A + B
No	C	D	C + D
	A + C	B + D	N

FIGURE 6–1 The 2 by 2 table.

information is known about each subject's exposure and disease status. That is, it is possible to cross-classify each subject with respect to exposure and disease and thereby fill in each of the interior cells of the 2 by 2 table. In the fourth category of observational studies, the ecologic study, the interior cell counts are not known, as will be discussed in the following section.

What is an ecologic study?

An ecologic study is one that examines a group as a unit of analysis. The ecologic approach differs from most study designs, which use an individual as the unit of analysis.

Example: A study of mortality from lung disease in different cities that are known to have differing levels of air pollution would comprise an ecologic study. The unit of analysis is a city.

Uses of ecologic studies: They can be used for generating hypotheses and also in analytic studies.

Limitations: The ecologic fallacy

Refer to the text for more details.

Ecologic Studies

As mentioned earlier, for cross-sectional, case-control, and cohort studies, data on exposure and disease are known at the level of the individual. In ecologic studies, the unit of analysis is the group. Here is an example: in the southern California basin, a geographic area that spans more than 200 miles (330 km) from the U.S. California border with Mexico to the city of Santa Barbara, concentrations of air pollutants vary greatly. The highest concentrations are in urban centers, such as central Los Angeles and sections of Long Beach near oil refineries and ports; conversely, air pollution levels are lowest in the coastal areas that are farthest from heavy industry. Suppose data were available on the average mortality and average particulate levels (one of the components of air pollution) during the year for each census tract in the basin. We could then assess the association between particulate pollution and mortality by plotting the mortality levels within each census tract. This hypothetical example illustrates one of the typical schemas for an ecologic study, which in this case uses a census tract, rather than individuals, as the unit of analysis. Table 6–3 provides additional examples of questions asked by ecologic studies.

Referring to Figure 6–1, you can see that the number of exposed persons (preferably the rate of exposure) and the number of cases (preferably the rate of disease) are known, but the number of exposed cases is not known. The number of nonexposed persons and noncases may be inferred also. Thus, the marginal totals are known, but the interior cells are not. As shown in Figure 6–2, the known information is surrounded by boxes.

This section covers two major types of ecologic studies: ecologic comparison studies and ecologic trend studies. *Ecologic comparison studies* (sometimes called

---

Table 6–3   Examples of Questions Investigated by Ecologic Studies

- Is the ranking of cities by air pollution levels associated with the ranking of cities by mortality from cardiovascular disease, adjusting for differences in average age, percent of the population below poverty level, and occupational structure?
- Have seat belt laws made a difference in motor vehicle fatality rates? This question could be addressed by comparing the motor vehicle fatality rates from years before and years after seat belt laws were passed.
- Are daily variations in mortality in Boston related to daily variations in particle air pollution, adjusting for season of year and temperature?
- What are the long-term time trends (1950–1995) for mortality from the major cancers in the United States, Canada, and Mexico?

Source: Adapted from *ERIC Notebook,* April 2000, Issue 12, pp. 1–2. Department of Veterans Affairs, Epidemiologic Research and Information Center at Durham, NC.

		Disease Status		
		Yes	No	Total
Exposure Status	Yes	A	B	A + B
	No	C	D	C + D
		A + C	B + D	N

FIGURE 6–2 Illustration of sample selection for an ecologic study.

cross-sectional ecologic studies) involve an assessment of the correlation between exposure rates and disease rates among different groups or populations over the same time period; usually there are more than 10 groups or populations. (Note that the term cross-sectional is defined in the next section.) The data on a disease may include incidence rates, prevalence, or mortality rates for multiple, defined populations. Data on rates of exposure also must be available on the same defined populations. Examples of exposure data include:

- measures of economic development (e.g., per capita income and literacy rate)
- environmental measures (e.g., mean ambient temperature, levels of humidity, annual rainfall, and levels of mercury or microbial contamination in water supplies)
- measures of lifestyle (e.g., smoking prevalence, mean per capita intake of calories, annual sales of alcohol, and number of memberships in health clubs)

The important characteristic of ecologic studies is that the level of exposure for each individual in the unit being studied is unknown. Although one may have to do considerable work to amass the data needed for such studies, ecologic studies generally make use of secondary data that have been collected by the government, some other agency, or other investigators. Thus, in terms of cost and duration, ecologic studies are clearly advantageous.

A second type of ecologic study, the *ecologic trend study,* involves correlation of changes in exposure with changes in disease over time within the same community, country, or other aggregate unit. For example, within the United States there has been a consistent downward trend in the incidence of and mortality from coronary heart disease. The exact reasons for the decline are unknown. A cynic, however, might assert that some organizations that have worked hard to achieve such results may find it desirable to claim responsibility (to ensure continued funding). Ecologic correlation data could be generated to support the claim that the downward trends reflect increased prescription of antihypertension medications or the number of coronary bypass surgeries performed.

A classic example of an ecologic correlation is the association between breast cancer and dietary fat.[4] Rates of breast cancer mortality and estimates of per capita dietary fat intake were collected for 39 countries. When presented graphically, the data led to a striking observation: Countries with high per capita intakes of dietary fat tended to be the same countries with high rates of breast cancer mortality (Figure 6–3).

A second example is a study of childhood lead poisoning in Massachusetts.[5] More than 200,000 children from birth through four years of age were screened at physicians' offices, hospitals, and state-funded screening sites, through nutritional supplementation programs, and by door-to-door screening in high-risk areas. Blood samples were drawn and analyzed for lead levels using standard procedures. Communities were the unit of analysis, the value for each being the proportion of screened children with high blood levels of lead. The severity of blood lead poisoning was correlated with indexes from U.S. census data. Community rates of lead poisoning were positively associated with a poverty index, the percentage of houses built before lead-based paints were banned, and the percentage of the community that was African American. Median per capita income was inversely associated with lead poisoning. This example was an ecologic study because the outcomes were measured on groups (summary rates of lead poisoning by community) and the exposures were measured on groups (based on census data). By identifying factors in communities associated with high rates of lead poisoning, this study provided data that may be relevant to the identification of high-risk communities where funding for screening may not be available.

Our third example of an ecologic study explores the unexpected inverse relationship found in the Seven Countries Study between mean systolic blood pressure levels and stroke mortality rates.[6] (An inverse relationship is the converse of a direct relationship: in a direct relationship, when a risk factor increases the outcome increases also; in an inverse relationship, the outcome decreases when

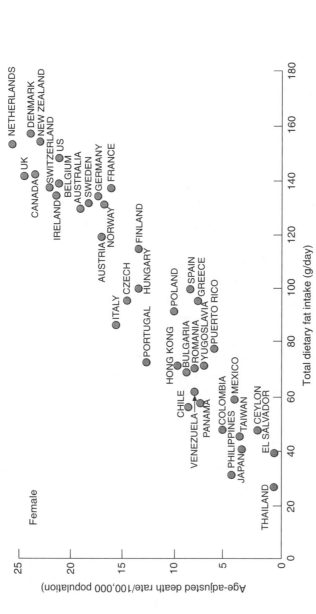

FIGURE 6–3   Ecologic correlation of breast cancer mortality and dietary fat intake. *Source:* Reprinted with permission from Carroll KK. Experimental evidence of dietary factors and hormone-dependent cancers. *Cancer Research,* Vol. 35, p. 3379, © 1975, American Association for Cancer Research.

the risk factor increases.) Thus, in the Seven Countries Study, investigators expected stroke mortality rates to increase as mean blood pressures levels increased, but the opposite relationship was found. Investigators obtained stroke mortality rates in a 25-year follow-up of 16 cohorts of men aged 40 to 59 in the United States, several European countries, and Japan. All age-eligible men in the targeted countries were followed from 1958 to 1964. At the population (ecologic) level, the association between mean entry-level blood pressure levels and mortality due to strokes over 25 years was inverse and strong. When the analyses were repeated at the individual level within cohorts, the association was strongly positive among most of the cohorts examined. Although the findings for the group level seemed to contradict those for the individual level analysis, this study provided an excellent example of the ecologic approach in which countries are the unit of analysis.

In summary, the ecologic approach has applications in a wide variety of situations. Some additional examples include: the effect of fluoridation of the water supply on hip fractures,[7] the association of naturally occurring fluoride levels and cancer incidence rates,[8] and the relationship between neighborhood or local area social characteristics and health outcomes.[9]

The preceding examples reveal some of the applications and merits of ecologic studies; the following discussion presents some of their disadvantages. One of these is known as the ecologic fallacy, a term that will be defined subsequently. Let us begin with a hypothetical illustration. For the sake of argument, suppose that we found the mortality rates for emphysema to be lower in central Los Angeles, California (a highly industrialized area), than they were in the desert resort of Palm Springs, California (a less industrialized area). We might conclude erroneously that areas with lower air pollution levels have higher emphysema mortality rates than do areas with higher air pollution levels. How could we explain this apparently contradictory finding? The answer lies in differentiating between lifelong residents and in-migrants (Figure 6–4).

After spending their working years in central Los Angeles, which is a major employment setting, some people migrate to Palm Springs during their retirement years, especially if they are afflicted with pulmonary difficulties. This retirement haven is also a magnet for in-migrants from northern industrialized cities throughout the United States. As Figure 6–4 shows, when we examine the composite emphysema mortality data (which do not disclose length of residence in Palm Springs), we may be misled into reaching an erroneous conclusion about the association between exposure and disease (refer to the bottom panel of the figure). This incorrect observation results from the ecologic fallacy: individuals'

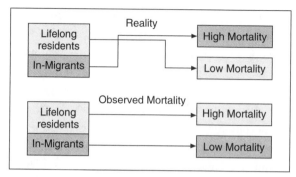

FIGURE 6–4 Example of ecologic fallacy. *Source:* Adapted from *ERIC Notebook*, April 2000, Issue 12, pp. 1–2. Department of Veteran Affairs, Epidemiologic Research and Information Center at Durham, NC.

levels of exposure to air pollution have not been specified. When degree of exposure is differentiated at the individual level by comparing in-migrants and lifelong residents of Palm Springs, the correct exposure and disease relationships become apparent (top panel of the figure). When those who have had long-term exposure to air pollution (in-migrants) are compared with lifelong residents with respect to emphysema mortality, the former have higher mortality.

We have seen that ecologic studies, which by definition use observations made at the group level, may not represent the exposure-disease relationship at the individual level. Hence, the term *ecologic fallacy* is defined as, "The bias that may occur because an association observed between variables on an aggregate level does not necessarily represent the association that exists at an individual level."[10]

To give a second illustration, consider the association between wearing hats and protection against sunburn, an example that can be viewed from the perspective of the individual and the group. Suppose that among a sample of 10 individuals there are 7 (70%) who have sunburned foreheads and 6 (60%) who wear hats when they go outside. At this point, we do not specify at the individual level who wore hats and who were sunburned. We specify only the overall percent of who wore hats and the percent of those who were sunburned, just as we would in an ecologic study. The similar proportion of hats and sunburns suggests that there is an association between the exposure (wearing hats) and disease (sunburn). The conclusion is illusory, however (Table 6–4).

To verify the error in this conclusion, note that among the six persons who wore hats outside, three were sunburned (50%). Among the remaining four per-

Table 6–4 Hypothetical Ecologic Relationship Between Hats and Sunburn

Person	Hat Wearer	Sunburned Head
1	Yes	Yes
2	Yes	Yes
3	Yes	Yes
4	No	Yes
5	Yes	No
6	No	Yes
7	Yes	No
8	No	Yes
9	Yes	No
10	No	Yes

sons who did not wear hats, however, all four (100%) had sunburned foreheads. Thus, the conclusion based on the association between hats and sunburns at the group level was incorrect.

The reader may infer from the hat-sunburned head example that aggregate data on populations may not apply to individuals. To cite still another example, although rates of breast cancer tend to be higher in countries in which fat consumption is high than in those in which fat consumption is low, one cannot be certain that the breast cancer cases had high fat intakes. One could draw a similar correlation between the number of cars in a country and breast cancer rates, yet few would be willing to provide it as evidence of a cause-effect relationship. Thus, more rigorous study designs in which data on exposure and disease are collected on individuals are desirable as further support.

Other limitations of the ecologic study also must be acknowledged. Imprecision in the measurement of exposure and disease makes accurate quantification of the exposure-disease associations difficult. The ability to adjust for the influence of extraneous variables is limited by the availability of such data and the analytic approaches for incorporating them.

In summary, despite the problems of the ecologic fallacy and other limitations, ecologic studies have earned a well-deserved place in epidemiologic research. They are quick, simple to conduct, and inexpensive. Thus, when little is known about the association between an exposure and disease, an ecologic study is a reasonable place to start if there are suitable data available. If the investigator's hypothesis is not supported, then few resources have been invested. In addition, when a disease is of unknown etiology, ecologic analyses represent a good approach for generating hypotheses.

Cross-Sectional Studies

The cross-sectional study (also termed prevalence study) is the first design to be covered in this chapter in which exposure and disease measures are obtained at the level of the individual. One starts by selecting a sample of subjects (N) and then determining the distribution of exposure and disease. Note that it is not imperative that a cross-sectional study include assessment of both exposure and disease. Some studies may be designed to provide only a measure of the burden of disease in a population, whereas others may focus exclusively on the distribution of certain exposures.

The features of this type of study design include a single period of observation (Figure 6–5). Exposure and disease histories are collected simultaneously but may include assessment of history of disease or exposures. The unit of observation and analysis in cross-sectional studies is the individual. The majority of data are collected for the first time, primarily for the purpose of the study, although they may be supplemented with secondary data, such as school records and medical records. Data from national surveys by the U.S. government are frequently used.

As mentioned earlier in this chapter, cross-sectional studies are typically descriptive in nature. Primarily, they provide quantitative estimates of the magnitude of a problem but do not measure the temporal ordering of cause and effect.[10] One could take two basic approaches to provide a measure of the severity of a public health problem: Collect data on each member of the population

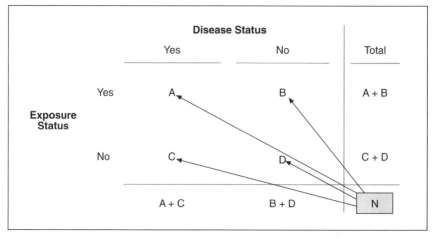

FIGURE 6–5   Illustration of subject selection in a cross-sectional study.

(i.e., a census, used frequently in prevalence studies); or take a sample of the population and draw inferences to the remainder. The more common method, however, is the second because in a shorter period of time, and much less expensively, one could derive reasonable estimates of the extent of a health problem through a survey on a subset of the population.

Sampling schemes for cross-sectional studies comprise two main types: probability samples and nonprobability samples. They are defined as follows[11(p. 15)]:

> A *probability sample* has the characteristic that every element in the population has a nonzero probability of being included in the sample. A *nonprobability sample* is one based on a sampling plan that does not have that feature.

Examples of probability samples include simple random samples, systematic samples, and stratified samples. Simple random samples refer to a type of sample in which each individual in the population (or other group) has an equal probability of being selected. Simple random samples require enumeration of all potential subjects before sampling, an expensive process that may not be feasible to implement. A systematic sample is, "The procedure of selecting according to some simple, systematic rule, such as all persons whose names begin with specified alphabetic letters, born on certain dates, or located at specified points on a master list."[10] Construction of a systematic sample does not necessarily require prior knowledge of the total number of sampling units. A sampling unit refers to "that element or set of elements considered for selection in some stage of sampling."[12(p. 198)] In epidemiologic research, a sampling unit is usually a specific person selected for the study. It is possible to perform systematic sampling at the same time as the sampling frame is being constructed, a feature that makes systematic sampling the most widely used of all sampling procedures.[11] ("A sampling frame is the actual list of sampling units from which the sample or some stage of the sample is selected."[12(p. 198)])

Suppose one wants to derive estimates of the magnitude of a health problem in a relatively small subset of the population. Simple random samples and systematic samples will not ensure that sufficient numbers of this subgroup will be represented for meaningful estimates to be derived. A stratified sampling approach requires that the population be divided into mutually exclusive and exhaustive strata; sampling is then performed within each stratum (strata are "distinct subgroups according to some important characteristic, such as age or socioeconomic status . . ."[10])

Nonprobability samples include quota samples and judgmental samples. An example of a quota sample design is one that requires interviewers to obtain information from a fixed number of subjects with particular characteristics regardless of their distribution in the population. A judgmental sample selects subjects on the basis of the investigator's perception that the sampled persons will be representative of the population as a whole. Nonrandom samples are not appropriate for cross-sectional studies because the reliability of the estimates derived from such samples cannot be evaluated.[11] Details on how to determine sample sizes and parameter estimates are beyond the scope of this book. The reader is referred to any of several excellent textbooks on the subject.[11,13]

Some examples of cross-sectional studies are now presented. Murray et al.[14] surveyed smokeless tobacco use among ninth graders in four school districts representative of the Minneapolis-St. Paul metropolitan area of Minnesota. A questionnaire was administered in the classroom during the fall of 1985 to estimate the prevalence of usage and to identify correlates of usage that might predict those teenagers who were at greater risk than their peers of using smokeless tobacco. The study revealed that nearly 63% of boys and 24% of girls had ever used smokeless tobacco, but only 18.5% of boys and 2.4% of girls had used it in the past week. Ethnicity also was associated with prevalence of usage, especially among boys. Self-reported prevalence ranged from a low among Asians and African Americans (21% and 22%, respectively), medium (45.5%) among whites, and high (60.8%) among Native Americans. The prevalence among boys from a two-parent household was 42.1%, 41.3% if only the mother lived at home, and 54.5% if the boy came from a father-only household. The smokeless tobacco use was much more common among cigarette smokers than among nonsmokers. Only 6% of nonsmoking girls reported using smokeless tobacco, in contrast to 16.4% of girls who smoked. A similar magnitude of difference was observed among the boys: 34.5% versus 56.1% for nonsmokers and smokers, respectively. Additional analyses revealed a clustering of unhealthy behaviors. For example, prevalence of smokeless tobacco use among subjects who did not drink, smoke cigarettes, or smoke marijuana was 6.9%. In contrast, the prevalence of smokeless tobacco use among respondents who drank alcoholic beverages, smoked cigarettes, and smoked marijuana was 50.8%, more than seven times higher.

The preceding example was based on a survey of schoolchildren from a single major metropolitan area. Prevalence studies may also be done with a much broader sampling frame. For example, a national survey of urology, general surgery, and family practice physician practices was conducted to estimate the annual number of vasectomies performed in the United States in 1991.[15] Possible health risks associated with vasectomy have generated considerable medical and scientific interest. The prevalence study permitted an estimate of the number of vasectomies performed (~493,500), the rate of vasectomies (10.3 procedures per 1,000 men aged 25 through 49), the specialist most likely to perform the procedure (urologist), and regional variation in the surgical approach. The prevalence survey generated several important questions to be answered in future studies, including the effectiveness of the various methods of sterilization and characteristics of men who elect to have the procedure performed.

Prevalence studies provide a source of hypotheses for more detailed etiologic studies, as with the example of teenage pregnancy, which is a significant public health issue because of its link with adverse outcomes including birth defects and social problems. Data from the California Birth Defects Monitoring Program for 1983 through 1988 were used to determine the prevalence of congenital malformations across the maternal age spectrum and to determine specific malformations that contributed to overall prevalence among mothers under the age of 20 years.[16] Results suggested a general J-shaped prevalence with maternal age: highest at young and old ages, and lowest at middle ages (Figure 6–6). Curiously,

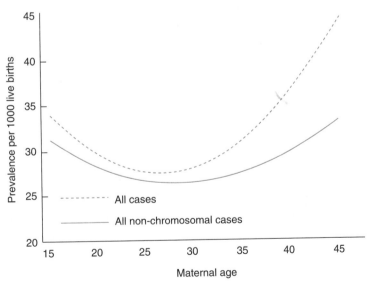

FIGURE 6–6 Prevalence of congenital malformations across maternal age: California, 1983–1986. *Source:* Reprinted from Croen LA, Shaw GM. Young maternal age and congenital malformations: a population-based study. *American Journal of Public Health*, Vol. 85, p. 711, with permission of the American Public Health Association, ©1995.

when examined by the race/ethnicity of the mother, the pattern was not apparent for African Americans. The investigators raised the question as to "whether the increased risk of malformations among young mothers is due to behavioral or developmental factors and when, relative to conception, these factors may be etiologically important."[16(p. 713)] The investigators' observations illustrated how a prevalence study could lead to important research hypotheses.

Fortunately, in recent years the birth rates among adolescents aged 15 to 19 years have been at record lows. The rate in 1991 was 61.8% per 1,000 females and declined to 41.1% per 1,000 females in 2004, a decrease of 33%.[17] This trend (identified by a prevalence study) supports the formulation of additional hypotheses to account for the decline in teenage pregnancy, e.g., that the decline may have been the result of abstaining from sexual intercourse or adopting responsible behavior such as use of effective birth control methods.

Prevalence surveys are useful for planning interventions. The historical neglect of the health needs of minority populations has begun to show signs of reversal. Hispanics (as you remember from Chapter 2 is the term used to describe many diverse cultural subgroups, such as Mexican Americans, Cuban Americans, and Puerto Ricans) represent the second largest minority group in the United States.[18] Data from the Hispanic Health and Nutrition Examination Survey and the second National Health and Nutrition Examination Survey were used to compare energy and macronutrient intakes among adult Mexican Americans, Cuban Americans, mainland Puerto Ricans, and non-Hispanics.[19] Important differences were identified among the major ethnic groups, suggesting that efforts to reduce the occurrence of chronic disease must incorporate the development of dietary recommendations and interventions targeted to each Hispanic group.

Repeated cross-sectional surveys can be used to examine trends in disease or risk factors that can vary over time. The Centers for Disease Control and Prevention used data on persons 12 through 19 years of age from the National Household Surveys on Drug Abuse, High School Seniors Surveys, and National Health Interview Surveys to examine the prevalence of cigarette smoking among U.S. adolescents.[20] Data were available from 1974 (1976 for the High School Seniors Surveys), 1980, 1985, and 1991. The results (Figure 6–7) suggest that overall smoking levels declined at all survey periods, but that there was notable variation by race, sex, and time period.

In general, the decline of smoking was most rapid between 1974 and 1980; the decline was faster for females than males and greater for African Americans than whites. Nelson et al.[20] concluded that the slowing of the trend toward lower

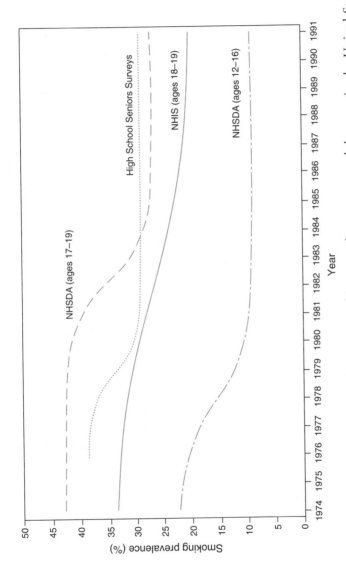

FIGURE 6–7 Overall weighted estimates of current smoking prevalence among adolescents in the United States, by survey, 1974–1991. *Source:* Reprinted from Nelson DE et al. Trends in cigarette smoking among U.S. adolescents, 1974–1991. *American Journal of Public Health,* Vol. 85, p. 36, with permission of the American Public Health Association, ©1995.

smoking prevalence was evidence of the success of increased tobacco advertising and promotional activities aimed at adolescents or inadequate antitobacco educational efforts.

These examples have been selected to illustrate a number of important applications of the cross-sectional study design. Perhaps the greatest utility of such studies is for collecting data to describe the magnitude and distribution of a health problem, data essential for planning health services and administering medical care facilities. The survey of smokeless tobacco use among ninth graders provided evidence that usage was quite common even at this early age, representing a significant public health problem. The foregoing example also demonstrated that cross-sectional studies permit assessment of a population's various characteristics; such assessment may help target appropriate interventions and educational materials. An example of such a characteristic would be the prevalence of single-parent households. The survey of vasectomies in the United States revealed that urologists perform most of the surgical procedures and that local anesthesia is typically used. Sometimes, repeated cross-sectional surveys examine quantitative factors that vary over time. Finally, prevalence studies may generate new etiologic hypotheses that can be tested in future studies.

The limitations of cross-sectional designs stem mainly from their relative lack of utility for studies of disease etiology. First, prevalent cases represent survivors: The study of prevalent cases makes it difficult to sort out factors associated with risk of disease from factors associated with survival, such as treatment and severity. For diseases in which onset is difficult to determine (e.g., mental disorders), however, prevalence is an acceptable substitute for incidence. In other situations, the study of existing cases is the only feasible and affordable strategy to test etiologic hypotheses. The second major limitation applies to the ability to study diseases of low frequency. Recall from Chapter 3 that the prevalence of disease in a population is proportional to the incidence of the disease times its duration. Therefore, even a large survey may yield but few cases of rare diseases or diseases with short duration. Third, because exposure and disease histories are taken at the same time in a cross-sectional study, one must be careful about the temporality issue (i.e., whether exposure or disease came first), making assertions about any apparent cause-effect relationship tenuous.

Case-Control Studies

The basic premise of analytic epidemiology is that disease does not occur randomly but rather in describable patterns that reflect the underlying etiology. This rationale certainly applies to case-control studies. Consider two groups, one in which everyone has the disease of interest (cases) and a comparable one in which everyone is free from the disease (controls). The case-control study seeks to identify possible causes of the disease by finding out how the two groups differ. That is, because disease does not occur randomly, the case group must have been exposed to some factor, either voluntarily (e.g., through diet, exercise, or smoking) or involuntarily (through such factors as cosmic radiation, air pollution, occupational hazards, or genetic constitution), that contributed to the causation of their disease. Therefore, a comparison of the frequency of exposure among cases and controls may permit inferences as to the basis for the difference in disease status. Case-control studies are a mainstay of epidemiologic research. From the standpoint of selection of study groups for research into disease etiology, one is going from effect to cause. In Figure 6–8, the column totals, denoted by boxes, represent the presence (i.e., cases) or absence (i.e., controls) of disease. In recent years, the case-control design has proven to be useful and efficient for evaluation of vaccine effectiveness,[21] treatment efficacy,[22] screening programs,[23] and outbreak investigations.[24]

The number of observation points for a case-control study is only one. Cases and controls are selected, and data are collected about past exposures that may have contributed to disease. As is true also of cross-sectional studies, the unit of observation and the unit of analysis are the individual. The method of data collection typically involves a combination of both primary and secondary sources. Usually the data on exposure are collected by the investigators, although one can

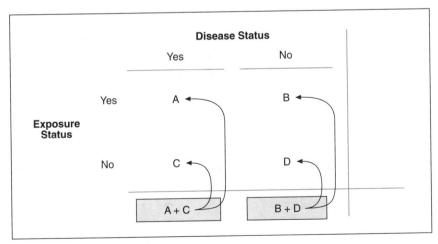

FIGURE 6–8   Illustration of selection in a case-control study.

easily imagine situations where valuable information might be obtained from medical, school, and employee records. Data on disease are often collected by someone other than the investigator, especially if one is making use of special registries or surveillance systems for case identification. In some situations, however, the investigator might conduct a population screening survey to identify suitable cases. Notice that Figure 6–8 does not include the marginal totals A + B, C + D, or a total N. Because one is taking only a subset of the total population, namely the cases and some number of controls, these marginal totals are meaningless.

Selection of Cases

Two tasks are involved in case selection: defining a case conceptually and identifying a case operationally.[25] The definition of a case is influenced by a number of factors, including whether there are standard diagnostic criteria, the severity of the disease, and whether the criteria to diagnose the disease are subjective or objective. At issue is misclassification. If the criteria are broad, the case group is more likely to include individuals who truly do not have the disease. Conversely, overly restrictive criteria may limit the number of subjects available for study. Although the selection criteria need to be weighed for each individual study, there is some evidence that the benefits of a more restrictive definition of a case outweigh the benefits of being overly inclusive.[26]

Sources of Cases

Once a case has been defined conceptually, one can then proceed to develop a strategy for case identification. The researcher's goal "is to ensure that all true cases have an equal probability of entering the study and that no false cases enter."[25(p. 8)] The ideal situation is to identify and enroll all incident cases in a defined population in a specified time period. For example, a tumor or disease registry or Vital Statistics Bureau may provide a complete listing of all available cases. The advantage of using incident cases is that, when all cases in a population are identified, there can be little question of their representativeness. In the real world, however, logistics or the lack of a suitable disease registry may restrict case selection to one or a few medical facilities. The main caveat in the selection of cases is the representativeness of the cases derived from special care facilities. Such institutions may receive only the most severe cases, ones in which the distribution of risk factors is atypical. Per the discussion in the last section on cross-sectional designs, prevalent cases make it difficult to separate characteristics that are causal or consequential. Additional benefits of studying incident (as opposed to prevalent) cases include subjects' better recall of past exposures and a reduced likelihood that exposure has changed as a consequence of the disease.

Selection of Controls

Suppose you have a strong and justified hypothesis about a new risk factor for a disease and want to conduct a case-control study. How should the controls be selected? To determine whether this risk factor is truly associated with the disease—not indirectly or incorrectly associated because of some third (confounding) factor—the ideal controls should have the same characteristics as the cases (except for the exposure of interest). That is, if the controls were equal to the cases in all respects other than disease and the hypothesized risk factor, one would be in a stronger position to ascribe differences in disease status to the exposure of interest. Taking this example one step further, imagine a study of childhood vaccination and an adult chronic disease in which the cases and controls were all the same age, the same sex, and the same race, worked at the same job, ate the same foods, were educated at the same schools, and had the same leisure activities. Speculate that the cases and controls were identical in every respect except for vaccinations in childhood; all of the cases were exposed and none of the controls was exposed. This situation would provide the most clear-cut evidence that an exposure was indeed a risk factor for the disease. Clearly, such an ideal selection of cases and controls is extremely unlikely to occur, but the point should be obvious: Cases are presumed to have a given disease because of an excess (or deficiency) of an exposure. To identify whether the exposure patterns of a group of cases are excessively high or excessively low, the investigator needs to know what exposure pattern should normally be expected. Selection of a group of disease-free individuals (controls) supposedly will reveal what a normal or expected level of exposure should be in the absence of disease.

Note, however, that controls are neither always nor necessarily disease free. To examine the specificity of an exposure-disease association, one might identify controls with a different disease, assuming that the illness has a different etiologic basis from the disease of interest. For example, a review of 106 cancer case-control studies identified nine that used controls who had a type of cancer that was different from that of the cases.[27]

The epidemiologist needs to be able to isolate the effect of the risk factor on the outcome from influences that emanate from the controls. For example, suppose that the cases and controls differ in demographic characteristics, such as age or socioeconomic status. These demographic factors could operate as rival explanations to account for observed outcomes. That is, the researcher would be unable to distinguish the effects of the risk factor from the influence of demographic factors. To overcome the potential impact of systematic case-control differences in demographic and other characteristics upon the outcome, the investigator can use matching. Two methods of matching are the use of matched pairs (individual matching) and frequency matching (group matching). Refer to Chapter 10 (section entitled, Three Prevention Strategies to Control Confounding) for an extended discussion of matching.

In addition to the problem of how to select the controls, a second issue is the number of controls to select. Estimating the number of controls is an aspect of statistical power (ability to identify a significant difference), a topic that is beyond the scope of this text. (For more information, refer to Chernick and Friis.[28]) However, here is a rule of thumb: epidemiologic researchers sometimes use an equal number of cases and controls (one-to-one ratio), a perfectly acceptable procedure. Preferably, researchers may select more controls than cases (up to a three-to-one or four-to-one ratio). When the ratio of controls to cases is at about a four-to-one ratio, statistical power of the design is maximal. A single case-control study also may use more than one control group, as in the case of hospital controls for hospitalized cases as well as community controls who represent a less selected group than do the controls from a hospital.

Sources of Controls

The general concept guiding the selection of controls is that they should come from the same population at risk for the disease or condition as the cases being studied. That is, one should ask, if a "control" had developed the outcome under investigation, would he or she have been ascertained as a case? Moreover, suitable controls should have the potential to become a case. For example, if you are conducting a study of ovarian cancer, women who have had bilateral oophorectomy (removal of their ovaries) would not be eligible as controls, since they could not develop ovarian cancer. Table 6–5 provides a guide for selection of controls who are comparable to the cases. Several options are available to the investigator regarding sources of controls. Each option has inherent strengths and weaknesses, advantages and disadvantages. The more common sources of controls are described below.

Population-Based Controls

Perhaps the best way to ensure that the distribution of exposure among the controls is representative of the exposure levels in the population is to select population-based controls. A method to identify such controls is to obtain a list

Table 6–5   Guide for Selection of Comparable Cases and Controls

Example	Cases	Controls
1	All cases diagnosed in the community	Sample of the general population in a community
2	All cases diagnosed in a sampled population	Noncases, in a sample of the general population, or a specified subgroup
3	All cases diagnosed in all hospitals in the community	Sample of persons who reside in the same neighborhood as cases
4	All cases from one or more hospitals	Sample of patients in one or more hospitals in the community who do not have the same or related diseases being studied
5	All cases from a single hospital	Sample of noncases from the same hospital
6	Any of the above	Spouses, relatives, or associates of cases

that contains names and addresses of most residents in the same geographic area as the cases. For example, a driver's license list would include most people between the ages of 16 and 65; a roster from The Centers for Medicare and Medicaid Services (the former Health Care Financing Administration) would be a good source for subjects over the age of 65. Tax lists, voting lists, and telephone directories may be useful, provided that their coverage of the population is complete or nearly complete. One then could randomly select controls from the total list, making sure to verify that selected persons met all exclusion criteria. Another method would be to select controls matched to the cases on variables such as age or sex. An approach that historically worked well in countries where most households have a telephone is random-digit dialing (RDD).[29] This technique uses a computer to generate randomly the last two to four digits of a telephone number for potential controls who have the same three-digit telephone prefix as the cases. The procedure is repeated until a suitable control is found. There is some evidence, however, that controls selected by RDD are better educated and more likely to be employed than survey controls.[30] In addition, increasing use of caller identifications on home telephones, inundation by telemarketers, and replacement of land telephones with cellular telephones have decreased the yield of this approach. As a response to the excessive number of calls from telemarketers, the Federal Trade Commission implemented the National Do Not Call Registry (DNC) on October 1, 2000. The DNC Registry does not apply to survey researchers and, consequently, does not limit their activities.

In comparison with other methods for selection of controls, the use of population-based controls is most likely to result in a control group that is representative of the exposure rate in the general or target population. Controls selected from the general population may have little incentive to participate in a research study, producing low participation rates and the need to contact more individuals to find an eligible control willing to participate. Consequently, the study becomes more expensive. Another consequence of low participation is that individuals who do ultimately agree to participate may be systematically different in the frequency of exposure than the target population they are intended to represent.

Patients from the Same Hospital as the Cases

For the reasons noted, a preferred approach is to conduct case-control studies in which both study groups are population based. When selection of population-based study groups is not feasible, however, cases may need to be derived from one or more major hospitals. Although hospital-based studies are inherently subject to greater potential for errors than population-based studies, their use is certainly justified when little information has been reported about a particular exposure-disease association or when a population-based case registry is not available. After the decision has been made to select cases from hospitals, it is perfectly appropriate to select hospital controls.

There are several practical advantages to using hospital controls. The study personnel who are already in the hospital to interview cases may achieve time efficiency by also interviewing controls. This time saving, plus the fact that hospital controls may be more likely than population controls to participate, ultimately equates to cost savings.

Perhaps the main difficulty of using hospital controls is trying to decide the diagnostic categories from which to select the controls. A second major limitation of hospital controls is that they may not be representative of the true exposure rates in the target population; after all, they were ill enough to require medical attention and motivated enough to seek it. Taken to the extreme, a possible category of controls is deceased persons. If cases were defined as individuals who had died from a particular cause, dead controls would permit testing of hypotheses regarding exposures and each cause of death.[25]

Relatives or Associates of Cases

Earlier in this chapter, we stated that the ideal control is a person free of the outcome of interest and similar in every respect to the case except for the exposure of interest. This objective is not only difficult to achieve but also difficult to evaluate. One approach to control indirectly for factors that will not be measured directly as part of the study is to select relatives, associates, or neighbors of cases as the control group. This strategy tends to be a good method to control for possible differences in socioeconomic status, education, or other characteristics assumed to be determinants of friendship or neighborhood.[25] At the same time, use of this category of controls is not without some disadvantages. Compared with the use of hospital controls, the method is more expensive and time consuming. Although one might intuitively expect "friend" controls to be highly cooperative, several investigators have noted that cases may be unwilling to provide the name of a friend to fill this role.[31,32] A greater problem is that one may end up controlling for an important (unidentified) risk factor that could no longer be evaluated.

Measure of Association

The objective of case-control studies is to identify differences in exposure frequency that might be associated with one group having the disease of interest and the other group not having it. Although several measures of association between exposure and disease can be calculated (covered in Chapter 9), at this point we introduce the most frequently calculated measure of effect. The guiding principle is to determine how much more (or less) likely the cases are to be exposed than the controls.

In Figure 6–9, first consider only the cases. The proportion of the cases exposed is A/(A + C). The proportion of cases not exposed is C/(A + C). The

		Disease Status	
		Yes	No
Exposure Status	Yes	A	B
	No	C	D
		A + C	B + D

FIGURE 6–9 Distribution of exposures in a case-control study.

odds of exposure, given that an individual is a member of the case group, are simply the ratio of these two proportions: $[A/(A + C)] \div [C/(A + C)]$. To simplify this expression, one inverts the second term and multiplies it by the first: $[A/(A + C)][(A + C)/C]$. The terms $(A + C)$ cancel out, and one is left with A/C; this term represents the odds of exposure among the case group. Repeating the same calculations, one determines that the odds of exposure among the control group are B/D. To evaluate whether the odds of exposure for the case group are different from the odds of exposure for the control group, we create a ratio of these two odds, or an *odds ratio* (OR): $(A/C) \div (B/D)$. Note that this can be more conveniently expressed as $(AD)/(BC)$, which is the cross-product of the cells from our 2 by 2 table. A calculation example is shown in Exhibit 6–1.

EXHIBIT 6–1

Sample Calculation of an Odds Ratio

Those of us who have a predilection for spicy foods have wondered about the health hazards associated with consumption of chili peppers. López-Carrillo et al.[33] conducted a population-based case-control study in Mexico City of the relationship between chili pepper consumption and gastric cancer risk. They reported that consumption of chili peppers was significantly associated with high risk for gastric cancer (age- and sex-adjusted OR = 5.49). Subjects for the study consisted of 220 incident cases and 752 controls randomly selected from the general population. Interviews produced information regarding chili consumption. In the present example, the data from this study are abstracted to illustrate how to calculate the OR.

Chili Pepper Consumption	Cases of Gastric Cancer	Controls
Yes	A = 204	B = 552
No	C = 9	D = 145

The OR (unadjusted for age and sex) is:

$$\frac{AD}{BC} = \frac{(204)(145)}{(552)(9)} = 5.95$$

Source: Data from López-Carrillo L, Avila MH, Dubrow R. Chili Pepper Consumption and Gastric Cancer in Mexico: A Case-Control Study, *American Journal of Epidemiology,* Vol 139, pp. 263–271, Johns Hopkins University, School of Hygiene and Public Health, © 1994.

The OR literally measures the odds of exposure of a given disease. An OR of 1.0 implies that the odds of exposure are equal among the cases and controls and suggests that a particular exposure is not a risk factor for the disease in this study. An OR of 2.0 indicates that the cases were twice as likely as the controls to be exposed. The implication of this OR, given proper consideration to the issues of causality, is that this particular exposure is a risk factor for the disease. More specifically, an OR of 2.0 implies that this particular exposure is associated with twice the risk of disease. Not all risk factors increase risk; a factor that is associated with lower risk of disease (i.e., a protective factor) would manifest as an OR of less than 1.0.

The reader is advised to interpret the OR with caution. The case-control study is retrospective in nature with only one period of observation. Therefore, rates (and consequently risk, which can be determined only from prospective studies) cannot be directly determined. The reason for this inability to determine rates and risks centers upon the way the study groups are assembled. Referring back to Figure 6–8, you can see that groups (A + B) and (C + D) do not represent the total populations exposed and not exposed to the factor. That is, there are no appropriate denominators for the population at risk, and therefore no way to directly determine disease rates. Under certain conditions, however, as noted below, the OR provides a good approximation of the risk associated with a given exposure:

- *The controls are representative of the target population.* The key issue is that the controls are representative of the target population in the frequency of the exposure of interest.
- *The cases are representative of all cases.* Cases should be typical with respect to severity and diagnostic criteria.
- *The frequency of the disease in the population is small.* Algebraically, the formula for relative risk approximates that of the OR when the number of cases is small relative to the population at risk. There is some debate over whether this assumption is necessary, however.

Table 6–6, which summarizes examples of case-control studies presented in this chapter, highlights the many uses of the case-control approach in such diverse areas as research on cancer, birth defects, heart disease, and infectious disease. (This list is by no means exhaustive.) Note that several of the research studies cited in Table 6–6 deal with cancer etiology. Many forms of cancer have unknown causation and low prevalence in the general population; for this reason, case-control studies are used frequently to investigate cancer etiology. For

---

Table 6–6   Examples of Research Conducted with Case-Control Studies

---

Cancer research
   Young women's cancers resulting from in utero exposure to diethylstilbestrol
   Smoking and invasive cervical cancer
   Chili pepper consumption and gastric cancer
   Green tea consumption and lung cancer
   Parental smoking and childhood cancer
   Efficacy of colonoscopic screening
   Cigarette tar yield and risk of upper digestive tract cancers
Birth defects research
   Maternal anesthesia and fetal development of birth defects
Heart disease research
   Passive smoking at home and risk of acute myocardial infarction
Infectious disease research
   Household antibiotic use and antibiotic resistant pneumococcal infection

---

example, the association between green tea consumption and lung cancer was the focus of a case-control study conducted in Shanghai, People's Republic of China.[34] A total of 649 incident cases of primary lung cancer diagnosed among women between early 1992 and early 1994 were selected from the Shanghai Cancer Registry. Investigators matched the cases to 675 control women selected at random and reported a significantly reduced risk of lung cancer (OR = 0.94) among women who consumed green tea and also did not smoke. The association was not significant among women who smoked.

To give another example from cancer etiology, we note that the case-control method is well suited to explore in greater detail unusual clinical observations based on a small number of cases. A classic historical example is exposure of female fetuses in utero to diethylstilbestrol (DES) and the development of vaginal adenocarcinoma as young women.[35] A sudden increase in the number of vaginal cancers of a rare histologic type at an atypical age led to a small case-control study that successfully identified maternal exposure to DES as the cause.

The preceding example may give the erroneous impression that case-control studies examine only a single exposure or a series of related exposures. In fact, especially when one is exploring a disease for which relatively little is known about the etiology, the exposure data being collected can cover a broad range of known and suspected factors. Consider the case-control study conducted by Brinton et al.[36] on cervical cancer. The cases included 480 patients with invasive cervical cancer diagnosed at 24 hospitals in five U.S. cities: Birmingham,

Chicago, Denver, Miami, and Philadelphia. All patients were between the ages of 20 and 74 years. A total of 797 population controls were identified through RDD. Two controls were matched to each case by using the variables of telephone exchange, race, and five-year age group. Women who had a previous hysterectomy were excluded. Data on cases and controls were collected through extensive home interviews that included questions on a variety of known and hypothesized risk factors, including smoking, sexual behavior, pregnancy history, menstrual history and hygiene practices, oral contraceptive use, medical history, diet, marital status, and family history.

A history of ever having smoked cigarettes was reported by 256 cases (61.4%) and 383 controls (48.1%). The corresponding OR was 1.7; when examined by currency of smoking, the ORs were 1.4 for ever-smokers and 1.9 for current smokers. There was evidence for a dose-response relationship: Compared with never-smokers, the ORs for those who smoked fewer than 10, 10 to 19, 20 to 29, and 30 or more cigarettes per day were 1.2, 1.6, 1.7, and 3.2, respectively.

Case-control studies have explored the relationship between tobacco use and cancers at various sites. Smoking is a risk factor for oral and throat (upper digestive tract) cancers; risk of these forms of cancer is thought to be associated with the concentration of tars in cigarettes. A case-control study conducted in Italy and Switzerland (with 749 cases and 1770 controls) confirmed an association between cigarette consumption and upper digestive tract neoplasms.[37] Investigators reported a direct relationship between the tar yield of cigarettes and such cancers. The ORs between current smokers and never-smokers were 6.1 for cigarettes with lower tar concentrations and 9.8 for cigarettes with higher tar concentrations.

The United Kingdom Childhood Cancer Study examined parental smoking behavior as a risk factor for childhood cancers.[38] The study included 3,838 children with cancer and 7,629 control children. Cancers were classified into four major groups: leukemia, lymphomas, central nervous system tumors, and other solid tumors. Information was collected on self-reported smoking habits of parents. Statistical analyses adjusted for factors such as parental age. In general, the study did not demonstrate that parental smoking was a significant risk factor for childhood cancers, although risk of one form of cancer (hepatoblastoma) was significant when both parents smoked (OR = 4.74).

Case-control studies have evaluated the efficacy of cancer screening programs.[39] The efficacy of colonoscopic screening and polypectomy for preventing colorectal cancer (CRC) was assessed in a small-scale case-control study.

The cases consisted of 40 asymptomatic persons diagnosed with CRC and 160 normal controls. Researchers selected subjects from a high-risk population of first-degree relatives of CRC patients. It was found that cases and controls varied in frequency of screening, with procedures such as screening colonoscopy occurring less frequently among the cases than among the controls.

The remainder of this section illustrates the use of case-control studies to investigate conditions other than cancer (e.g., heart disease, birth defects, infectious disease). For example, exposure to side-stream cigarette smoke has been hypothesized to be a risk factor for heart disease. A study conducted in Argentina examined the risk associated with passive smoking and acute myocardial infarction (AMI).[40] Both cases ($n = 336$) and controls ($n = 446$) consisted of never-smokers admitted to the same network of hospitals. Cases were patients with AMI; controls were patients admitted with acute disorders unrelated to smoking or known to be risk factors for AMI. Trained interviewers administered a structured questionnaire that contained items on smoking by close relatives, such as children and spouses. The risk of AMI was significantly associated with passive smoking; the ORs ranged upward of 1.68 depending on the contrast category (e.g., numbers of relatives who smoked and the number of cigarettes smoked).

Regarding the use of case-control studies to explore risk of birth defects, an example is the report based on a record linkage of Swedish health care registries. This research identified six infants with neural tube defects (NTDs) born to mothers who had undergone surgery in the first trimester of pregnancy when only 2.5 were expected.[41] The observation was evaluated in more detail by investigators at the Centers for Disease Control and Prevention.[42] Cases were infants with major central nervous system defects, including NTDs (anencephaly, spina bifida, and encephalocele), microcephaly, and hydrocephaly (hydrocephalus) ascertained through the population-based surveillance system known as the Metropolitan Atlanta Congenital Defects Program. Controls were a 1% random sample of infants born in the same geographic region over the same time period. Trained interviewers, blinded to the case-control status of the infant, collected data from the mothers by telephone. (See Chapter 8 for information on blinding.) Maternal anesthesia exposure immediately before becoming pregnant or during the first three months of gestation was ascertained. Data were collected from the mothers of 694 case infants and the mothers of 2,984 control infants. There were no differences between mothers of the cases and controls with respect to mean age, parity, smoking status, use of alcohol-containing beverages, weight gain during pregnancy, or education. Maternal exposure to general anesthesia during the first trimester, however, was reported by 1.7% of case mothers versus only 1.1% of control mothers. This equates to an OR of 1.7, with a 95% confidence interval (CI) of 0.8 to 3.3. Because the 95% CI includes the null value of 1.0, the results are consistent with the hypothesis of no association. Further analysis of the data revealed that a stronger association was evident for one subtype of defect, hydrocephalus (OR, 3.8; 95% CI, 1.6–9.1). Thus, the mothers of infants with hydrocephalus were nearly four times as likely to have reported early exposure to general anesthesia as mothers of infants without congenital malformations, an association that does not appear to be due to chance alone. When multiple defects were considered, stronger associations were identified. For example, there were eight infants with both hydrocephalus and eye defects. Three of the mothers of these eight infants (37.5%) reported general anesthesia exposure, an odds of exposure 39.6 times greater (95% CI, 7.5–209.2) than among control mothers. These intriguing data warrant additional research to determine why the surgeries were performed as well as the types of surgeries, premedications for surgery, and use of general anesthesia and whether there were complications during or after the surgery.

Case-control studies are often the method of choice in infectious disease research. Outbreaks of new and unusual diseases, such as toxic shock syndrome, anthrax, and even occurrence of antibiotic-resistant organisms, may be explored fruitfully by applying case-control methods. A case-control study examined the issue of whether a person's risk of antibiotic-resistant infection is increased if a member of that person's family is exposed to antibiotics.[43] These data were derived from patients enrolled in health maintenance organizations in western Washington State and northern California. The study outcome was affliction with penicillin nonsusceptible pneumococcal disease (143 cases) versus penicillin susceptible disease (79 controls). A significant association between antibiotic use within two months prior to diagnosis and antibiotic resistance was found. Use of antibiotics by other family members within four months prior to diagnosis was not related to antibiotic resistance.

Summary of Case-Control Studies

In this section we have indicated the numerous attractive features of case-control studies. Compared with large-scale surveys or prospective studies, case-control studies tend to be smaller in size: hundreds to thousands of subjects versus thousands to tens of thousands. As such, they are relatively quick and easy to complete as well as cost effective. The smaller sample size increases the likelihood that a case-control study will be repeated. In fact, because consistency is critical to epidemiologic research, it is highly desirable that several investigators repeat studies of a particular outcome in different populations. Although progression from case-control studies to a cohort study may be a logical pursuit, prospective studies are not feasible for some exposures and outcomes; a meaningful cohort study of a rare disease would require a large study group, a long period of follow-up, or both. In comparison with cohort studies, case-control studies are particularly useful for investigations into the etiology of rare diseases.

Limitations of the case-control design include the uncertainty of the exposure-disease time relationship and the inability to provide a direct estimate of risk. It is frequently difficult to determine the representativeness of the cases and controls selected for study, and there is a real possibility of introduction of errors in selection of subjects, measurement of exposures, and analysis. If the exposure is rare in the population, then case-control studies may be inefficient. That is, despite a large number of cases, one may still end up with few exposed cases. For a more detailed coverage of case-control studies, the reader is referred to the textbook by Schlesselman.[44] An entire issue of *Epidemiologic Reviews* was devoted to this topic.[45]

Conclusion

This chapter provided an overview of major study designs that are used in epidemiology. The authors noted that study designs differ in a number of key respects, including the unit of observation, the unit of analysis, the timing of exposure data in relation to occurrence of disease end point, complexity, rigor, and amount of resources required. Some studies are designed to infer etiology; others are designed to affect parameters of health. Study designs differ with respect to control overexposure and the ability to assign subjects to study conditions. Two major categories of study design exist: observational and experimental. This chapter presented three major types of observational designs: ecologic, cross-sectional, and case-control. The measure of effect used in case-control studies, OR, was illustrated. Chapter 7 provides information on the other major observational design used in epidemiology—the cohort study—and its corresponding measure of effect, relative risk. Chapter 8 covers the use of experimental designs in public health. Chapter 9 expands on the two measures of effect used in observational study designs and presents several ways to summarize the results of epidemiologic studies.

Study Questions and Exercises

1. Define in your own words the following terms:
   a. ecologic study
   b. ecologic comparison study
   c. ecologic trend study
   d. ecologic fallacy
   e. cross-sectional study
   f. case-control study
2. Compare ecologic, cross-sectional, and case-control studies with respect to their strengths and weaknesses, and advantages and disadvantages.
3. The following question lists examples of observational studies. Indicate the type of study design that is being described.
   a. A study examined the effect of hormone replacement therapy on cancer; cancer cases were identified by using a cancer registry in northern California. Controls were selected from a random sample of Bay Area cities.
   b. Data from the Behavioral Risk Factor Survey were used in a secondary data analysis to examine the effect of income inequality and race on preventive health practices.
   c. The level of unemployment was used as a measure of economic distress in Germany. Researchers examined the association between distress and general anxiety syndrome across states (e.g., Saxony) in Germany.
4. What are the differences between probability and non-probability samples used in cross-sectional designs?
5. You are interested in conducting a case-control study of childhood leukemia and exposure to environmental toxins in utero. Describe how you would select cases and controls for this study and how you would define exposure and outcome factors. How could the same problem be investigated using an ecologic study design?
6. Describe the advantages and disadvantages of each of the following types of controls in a case-control study:
   a. Population-based
   b. Hospital cases
   c. Relatives

7. Calculate the OR for the following 2 by 2 table:

	Outcome	
	Yes	No
Factor		
Yes	37	68
No	24	121

8. An investigator wanted to determine whether vitamin deficiency was associated with birth defects. By reviewing the birth certificates during a single year in a large U.S. county, the researcher located 189 infants born with NTDs. A total of 600 other births were selected at random from the certificates. Mothers were given a dietary questionnaire. Among mothers who gave birth to an infant with an NTD, 84 reported no use of supplementary vitamins; a total of 137 control mothers did not use a vitamin supplement. Construct the appropriate 2 by 2 table and calculate the OR between vitamin use and NTDs.

9. The association between job-related exposure to welding fumes and chronic obstructive pulmonary disease (COPD) was explored in a case-control study. The following data were reported for 399 COPD patients: 37 currently employed as welders; the remainder had no occupational exposure. Among 800 controls, 48 were employed as welders. Set up a 2 by 2 table and calculate the OR.

10. Hypothesize that cell phone use by drivers is related to fatal automobile accidents. Design a hypothetical case-control study, giving attention to the following points: definition of the outcome, selection of controls, and difficulties in conducting such a study.

11. Why would you exclude as controls in a case-control study of gynecologic cancer women who cannot develop the disease?

12. The following ORs are reported for several hypothetical examples. Give your interpretation of the results, assuming all results are statistically significant unless otherwise specified.

   a. OR (low-fat diet and colon cancer) = 0.6
   b. OR (aerobic exercise and dental caries) = 1 (not significant)
   c. OR (exposure to side-stream cigarette smoke and lung cancer) = 1.3
   d. OR (infectious disease of the pelvis and ectopic (tubal) pregnancy) = 3.0

13. A random-digit dialed survey conducted in the City of Long Beach, California, reported that a greater proportion of nonsmokers endorsed a

ban on smoking in alcohol-serving establishments than did smokers. What type of study design was this?

14. Case-control studies allow the investigator to examine only one outcome at a time, but they permit examination of several different exposures at a time. Select a disease or other health outcome with which you are familiar and see how many potential exposures you can identify.

15. How would you design an ecologic study to investigate the following problems? How might the ecologic fallacy come into play in each situation?
    a. lung disease and air pollution
    b. birth defects and hazardous waste
    c. cancer and radiation leakage from a power plant

References

1. Kleinbaum DG, Kupper LL, Morgenstern H. *Epidemiologic Research: Principles and Quantitative Methods.* Belmont, CA: Lifetime Learning; 1982.

2. Valls V, Lozano MS, Yanez R, et al. Use of safety devices and the prevention of percutaneous injuries among healthcare workers. *Infect Control Hosp Epidemiol.* 2007;28:1352–1360.

3. Garrard J, Chen V, Dowd B. The impact of the 1987 federal regulations on the use of psychotropic drugs in Minnesota nursing homes. *Am J Public Health.* 1995;85:771–776.

4. Carroll KK. Experimental evidence of dietary factors and hormone-dependent cancers. *Cancer Res.* 1975;35:3374–3383.

5. Sargent JD, Brown MJ, Freeman JL, Bailey A, Goodman D, Freeman DH. Childhood lead poisoning in Massachusetts communities: its association with sociodemographic and housing characteristics. *Am J Public Health.* 1995;85:528–534.

6. Menotti A, Blackburn H, Kromhout D, et al. The inverse relation of average population blood pressure and stroke mortality rates in the seven countries study: a paradox. *Eur J Epidemiol.* 1997;13:379–386.

7. Jacobsen SJ, O'Fallon WM, Melton LJ 3rd. Hip fracture incidence before and after the fluoridation of the public water supply, Rochester, Minnesota. *Am J Public Health.* 1993;83:743–745.

8. Steiner GG. Cancer incidence rates and environmental factors: an ecological study. *J Environ Pathol Toxicol Oncol.* 2002;21:205–212.

9. Pickett KE, Pearl M. Multilevel analyses of neighbourhood socioeconomic context and health outcomes: a critical review. *J Epidemiol Community Health.* 2001;55:111–122.

10. Last JM, ed. *A Dictionary of Epidemiology,* 4th ed. New York, NY: Oxford University Press; 2001.

11. Levy PS, Lemeshow S. *Sampling for Health Professionals.* Belmont, CA: Lifetime Learning; 1980.

12. Babbie E. *The Practice of Social Research*, 6th ed. Belmont, CA: Wadsworth; 1992.

13. Kish L. *Survey Sampling*. New York, NY: Wiley; 1965.

14. Murray DM, Roche LM, Goldman AI, Whitbeck J. Smokeless tobacco use among ninth graders in a North-Central metropolitan population: cross-sectional and prospective associations with age, gender, race, family structure, and other drug use. *Prev Med.* 1988;17:449–460.

15. Marquette CM, Koonin LM, Antarsh L, Gargiullo PM, Smith JC. Vasectomy in the United States, 1991. *Am J Public Health.* 1995;85:644–649.

16. Croen LA, Shaw GM. Young maternal age and congenital malformations: a population-based study. *Am J Public Health.* 1995;85:710–713.

17. Martin JA, Hamilton BE, Sutton PD, et al. Births: Final data for 2004. *National Vital Statistics Reports.* 2006;55(1). Hyattsville, MD: National Center for Health Statistics.

18. U.S. Bureau of the Census. U.S. population estimates, by age, sex, race and Hispanic origin: 1980 to 1991. In: *Current Population Reports.* Washington, DC: Government Printing Office; 1993:P25–P1095.

19. Loria CM, Bush TL, Carroll MD, et al. Macronutrient intakes among adult Hispanics: a comparison of Mexican Americans, Cuban Americans, and Mainland Puerto Ricans. *Am J Public Health.* 1995;85:684–689.

20. Nelson DE, Giovino GA, Shopland DR, Mowery PD, Mills SL, Eriksen MP. Trends in cigarette smoking among U.S. adolescents, 1974 through 1991. *Am J Public Health.* 1995;85:34–40.

21. Comstock GW. Evaluating vaccination effectiveness and vaccine efficacy by means of case-control studies. *Epidemiol Rev.* 1994;16:77–89.

22. Selby JV. Case-control evaluations of treatment and program efficacy. *Epidemiol Rev.* 1994;16:90–101.

23. Weiss NS. Application of the case-control method in the evaluation of screening. *Epidemiol Rev.* 1994;16:102–108.

24. Dwyer DM, Strickler H, Goodman RA, Armenian HK. Use of case-control studies in outbreak investigations. *Epidemiol Rev.* 1994;16:109–123.

25. Lasky T, Stolley PD. Selection of cases and controls. *Epidemiol Rev.* 1994;16:6–17.

26. Brenner H, Savitz DA. The effects of sensitivity and specificity of case selection on validity, sample size, precision, and power in hospital-based case–control studies. *Am J Epidemiol.* 1990;132:181–192.

27. Linet MS, Brookmeyer R. Use of cancer controls in case-control studies. *Am J Epidemiol.* 1987;125:1–11.

28. Chernick MR, Friis RH. *Introductory Biostatistics for the Health Sciences: Modern Applications Including Bootstrap.* Hoboken, NJ: John Wiley & Sons, Inc.; 2003.

29. Hartge P, Brinton LA, Rosenthal JF, et al. Random digit dialing in selecting a population-based control group. *Am J Epidemiol.* 1984;120:825–833.

30. Olson SH, Kelsey JL, Pearson TA, et al. Evaluation of random digit dialing as a method of control selection in case-control studies. *Am J Epidemiol.* 1992;135: 210–222.

31. Shaw GL, Tucker MA, Kase RG, et al. Problems ascertaining friend controls in a case-control study of lung cancer. *Am J Epidemiol.* 1991;133:63–66.

32. Jones S, Silman AJ. Re: "Problems ascertaining friend controls in a case-control study of lung cancer." *Am J Epidemiol.* 1991;134:673–674.

33. López-Carrillo L, Avila MH, Dubrow R. Chili pepper consumption and gastric cancer in Mexico: a case-control study. *Am J Epidemiol.* 1994;139:263–271.

34. Zhong L, Goldberg MS, Gao Y-T, et al. A population-based case-control study of lung cancer and green tea consumption among women living in Shanghai, China. *Epidemiology.* 2001;12:695–700.

35. Herbst AL, Scully RE. Adenocarcinoma of the vagina in adolescence. *Cancer.* 1970;25:745–757.

36. Brinton LA, Schairer C, Haenszel W, et al. Cigarette smoking and invasive cervical cancer. *JAMA.* 1986;255:3265–3269.

37. Gallus S, Altieri A, Bosetti C, et al. Cigarette tar yield and upper digestive tract cancers: case-control studies from Italy and Switzerland. *Ann Oncol.* 2003;14:209–213.

38. Pang D, McNally R, Birch JM. Parental smoking and childhood cancer: results from the United Kingdom Childhood Cancer Study. *Br J Cancer.* 2003;88:373–381.

39. Niv Y, Dickman R, Figer A, et al. Case-control study of screening colonoscopy in relatives of patients with colorectal cancer. *Am J Gastroenterol.* 2003;98:486–489.

40. Ciruzzi M, Pramparo P, Esteban O, et al. Case-control study of passive smoking at home and risk of acute myocardial infarction. *J Am Coll Cardiol.* 1998;31:797–803.

41. Kallen B, Mazze RI. Neural tube defects and first trimester operations. *Teratology.* 1990;41:717–720.

42. Sylvester GC, Khoury MJ, Lu X, Erickson JD. First-trimester anesthesia exposure and the risk of central nervous system defects: a population-based case-control study. *Am J Public Health.* 1994;84:1757–1760.

43. Kwan-Gett TS, Davis RL, Shay DK, et al. Is household antibiotic use a risk factor for antibiotic-resistant pneumococcal infection? *Epidemiol Infect.* 2002;129:499–505.

44. Schlesselman JJ. *Case-Control Studies: Design, Conduct, Analysis.* New York, NY: Oxford University Press; 1982.

45. Armenian HK, ed. Applications of the case-control method. *Epidemiol Rev.* 1994;16(1).

CHAPTER 7

Study Designs: Cohort Studies

LEARNING OBJECTIVES

By the end of this chapter the reader will be able to:

- differentiate cohort studies from other epidemiologic study designs
- list the main characteristics, advantages, and disadvantages of cohort studies
- describe at least three research questions that lend themselves to cohort studies
- calculate and interpret a relative risk
- give three examples of published studies discussed in this chapter

CHAPTER OUTLINE

I. Introduction
II. Cohort Studies Defined
III. Sampling and Cohort Formation Options
IV. Temporal Differences in Cohort Designs
V. Practical Considerations
VI. Measures of Interpretation and Examples
VII. Summary of Cohort Studies
VIII. Comparisons of Observational Designs
IX. Conclusion
X. Study Questions and Exercises

Introduction

Chapter 6 provided an overview of types of epidemiologic study designs as well as key features of each type, and distinctions between the experimental and observational approaches. In addition, three observational study designs were discussed in detail: ecologic, cross-sectional, and case-control designs.

A distinguishing feature of each type of study design—whether observational or experimental—is the temporality of data collection with respect to exposure and disease. The term *temporality* refers to the timing of information gathering, that is, whether the information about cause and effect was assembled at the same time point or whether information about the cause was garnered before or after the information about the effect.

Cross-sectional and case-control study designs (and many types of ecologic study designs) are premised upon exposure information and disease information that are collected at the same time. Although this strategy is efficient for generating and testing hypotheses, the strategy does lead to almost unavoidable challenges regarding interpretation of results. In particular, cross-sectional studies present difficulties in distinguishing the causes (e.g., certain exposures) from the consequences (e.g., certain outcomes) of the disease, especially if the outcome marker is a biological or physiological parameter. Similarly, case-control studies may raise concerns that recall of past exposures differs between the cases (i.e., those study participants who have the disease or outcome of interest) and the controls (those study participants who do not). In addition, although investigators may query subjects about exposures that took place many years in the past, there has been no actual lapse of time between measurement of exposure and disease. Chapter 10 (in the section titled "Factors That Contribute to Systematic Errors") presents more information regarding these issues. Finally, none of the designs discussed in Chapter 6 is especially well suited for exposures that are uncommon in the population. Chapter 7 elaborates on one of the most powerful epidemiologic designs—the cohort study—which overcomes many of the foregoing problems associated with temporality of data collection and rare exposures.

Cohort Studies Defined

Cohorts and Cohort Effects

A *cohort* is defined as a population group, or subset thereof (distinguished by a common characteristic), that is followed over a period of time. The term *cohort* is said to originate from the Latin *cohors,* which is one of 10 divisions of an ancient

Roman military legion. The common characteristic may be either that the group members experience an exposure associated with a specific setting (e.g., an occupational cohort or a school cohort) or that they share a nonspecific exposure associated with a general classification (e.g., a birth cohort, defined as being born in the same year or era). For example, people who belong to the same birth cohort may be exposed to similar environmental and societal changes, whereas those who belong to different birth cohorts may grow up exposed to dissimilar environmental conditions that are reflected in differences in health outcomes. The influence of membership in a particular cohort is known as a cohort effect.

The term *cohort analysis* refers to "the tabulation and analysis of morbidity or mortality rates in relationship to the ages of a specific group of people (cohort) identified at a particular period of time and followed as they pass through different ages during part or all of their life span."[1] Wade Hampton Frost helped to draw attention to the method of cohort analysis, even though he did not originate this methodology.[2] Table 7–1 reproduces Frost's data. "To illustrate cohort analysis, Frost first arranged tuberculosis mortality rates from Massachusetts . . . in a table with age on one axis and year of death on the other . . . Arranged in this way, one could quickly see the age-specific mortality for each of the available years on one axis, and the time trend for each age group on the other. What proved to be most interesting in this instance were the rates in the cells of the table that lay on the diagonals, starting with the youngest ages and earliest years. These 'diagonal rates' were analogous to tuberculosis mortality rates . . . experienced by each cohort of persons as they simultaneously aged and passed through time."[2(pp. 9–10)]

Table 7–1 shows that the 1880 mortality rates from tuberculosis were high among males aged zero to four and five to nine years—the highest rates occurring among the cohort aged zero to four years—when compared with mortality for the cohort as it aged. You can confirm this observation by tracing along the diagonal shown in the table. With respect to 1890 and subsequent decades, the groups that were zero to four and five to nine years of age in 1880 are combined as one moves along the diagonal. In comparison to 1880, mortality rates for that same cohort were lower during subsequent points of observation; however, during 1900 and 1910 they were higher than in 1890 and then declined again. The mortality pattern was similar for the female cohort that was aged zero to four years and five to nine years in 1880.

Another example of a cohort effect is the use of tobacco products in the United States (Figure 7–1). A low proportion ($< 5\%$) of the population smoked cigarettes around the early 1900s. As a result of widespread distribution of free

Table 7-1 Death Rates per 100,000 from Tuberculosis, All Forms, for Massachusetts, 1880 to 1930, by Age and Sex, with Rates for Cohort of 1880 Indicated

Age	1880	1890	1900	1910	1920	1930
Male						
0–4	760	578	309	209	108	41
5–9	43	49	31	21	24	11
10–19	126	115	90	63	49	21
20–29	444	361	288	207	149	81
30–39	378	368	296	253	164	115
40–49	364	336	253	253	175	118
50–59	366	325	267	252	171	127
60–69	475	346	304	246	172	95
70+	672	396	343	163	127	95
Female						
0–4	658	595	354	162	101	27
5–9	71	82	49	45	24	13
10–19	265	213	145	92	78	37
20–29	537	393	290	207	167	92
30–39	422	372	260	189	135	73
40–49	307	307	211	153	108	53
50–59	334	234	173	130	83	47
60–69	434	295	172	118	83	56
70+	584	375	296	126	68	40

Source: Reproduced with permission. Frost WH. The Age Selection of Mortality from Tuberculosis in Successive Decades. *Am J Epidemiol*, 1995, Vol 141, p. 95. © The Johns Hopkins University School of Hygiene and Public Health.

cigarettes to the troops during World War I, however, the prevalence of smoking in the population began to increase gradually, reaching a peak in the 1960s.[3] When smoking first became popular, the age at which the habit was initiated varied greatly; that is, there were considerable differences according to age, sex, and education levels.

Although some people began smoking as young adults, a large number of people adopted the habit much later in life. Over the years, more and more people took up smoking and commenced smoking earlier in life. This trend is depicted graphically in Figure 7–2. One of the net effects was a shift in the distribution of the age of onset of lung cancer.[4] Consider, for example, the birth cohort of 1850. If smoking prevalence in this cohort was similar to that of the general population, then most individuals did not begin smoking until around 1915, when the average cohort member was in his or her 60s. Because there is a delay between the onset of smoking and the development of cancer, these individuals would not develop cancer for 10 years or more, perhaps around the age of

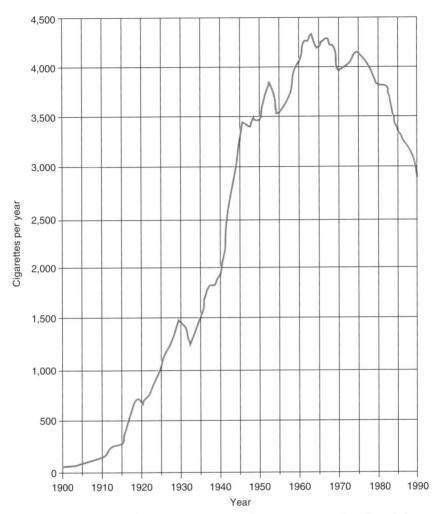

FIGURE 7–1 United States per capita tobacco consumption for adults aged 18 and older (1900–1990). *Source:* Reprinted from *Strategies to Control Tobacco Use in the United States: A Blueprint for Public Health Action in the 1990s.* Washington, DC: National Cancer Institute, National Institutes of Health; Publication No. 92-3316. 1992:75.

70. In contrast, individuals born in 1890 were only 20 when smoking became popular. As a result, a greater proportion of this age cohort would have started smoking at an earlier age, so the distribution of the entire age at onset curve for lung cancer would be shifted toward earlier ages. The more traditional approach of examining trends through repeated cross-sectional surveys leads to a distorted

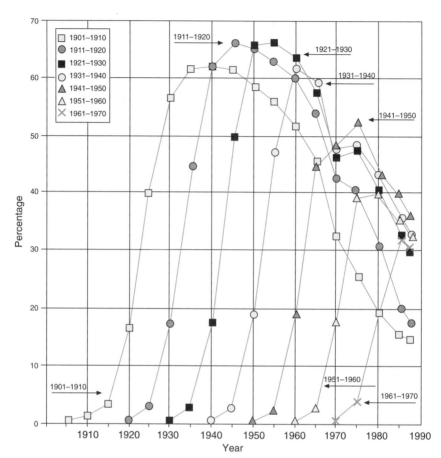

FIGURE 7–2 Changes in prevalence of cigarette smoking among successive birth cohorts of U.S. men, 1900–1987. *Source:* Reprinted from *Strategies to Control Tobacco Use in the United States: A Blueprint for Public Health Action in the 1990s.* Washington, DC: National Cancer Institute, National Institutes of Health; Publication No. 92-3316. 1992:82.

impression of the smoking-cancer association. In particular, it leads to an underestimation of the past smoking behavior of the older segments of the current population. That is because smoking behavior (age at initiation and total duration) is greatly influenced by the calendar year of birth.

Table 7–2 demonstrates a final example of a cohort effect, this time for lung cancer death rates in the United Kingdom and the United States.[5] The table presents the midpoint of birth cohorts on the Y-axis (left side) and the midpoint of five-year age groups on the X-axis (across the top). From the table, one is able

Table 7–2 Lung Cancer Death Rate per 100,000 for the United Kingdom and United States

Age (Midpoint of 5-year Age Group)
United Kingdom

Midpoint of Birth Cohort	32.5	37.5	42.5	47.5	52.5	57.5	62.5	67.5	72.5	77.5	82.5
1873											167.30
1878										243.01	259.83
1883									305.25	377.48	391.85
1888								329.25	431.62	506.16	509.23
1893							289.47	428.10	538.81	650.73	679.95
1898						219.13	353.38	512.62	662.33	764.63	812.65
1903					126.17	232.18	374.27	528.11	682.74	796.69	832.76
1908				59.72	125.16	228.23	369.44	514.73	655.69	756.35	767.28
1913			24.87	57.76	120.75	215.69	344.15	479.32	616.24	678.27	669.39
1918		9.78	25.00	55.08	111.60	202.32	316.22	437.96	553.20	592.54	
1923	3.76	9.47	22.38	53.96	106.37	184.94	294.74	402.30	475.24		
1928	3.53	9.06	21.01	46.80	92.11	158.66	245.40	326.52			
1933	2.80	6.29	16.30	36.15	69.26	122.78	184.53				
1938	2.49	5.90	12.96	29.62	59.51	102.18					
1943	2.24	4.97	11.24	26.26	49.74						
1948	1.56	4.07	9.72	20.74							
1953	1.09	3.13	8.02								
1958	0.77	2.13									
1963	0.65										

United States

	32.5	37.5	42.5	47.5	52.5	57.5	62.5	67.5	72.5	77.5	82.5
1873											116.80
1878										138.60	176.30
1883									148.90	199.60	222.60
1888								157.80	232.20	268.30	325.40
1893							135.50	219.70	302.60	380.60	431.60
1898						95.90	180.70	277.30	371.00	464.00	477.70
1903					58.20	114.92	199.88	306.95	418.93	502.80	543.33
1908				30.40	68.71	127.55	228.01	329.42	458.80	546.20	584.96
1913			11.60	31.79	76.79	152.13	244.30	359.11	470.70	565.40	580.60
1918		4.90	13.99	38.61	84.32	150.01	255.74	367.06	485.89	529.90	
1923	1.70	5.73	17.26	44.03	90.91	162.93	262.46	374.07	470.90		
1928	1.97	7.05	21.54	47.86	95.28	167.41	268.18	359.60			
1933	2.00	7.34	19.30	45.44	86.59	159.35	233.60				
1938	2.03	6.15	17.43	40.26	80.52	132.70					
1943	1.80	5.29	15.19	34.64	66.10						
1948	1.12	4.32	11.63	26.20							
1953	0.98	3.85	9.50								
1958	1.16	3.30									
1963	1.20										

Source: Adapted from National Cancer Institute. *Risks Associated with Smoking Cigarettes with Low Machine-Measured Yields of Tar and Nicotine,* p. 128. Smoking and Tobacco Control Monograph No. 13, NIH Pub. No. 02-5074. Bethesda, MD: U.S. Department of Health and Human Services, National Institutes of Health, National Cancer Institute; October 2001.

to infer cohort effects as a particular cohort ages and also can compare mortality between the two regions. For example, the respective lung cancer death rates per 100,000 of the 1923 cohort at age 32.5 years are 3.76 and 1.70. The cohort effect can be traced along a diagonal: the respective rates at the intersection of year 1928 and age 37.5 years are 9.06 and 7.05. The overall trend shown in the table is for age-specific lung cancer death rates to start at lower levels in the United States but then show more rapid increases than in the United Kingdom, perhaps due to differences in age of initiation of smoking, particularly among males.

Life Table Methods

According to Chernick and Friis, "Life tables give estimates for survival during time intervals and present the cumulative survival probability at the end of the interval."[6(p. 339)] We are able to construct life tables in order to portray the survival times of patients in clinical trials. (Clinical trials are discussed in Chapter 8.) For the U.S. population, the National Center for Health Statistics produces life tables known as periodic life tables.[7] Two major types of life tables exist: cohort life tables and period (or current) life tables. A *cohort life table* shows the mortality experience of all persons born during a particular year, such as 1900.

A *period life table* gives an overview of the present mortality experience of a population and shows projections of future mortality experience. The term *life expectancy* refers to the number of years that a person is expected to live, at any particular year. With respect to a year of interest (e.g., 2000), a period life table enables us to project the future life expectancy of persons born during the year as well as the remaining life expectancy of persons who have attained a certain age. Table 7–3 in Exhibit 7–1 shows an abridged life table for the total U.S. population in 2000. From the table, you can see (column e_x) that the life expectancy at birth (0–1 years) was 76.9 years and at age 79–80 years was 9.1 years. As noted in Chapter 4, life expectancy varies greatly from one country to another. For more information about life table methods, refer to Chernick and Friis.[6]

There are additional ways to describe the mortality experience of the population. One measure, which takes into account the effect of premature death caused by diseases, is known as *years of potential life lost (YPLL)*.[8] For example, we might assume that the average person lives until age 65. If an individual succumbs at age 60, that person has lost five years of life. YPLL is computed by summing years of life lost for each individual in a population such as the United States for a specific cause of mortality (Figure 7–3). Another measure is disabil-

EXHIBIT 7-1

Illustration of a Life Table

Table 7-3   Life Table for the Total Population: United States, 2000 (Abridged)

Age	Probability of dying between ages x to x+1 q_x	Number surviving to age x l_x	Number dying between ages x to x+1 d_x	Person-years lived between ages x to x+1 L_x	Total number of person-years lived above age x T_x	Expectation of life at age x e_x
0–1	0.006930	100,000	693	99,392	7,686,810	76.9
1–2	0.000517	99,307	51	99,281	7,587,418	76.4
2–3	0.000347	99,256	34	99,238	7,488,137	75.4
3–4	0.000243	99,221	24	99,209	7,388,898	74.5
4–5	0.000202	99,197	20	99,187	7,289,689	73.5
5–6	0.000189	99,177	19	99,168	7,190,502	72.5
6–7	0.000177	99,158	18	99,150	7,091,334	71.5
7–8	0.000167	99,141	17	99,132	6,992,185	70.5
8–9	0.000154	99,124	15	99,117	6,893,052	69.5
9–10	0.000137	99,109	14	99,102	6,793,936	68.6
10–11	0.000125	99,095	12	99,089	6,694,833	67.6
11–12	0.000130	99,083	13	99,077	6,595,744	66.6
12–13	0.000170	99,070	17	99,062	6,496,668	65.6
13–14	0.000253	99,053	25	99,041	6,397,606	64.6
14–15	0.000366	99,028	36	99,010	6,298,565	63.6
15–16	0.000491	98,992	49	98,968	6,199,555	62.6
16–17	0.000607	98,943	60	98,913	6,100,587	61.7
17–18	0.000706	98,883	70	98,848	6,001,674	60.7
18–19	0.000780	98,814	77	98,775	5,902,826	59.7
19–20	0.000833	98,736	82	98,695	5,804,051	58.8
20–21	0.000888	98,654	88	98,610	5,705,355	57.8
67–68	0.018933	79,406	1,503	78,655	1,305,916	16.4
68–69	0.020701	77,903	1,613	77,097	1,227,262	15.8
69–70	0.022663	76,290	1,729	75,426	1,150,165	15.1
70–71	0.024673	74,561	1,840	73,641	1,074,739	14.4
71–72	0.026741	72,722	1,945	71,749	1,001,098	13.8
72–73	0.029042	70,777	2,056	69,749	929,349	13.1
73–74	0.031663	68,721	2,176	67,633	859,600	12.5
74–75	0.034588	66,545	2,302	65,395	791,966	11.9
75–76	0.037675	64,244	2,420	63,034	726,571	11.3
76–77	0.040886	61,823	2,528	60,560	663,538	10.7
77–78	0.044437	59,296	2,635	57,978	602,978	10.2
78–79	0.048530	56,661	2,750	55,286	545,000	9.6
79–80	0.053313	53,911	2,874	52,474	489,714	9.1

continues

EXHIBIT 7–1 *continued*

Explanation of the columns of the life table

Column 1—age (x to x + 1): This column shows the age interval between the two exact ages indicated. For instance, "20–21" means the 1-year interval between the 20th and 21st birthdays.

Column 2—Probability of dying (q_x): This column shows the probability of dying between the ages x to x +1. For example, in the age interval 20–21 years, the probability of dying is 0.000888. The "probability of dying" column forms the basis of the life table; all subsequent columns are derived from it.

Column 3—number surviving (l_x): This column shows the number of persons from the original cohort of 100,000 live births, who survive to the beginning of each age interval. For information regarding how this cohort is constructed, refer to the original document. Thus, out of 100,000 persons born alive, 99,307 will complete the first year of life and enter the second; 99,095 will reach age 10; 98,654 will reach age 20; and 53,911 will live to age 79.

Column 4—number dying (d_x): This column shows the number dying in each successive age interval out of the original 100,000 live births. For example, out of 100,000 persons born alive, 693 will die in the first year of life; 88 between ages 20 and 21; and 2,874 will die between ages 79 and 80. Each figure in column 4 is the difference between two successive figures in column 3.

Column 5—Person-years lived (L_x): This column shows the number of person-years lived by the life table cohort within an age interval x to x +1. Each figure in column 5 represents the total time (in years) lived between two indicated birthdays by all those reaching the earlier birthday. Thus, the figure 98,610 for the total population in the age interval 20–21 is the total number of years lived between the 20th and 21st birthdays by the 98,654 (column 3) persons who reached their 20th birthday out of 100,000 persons born alive.

Column 6—Total number of person-years lived (T_x): This column shows the total number of person-years that would be lived after the beginning of the age interval x to x +1 by the life table cohort. For example, the figure 5,705,355 is the total number of years lived after attaining age 20 by the 98,654 persons reaching that age.

Column 7—Expectation of life (e_x): The expectation of life at any given age is the average number of years remaining to be lived by those surviving to that age on the basis of a given set of age-specific rates of dying. Thus, the average remaining lifetime for persons who reach age 20 is 57.8 years.

For more information regarding how the numbers shown in the table are calculated, refer to the original source. ▮

Source: Adapted from Arias E. United States Life Tables, 2000, *National Vital Statistics Reports*, Vol 51, No 3, pp. 2–3, 7–8, 2002, National Center for Health Statistics.

ity-adjusted life years (DALYs), which adds the time a person has a disability to the time lost to early death.[9] Thus, one DALY indicates one year of life lost to the combination of disability and early mortality. Chapter 15 provides additional coverage of DALYs.

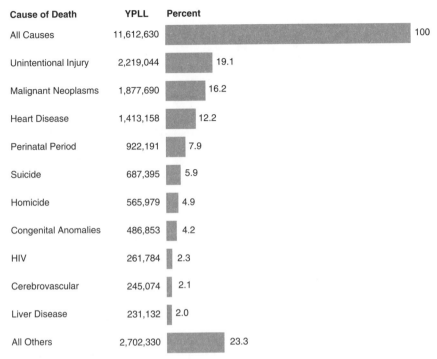

Cause of Death	YPLL	Percent
All Causes	11,612,630	100
Unintentional Injury	2,219,044	19.1
Malignant Neoplasms	1,877,690	16.2
Heart Disease	1,413,158	12.2
Perinatal Period	922,191	7.9
Suicide	687,395	5.9
Homicide	565,979	4.9
Congenital Anomalies	486,853	4.2
HIV	261,784	2.3
Cerebrovascular	245,074	2.1
Liver Disease	231,132	2.0
All Others	2,702,330	23.3

FIGURE 7–3 Years of potential life lost (YPLL) before age 65, 2004 United States, all races, both sexes, all deaths. *Source:* Centers for Disease Control and Prevention, National Center for Injury Prevention and Control, Web-based Injury Statistics Query and Reporting System, WISQARS YPLL Report. Available at: http://webappa.cdc.gov/sasweb /ncipc/ypll10.html. Accessed November 5, 2007.

Survival Curves

In addition to life tables, one of the methods for portraying survival times is to use survival curves. Take the case of a small-scale clinical study. In order to construct a survival curve, the following information would be required about each subject: time of entry into the study, time of death (or other outcome), and status of the patient at that time (either dead or censored, which may mean that the patient is lost to follow-up).

Consider a simple example in which 15 subjects were followed over 36 months and all entered the study at the same time (Figure 7–4).[10] A total of nine subjects died at different points during the study. Each step of the curve indicates the death(s) of one or more patients. The steep drop at 19 months is caused by

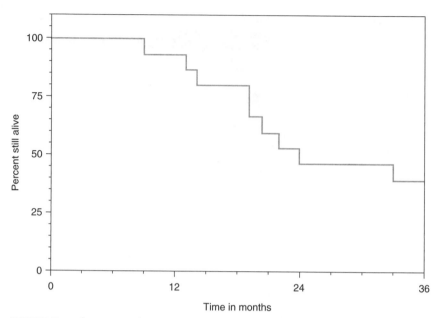

FIGURE 7–4   A simple survival curve. *Source:* Reprinted with permission from Motulsky H. *Intuitive Biostatistics.* New York, NY: Oxford University Press, Inc., 1995. Available at: http://www.graphpad.com/www/book/survive.htm. Accessed October 30, 2007.

the death of two patients. The foregoing section provided an extremely simplified example of a survival curve. In practice, the process of constructing survival curves may be much more complicated. Survival curves have numerous applications in research on infectious diseases, clinical trials, occurrence of psychiatric disorders, and many other situations. For more detailed information, consult Chernick and Friis.[6]

Cohort Studies

The bases for forming a cohort are almost limitless with regard to the unifying feature, but the rationale for studying a particular cohort should be guided by the scientific question of interest, rather than mere availability of a group for study. Also known as a prospective or longitudinal study, a cohort study is distinguished from other observational research designs by the fact that it starts with a group of subjects who lack a positive history of the outcome of interest and are at risk for the outcome. From the standpoint of selecting study groups, cohort studies can be thought of as going from cause to effect. That is, the exposure(s) of interest is(are) determined for each member of the cohort at baseline or time of study; then the group is followed through time to document the incidence of an outcome among the exposed and nonexposed members. Possible outcome measures include the incidence of disease (cohort studies measure disease incidence directly), mortality, health status, and certain biological parameters, which are examined for changes that occur as a result of exposure to a risk factor.

In contrast to other observational designs, an additional characteristic of cohort studies is that they include at least two observation points: one to determine exposure status and eligibility and a second (or more) to determine the number of incident cases that developed during follow-up. This feature (i.e., two or more observation points) permits the calculation of disease rates, which cannot be obtained with only a single time point of observation. In cohort studies, the individual forms the unit of observation and the unit of analysis, as is also true of cross-sectional studies and case-control studies. Cohort studies almost always involve the collection of primary data, although secondary data sources are used sometimes for both exposure and disease assessment.

Sampling and Cohort Formation Options

Although all cohort studies share certain common features, such as measurement of exposure before disease onset and at least two periods of observation, some types of cohort studies differ from one another. We make note of these differences now, because they have implications for the measures of association that can be calculated with the data generated. (Measures of association used in cohort studies will be discussed in more detail in Chapter 9.) One of the differences is the sampling strategy used to define the cohort; these two strategies are population-based samples and exposure-based samples.

Population-Based Cohort Studies

In *population-based cohort studies,* the cohort includes either an entire population or a representative sample of the population. As illustrated in Figure 7–5, a population-based cohort study starts with N; the total of exposed (A + B) and nonexposed (C + D) subjects is determined as part of the research process. Population-based cohorts have been used in studies of coronary heart disease (CHD). Perhaps the best known cohort study of CHD was initiated in 1948 in

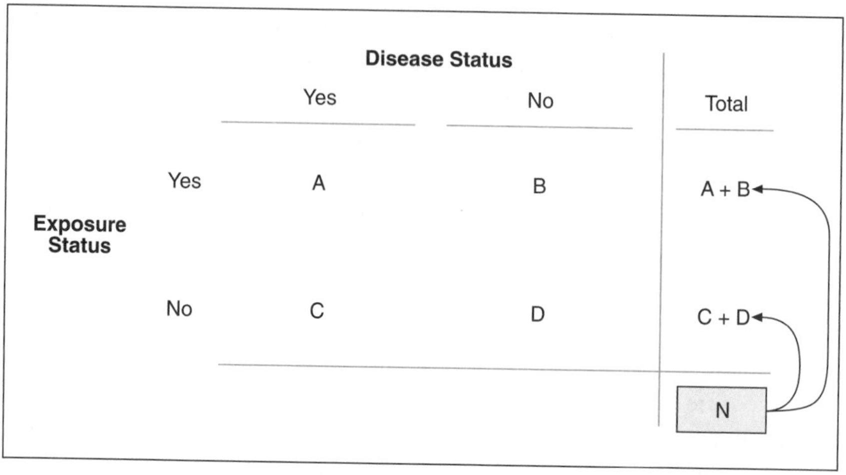

FIGURE 7–5   Illustration of sample selection in a one-sample cohort study.

Framingham, Massachusetts.[11] When the study commenced, the town had a population of 28,000; the study design called for a random sample of 6,500 from the targeted age range of 30 to 59 years. This sample, representative of the population, was followed subsequently for changes in risk factors and incidence of disease.

An example of a cohort based on an entire population comes from the city of Tecumseh, Michigan, which was selected to examine the contribution of environmental and constitutional factors to the maintenance of health and the origins of illness. Begun in 1959–1960, the Tecumseh study successfully enrolled 8,641 persons, 88% of the community residents.[12] For some applications, cohort studies may be larger than a given community. The Iowa Women's Health Study, described earlier in Chapter 3, included a random sample of 41,837[13] women between the ages of 55 and 69 in 1986 in the entire state.

The important point to remember is that these cohorts—Framingham, Tecumseh, and Iowa—were not heterogeneous in terms of their exposures nor were they selected because of a particular exposure (or risk factor) for disease. Consequently, the frequency of the exposures within the cohort was expected to be representative of the target population. Thus, in a population-based cohort study the proportion of the population exposed can be determined either directly (when the entire population has been selected) or indirectly (when a known fraction of the population has been selected). Let us explain how exposure could be determined.

With a population-based cohort, exposures are unknown until the first period of observation when exposure information is collected. For example, after administration of questionnaires, collection of biologic samples, clinical examinations, or physiologic testing, the cohort can be divided into two or more exposure categories as a result of what is learned from the subjects. For a simple dichotomy (i.e., exposed versus nonexposed), the nonexposed subjects become an internal comparison group. Sometimes, exposure may be categorized along a continuum, called a *continuous variable*, which is a type of variable that has an infinite set of possible values within a specified range. (Blood pressure measurements represent a continuous variable, whereas the designation of exposed/nonexposed forms a dichotomy that signifies a discrete variable.) For a continuous variable, such as certain dietary intake measures or blood pressure, one typically constructs multiple levels of exposure. A statistical procedure is used to subdivide the exposure variable into quantiles, which are divisions of a distribution into equal, ordered subgroups[1] (e.g., quartiles or quintiles). These subdivisions are then used to define the levels of exposure. Subjects in one of the extreme categories, such as the upper or lower quintile, serve as the comparison (or referent) category. The incidence rate among this referent category becomes the expected rate of disease occurrence.

Exposure-Based Cohort Studies

One often hears about the touted superiority of population-based studies. Indeed, this sampling feature has benefits regarding generalizability of results and the measures of effect that can be estimated. However, population-based cohort designs (or case-control studies, for that matter) are not efficient for rare exposures. This assertion can be illustrated best with an example. Suppose that experiments with animals provided evidence that exposure to lead causes long-term neurologic toxicity. The amounts of lead used were much greater than those found in most human exposures. Certain occupational groups, however, such as those involved in battery production, might have sufficient occupational exposure to incur significant health risks. Although one could consider using a case-control study, because the proportion of the population employed in the battery manufacturing industry is low, there would likely be few cases or controls with exposure in the study sample. An alternative approach might be to assemble an exposure-based cohort of employees in battery production factories, quantify levels of exposure using job titles and assignments, and determine incidence rates of neurotoxicity.

Comparison (Nonexposed) Group

Cohort studies involve the comparison of disease rates between exposed and nonexposed groups. Continuing with our example of neurotoxicity and lead exposure among workers in the battery manufacturing industry, there are essentially three options in defining the comparison group. First, it may be that certain workers within the industry have no exposure to lead. For example, sales staff, secretaries, and management may have significantly less (or more) exposure to lead than factory workers. Thus, an internal comparison would be possible (exposed vs. nonexposed) within the factory or factories under investigation. However, consider the situation in which everyone in the factory or industry is exposed to lead, and a nonexposed group could not be identified. The second option would therefore be the construction of a nonexposed group from a separate industrial cohort, similar in demographics and geography to the battery factory, but without lead exposure. A third option would be to compare disease rates among workers in the battery manufacturing industry with available population rates. Because population rates are summary rates, however, perhaps only specific to age-, sex-, and race-defined subgroups, they may have limited utility in some situations.

Consider the example of a cohort study of lung cancer among uranium ore miners. Careful attention is paid to collection of data on other exposures that contribute to lung cancer risk, including use of tobacco products and diet. In fact, in this population a high percentage of the cohort consists of current smokers. Population rates of lung cancer, however, are based on the entire population. They are not adjusted for smoking, nor are smoking status-specific rates available. In this situation, because of the smoking levels alone, comparison of lung cancer rates among the miners with population lung cancer rates would not be informative.

Except in certain circumstances, the use of special exposure groups to form study groups precludes determination of the proportion of the target population exposed; as a result this design limits the public health inferences (generalization to a larger population). As shown in Figure 7–6, such designs typically involve select subgroups with known exposures, for example, an exposed cohort (A + B) and a nonexposed, comparison cohort (C + D). Thus, in most situations the cohort members are homogeneous with respect to exposure, and because of the selection procedure, the frequency of exposure in the population cannot be determined.

Additional examples of exposure-based cohorts include:

- Prepaid medical care plans, such as Kaiser Permanente or Group Health of Puget Sound, keep detailed medical information about a potentially large number of readily accessible subjects and maintain regular contact for fol-

		Disease Status		
		Yes	No	Total
Exposure Status	Yes	A	B	A + B
	No	C	D	C + D

FIGURE 7–6 Illustration of sample selection in a multisample cohort study.

low-up information. In this case, the cohort is defined by insurance membership and the exposure of interest may be some medical condition or test recorded in the medical record.

- Physicians, nurses, and other health professionals have been the focus of several cohort studies. Because these individuals typically belong to national organizations (e.g., the American Medical Association), they are often easier to follow over the long term than other occupational groups. Their knowledge of disease makes them good respondents for surveys; they can be expected to report previous medical conditions and recent diagnoses reliably.
- Childhood cancer survivors are becoming increasingly common, due mainly to remarkable improvements in therapy. The Childhood Cancer Survivor Study[14] represents the largest (> 14,000 five-year survivors initially diagnosed between 1970 and 1986 from 25 centers) and most extensively characterized cohort of childhood and adolescent cancer survivors in North America. It serves as a resource for addressing important issues, such as risk of second malignancies, endocrine and reproductive outcome, cardiopulmonary complications, and psychosocial implications, among this unique and ever-growing population.
- Veterans, because of the benefits they receive from the U.S. government, usually remain in contact with the relevant agency, making long-term follow-up feasible.

- College graduates are a final example of special resource groups that have been investigated in several noteworthy epidemiologic studies (later in this chapter we will cover in detail findings from a longitudinal study of Harvard alumni[15]).

Outcome Measures in Cohort Studies

In a previous section, we mentioned that although many cohort studies gather information on the incidence of disease as the principal outcome measure, several other types of outcomes may be assessed. Table 7–4 illustrates types of outcomes used for cohort studies and lists three categories of outcomes: discrete events, levels of disease markers, and changes in disease markers.[16] Discrete events cover single events and multiple occurrences, an example of the former being death and the first occurrence of a disease such as cancer, and the latter referring to repeated occurrence of disease such as recurrent heart disease (heart attacks) or strokes. Examples of discrete measures include the age-standardized annual death rate, annual age-specific death rates, and the cumulative incidence of disease of specific time intervals (e.g., five years).

Cohort studies that include multiple occurrences outcomes involve the repeated assessment of these outcomes over time. The multiple occurrences can involve discrete events, as in the case of repeated heart attacks or changes in sta-

---

Table 7–4 Types of Outcomes for Cohort Studies

Discrete events
  Single events
    Mortality
    First occurrence of a disease or health-related outcome
      Incidence (density)
      Cumulative incidence (risk)
      Ratios (incidence density and cumulative incidence)
  Multiple occurrences:
    Of disease outcome
    Of transitions between states of health/disease
    Of transitions between functional states
Level of a marker for disease or state of health
Change in a functional/physiologic/biochemical/anatomical marker for disease or health
  Rate of change
    Patterns of growth and/or decline
    "Tracking" of markers of disease/health
  Change in level with time (age)

Source: Adapted with permission from Tager IB. Outcomes in cohort studies. *Epidemiologic Reviews.* 1998, Vol 20, p. 16.

tus of outcome markers. Research questions may address the association between changes in risk markers over time and health status, studies of the effects of aging on the natural history of disease, and transitions of health status, such as the shift to functional disability among some elderly persons.

Temporal Differences in Cohort Designs

Although the basic feature of all cohort studies is measurement of exposure and follow-up for disease, there are several variations in cohort designs that depend on the timing of data collection on exposure and outcomes. These variations are prospective and retrospective cohort studies.

Prospective Cohort Studies

A *prospective cohort study* is purely prospective in nature and is characterized by determination of exposure levels at baseline (the present) and follow-up for occurrence of disease at some time in the future (Figure 7–7). The sampling strategy may be population-based or defined by a special exposure of interest. There are numerous advantages to prospective studies:

- Prospective cohort studies enable the investigator to collect data on exposures. The collection of exposure information at baseline may result in the most direct and specific test of the study hypothesis. Examples include assessment of diet, physical activity, alcohol use, occupation, coping skills, and quality of life, each of which can be assessed with a few specific items or a comprehensive battery of items.

Design	Past	Present	Future
Prospective		E ⟶	D
Retrospective	E ⟶	D	
Historical prospective	E ⟶	E ⟶	D

FIGURE 7–7 Cohort design options on timing of data collection. E, exposure; D, disease.

- The size of the cohort to be recruited is under greater control by the investigators than is the size of a retrospective cohort (see next section). Cohort studies that rely on historical records are sometimes fixed in size.
- Biological and physiological assays can be performed with decreased concern that the outcome will be affected by the underlying disease process. Examples include measures of serum factors or nutrient levels, and medical examinations (e.g., specific functional tests, antibody titers, or cholesterol levels).
- Direct measures of the environment (e.g., indoor radon levels, electromagnetic field radiation, cigarette smoke concentration, or chlorination byproducts in the water supply) can be made in order to define exposures precisely.

Retrospective Cohort Study

Despite the substantial benefits of prospective cohort studies, investigators must wait for cases to accrue while conducting such a study. Depending upon the size of the cohort and the prevalence of a disease in the population, several years could elapse before meaningful analyses are feasible. An alternative is a *retrospective cohort study* that makes use of historical data to determine exposure level at some baseline in the past; "follow-up" for subsequent occurrences of disease between baseline and the present is performed. A design that makes use of both retrospective (to determine baseline exposure) and prospective (to determine disease incidence in the future) features is the *historical prospective cohort study* (also known as an *ambispective cohort study*).

There are several advantages to retrospective cohort studies:

- In a relatively short period of time, a significant amount of follow-up data may be accrued. For example, Sellers et al.[17] performed a follow-up beginning in 1991 of a cohort of 426 families originally ascertained between 1944 and 1952 at the Dight Institute of Genetics at the University of Minnesota. Three-generation pedigrees were constructed at baseline with data collected from mothers, aunts, sisters, and daughters of breast cancer patients. Records of breastfeeding, reproductive history, and validated occurrences of cancer were stored. Thus, when the family members were recontacted and interviewed regarding subsequent occurrences of cancer, almost 50 years of follow-up was completed during a five-year period of funding.

● The amount of exposure data collected can be quite extensive and can be available to the investigator at minimal cost. For example, Hartmann and colleagues[18] at the Mayo Clinic, using an index of surgical procedures, were able to construct a cohort of women who received prophylactic mastectomy between 1963 and 1986. Details were available in the medical record on type of surgery, age at surgery, family history of cancer, and complications following surgery. Follow-up through 1997 was performed to identify subsequent occurrences of breast cancer. Analyses based on a median 14 years of follow-up were possible, even though the actual study took less than five years to complete.

Many beginning epidemiology students find the distinction between case-control studies and retrospective cohort studies difficult to grasp. The nuances may be subtle but are noteworthy. Recall that case-control studies begin with ascertainment of study subjects on the basis of disease status. Data are then collected regarding exposures that occurred prior to disease onset. Because there is only one time point of observation, there is no longitudinal component and disease rates cannot be computed. Retrospective cohort studies begin with exposure, although these measurements occurred sometime in the past. The subsequent occurrence of disease, perhaps supplemented with additional exposure assessments, is the primary focus of research activity. A retrospective cohort study incorporates an entire cohort of study subjects, whereas a case-control study involves identified cases and controls only.

Practical Considerations

Given the considerable advantages of cohort studies over other observational study designs, some readers may wonder why cohort studies are not the only designs used. In this next section, we provide a brief answer under the unifying theme of practical considerations. Such considerations include availability of exposure data, size and cost of the cohort used, data collection and data management, follow-up issues, and sufficiency of scientific justification.

Availability of Exposure Data

Although development of prospective cohort studies may leverage data collected for other reasons besides the cohort study itself, the quality and extent of historical exposure data are absolutely essential for retrospective cohort studies. In most situations, investigators will find themselves trying to weigh the trade-offs between a retrospective study design—with its associated benefits of more immediate follow-up time—versus the value of collecting the primary exposure data in the most ideal manner in a prospective cohort design. There are no simple rules to guide this decision, which must be carefully evaluated for each particular research question.

Size and Cost of the Cohort

From a scientific standpoint there is little question that the larger the size of the cohort, the greater the opportunity to obtain answers in a timely manner. For a fixed rate of disease or outcome, only by increasing the denominator can the number of cases be increased during an interval. Of course, there is a direct relationship between size and cost, and resource constraints typically influence design decisions. One approach to design cohorts with the greatest future value is to focus initial development on the collection of risk factor data and biological samples, with subsequent (future) or parallel (nested studies) grants to obtain funding for analyses of the samples. For example, Zheng and colleagues[19] obtained funding to establish the Shanghai Women's Cohort Study of 75,000 women by limiting activities during the first five years to collection of diet and risk factor data, blood samples, tissue blocks, and urine samples. To keep costs within funding limits, initial aims did not focus on assays of the biological specimens. Subsequent renewal of the funding for that study was obtained to begin testing hypotheses related to hormone metabolism (urine), growth factor levels (serum), and genetic polymorphisms (DNA from lymphocytes in the blood).

Data Collection and Data Management

An axiom of epidemiologic research design is that larger studies necessarily are more demanding than smaller ones with regard to challenges in data collection and data management. Coordination of activities in the field is especially complex when multiple sites are necessary for recruitment. Additional challenges may arise from data entry, especially if individual sites enter their own data for transmittal to the coordinating center. In these situations, explicit protocols for quality control (e.g., double entry of data, and scannable forms) should be considered in the design and implementation stage. The organizational and administrative burdens are increased even further when there are multiple levels of data collection (such as telephone interviews, mail-out questionnaires, consent forms to access medical records, and collection of biological samples) at multiple time periods (especially when active follow-up is needed). Cohort study research protocols may require elaborate data-management systems to monitor the status of the various components of data collection. Such management systems support individuals in the field who are charged with the multifaceted components as well as study managers and investigators who monitor overall progress. Management of data from cohort studies can be incredibly challenging and should be considered when staffing needs are being defined. Challenges arise from data collected from multiple sources, merging of files, and "cleaning" of data files. Cleaning is necessary in the case of missing values, out-of-range entries, and inconsistencies (e.g., someone responds that they never smoke but subsequently report a habit of 2 packs per day). These issues are not peculiar to cohort studies, because cross-sectional surveys and case-control studies can be quite large, too. However, the relative inefficiency of cohort studies for investigation of rare diseases means that they are typically larger than other designs.

Follow-up Issues

The value of cohort studies can be realized only if an effective system can be implemented to follow the cohort for subsequent occurrence of disease or other outcomes. It may be helpful at this time to distinguish between active versus passive follow-up.

Active follow-up denotes the situation in which the investigator, through direct contact with the cohort, must obtain data on subsequent incidence of the outcome (disease, change in risk factor, change in biological marker). Such contact may be accomplished through follow-up mailings, phone calls, or written invitations to return to study sites/centers for subsequent medical evaluation and, in some cases, biospecimen collection. Follow-up requires a substantial amount of effort, especially for large cohorts. For instance, the Minnesota Breast Cancer Family Study[20] follows up on study participants with a mailed survey, a reminder postcard 30 days later, a second survey, and a telephone call to nonresponders. In the present era of telephone technology—answering machines, caller identification, and automated telemarketing solicitations—active follow-up is becoming increasingly labor intensive and oftentimes frustrating, especially in our mobile society where addresses change often. For some cohort studies, however, a persistent and labor-intensive effort is the only option for follow-up.

Contrast the foregoing scenario with passive follow-up, which does not require direct contact with cohort members. Passive follow-up is possible when databases containing the outcomes of interest are collected and maintained by organizations outside the investigative team. Epidemiologists sometimes are able to achieve record linkage between databases and the study cohort. An excellent example amenable to passive follow-up is cancer, for which the federal and many state governments mandate reporting. The Iowa Women's Health Study[13] (described earlier in Chapter 3) is able to conduct follow-up for cancer incidence within the state in this manner.

Passive follow-up is clearly not an option for many diseases. The only endpoint for which there is universal coverage is death; the National Center for Health Statistics collects mortality data, which are made available to the scientific community through the National Death Index (NDI). The success of linkage to the NDI depends upon the extent of demographic information collected on participants. Social Security numbers are the most effective data element for linkage. If Social Security numbers are unavailable, record linkage sometimes is possible for persons who have uncommon last names.

Sufficiency of Scientific Justification

The preceding sections emphasized that the establishment of a cohort study requires major investments in resources (time, money, and energy). Thus, there should be considerable scientific rationale for a cohort study. This rationale should be grounded on prior research from various perspectives: study designs other than cohort studies; several different investigators; and several different study populations. Additional justification for cohort studies may come from laboratory experiments or animal studies. Furthermore, the situation in which investigators would like to explore more than one outcome from a particular exposure provides one of the greatest justifications for a cohort study. Because of the nature of case-control studies, only a single outcome can be investigated at a time. Cohort studies are the only observational study design that permits examination of multiple outcomes at the level of the individual within a single study. Consider as an example the complex issue of hormone replacement therapy (HRT). Numerous epidemiologic studies have noted that HRT is associated with a slight, but detectable, increased risk of breast cancer. In fact, recommendations have been published in leading medical journals for the avoidance of HRT among women at elevated risk of breast cancer because of a family history.[19] Complicating such a recommendation is the observation from other epidemiologic studies that have associated HRT with a number of health benefits, including lower risks of CHD,[21,22] osteoporosis,[23,24] and Alzheimer's disease (AD).[25] However, a study published in mid-2003 reported increased rates of dementia among older women on combination hormone replacement therapy (see box). The pros and cons of HRT use can be examined within an appropriately designed cohort study[26] with measures of HRT collected at baseline and a follow-up protocol designed to collect data on the multiple outcomes of interest.

Hormone Replacement Therapy

Rates of Dementia Increase Among Older Women on Combination Hormone Therapy

Older women taking combination hormone therapy had twice the rate of dementia, including Alzheimer's disease (AD), compared with women who did not take the medication, according to new findings from a memory substudy of the Women's Health Initiative (WHI). The research, part of the Women's Health Initiative Memory study (WHIMS) and reported in the May 28, 2003, *Journal of the American Medical Association* (JAMA), found the heightened risk of developing dementia in a study of women 65 and older taking Prempro™, a particular form of estrogen plus progestin hormone therapy.

The study also found that the combination therapy did not protect against the development of Mild Cognitive Impairment, or MCI, a form of cognitive decline less severe than dementia.

'Because of possible harm in some areas and lack of a demonstrated benefit in others, we have concluded that combination hormone therapy should not be prescribed at this time for older, postmenopausal women to maintain or improve cognitive function,' says . . . [a government official affiliated with the National Institutes of Health]. ■

Source: Reprinted from National Institutes of Health, National Institute on Aging. *NIH News,* May 27, 2003. Available at: http://www.nih.gov/news/pr/may2003/nia-27.htm. Accessed October 29, 2007.

Measures of Interpretation and Examples

In the simplest case of two levels of exposure (yes/no), two incidence rates are calculated. The relative risk is defined as the ratio of the risk of disease or death among the exposed, to the risk among the unexposed.[1] Recall from Chapter 3 that risk is estimated in epidemiologic studies only by the cumulative incidence.

When the relative risk is calculated with incidence rates or incidence density, then the term *rate ratio* is more precise.

$$\text{Relative risk} = \frac{\text{Incidence rate in the exposed}}{\text{Incidence rate in the nonexposed}}$$

Using the notation from the 2 by 2 table (Figure 6–1), the relative risk can be expressed as $[A/(A + B)] \div [C/(C + D)]$. A sample calculation is shown in Exhibit 7–2.

Some comments regarding interpretation of relative risk are in order. A relative risk of 1.0 implies that the risk (rate) of disease among the exposed is no different from the risk of disease among the nonexposed. A relative risk of 2.0 implies that risk is twice as high, whereas a relative risk of 0.5 indicates that the exposure of interest is associated with half the risk of disease.

EXHIBIT 7–2

Sample Problem: Relative Risk

The following is an example of how to use a fourfold table for calculation of relative risk. Deykin and Buka[27] studied suicide ideation and attempts in a population of chemically dependent adolescents believed by the researchers to be a group at high risk for self-destructive behavior. Boys who had been exposed to physical or sexual abuse and who stated that a report of abuse or neglect had been filed with authorities were more likely than boys who were absent such exposures to have made a suicide attempt. The data for history of sexual abuse among the boys are charted below:

History of Sexual Abuse	Suicide Attempt	No Suicide Attempt	Totals
Yes	A = 14	B = 9	A + B = 23
No	C = 49	D = 149	C + D = 198

Relative risk (14/23)/(49/198) = 0.609/0.247 = 2.46

Source: Data from Deykin EY, Buka SL. 1994. Suicidal ideation and attempts among chemically dependent adolescents. *American Journal of Public Health.* Vol 84, pp. 634–639; American Public Health Association, © 1994. The fourfold table was constructed by the authors from these data and from the percentage of suicide attempts reported for boys with a positive history and boys with a negative history of sexual abuse. Deykin and Buka reported 60.9% and 24.8% attempting suicide, respectively, and a relative risk of 2.4.

Examples of Cohort Studies

Table 7–5 presents examples of major cohort studies, including when they were initiated, their main focus, study population, measurement of exposure at baseline and follow-up, and frequency of exposure follow-up. More detailed coverage of some of these studies is provided in this chapter and throughout the text. Exhibit 7–3 showcases four cohort studies that concern women's health.

The remainder of this section provides examples of cohort studies built upon a common research theme: physical activity and CHD. The idea that physical activity is beneficial to humans is certainly not a new one. In *The Dialogues*, Timeus tells Socrates that, "Moderate exercise reduces to order, according to their affinities, the particles and affections which are wandering about the body."[28(p. 405)] Two thousand years later, experts still are unable to agree on how much or how often exercise is needed or whether habitual physical activity (as opposed to exercise) is sufficient to maintain one's health. The rediscovery of the potential importance of physical activity was spurred by a landmark study of British transportation workers by Morris and colleagues in 1953.[29] Hoping to uncover "social factors which may be favourable or unfavourable to its occurrence,"[29(p. 1053)] the investigators conducted a study of roughly 31,000 men aged 35 to 64. Rates of angina pectoris, coronary thrombosis, and sudden death were obtained for drivers, conductors, and underground railway workers. Conductors, whose job was physically more demanding than that of the other two groups, had significantly lower rates of CHD. The proposition that physical activity might be protective generated tremendous interest and spurred numerous investigations to confirm and refine the hypothesis.

The first example is a retrospective cohort study of railroad workers.[30] The cohort included 191,609 railroad industry employees in the United States between the ages of 40 and 64.[30] The "exposure" was work-related physical activity. Based on job descriptions, three groups were formed: clerks, switchmen, and section men, with activity levels of low, moderate, and heavy, respectively. With any cohort study that entails long periods of follow-up, a legitimate concern is whether exposures at the baseline period change over time, resulting in exposure misclassification. One advantage of using the railroad industry for this study was that the labor contracts between management and the brotherhoods contained seniority provisions that prevented a man from carrying his seniority from one job to another job controlled by a separate brotherhood. Because seniority brings benefits in terms of privileges and income, job changes associated with a switch to a different labor contract were uncommon. Follow-up for CHD end points was accomplished through the Railroad Retirement Board, which maintained an

Table 7-5   Examples of Major Cohort Studies

Study [Year Begun]	Main Focus	Study Population [Sample Size]	Baseline Exposure Instruments*	Follow-Up Exposure Instruments*	Frequency of Exposure Follow-up
The Framingham Heart Study [1948]	Risk factors for cardiovascular disease	Residents of Framingham, MA, ages 28–62 years [n = 5,209]	Interview, clinic examination (PE, lab, tests)	Interview, clinic examination (PE, lab, tests)	Every 2 years
Colorado Plateau Uranium Miners Study [1950]	Occupational risk factors for cancer	White, male underground uranium miners, Colorado Plateau [n = 3,415]	Clinic examination (PE), questionnaire, environmental measures (airborne radiation)	Questionnaire (in-person or mailed), environmental measures (airborne radiation)	Triennial
American Cancer Society: Cancer Prevention Study 1 [1959]	Cigarette smoking and cancer mortality	U.S. men and women aged 30 years and older [n = 1,045,087]	Self-administered questionnaire delivered by volunteers	Self-administered questionnaire	Every 2 years
The Alameda County Study [1965]	Factors associated with health and mortality	Residents of Alameda County, CA, ages 16–94 years [n = 6,928]	Mailed questionnaire; telephone interview or home interview of nonrespondents	Mailed questionnaire; telephone interview or home interview of nonrespondents	At years 9, 18, and 29
Honolulu Heart Program 12 [1965]	Coronary heart disease and stroke in men of Japanese ancestry	Men of Japanese ancestry living on Oahu, HI, ages 45–65 years [n = 8,006]	Mailed questionnaire, interview, clinic examination (PE, lab, tests)		
The Oral Contraception Study of the Royal College of General Practitioners [1968]	Oral contraceptive use and cancer	Married premenopausal British women [n = 47,000]	Medical form completed by physician based on patient interview or medical record	Same	Every 6 months
Nurses' Health Study [1976]	Originally oral contraceptive use and cancer, expanded to women's health	Married female U.S. registered nurses ages 30–55 years [n = 121,700]	Mailed questionnaire	Mailed questionnaire Lab (toenail sample) Lab (home blood draw)	Every 2 years At year 6 At year 13

continues

Study	Topic	Population	Measures (baseline)	Measures (follow-up)	Schedule
Port Pirie Cohort Study [1979]	Lead exposure and child development	Infants born in Port Pirie, South Australia, 1979–1982 [n = 723]	Lab (blood samples from pregnant mother and umbilical cord at birth)	Lab (blood samples)	At 6,15, and 24 months, annually up to 7 years, and at 11–13 years
Multicenter AIDS Cohort Study [1984]	Risk factors for HIV in gay men	U.S. homosexual men ages 18–70 years [n = 4,954]	Clinic examination (PE, lab), self-administered questionnaire, interview	Clinic examination (PE, lab), self-administered questionnaire, interview	Every 6 months
Coronary Artery Risk Development in Young Adults (CARDIA) [1985]	Risk factors for coronary heart disease in young adults	Black and white U.S. men and women ages 18–30 years [n = 5,115]	Telephone interview, clinic examination (PE, lab, tests), self-administered questionnaire, interview	Clinic examination (PE, lab, tests), self-administered questionnaire, interview	At years 2, 5, and 7
New York University Women's Health Study [1985]	Endogenous hormones and risk of breast cancer	New York women ages 35–65 years [n = 14,291]	Lab, self-administered questionnaire	Lab	Annual
Iowa Women's [Health] Study [1986]	Cancer in women	Iowa women ages 55–69 years [n = 41,837]	Mailed questionnaire with self body girth measures	None	
Study of Osteoporotic Fractures [1986]	Risk factors for fractures	Nonblack U.S. women aged 65 years and older [n = 9,704]	Questionnaire, clinic examination (PE, tests), abstraction (medication labels)	Questionnaire / Clinic examination (PE, tests)	Year 1 / Year 2
Cardiovascular Health Study (CHS) [1989]	Risk factors for cardiovascular disease in older adults	U.S. men and women aged 65 years and older [n = 5,201]	Home interview, clinic examination (PE, lab, tests), questionnaire, abstraction (medication labels)	Clinic examination (PE, tests), questionnaire, abstraction (medication labels) / Clinic examination (lab) and all of above	Annual / Triennial

continues

Table 7-5 *continued*

Study [Year Begun]	Main Focus	Study Population [Sample Size]	Baseline Exposure Instruments*	Follow-Up Exposure Instruments*	Frequency of Exposure Follow-up
Women's Health Initiative (WHI) Observational Study [1994]	Women's health	U.S. women, ages 50–79 years [n = 100,000]	Telephone interview, clinic examination (PE, lab, tests), interview, self-administered questionnaire, abstraction (medication labels)	Mailed questionnaire Clinic examination (PE, lab, tests), abstraction (medication labels), self-administered questionnaire	Annual At year 3

*Exposure instruments definitions: PE, physical examination or physical measures, such as anthropometrics, strength, etc.; lab, measures in blood and other specimens; tests, medical tests, such as electrocardiography, treadmill, bone mineral density, etc.; abstraction, abstraction of medication information from medication labels, medical record abstraction; environmental measures, measures in the environment (air or water); questionnaire, either self-administered or interviewer-administered (not explicitly stated); and interview, interviewer-administered questionnaire.

Source: Adapted with permission from White E, Hunt JR, Casso D. Exposure measurement in cohort studies: the challenges of prospective data collection. *Epidemiologic Reviews*, Vol 20, No 1, pp. 44–45, 1998.

EXHIBIT 7-3

Four Cohort Studies That Investigate Women's Health

Nurses' Health Study: Affiliated investigators, housed at Brigham and Women's Hospital in Boston, mailed questionnaires beginning in 1976 to 170,000 nurses who resided in the 11 most populous U.S. states. Nurses (approximately $n = 122,000$ responding) were selected because they were knowledgeable about the technically worded questionnaire items and motivated to remain over the long term in the cohort study. The aim of Frank Speizer, the study's originator, was to examine the long-term potential consequences of use of oral contraceptives. Mailed every two years, the original questionnaire searched for the occurrence of various diseases and also probed health-related topics, such as smoking, hormone use, and menopausal issues. A later phase of the project initiated in 1980 was expanded to include diet and quality of life topics. A subset of the cohort submitted toenail samples (used for mineral analyses) and blood samples, employed in studies of biomarkers. In 1989, Dr. Walter Willett started the Nurses' Health Study II, which focused on oral contraceptive use, diet, and lifestyle risk factors in a population younger that the original Nurses' Health Study cohort. The Nurses' Health Study has generated an impressive list of scientific publications and many fundamental contributions to the store of health knowledge.[1]

Women's Health Initiative (WHI): The WHI, begun in 1991, concentrates on the major causes of death, disability, and frailty among postmenopausal women: coronary heart disease, breast and colorectal cancer, and osteoporotic fractures. Two major goals of the WHI are to provide estimates of the extent to which known risk factors predict heart disease, cancers, and fractures and to identify new risk factors for these and other diseases in women. One of the largest preventive studies of its kind in the United States, the WHI lasted 15 years. The WHI encompassed three major components: a randomized clinical trial for disease prevention, a study of community approaches to developing healthful behaviors, and an observational study (OS). The OS followed more than 93,000 postmenopausal women between the ages of 50 to 79 over an average of nine years. The respondents completed periodic health forms and visited a

continues

EXHIBIT 7–3 *continued*

clinic three years after enrollment.[2] The data and stored biological specimens collected from study participants are expected to serve as a resource for continued analyses. The WHI Extension Study currently is funded through 2010.[3]

Study of Osteoporotic Fractures: From September 1986 to October 1987, this prospective cohort study enrolled 9,704 women aged 65 years of age and older. Subjects were selected from the rosters of four clinical centers: The Kaiser-Permanente Center for Health Research, Portland, OR; the University of Minnesota, Minneapolis; the University of Maryland, Baltimore; and the University of Pittsburgh. The University of California, San Francisco, acted as the research coordinating center. Investigators administered questionnaires, interviews, and examinations to obtain information on anthropometric characteristics, estrogen use, and medical history. Follow-up measures included the incidence of fractures, validated by radiographic reports.[4]

Iowa Women's Health Study: See Chapter 3, Exhibit 3–2. ▪

Sources: Adapted from [1]http://www.channing.Harvard.edu/nhs/, accessed October 29, 2007; [2]http://www.nhlbi.nih.gov/whi/, accessed October 29, 2007; [3]The Women's Health Initiative, *WHI Matters*, Vol 11, 2006, p. 1; [4]Sellmeyer DE, Stone KL, Sebastian A, et al. A high ratio of dietary animal to vegetable protein increases the rate of bone loss and the risk of fracture in postmenopausal women. *American Journal of Clinical Nutrition.* 2001;73:118–122.

account for each man employed by any interstate railroad in the United States. Because the retirement and disability benefits to members were greater than those received from Social Security, follow-up rates were high. Members' deaths that were not detected by the board occurred almost exclusively among men who left the industry completely; the investigators estimated that this number was only 11 to 12 per 1,000 workers.

Average annual age-adjusted mortality rates of CHD per 1,000 men were calculated among men who had accumulated 10 years of service by the end of 1951 and were employed in 1954. Mortality rates per 1,000 were 5.7, 3.9, and 2.8 for clerks, switchmen, and section men, respectively. If one considers the rates among the sedentary clerks as the reference, then the relative risk of CHD death for the moderately active switchmen was 0.68, and 0.49 for the very active section men.

Although the study findings supported the hypothesis that physical activity is protective for CHD, there were some limitations inherent in the historical exposure data. In this particular situation, few data were available on other risk factors that might underlie the observed association. For example, no information was available about smoking, body mass index, blood pressure, family history of CHD, and hypertension. Therefore, additional studies were warranted.

The second example is of an ambispective (or historical prospective) cohort study. Reported by Paffenbarger and colleagues in 1984,[15] the study examined a history of athleticism and CHD in a cohort of male Harvard alumni from 1916 to 1950 (N = 16,936). Exposure assessments occurred at two time periods: a historical measure of physical activity based on college archives of student health and athletics, and a questionnaire mailed in 1962 or 1966 for which the response rate was 70%. The alumni questionnaire assessed post-college physical exercise, other elements of lifestyle, health status, and histories of parental disease. The assessment of physical activity included the number of stairs climbed per day, the number of city blocks or equivalent walked each day, and sports actively played (in hours per week). Responses were used to estimate kilocalories of energy expenditure per week. Follow-up of the cohort was achieved through questionnaires mailed in 1972 by the alumni office. The first questionnaire ascertained self-reports of physician-diagnosed CHD events. The second questionnaire, mailed in the same year to the survivors of the deceased cohort members, ascertained dates of death. Weekly updates of death lists by the alumni office provided the means to obtain death certificates for causes. To account for the varying amount of follow-up, person-years of observation were calculated. Heart attack rates were computed according to activity level as a student and as an alumnus. Men who participated in fewer than five hours per week of intramural sports as a student and fewer than 500 kilocalories per week of leisure time activity as an alumnus were designated as the reference group (85.5 per 10,000 person-years). Men who were college varsity athletes but became sedentary as adults had the same rate of first CHD attacks (relative risk, 1.0) as the reference group. In contrast, men who were active as adults (2,000+ kilocalories per week) had a much-reduced risk of CHD, regardless of whether they had been sedentary or active as students.

The third and final example study is purely prospective in nature. Peters et al.[31] designed a study to address one of the major concerns of the previous body of literature on the subject of physical activity (occupational or leisure). Most occupational physical activity is not of sufficient intensity or duration to affect cardiorespiratory fitness. Exercise physiologists argued that physical fitness, not physical activity, was the appropriate and relevant exposure. A cohort of 2,779 firefighters and police officers in Los Angeles County between the ages of 35 and 55 was established. In contrast to the two previous studies, which based exposure levels on job title or questionnaires, level of physical work capacity was determined by use of a bicycle ergometer. The cohort was divided into two exposure categories based on a median split (the 50% point in a distribution). Measurements were taken also on a number of other risk factors, including blood pressure, relative weight, family history, cholesterol, and skinfold measurements. Follow-up for heart attacks was accomplished using county workers' compensation files, death certificates, and medical records; person-years of observation were tabulated. Because heart attacks and an expensive hospital stay were fully reimbursable by insurance, coverage was thought to be complete. Analyses were performed to control for smoking, obesity, blood pressure, cholesterol, family history, relative weight, and physical activity. Results suggested that the least physically fit had more than a twofold greater risk of heart attacks than the most physically fit. Risk was especially prominent (relative risk, 6.6) for those who had at least two additional risk factors (smoking, high serum cholesterol, or high blood pressure).

Nested Case-Control Studies

Although this section would seem to be more logically placed with Chapter 6 (case-control studies), an understanding of nested case-control studies requires an understanding of cohort studies. A *nested case-control study* is defined as a type of case-control study ". . . in which cases and controls are drawn from the population in a cohort study."[1] For example, suppose we have data from an ongoing cohort study of the relationship between use of birth control pills and breast cancer. The population of the cohort study would comprise both exposed and nonexposed persons; the former and latter would consist of women who do and do not take birth control pills, respectively. To perform a nested case-control study, the investigator would select a subset of the population from the cohort study; this subset would comprise the controls. The cases of breast cancer identified from the cohort study would comprise the cases in the case-control study. Figure 7–8 contrasts a cohort study with a nested case-control study.

What are the advantages of a nested case-control study? This design provides a degree of control over confounding factors, because exposure information and other data have been collected during the course of the cohort study. Another

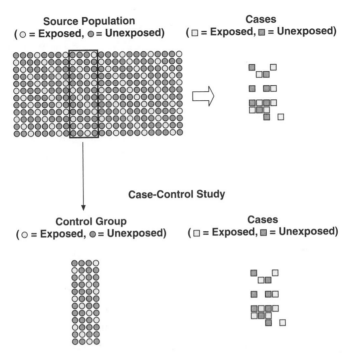

FIGURE 7–8 Illustration of cohort and nested case-control studies. *Source:* Reprinted with permission from Rothman KJ. *Epidemiology: An Introduction.* New York: NY: Oxford University Press; 2002, p. 74.

advantage relates to the reduced cost of collecting detailed exposure information from a subset of the cohort only; this procedure obviously would be less costly than obtaining information from every single person in the cohort.

An example of a nested case-control study is an investigation of suicide among electric utility workers. The study examined the association between exposure to extremely low-frequency magnetic fields and suicide.[32] Cases (536 deaths from suicide) and controls (*n* = 5,248) were selected from a cohort of 138,905 male utility workers. Findings supported an association between occupational exposure to electromagnetic fields and suicide.

A second example comes from Dearden et al.,[33] who conducted a case-control study that aimed to identify factors associated with teen fatherhood. Data came from the National Child Development Study, a longitudinal investigation of all children born in Great Britain between March 3 and March 9, 1958. This type of design, in which a subset of members from a larger cohort study is selected for analysis, was a nested case-control study. Data were collected at birth and at 7, 11, 16, and 23 years of age[34]; information about fatherhood status was available on 5,997 males. Cases were defined as teens who had fathered a child before their 20th birthday ($n = 209$). Controls, selected from the same follow-up group, were divided into two groups: 844 nonteen fathers (those who became fathers between the ages of 20 and 23), and 798 nonfathers (those who had no children by age 23). Teen fathers were found to be three times as likely as nonfathers to engage in lawbreaking behavior and to be absent from school, three to four times as likely to show signs of aggression, and eight times as likely to leave school at age 16.

Summary of Cohort Studies

Cohort studies have several clearly identified strengths. The cohort study is the first observational study design covered that permits direct determination of risk. Because one starts with disease-free subjects, this design provides stronger evidence of an exposure-disease association than the case-control scheme. In addition, cohort studies provide evidence about lag time between exposure and disease. In comparison with case-control studies, which have a greater potential for error, cohort studies facilitate generalization of findings. A tremendous advantage of cohort studies is that, if properly designed and executed, they allow examination of multiple outcomes. While case-control studies may not be efficient for exposures that are rare in the population, cohort studies are able to increase the efficiency for rare exposures by selecting cohorts with known exposures (such as certain occupational groups).

The main limitation of cohort studies, at least for those that are purely prospective, is that they take considerable effort to conduct. Because they are almost always larger than case-control studies, more time is required to collect the exposure information. Additional time passes while one waits for the outcomes to occur. The amount of time required to accumulate sufficient end points for meaningful analysis can be reduced by increasing the size of the cohort, but this increase has to be balanced against the longer time to assemble and measure the cohort as well as the increased financial costs. Given the large size of cohort studies and the need for multiple observation points, they are more difficult to implement and carry out than other observational designs, especially for rare diseases. Loss to follow-up can be a significant problem, limiting the sample size for analysis and raising questions about the results if loss is too high. With long-term follow-up, some exposures may change over time. This misclassification of exposure would attenuate the estimates of the relative risk. It is even conceivable that participation in the study itself may lead to changes in exposure. For example, suppose the investigator recruits a cohort to study the association of dietary fat and disease. As a result of participation, subjects' motivation to learn more about the hypothesis may subsequently lead to adoption of a low-fat diet. Ethical issues arise if good data already indicate that a particular exposure is harmful and one does nothing to intervene with at-risk subjects. Despite these limitations, the cohort study design is an important and valuable tool. For an in-depth coverage of cohort studies, refer to Samet and Munoz.[35]

Comparisons of Observational Designs

Chapters 6 and 7 have covered all of the major types of observational study designs used in public health practice. Table 7–6 summarizes these designs by giving a comparison of their characteristics, advantages, and disadvantages.

Conclusion

Chapter 7 has covered the cohort study, one of the most powerful epidemiologic study designs. We noted that cohort studies overcome many of the problems associated with temporality of data collection and rare exposures. Both the term cohort and the method of cohort analysis were defined. We provided several examples of cohort analyses, including Frost's tabular data on tuberculosis mortality. Related to cohort analyses are life tables and survival curves, which, respectively, estimate and graphically portray survival (often of patients in clinical trials) over time.

The remainder of the chapter focused on methods associated with cohort studies. Population-based cohort studies were distinguished from exposure-based cohort studies. We also presented methods for the selection of comparison groups in cohort studies. Other issues included types of outcome measures, temporal differences in designs, and practical considerations in the operation of cohort studies. Relative risk, a measure of interpretation, was defined and illustrated. Finally, the chapter concluded with many examples of cohort studies, a review of the related topic of nested case-control studies, and a comparison of OS designs.

Table 7-6   Comparisons of Observational Study Designs

		Name of Study Design		
Study Attribute	**Ecologic**	**Cross-Sectional**	**Case-Control**	**Cohort**
Type of Study	Descriptive and analytic	Descriptive	Analytic	Analytic
Number of Observations	Single point of observation (ecologic comparison study)	Single point of observation. Collect exposure and disease histories simultaneously.	Single point of observation.	Outcome determined prospectively. Exposure determined at baseline.
Information on Directionality of Exposure	Usually unknown	Unknown whether disease or exposure came first.	Exposure information collected retrospectively.	Exposure information collected at baseline. Outcome information collected prospectively.
Data Sources/Collection Methods	Existing data, such as mortality rates.	Data from sample surveys. May also use secondary data, i.e., school records, national surveys.	Primary data from surveys of patients. Secondary data, e.g., from disease registries, medical records.	Primary data for exposure and outcome. Some cohort designs use secondary data.
Unit of Observation	The group	The individual	The individual	The individual
Measures used	Correlation, chi-square	Prevalence estimates	Odds ratio	Relative risk
Advantages	Quick and easy to conduct. Inexpensive.	Can be completed within a short time frame. Inexpensive.	Often smaller in size than prospective studies. Quick and easy to complete. Cost effective. Useful for studying rare diseases.	Permit direct determination of risk. Provide stronger evidence of exposure-disease associations than other observational designs. Useful for studying rare exposures.

continues

Disadvantages	Ecologic fallacy. Imprecise measurement of exposure-disease relationships.	Should not be used for studying disease etiology. Not useful for diseases of low frequency. Exposure-disease temporality not ascertained.	Uncertainty of the exposure-disease relationship. Inability to provide direct estimate of risk. Not useful for rare exposures. Recall bias.	Lengthy to conduct. Attrition. Difficult to carry out. Selection bias. Difficult to use with rare diseases.
Applications	Test specific etiologic hypotheses. Develop new etiologic hypotheses. Suggest mechanisms of causation. Identify new methods for disease prevention.	Depict mortality and morbidity from specific diseases. Generate hypotheses. Plan interventions. Describe the magnitude and distribution of a health problem. Assist in planning health services.	Infectious disease outbreak investigation. Chronic disease investigation when etiology unknown. Hypothesis testing.	Studies of chronic disease etiology Risk estimation. Hypothesis testing.
Examples	Association between breast cancer mortality and dietary fats. Air pollution and mortality by cities.	Prevalence of smokeless tobacco use among school-children. Number of vasectomies. Prevalence of congenital malformations.	Association between chili pepper consumption and gastric cancer risk. Anesthesia and neural tube defects. Smoking and cervical cancer.	Physical activity and coronary heart disease mortality. Child abuse and suicide. Exposure to toxic materials and mortality among workers.

Study Questions and Exercises

1. Define in your own words the following terms:
   a. Cohort
   b. Cohort effect
   c. Population-based cohort
   d. Exposure-based cohort
   e. Comparison groups in cohort studies
   f. Prospective cohort study
   g. Retrospective cohort study
   h. Ambispective cohort study

2. What are secular trends and cohort effects? Explain the relationship between these two terms.

3. Explain what is meant by the term relative risk and explain how it is used in cohort studies.

4. Describe the essential differences between life tables and survival curves.

5. A cohort study was conducted to study the association of coffee drinking and anxiety in a population-based sample of adults. Among 10,000 coffee drinkers, 500 developed anxiety. Among the 20,000 non-coffee drinkers, 200 cases of anxiety were observed. What is the relative risk of anxiety associated with coffee use?

6. How is a case-control study different from a retrospective cohort study? List the key criteria that, in general, would influence you to select one approach over the other.

7. Are relative risks of 2.0 and 0.5 the same or different in strength of association?

8. Cohort studies have some advantages over case-control studies in terms of the confidence with which their results are viewed. Suppose there have been four case-control studies of an exposure-disease association and that the range of the odds ratios is from 28.0 to 49.0. Would you advocate a cohort study? Justify your answer.

9. Cohort studies allow the investigator to examine multiple outcomes and multiple exposures. Consider the following three exposures: smoking, low vitamin D intake, and severe cold weather. How many different outcomes could you examine in a cohort study that measured all three exposures at baseline?

10. High rates of follow-up are essential to the validity of cohort studies. What are some approaches that can be employed to ensure compliance when linkage to a central disease registry is not an option?

11. Summarize the strengths and weaknesses and advantages and disadvantages of the various types of observational study designs: ecologic, cross-sectional, case-control, and cohort.

12. Describe how you would conduct a nested case-control study of low socioeconomic status as a risk factor for teenage pregnancy.

13. Explain what is meant by the statement that cohort studies overcome the problem of temporality, which is not addressed by other types of observational study designs.

14. What are some of the practical issues that influence the design of a cohort study?

15. Discuss some of the possible outcomes for cohort studies, distinguishing between discrete events and disease markers.

References

1. Last JM. *A Dictionary of Epidemiology*, 4th ed. New York: Oxford University Press; 2001.

2. Comstock GW. Cohort analysis: W.H. Frost's contributions to the epidemiology of tuberculosis and chronic disease. *Soz Präventivmed.* 2001;46:7–12.

3. Tolley HD, Crane L, Shipley N. Smoking prevalence and lung cancer death rates. In: *Strategies To Control Tobacco Use in the United States: A Blueprint for Public Health Action in the 1990s.* Bethesda, MD: National Institutes of Health; 1991.

4. National Center for Health Statistics. Mortality from diseases associated with smoking, United States, 1950–64. *Mon Vital Stat Rep.* 1966;20.

5. National Cancer Institute. *Risks Associated With Smoking Cigarettes With Low Machine-Measured Yields of Tar and Nicotine.* Smoking and Tobacco Control Monograph No. 13. NIH Pub. No. 02-5074. Bethesda, MD: U.S. Department of Health and Human Services, National Institutes of Health, National Cancer Institute; October 2001.

6. Chernick MR, Friis RH. *Introductory Biostatistics for the Health Sciences: Modern Applications Including Bootstrap.* Hoboken, NJ: John Wiley & Sons, Inc.; 2003.

7. Arias E. United States Life Tables, 2000. *National Vital Statistics Reports.* Hyattsville, MD: National Center for Health Statistics; 2002:51, No. 3.

8. Gordis L. *Epidemiology*, 3rd ed. Philadelphia, PA: Elsevier Saunders; 2004.

9. World Health Organization. Disability adjusted life years (DALY). Available at: http://www.who.int/healthinfo/boddaly/en/index.html. Accessed October 30, 2007.

10. Motulsky H. *Intuitive Biostatistics.* New York: Oxford University Press; 1995. Available at: http://www.graphpad.com/www/book/survive.htm. Accessed October 29, 2007.

11. Dawber TR, Meadors GF, Moore FE. Epidemiological approaches to heart disease: the Framingham Study. *Am J Public Health.* 1951;41:279–286.

12. Francis T Jr., Epstein FH. Survey methods in general populations: Tecumseh, Michigan. In: Acheson RM, ed. *Comparability in International Epidemiology.* Princeton, NJ: Milbank Memorial Fund; 1965:333–342.

13. Bisgard KM, Folsom AR, Hong C-P, Sellers TA. Mortality and cancer rates in nonresponders to a prospective study in older women: 5-year follow-up. *Am J Epidemiol.* 1994;139:990–1000.

14. Robison LL, Mertens AC, Boice JD, et al. Study design and cohort characteristics of the Childhood Cancer Survivor Study: a multi-institutional collaborative project. *Med Pediatr Oncol.* 2002;38:229–239.

15. Paffenbarger RS, Hyde RT, Wing AL, Steinmetz CH. A natural history of athleticism and cardiovascular health. *JAMA.* 1984;252:491–495.

16. Tager IB. Outcomes in cohort studies. *Epidemiol Rev.* 1998;20:15–28.

17. Sellers TA, King RA, Cerhan JR, et al. Fifty-year follow-up of cancer incidence in a historical cohort of Minnesota Breast Cancer Families. *Cancer Epidemiol Biomarkers Prev.* 1999;12:1051–1057.

18. Hartmann LC, Schaid DJ, Woods JE, et al. Efficacy of bilateral prophylactic mastectomy in women with a family history of breast cancer. *N Engl J Med.* 1999; 340:77–84.

19. Zheng W, Chow WH, Yang G, et al. The Shanghai Women's Health Study: rationale, study design, and baseline characteristics. *Am J Epidemiol.* 2005;162:1123–1131.

20. Hoskins KF, Stopler JE, Calzone KA, et al. Assessment and counseling for women with a family history of breast cancer. A guide for clinicians. *JAMA.* 1995;273: 577–585.

21. Hu FB, Grodstein F. Postmenopausal hormone therapy and the risk of cardiovascular disease: The epidemiologic evidence. *Am J Cardiol.* 2002;90(suppl):26F–29F.

22. Psaty BM, Heckbert SR, Atkins D, et al. A review of the association of estrogens and progestins with cardiovascular disease in postmenopausal women. *Arch Intern Med.* 1993;153:1421–1427.

23. Nelson HD, Humphrey LL, Nygren P, et al. Postmenopausal hormone replacement therapy: scientific review. *JAMA.* 2002;288:872–881.

24. Lobo RA. Benefits and risks of estrogen replacement therapy. *Am J Obstet Gynecol.* 1995;173:782–789.

25. Kawas C, Resnick S, Morrison A, et al. A prospective study of estrogen replacement therapy and the risk of developing Alzheimer's disease: the Baltimore Longitudinal Study of Aging. *Neurology.* 1997;48:1517–1521.

26. Sellers TA, Mink PJ, Anderson KE, et al. The role of hormone replacement therapy in the risk for breast cancer and total mortality in women with a family history of breast cancer. *Ann Intern Med.* 1997;127:973–980.

27. Deykin EY, Buka SL. Suicidal ideation and attempts among chemically dependent adolescents. *Am J Public Health.* 1994;84:634–639.

28. Fox SM III, Naughton JP, Haskell WL. Physical activity and the prevention of coronary heart disease. *Ann Clin Res.* 1971;3:404–432.

29. Morris JN, Heady JA, Raffle PAB, et al. Coronary heart disease and physical activity of work. *Lancet.* 1953;2:1053–1120.

30. Taylor HL, Klepetar E, Keys A, et al. Death rates among physically active and sedentary employees of the railroad industry. *Am J Public Health.* 1962;10:1697–1707.

31. Peters RK, Cady LD Jr., Bischoff DP, et al. Physical fitness and subsequent myocardial infarction in healthy workers. *JAMA.* 1983;249:3052–3056.

32. van Wijngaarden E, Savitz DA, Kleckner RC, et al. Exposure to electromagnetic fields and suicide among electric utility workers: A nested case-control study. *West J Med.* 2000;173:94–100.

33. Dearden KA, Hale CB, Woolley T. The antecedents of teen fatherhood: a retrospective case-control study of Great Britain youth. *Am J Public Health.* 1995;85:551–554.

34. Shepherd PM. The National Child Development Study: An Introduction to the Background to the Study and the Methods of Data Collection (Working Paper I, National Child Development Study User Support Group). London, UK: City University, Social Statistics Unit; 1985.

35. Samet JM, Munoz A, eds. Cohort studies. *Epidemiol Rev.* 1998;20(1).

CHAPTER 8

Experimental Study Designs

LEARNING OBJECTIVES

By the end of this chapter the reader will be able to:

- state how study designs compare with respect to validity of causal inference
- distinguish between a controlled experiment and a quasi-experiment
- describe the scope of intervention studies
- define the term *controlled clinical trials* and give examples
- explain the phases in testing a new drug
- discuss *blinding* and *crossover* in clinical trials
- define what is meant by *community trials*
- discuss ethical aspects of experimentation with human subjects

CHAPTER OUTLINE

I. Introduction
II. Hierarchy of Study Designs
III. Intervention Studies
IV. Clinical Trials
V. Community Trials
VI. Conclusion
VII. Study Questions and Exercises

Introduction

In Chapters 6 and 7, we covered observational study designs. Chapter 8 focuses on experimental and quasi-experimental designs. We examine how these study designs differ from observational studies as well as their unique advantages and disadvantages.

Modern epidemiologists often equate experimental epidemiology with randomized controlled clinical trials.[1] In the field of epidemiology, experimental designs are typically implemented as intervention studies, either controlled experiments or quasi-experiments. We begin by taking an in-depth look at the two categories of intervention studies, which are clinical trials and community trials. The authors provide examples of each type as well as a discussion of ethical aspects of human experimentation. Next, the authors take up the related topic of special considerations such as sample selection and crossover designs. The chapter concludes with a discussion of methods for evaluating the outcomes of community interventions.

Hierarchy of Study Designs

Chapters 6 and 7 identified strengths and weaknesses of observational studies for descriptive and analytic epidemiology, especially with respect to our confidence in inferring causation of disease. These assertions are summarized in Exhibit 8–1, which ranks study designs according to their validity.

Exhibit 8–1 also includes experimental designs (i.e., randomized clinical trials, which are covered in the present chapter). As Exhibit 8–1 indicates, all of the study designs from case studies to prospective cohort studies may be considered less powerful for etiologic inference than randomized clinical trials. The latter are generally regarded as the most scientifically rigorous method of hypothesis testing available in epidemiology. The emphasis is on rigor and not feasibility, for as we shall learn subsequently, not all research situations permit the use of this design.

Experimental designs, including clinical trials, enable us to overcome some of the deficiencies inherent in observational designs. The use of experimentation to derive knowledge about the causes of disease has intuitive appeal. In a controlled clinical trial, by exercising control over who will receive the exposure as well as the level of the exposure, the investigator more confidently may attribute cause and effect to associations than in nonexperimental designs.

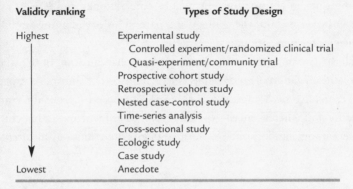

EXHIBIT 8–1

Validity for Etiologic Inference According to Study Designs

Validity ranking	Types of Study Design
Highest	Experimental study
	Controlled experiment/randomized clinical trial
	Quasi-experiment/community trial
	Prospective cohort study
	Retrospective cohort study
	Nested case-control study
	Time-series analysis
	Cross-sectional study
	Ecologic study
	Case study
Lowest	Anecdote

Source: Adapted from Künzli N, Tager IB. The semi-individual study in air pollution epidemiology: a valid design as compared to ecologic studies, *Environmental Health Perspectives*, Vol 105, No 10, p. 1079, 1997, National Institute of Environmental Health Sciences, U.S. Department of Health and Human Services.

Ranked immediately below controlled experiments are quasi-experiments.[2] As noted in Chapter 6, the investigator is unable to randomly allocate subjects to the conditions (intervention or control) of a quasi-experimental study. As a result, there may be contamination across the conditions of the study. It becomes more difficult to differentiate between the effects of the intervention and the control conditions than in a controlled experiment. (Of course, it also is possible for contamination to occur in a clinical trial.)

The reader should not conclude that experimental designs (i.e., randomized controlled trials [RCTs]) are always the most appropriate design for investigating the causes of disease. Experimental designs are not necessarily appropriate for testing all conceivable hypotheses, such as those in the fields of occupational and environmental health. To give an example, an epidemiologist might want to examine the relative contributions of smoking and radon exposure to lung cancer among uranium miners. For ethical reasons, this investigation could not be conducted as an experimental study because it would involve deliberate exposure of subjects to agents suspected of being harmful. An observational study design is the only realistic approach in this scenario. In the following sections, we explore in greater detail the designs that we introduced previously.

Intervention Studies

Intervention studies are employed to test the efficacy of a preventive or thera-peutic measure. In comparison, the goal of observational studies is to generate enough knowledge about the etiology and natural history of a disease to formu-late strategies for prevention.

Recall the two basic facets of research designs: manipulation of the study fac-tor and randomization of study subjects (see Table 6–1). Controlled experimen-tal studies involve randomization of subjects to exposures under the control of the investigator, whereas quasi-experimental studies involve external control of exposure without randomization. Both strategies are employed in intervention studies.

Intervention Designs Include:

- Controlled clinical trials (focus on the individual)
- Community interventions (focus on the group or community)

Note: Controlled clinical trials may be conducted both at the individual and community levels (for narrowly defined outcomes).

Broadly defined, there are two types of intervention designs: clinical trials and community trials. The key difference between the two types of intervention is that in clinical trials the focus is individuals, whereas the focus of community tri-als is groups or community outcomes. This difference in focus limits the types of interventions that are possible under each approach. Clinical trials are usually tightly controlled in terms of eligibility, delivery of the intervention, and moni-toring of outcomes. The duration of clinical trials ranges from days to years. Participation is generally restricted to a highly selected group of individuals: commonly volunteers who have been diagnosed with a disease; volunteers who are screened subjects at high risk for disease; or other types of volunteers who may be interested in participating in the clinical trial and are deemed eligible for such participation. The RCT is most appropriate for testing narrow hypotheses regarding vaccines, treatments, or individuals' behavior change.[2] An example of behavior change is elimination of tobacco use among smokers. A clinical trial is not the most applicable design for complex interventions.

Usually, community trials cannot exert rigid control over members of the group or community, are typically delivered to all members rather than narrowly defined subsets, tend to be of longer duration, and usually involve primary prevention efforts. Thus, RCTs at the community level can be used only in special situations when there is a simple intervention (i.e., a response to a vaccine) and there is a sufficient number of communities to involve in the experiment.[2]

Clinical Trials

The concepts of clinical trials have a venerable history that spans a time period from early biblical and Greek references to increasing activity during the eighteenth and nineteenth centuries to present methodologic sophistication.[3] The first efforts were not formal clinical trials, as we know them today; however, the attempts at experimentation led the way to contemporary methods. For example, in 1537 Ambroise Paré applied an experimental treatment for battlefield wounds that used what he called a "digestive" made from turpentine, rose oil, and egg yolks. He observed that this concoction was more effective in treating wounds than the application of boiling oil, the standard treatment of the day. Later, in 1600, the East India Shipping Company found that lemon juice protected sailors from scurvy by comparing sailors on a ship supplied with lemon juice with sailors on ships that were not supplied. James Lind, in 1747, was credited with designing one of the first experiments that used a concurrently treated control group.[3] His experiment involved feeding 12 sailors who were suffering from scurvy six different types of diets; Lind noted that sailors who received citrus fruits had the best recovery from their malady.

Other pioneering landmarks in the development of clinical trials include Jenner's efforts to develop a smallpox vaccine in the late eighteenth century and experiments with anesthetics, such as ether and chloroform, in the mid-nineteenth century. While the earliest planned experiments were carried out without the benefit of a control or comparison, subsequent research contributed to the development of control treatments and randomization. More recent historical developments have included the use of multicenter trials in which the results from several researchers are pooled. Multicenter trials have been instrumental in the development of treatments for infectious diseases (e.g., polio) and recently in chronic diseases that are of noninfectious origin (Exhibit 8–2).

"A clinical trial is a planned experiment designed to assess the efficacy of a treatment in man by comparing the outcomes in a group of patients treated with

EXHIBIT 8-2

The Why, What, When, and Where of Clinical Trials

We've all taken medication. It may have been in the form of over-the-counter cough medicine or prescription pills to treat chronic conditions such as diabetes. But how did researchers discover if the medicine is effective, if it's safe, and if there are any potential side effects?

Testing and evaluating drugs is serious business, and clinical trials are right at the center of the process, according to Dorothy Cirelli, chief of the Patient Recruitment and Referral Center at the National Institutes of Health (NIH), U.S. Department of Health and Human Services (HHS). "Medical advances would not occur without clinical trials," she said.

Well known as a world leader in medical research, NIH developed the first treatment for the human immunodeficiency virus (HIV) as well as innovative therapies for breast cancer, leukemia, and lymphoma. For over a century, the agency has conducted clinical studies that explore the nature of illnesses. Clinical studies are currently under way for nearly every kind of cancer, HIV, cardiovascular disease, diabetes, obesity, and many other conditions both common and rare.

There are several types of clinical trials. By far the largest number test new drugs. Prevention studies look at drugs or lifestyle changes that may help prevent disease. Diagnostic studies look at ways of detecting or finding out more about disease. Treatment studies may monitor new drugs or evaluate new combinations of established treatments.

The Food and Drug Administration (FDA), another HHS agency, is responsible for reviewing the scientific work of drug developers and implementing a rigorous drug approval process. The FDA, which some have called the world's largest consumer protection agency, works to protect the public by ensuring that products are safe, effective, and labeled for their intended use.

From Animals to Humans: Every year, hundreds of clinical trials are conducted at medical centers across the country. Drugs must be studied in properly controlled trials in order to determine if they work for a specific purpose. Drugs that have not been previously used in humans must

continues

EXHIBIT 8-2 *continued*

undergo preclinical test-tube analysis and/or animal studies involving at least two mammals to determine toxicity.

The toxicity information is then used to make risk/benefit assessments, and determine if the drug is acceptable for testing in humans.

NIH or the company developing the drug must conduct studies to show any interaction between the body and the drug. In addition, researchers must provide the FDA with information on chemistry, manufacturing, and controls. This ensures the identity, purity, quality, and strength of both the active ingredient and the finished dosage form.

The sponsor of the proposed new drug then develops a plan for testing the drug in humans. The plan is submitted to the FDA with information on animal testing data, the composition of the drug, manufacturing data, qualifications of its study investigators, and safety of the people who will participate in the trial. This information forms what is known as the Investigational New Drug Application (IND).

The entire drug development process is lengthy and expensive. On average it takes about 10 years to complete. But it is an effective system that generally protects the public from dangerous and ineffective drugs. ■

Source: Reprinted from Brooks J. Clinical trials: how they work, why we need them. In: *Closing the Gap*, December 1997/January 1998, pp. 1–2. Washington, DC: Office of Minority Health, Public Health Service, U.S. Department of Health and Human Services.

the test treatment with those observed in a comparable group of patients receiving a control treatment, where patients in both groups are enrolled, treated, and followed over the same time period."[3(p. 3)] Therefore, one starts by determining eligibility of potential subjects. Eligibility rules must be carefully defined and rigidly enforced. Criteria for inclusion will vary by the type and nature of the intervention proposed. Once eligible subjects agree to participate, they are then randomly assigned to one of the study groups. Figure 8–1 illustrates a single intervention and single control (or placebo) arm of a trial, yet more than one experimental intervention can be run in parallel.

Prophylactic and Therapeutic Trials

A prophylactic trial is designed to evaluate the effectiveness of a substance (such as a vaccine against measles or polio) or a prevention program (such as vitamin

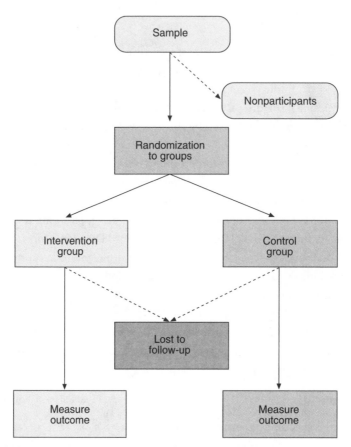

FIGURE 8–1   Schematic diagram of a clinical trial.

supplementation or patient education) that is used to prevent a disease. A therapeutic trial involves the study of curative drugs or a new surgical procedure to
evaluate how well they bring about an improvement in the patient's health. One
group is designated as the control arm of the trial; these subjects would receive
the standard of care (for a surgery or drug trial), a placebo (for a vitamin trial), or
no intervention (for the patient education trial). Some patient education programs might use individual or group counseling in the intervention group and
provide control participants with an informational brochure—the usual method
of education.

Outcomes of Clinical Trials

Outcomes, or results of a clinical trial, are referred to as clinical end points. To assess the results, investigators compare rates of disease, death, recovery, or other appropriate outcome. The outcome of interest is measured in the intervention and control arms of the trial to evaluate efficacy. We have previously noted that the outcome of a clinical trial must be measured in a comparable manner in both the intervention and control conditions.

For some drugs, such as antihypertensive agents, it may not be feasible to conduct randomized large clinical trials that evaluate major clinical end points, such as strokes or myocardial infarctions.[4] As an alternative, surrogate end points may be used in small short-term trials. A surrogate end point for drug therapy in hypertension would be measures of subclinical disease or physical measures, including reduction of blood pressure.

Examples of Clinical Trials

The first example of a clinical trial is the double-blind Medical Research Council Vitamin Study.[5] Neural tube defects (NTDs; e.g., anencephaly, spina bifida, or encephalocele) are among the most severe congenital malformations. The possibility that folic acid (a B vitamin) might be involved was raised as early as 1964.[6] Preliminary interventions had been promising but not conclusive. Therefore, a randomized trial was conducted at 33 centers in seven countries. The trial examined whether vitamin supplementation around the time of conception could prevent NTDs. The supplements used were folic acid or a mixture of seven other vitamins: A, D, B_1, B_2, B_6, C, and nicotinamide. Eligible subjects included women who were planning a pregnancy, had had a previous child with an NTD, and were not already taking vitamin supplements. A total of 1,817 women were randomized into one of four groups: folic acid, other vitamins, both, or neither. Subjects did not know to which group they were assigned. To monitor possible toxicity associated with the supplementation, recording forms were provided to all subjects. Of those randomized, 1,195 gave birth to a child with a known outcome. Whenever an NTD was reported, independent corroboration was sought. Classification was made without knowing to which group the mother had been randomized.

The rate of NTDs among women receiving folic acid (alone or in combination with other vitamins) was 1% (5 out of 514). The rate among those allocated to the other groups (other vitamins or nothing) was 3.5%, yielding a relative risk of 0.28 (95% confidence interval [CI], 0.12–0.71). The rate among women in the other vitamin-only group was only slightly lower than the rate among the women receiving nothing (relative risk, 0.80; 95% CI, 0.32–1.72). The trial results were regularly monitored. By April 12, 1991, the difference between the folic acid-supplemented group and the others was firmly established by case 27. The data-monitoring committee recommended that the trial be stopped; the steering committee agreed. The authors of the report[5] concluded that folic acid supplementation could now be recommended for all women who had a previously affected pregnancy. Furthermore, they suggested that public health measures should be taken to ensure that all women of childbearing age receive adequate dietary folic acid and that consideration should be given to fortification of staple foods with it.

Another application of clinical trials is to evaluate the effectiveness of education efforts to prevent the spread of sexually transmitted diseases (STDs). The factors that contribute to an increased risk of STDs are multiple and complex and include social, behavioral, and environmental influences. Efforts to reduce the incidence of STDs among inner-city residents are especially difficult, given the fact that most education efforts are relegated to public clinics. Because the clinics often have limited resources, educational programs must be delivered by staff who may be inadequately trained in prevention and unprepared to provide information and skills to culturally diverse populations. O'Donnell and colleagues[7] conducted a clinical trial of video-based educational interventions on condom acquisition among men and women seeking services at a large STD clinic in South Bronx, New York. A total of 3,348 African-American and Hispanic male and female patients were assigned to one of three arms: video only, video plus interactive session, or control. The videos were 20 minutes in length, culturally appropriate, and designed to model appropriate strategies for overcoming barriers to consistent condom use. A proxy measure of condom use was employed. After clinic services and participation in the assigned treatment group, subjects were given coupons for free condoms at a nearby pharmacy. The rate of redemption of coupons for condoms was 21.2% among patients who received no intervention, 27.6% among patients who received video alone, and 36.9% among patients who received video plus interactive group sessions. O'Donnell et al. pointed out that because of the high prevalence of STDs in the population served by public clinics, the observed increases in the number of people practicing safer sex could have a significant impact on public health.

Blinding (Masking)

Objectivity of the data is a major concern regarding clinical trials. For example, some clinical trials make use of volunteers who are extremely grateful for the opportunity to participate. At the same time, the investigator may assess the trial's outcome by determining the participants' subjective impressions, for example, by means of a self-report questionnaire. This evaluation method may tend to overstate the intervention's clinical responses and benefits. Furthermore, subjects who learn that they had been randomized to the placebo arm of the trial may not wish to continue participation. For these reasons, a commonly used approach is a single-blind design. (A synonym for the term *blinding* is *masking*.) In this design, the subject is unaware of group assignment. Informed consent is obtained before assignment, and the experimenter must treat and monitor all groups in a similar manner. Another concern and potential for problems lies in how the experimenter assesses the trial's outcome. This concern is especially warranted if the trial evaluates a new drug, the drug's manufacturer is financing the trial, and/or those performing the evaluations stand to benefit if the new drug is shown to be more effective than existing medications. To reduce the likelihood of biased assessment, an approach called a double-blind design is used; neither the subject nor the experimenter is aware of group assignment. For example, in a clinical trial of a new drug, one way to implement such a procedure is to have the placebo or treatment agents come in a preassigned container, the contents of which are unknown to the investigator and subjects at the time of the trial. All subjects are then treated and monitored in a similar manner.

Phases of Clinical Trials

Phases in a clinical trial refer to the stages that must occur in the development of a vaccine, drug, or treatment before it can be licensed for general use. A long and arduous process is required to bring a vaccine from the laboratory setting to eventual licensing,[8] and the same may be said for licensing of new drugs. The process of bringing a new vaccine to market requires the balance between protecting the public from a potentially deleterious vaccine and satisfying urgent needs for new vaccines. To illustrate, while researchers have devoted a great deal of attention to producing a vaccine for HIV, the problems in perfecting such a vaccine have been daunting. Generally, licensing of a vaccine requires a phase I, phase II, and phase III evaluation. A description of these steps for the development of a new vaccine is in Exhibit 8–3.

EXHIBIT 8–3

Stages in the Development of a Vaccination Program

Pre-licensing evaluation of vaccine

- Phase I trials: Safety in adult volunteers
- Phase II trials: Immunogenicity and reactogenicity in the target population
- Phase III trials: Protective efficacy

Postlicensing evaluation

- Safety and efficacy of vaccine
- Disease surveillance
- Serologic surveillance
- Measurement of vaccine coverage

Source: Reprinted from Begg N, Miller E. Role of Epidemiology in Vaccine Policy. In *Vaccine,* Vol 8, p. 180. © 1990, with permission from Elsevier.

In the evaluation of vaccines, phase I trials involve testing the new vaccine in adult volunteers, typically fewer than 100. Upon successful demonstration of a response in a small-scale study among the volunteers (e.g., antibody formation in response to a vaccine), the testing proceeds to phase II. This phase expands the testing to a group of approximately 100 to 200 subjects who are selected from the target population for the vaccine. Antibody responses and clinical reactions to the vaccine are examined. There may be a double-blind design with random allocation to study or placebo conditions. The third phase, which is used to assess protective efficacy in the target population, is the main test of the vaccine. Vaccine efficacy refers to the reduction in the incidence rate of a disease in a vaccinated population compared with an unvaccinated population.[8] After phase III testing has been completed, a license to manufacture the vaccine may be granted. Postlicensing evaluations of the vaccine need to continue to monitor its safety and efficacy.

The phases for testing an anticancer drug follow a similar pattern (Table 8–1). Laboratory studies in vitro and in vivo among animals may have suggested a new agent that has promising antitumor action. Phase I consists of testing the agent among human subjects. Phase II is concerned with testing the efficacy of the

Table 8–1 A Description of Clinical Trials for a Cancer Drug

Phase	Goals	Objectives
I	Initial testing in humans following animal studies. Organized as escalating dose trials in which subjects are entered into a series of progressively higher dosage levels until life-threatening, irreversible, or fatal toxicity is experienced.	Identify dose-limiting toxicities. Establish maximally tolerated dose; optimal dosage range. Describe pharmacology of agent (e.g., metabolism, distribution, excretion).
II	Testing in selected tumor types ranging from highly chemosensitive to chemo-resistant.	Determine activity and therapeutic efficacy in a range of tumor types. Validate toxicity and dosage data.
III	Randomized trial comparing new therapy with existing therapies in terms of duration and quality of survival. Trial may have multiple study arms and involve sample stratification.	Determine value of new therapy in relation to existing therapies. Generate and publish recommendations for the medical community.

Source: Adapted from Engelking C. Clinical trials: impact evaluation and implementation consideration. *Seminars in Oncology Nursing,* Vol 8, No 2, p. 149. © 1992, W.B. Saunders Company.

drug with various tumor types. At the conclusion of phase III trials, much information has been gathered about the agent.[9] In practice, some clinical trials may have more than three phases.

The lengthy process that is required to bring a new drug, vaccine, or treatment to the healthcare marketplace not only helps to protect the consumer, but also delays bringing needed pharmaceutical agents to critically ill patients. Because of demands that advocacy groups have made on government agencies, proposals have been made to shorten the lead time to make new drugs more rapidly available. These legislative and policy modifications are intended to bring more speedy relief to patients who are afflicted with conditions such as acquired immune deficiency syndrome (AIDS) and cancer.

Randomization

The method of choice for assigning subjects to the treatment or control conditions of a clinical trial is randomization. Researchers must be very concerned about errors that might be introduced when some other method of subject assignment is used. In nonrandom assignment, any observed differences between study arms might simply reflect differences observed among participants of the trial. There are two general methods for randomization of subjects to the conditions of the trial, known as fixed and adaptive randomization.[3] Fixed randomization is easier to perform than adaptive randomization. However, a full discussion of them is beyond the scope of this text. The general concept of fixed randomization is that once subjects have been selected, pass the eligibility determination, and agree to participate they have an equal probability of being assigned to the intervention or control arm. The simplest form of randomization is the "flip of a coin," but more elaborate protocols that employ random numbers tables or computer algorithms are typically used. As part of randomization in some trials, subjects are stratified in order to improve comparability among conditions. For example, in order to control for sex and age differences, equal proportions of gender and age groups are included in the treatment and control groups. For randomization to be fully effective, a reasonably large number of subjects must be enrolled in order to obtain equal distributions of demographic and other variables in the study conditions. For the sake of illustration, a study with only two men and two women would have too few subjects, because random assignment could result in each study arm having only one gender, e.g., one group with all men and the other with all women.

Crossover Designs

A treatment crossover refers to, "any change of treatment for a patient in a clinical trial involving a switch of study treatments."[3(p. 306)] These crossovers may be planned or unplanned. To illustrate, the protocol may specify in advance that a patient or group of subjects may be switched from one treatment condition to another treatment condition during the course of the trial and after a predetermined period of follow-up. Sometimes, in such crossovers, the patient is said to serve as his or her own control. An unplanned crossover refers to a switch of patients to different treatment conditions for various reasons. For example, patients in a coronary bypass treatment may have misgivings about this invasive surgical procedure, or patients in a medical care group may require surgical treatment because of deterioration in their condition.[10]

Ethical Aspects of Experimentation with Human Subjects

Miké and Schottenfeld[11] identified some of the ethical issues surrounding experimentation with human subjects, particularly with respect to clinical trials. These issues include informed consent, withholding treatment known to be effective, protecting the interests of the individual patient, monitoring for toxicity and side effects, and deciding when to withdraw a patient from the study.

The ethical aspects of experimentation with human subjects are capable of generating much heated debate and strong emotional responses. It is generally agreed that the benefits of participation in an experimental study must clearly outweigh any possible risks to the subject. One side of the issue is that human experimentation, especially with drugs, may bring about certain iatrogenic reactions (adverse effects caused by the medications) that could have been avoided had the subject not participated in the experiment. The other viewpoint is that an experimental design (i.e., being in a control condition) requires that medication be withheld from people who might benefit from it. The problem of iatrogenic reactions may be circumvented through experimental studies with animals, although animal models may not apply directly to human beings.

In order to address both of these issues—the withholding of needed medication and the possibility of adverse effects from the medication—experimental drug trials use what is known as a sequential design. Let us consider a clinical trial to evaluate a new drug. In contrast with a sequential design, many drug trials use a preestablished number of subjects who are assigned a priori to the study and control conditions. The results of the trial are evaluated after all subjects have been assigned to the conditions of the trial, usually after an extended period of time. In a sequential design, investigators continuously monitor results and add subjects, i.e., there is no preestablished number of subjects. The trial is interrupted as soon as the results are statistically significant and either confirm or reject a positive outcome for the drug being tested. If the drug produces improvement in the patients' conditions, it then becomes available for use by members of the control group as well (or the drug is discontinued if it is found to produce adverse effects). In addition, in some clinical trials, experimental therapies are evaluated only on patients for whom all other treatments have failed.

There has been increasing interest in developing rigorous evaluations of psychological therapy interventions.[12] Selection of appropriate control subjects in such evaluations poses ethical concerns for subjects in placebo or no-treatment conditions. One concern relates to withholding benefits that might accrue from a psychosocial intervention. This concern is similar to the ethical issue of withholding an effective drug from a needy control patient. Another issue is finding a control group that is sufficiently comparable to the study group for which the intervention is being evaluated.

The NIH have instituted a policy "…that requires oversight and monitoring of all intervention studies to ensure the safety of participants and the validity and integrity of the data."[13] This goal is accomplished through the use of a data and safety monitoring board (DSMB) composed of an independent group of experts who advise investigators and funding agencies. For example, in the case of the Division of Microbiology and Infectious Diseases (DMID), "The primary responsibilities of the DSMB are to 1) periodically review and evaluate the accumulated study data for participant safety, study conduct and progress, and, when appropriate, efficacy, and 2) make recommendations to DMID concerning the continuation, modification, or termination of the trial."[14] Although phase III clinical trials are required to have a DSMB, phase I and phase II trials, in certain circumstances, also may require them.

As part of their participation in a clinical trial, study subjects are required to give informed consent by signing an informed consent document. This document describes the risks and benefits of participating in the study and discloses the purpose of the clinical trial, how long it will last, and the procedures involved.[15] Upon receiving full information about the trial, a potential study subject is in a position to decide whether or not to participate. Chapter 16 gives additional coverage of ethical issues in clinical trials and epidemiology in general.

Reporting of the Results of Clinical Trials

The results of an RCT may impact patient care greatly.[16] Readers of the results of a RCT need to comprehend key aspects of the trial—design, conduct, and analysis—as well as to determine the generalizability of its findings. To meet that need, a panel of experts developed the CONSORT statement.[17] The acronym CONSORT stands for Consolidated Standards of Reporting Trials. The current revision guides the reporting of randomized trials by providing a 22-item checklist and a flowchart, to be used by those who review, write, and assess the findings from a RCT. One of the main aims of CONSORT is to help authors optimize the quality of their reports of simple RCTs. Figure 8–2 is a CONSORT flowchart, which describes the flow of subjects through the phases of a RCT.

Summary of Clinical Trials

This brief overview of clinical trials reveals a number of their strengths. As opposed to the several varieties of observational studies, clinical trials provide the greatest control over the study situation. The investigator has the ability to control the amount of exposure (e.g., drug dosage), the timing and frequency of the exposure, and the period of observation for end points. For large trials, the ability to randomize subjects to study assignments reduces the likelihood that the

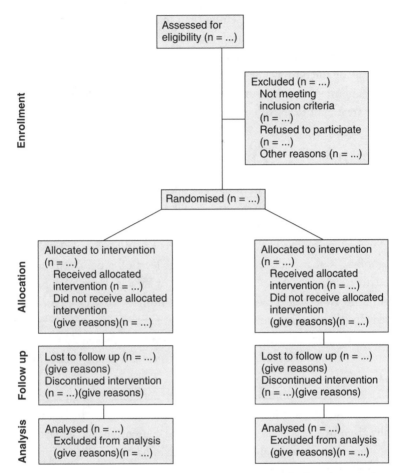

FIGURE 8–2 Flow diagram of the progress through the phases of a randomized trial. *Source:* Reprinted with permission from Moher D, Schultz KF, Altman DG. The CONSORT statement: revised recommendations for improving the quality of reports of parallel-group randomized trials. *Lancet.* 2001;357:1193.

groups will differ significantly with respect to the distribution of risk factors that might influence the outcome.

Clinical trials have several limitations. In particular, one of these is the very thing that was cited as an advantage: The setting for delivery and evaluation of the treatment tends to be artificial, so that the experimenter may find it difficult to determine whether the treatment would work well in the larger community or for unselected patient populations. Obviously, there is necessarily less control over all factors in a community setting than in a clinical trial. A second disadvantage is that adherence to protocols may be difficult to enforce, especially if the treatment produces undesirable side effects and presents a significant burden to the subjects. By the time a clinical trial is conducted, fairly good evidence usually exists in support of the exposure-disease association; withholding a potentially beneficial treatment from the control arm presents an ethical dilemma.

Community Trials

Although clinical trials play an important role in efforts to improve health and the delivery of medical care, they are limited in terms of the scope of their potential impact. Because they require such great control over subjects, they are not typically employed to evaluate the potential efficacy of large-scale public health interventions. Rather, intervention trials at the level of entire communities are needed to determine the potential benefit of new policies and programs. According to Rossi and Freeman, an intervention is "Any program or other planned effort designed to produce changes in a target population."[18(p. 15)] Note that the word community as used here is not meant to be taken literally. A community may well be some other defined unit, such as a county, state, or school district.

Like clinical trials, community trials start by determining eligible communities and their willingness to participate. Permission to enroll the community is typically given by someone capable of providing consent, such as a mayor, governor, or school board. To be able to evaluate the impact of a program properly, it is desirable to have some baseline measures of the problem to be addressed in the intervention and control communities. Such measures may include, for example, disease prevalence or incidence; knowledge, attitudes, and practice; or purchase of lean relative to fatty cuts of meat. After the relevant baseline measures have been taken, communities are randomized to receive or not receive the intervention. Both study assignments are followed for a period of time, and the outcomes of interest are measured (Figure 8–3).

Years of etiologic research on atherosclerotic disease have contributed greatly to our understanding of risk factors for the disease. Many of these risk factors, such as elevated levels of serum cholesterol and low-density lipoprotein, can be reduced by lowering intake of dietary fat and cholesterol; cigarette smokers can quit; and hypertensive individuals can lower their body weight, exercise more, or use appropriate medication. By the 1970s, enough was known about these risk factors and their potential for modification that a number of community inter-

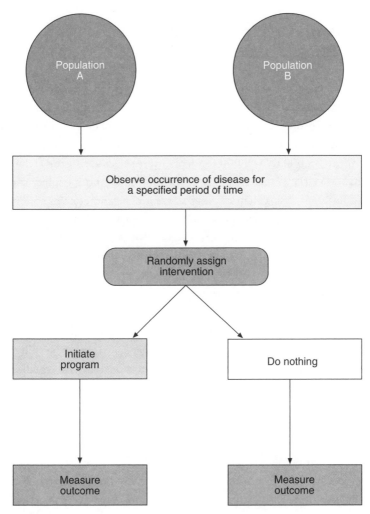

FIGURE 8–3 Schematic diagram of a community trial.

ventions were tested; a few of these interventions include the North Karelia Project, the Minnesota Heart Health Program, and the Stanford Five-City Project (Exhibit 8–4 and Figure 8–4).

As another example of a community trial, the design and methods of the Pawtucket Heart Health Program are described.[19] Nine cities in Rhode Island that met certain size and population stability criteria were identified. Pawtucket was randomly selected for the intervention, and an unnamed city with similar sociodemographic characteristics was chosen as the comparison city. The focus of

EXHIBIT 8-4

Stanford Five-City Project Design, Methods, and Results

The Stanford Five-City Project was a major community trial designed to lower risk of cardiovascular diseases. Two treatment cities (Monterey and Salinas) and two control cities (Modesto and San Luis Obispo), located in northern California and ranging in size from 35,000 to 145,000 residents, were selected for study (the fifth city, Santa Maria, was included only for morbidity and mortality surveillance). Random assignment of cities to treatment and control conditions was precluded by constraints on community selection, particularly concerning independent media markets (Figure 8–4).

The intervention was a six-year, integrated, comprehensive, community-wide multifactor risk reduction education program. The interventions had multiple target audiences and used multiple communication channels and settings. Before the intervention began, data from a baseline population survey were used to develop an overview of knowledge, attitudes, and behavior in treatment communities. The audience was segmented by age, ethnicity, socioeconomic status, overall cardiovascular risk, media use, organizational membership, and motivation to change behavior. Formative evaluation with these audience subgroups was used to refine educational strategies, programs, and materials. [Formative evaluation is defined later in this chapter.] Social learning theory guided the development of educational materials.

To evaluate the effect of the intervention on cardiovascular risk factors, four independent cross-sectional surveys of randomly selected households and four repeated surveys of a cohort were conducted. All persons from households randomly chosen from commercial directories, age 12 to 74 years, were eligible for recruitment into the survey. Eligible persons were contacted by mail, telephone, and in person, and they were invited to attend survey centers located in the four cities. Trained health professionals interviewed participants about their demographic background, health knowledge, cardiovascular risk-related attitudes and behavior, including a 24-hour diet recall, and medical history. Weight was measured using a balance beam, and blood pressure was measured using a semiautomated

continues

cuff, after which venous blood samples were drawn for determination of total and high-density lipoprotein cholesterol concentrations. Prior fasting was not required. Cigarette smoking status was confirmed with biochemical testing.

Morbidity and mortality rate data are still being collected and have yet to be analyzed. However, changes in risk factors have been reported. These risk factor results . . . [showed] . . . changes during the six-year educational intervention in the individuals surveyed in the treatment towns compared with the control towns. With the exception of obesity, as measured by body mass index, risk factor changes were in healthful directions in both treatment and control towns, the changes in treatment towns exceeded those in control towns, and there was general consistency of these treatment-control differences across risk factors and in both the cohort and serial cross-sectional surveys. ■

Source: Reprinted with permission from Fortmann SP et al. Community intervention trials: reflections on the Stanford Five-City Project experience. *American Journal of Epidemiology,* Vol 142, No 6, pp. 579–580, © 1995, The Johns Hopkins University School of Hygiene and Public Health.

the intervention was to help individuals adopt new, healthy behaviors and to create a supportive physical and behavioral environment. The program targeted three dimensions of activities: risk factors (e.g., elevated blood cholesterol, elevated blood pressure, and smoking), behavioral change (e.g., training, aid in development of social support, and maintenance strategies), and community activation (achieving goals while working through community groups and organizations). During a seven-year intervention period, "over 500 community organizations were involved at some level. These included all 27 public and private schools, most religious and social organizations and larger work sites, all supermarkets and many smaller grocery stores, 19 restaurants, and most departments of city government. In addition, a total of 3,664 individuals volunteered to assist in program delivery."[20(p. 778)] Efforts to create a supportive environment included identification of low-fat foods in grocery stores, installation of an exercise course, nutrition programs at the public library, and highlights of heart-healthy selections on restaurant menus. Efforts to permeate the community, its organizations, and social groupings placed particular emphasis on behavior change, low cost, ease of adoption, and visibility.

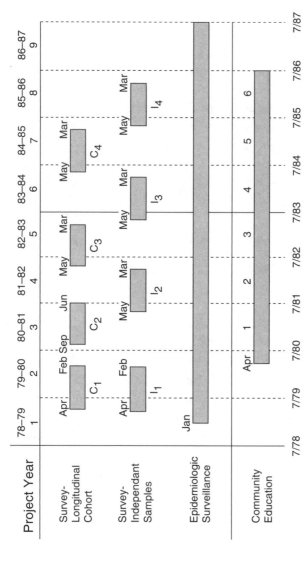

FIGURE 8–4 Design of the nine-year Stanford Five-City Project, encompassing the initial surveys and the intervention. The project was subsequently extended to 18 years, including four years of education maintenance activity (to 1990) and six additional years of surveillance (through 1992). C_1–C_4, cohorts 1–4; I_1–I_4, independent samples 1–4. *Source:* Reprinted with permission from Fortmann SP et al., Community intervention trials: reflections on the Stanford Five-City Project experience, *American Journal of Epidemiology,* Vol 142, No 6, p. 579, © 1995, The Johns Hopkins University School of Hygiene and Public Health.

Evaluation of the community intervention included cross-sectional surveys in the intervention and control communities at baseline, four times over the course of the intervention, and after the intervention was completed. There was some evidence of lower mean cholesterol and blood pressure levels in Pawtucket, with significantly lower projected disease rates. According to the authors of the report, however, "The hypothesis that projected cardiovascular disease risk can be altered by community-based education gains limited support from these data. Achieving cardiovascular risk reduction at the community level was feasible, but maintaining statistically significant differences between cities was not."[20(p. 777)]

The Community Intervention Trial for Smoking Cessation was conducted as a multicenter project beginning in 1989. The project sought to reach cigarette smokers and bring about long-term cessation of the habit.[21] This intervention trial involved 11 matched pairs of communities throughout the United States and Canada and was believed to affect more than 200,000 adult smokers.

The Community Clinical Oncology Program, begun in 1983, is sponsored by the National Cancer Institute.[22] As part of a larger clinical trials network, it is designed to evaluate the efficacy of new chemopreventive agents for cancer. In 1987, cooperative groups were formed that consisted of an administrative core, statistical center, member institutions, and affiliated physicians. These cooperative groups and the clinical trials network have been involved in such cancer prevention and control research activities as the implementation of the Tamoxifen and Finasteride Prevention Trials.

We point out that there are many other examples of community trials. In recent times, community-based interventions have been conducted for the purpose of HIV prevention. Many of these interventions may be characterized as rigorous and theory based with multi-arms, multi-sites, or using multiple outcome measures. An illustration of a multi-site study was a randomized controlled community trial that evaluated the impact of an HIV/AIDS prevention program in Tanzania.[23] Prevention programs were adopted in Arusha and Kilimanjaro, neighboring areas in Tanzania. The target study sites were all public primary schools, which were stratified for random assignment to intervention or comparison conditions. Investigators reported that intervention groups showed a significant increase in knowledge of AIDS information and had significantly more positive attitudes toward people with AIDS relative to the comparison groups. Another example of an AIDS-related community trial is shown in Exhibit 8–5.

EXHIBIT 8–5

Project RESPECT

Project RESPECT is an example of a randomized controlled trial for prevention of HIV and other STDs.[24] The trial sought to establish the efficacy of several counseling methods for reducing high-risk sexual behaviors. This effort involved collaboration among a clinic in Long Beach, California, as well as four other inner-city clinics across the United States.

The project had four interventions. In a study that has several different interventions, each type is called an arm. The four arms of project RESPECT were enhanced counseling (arm 1), brief counseling (arm 2), and didactic messages (arms 3 and 4). Arms 1 through 3 were followed up actively after enrollment with periodic questionnaires and STD tests for one year. Outcome measures were use of condoms and new occurrence of STDs.

The study sample comprised a total of 5,758 HIV-negative heterosexual patients (14 years of age and older) who presented at the five STD clinics for examinations. Project investigators randomly assigned subjects to one of the four arms of the trial (with approximately equal numbers of subjects in each arm). The results of this study demonstrated that brief counseling sessions for risk reduction (as opposed to didactic sessions) are effective in increasing condom use and preventing the occurrence of new STDs. ∎

Summary of Community Trials

Community trials are crucial because they represent the only way to estimate directly the realistic impact of a change in behavior or some other modifiable exposure on the incidence of disease. They are inferior to clinical trials with respect to the ability to control entrance into the study, delivery of the intervention, and monitoring of outcomes. With clinical trials one can potentially randomize a large enough number of subjects to ensure that the study groups are comparable with respect to both measured and unmeasured variables. This statement is less true of community trials; fewer study units (e.g., communities or subjects) are capable of being randomized. Accordingly, the likelihood remains that the intervention and control communities may differ with respect to racial composition, education level, age distribution, or some other unmeasured variable. In a dynamic population, residents who received the intervention may move away, and people may move into the community after the intervention has begun; such shifting in the composition of the study population may lead to loss of effect. If there are significant secular trends with respect to the prevalence of the exposure being modified, then it may be extremely difficult to demonstrate an effect of the intervention. For example, the prevalence of cigarette smoking among U.S. adults is decreasing irrespective of specific interventions in a given community. A related phenomenon is that of nonintervention influences. Continuing with the example of cigarette smoking, suppose the American Cancer Society decides to implement a national stop-smoking campaign characterized by television, radio, and newspaper messages. Its ability to succeed can affect both control and treatment communities involved in an intervention.

Evaluation of Community Interventions

The benefit of an intervention should never be assumed. Rather, it is important for the investigator to quantify and properly evaluate whether a program has achieved its intended results. Evaluations may be undertaken for a variety of reasons, and the form of the evaluation must obviously follow the function. A thorough coverage of evaluation is beyond the scope of this book. The reader is referred to the text by Rossi and Freeman[18] for greater detail. It is our intent to provide an overview as well as some of the specifics germane to assessment. We note that evaluation is, ideally, a continuing activity that comprises four stages following in sequence: formative, process, impact, and outcome (Exhibit 8–6). The examples that we have provided in this chapter apply mostly to impact evaluation.

In most instances, community interventions make use of quasi-experimental designs because random selection of individual study subjects often is not possible in such interventions. Referring to Table 6–1, you will see that quasi-experimental designs permit manipulation of the study factor but do not permit random assignment of study subjects. Community interventions may involve the random selection of entire communities or other units, but this method of sample selection is not equivalent to random selection of individual subjects. The following section describes four major variations on quasi-experimental designs: posttest only; pretest/posttest; pretest/posttest/control; and Solomon four-group. Table 8–2 gives an overview of these four quasi-experimental designs.

Posttest

One approach to evaluation is simply for the researcher to make observations only after the program has been delivered. The U.S. educational system typically

EXHIBIT 8–6

The Four Stages of Evaluation

Formative Evaluation: "a way of making sure program, plans, procedures, activities, materials, and modifications will work as planned. Begin formative evaluation as soon as the idea for a program is conceived."

Process Evaluation: Its purpose "is to learn whether the program is serving the target population as planned and whether the number of people being served is more or less than expected. Begin process evaluation as soon as the program goes into operation."

Impact Evaluation: Measures "whatever changes the program creates in the target population's knowledge, attitudes, beliefs, or behaviors." Requires collection of baseline information before the program starts and subsequent data after first encounter with the target group. Informs program planners whether they are making progress toward goals.

Outcome Evaluation: "For ongoing programs…, conduct outcome evaluations at specified intervals…For one-time programs conduct outcome evaluation after the program is finished. The purpose is to learn how well the program has accomplished its ultimate goal." ■

Source: Adapted from Thompson NJ, McClintock HO. *Demonstrating Your Program's Worth: A Primer on Evaluation for Programs to Prevent Unintentional Injury.* 1998, pp. 21–22. Atlanta, GA: National Center for Injury Prevention and Control, Centers for Disease Control and Prevention.

Table 8–2　Overview of Quasi-Experimental Study Designs

Type of Study Design	Group(s)	Pretest	Intervention	Posttest
Posttest only (has only one group)	Intervention	O	X	X
Pretest/Posttest (has only one group)	Intervention	X	X	X
Pretest/Posttest/Control (has two groups)	Intervention	X	X	X
	Control	X	O	X
Solomon Four-Group (has four groups)	Intervention 1	X	X	X
	Intervention 2	O	X	X
	Control 1	X	O	X
	Control 2	O	O	X

Note. O = not used; X = used.

follows the pattern for evaluation of classroom instruction. Students enter a class, endure lectures and presentations from the instructor, and then complete examinations to demonstrate that they have acquired knowledge. The advantage of this evaluation method is that it makes explanation of results easy. The obvious limitation is that there is usually no measure for baseline comparison. Perhaps the students who score highest on examinations came into the class with greater prior knowledge of the subject. In a similar vein, an evaluation of the effectiveness of a community program to increase consumption of fresh fruits and vegetables (a posttest-only design) would be unable to determine whether eating habits had actually changed.

Pretest/Posttest

In view of the criticisms leveled at the posttest-only design, one way to improve the evaluation is simply to add a baseline period of observation. The intervention and posttest observations would still be done. By making observations before and after the program is put into effect, one can measure change relative to baseline.

Pretest/Posttest/Control

Although the pretest/posttest design is better than the posttest-only design, the limitation of the former is that there is no measure of external influences that might induce changes in both study groups. One approach to address this deficiency is to add a control group that does not receive the intervention. Observations are made in both intervention and control groups before and after the program. Thus, the effect of any external influences can be estimated by any measured changes that occur in the nonintervention group. The "true" effect of the intervention therefore would be the "observed effect" in the intervention group minus the "nonintervention effect" from external factors as measured in the control group.

Solomon Four-Group Assignment

As alluded to earlier in this chapter, the mere fact that individuals are observed may result in behavior change. In a famous experiment designed to determine the effects of varying light intensity on the productivity of women assembling small electronic parts,[25] it was observed that a change, whether positive or negative, in the intensity of illumination produced an increase in worker productivity.

The investigators reasoned that the workers took the fact that they had been singled out as an experimental group and given a great deal of attention as evidence that the firm was interested in their personal welfare. Termed the *Hawthorne effect* (after the site where the experiment was conducted), the phenomenon is not specific to social experiments but applies to any circumstance that involves human subjects. This is the basis for the placebo control in clinical trials of pharmacologic agents.

One possible solution to the problem of the Hawthorne effect is to design a study that includes four equivalent groups: two intervention and two control groups. Two are observed before and after the program, and the other two are observed only after the program. Thus, one has the pretest/posttest/control design with two additional arms, neither of which had a pretest observation. This design allows one to determine the effect of both the treatment and the observations. Although the Solomon four-group assignment has been used extensively in social science and educational research, epidemiologists seldom employ it. An obvious reason for its limited use is the increased cost inherent in adding two additional study arms. Furthermore, a reanalysis of the Hawthorne experiment cast considerable doubt on whether the work actually demonstrated any observation effect at all[26]; some researchers believe that such an effect is probably rare.[18]

Miscellaneous Issues

Several other issues apply to the design of experiments: external validity, statistical power, and noncompliance. We have already considered external validity in Chapter 5. This term refers to the ability to generalize the results of the clinical or community trial to a target population beyond the subjects of the study. External validity is very much connected with the manner in which the study subjects have been selected (e.g., white, middle-class men only, or a more diverse sample). Findings from a controlled clinical trial of a new medication using a sample that has limited demographic composition, such as all white men, can be generalized only to a similarly narrow target population. As a result, the research community is required to increase the diversity of human subjects who participate in epidemiologic studies.

The issue of statistical power is linked to the size of the samples selected for the various conditions of the intervention. It refers to the ability of the study design to detect the hypothesized outcomes of the study. Studies that have larger samples in comparison to smaller samples have greater statistical power and

reduced measurement error; of course, larger samples are more costly to collect than smaller samples.

Finally, noncompliance is a factor in experimental study design that has the potential to vitiate or nullify the effects of the intervention. For example, if the subjects in a randomized controlled clinical trial do not take a prescribed medication, the outcome of the trial may be reduced or may not be detectable. Table 8–3 summarizes intervention studies (comparisons of clinical trials and community trials).

Table 8–3 Summary of Intervention Studies (Clinical Trials versus Community Trials)

Clinical Trials	Community Trials
Prospective study that often uses a true experimental design.	Prospective study that often uses a quasi-experimental design.
Used for testing new medications, procedures (therapeutic trials), and substances to prevent disease (prophylactic trials).	Designed to produce changes (especially health-related) in a target population.
Focused on the individual.	Focused on the community, school district, county or state.
Randomization of subjects to the exposure (treatment or control conditions), in order to promote comparability of subjects with respect to measured and unmeasured variables.	Fewer study units can be randomized to the study conditions. Intervention and control communities may differ with respect to race, education, age, and other unmeasured variables.
Manipulation (external control of exposure) is possible.	Manipulation (external control of exposure) is possible.
Duration ranges from days to years (in the case of some trials).	Generally longer time duration than clinical trials.
Strict human subject protocol to regulate eligibility of subjects; informed consent to participate required.	Informed consent of participating subjects required for collection of baseline, outcome, and other information.
Participation restricted to a highly selected group of individuals with disease, at high risk for disease, or volunteers.	Participation involves all members of a targeted community; intervention is applied more generally than in a clinical trial.
Tightly controlled in terms of eligibility, delivery of intervention (treatment), and monitoring of outcome.	Less rigid control over intervention in comparison to clinical trials.
Appropriate for testing narrow hypotheses, such as those related to vaccine treatment testing and evaluating new drugs.	Appropriate for determining the potential benefit of new policies and programs, such as those related to health.

continues

Table 8–3 *continued*

Clinical Trials	Community Trials
Usually two groups (experimental and control) are compared in terms of an outcome.	Baseline measures taken in the intervention and control communities with follow-up at the end of the intervention.
Outcomes of clinical trials (clinical end points): compare rate of disease, death, recovery; outcome of interest is measured in the intervention and control arms of the trial to evaluate efficacy.	Outcomes of community trials: programs may be evaluated according to the four stages of evaluation: formative, process, impact, and outcome. Pre- and posttest measures compared.
Advantages: provide general control over the study situation with respect to amount of exposure, timing, frequency, and period of observation.	Advantages: estimate realistically the impact of behavior change or other modifiable exposure in the incidence of disease.
Disadvantages: Artificial setting of the treatment delivery and evaluation result in lack of generalizability (external validity). Difficulty of adherence to a protocol when trial produces side effects or preliminary results show it to be efficacious.	Disadvantages: loss of effect may occur due to the shifting in the study population composition. Secular trends in respect to prevalence of the exposure being modified make it difficult to determine the effect of the intervention.
Blinding and double blinding are used to promote objectivity.	Blinding and double blinding not generally used.
Variations: crossover design, a switch of treatments for the study patients.	Variations: posttest only, pretest/posttest, pretest/posttest/control, and the Solomon four-group assignment
Examples: the folic acid randomized clinical trial; effectiveness of education efforts to reduce STDs. Refer to text.	Examples: the Pawtucket Heart Healthy Program; Project Respect. Refer to text.

Conclusion

This chapter has provided an overview and description of experimental study designs, both controlled experiments and quasi-experiments, which usually take the form of interventions in the field of epidemiology. Examples of intervention studies covered were clinical trials and community trials. The distinction between the two is that clinical trials focus upon individuals and community trials upon the group. While both clinical trials and community trials can take the form of controlled experiments, community trials, because of their complexity, are often conducted as quasi-experimental designs. Related to the types of study designs is their hierarchy with respect to ability to generate causal inferences. Other issues covered in this chapter were the applications and phasing of clinical trials as well as randomization and crossover designs.

Study Questions and Exercises

1. Define the following terms:
   a. Experimental study
   b. Quasi-experimental study
   c. Intervention study
   d. Controlled clinical trial

2. Compare and contrast the two categories of intervention studies (controlled clinical trials vs. community interventions) discussed in this chapter. What are some advantages and disadvantages of controlled experimental designs in comparison to quasi-experimental designs?

3. Explain the purposes of blinding and randomization in clinical trials.

4. Describe the phases of a clinical trial to license a vaccine or new medicine.

5. What is meant by a crossover design? Distinguish between a planned and unplanned crossover.

6. Can you foresee ethical problems that might arise in the development of new pharmaceutical agents for HIV?

7. What are some of the design strategies that are used to improve the validity of community trials?

Questions 8 and 9 pertain to Chapters 6, 7, and 8.

8. Epidemiologic studies of the role of a suspected factor in the etiology of a disease may be observational or experimental. The essential difference between experimental and observational studies is that in experimental studies: (Choose one answer.)
   a. The study and control groups are equal in size.
   b. The study is prospective.
   c. The study and control groups are always comparable with respect to all factors other than the exposure.
   d. The investigator determines who shall be exposed to the suspected factor and who shall not.
   e. Controls are used.

9. From the descriptions provided, identify the type of study design that is being described:
   a. Smoking histories are obtained from all patients entering a hospital who have lip cancer and are compared with smoking histories of patients with cold sores who enter the same hospital.

b. The entire population of a given community is examined, and all who are judged free of bowel cancer are questioned extensively about their diet. These people are then followed for several years to see whether their eating habits will predict their risk of developing bowel cancer.

c. To test the efficacy of vitamin C in preventing colds, army recruits are randomly assigned to two groups: one given 500 mg of vitamin C daily, and one given a placebo. Both groups are followed to determine the number and severity of subsequent colds.

d. The physical examination records of the incoming first-year class of 1935 at the University of Minnesota are examined in 1980 to see whether the freshmen's recorded height and weight at the time of admission to the university were related to their chance of developing coronary heart disease by 1981.

e. Fifteen hundred adult men who worked for Lockheed Aircraft were initially examined in 1951 and were classified by diagnostic criteria for coronary artery disease. Every three years they have been reexamined for new cases of the disease; attack rates in different subgroups have been computed annually.

f. A random sample of middle-aged sedentary women was selected from four census tracts, and each subject was examined for evidence of osteoporosis. Those found to have the disease were excluded. All others were randomly assigned to either an exercise group, which followed a two-year program of systematic exercise, or a control group, which had no exercise program. Both groups were observed semiannually for incidence of osteoporosis.

g. Questionnaires were mailed to every 10th person listed in the city telephone directory. Each person was asked to provide his or her age, sex, and smoking habits and to describe the presence of any respiratory symptoms during the preceding seven days.

References

1. Last JM, ed. *A Dictionary of Epidemiology*, 4th ed. New York: Oxford University Press; 2001.
2. Susser M. Some principles of study design for preventing HIV transmission: rigor or reality. *Am J Public Health*. 1996;86:1713–1716.
3. Meinert CL. *Clinical Trials: Design, Conduct, and Analysis*. New York: Oxford University Press; 1986.
4. Psaty BM, Siscovick DS, Weiss NS, et al. Hypertension and outcomes research: from clinical trials to clinical epidemiology. *Am J Hypertens*. 1995;9:178–183.

5. Medical Research Council Vitamin Study Research Group. Prevention of neural tube defects: results of the Medical Research Council Vitamin Study. *Lancet.* 1991;338: 131–137.

6. Hibbard BM. The role of folic acid in pregnancy with particular reference to anaemia, abruption, and abortion. *J Obstet Gynaecol Br Commonw.* 1964;71:529–542.

7. O'Donnell LN, San Doval A, Duran R, O'Donnell C. Video-based sexually transmitted disease patient education: its impact on condom acquisition. *Am J Public Health.* 1995;85:817–822.

8. Begg N, Miller E. Role of epidemiology in vaccine policy. *Vaccine.* 1990;8:180–189.

9. Engelking C. Clinical trials: impact evaluation and implementation considerations. *Semin Oncol Nurs.* 1992;8:148–155.

10. Gordis L. *Epidemiology.* 3rd ed. Philadelphia, PA: Elsevier Saunders; 2004.

11. Miké V, Schottenfeld D. Observations on the clinical trial. *Clin Bull.* 1972;2: 130–135.

12. Schwartz CE, Chesney MA, Irvine MJ, Keefe FJ. The control group dilemma in clinical research: applications for psychosocial and behavioral medicine trials. *Psychosom Med.* 1997;59:362–371.

13. National Institutes of Health. Further guidance on a data and safety monitoring for phase I and phase II trials. Notice: OD-00-038, June 5, 2000. Available at: http://grants.nih.gov/grants/guide/notice-files/NOT-OD-00-038.html. Accessed November 22, 2007.

14. National Institutes of Health, National Institute of Allergy and Infectious Diseases, Division of Microbiology and Infectious Diseases. Policy and Guidelines for Data and Safety Monitoring. Available at: http://www3.niaid.nih.gov/research/resources/DMIDClinRsrch/PDF/dsm_pol_guide.pdf. Accessed November 22, 2007.

15. U.S. National Institutes of Health. An Introduction to Clinical Trials. Available at: http://clinicaltrials.gov/ct/info/whatis. Accessed October 30, 2007.

16. Begg C, Cho M, Eastwood S, et al. Improving the quality of reporting of randomized controlled trials: the CONSORT statement. *JAMA.* 1996;276:637–639.

17. Moher D, Schultz KF, Altman DG. The CONSORT statement: Revised recommendations for improving the quality of reports of parallel-group randomized trials. *Lancet.* 2001;357:1191–1194.

18. Rossi PH, Freeman HE. *Evaluation: A Systematic Approach,* 4th ed. Newbury Park, CA: Sage; 1989.

19. Carleton RA, Lasater TM, Assaf A, Lefebvre RC, McKinlay SM. The Pawtucket Heart Health Program, I: an experiment in population-based disease prevention. *R I Med J.* 1987;70:533–538.

20. Carleton RA, Lasater TM, Assaf AR, Lefebvre RC, McKinlay SM. The Pawtucket Heart Health Program: community changes in cardiovascular risk factors and projected disease risk. *Am J Public Health.* 1995;85:777–785.

21. COMMIT Research Group. Community Intervention Trial for Smoking Cessation (COMMIT): summary of design and intervention. *J Natl Cancer Inst.* 1991;83: 1620–1628.

22. Kaluzny AD, Warnecke RB, Lacey LM, et al. Cancer prevention and control within the National Cancer Institute's clinical trials network: lessons from the Community Clinical Oncology Program. *J Natl Cancer Inst.* 1993;85:1807–1811.

23. Klepp K, Ndeki SS, Leshabari MT, Hannan PJ, Lyimo BA. AIDS education in Tanzania: Promoting risk reduction among primary school children. *Am J Public Health.* 1997;87:1931–1936.

24. Kamb ML, Fishbein M, Douglas JM, et al. Efficacy of a risk-reduction counseling to prevent human immunodeficiency virus and sexually transmitted diseases: a randomized controlled trial. *JAMA*. 1998;280:1161–1167.
25. Roethlisberger FJ, Dickson W. *Management and the Worker*. Cambridge, MA: Harvard University Press; 1939.
26. Franke RH, Kaul JD. The Hawthorne experiments: first statistical interpretation. *Am Sociol Rev*. 1978;43:623–642.

Measures of Effect

LEARNING OBJECTIVES

By the end of this chapter the reader will be able to:

- explain the meaning of absolute and relative effects
- calculate and interpret the following measures: risk difference, population risk difference, etiologic fraction, and population etiologic fraction
- define the role of statistical tests in epidemiologic research
- apply five criteria for evaluation of epidemiologic associations

CHAPTER OUTLINE

I. Introduction
II. Absolute Effects
III. Relative Effects
IV. Statistical Measures of Effect
V. Evaluating Epidemiologic Associations
VI. Models of Causal Relationships
VII. Conclusion
VIII. Study Questions and Exercises

Introduction

One of the major challenges to an epidemiologist is presentation of research findings in a meaningful and interpretable manner. Much of the basic vocabulary ("epi-speak") for presentation of data and results was defined in Chapter 3. As part of the presentation on study designs in Chapters 6 and 7, the terms *odds ratios (OR)* and *relative risk (RR)* were defined and illustrated. The purpose of this chapter is to extend the discussion begun in Chapter 6 by introducing several additional measures that are useful when one is attempting to evaluate the potential implications of an exposure-disease association. For the science of public health, the ability to extrapolate the health ramifications for the larger population from the findings of individual studies is critical to the planning of programs and delivery of resources. A knowledge of the measures presented in this chapter will facilitate planning and evaluation of proposed interventions. We also demonstrate that the exposure-disease association can have quite different implications for risk to the individual and impact upon the population.

Absolute Effects

One of the simplest ways to compare the disease burden in two groups is to calculate the absolute difference in disease frequency. This type of comparison also is referred to as a difference measure of association, or attributable risk.[1] An absolute effect may be based on differences in incidence rates, cumulative incidence, prevalence,[2] or mortality.[3] An attributable risk is also known as a rate difference or risk difference.[2,4]

Risk Difference

I_e = Incidence rate of disease in exposed group

I_{ne} = Incidence rate of disease in nonexposed group

Recall from Chapter 2 the discussion about causality in epidemiology. Rothman's comments are particularly relevant:

> A *cause* is an act or event or a state of nature which initiates or permits, alone or in conjunction with other causes, a sequence of events resulting in an *effect*. A cause which inevitably produces the effect is *sufficient*. The inevitability of disease after a

sufficient cause calls for qualification: disease usually requires time to become manifest, and during this gestation, while disease may no longer be preventable, it might be fortuitously cured, or death might intervene . . . Most causes that are of interest in the health field are components of sufficient causes but are not sufficient in themselves . . . Causal research focuses on components of sufficient causes, whether necessary or not.[5(p. 588)]

Along the lines of Rothman's statements, it is asserted elsewhere in this book that many chronic diseases, for example, coronary heart disease (CHD), result not from a single exposure but rather from the combined influences of several exposures, such as environmental and lifestyle factors, that operate over a long time period. Therefore, removal of only one of the exposures (e.g., high serum cholesterol) that leads to a chronic disease (i.e., CHD) would not result in complete elimination of the disease; other risk factors would still be operative and contribute to the rate of disease. One approach to estimate the realistic potential impact of removing an exposure from the population is to calculate the risk difference in disease frequency (i.e., incidence rates) between the exposed and the nonexposed groups. According to Rothman, a risk difference "represents the incidence rate of disease with the exposure as a component cause."[2(p. 35)]

> *Risk difference:* The difference between the incidence rate of disease in the exposed group (I_e) and the incidence rate of disease in the nonexposed group (I_{ne}); risk difference = $I_e - I_{ne}$.[4]

As mentioned earlier, the measure of disease frequency used in the determination of absolute effects may be incidence density, cumulative incidence, prevalence, or mortality. Thus, to be perfectly accurate, when the measure of disease frequency is cumulative incidence, the term *risk difference* could be used. When incidence density measures are used as the measure of disease frequency, the term *rate difference* is most appropriate. For prevalence and mortality, the most precise terms would be *prevalence difference* and *mortality difference*, respectively. Regardless of the measure of disease frequency used, the basic concept of absolute effects is the same: The measure of disease frequency among the nonexposed group is subtracted from the measure of disease frequency among the exposed group.

As an example, hip fractures pose a significant public health burden for the aged population. In 2002, there were an estimated 44 million U.S. adults with osteoporosis or low bone mass.[6] Investigators at the Mayo Clinic in Rochester,

Minnesota, examined seasonal variations in fracture rates, comparing the rates during winter with those during summer.[7] For women younger than age 75, the incidence I_e of fractures per 100,000 person-days was highest in the winter (0.41), and the incidence I_{ne} was lowest in the summer (0.29). The risk difference between the two seasons ($I_e - I_{ne}$) was 0.41 − 0.29, or 0.12 per 100,000 person-days.

Population Risk Difference

> I_p = Overall incidence rate of disease in a population
> P_e = Proportion of the population exposed
> P_{ne} = Proportion of the population not exposed

Population risk difference is defined as a measure of the benefit to the population derived by modifying a risk factor. This measure addresses the question of how many cases in the whole population can be attributed to a particular exposure. To understand fully the concept of population risk difference, consider that the incidence rate (risk) of disease in the population (denoted by the symbol I_p), for the simplest case of a dichotomous exposure (exposed or nonexposed), is made up of four components: the incidence rate (risk) of disease in the exposed group (I_e); the incidence rate (risk) of disease in the nonexposed group (I_{ne}); the proportion of the population exposed (P_e); and the proportion of the population not exposed (P_{ne}). The nonexposed group is sometimes called the reference group. The relationship among the four components may be expressed by the following formula:

$$I_p = (I_e)(P_e) + (I_{ne})(P_{ne})$$

Ignore, for the moment, the proportion exposed (P_e) and the proportion not exposed (P_{ne}). If one were to remove the effects of exposure associated with higher rates of disease, the overall rate of disease in the population then would be expected to decrease to the rate observed among the nonexposed, or reference, group. Thus, subtraction of the rate (risk) of disease among the nonexposed (I_{ne}) from the rate of disease among the population (I_p) provides an indication of the potential impact of a public health intervention designed to eliminate the harmful exposure.

> *Population risk difference:* The difference between the rate (risk) of disease in the nonexposed segment of the population (I_{ne}) and the overall rate (I_p).

Just as for the risk difference, the measures of disease frequency used to calculate population risk differences may be generalized to include the cumulative incidence (risk), incidence density (rates), prevalence, or mortality. Remember: Risk difference is the risk in the exposed minus the risk in the nonexposed; population risk difference is the risk in the population minus the risk in the nonexposed subset of the population.

As another example, nonsteroidal anti-inflammatory drugs (NSAIDs) are the most frequently used drugs in the United States and have been estimated to cost about $6.5 billion annually.[8] To examine the association of NSAID usage and peptic ulcer disease among elderly persons, Smalley et al.[9] determined the incidence rate of serious ulcer disease among users and nonusers of NSAIDs. The study was based on 103,954 elderly Tennessee Medicaid recipients followed from 1984 to 1986. A total of 1,371 patients were hospitalized with peptic ulcer disease after 209,068 person-years of follow-up. The incidence (density) rate of peptic ulcer disease in the study population (I_p) was calculated to be 6.6 per 1,000 person-years [(1,371/209,068) × 1,000]. The rate (I_{ne}) among nonusers of NSAIDs was only 4.2 per 1,000 person-years. The population risk difference ($I_p - I_{ne}$) was 6.6 − 4.2, or 2.4 per 1,000 person-years. The risk difference may be computed also: It was known that the observed incidence rate (I_e) of peptic ulcer disease among users of NSAIDs was 16.7 per 1,000 person-years. Therefore, the risk difference ($I_e - I_{ne}$) was 16.7 − 4.2, or 12.5 per 1,000 person-years.

Relative Effects

Interpretation of the absolute measures of effect can sometimes be enhanced when expressed relative to a baseline rate. For example, RR (discussed in Chapter 7) provides an estimate of the magnitude of an association between exposure and disease.[4] Such a ratio also can be described as a relative effect. Note that all relative effects contain an absolute effect in the numerator.

Previously, we defined RR as the ratio of the cumulative incidence rate in the exposed (I_e) to the cumulative incidence rate in the nonexposed (I_{ne}), or I_e/I_{ne}. This is actually a simplification of the true formula for RR, in which the numerator is $I_e - I_{ne}$ (the risk difference). If one divides both terms in the numerator by I_{ne}, one is left with the formula $(I_e/I_{ne}) - (I_{ne}/I_{ne})$. The first term, I_e/I_{ne}, was previously defined as the RR. Because any number (or variable) divided by itself is 1, the second term becomes 1, and the expression becomes RR $- 1$. Typically the $- 1$ is ignored. Occasionally, however, one may encounter statements such as "30% greater risk among the exposed"; this statement implies that the RR ratio of I_e/I_{ne} is 1.3 but that the 1 has been subtracted. The interpretation is exactly the same. RRs between 1.0 and 2.0 sound bigger when stated as a percentage, however (e.g., 1.3 vs. 30%).

Etiologic Fraction

One of the conceptual difficulties with RR is that the rate of disease in the referent (nonexposed) group is not necessarily 0. In fact, for a common disease that is theorized to have multiple contributing causes, the rate may still be quite high in the referent group as a result of other causes in addition to the exposure of interest. One implication of multiple contributing causes is that, even in the absence of exposure to the single factor of interest, a number of cases still would have developed among the nonexposed population. An approach to estimating the effects due to the single exposure factor is to compute the *etiologic fraction*. It is defined as the proportion of the rate in the exposed group that is due to the exposure. Also termed attributable proportion or attributable fraction, it can be estimated by two formulas. To estimate the number of cases among the exposed that are attributable to the exposure, one must subtract from the exposed group those cases that would have occurred irrespective of membership in the exposed population.

$$\text{Etiologic fraction} = \frac{(I_e - I_{ne})}{I_e} \qquad \text{(Eq. 1)}$$

Note that the difference between Equation 1 and RR is the rate in the denominator, I_e instead of I_{ne}. The numerator represents an acknowledgment that not all the cases among the exposed group can be fairly ascribed to the exposure; some fraction would have occurred anyway, and this fraction is estimated by the rate in the nonexposed. This formula can be applied to data from cohort or cross-sectional studies. The appropriate measures of disease frequency must be utilized: cumulative incidence, incidence density, or mortality from cohort studies or prevalence of disease from cross-sectional studies.

With a little arithmetic, it is possible to express Equation 1, the formula for etiologic fraction, in another convenient form. If one considers Equation 1 as two separate fractions, one obtains $1 - (I_{ne}/I_e)$. Note that (I_{ne}/I_e) is merely the reciprocal of the original definition of RR. Thus, one is left with $1 - (1/RR)$. If one expresses the 1 as RR/RR, the formula requires only an estimate of RR, obviously beneficial for those situations in which the actual incidence rates are unknown (Equation 2). Thus, this formula may be applied when the data at hand, whether from a report or a published article, include only the summary measures. More important, because the OR provides an estimate of RR, this formula is applicable to data from case-control studies.

$$\text{Etiologic fraction} = \frac{(RR - 1)}{RR} \qquad \text{(Eq. 2)}$$

For example, what fraction of peptic ulcer disease in elderly persons is attributable to NSAIDs? Recall from the previous example that I_{ne} was 4.2 and I_e was 16.7 per 1,000 person-years.[9] The risk difference was computed to be 16.7 − 4.2, or 12.5 per 1,000 person-years. The etiologic fraction from Equation 1 is 12.5 ÷ 16.7, or 74.9%. Thus, roughly three-fourths of the cases of peptic ulcer disease that occurred among NSAID users were attributed to that exposure.

To demonstrate that both formulas are equivalent, one may compute the etiologic fraction using Equation 2. To do this, one must first compute the RR. In this example the answer is 16.7 ÷ 4.2, or 3.98. The etiologic fraction is therefore 2.98 divided by 3.98. Both formulas should yield the same answer, an outcome that the reader may wish to verify.

In general, low RRs equate to a low etiologic fraction, and high RRs equate to a high etiologic fraction. A reasonable question to ask at this point is: What does risk difference reveal beyond what one could already infer from the RR? Perhaps this question is best answered with an illustration. Take the case of two diseases, A and B, and two exposure factors, X and Y. The rate of disease A is 2 per 100,000 per year among individuals exposed to factor X and 1 per 100,000 per year among those not exposed to factor X. The rate of disease B is 400 per 100,000 per year among individuals exposed to factor Y and 200 per 100,000 per year among those not exposed to factor Y. Therefore, for either disease the RR associated with the relevant exposure is 2 (i.e., 2 ÷ 1 or 400 ÷ 200). Exposure factors X and Y both appear to pose a significant health hazard, a doubling of risk of disease. Consider what is obtained by examining the risk difference: For disease A the risk difference is 2 − 1 or 1 per 100,000 per year, and for disease B the risk difference is 400 − 200 or 200 per 100,000 per year. Although the RRs for factor X and factor Y are the same, the risk differences for the two factors are quite disparate. If one were to design an intervention to improve public health, the RRs for factors X and Y would not be terribly informative. The risk difference calculations would suggest, however, that control of exposure Y might pay greater dividends than control of exposure X (ignoring, for the moment, critical issues such as cost and feasibility).

Population Etiologic Fraction

As we have seen, from the perspective of those with a disease, the etiologic fraction gives an indication of the potential benefit of removing a particular exposure to a putative disease factor. That is, does a particular exposure account for 5% of the etiology of the disease or 95%? An alternative perspective to consider is that of the population. The population etiologic fraction provides an indication of the effect of removing a particular exposure on the burden of disease in the population. A possible scenario is one in which a dichotomous (present or absent) exposure factor is associated with risk of disease and 25% of the population is exposed to the factor. As was pointed out earlier, the total rate of disease in the population may be thought of as a weighted average of the rate of disease among the 25% of the population exposed and the rate of disease among the 75% of the population not exposed (the concept of weighted average was applied, in Chapter 3, to the direct method of age adjustment). If the offending exposure is reduced, the lower limit of disease rate that can be achieved is the background rate observed among the nonexposed segment of the population. Again, two formulas for the population etiologic fraction will be presented.

The population etiologic fraction (also termed the attributable fraction in the population) represented by Equation 3 is the proportion of the rate of disease in the population that is due to the exposure. It is calculated as the population risk difference divided by the rate of disease in the population.

$$\text{Population etiologic fraction} = \frac{(I_p - I_{ne})}{I_p} \qquad \text{(Eq. 3)}$$

As an example, consider again the study of NSAIDs and peptic ulcer disease among elderly persons.[9] I_{ne} was 4.2, I_p was 6.6 per 1,000 person-years, and the population risk difference was computed to be 6.6 − 4.2, or 2.4 per 1,000 person-years. For this example, the population etiologic fraction is (2.4/6.6) × 100 = 36.4%. Therefore, if everyone in the population stopped taking NSAIDs, the rate of peptic ulcer disease would decrease by more than one-third. Notice that compared with the etiologic fraction of those with the disease, this value of 36.4% is far less than the etiologic fraction of 74.9%.

When the incidence rate in the population is unknown, an alternative formula (Equation 4) may be applied. This formula requires information about two components: the RR of disease associated with the exposure of interest, and the prevalence of the exposure in the population (P_e).

$$\text{Population etiologic fraction} = \frac{P_e(\text{RR} - 1)}{P_e(\text{RR} - 1) + 1} \times 100 \quad \text{(Eq. 4)}$$

Case-control studies do not allow an estimation of disease rates in the total population or in the nonexposed population and, therefore, the Equation 3 population etiologic fraction cannot be used. Equation 4, however, lends itself to interpretation of data from case-control studies because the OR can be substituted for RR. The missing piece of information is the prevalence of the exposure in the population. Recall from Chapter 6 (selection of controls in a case-control study) that the purpose of a control group is to provide an estimate of the expected frequency of the exposure of interest. With certain assumptions, the frequency of exposure among the control group can be used to approximate the overall frequency of exposure in the population.

Example 1: Given that the prevalence (P_e) of current NSAID use in the study by Smalley et al.[9] was 0.13, compute the population etiologic fraction using Equation 4. The RR had been previously determined to be 3.98. Plugging the values for RR and P_e into Equation 4, one obtains:

$$\frac{0.13(3.98 - 1)}{0.13(3.98 - 1) + 1} \times 100 = \frac{0.387}{1.387} \times 100 = 27.9\%$$

This answer is slightly lower than the results obtained by using Equation 3 for the population etiologic fraction because the prevalence figure P_e did not include former or indeterminate users of NSAIDs. Mathematically the two formulas yield the same result, however.

Example 2: Suppose you are dealing with an exposure that confers a high RR for disease (e.g., RR = 20), but the prevalence (P_e) of the exposure in the population is low (e.g., 1 per 100,000). Compare the etiologic fraction with the population etiologic fraction using these data. Compute the etiologic fraction using Equation 2. We obtain:

$$\frac{20 - 1}{20} \times 100 = 95\%$$

From Equation 4, we obtain:

$$\frac{0.00001(20 - 1)}{0.00001(20 - 1) + 1} \times 100 = 0.019\%$$

Thus, 95% of the cases that occurred among the exposed were attributable to the exposure. Because the exposure was rare in the population, however, it contributed little to the total disease rate.

These two examples illustrate that the impact of an exposure on a population depends upon:

- the strength of the association between exposure and resulting disease
- the overall incidence rate of disease in the population
- the prevalence of the exposure in the population

One may also infer that exposures of high prevalence and low RR can have a major impact on public health. Chapter 2 provided an example of an individual's slight risk of cardiovascular disease mortality associated with a high serum cholesterol level; that is, the etiologic fraction was low. Because a substantial proportion of the population has high cholesterol, however (i.e., has a high prevalence of hypercholesterolemia), the benefit to the population from reducing cholesterol could be substantial. In contrast, the foregoing example of a rare exposure with a high RR for disease demonstrates that a single exposure factor can account for the vast majority of cases of disease among the exposed but that removal of that particular exposure from the population will have little impact on the overall incidence of disease.

Statistical Measures of Effect

In addition to the preceding methods of expressing epidemiologic study results (absolute and relative effects), epidemiologists frequently employ and rely on statistical tests to help interpret observed associations. An illustration of statistical tests arises from a study of the effects of passive smoking (by parents) on the prevalence of wheezing respiratory illness among their children.[10] The results indicate that mothers who smoked at the time of the survey were 1.4 times more likely to report wheezing respiratory illness among their children than mothers who did not smoke. The reasons for this outcome may be as follows:

1. Passive smoking by a parent does, in fact, increase children's risk of wheezing respiratory illness.
2. Some additional exposure has not been properly allowed for in the analysis.
3. The results represent nothing more than a chance (random) finding.

Only after options 2 and 3 have been ruled out can one reasonably conclude that passive smoking increases children's risk of wheezing respiratory illness.

Significance Tests

Underlying all statistical tests is a null hypothesis, usually stated as, "There is no difference in population parameters among the groups being compared." The parameters may consist of the prevalence or incidence of disease in the population. For example, the prevalence or incidence might represent an actual count of cases of disease identified by surveillance programs, or by other means such as positive serological evidence of infection from elevated antibody titers (discussed in Chapter 12). A discussion of the particular statistical test to be employed, the choice of which is determined by a number of considerations, is beyond the scope of this book. Suffice it to say that, in deciding whether to fail to reject or to reject the null hypothesis, a test statistic is computed and compared with a critical value obtained from a set of statistical tables. The significance level is the chance of rejecting the null hypothesis when, in fact, it is true.

The P Value

The P value indicates the probability that the findings observed could have occurred by chance alone. The converse is not true: A nonsignificant difference is not necessarily attributable to chance alone. For studies with a small sample size, the sampling error is likely to be large, which may lead to a nonsignificant test even when the observed difference is caused by a real effect.

Confidence Interval

A confidence interval (CI) is a statistical measure that is considered by many epidemiologists to be more meaningful than a point estimate; the latter is a single number—for example, a sample mean, an incidence rate, or an RR—that is used to estimate a population parameter. A CI is expressed as a computed interval of values that, with a given probability, contains the true value of the population parameter.[11] The degree of confidence is usually stated as a percentage; the 95% CI is commonly used. Although it is beyond the scope of this book to demonstrate how to construct CIs, it is important, nonetheless, to know how to interpret them. A CI can be interpreted as a measure of uncertainty about a parameter estimate (e.g., a mean, OR, RR, or incidence rate).

- In terms of utility, a 95% CI contains the "true" population estimate 95% of the time.
- Thus, if one samples a population 100 times, the 95% CI will contain the true estimate (i.e., the population parameter) 95 times. Alternatively, if one were to repeat the study 100 times, one would observe the same outcome 5 times just by chance.
- CIs are influenced by the variability of the data and the sample size.

The hypothetical example presented in Table 9–1 reports the OR for a case-control study with three different sample sizes. The exposure, disease, study population, and survey instrument are the same in all three cases. In fact, everything is identical except for the size of the study groups.

Perhaps the first sample size was obtained for a small-scale pilot study. Twenty cases and 20 controls are included. An OR of 2 is observed, but the 95% CI

Table 9–1 Odds Ratios, *P* Values, and 95% Confidence Intervals for a Case-Control Study with Three Different Sample Sizes

Parameter Computed	Sample Size		
	20	50	500
OR	2.0	2.0	2.0
P	0.50	0.20	0.001
95% CI	0.5, 7.7	0.9, 4.7	1.5, 2.6

includes 1; the results are therefore consistent with no association. Suppose, alternatively, that one is able to study 50 per group instead of only 20. The same point estimate of association is observed, and the 95% CI also includes the null value of 1. The degree of precision of the magnitude of the OR is improved; the interval is narrower, but the results are still not statistically significant. In the final scenario there are unlimited resources, and one is able to study 500 individuals in each group. With this extra effort and expense, the same study results are obtained: an OR of 2. The larger sample size has allowed for a more precise estimate of the effect to be obtained (the 95% CI is narrower). The outcome is now statistically significant, as the null value of 1 is now excluded from the 95% CI for the OR. The point to be made is that the estimate of an effect from an epidemiologic study is not necessarily incorrect just because the sample size is small; a small sample size merely may not produce precise results (i.e., there is a wide CI around the estimate of effect).

Clinical Versus Statistical Significance

The preceding discussion of statistical significance should suggest to the reader that *P* values are only a part of the evaluation of the validity of epidemiologic data.

One also should be aware of an important caveat of large sample sizes: Small differences in disease frequency or low magnitudes of RR may be statistically significant. Such minimal effects may have no clinical significance, however. For example, suppose an investigator conducted a survey among pregnant women in urban and suburban populations to assess folic acid levels. Furthermore, suppose that there were 2,000 women in each group, that the average folic acid levels differed by 1.3%, and that this difference was statistically significant. In this example, the sample size was large enough to detect subtle differences in exposure; biologically and clinically, such small differences may be quite insignificant.

The converse of the large sample size issue is that, with small samples, large differences or measures of effect may be clinically important and worthy of additional study. Thus, mere inspection of statistical significance could cause oversight. The lack of statistical significance may simply be a reflection of insufficient statistical power to detect a meaningful association. Statistical power is defined as, "The ability of a study to demonstrate an association if one exists. The power of a study is determined by several factors, including the frequency of the condition under study, the magnitude of the effect, the study design, and sample size."[11] One example of the magnitude of the effect is how large a relative risk is found, that is, whether RR = 1, 5, or 10.

Another problem inherent in the use of statistical significance testing is that it may lead to mechanical thinking. In his Cassel Memorial Lecture to the Society for Epidemiologic Research Annual Meeting in June 1995, Rothman[12] noted that John Graunt's famous epidemiologic contributions were made in the absence of a knowledge of statistical significance testing.

Evaluating Epidemiologic Associations

The ability to evaluate critically epidemiologic associations reported in the literature is a realistic and attainable goal for the public health practitioner. Although the basic skills to perform such an evaluation are covered in this book, there is no substitute for practice. As an aid to the reader, five key questions that should be asked are presented below.

Could the Association Have Been Observed by Chance?

The major tools that are used to answer this question are statistical tests. Although any public health practitioner should have a basic understanding of biostatistics, he or she should not underestimate the value of a competent biostatistician as a source of help.

Could the Association Be Due to Bias?

The term *bias*, which refers to systematic errors, is discussed in detail in Chapter 10. At this point it is sufficient to say that one should critically evaluate how the study groups were selected, how the information about exposure and disease was collected, and how the data were analyzed. Errors at any of these stages may lead to results that are not valid.

Could Other Confounding Variables Have Accounted for the Observed Relationship?

Confounding refers to the masking of an association between an exposure and an outcome because of the influence of a third variable that was not considered in the design or analysis. The issue of confounding and how to control it is covered in Chapter 10. Based on one's understanding of the natural history and epidemiology of a disease, one needs to consider whether important known confounding factors have been omitted from the study.

To Whom Does This Association Apply?

Although population-based samples are important in epidemiologic research, and although these sampling procedures enhance the likelihood of generalizability of results, they do not guarantee such an outcome. Furthermore, in some situations a great deal can be learned from an unrepresentative study sample. If a study has been properly conducted among a certain stratum of the population, for example, white women between the ages of 55 and 69 who live in the state of Iowa, then one could certainly generalize to other white women who live in the Midwest. If the diets of the women in Iowa are indicative of the diets of American women of this age group, however, then any observed diet-disease associations may apply to a much broader population.

In addition to the representativeness of the sample, many investigators believe that participation rates are crucial to the validity of epidemiologic findings. Participation rates, the percentage of a sample that completes the data collection phase of a study, must be at a sufficiently high level. For example, some top-tier public health journals may not publish a report in which the participation rate was less than 70%. Ironically, high participation rates do not necessarily ensure generalizability, and in certain circumstances generalizability may be high even if participation rates are low. Consider a study of a potential precursor of colorectal cancer: the rate of proliferation of cells in the rectal mucosa. Measurement of the proliferation rate of the rectal epithelium requires a punch biopsy, obtainable as part of a sigmoidoscopy or colonoscopy procedure. Suppose one conducts a case-control study of patients with adenomatous polyps (a known precursor of colorectal cancer) and controls free from colon polyps or cancer. Cases are found to have significantly higher rates of rectal cell proliferation than the controls. Because of the invasive nature of the procedure, however, the participation rates are only 10% among the eligible cases and 5% among eligible controls. Does this necessarily mean that the findings cannot be generalized? The key issue is whether the exposure of interest influenced the decision process of the eligible cases and controls to participate. In this example, it is difficult to imagine how an unmeasured characteristic, such as the rate of rectal cell proliferation, could possibly influence participation. Therefore, despite participation rates that usually would be regarded as unacceptable, one may still be able to generalize the findings, especially the underlying biology, to a broader population.

Does the Association Represent a Cause-and-Effect Relationship?

The answer to this question is determined by careful consideration of each of the criteria of causality that were identified and described in Chapter 2: strength of the association, temporality, dose-response, consistency, biologic plausibility, specificity, analogy, and coherence. Refer to Chapter 2 to review these concepts.

Models of Causal Relationships

Drawing upon the concepts presented earlier in the chapter, this section introduces models of disease causation. Relationships between suspected disease-causing factors and outcomes fall into two general categories: not statistically associated and statistically associated.[13] Among statistical associations are noncausal and causal associations. Possible types of associations are formatted in Figure 9–1.

We have already considered the role of statistical significance in evaluating an association and noted that evaluation of statistical significance is used to rule out the operation of chance in producing an observed association; a non-statistically associated (independent) relationship is shown in box A of the diagram (left side).

As shown in Figure 9–1, a statistical association may be either noncausal or causal. What is meant by a noncausal (secondary) association? Suppose factor C is related to disease outcome A. The association may be due to the operation of a third factor B that is related to both C and A. Thus, the association between C and A is secondary to the association of C with B and C with A. For example, periodontal disease (C) is associated with chronic obstructive pulmonary disease (A).[14] One possible explanation for this association is the secondary association

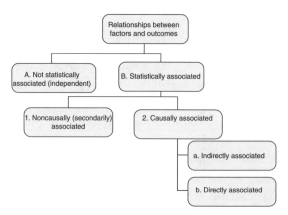

FIGURE 9–1   Map of possible associations between disease-causing factors and outcomes. *Source:* Data are from MacMahon B, Pugh TF. *Epidemiology Principles and Methods.* Boston: Little, Brown and Company; 1970.

of smoking (B) with both periodontal disease (C) and chronic obstructive pulmonary disease (A). This model suggests that the increased risk of chronic obstructive pulmonary disease associated with periodontal disease is related to the role that smoking may play as a co-factor in both conditions. Here is a map of a secondary association: C ← B → A.[11]

With respect to causal associations, the relationship between factor and outcome may be indirect or direct. An indirect causal association involves the operation of an intervening variable, which is a variable that falls in the chain of association between C and A. An illustration of an indirect association is the postulated relationship between low education levels (C) and obesity (A) among men.[15] Men who have lower education levels tend to be more obese than those who have higher education levels. It is plausible that the relationship between C and A operates through the intervening variable of lack of leisure time physical activity (B). An indirect association involves an intervening variable in the association between C and A. This relationship may be formatted as follows: C → B → A.[11] Note that the arrow between C and B has been reversed in contrast with an indirect noncausal association.

Multiple Causality

The foregoing section provided models of causality that employ more than one factor. As stated earlier in this chapter, the measure *risk difference* implies multivariate causality by isolating the effects of a single exposure from the effects of other exposures. The example on NSAIDs examined the difference between risk of peptic ulcer among users and non-users of NSAIDs, where the risk difference was 12.5 per 1,000 person-years. The risk of peptic ulcer caused by other exposures was 4.2 per 1,000 person-years.

The issue of disease causality is exceedingly complicated. To describe exposure–disease relationships, epidemiologists have developed complex models of disease causality. These models acknowledge the multifactor causality of diseases, even those that seem to have "simple" infectious agents. Often, these models involve an ecologic approach by relating disease to one or more environmental factors. "The requirement that more than one factor be present for disease to develop is referred to as *multiple causation* or *multifactorial etiology*."[16(p. 27)] Examples of several influential models are the:

- epidemiologic triangle (see Chapter 12)
- web of causation
- wheel
- pie model

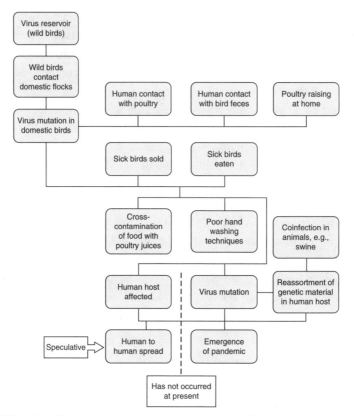

FIGURE 9–2   The web of causation for avian influenza.

Web of Causation

The web of causation is a "metaphor for the complex, multifactorial causation of disease, such as coronary heart disease."[11] The web of causation implicates broad classes of events and represents an incomplete portrayal of reality.[13] Although the web of causation for most diseases is complex, one may not need to understand fully the causality of any specific disease in order to prevent it. An example of the web of causation of avian influenza is provided in Figure 9–2. Follow the infection of the human host from the virus reservoir in wild birds. As of 2007, the virus had not mutated into a form that could be spread readily from person to person.

Wheel Model

The wheel model is similar to the epidemiologic triangle and web of causation with respect to involving multiple causality (Figure 9–3). Observe that the model

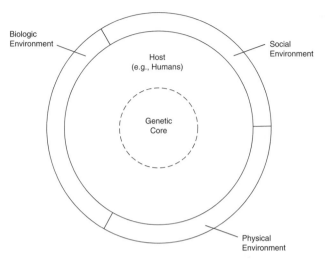

FIGURE 9–3 The wheel model of man-environment interactions. *Source:* Modified with permission from Mausner JS, Kramer S, *Mausner & Baun Epidemiology—An Introductory Text,* 2nd ed. Philadelphia: W.B. Saunders Company; 1985, p. 36.

explains the etiology of disease by calling into play host and environment interactions. Environmental components are biologic, social, and physical. The circle designated as "host" refers to human beings or other hosts affected by a disease. The circle called "genetic core" acknowledges the role that genetic factors play in many diseases. The wheel model deemphasizes specific agent factors and, instead, differentiates between host and environmental factors in disease causation. The biologic environment is relevant to infectious agents, by taking into account the environmental dimensions that permit survival of microbial agents of disease.

A wheel model may be used to account for the occurrence of childhood lead poisoning.[16] In this example, preschool children are typical hosts. The physical environment provides many opportunities for lead exposure from lead-based paint in older homes, playground equipment, candy wrappers, and other sources. Some children ingest paint chips from peeling surfaces as a result of pica, the predilection to eat nonfood substances. Because lead-based paints often are located in poorer neighborhoods that have substandard housing, the social environment is associated with childhood poisoning. Limited access to medical care in such communities may restrict screening of preschool children for lead exposure. Elimination of childhood lead poisoning requires visionary public health leadership to advocate for detection of lead-based paints and other sources of environmental lead exposure as well as the implementation of screening programs. Such efforts will help to protect vulnerable children against the seque-lae of lead poisoning.

Pie Model

Another model of multiple causality (multicausality) is the causal pie model.[17] As Figure 9–4 shows, the model indicates that a disease may be caused by more than one causal mechanism (also called a sufficient cause), which is defined as "a set of minimal conditions and events that inevitably produce disease."[17(p. S144)] Each causal mechanism is denoted in Figure 9–4 by the numerals I through III. An example of different causal mechanisms for a disease is provided by the etiology of lung cancer: lung cancer caused by smoking; lung cancer caused by exposure to ionizing radiation; and lung cancer caused by inhalation of carcinogenic solvents in the workplace.

Rothman and Greenland note that, "A given disease can be caused by more than one causal mechanism, and every causal mechanism involves the joint action of a multitude of component causes."[17(p. S145)] The component causes, or factors, are denoted by the letters shown within each pie slice. A single letter indicates a single component cause. A single component could be common to each causal mechanism (shown by the letter A that appears in each pie); in other cases, the component causes for each causal mechanism could be different for each mechanism (shown by the letters that differ across the pies). Returning to the lung cancer example, a common factor that could apply to all causal mechanisms for lung cancer is a genetic predisposition for cancer. Several other compo-

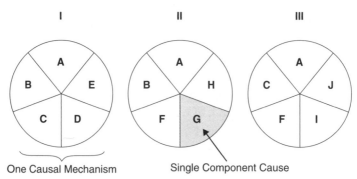

FIGURE 9–4 Three sufficient causes of disease. *Source:* From Rothman KJ, Greenland S. Causation and causal inference in epidemiology. *Am J Public Health.* 2005; Vol 95, p. S145. Reprinted with permission from the American Public Health Association.

nent causes might be different for each causal mechanism involved in the etiology of lung cancer.

In models of multicausality, most of the identified component causes are neither necessary nor sufficient causes (defined in the section on absolute effects). Accordingly, it is possible to prevent disease when a specific component cause that is neither necessary nor sufficient is removed; nevertheless, when the effects of this component cause are removed, cases of the disease will continue to occur.

Conclusion

This chapter covered two new measures of effect—absolute and relative effects—that may be used as aids in the interpretation of epidemiologic studies. In addition, the chapter presented guidelines that should be taken into account when one is interpreting an epidemiologic finding. Absolute effects, the first variety of which is called risk differences, are determined by finding the difference in measures of disease frequency between exposed and nonexposed individuals. A second type of absolute effect, called population risk difference, is found by computing the difference in measures of disease frequency between the exposed segment of the population and the total population. Relative effects are characterized by the inclusion of an absolute effect in the numerator and a reference group in the denominator. One type of relative effect, the etiologic fraction, attempts to quantify the amount of a disease that is attributable to a given exposure. The second type of relative effect, the population etiologic fraction, provides an estimate of the possible impact on the population rates of disease that can be anticipated by removal of the offending exposure. With respect to interpretation of epidemiologic findings, one should be cognizant of the influence of sample size upon the statistical significance of the results. Large sample sizes may lead to clinically unimportant, yet statistically significant, results; small sample sizes may yield statistically nonsignificant results that are clinically important. Therefore, we presented a series of five questions that should be asked when one attempts to interpret an epidemiologic observation. The chapter closed with a discourse on causal models, which may be particularly instructive when trying to interpret epidemiologic data.

Study Questions and Exercises

1. Calculate the etiologic fraction when the RR for disease associated with a given exposure is 1.2, 1.8, 3, and 15.

2. The impact of an exposure on a population does not depend upon:
   a. the strength of the association between exposure and disease
   b. the prevalence of the exposure
   c. the case fatality rate
   d. the overall incidence rate of disease in the population

The next seven questions (3–9) are based on the following data: The death rate per 100,000 for lung cancer is 7 among nonsmokers and 71 among smokers. The death rate per 100,000 for coronary thrombosis is 422 among nonsmokers and 599 among smokers. The prevalence of smoking in the population is 55%. (Refer to Chapter 7 for formulas for RR.)

3. What is the RR of dying of lung cancer for smokers versus nonsmokers?
4. What is the RR of dying of coronary thrombosis for smokers versus nonsmokers?
5. What is the etiologic fraction of disease due to smoking among individuals with lung cancer?
6. What is the etiologic fraction of disease due to smoking among individuals with coronary thrombosis?
7. What is the population etiologic fraction of lung cancer due to smoking?
8. What is the population etiologic fraction of coronary thrombosis due to smoking?
9. On the basis of the RR and etiologic fractions associated with smoking from lung cancer and coronary thrombosis, which one of the following statements is most likely to be correct?
   a. Smoking seems much more likely to be causally related to coronary thrombosis than to lung cancer.
   b. Smoking seems much more likely to be causally related to lung cancer than to coronary thrombosis.
   c. Smoking seems to be equally causally related to both lung cancer and coronary thrombosis.
   d. Smoking does not seem to be causally related to either lung cancer or coronary thrombosis.
   e. No comparative statement is possible between smoking and lung cancer or coronary thrombosis.
10. A cohort study was conducted to investigate the association between coffee consumption and anxiety in a population-based sample of adults. The data are presented in Appendix 9.

a. What is the RR of anxiety associated with coffee use?

b. Calculate the risk (rate) difference.

c. What is the etiologic fraction?

d. Determine the population etiologic fraction.

References

1. Kelsey JL, Thompson WD, Evans AS. *Methods in Observational Epidemiology.* New York: Oxford University Press; 1986.

2. Rothman KJ. *Modern Epidemiology.* Boston: Little, Brown; 1986.

3. Kleinbaum DG, Kupper LL, Morgenstern H. *Epidemiologic Research: Principles and Quantitative Methods.* Belmont, CA: Lifetime Learning; 1982.

4. Hennekins CH, Buring JE. *Epidemiology in Medicine.* Boston: Little, Brown; 1987.

5. Rothman KJ. Causes. *Am J Epidemiol.* 1976;104:587–592.

6. National Osteoporosis Foundation. *America's Bone Health: The State of Osteoporosis and Low Bone Mass in Our Nation.* Washington, DC: National Osteoporosis Foundation; 2002.

7. Jacobsen SJ, Sargent DJ, Atkinson EJ, O'Fallon WM, Melton LJ III. Population-based study of the contribution of weather to hip fracture seasonality. *Am J Epidemiol.* 1995;141:79–83.

8. Laine I. GI risk and risk factors of NSAIDs. *J Cardiovas Pharmacol.* 2006;47(Suppl 1): S60–66.

9. Smalley WE, Ray WA, Daugherty JR, Griffin MR. Nonsteroidal anti-inflammatory drugs and the incidence of hospitalizations for peptic ulcer disease in elderly persons. *Am J Epidemiol.* 1995;141:539–545.

10. Stoddard JJ, Miller T. Impact of parental smoking on the prevalence of wheezing respiratory illness in children. *Am J Epidemiol.* 1995;141:96–102.

11. Last JM, ed. *A Dictionary of Epidemiology,* 4th ed. New York: Oxford University Press; 2001.

12. Rothman gives Cassel Memorial Lecture at SER. *Epidemiol Monit.* 1995;16:1.

13. MacMahon B, Pugh TF. *Epidemiology Principles and Methods.* Boston: Little, Brown; 1970.

14. Hyman JJ, Reid BC. Cigarette smoking, periodontal disease, and chronic obstructive pulmonary disease. *J Periodontol.* 2004;75:9–15.

15. Ward H, Tarasuk V, Mendelson R. Socioeconomic patterns of obesity in Canada: Modeling the role of health behaviour. *Appl Physiol Nutr Metab.* 2007;32:206–216.

16. Mausner JS, Kramer S. *Mausner & Bahn Epidemiology: An Introductory Text,* 2nd ed. Philadelphia: Saunders; 1985.

17. Rothman KJ, Greenland S. Causation and causal inference in epidemiology. *Am J Public Health.* 2005;95:S144–S150.

Appendix
9

Cohort Study Data for Coffee Use and Anxiety

Table 9A-1

Coffee Use	Anxiety		
	Yes	No	Total
Yes	500	9,500	10,000
No	200	19,800	20,000

Data Interpretation Issues

LEARNING OBJECTIVES

By the end of this chapter the reader will be able to:

- distinguish between random and systematic errors
- state and describe three main sources of bias
- identify techniques to reduce bias at the design and analysis phases of a study
- define what is meant by the term *confounding* and provide three examples
- describe the methods that can be used to control confounding

CHAPTER OUTLINE

I. Introduction
II. Validity of Study Designs
III. Sources of Error in Epidemiologic Research
IV. Techniques to Reduce Bias
V. Methods to Control Confounding
VI. Bias in Analysis and Publication
VII. Conclusion
VIII. Study Questions and Exercises

Introduction

As Exhibit 10–1 suggests, findings from epidemiologic studies are often quite newsworthy. One of the real dangers of obtaining epidemiologic information solely from media reports, however, is the selective nature of the coverage; the media may focus on the one positive result among a larger quantity of negative data. Another more troubling issue is whether the study being reported was even scientifically valid. One must not only understand the study's results and implications, but also be able to evaluate critically the study's design and methodology, a task that requires considerably greater knowledge and skills than merely assimilating the findings. Despite the peer review process adopted by scientific journals, methodologically flawed studies do appear in print and do attract media attention. One cannot assume that just because a study was published in a reputable journal the findings should not be questioned.

Where do possible deficiencies in media reports and published research leave the public health practitioner? To gain a more complete picture of any particular report, one really should retrieve and read the original article firsthand. More important, one should have the basic skills to evaluate critically the report as to selection of study subjects, measurement of exposure and outcome, analysis of data, and interpretation of results. This chapter provides a foundation for such skills.

Validity of Study Designs

The validity of a study is defined as "The degree to which the inference drawn from a study, [is] warranted when account is taken of the study methods, the representativeness of the study sample, and the nature of the population from which it is drawn."[1] Study validity embodies two components: internal and external validity.

Internal Validity

A study is said to have internal validity when there have been proper selection of study groups and a lack of error in measurement. The goal is to be able to ascribe any observed effect to the exposure under investigation. Thus, the manner of selection of cases and controls, or exposed and nonexposed groups, must be critically reviewed. Maintenance of internal validity also necessitates appropriate measurement of the following:

EXHIBIT 10–1

Press Coverage: Leaving Out the Big Picture

In the past . . . years, thorough readers of the *Los Angeles Times* would have learned about an extraordinary range of potential cancer causes. Among these putative hazards of modern life are hot dogs, breast implants, dioxin, stress, asbestos, allergy drugs, gas leaks, living in Orange County, tubal ligation, sunscreen, Asian food, pesticides, vasectomy, liquor, working in restaurants, Retin-A, vegetables, dietary fat, delayed child-bearing, impurities in meat, and lesbianism. This litany of fear was accompanied by a similar, although shorter, series of reports on dietary habits and lifestyles that may reduce cancer risk. Parallel coverage appeared in other newspapers and magazines and on television. To many scientists, though, the media would do well to curb its appetite for such news.

The problem, many researchers say, is that journalists often misunderstand the context of the research. Because of the limitations of risk factor epidemiology, most individual studies cannot produce authoritative findings. "Articles published in medical journals are often misconstrued by the lay press to be more definitive than they really are," says Larry Freedman, a biostatistician at the National Cancer Institute. "Broccoli prevents cancer, garlic prevents cancer—all these things do appear in the literature. But epidemiologists understand very well that these studies are far from definitive. It's only when a body of evidence exists over many, many studies that epidemiologists should really get serious about giving the public advice."

Instead of presenting surveys of the big, evolving picture, he and others say the media tend to report each new study in isolation, as a new breakthrough. Such reporting, some scientists say, is encouraged by press releases put out by journals and researchers' institutions. But whoever is to blame, says Noel Weiss, an epidemiologist at the University of Washington, Seattle, the result is "just too many false alarms. When we do have a serious message, I fear it won't be heeded because of the large number of false messages." ■

Source: Reprinted with permission from Charles C. Mann. Press Coverage: Leaving Out the Big Picture, *Science*, Vol 269, p. 166. © 1995 American Association for the Advancement of Science.

- *Exposure.* Was characterization of exposure based on a questionnaire? If so, was the questionnaire administered in person or as a telephone survey, or was it mailed to the study participant for self-administration? To illustrate, the investigator may collect some types of data with reasonable accuracy by using mailed questionnaires, but careful probing that can be achieved only through in-person interviews may be required to collect other types of data. Were the instruments validated? It is important to know whether the questionnaires used actually measured what they purported to measure. Is the reliability known? If the instrument were administered to the same individual on separate occasions, would it provide the same response? Were biologic samples collected to quantify exposure? If so, were the procedures to collect the samples standardized according to timing of collection? For example, suppose you were interested in urinary hormone levels of premenopausal women. It would be important to know whether the samples were all collected during the same phase of the menstrual cycle. Were the laboratory assays used appropriate? Although it is not possible to cover all variations on the theme, this brief overview indicates some of the types of questions that should be pondered with respect to exposure assessment.

- *Outcome.* Whether the outcome of interest is a particular disease, behavior, or intermediate marker, the criteria used to define the outcome should be fully described. Was the outcome based solely on self-report, or was an examination performed by trained health professionals according to a standard protocol? How were the subjects with and without the outcome of interest identified? Were all eligible subjects successfully located? Did a high proportion participate? If the study was prospective in nature, were all end points identified? Was there loss to follow-up? Clearly, a number of important considerations pertain to assessment of the outcome and the formation of the study groups.

- *Association between exposure and disease.* The two preceding categories reflect aspects of measurement of exposure and outcome; this category relates to assessment of the association between them by raising the following questions: Were the data properly analyzed? Was adjustment made for extraneous factors that might influence the results? Some types of data analysis require certain assumptions about the nature (distribution) of the data. Were the assumptions tested? Do they appear reasonable given the context of the study? Are there crucial analyses that appear to have been omitted?

External Validity

The preceding section discussed internal validity, a requirement that must be satisfied for a study to have external validity. External validity is a more encompassing process than the ability to extrapolate from a sample population to a target population. External validity implies the ability to generalize beyond a set of observations to some universal statement. According to Last, "A study is externally valid, or generalizable, if it can produce unbiased inferences regarding a target population (beyond the subjects in the study). This aspect of validity is only meaningful with regard to a specified external target population."[1]

The basic process of generalizing study results is neither mechanical nor statistical, for one must understand which conditions are relevant or irrelevant to the generalization. Although representativeness of the sample is a condition of external validity, generalizability also is independent of how representative of the target population the study groups are; this statement applies particularly when one uses epidemiology to improve understanding about the biologic basis of a disease.

An example is a feeding study designed to evaluate the utility of plasma carotenoids (compounds found in plant foods thought to have anticarcinogenic properties) as a marker of vegetable intake.[2] Subjects (volunteers who agreed to participate) were randomized into a crossover feeding study of four experimental diets of nine days each. Thus, after spending nine days consuming a particular experimental diet, the participants were "crossed over" to one of the other diets. It should be noted that volunteers for health studies tend to be more educated and health conscious than the general population. In this particular study, however, 11 exclusion criteria were applied to restrict the pool of volunteers. These included a medical history of gastrointestinal disorders, food allergies, weight loss or gain greater than 4.5 kg within the past year, major changes in eating habits within the past year, exercise regimens requiring significant short-term dietary changes, antibiotic use within the past three months, body weight greater than 130% of ideal, current treatment for a diagnosed disease, alcohol intake greater than two drinks per day, oral contraceptive use, and unwillingness to consume all foods provided in the study. Although these exclusion criteria greatly improved the internal validity of the study, they might have decreased the generalizability of the study if the subjects enrolled were physiologically atypical with respect to how their plasma carotenoid levels responded to a high-vegetable diet.

The preceding example reaffirms the notion that clinical trials are often initially based on a highly selected subgroup of patients. Nonetheless, the information gleaned from such trials often can be generalized to a much broader category of patients.

Sources of Error in Epidemiologic Research

In the context of epidemiologic research, one should consider two categories of error: random and systematic. Random errors reflect fluctuations around a true value of a parameter (such as a rate or a relative risk) because of sampling variability. They can occur as a result of poor precision, sampling error, or variability in measurement. Systematic errors refer to measurement biases.

Factors That Contribute to Random Error

Poor Precision

This type of random error occurs when a study factor is not measured sharply. Consider the analogy of aiming a rifle at a target that is not in focus. The target may correctly yield the proper direction in which one should be aiming, but the blurry picture makes it difficult to hit the bull's-eye, causing bullets to scatter all over the target. Increasing the sample size of a study or the number of measurements will yield greater precision. For example, in the Bogalusa Heart Study, a prospective study of the early natural history of cardiovascular disease in a small, rural Louisiana community, an average of six blood pressure readings was used to characterize an individual child's blood pressure.[3] Each child was randomly assigned to two of three trained observers who each made three independent blood pressure measurements. By taking the average of six readings, the random error was reduced, thereby improving precision.

Sampling Error

In the field of epidemiology, one wishes to make inferences about a target population without necessarily having to measure each member of the target population. The target population may be the general population of the entire United States or a specified subset, such as residents of California, children aged 5 to 9, African Americans, or Hmong residents of the Minneapolis-St Paul area of Minnesota. For this reason, one typically selects samples from the target population that are of a more manageable size for study than would occur if every member of the target population were examined.

Sampling error is a type of error that arises when values (statistics) obtained for a sample differ from the values (parameters) of the parent population. Sampling error is relevant to all types of epidemiologic studies: cross-sectional, case-control, cohort, or intervention. For example, when one conducts a case-control study of colorectal cancer in the state of Utah, the study group of cases may be considered a sample of all cases of colorectal cancer in the United States. When one draws a sample from a larger population, the possibility always exists that the sample selected is not representative of the target population. Nonrepresentative samples may occur without any intention or fault of the investigators even if subjects are randomly selected. To a certain extent, sampling error may be thought of as just plain bad luck of the draw, just as there can be an unusual run of cards in poker or run of colors in a roulette game. Although there is no way to prevent a nonrepresentative sample from occurring, increasing the size of the sample can reduce the likelihood of its happening.

Variability in Measurement

The validity of a study will be enhanced greatly if the data that are collected are objective, reliable, accurate, and reproducible. Even under the best of circumstances, however, errors in measurement can and do occur. For example, the Bogalusa Heart Study investigators were concerned about the stability of laboratory measures over long periods of time.[3] To determine consistency in measurement, a blind sample from randomly selected individuals was included when samples of blood were sent to the laboratory for analysis. In fact, perfect agreement was rarely achieved despite the fact that the same procedures were used and the samples were from the same individuals and collected at the same time. The lack of agreement in results from time to time reflects random error inherent in the type of measurement procedure employed.

Factors That Contribute to Systematic Errors

Bias (Systematic Errors)

"Deviation of results or inferences from the truth, or processes leading to such deviation. Any trend in the collection, analysis, interpretation, publication, or review of data that can lead to conclusions that are systematically different from the truth."[1]

A much more serious problem for the validity of a study than random errors is systematic errors, or bias. As the definition of bias given above implies, systematic errors can be introduced at any point in an investigation. These errors can be conveniently grouped into three broad categories: selection bias, information bias, and confounding.

Selection Bias

Selection bias arises when the relation between exposure and disease is different for those who participate and those who would be theoretically eligible for study but do not participate.[4] Such bias may occur during the follow-up period of a study, during the period of recruitment for the study, or even before the study begins. For example, the healthy worker effect represents a source of bias that may occur when only employed individuals, such as an occupational cohort, are eligible for a study. Workers typically are relatively healthy people who have had the opportunity to find and maintain employment. Physically or mentally disabled individuals may not have enjoyed a similar opportunity and thus would not be represented in the study.

As another example, recall the Iowa Women's Health Study, described in Chapter 3. The target population consisted of women between the ages of 55 and 69. From the total eligible pool of licensed female drivers, a 50% random sample of women in this age range was selected.[5] Not all age-eligible subjects were identified using this method because only 94% of women in this age category actually had a valid Iowa driver's license and thus the potential to participate. Data were available on the self-reported height and weight of all participants and nonparticipants from the driver's license data tape provided by the state motor vehicle agency. These data from respondents and nonrespondents provided a rare opportunity to examine possible selection bias. It was found that respondents were on average three months younger and 0.38 kg/m^2 lighter than nonrespondents. Based on 1980 census data, respondents were slightly more likely than nonrespondents to live in rural, less affluent counties. One advantage of conducting the study in Iowa is that one's driver's license number is the same as one's Social Security number. This circumstance facilitated efficient record linkage with the State Health Registry for documentation of subsequent cancer occurrence. Bisgard et al.[6] compared the rates of cancer incidence and mortality between respondents and nonrespondents. Results suggested greater occurrence of smoking-associated diseases among the nonrespondents, a finding consistent with a lower response rate of smokers to a health survey.

Information Bias

Information bias is a kind of bias introduced as a result of measurement error in assessment of both exposure and disease. One example of information bias is *recall bias*, which denotes a phenomenon whereby cases may be more likely to recall past exposures than controls. Suppose that in a study of childhood leukemia, mothers are interviewed regarding drug use during pregnancy. Mothers of cases are likely to have spent considerable periods of time pondering their children's illness. Although the frequency of exposure may actually be equivalent in both study groups, better recall among the cases than among the controls would yield positive evidence of an association. A special case of recall bias is recollection of a family history of disease, labeled family recall bias.[7] Cases learn of a family history of a disease from relatives after the diagnosis is made. As a result of family recall bias, data on the occurrence of the same disease among family members is likely to be more complete among cases than among controls. Although the true prevalence of the disease among family members of cases and controls may be similar, this bias would give the appearance of a higher prevalence among cases.

Interviewer/abstractor bias can occur when well-intentioned interviewers probe more thoroughly for an exposure in a case than in a control. Similarly, an abstractor may pore over records more thoroughly to identify an exposure in a case than in a control.

Prevarication (lying) bias is a type of information bias that may occur when participants have ulterior motives for answering a question and thus may underestimate or exaggerate exposures. For example, questions asked of married, apparently heterosexual men with acquired immune deficiency syndrome may not necessarily reveal past homosexual behavior. Surveys of individuals who have drinking disorders or members of religious groups that disallow alcohol use may yield false responses.

Information bias may occur also in relation to ascertainment of health outcomes. Consider again the Iowa Women's Health Study cohort of postmenopausal women. One of the exposures of interest was a positive family history of selected cancers, especially breast cancer. The National Cancer Institute (NCI) recommends the use of screening mammography for the early detection of breast cancer; the NCI argues that although mammography is imperfect, it is the best available tool for breast cancer screening. Nevertheless, according to data from the 2001 Behavioral Risk Factor Survey, the frequency (83%) of receiving mammograms among women peaked in the age category 55 to 59. Thereafter, it declined among women 60 years of age and older.[8] A positive family history of breast cancer is an established risk factor for the disease, however, and some data suggest that women with a known family history of the disease are more likely to be administered mammograms than women with a negative history of the disease.[9] Accordingly, a physician who knows of a patient's family history of breast cancer may refer the patient for a mammogram, increasing the likelihood of detecting a malignancy in the exposure group of interest.

Confounding

Confounding is the term used to describe distortion of the estimate of the effect of an exposure of interest because it is mixed with the effect of an extraneous factor. According to Susser, a confounding variable is "an independent variable that varies systematically with the hypothetical causal variable under study. When uncontrolled, the effects of a confounding variable cannot be distinguished from those of the study variable."[10(p. 95)] According to a good working definition, confounding occurs when the crude and adjusted measures of effect are not equal. Formal statistical tests can be performed to evaluate the statistical significance of a confounder. A reasonable rule of thumb is that a change in the estimate of effect by at least 10% when crude and adjusted measures of effect are compared suggests the influence of a confounder.

Although the categories of error (selection bias, information bias, and confounding) are not mutually exclusive, only confounding, practically speaking, can be controlled in the data analysis. To be a confounder, the extraneous factor must satisfy the following three criteria:

1. be a risk factor for the disease (not necessarily causal, but at least a marker for the actual cause of the disease)
2. be associated with the exposure under study in the population from which the cases derive (e.g., smoking would not be a confounder in an occupational cohort study if unassociated with occupational exposure; on the other hand, age might be a confounder because old persons are likely to have more exposure than younger ones).
3. not be an intermediate step in the causal path between exposure and disease

An excellent illustration of confounding is known as Simpson's paradox.[11] A man enters a shop to buy a hat and sees two tables, each with 30 hats. At the first table he determines that 90% of the black hats fit but only 85% of the gray hats fit. Over at the second table he notices that, similar to the first table, a greater proportion of black hats than gray hats fits (15% vs. 10%). Unfortunately, the shop is closing and the man is forced to return the next day. Much to his chagrin, when he returns he sees that the store clerk has placed all 60 of the hats on a single table. Although on the previous day the greatest proportion of hats that fit at each table were black in color, he soon discovers that, now that all the hats have been mixed together on the same table, 60% (18 of 30) of the gray hats fit but only 40% (12 of 30) of the black hats fit (Table 10–1).

This intriguing example is neither obvious nor intuitive. Confounding can be equally vexing; sometimes associations can be so distorted that even the direction is reversed.[12] An example of confounding is the positive association between air pollution and bronchitis. Air pollution varies directly and systematically with urban density and overcrowding, factors that may facilitate the spread of respiratory-associated diseases, such as bronchitis. In this situation, crowding represents a confounding variable.

Another example is the inverse relation between coronary heart disease (CHD) mortality and altitude described by Buechley et al.[13] Some investigators had reported that populations residing at high altitudes had lower heart disease mortality because of the protective effect of adaptation to reduced oxygen tension. A confounding variable that had not been previously accounted for was ethnicity: Hispanics in New Mexico tended to live at higher altitudes and to have lower CHD rates than other ethnic groups. Thus, there was an apparent association between altitude and CHD mortality because of unrecognized differences in ethnic composition of the regions being compared.

A more complicated example is obesity and lung cancer. Obesity has been associated with an increased risk of cancer at a number of sites. A notable exception appears to be lung cancer, for which several studies have suggested a modest inverse association.[14,15] Cigarette smoking is directly associated with lung cancer risk, however, and inversely associated with body mass index, which is a measure

Table 10–1   An Analogy to Confounding: Simpson's Paradox

Table	Hat Color	Total Number	Number that Fit	Percent that Fit
1	Black	10	9	90%
	Gray	20	17	85%
	Black	20	3	15%
2	Gray	10	1	10%

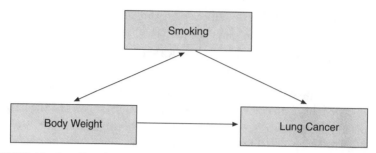

FIGURE 10–1   Graphic representation of how smoking confounds the body weight-lung cancer association

of obesity.[16] A careful analysis of the obesity-lung cancer association with proper control for the confounding effect of tobacco exposure suggested that the previous observations were spurious.[17] A pictorial representation of the model is presented in Figure 10–1.

Summary

To recapitulate, error can be introduced into an epidemiologic study at many stages. An overview of these sources of error is depicted in Figure 10–2.

Techniques to Reduce Bias

A variety of methods are available to reduce or prevent the occurrence of bias in epidemiologic research. Some guidelines that may help prevent selection bias are as follows:

- Develop an explicit (objective) case definition.
- Enroll all cases in a defined time and region.
- Strive for high participation rates (incentives).
- Take precautions to ensure representativeness.
- For cases:
  1. Ensure that all medical facilities are thoroughly canvassed.
  2. Develop an effective system for case ascertainment.
  3. Consider whether all cases require medical attention; consider possible strategies to identify where else the cases might be ascertained.

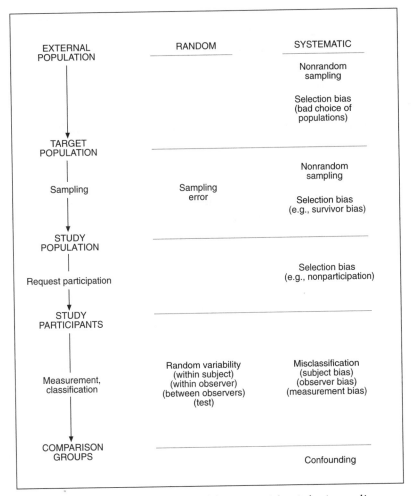

FIGURE 10–2 Sources of error and bias in epidemiologic studies

- For controls:
  1. Try to compare the prevalence of the exposure with other sources to evaluate credibility.
  2. Attempt to draw controls from a variety of sources.

One way to prevent nonrepresentative sampling of eligible cases is to develop—before data collection—explicit definitions about what constitutes a case. Study personnel should be trained to follow the guidelines irrespective of the exposure status of the case. There can be no doubt about the representativeness of the cases if all cases in the target population are selected for study.

Definition of the number of cases eligible by time period and geographic region, for example, a three-year period in a five-state area, gives precision to the denominator. An established case registry facilitates the identification of cases; if a registry is not available, a surveillance network of medical facilities where patients would be seen should be established, and all such facilities should be enrolled. Health conditions that do not universally motivate afflicted persons to seek medical attention raise a special concern for the investigator; those individuals who present for medical care may represent only the most severe cases who are atypical with respect to their exposure patterns.

Low participation rates always raise concerns about the validity and generalizability of a study. One approach to enhance participation is to use incentives. These may take the form of T-shirts, key chains, buttons, stickers, coupons for discounts on healthful food choices, free medical evaluation, and even monetary compensation.

Techniques to reduce information bias include the following:

- Use memory aids and validate exposures.
- Blind interviewers as to subjects' study status.
- Provide standardized training sessions and protocols.
- Use standardized data collection forms.
- Blind participants as to study goals and participants' classification status.
- Try to ensure that questions are clearly understood through careful wording and pretesting.

The problem of recall bias can be reduced by using memory aids to prompt for responses. For example, when one is conducting an interview of subjects to determine foods eaten over the previous day (a 24-hour recall), it is helpful to structure the interview to refer to particular meals and snack times. The use of food models to indicate portion sizes can help quantify intakes, and posters of commonly eaten snack foods are useful reminders. Studies of oral contraceptive use have utilized pictures of the pill dispensers to help subjects identify brand names and formulations.

Although a study staff committed to the research is an asset, well-intentioned interviewers or abstractors may introduce bias in data collection. Whenever possible, staff should be blinded as to the status of the study subjects: case versus noncase, exposed versus nonexposed. In some situations, it also may be desirable to blind the subjects themselves to the true goals of the study. This strategy can help reduce the likelihood of subjects providing responses to please the investigator, attempting to anticipate the "correct" answer to a given question, or producing what they consider socially desirable answers. Clearly, biases introduced by the study subjects are less of an issue when the exposure is a biologic factor that cannot be purposely changed by the subject. One situation in which biases from study subjects might be an issue, however, would be if the biases influenced their decision to participate. Although ethical conduct of research on humans dictates that subjects be informed of the reason for the study and the basis for their invitation to participate, the specific hypothesis to be tested need not be revealed. Development of standardized data collection forms and survey instruments helps ensure that complete data are collected on all subjects in a uniform manner.

Methods to Control Confounding

There are two general approaches to control for confounding. Prevention strategies represent an attempt to control confounding through the study design itself. Analysis strategies seek to control confounding through the use of statistical analysis methods.

Control of Confounding

Prevention strategies
- Randomization
- Restriction
- Matching

Analysis strategies
- Stratification
- Multivariate techniques

Three Prevention Strategies to Control Confounding

The first prevention strategy is randomization of study subjects. The intended net effect is to ensure equal distributions of the confounding variable in each exposure category. This strategy is an extremely efficient approach with a number of clearly defined advantages. Randomization of subjects, if the sample size is sufficiently large, provides control of all factors known and unknown. It is a fairly convenient method, is inexpensive, and permits straightforward data analysis. The primary disadvantages are that randomization can be applied only to intervention studies when investigators have control over the exposure and are able to assign subjects to study groups. Even then, randomization works well only for large sample sizes. If the number of subjects is small, a chance remains that the distribution of confounding variables will be dissimilar across study groups.

The second prevention strategy, restriction of admission criteria, may prohibit variation of the confounder in the study groups. For example, if age is thought to be a potential confounder, the study could simply be restricted to subjects within a narrow age category. Restriction is extremely effective in providing complete control of known confounding factors; it shares with randomization the virtues of being convenient and inexpensive and permitting relatively easy data analysis compared with some of the alternatives. The difficulties encountered with restriction include the distinct possibility that there may still be residual confounding if restrictions are not sufficiently narrow. Moreover, restriction will not address problems created by unknown confounding. From a practical standpoint, restriction may shrink the pool of available subjects to an unacceptably low level. Depending on the health problem studied, one may not be able to generalize the results beyond restricted categories.

Matching of subjects in the study groups according to the value of the suspected or known confounding variable to ensure equal distributions is the third prevention strategy; an example of a potential confounding variable that might be controlled using matching is age. Several types of matching are available. In frequency matching, the number of cases with the particular match characteristics is tabulated. For example, if one is matching on five-year age groups, a frequency distribution of the cases by age group would be generated. Each five-year age group is called an age stratum. A *stratum* is a homogeneous population subgroup, such as that characterized by a narrow age range, e.g., a five-year age group. Controls are then selected until the required number of controls for each stratum has been acquired. If the controls are to be studied concurrently with the cases, one can generate an expected frequency of cases for each matching stratum based on previously observed rates. Another type of matching is individual matching, the pairing of one or more controls to each case based on similarity of one or several variables, for example, sex or race.

The use of matching to control confounding has a number of clear advantages. In terms of sample size requirements for follow-up studies, matching is efficient in that fewer subjects are required than in unmatched studies of the same hypothesis.[11] Matching also may enhance the validity of a follow-up study. Despite these advantages, matching can be costly, often requiring extensive searching and recordkeeping to find matches. For example, Ross and colleagues[18] conducted a case-control study of renal cancer to evaluate the potential role of analgesics in carcinogenesis. A total of 314 cases of incident cancer of the renal pelvis were identified through the Cancer Surveillance Program. Of these, 61 died before contact, 20 refused to be interviewed, and another 30 were prohibited from participating by the attending physician, leaving 203 cases. Controls were matched to cases on birth date (65 years), race, sex, and neighborhood. A predetermined walking algorithm, starting with the residence of the case, was applied for the selection of controls. The procedure continued until a suitable control was found or until 40 houses had been approached. Successful matches were found for 187 (92%) of the cases, and an average of 22 household units were approached per case to find an appropriate control.

For case-control studies, matching may introduce confounding rather than control for it. Confounding typically occurs by matching subjects on factors associated with exposure but then ignoring the matching in the analysis stage. The result is often an estimate of effect that is biased toward the null value (i.e., an odds ratio of 1). When one matches subjects on a potential confounder, that particular exposure variable can no longer be evaluated with respect to its contribution to risk; the distribution of the exposure variable is constrained to be similar (perhaps even identical) in both groups. When one matches on several factors, such as age, sex, and neighborhood, there is a danger of making the study groups so similar that one essentially has matched oneself out of business; this problem sometimes is called overmatching. That is, the exposure that is associated with the outcome of interest (not the confounder) becomes equivalent in the two study groups, and no meaningful associations are identified. Depending on how imprecise the matching variables are, one also can have residual confounding. For example, in a nested case-control analysis of alcohol and lung cancer risk in the Iowa Women's Health Study cohort, cases and noncases were matched on pack-years of smoking.[19] Careful inspection of the data revealed that within strata of pack-years cases tended to have slightly higher mean exposure levels than noncases.

Two Analysis Strategies to Control Confounding

Although it can be somewhat more comforting to conduct a study in which the potential for known confounding can be addressed in the design phase, issues of cost and feasibility may make it necessary instead to address confounding in the analysis stage. Furthermore, attempts to minimize confounding in the design phase obviously can be done only for known confounders. Often the presence of a confounding factor is not observed or detected until analyses are underway, making analysis strategies for dealing with confounding important tools indeed.

The first analysis strategy, stratification, occurs when analyses are performed to evaluate the effect of an exposure within strata (levels) of the confounder. A general approach is to define homogeneous categories or narrow ranges of the confounding variable. One can then combine stratum-specific effects into an overall effect by standard statistical principles and methods (e.g., the Mantel-Haenszel procedure).[20] There are three advantages to this approach. First, performing analyses within strata is a direct and logical strategy. Second, there are minimum assumptions that must be satisfied for the analyses to be appropriate. Third, the computational procedure is quite straightforward.

The difficulties with stratification arise in several areas. The basic process of stratification of the data may result, unfortunately, in small numbers of observations in some strata. When dealing with a continuous variable or an ordinal variable with a relatively large number of categories, one is faced with a variety of ways to form strata. Knowing or deciding which cut points are most appropriate may be difficult. If several confounding factors must be evaluated, necessitating stratification across two or more variables, each of which may have multiple levels, one can easily run into difficulty in interpretation. Finally, from a statistical standpoint, categorization almost always results in loss of information.

The second analysis strategy involves multivariate techniques in which computers are used to construct mathematical models that describe simultaneously the influence of exposure and other factors that may be confounding the effect. This strategy tends to be more feasible with smaller numbers of study subjects than stratification, although multivariate techniques generally require large sample sizes. Another advantage of this tactic pertains to the use of continuous versus categoric variables in the analysis of confounding. When factors that must be controlled are entered into the models as continuous variables, the problem of creating categoric variables is obviated. Continuous variables may be converted to categoric variables by establishing cut points for categories. The epidemiologist may be faced with theoretical difficulties in knowing or deciding where to form such cut points. Another major advantage of multivariate modeling is that it allows for simultaneous control of several exposure variables in a single analysis.

The main disadvantage of multivariate techniques is their great potential for misuse. There are some restrictive assumptions about the distribution of the data that should be, but are not always, examined. The choice of the model may be difficult, especially when the investigator is faced with a large number and wide variety of variables that could be selected. The widespread availability and user-friendly nature of commercial computer software make the method accessible to some data analysts who may not have had adequate instruction in its appropriate applications. When they are misapplied, multivariate techniques have the potential to contribute to incorrect model development, misleading results, and inappropriate interpretation of the effects of hypothesized confounders.

Bias in Analysis and Publication

Although not a reflection of errors in selection, measurement, or analysis (confounding), it is important to consider another source of bias that can have a profound influence. This type of bias is presented in a separate section of the chapter because it is generally outside the control of individual investigators. Publication bias is a phenomenon that occurs because of the influence of study results on the chance of publication. In particular, studies with positive results are more likely to be published than studies with negative results,[21] and to be published more quickly.[22,23] The net effect is a preponderance of false-positive results in the literature. The bias is compounded when published studies on a topic are subjected to meta-analysis. These tend to give an even greater air of importance because of the intent to summarize and synthesize a large number of studies on a given topic. Moreover, meta-analyses of observational studies may be used as the rationale for large clinical trials. Recent comparisons of results from meta-analyses and subsequent randomized clinical trials confirm that results cannot be accurately predicted roughly 35% of the time.[24] This deficiency raises the question of whether meta-analyses should include unpublished data. Crowther and Cook[25] pointed out that the inclusion of unpublished data in systematic literature reviews such as meta-analyses is controversial. Although these reviews may be affected by publication bias, inclusion of unpublished data may lower the quality of the meta-analysis itself.

Although each of us as public health professionals adheres to a professional code of conduct and integrity in the work that we do, we cannot control the actions of our peers. In these days of "publish or perish" pressures within academia, and the increasing collaboration of universities with private businesses in sponsored research, not all actions are above reproach even though they are not necessarily fraudulent. Thus one must have a dose of skepticism about what appears in the literature. For example, one may have difficulty in ascertaining whether or not study results from an observational study were tests of a priori hypotheses or post hoc analyses masqueraded as such. This conundrum is particularly worrisome in these days of large data sets, powerful analysis packages, and high-speed computers. Readers of the literature may have difficulty telling whether or not reported results were merely the product of "data dredging" and actually only a chance observation that would be most difficult to replicate.

Further raising the cloud of suspicion is the habit of deleting certain study subjects because they are considered outliers, or when a number of cut points are considered in the analysis and only the ones that yield statistically significant results are presented. Unfortunately, although most scientific journals have a peer review process, such actions are exceedingly difficult to detect. Moreover, there are tendencies for editors to make their decisions on suitability for publication based on the direction or strength of the study findings.[26]

Conclusion

The ability to evaluate critically sources of error in epidemiologic research is necessary not only to interpret properly the plethora of media reports, but also to design and analyze studies. Two main types of research errors must be considered: random errors, which occur because of sampling error, lack of precision, and variability in measurement; and systematic errors (bias), which occur through selection of subjects, collection of information about exposure and disease, and confounding. This chapter presented a number of techniques to reduce bias and introduced some helpful methods to control confounding. Prevention strategies include randomization of subjects into exposure groups, restriction of admission criteria, and matching subjects on the potential confounder. Analysis strategies include stratification and multivariate modeling.

Study Questions and Exercises

1. In a study to determine the incidence of a chronic disease, 150 people were examined at the end of a three-year period. Twelve cases were found, giving an incidence rate of 8%. Fifty other members of the initial cohort could not be examined; 20 of these 50 could not be examined because they died. Does this loss of subjects to follow-up represent a source of bias that may have affected the study results?

2. A case-control study was carried out in which 120 of 200 cases of stomach cancer and 50 of 200 control subjects gave a history of exposure to radiation. In further analysis, however, the investigators noticed that 50% of the cases but only 25% of the controls were men. What would be a

practical and efficient way to eliminate differences between cases and controls with respect to sex?

3. Two automated blood cell counters are tested twice using a prepared suspension of leukocytes containing 8,000 cells/mm^3. The cell counts by device A are 8,400 cells/mm^3 the first time and 8,350 cells/mm^3 the second. Device B's counts are 8,200 and 7,850 cells/mm^3, respectively. Which device (A or B) gives leukocyte counts with greater validity? Which device gives leukocyte counts with greater reliability?

4. You are planning a case-control study of lung cancer to test the hypothesis that vegetable consumption is protective against lung cancer. Would you match on smoking? Explain your answer.

5. A follow-up study was conducted of 3,000 military troops deployed at an atomic test site in Nevada to detect the occurrence of leukemia. A total of 1,870 persons were successfully traced by the investigators, and an additional 443 contacted the investigators on their own as a result of publicity about the study. Four cases of leukemia occurred among the 1,870 individuals traced by the investigators, and an additional four occurred among those individuals who contacted the investigators on their own. Could interpretation of the study results be subject to bias?

6. You are conducting a study of insulin resistance and its relationship to body weight. Using a weight scale as your instrument to measure body weight, you find the scale always reads 30 kg regardless of who is standing on it. Discuss the validity and reliability of the scale.

Questions 7 through 10 are multiple choice. Select the correct answer from the options that follow each question.

7. You are investigating the role of physical activity in heart disease, and your data suggest a protective effect. While presenting your findings, a colleague asks whether you have thought about confounders, such as factor X. Under which of the following conditions could this factor have confounded your interpretation of the data?

   a. It is a risk factor for some other disease, but not heart disease.

   b. It is a risk factor associated with the physical activity measure and heart disease.

   c. It is part of the causal pathway by which physical activity affects heart disease.

   d. It has caused a lack of follow-up of test subjects.

   e. It may have blinded your study.

8. Surgeons at hospital A report that the mortality rate at the end of a one-year follow-up after a new coronary bypass procedure is 15%. At hospital B, the surgeons report a one-year mortality rate of 8% after the same procedure. Before concluding that the surgeons at hospital B had vastly superior skill, which of the following possible confounding factors would you examine?

   a. the severity (stage) of disease of the patients at the two hospitals at baseline
   b. the start of the one-year follow-up at both hospitals (after operation vs. after discharge)
   c. differences in postoperative care at the two hospitals
   d. equality of follow-up for mortality
   e. all of the above

9. Which of the following is not a method to control for the effects of confounding?

   a. randomization
   b. stratification
   c. matching
   d. blinding

10. The strategy that will not help reduce selection bias is:

   a. development of an explicit case definition
   b. the use of incentives to encourage high participation
   c. a standardized protocol for structured interviews
   d. enrollment of all cases in a defined time and region

References

1. Last JM, ed. *A Dictionary of Epidemiology*, 4th ed. New York, NY: Oxford University Press; 2001.
2. Martini MC, Campbell DR, Gross MD, Grandits GA, Potter JD, Slavin JL. Plasma carotenoids as biomarkers of vegetable intake: the University of Minnesota Cancer Prevention Research Unit Feeding Studies. *Cancer Epidemiol Biomarkers Prev.* 1995;4: 491–496.
3. Berenson GS, McMahan CA, Voors AW, et al. *Cardiovascular Risk Factors in Children: The Early Natural History of Atherosclerosis and Essential Hypertension.* New York, NY: Oxford University Press; 1980.
4. Greenland S. Response and follow-up bias in cohort studies. *Am J Epidemiol.* 1977;106:184–187.
5. Folsom AR, Kaye SA, Potter JD, et al. Association of incident carcinoma of the endometrium with body weight and fat distribution in older women: early findings of the Iowa Women's Health Study. *Cancer Res.* 1989;49:6828–6831.

6. Bisgard KM, Folsom AR, Hong C-P, Sellers TA. Mortality and cancer rates in nonrespondents to a prospective study of older women: 5-year follow-up. *Am J Epidemiol.* 1994;139:990–1000.

7. Sackett DL. Bias in analytic research. *J Chronic Dis.* 1979;32:51–63.

8. Jerant AF, Franks P, Jackson JE, Doescher MP. Age-related disparities in cancer screening: analysis of 2001 behavioral risk factor surveillance system data. *Ann Fam Med.* 2004;2:481–487.

9. Liu X, Sennett C, Legorreta AP. Mammography utilization among California women age 40–49 in a managed care environment. *Breast Cancer Res Treat.* 2001;67:181–186.

10. Susser M. *Causal Thinking in the Health Sciences.* New York, NY: Oxford University Press; 1973.

11. Rothman KJ. *Modern Epidemiology.* Boston, MA: Little, Brown; 1986.

12. Rothman KJ. A pictorial representation of confounding in epidemiologic studies. *J Chronic Dis.* 1975;28:101–108.

13. Buechley R, Key C, Morris D, et al. Altitude and ischemic heart disease in tricultural New Mexico: an example of confounding. *Am J Epidemiol.* 1979;109:663–666.

14. Kabat GC, Wynder EJ. Body mass index and lung cancer risk. *Am J Epidemiol.* 1992;135:769–774.

15. Knekt P, Heliovaara M, Rissanen A, et al. Leanness and lung cancer risk. *Int J Cancer.* 1991;49:208–213.

16. Rigotti NA. Cigarette smoking and body weight. *N Engl J Med.* 1989;320:931–933.

17. Drinkard CR, Sellers TA, Potter JD, et al. Association of body mass index and body fat distribution with risk of lung cancer in older women. *Am J Epidemiol.* 1995;142:600–607.

18. Ross RK, Paganini-Hill A, Randolph J, Gerkins V, Henderson BE. Analgesics, cigarette smoking, and other risk factors for cancer of the renal pelvis and ureter. *Cancer Res.* 1989;49:1045–1048.

19. Potter JD, Sellers TA, Folsom AR, McGovern PG. Alcohol, beer and lung cancer in postmenopausal women: the Iowa Women's Health Study. *Ann Epidemiol.* 1992;2:587–595.

20. Mantel N, Haenszel W. Statistical aspects of the analysis of data from retrospective studies of disease. *J Natl Cancer Inst.* 1959;22:719–748.

21. Begg CB, Berlin JA. Publication bias and dissemination of clinical research. *J Natl Cancer Inst.* 1989;81:107–115.

22. Stern JM, Simes RJ. Publication bias: evidence of delayed publication in a cohort study of clinical research projects. *Br Med J.* 1997;315:640–645.

23. Ioannidis JP. Effect of the statistical significance of results on the time to completion and publication of randomized efficacy trials. *JAMA.* 1998;279:281–286.

24. LeLorier J, Gregoire G, Benhaddad A, Lapierre J, Derderian F. Discrepancies between meta-analyses and subsequent large randomized, controlled trials. *N Engl J Med.* 1997;337:536–542.

25. Crowther MA, Cook DJ. Trials and tribulations of systematic reviews and meta-analyses. *Hematology.* 2007:493–497.

26. Dickersin K. The existence of publication bias and risk factors for its occurrence. *JAMA.* 1990;263:1385–1389.

Screening for Disease in the Community

LEARNING OBJECTIVES

By the end of this chapter the reader will be able to:

- define and discuss reliability and validity, giving differentiating characteristics and interrelationships
- identify sources of unreliability and invalidity of measurement
- define the term *screening* and list desirable qualities of screening tests
- define and discuss sensitivity and specificity, giving appropriate formulas and calculations for a sample problem
- identify a classification system for a disease

CHAPTER OUTLINE

I. Introduction
II. Screening for Disease
III. Appropriate Situations for Screening Tests and Programs
IV. Characteristics of a Good Screening Test
V. Evaluation of Screening Tests
VI. Sources of Unreliability and Invalidity
VII. Measures of the Validity of Screening Tests
VIII. Effects of Prevalence of Disease on Screening Test Results

IX. Relationship Between Sensitivity and Specificity
X. Evaluation of Screening Programs
XI. Issues in the Classification of Morbidity and Mortality
XII. Conclusion
XIII. Study Questions and Exercises

Introduction

The public health field has increasingly recognized the importance of screening programs for the secondary prevention of morbidity and mortality. Efforts to control diseases by early detection through screening have led to a basic change in the nature of medical practice from an exclusive focus upon a small number of ill persons to a targeting of large numbers of asymptomatic persons.[1] Screening programs for coronary heart disease risk factors have elicited the public's awareness of hypertension control and dietary components of hypercholesterolemia. Breast cancer screening by mammography for early malignancies may contribute to the high five-year survival rates for this cancer site. According to research findings, breast cancer screening is efficacious for women 50 years of age and older. Exhibit 11–1 describes one opinion regarding the current debate over the effectiveness of screening women who are in the 40- to 49-year-old age group. This chapter discusses screening for disease in the population, including reliability and validity of measures, concepts and terminology of screening, sensitivity, and specificity as well as positive and negative predictive values.

Screening for Disease

A tenet of public health is that primary prevention of disease is the best approach. If all cases of disease cannot be prevented, however, then the next best strategy is early detection of disease in asymptomatic, apparently healthy individuals. *Screening* is defined as the presumptive identification of unrecognized disease or defects by the application of tests, examinations, or other procedures that can be applied rapidly. The qualifier *presumptive* is included in the definition to emphasize the preliminary nature of screening; diagnostic confirmation is required, usually with the benefit of more thorough clinical examination and addi-

EXHIBIT 11-1

Should Women Aged 40 Through 49 Years Receive Routine Mammography Screening?

One of the more remarkable aspects of the efforts to promote breast cancer screening has been the influence of rigorously conducted research. From an epidemiologic standpoint, the sequence of events could not have been better orchestrated.

In the 1950s and early 1960s, mammography emerged as a procedure that could lead to the detection of breast cancer at an earlier stage of the disease than could be detected in general clinical practice. This raised the question of whether mammography could be an effective screening tool when applied in the population at large. . . .

The HIP trial (initiated in 1963 at the Health Insurance Plan of Greater New York with contract support from the National Cancer Institute) enrolled women aged 40 through 64 years for annual screening; the control group continued to receive usual care.[2]

Thirty years of randomized controlled trials, diverse in content and design, have been conducted in various parts of the world.[3] . . . Case-control and quasi-experimental studies have added to the information about the value of mammography. During the 1970s, the Breast Cancer Detection Demonstration Project in the United States demonstrated that mammography screening had increased the capability to detect breast cancer early among young and older women; additional improvements in mammography have occurred since then. . . .

. . .guidelines from the National Cancer Institute (NCI), American Cancer Society, and other organizations . . . specify mammography screening every year or two for women aged 40 through 49 years and every year for women aged 50 years and older, and clinical breast examinations every year for all women aged 40 and older. . . . The results of the randomized controlled trials suggest that the guidelines should be changed.

One might best summarize the current situation by using the data from randomized controlled trials presented at the International Workshop on Screening for Breast Cancer in February 1993.[4] The task force charged with drawing conclusions that might affect screening guidelines found as

continues

EXHIBIT 11–1 *continued*

follows: . . . The benefits of mammography screening for women aged 40 through 49 years are uncertain; the evidence from trials is "consistent in showing no benefit 5–7 years after entry (to screening), an uncertain, and, if present, marginal benefit at 10 to 12 years." In short, the value of mass mammography screening at these ages is judged to be questionable on the basis of currently available information . . .

The NCI statement that was released in early December 1993, "Updating the Guidelines for Breast Cancer Screening," calls attention to the controversy about routine screening mammography for women aged 40 through 49 and the lack of convincing evidence on any reduction of breast cancer mortality related to screening in this age group. . . . New guidelines would emphasize mammography screening at 1- to 2-year inter- vals for women aged 50 years and older; for asymptomatic women aged 40 through 49 years, the guidelines would emphasize that patients and health care professionals should together discuss the uncertainty of the benefits, along with the risk factors, of mammography screening.

There will be voices raised against a change that focuses routine mam- mography screening on women aged 50 and older, just as there are chal- lenges (albeit less frequent) to screening at any age. But in making decisions on mammography screening for millions of women, we need to continue to rely on evidence from research, and the uncertainty of the available evidence for women aged 40 through 49 calls for a change in guidelines that excludes these women from programs for mass, routine screening with mammography. ■

Source: Reprinted from Shapiro S. The call for change in breast cancer screening guidelines. *American Journal of Public Health,* Vol 84, No 1, pp. 10–11, with permission of the American Public Health Association, © 1994.

[Authors' note: More than a decade since this statement was written, the guidelines for peri- odic screening mammography continue to evolve. Not only is the American College of Physicians a proponent of additional research on screening methods, but also the College rec- ommends periodic assessment of risk, informing patients of possible benefits and harms, and consideration of a woman's preferences and risk profile.*]

*Qaseem A, Snow V, Sherif K, et al. Screening mammography for women 40 to 49 years of age: a clinical practice guideline from the American College of Physicians. *Ann Intern Med.* 2007;146:511–515.

tional tests. Some screening programs are conducted on an ad hoc basis to screen interested and concerned individuals for specific health problems, such as hypertension, cervical cancer, or sickle-cell disease. An example of an ad hoc screening program would be administration of a free thyroid test (serum level of thyroxine) to passersby in a shopping center or members of a senior citizens center.[5] Other screening programs may be applied on a mass basis to almost all individuals in the population; an example is screening for phenylketonuria (PKU) among all neonates.

It should be noted that screening differs from diagnosis, which is the process of confirming an actual case of a disease.[6,7] As a result of diagnosis, medical intervention, if appropriate, is initiated. Diagnostic tests are used in follow-up of positive screening test results (e.g., phenylalanine loading test in children positive on PKU screening) or directly for screening (e.g., fetal karyotyping in prenatal screening for Down syndrome). For example, if a thyroid test is administered to determine an exact cause of a patient's illness, it would then be a diagnostic test.[5] The thyroid test also could be a screening test, however, as will be demonstrated subsequently.

Multiphasic Screening

Although screening programs can be restricted to early detection of a single disease, a more cost-effective approach is to screen for more than one disease. *Multiphasic screening* is defined as the use of two or more screening tests together among large groups of people.[8] The multiphasic screening examination may be administered as a preemployment physical, and successfully passing the examination may be a necessary condition for employment in the organization. As a benefit of employment, some large companies repeat the screening examination on an annual basis and direct suggestive findings to the employee's own physician while maintaining confidentiality of the results. Typical multiphasic screening programs assess risk factor status as well as individual and family history of illness, and they also collect physiologic and health measurements. Multiphasic screening also is a cornerstone of health maintenance organizations, such as Kaiser Permanente and Group Health Incorporated.

Mass Screening and Selective Screening

Mass screening (also known as population screening) refers to screening of total population groups on a large scale, regardless of any a priori information as to whether the individuals are members of a high-risk subset of the population.

Selective screening, sometimes referred to as targeted screening, is applied to subsets of the population at high risk for disease or certain conditions as the result of family history, age, or environmental exposures. It is likely to result in the greatest yield of true cases and represents the most economical utilization of screening measures. For example, screening tests for Tay-Sachs disease might be applied to individuals of Jewish extraction whose ancestors originated in Eastern Europe because this group has a higher frequency of the genetic alteration.

Mass Health Examinations

Several other activities are similar to screening but differ in one or more critical respects. Population or epidemiologic surveys aim to elucidate the natural history, prevalence, incidence, and duration of health conditions in defined populations.[8] The purpose of such surveys is to gain new knowledge regarding the distribution and determinants of diseases in carefully selected populations. Thus, they are not considered screening because they imply no immediate health benefits to the participants.[9]

Epidemiologic surveillance, defined in Chapter 1, aims at the protection of community health through case detection and intervention (e.g., tuberculosis control).[10] It refers to the continuous observation of the trends and distribution of disease incidence in a community or other population over time to prevent disease or injury.[11] Sources of data for surveillance include morbidity and mortality reports, for example, those reported by the Centers for Disease Control and Prevention. Surveillance activities detected an increase in tuberculosis in the United States as well as an increase in measles cases; subsequently, the latter disease was brought under control by stepped-up immunization of children. Surveillance programs are used for detection and control of conditions ranging from infectious diseases to injuries to chronic diseases.

Case finding, also referred to as opportunistic screening, is the utilization of screening tests for detection of conditions unrelated to the patient's chief complaint.[5,12] An example would be administration of a screen for colon cancer to a patient who came to a physician complaining of pharyngitis.

Appropriate Situations for Screening Tests and Programs

A number of criteria must be considered carefully before a decision is made to implement a screening program.[8] Although the ideal situation is one in which all

EXHIBIT 11–2

Appropriate Situations for Screening

Social: The health problem should be important for the individual and the community. Diagnostic follow-up and intervention should be available to all who require them. There should be a favorable cost-benefit ratio. Public acceptance must be high.

Scientific: The natural history of the condition should be adequately understood. Identification should occur during prepathogenesis with sufficient lead time (see text for definition of *lead time*). There is sound case definition in addition to a policy regarding whom to treat as patients. A knowledge base exists for the efficacy of prevention and the occurrence of side effects. The prevalence of the disease or condition is high.

Ethical: The provider initiates the service and, therefore, should have evidence that the program can alter the natural history of the condition in a significant proportion of those screened. Suitable, acceptable tests for screening and diagnosis of the condition as well as acceptable, effective methods of prevention are available. ■

Source: Data are from Wilson JMG, Jungner F. Principles and practice of screening for disease, *Public Health Papers*, No. 34, World Health Organization, 1968; and from Cochrane AL, Holland WW. Validation of screening procedures. *British Medical Bulletin*, Vol 27, pp. 3–8, Churchill Livingstone; 1971.

criteria are satisfied, numerous examples can be cited to illustrate how screening programs that violate one or more of these issues can still be extremely valuable (Exhibit 11–2).

Social

Of major importance is the magnitude of the health problem for which screening is being considered. Magnitude is relevant in a number of dimensions: to the community, in terms of economics, and medically. From the community perspective, the disease or outcome must be viewed as a major health problem. This means that there is general consensus that the health problem is of sufficiently high priority as to justify the commitment of resources to implement and carry out the program. Furthermore, acceptance of the program by the public must be high. For example, an effective screening test for a major health problem will not necessarily result in an effective screening program if the public refuses to participate.

Although it may be tempting to do so, one must not automatically assume that screening programs are beneficial. Early detection efforts, if they are to be successful over the long run, must be cost-effective. Thus, one must consider the costs of the test itself, the costs of follow-up examinations, and the costs of treatments avoided. The most clear-cut evidence of cost-effectiveness manifests itself when the cost of the program itself is more than offset by the savings of more expensive treatment that would have been necessary had the condition advanced to a more serious stage. Oftentimes this may not be the case, however, and one must consider as benefits improvements in quality of life and the value of years of life saved. Negative costs should be considered also: There are emotional costs to healthy individuals who are falsely labeled as ill by a screening test and emotional costs to individuals (and their loved ones) who are diagnosed early and yet die quickly anyway.

An obvious determinant of the cost-benefit ratio of a screening program is the current cost to the medical community in the absence of screening. How much money is being spent to treat individuals with the disease? How many hospital beds are being utilized? What is the number of health personnel assigned to the problem? Diseases and conditions that are costly to treat may still be considered for early detection even if the scientific justification for screening is weaker than for a disease that represents less of a medical burden.

Scientific

Early detection efforts are most likely to be successful when the natural history of the disease is known. This knowledge permits identification of early stages of disease and appropriate biologic markers of progression. For example, it is known that individuals with high cholesterol and high blood pressure are at increased risk for coronary heart disease. Because these risk factors precede onset of an acute myocardial infarction, identification of such high-risk individuals may lead to medical intervention (changes in diet, exercise, weight loss, or use of drugs) to prevent the disease. This example illustrates that there also should be good tests (screening and diagnostic) to measure blood pressure and blood cholesterol and that effective treatment should be available.

Ethical

It is most desirable to implement screening programs for diseases that—when diagnosed early—have their natural history altered, that is, for which effective treatment is available. Note, however, that screening is sometimes done for diseases for which effective treatment is not available. For example, we are yet without a cure for acquired immune deficiency syndrome. Screening is nonetheless important to prevent spread of the disease from infected to uninfected individuals and to improve the prognosis of those who may be affected. For those diseases for which effective treatments are available, it is important to consider the capacity of the medical community to handle the increased number of individuals requiring definitive diagnoses. Suppose a volunteer organization decides to offer a free health screening for high cholesterol at the local community center and that 10,000 citizens attend. Suppose further that 1,000 citizens are found to have high cholesterol. These individuals are mailed a letter informing them of their results with the suggestion to see their physician for further evaluation. A number of ethical issues can be envisioned. What if physicians in the local medical community are unable to accommodate the sudden increased demand for their services? What if these individuals lack medical insurance and have no physician?

Characteristics of a Good Screening Test

There are five attributes of a good screening test: simple, rapid, inexpensive, safe, and acceptable[8,9,13]:

1. *Simple:* The test should be easy to learn and perform. One that can be administered by nonphysician medical personnel will necessarily cost less than one that requires years of medical training.

2. *Rapid:* The test should not take long to administer, and the results should be available soon. The amount of time required to screen an individual is directly related to the success of the program: If a screening test requires only five minutes out of a person's schedule, it is likely to be perceived as being more valuable than one that requires an hour or more. Furthermore, immediate feedback is better than a test in which results may not be available for weeks or months. Results of a blood pressure screening are usually known immediately; results of a screen for high cholesterol must await laboratory analysis. Fortunately, much progress is being made in the development of rapid screening tests for many conditions.

3. *Inexpensive:* As discussed earlier, cost-benefit is an important criterion to consider in the evaluation of screening programs. The lower the cost of a screening test, the more likely it is that the overall program will be cost beneficial.

4. *Safe:* The screening test should not carry potential harm to screenees.

5. *Acceptable:* The test should be acceptable to the target group. An effective protocol has been developed to screen for testicular cancer, but acceptance rates among men have not been as high as for a similar procedure, mammography, among women.

Evaluation of Screening Tests

Recall that the purpose of a screening test is to classify individuals as to whether they are likely to have disease or be disease-free. To do this, a measuring instrument or combination of instruments is required. Examples of such instruments are clinical laboratory tests, a fever thermometer, weighing scales, and standardized questionnaires. The preceding section made no mention of the important issue of how well the screening test should actually work. This complex subject requires the introduction of several new concepts. The first and second of these concepts are reliability and validity.

Reliability

Reliability, also known as precision, is the ability of a measuring instrument to give consistent results on repeated trials. According to Morrison, reliability of a test refers to "its capacity to give the same result—positive or negative, whether correct or incorrect—on repeated application in a person with a given level of disease. Reliability depends on the variability in the manifestation on which the test is based (e.g., short-term fluctuation in blood pressure), and on the variability in the method of measurement and the skill with which it is made."[1(p. 10)]

Repeated measurement reliability refers to the degree of consistency between or among repeated measurements of the same individual on more than one occasion. For example, if one were to measure the height of an adult at different times, one would expect to observe similar results. That is because, in part, one's true value of height is relatively constant (although we are actually slightly shorter at the end of the day than we were at the beginning!). There also might be slight errors in measurement from one occasion to another, however; some measurements overestimate and others underestimate the true value. Although one might expect to measure height reliably, other measures, such as blood pressure, may be much more unreliable than height. Technicians' skills in the measurement of blood pressure, slight variations in the calibration of the manometer cuff, and variability in subjects' true blood pressure levels from one occasion to another all affect the reliability of blood pressure measurements.

Internal consistency reliability evaluates the degree of agreement or homogeneity within a questionnaire measure of an attitude, personal characteristic, or psychologic attribute. For example, a researcher may be interested in studying the relationship between general anxiety level and peptic ulcer. A multi-item paper-and-pencil measure for general anxiety may be utilized in the research. The Kuder-Richardson reliability coefficient measures the internal consistency reliability of this type of measure.[14] It is based on the average intercorrelation of a set of items in a multi-item index. Chronbach's α coefficient is used also to measure internal consistency reliability; an α value of 0.7 or greater is believed to indicate satisfactory reliability and suggests that a set of items is measuring a common dimension.[15] These two reliability measures are particularly applicable to epidemiologic research that uses survey measures, such as interviews or self-report questionnaires.

Interjudge reliability refers to reliability assessments derived from agreement among trained experts. The ratings of psychiatrists in psychiatric research, for example, may be used to measure an individual's degree of psychiatric impairment. To obtain an estimate of the reliability of the rating procedure, the average percentage of agreement of the judges who are rating an attribute may be calculated.

There are several ways to express the reliability (precision) of a set of measurements.[13] One is to obtain repeated measurements of an attribute for a single person and then obtain the standard deviation of the measurements, known as the standard error of measurement. A second is the reliability coefficient, which is an indicator of repeated measurement reliability. It is a correlation coefficient that quantifies the degree of agreement between measurements taken on two different occasions.

Reliability types:	**Validity types:**
Repeated measurements	Content
Internal consistency	Criterion-referenced
Interjudge	Predictive
	Concurrent
	Construct

Validity

Also known as accuracy, *validity* is the ability of a measuring instrument to give a true measure (i.e., how well it measures what it purports to measure).[16] Validity can be evaluated only if an accepted and independent method exists for confirming the test measurement. Validity is an important component of epidemiologic research, including areas outside screening. Variations on the theme of validity are presented in the next few sections. The issues discussed extend beyond the role of validity in screening for a disease. However, they may be applicable to screening for high-risk behaviors.

Content validity is often used to measure the validity of survey instruments or paper-and-pencil measures. *Content validity* "refers to the degree to which a measure covers the range of meanings included within the concept."[17(p. 133)] It concerns the extent to which the items in a questionnaire seem to be valid for measuring the domain of the phenomenon that they are supposed to measure; that is, the measurement includes and fully covers all the aspects of the dimension being measured. For example, the content validity of a test of mechanical aptitude would measure whether the test contains items that cover a full range of mechanical abilities. This type of validity also is referred to as rational or logical validity.[13]

Criterion-referenced validity generally refers to validity that is found by correlating a measure with an external criterion of the entity being assessed.[7] The external standard used to assess validity is called the *validity criterion*. The two types of criterion-referenced validity are predictive validity and concurrent validity. Predictive validity denotes the ability of a measure to predict some attribute or characteristic in the future. To illustrate this type of validity, consider the association between type A behavior and coronary heart disease. Researchers attempted to demonstrate the validity of the type A measure through its positive correlations with future incidence of coronary heart disease. The future outcome that was predicted by the type A measure was the validity criterion. Predictive validity also is called *empirical* or *statistical validity*. Similar to predictive validity is concurrent validity, which refers to validity measurement by correlating a measure with an alternative measure of the same phenomenon taken at the same point in time; typically the concurrent validating criterion is more cumbersome than the new measure. Much work has been devoted to self-administered measures of mental health characteristics for use in epidemiologic studies. An example would be the validation of a self-administered depressive symptoms questionnaire against the criterion of psychiatric diagnosis.

Construct validity refers to the degree to which the measurement agrees with the theoretical concept being investigated.[7] Construct validity involves the confirmation of a theoretical construct, such as anxiety. In designing a paper-and-pencil test of anxiety, the investigator would first need to specify what types of behavior are associated with anxiety. Then the investigator would compose items that measure these behaviors and demonstrate that they are consistent with a theoretical conception of anxiety. Construct validity is concerned primarily with the meaning of the items in a measure[14] and whether the measure is associated logically with other variables specified in a theoretical framework.[17] Construct validity is important to epidemiologic measures, such as scales of depressive symptomatology.

Interrelationships Between Reliability and Validity

Figure 11–1 is designed to assist the reader in differentiating between reliability and validity, and in understanding how the two terms are interrelated. In part A, the periphery of the target shows a measure that is highly reliable but invalid. Bullets have hit the target in the same general area (i.e., have clustered around the same general area) but have missed the bull's-eye (center) of the target. Figure 11–1B shows a measure that is neither reliable nor valid. The bullets have scattered randomly around the target and have not consistently hit the bull's-eye. Part C of the figure illustrates a measure that is both reliable and valid. The bullets have consistently hit the bull's-eye and also cluster in the same general area. Thus, it is possible for a measure to be highly reliable but invalid. Reliability means only that the same measurement results are being reproduced on repeated occasions. Conversely, however, it is not possible for a measure to be valid but unreliable. If the measure consistently hits the bull's-eye on repeated occasions, then the measure is, by definition, both reliable and valid.

Sources of Unreliability and Invalidity

Measurement bias refers to constant errors that are introduced by a faulty measuring device and tend to reduce the reliability of measurements. For example, a

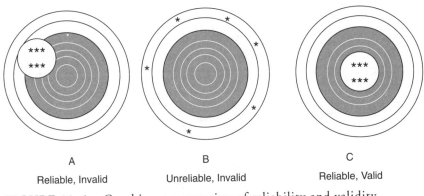

A	B	C
Reliable, Invalid	Unreliable, Invalid	Reliable, Valid

FIGURE 11–1 Graphic representation of reliability and validity

blood pressure manometer may be miscalibrated so that it consistently underestimates or overestimates true blood pressure values. Psychiatrists and clinicians also might introduce measurement biases in their judgments, which would be revealed if one rater had an average group of judgments that was higher than the mean ratings of other judges.

The halo effect is another kind of bias that affects the validity of questionnaire measurements. An illustration is completion of a checklist evaluation of an employee by a supervisor who has formed a general opinion about the employee. The supervisor might tend to evaluate all items of behavior in the same general direction without carefully rating specific aspects of the employee's behavior.

Social desirability effects are biases introduced when a respondent answers questions in a manner that corresponds to what may be the prevailing socially desired mode of behavior. For example, teenage boys might respond to an interviewer's questions about sexual behavior by exaggerating the frequency of sexual activity because this would be a socially desirable response among some peer groups. The factor of social desirability tends to affect the validity of questionnaire responses.

Measures of the Validity of Screening Tests

In the context of screening, there are four measures of validity that must be considered: sensitivity, specificity, predictive value (+), and predictive value (−). Figure 11–2 represents a sample of individuals who have been examined with both a screening test for disease (rows) and a definitive diagnostic test (columns). Thus, we are able to determine how well the screening test performed in identifying individuals with disease.

- *Sensitivity:* the ability of the test to identify correctly all screened individuals who actually have the disease. In Figure 11–2, a total of a + c individuals were determined to have the disease, according to some established gold standard, a definitive diagnosis that has been determined by biopsy, surgery, autopsy, or other method[5] and has been accepted as the standard. Sensitivity is defined as the number of true positives divided by the sum of true positives and false negatives. Suppose that in a sample of 1,000 individuals there were 120 who actually had the disease. If the screening test correctly identified all 120 cases, the sensitivity would be 100%. If the screening test was unable to identify all individuals who should be referred for definitive diagnoses, then sensitivity would be less than 100%.

Test Result		Condition According to Gold Standard			
		Present	Absent	Total	
	Positive	a = True positives	b = False positives	a + b	Predictive Value (+) $\frac{a}{a+b}$
	Negative	c = False negatives	d = True negatives	c + d	Predictive Value (−) $\frac{d}{c+d}$
	Total	a + c	b + d		Grand Total a + b + c + d
		Sensitivity $\frac{a}{a+c}$	Specificity $\frac{d}{b+d}$		

FIGURE 11–2 Fourfold table for classification of screening test results. Definitions: True Positives are individuals who both have been screened positive and truly have the condition; false positives are individuals who have been screened positive but do not have the condition; false negatives are individuals screened negative who truly have the condition; and true negatives are individuals who both have been screened negative and do not have the condition.

- *Specificity:* the ability of the test to identify only nondiseased individuals who actually do not have the disease. It is defined as the number of true negatives divided by the sum of false positives and true negatives. If a test is not specific, then individuals who do not actually have the disease will be referred for additional diagnostic testing.
- *Predictive value (+):* the proportion of individuals screened positive by the test who actually have the disease. In Figure 11–2, a total of a + b individuals were screened positive by the test. Predictive value (+) is the proportion a/(a + b) who actually have the condition, according to the gold standard.
- *Predictive value (−):* an analogous measure for those screened negative by the test; it is designated by the formula d/(c + d).

Note that the only time these measures can be estimated is when the same group of individuals has been examined using both the screening test and the gold standard. According to McCunney:

> False positive results are inherent in most laboratory reference limits, simply because of the manner by which those limits are established. People whose results are beyond 2 standard deviations from the mean are by definition "abnormal." In general, 1 out of 20 "well people" have an abnormal test result—without evidence of illness . . . the rates of false positive results reported from a variety of health fairs [range from approximately 3% for blood chemistry tests for iron to over 20% for triglycerides].[18(p. 299)]

The accuracy of a screening test is found by the following formula: (a + d)/(a + b + c + d). Accuracy measures the degree of agreement between the screening test and the gold standard. A sample calculation for accuracy as well as sensitivity, specificity, and predictive value is shown in Exhibit 11–3.

Effects of Prevalence of Disease on Screening Test Results

Sensitivity and specificity are stable properties of screening tests and, as a result, are unaffected by the prevalence of a disease. Predictive value, however, is very much affected by the prevalence of the condition being screened. Many screening tests are validated upon groups that have a contrived prevalence of disease (e.g., approximately 50%). This prevalence would usually be higher than what is found in clinical practice.[5]

In Table 11–1, the cells of a 2 by 2 table have been arranged horizontally. Sensitivity and specificity are stable properties of screening tests that remain constant across groups that have different prevalences of disease. The data from Exhibit 11–3 have been transposed to row A. Sensitivity and specificity were pre-

Sample Calculation of Sensitivity, Specificity, and Predictive Value

Suppose the following data are obtained from a screening test applied to 500 people:

| Screening Test Result | Condition according to gold standard | | |
	Positive	Negative	Total
Positive	a = 240	b = 25	a + b = 265
Negative	c = 15	d = 220	c + d = 235
Total	a + c = 255	b + d = 245	a + b + c + d = 500

Sensitivity = $a/(a + c)$ = $(240/255) \times 100$ = 94.1%

Specificity = $d/(b + d)$ = $(220/245) \times 100$ = 89.8%

Predictive Value (+) = $a/(a + b)$ = $(240/265) \times 100$ = 90.6%

Predictive Value (−) = $d/(c + d)$ = $(220/235) \times 100$ = 93.6%

Prevalence = $(a + c)/(a + b + c + d)$ = $(255/500) \times 100$ = 51%

Accuracy = $(a + d)/(a + b + c + d)$ = $(460/500) \times 100$ = 92%

viously calculated to be 94.1% and 89.8%, respectively. The prevalence of disease was 51%. In row B, the prevalence of disease is 10%. The number of cases of disease (a + c) in row B is found by multiplying $500 \times 0.10 = 50$. The number of true positives (a) is the number of cases of disease multiplied by the sensitivity of the test: $50 \times 0.94 = 47$. The number of true negatives (d) is the number of diagnosed negatives multiplied by the specificity of the test: $450 \times 0.90 = 405$. The numbers of false negatives (c) and false positives (b) are found by subtraction (3 and 45, respectively). For row B, the predictive value (+) is $[a/(a + b)] \times 100 = 51.1\%$, and the predictive value (−) is $[d/(c + d)] \times 100 = 99.3\%$. Thus, when the values for sensitivity and specificity found in row A are applied to the data in row B, among a group of people who have a 10%

Table 11–1 Effects of Disease Prevalence on the Predictive Value of a Screening Test

| | Cell Values | | | Total | | No. of Cases of Disease | Predictive | Predictive |
Row	a	b	c	d	(a + b + c + d)	Prevalence	(a + c)	Value (+)	Value (−)
A	240	25	15	220	500	51%	255	90.6%	93.6%
B	47	45	3	405	500	10%	50	51.1%	99.3%

prevalence of disease, the predictive value (+) decreases to 51.1% and the predictive value (−) increases to about 99%.

When the prevalence of a disease falls, the predictive value (+) falls and the predictive value (−) rises. The clinical implications of low predictive value (+) are that any individual who has a positive screening test would have low probability of having the disease; an invasive diagnostic procedure would probably not be warranted for this patient. Table 11–1 demonstrates the effects of changing the prevalence of disease upon predictive values. When the prevalence of disease drops from about 51% to 10%, the predictive value (+) drops from about 91% to 51%, and the predictive value (−) increases from about 94% to 99%.

Relationship Between Sensitivity and Specificity

Figure 11–3 illustrates the relationship between sensitivity and specificity. When the screening test result is a continuous or ordered variable with several levels, then the choice for a cut point that discriminates optimally between suspected diseased and normal individuals is a trade-off. Figure 11–3 demonstrates the effects of choosing various cut points. The figure shows a hypothetical distribution of trait values (e.g., fasting blood glucose, an indicator of diabetes) for normals and a distribution curve for the diseased population that overlaps the curve for the normal population. For example, fasting blood glucose levels may approximate the normal distribution with a mean of 100 mg/dL. A subject may have an elevated glucose level in the high range for a population (e.g., 120 mg/dL) and not be diabetic. Some diabetic individuals who are at the lower end of the curve for the diseased group also may have glucose levels in the high normal range. Thus, the two distributions may overlap: Some nondiseased individuals may have elevated glucose levels, and some diseased individuals may have glucose levels in the lower ranges for the abnormal group. The cut point may be set at B to maximize both sensitivity and specificity. If the cut point is moved to A by lowering the specific blood glucose level that is to be classified as abnormal, almost all of the individuals who have the disease will be screened as positive, and sensitivity will approach 100%. Specificity will be lowered because more of the nondiseased individuals will be classified as diseased. By moving the cut point to C, which represents a higher blood glucose level than point A or B, specificity will be increased at the expense of sensitivity.

Another example of establishing a cut point to distinguish between diseased and nondiseased people is setting the referral criteria for screening for glaucoma.[19] By using the criterion of 15 mm Hg intraocular pressure, the sensitivity

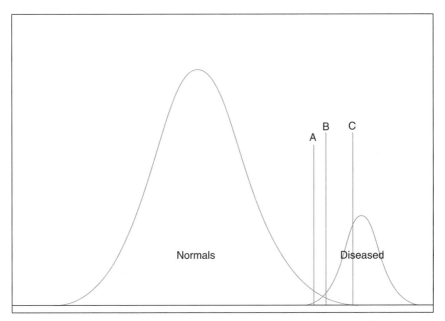

FIGURE 11–3   Interrelationship between sensitivity and specificity

of the screening test would be high, and few persons with glaucoma would be missed. At the same time, many persons who did not have the disease would be incorrectly classified. If a high referral point were selected (e.g., 33 mm Hg), the majority of those without glaucoma would not be referred, but many with the disease would be missed by the screening test. Thus, this example demonstrates that sensitivity and specificity are complementary. "The key to a successful screening is to balance the referral criteria so that both the overreferrals and underreferrals are minimized."[19(p. 360)]

In summary, if one wishes to improve sensitivity, the cut point used to classify individuals as diseased should be moved farther in the range of the nondiseased. To improve specificity, the cut point should be moved farther in the range typically associated with the disease. There are a number of additional procedures that can improve both sensitivity and specificity:

- *Retrain screeners:* If the test requires human assessment (e.g., blood pressure readings), then improving the precision of measurement through additional training sessions will reduce the amount of misclassification.
- *Recalibrate screening instrument:* For those tests that utilize technology (e.g., a weighing device or a densitometer), it may be possible to reduce the amount of imprecision through refinement of the methodology.

- *Utilize a different test:* In some situations there may be more than one way to measure the outcome of interest. Suppose there are two laboratory assays available to quantify serum cholesterol. If one assay performs poorly (low reliability and validity), it may be possible to replace it with a better assay.
- *Utilize more than one test:* Because of the variability in some measures, it is easy to misclassify an individual as high or low. By taking more than one measure of blood pressure and averaging the results, the ability to label an individual correctly as hypertensive will be improved, resulting in better measures of sensitivity and specificity.

Evaluation of Screening Programs

Despite the intuitive appeal of screening programs, their utility should never be assumed. Rather, it is imperative that they be evaluated with the same rigor used to identify risk factors in the pathogenesis of disease. The ideal design is a randomized controlled trial. Under this approach, subjects are randomized either to receive the new screening test or program or to receive usual care. If the disease of interest is fatal, then the appropriate end point would be differences in mortality between the two groups. For nonfatal diseases (e.g., cataracts), differences in incidence between the screened and nonscreened populations should be estimated. Another approach, although less rigorous, is to conduct ecologic time trend studies in geographic areas with and without screening programs. Finally, the case-control method can be applied also: Cases are fatal (or likely to be fatal) cases of the disease, controls are nonfatal cases of the disease, and the exposure is participation in a screening program. Regardless of the approach that is taken, evaluation of screening programs is subject to several types of bias that have not yet been described fully in this chapter. Figure 11–4 depicts the natural history of disease in relation to the time of diagnosis.

Suppose the disease begins at time A and results in death at time D. A case detected as the result of screening may be picked up at time B, whereas a case that is picked up as a result of clinical signs and symptoms may not be detected until time C.

- *Lead time bias:* the perception that the screen-detected case has a longer survival simply because the disease was identified earlier in the natural history of the disease. Thus, although these two individuals had identical dates of onset and death, there is an apparent increase in survival for the

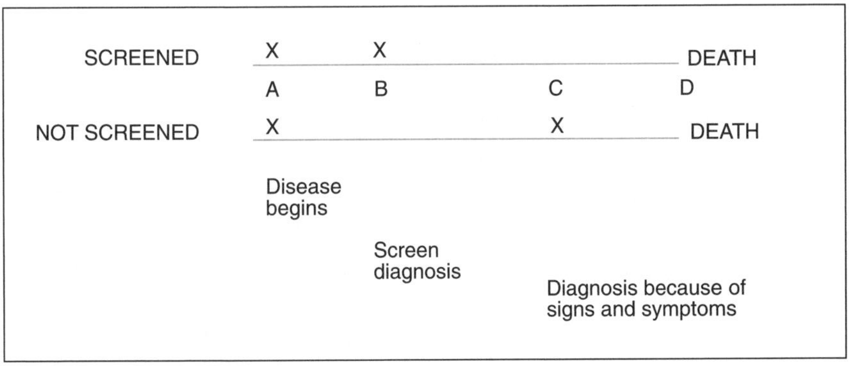

FIGURE 11–4   Natural history of disease in relation to time of diagnosis. C to D, survival time for unscreened case; B to D, survival time for screened case; B to C, lead time.

screen-detected case. The extent of this bias is estimated as the difference between time periods B and C.

- *Length bias:* used particularly with respect to certain cancer screening programs. In illustration, tumors that are detected by a screening program tend to be slower growing and hence have an inherently better prognosis than tumors that are more rapidly growing and are detected as a result of clinical manifestation.

- *Selection bias:* Although this topic was covered as an aspect of study designs, selection bias also is relevant to the evaluation of screening programs. In particular, individuals who are motivated enough to participate in screening programs may have a different probability of disease (as a result of other healthy behaviors) than individuals who refuse participation.

In conclusion, the foregoing section has discussed a number of factors that need to be taken into account in the evaluation of screening tests. Indeed, many of the issues remain controversial, as noted in Exhibit 11–4 for the prostate-specific antigen (PSA) test.

Issues in the Classification of Morbidity and Mortality

The central theme of this chapter has been screening for disease in the community and the related topics of reliability and validity of measurement. Schemes

Controversies in Screening

EXHIBIT 11–4

As an example of why it is important to evaluate the potential outcomes of new screening modalities, consider the case of PSA. As a marker, PSA is potentially useful for early detection of prostate cancer (as a form of adenocarcinoma). In venous blood samples, PSA levels greater than 10 ng/mL are associated with a positive predictive value of 66% for adenocarcinoma. For PSA levels between 4 and 10 ng/mL, the positive predictive value for adenocarcinoma declines to approximately 24%.[20] There is a complementary increment in false negative rates. Consequently, such high false negative rates tend to correspond with demands for biopsies as definitive diagnoses. The establishment of age-specific reference ranges[21] represents one approach to improve sensitivity while holding specificity constant, with a corresponding effect on positive and negative predictive values.

Prostate cancer is a disease for which incidence rates at autopsy are much higher than incidence rates based on clinical diagnoses. Anywhere from 40% to 80% of 90-year-old men will have pathologic evidence of prostate cancer at death, even if they had never been diagnosed with the disease.[22] Among elderly men all forms of cancer are much more prevalent than among younger men. Clinical medicine is unable to resolve the ethical issue of which type of cancer men should die with versus die from. The importance of the distinction arises from the risks of complications associated with surgical treatment of prostate cancer. These risks, for example, impotence and incontinence, have significant effects on quality of life. Thus, it is important to consider the negative effects of screening (unnecessary treatment) as well as the positive. Moreover, screening may incur significant financial burdens for patients; by some estimates, an ultrasound-guided biopsy and pathologic examination of the tissue cost approximately $1,000 during the 1990s.[23]

Recent mathematical modeling based on SEER data and estimates of PSA screening rates have lead to the conclusion that the use of PSA as a screening marker is responsible for 45% to 75% of the observed decline in prostate cancer.[24] In addition, the widespread adoption of PSA since its introduction in the 1980s makes conduct of a randomized controlled clinical trial

continues

EXHIBIT 11–4 *continued*

extremely difficult. Although such trials are now underway, decades will probably elapse before definitive answers are at hand.

The controversies surrounding PSA argue for the utility of careful observational research. For example, Jacobsen et al.[25] studied the incidence of prostate cancer in Olmsted County, Minnesota, and concluded that the recent increases in prostate cancer incidence are due to increased utilization of PSA, and that early detection efforts may be effective in identifying more early-stage cancers. Recent downward trends in prostate cancer mortality are the first suggestive evidence that PSA might be achieving the desired ends of any early detection program.

for the nomenclature and classification of disease are central to the reliable measurement of the outcome variable in epidemiologic research. The terms *nomenclature* and *classification* are defined as follows: A nomenclature is a highly specific set of terms for describing and recording clinical or pathologic diagnoses to classify ill persons into groups. A system of nomenclature must be extensive so that all conditions encountered by the practitioner in a particular health discipline can be recorded. Classification, in contrast, lends itself to the statistical compilation of groups of cases of disease by arranging disease entities into categories that share similar features.[26]

The classification systems used are in some cases purely arbitrary because they are determined by the function that is to be served by classification; nevertheless, all practitioners in a discipline need to have at their disposal a standardized system for classification of diseases. Many classification systems for diseases are theoretically possible; they might be based upon age, circumstance of onset, geographic location, or some other factor connected with the purpose for which they are to be used. The categories of disease should be general so that there will be a limited number of categories that take into account all the diseases that might be encountered. The use of general categories facilitates the epidemiologic study of disease phenomena by giving rise to groups of interrelated morbid conditions. The classifications of disease must be distinct so that a disease falls into only one category of the classification system. Each category of the classification system must refer to diseases that are sufficiently frequent to permit several cases of disease to fall into the category. Otherwise, there would be an excessively detailed list of categories to contain the range of morbid conditions.

Finally, a well-devised classification system permits standardization across different agencies and even countries so that comparisons in morbidity and mortality from disease can be made.

Two types of criteria are used for the classification of ill persons: causal and manifestational.[26] It is possible to classify cases of disease according to a causal basis (e.g., tuberculosis or syphilis) or according to manifestation (e.g., affected anatomic site: hepatitis or breast cancer). Epidemiologic research relies primarily on manifestational criteria for classification in the hope that there will be a strong enough connection with causal factors to make possible etiologic studies.[26]

One example of a classification system is the *Diagnostic and Statistical Manual of Mental Disorders,* now in its fourth revision; it provides for standardization of the classification of psychiatric diagnoses.[27] A second example, which was introduced in Chapter 5 and is one of the most widely used systems for the classification of diseases, is the *International Statistical Classification of Diseases and Related Health Problems,* now in its tenth revision (ICD-10).[28] The ICD is sponsored by the World Health Organization (Collaborative Centers for Classification of Diseases). It is designed for varied uses: for both clinical and general epidemiologic purposes and for the evaluation of health care. The ICD-10 spans three volumes; volume 1 provides classification of diseases into three- and four-character levels (an alphanumeric coding scheme replaces the previous numeric one).

Conclusion

This chapter discussed terminology related to the quality of measures employed in epidemiology. Measurement is a crucial issue because even the most carefully designed study may yield spurious results if premised upon faulty measures. Topics covered in this chapter included reliability and validity, screening for disease, and methods for the classification of diseases. Formulas and examples for calculation of sensitivity, specificity, and predictive value were provided. The effect of prevalence of disease upon predictive value was discussed also.

Study Questions and Exercises

1. Are you able to define the following?
   a. reliability
   b. validity

c. precision
d. accuracy
e. sensitivity
f. specificity
g. predictive value (+) and predictive value (−)

2. What factors should govern the selection and use of a screening instrument by a health clinic?

3. What is the relationship between reliability and validity? Is it possible for a measure to be reliable and invalid? Conversely, is it possible for a measure to be unreliable and valid?

4. Assume that the fasting blood level of a lipid is normally distributed in the population of people who do not have disease "X." There is a smaller distribution curve of the fasting blood levels of this lipid, which also is normal in shape, for the population of persons who have disease "X," and the curve overlaps the upper end (right side) of the curve for people without the disease. Draw distribution curves for the diseased and nondiseased populations and discuss the effects upon sensitivity and specificity of setting the cut point for disease and nondisease at various positions on the two overlapping curves.

5. How does the predictive value of a screening test vary according to the prevalence of disease?

6. A serologic test is being devised to detect a hypothetical chronic disease. Three hundred individuals were referred to a laboratory for testing. One hundred diagnosed cases were among the 300. A serologic test yielded 200 positives, of which one-fourth were true positives. Calculate the sensitivity, specificity, and predictive value of this test. (*Hint:* After setting up the appropriate 2 by 2 table, find missing data by subtraction. The numbers for the cells should then correspond to the numbers shown in Appendix 11.)

7. A new test was compared with a gold standard measurement with the following results:

New Test	Gold Standard	
	+	−
+	18	2
−	8	72

What are the sensitivity and specificity?

8. Using the data from question 7, what is the predictive value (+) and the predictive value (−)?
9. A test-retest reliability study of the new test was conducted with the following results:

Retest	Test +	−
+	80	9
−	8	3

What is the percentage agreement (accuracy)?
10. The prevalence of undetected diabetes in a population to be screened is approximately 1.5%, and it is assumed that 10,000 persons will be screened. The screening test will measure blood serum glucose content. A value of 180 mg% or higher is considered positive. The sensitivity and specificity associated with this screening test are 22.9% and 99.8%, respectively.
    a. What is the predictive value of a positive test?
    b. What is the predictive value of a negative test?

References

1. Morrison AS. *Screening in Chronic Disease*. New York, NY: Oxford University Press; 1985.
2. Shapiro S, Venet W, Strax P, Venet L. *Periodic Screening for Breast Cancer: The Health Insurance Plan Project and Its Sequelae, 1963–1986*. Baltimore, MD: Johns Hopkins University Press; 1988.
3. Hurley SF, Kaldor JM. The benefits and risks of mammographic screening for breast cancer. *Epidemiol Rev*. 1992;14:101–129.
4. Fletcher SW, Black W, Harris R, Rimer BK, Shapiro S. Report of the International Workshop on Screening for Breast Cancer. *J Natl Cancer Inst*. 1993;85:1644–1656.
5. Haynes RB. How to read clinical journals, II: to learn about a diagnostic test. *Can Med Assoc J*. 1981;124:703–710.
6. Commission on Chronic Illness. *Chronic Illness in the United States: Prevention of Chronic Illness*. Cambridge, MA: Harvard University Press; 1957:1.
7. Last JM, ed. *A Dictionary of Epidemiology*, 4th ed. New York, NY: Oxford University Press; 2001.
8. Wilson JMG, Jungner F. *Principles and Practice of Screening for Disease*. Public Health Paper 34. Geneva, Switzerland: World Health Organization; 1968.
9. Sackett DL, Holland WW. Controversy in the detection of disease. *Lancet*. 1975;2:357–359.
10. World Health Organization. *Mass Health Examinations*. Public Health Paper 45. Geneva, Switzerland: World Health Organization; 1971.

11. Halperin W, Baker EL Jr. *Public Health Surveillance.* New York, NY: Van Nostrand Reinhold; 1992.
12. Beaglehole R, Bonita R, Kjellström T. *Basic Epidemiology.* Geneva, Switzerland: World Health Organization; 1993.
13. Cochrane AL, Holland WW. Validation of screening procedures. *Br Med Bull.* 1971;27:3–8.
14. Thorndike RL, Hagen E. *Measurement and Evaluation in Psychology and Education,* 2nd ed. New York, NY: Wiley; 1961.
15. Abramson JH. *Survey Methods in Community Medicine,* 4th ed. New York, NY: Churchill Livingstone; 1991.
16. Weiss NS. *Clinical Epidemiology: The Study of the Outcome of Illness.* New York, NY: Oxford University Press; 1986.
17. Babbie E. *The Practice of Social Research,* 6th ed. Belmont, CA: Wadsworth; 1992.
18. McCunney RJ. Medical surveillance: principles of establishing an effective program. In: McCunney RJ, ed. *Handbook of Occupational Medicine.* Boston, MA: Little, Brown; 1988:297–309.
19. Myrowitz E. A public health perspective on vision screening. *Am J Optom Physiol Opt.* 1984;61:359–360.
20. Catalona WJ, Smith DS, Ratliff TL, et al. Measurement of prostate-specific antigen in serum as a screening test for prostate cancer. *N Engl J Med.* 1991;324:1156–1161.
21. Oesterling JE, Jacobsen SJ, Chute CG, et al. Serum prostate-specific antigen in a community-based population of healthy men. *JAMA.* 1993;270:860–864.
22. Sheldon CA, Williams RD, Fraley EE. Incidental carcinoma of the prostate: review of the literature and critical reappraisal of classification. *J Urol.* 1980;124:626–631.
23. Oesterling JE, Jacobsen SJ, Cooner WH. The use of age-specific reference ranges for serum prostate specific antigen in men 60 years old or older. *J Urol.* 1995; 153:1160–1163.
24. Etzioni R, Tsodikov A, Mariotto A, et al. Quantifying the role of PSA screening in the US prostate cancer mortality decline. *Cancer Causes Control.* 2007 Nov 20.
25. Jacobsen SJ, Katusic SK, Bergstralh EJ, et al. Incidence of prostate cancer diagnosis in the eras before and after serum prostate-specific antigen testing. *JAMA.* 1995; 274:1445–1449.
26. MacMahon B, Pugh TF. *Epidemiology Principles and Methods.* Boston, MA: Little, Brown; 1970.
27. American Psychiatric Association. *Diagnostic and Statistical Manual of Mental Disorders,* 4th ed. Text Revision: DSM-IV-TR. Washington, DC: American Psychiatric Association; 2000.
28. World Health Organization. *International Statistical Classification of Diseases and Related Health Problems,* 2nd ed. 10th revision. Geneva, Switzerland: World Health Organization; 2004.

APPENDIX
11

Data for Problem 6

Given	Find by Subtraction
Total = 300	Total − (TP + FN) = FP + TN = 300 − 100 = 200
TP + FN = 100	FP = (TP + FP) − TP = 200 − 50 = 150
TP + FP = 200	FN = (TP + FN) − TP = 100 − 50 = 50
TP = 50	TN = (FP + TN) − FP = 200 − 150 = 50

TP, true positive; FN, false negative; FP, false positive; TN, true negative.

CHAPTER 12

Epidemiology of Infectious Diseases

LEARNING OBJECTIVES

By the end of this chapter the reader will be able to:

- state modes of infectious disease transmission
- define three categories of infectious disease agents
- identify the characteristics of agents, such as infectivity, pathogenicity, virulence, and incubation period
- define quantitative terms used in infectious disease outbreaks
- describe the procedure for investigating a disease outbreak

CHAPTER OUTLINE

I. Introduction
II. Agents of Infectious Disease
III. Characteristics of Infectious Disease Agents
IV. Host
V. The Environment
VI. Means of Transmission: Directly or Indirectly from Reservoir
VII. Measures of Disease Outbreaks
VIII. Procedures Used in the Investigation of Infectious Disease Outbreaks

IX. Epidemiologically Significant Infectious Diseases in the Community
X. Conclusion
XI. Study Questions and Exercises

Introduction

Controlling infectious diseases is one of the most familiar applications of epidemiology at work in the community. Although there have been many advances in the prevention and treatment of infectious diseases, they remain significant causes of morbidity and mortality for the world's population in developed as well as developing countries. In the United States, pneumonia-influenza was the eighth leading cause of death in 2004.[1] From the world perspective, infections are the leading cause of death of children and young adults.[2] Additionally, diseases such as cancer (e.g., cervical cancer, some forms of liver cancer, and bladder cancer) are associated with infectious agents. Due to increasing world travel, passengers who are infected with a dangerous or exotic infectious disease can transmit the condition from a remote corner of the globe to a crowded city within the time span of a long-distance plane flight.

Other venues for outbreaks of infectious diseases are institutional settings; estimates suggest that approximately 4.5 per 100 patients admitted to U.S. hospitals experience nosocomial (hospital- or healthcare unit-acquired) infections, which range from wound infections to pneumonia to bloodstream infections.[3] About 100,000 of the estimated 1.7 million hospital-acquired infections are fatal. Also, infectious disease outbreaks occur in children's day care centers and residential settings for the developmentally disabled.[4] Another problem that is commanding the attention of public health practitioners is the spread of antibiotic-resistant staphylococcus infections into the community.

Let us consider one of the models—the epidemiologic triangle—that is used to explain the occurrence of disease outbreaks such as those that occur in institutional settings and the community at large. The epidemiologic triangle recognizes three major factors—agent, environment, and host—in the pathogenesis of disease. It is a venerable model that has been used for many decades, and epidemiologists still refer to it frequently.[5] The epidemiologic triangle (Figure 12–1) provides one of the fundamental public health conceptions of disease causality.

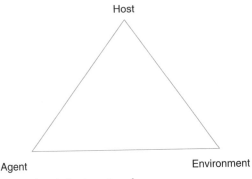

FIGURE 12–1 Epidemiologic triangle.

This model is particularly well suited to an explanation of the etiology of infectious diseases, although the current view regarding etiology of infectious diseases involves more complex multivariate causality as well. This chapter discusses how agent, host, and environment relate to the key topics in infectious disease epidemiology: methods for transmission of disease agents and specific outcomes, including foodborne illness and the major infectious diseases. Methods for investigation and control of epidemics also include examination of agent, host, and environment factors. Figure 12–2 presents one approach to categorizing the specific infectious diseases to be examined.

Agents of Infectious Disease

The study of biologic agents is the province of microbiology and will not be reviewed in detail in this book. Rather, a brief overview of some of the major biologic agents and the diseases associated with them is presented. Our goal is to demonstrate how epidemiologists describe the frequency of diseases caused by infectious disease agents in populations and how they attempt to discover and control mechanisms of transmission. In relation to infectious diseases, an agent must be present for an infection to occur. Microbial agents include the following:

- *Bacteria:* In the United States and Europe, bacterial diseases were among the leading killers during the 19th century. Antibiotics and improvements in medical care have helped to control some of these killers. Nevertheless, bacteria remain significant causes of human illness. Examples of diseases caused by bacteria are tuberculosis (TB), salmonellosis, and streptococcal infections (e.g., strep throat and necrotizing fasciitis). Of particular

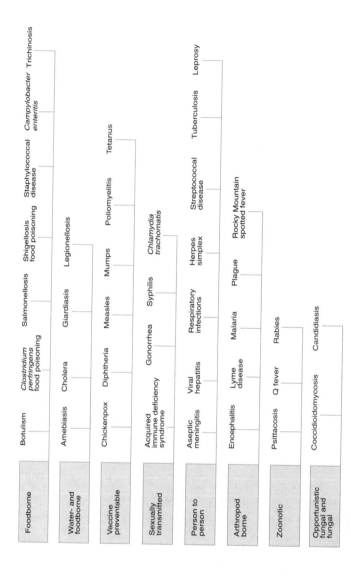

FIGURE 12–2 Epidemiologically significant infectious diseases (a partial list). The term *vaccine-preventable diseases* is used by the CDC. Although some categories overlap, they are helpful for didactic purposes. *Source:* Data are from Last JM, Wallace RB, eds., *Maxcy-Rosenau-Last: Public Health and Preventive Medicine*, 13th ed. pp. xix–xxi, Appleton & Lange, 1992; and from the Centers for Disease Control and Prevention, Reported vaccine-preventable diseases—United States, 1993; and the Childhood Immunization Initiative. *MMWR.* Vol 43, p. 57, February 4, 1994.

concern is the growing emergence of bacterial strains that are resistant to antibiotics (e.g., methicillin-resistant *Staphylococcus aureus*).

- *Viruses and rickettsia:* Examples of diseases caused by viruses include viral hepatitis A, herpes simplex, influenza, and viral meningitis (aseptic meningitis). Rickettsial agents produce Q fever, Rocky Mountain spotted fever, and rickettsialpox.
- *Fungi:* Examples of fungal diseases are San Joaquin Valley fever (one of the endemic mycoses—diseases caused by fungi—also called coccidioidomycosis), blastomycosis, ringworm (tinea capitis), and athlete's foot (tinea pedis). Opportunistic mycoses, which impose an increasing threat to immunocompromised patients, include candidiasis, cryptococcosis, and aspergillosis.[6]
- *Protozoa:* These organisms are responsible for malaria, amebiasis, babesiosis, cryptosporidiosis, and giardiasis.
- *Helminths:* These organisms (found most frequently in moist, tropical areas) include intestinal parasites—roundworms (which produce ascariasis), pinworms, and tapeworms—as well as the organisms that cause trichinellosis (trichinosis; infectious agent *Trichinella spiralis*). Another well-known helminth, *Schistosoma mansoni* (and several other species), is responsible for schistosomiasis, sometimes known as snail fever, which occurs in Africa (e.g., along the Nile River) and in South America (Brazil, Surinam, and Venezuela), China, Japan, and many other areas. The infectious agents responsible for schistosomiasis are not indigenous to North America.[7]
- *Arthropods:* One of the largest classes of living things, arthropods act as insect vectors that carry a disease agent from its reservoir to humans. Mosquitoes, ticks, flies, mites, and other insects of this type are examples of arthropod vectors that transmit a number of significant human diseases, such as malaria, encephalitis, Rocky Mountain spotted fever, trypanosomiasis, and leishmaniasis.

Characteristics of Infectious Disease Agents

- Infectivity
- Pathogenicity
- Virulence
- Toxigenicity
- Resistance
- Antigenicity

The following characteristics influence when an infectious disease agent will be transmitted to a host, whether it will produce disease, the severity of disease, and the outcome of infection.

- *Infectivity* refers to the capacity of the agent to enter and multiply in a susceptible host and thus produce infection or disease. Polio and measles are diseases of high infectivity. The secondary attack rate (discussed later in this chapter) is used to measure infectivity.
- *Pathogenicity* refers to the capacity of the agent to cause disease in the infected host. Measles is a disease of high pathogenicity (few subclinical cases), whereas polio is a disease of low pathogenicity (most cases of polio are subclinical). A measure of pathogenicity is the proportion of infected individuals with clinically apparent disease.
- *Virulence* refers to the severity of the disease (i.e., whether severe clinical manifestations are produced). The rabies virus, which almost always produces fatal disease in humans, is an extremely virulent agent. A measure of virulence is the proportion of total cases that are severe. If the disease is fatal, virulence can be measured by the case fatality rate (CFR).
- *Toxigenicity* refers to the capacity of the agent to produce a toxin or poison. The pathologic effects of agents for diseases such as botulism and shellfish poisoning result from the toxin produced by the microorganism rather than from the microorganism itself.
- *Resistance* refers to the ability of the agent to survive adverse environmental conditions. Some agents are remarkably resistant (e.g., the agents responsible for coccidioidomycosis and hepatitis) and others are extremely fragile (e.g., the gonococcus and influenza viruses). *Note:* The term resistance also is applied to the host.
- *Antigenicity* refers to the ability of the agent to induce antibody production in the host. A related term is *immunogenicity*, which refers to an infection's ability to produce specific immunity.[5] Agents may or may not induce long-term immunity against infection. For example, repeated reinfection is common with gonococci, whereas reinfection with measles virus is thought to be rare.

Host

Although it was stated earlier that an agent must be present for an infectious disease to develop, it is not a sufficient cause. That is, the agent must be capable of infecting a host. The host, after exposure to an infectious agent, may progress through a chain of events leading from subclinical (inapparent) infection to an active case of the disease. The end result may be complete recovery, permanent disability, disfigurement, or death. For example, the common cold is usually self-limiting, and a complete recovery can be expected. Smallpox at one time was greatly feared because of its high morbidity and mortality. A small proportion of untreated cases of Group A streptococcal infection (β hemolytic) may produce the incapacitating sequelae of rheumatic fever and nephritis. Other examples of variation in the severity of illness are shown in Figure 12–3, which demonstrates that a large proportion of TB cases are inapparent and that a small proportion are fatal. Measles virus produces a large proportion of cases with moderately severe illness. Some of the highly infectious virulent agents, such as the rabies virus, almost invariably cause death.

The ability to cause infection is determined by a number of factors; some are properties of the host. An important determinant of the degree of infection and the corresponding disease severity is the host's ability to fight off the infectious agent. This ability comprises two broad categories: nonspecific defense mechanisms and disease-specific defense mechanisms.

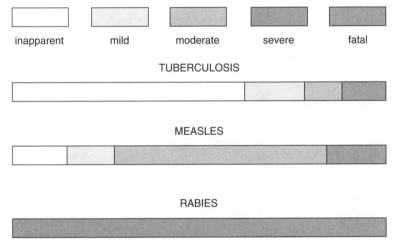

FIGURE 12–3 Variation in the severity of illness. Infectious diseases can result in a variety of effects ranging from no clinically detectable disease to fulminating symptoms and death. *Source:* Adapted from Mausner JS, Kramer S. *Mausner & Bahn Epidemiology—An Introductory Text,* 2nd ed. p. 265, with permission from Elsevier, © 1985.

Nonspecific Defense Mechanisms

The human body is equipped with a number of means to reduce the likelihood that an agent will penetrate and cause disease. Most environmental agents are unable to enter the body because of the protection afforded by our skin. Similarly, the mucosal surfaces also afford protection against foreign invaders. Tears and saliva can be thought of as a means to wash away would-be infectious agents. The high pH of our gastric juices is lethal to many agents that manage to enter the body via ingestion. The immune system is also highly developed to ingest, via phagocytes and macrophages, infectious agents.

Although the foregoing examples of nonspecific mechanisms are important in determining host susceptibility, several other factors influence host responses to infectious agents. As we age, the ability of our nonspecific defense mechanisms to fend off agents may decrease (e.g., through reduced immune function). The nutritional status of the host also may be critical because, in comparison to those who have adequate nutrition, malnourished individuals may be less able to fight off infections. Genetic factors are involved also, as illustrated by the clear differences in individuals' reactions to a mosquito bite, for example. Some may demonstrate little or no reaction, whereas others may develop a large welt at the site.

Disease-Specific Defense Mechanisms

Disease-specific defenses include immunity against a particular agent. Immunity refers to the resistance of the host to a disease agent. Immunity to a disease may be either natural or artificial, active or passive:

- *Active:* A disease organism causes the potential host's immune system to create antibodies against the disease.[8]
- *Passive:* A preformed antibody is administered to a recipient; the immunity is usually of short duration (half-life, 3 to 4 weeks) for immune globulin (gamma globulin) derived from the pooled plasma of adults.[8]
- *Natural, active:* This type of immunity, also called natural immunity, results from an infection by the agent. For example, a patient develops long-term immunity to measles because of a naturally acquired infection.[8]
- *Artificial, active:* This type of immunity, also called vaccine-induced immunity, results from an injection with a vaccine that stimulates antibody production in the host.[8] All or part of a microorganism or a modified part of that microorganism is administered to invoke an immunologic response. The response mimics the natural infection but presents little or no risk to the recipient.

- *Natural, passive:* Preformed antibodies during pregnancy are transferred across the placenta to the fetal bloodstream to produce short-term immunity in the newborn.
- *Artificial, passive:* Preformed antibodies against a specific disease are administered to an exposed individual to confer protection against a disease. An example is prophylaxis against hepatitis for individuals at risk.

The Environment

The environment refers to the domain in which the disease-causing agent may exist, survive, or originate. The external environment is the sum total of influences that are not part of the host and comprises physical, climatologic, biologic, social, and economic components. The physical environment includes weather, temperature, humidity, geologic formations, and similar physical dimensions. Contrasted with the physical environment is the social environment, which is the totality of the behavioral, personality, attitudinal, and cultural characteristics of a group of people. Both these facets of the external environment have an impact on agents of disease and potential hosts because the environment may either enhance or diminish the survival of disease agents and may serve to bring agent and host into contact.

The environment may act as a reservoir or niche that fosters the survival of infectious disease agents. The reservoir may be a part of the physical environment or may reside in animals or insects (vectors) or other human beings (human reservoir hosts). As an example of an environmental reservoir, contaminated water supplies or food may harbor infectious disease agents that cause typhoid, cholera, and many other illnesses. Fungal disease agents that may reside in the soil produce coccidioidomycosis (San Joaquin Valley fever). Infectious diseases that have vertebrate animal reservoirs and are potentially transmissible to humans under natural conditions are called the zoonoses.[9] Examples are rabies and plague. Some diseases have only humans as the reservoir; notable among these is smallpox, which has been successfully eradicated because the virus apparently does not survive outside the human reservoir. Other diseases, for example typhoid fever, may induce a chronic carrier state in some individuals who are not symptomatic for the disease but who have the capacity to transmit it to other susceptible individuals. A famous case was Typhoid Mary, a New York City area cook in the early 20th century who was a notorious and unwitting typhoid carrier.

Means of Transmission: Directly or Indirectly from Reservoir

Figure 12–4 illustrates the phases involved in the transmission of an infectious disease, which may be transmitted either directly or indirectly.

Direct Transmission

Direct transmission of diseases refers to spread of infection through person-to-person contact, as in the spread of sexually transmitted diseases, influenza, and acute respiratory infections. Portals of exit, defined as sites where infectious agents may leave the body, include the respiratory passages, the alimentary canal, the openings in the genitourinary system, and skin lesions (Table 12–1). Additional portals of exit may be made available through insect bites, the drawing of blood, surgical procedures, and accidents. For the chain of transmission to be continued, the portal of exit must be appropriate to the particular agent. To produce infection, the agent must exit the source in sufficient quantity to survive in the environment and to overcome the defenses surrounding the portals of entry in the new host. To be transmitted to a host, the agent requires a locus of access to the human body known as the portal of entry. The portals of entry consist of the respiratory system for such diseases as influenza and the common cold; the mouth and digestive system for diseases such as hepatitis A or staphylococcal food poisoning, and the mucous membranes or wounds in the skin for other types of disease.

Inapparent Infection

A subclinical or inapparent infection is one that has not yet penetrated the clinical horizon (i.e., does not have clinically obvious symptoms). Nevertheless, it is of epidemiologic significance because asymptomatic individuals could transmit the disease to other susceptible hosts. Isolation of infected individuals is more likely to occur when the infectious disease is clinically apparent (i.e., when the ratio of apparent to inapparent cases is high). To determine whether an infection has taken place in both symptomatic and asymptomatic individuals, one may search for serologic evidence of infection. An elevated blood antibody level (elevated antibody titer) suggests previous exposure and infection by the disease agent. For example, hepatitis A (infectious hepatitis) often is manifested as a subclinical infection in nursery school children, who may transmit the disease even though they do not have clinical symptoms. The infectious process may be tracked by

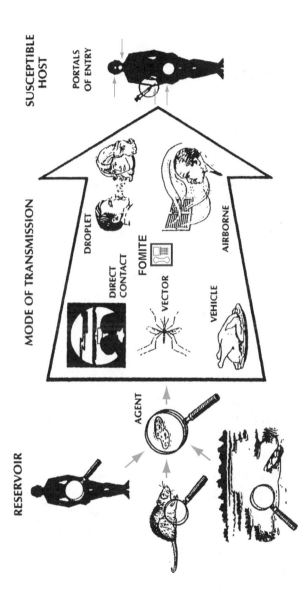

FIGURE 12–4   The chain of infection. *Source:* Centers for Disease Control and Prevention. *Principles of Epidemiology,* 2nd ed. Atlanta, GA: CDC; 1998, p. 45.

Table 12-1 Correspondence Between Portal of Exit (Escape) Mode of Transmission and Portal of Entry

Portal of Exit	Mode of Transmission	Portal of Entry	Type of Disease
Respiratory secretions	Airborne droplets, fomites	Respiratory tract	Common cold, measles
Feces	Water, food, fomites, flies	Alimentary tract	Typhoid, poliomyelitis
Lesions, exudate	Direct contact, fomites, sexual intercourse	Skin, genital membranes	Carbuncles, syphillis, gonorrhea
Conjunctival exudate	Fomites, flies	Ocular mucous membrane	Trachoma
Blood	Bloodsucking arthropod vector	Skin (broken)	Malaria, yellow fever, epidemic typhus

Source: Modified from Fox JP, Hall CE, Elvebach LR. *Epidemiology: Man and Disease.* New York: The Macmillan Company, 1970, p. 63.

monitoring blood antibody and enzyme responses to infection with hepatitis A virus (HAV). The epidemiologist and clinician may often conclude that infection has taken place by noting antibody and enzyme increases for hepatitis A after an appropriate incubation period.

Incubation Period

The *incubation period* is the time interval between exposure to an infectious agent and the appearance of the first signs or symptoms of disease. During this interval, the infectious organism replicates within the host. The incubation period is often a fixed period of hours, days, or weeks for each disease agent, and provides a clue to the time and circumstance of exposure to the agent. It is common practice for the epidemiologist to take into account the incubation period when attempting to fix the source of an infectious disease outbreak. For example, the incubation period for measles (rubeola) is most commonly 10 days, but it ranges from 7 to 18 days and requires about two weeks for a rash to appear. Another example is outbreaks of foodborne illness, in which the incubation period helps determine the etiologic agent.

Herd Immunity

The term *herd immunity* refers to the immunity of a population, group, or community against an infectious disease when a large proportion of individuals are immune (through either vaccinations or past infections). Herd immunity can oc-cur when immune persons prevent the spread of a disease to unimmunized indi-viduals; herd immunity confers protection to the population even though not every single individual has been immunized. For example, herd immunity against rubella may require that 85% to 90% of community residents are im-mune; for diphtheria it may be only 70%.

Generation Time

The term *generation time* relates to the time interval between lodgment of an in-fectious agent in a host and the maximal communicability of the host. The gen-eration time for an infectious disease and the incubation time may or may not be equivalent. For some diseases, the period of maximum communicability pre-cedes the development of active symptoms. An example of such a condition is mumps. The period of maximum communicability precedes the swelling of sali-vary glands by about 48 hours.[5] There is another distinction between incubation period and generation time. The term *incubation period* applies only to clinically apparent cases of disease, whereas the term *generation time* applies to both inap-parent and apparent cases of disease. Thus, generation time is utilized for de-scribing the spread of infectious agents that have a large proportion of subclinical cases.

Colonization and Infestation

It is important to emphasize that not all exposures to agents lead to illness. *Colonization* refers to the situation where an infectious agent may multiply on the surface of the body without invoking tissue or immune response. Infestation describes the presence of a living infectious agent on the body's exterior surface, upon which a local reaction may be invoked. Thus, the full spectrum of disease in the community setting may involve much more than individuals presenting with clinical symptoms.

Iceberg Concept of Infection

The iceberg concept of infection posits that the tip of the iceberg, which corre-sponds to active clinical disease, accounts for a relatively small proportion of hosts' infections and exposures to disease agents. Figure 12–5 demonstrates that most infections are subclinical and that in a substantial number exposure to a disease agent may not produce any infection or cell entry.

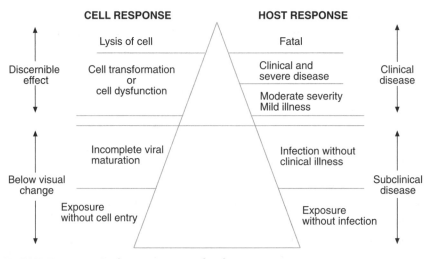

FIGURE 12-5   Iceberg concept of infection.

Inapparent/Apparent Case Ratio

Table 12–2 illustrates the wide variation in clinical presentation of viral infections. Although the vast majority of polio infections do not produce severe disease, the opposite is true for rabies, where reportedly only one infected case (in the absence of timely administration of rabies prophylaxis) has survived. The percentage of apparent clinical cases for hepatitis A increases from childhood to adulthood. Epstein-Barr virus and influenza among young adults as well as childhood measles produce a high percentage of clinical cases.

Indirect Transmission

Indirect transmission involves the spread of infection through an intermediary source: vehicles, fomites, or vectors. Examples of vehicle transmission of disease are contaminated water, infected blood on used hypodermic needles, and food. A fomite is an inanimate object—such as a doorknob or clothing—that is laden with disease-causing agents. Contamination refers to the presence of a living infectious agent in or on an inanimate object. A vector is an animate, living insect or animal that is involved with transmission of the disease agent. Arthropod vectors, such as flies and mosquitos, may sometimes form a component of the life cycle of the disease agent. For example, the *Anopheles* mosquito is essential to the survival of infectious agents for malaria (e.g., *Plasmodium vivax*); if the former is

Table 12–2 Examples of Subclinical/Clinical Ratio for Viral Infections (Inapparent/Apparent Ratio)

Virus	Clinical Features	Age at Infection	Estimated Ratio	Clinical Cases
Polio	Paralysis	Child	± 1,000:1	0.1% to 1%
Epstein-Barr	Mononucleosis	1 to 5 years	> 100:1	1%
		6 to15 years	10:1 to 100:1	1% to 10%
		16 to 25 years	2:1 to 3:1	50% to 75%
Hepatitis A	Icterus	< 5 years	20:1	5%
		5 to 9 years	11:1	10%
		10 to 15 years	7:1	14%
		Adult	1.5:1	80% to 95%
Rubella	Rash	5 to 20 years	2:1	50%
Influenza	Fever, cough	Young adult	1.5:1	60%
Measles	Rash, fever	5 to 20 years	1:99	> 99%
Rabies	Central nervous system symptoms	Any age	< 1:10,000	>>>> 99%

eradicated, the frequency of malaria cases diminishes. Control of arthropod vectors may be an effective means of limiting outbreaks of vector-borne diseases, such as malaria.

Measures of Disease Outbreaks

Attack Rate

In Chapter 3, we defined an incidence rate as the number of new cases of disease per unit population per unit time. Similar to an incidence rate, an *attack rate* is used when the occurrence of disease among a population at risk increases greatly over a short period of time, often related to a specific exposure. In addition, the disease rapidly follows the exposure during a fixed time period because of the nature of the disease process.[10] Thus, the term *attack rate* is frequently used to describe the occurrence of foodborne illness, infectious diseases, and other acute epidemics. The formula for attack rate is shown below. The numerator consists of people who are ill as a result of exposure to the suspected agent, and the denominator consists of all people, whether well or ill, who were exposed to the agent during a time period. A time interval during which exposure occurred is an important element of the definition and often is defined arbitrarily. The attack rate is often expressed as a percentage.

$$\text{Attack rate} = \frac{\text{Ill}}{(\text{Ill} + \text{Well})} \times 100 \text{ during a time period}$$

Table 12–3 provides an example for calculating attack rates for an outbreak of foodborne illness and for identifying food items that might have caused the outbreak. In a hypothetical outbreak of foodborne illness, several foods were implicated. Table 12–3 shows the method to calculate the attack rate for a specific food item. Food X demonstrated 77% attack rates among those who ate and 64% attack rates among those who did not eat the food. In order to identify foods suspected of producing an outbreak, the following procedure is recommended.

First, a list of all foods consumed during the outbreak is compiled. Next, the persons involved in the outbreak are categorized in two columns: A (ate the food) and B (did not eat the food). One calculates the attack rate among those in categories A and B by dividing the number of ill persons by the total number of persons and multiplying the result by 100. For example, the attack rate in column A is (10/13) × 100 = 77%. After calculating the attack rate, one finds the difference in attack rates (A − B) between those who ate and those who did not eat the food, in this case 13% (77% − 64%). One would repeat this process for each of the foods that were suspected in the outbreak of foodborne illness. Those foods that have the greatest difference in attack rates may be the foods that were responsible for illness. To complete the investigation, additional studies, including cultures and laboratory tests, might be required. In the foregoing situation, "time" is the estimated time interval during which the outbreak occurred—from exposure through appearance of all associated cases of disease. An example is given in the study questions and exercises at the end of the chapter.

Table 12–3　Data to Illustrate Calculation of Attack Rates for Food X

A (ate the food)				B (did not eat the food)			
Ill	Not Ill	A Total	Attack Rate	Ill	Not Ill	B Total	Attack Rate
10	3	13	77%	7	4	11	64%

Secondary Attack Rate

The secondary attack rate yields an index of the spread of a disease within a household or similar circumscribed unit (Exhibit 12–1). The *secondary attack rate* is defined as "the number of cases of an infection that occur among contacts within the incubation period following exposure to a primary case in relation to the total number of exposed contacts; the denominator is restricted to susceptible contacts when these can be determined. The secondary attack rate is a measure of contagiousness and is useful in evaluating control measures."[9(p. 165)] For example, a case of measles brought into a family may spread from the initial case to other members. Table 12–4 provides data for calculation of a secondary attack rate for the hypothetical spread of measles (rubeola) in a military barracks housing Reserve Officers' Training Corps summer cadets. The two initial cases occurred at the beginning of the military summer program and were presumed to have resulted from exposure outside the military base. Of the two initial cases, the case that came to the attention of public health authorities is called the index case.[5] The other case could be considered a coprimary case. This term refers to a case that is related to the index case so closely in time that it is thought to belong to the same

---

EXHIBIT 12–1

Secondary Attack Rate

The secondary attack rate refers to the spread of disease in a family, household, dwelling unit, dormitory, or similar circumscribed group.

$$\text{Secondary Attack Rate (\%)} = \frac{\text{Number of new cases in group} - \text{initial case(s)}}{\text{Number of susceptible persons in the group} - \text{initial case(s)}} \times 100$$

Initial case(s) = Index case(s) + coprimaries
Index case(s) = Case that first comes to the attention of public health authorities
Coprimaries = Cases related to index case so closely in time that they are considered to belong to the same generation of cases

Source: Adapted from Mausner JS, Kramer S. *Mausner & Bahn Epidemiology–An Introductory Text*, 2nd ed. WB Saunders, © 1985, with permission from Elsevier.

Table 12–4 Hypothetical Secondary Attack Rate Data for Military Cadets

Number of Cadets In Barracks		Number of Initial Cases		Number of Secondary Cases	
Unimmunized	Immunized	Unimmunized	Immunized	Unimmunized	Immunized
14	6	2	0	8	0

generation of cases as the index case. The eight secondary cases occurred approximately 10 to 12 days after measles symptoms were observed in the index cases. The total number of new cases in the group was 10 (initial cases plus secondary cases). The secondary attack rate was $[(10 - 2)/(14 - 2)] \times 100 = 66.7\%$.

Here is a second example of how to calculate a secondary attack rate:

"Seven cases of hepatitis A occurred among 70 children attending a child care center. Each infected child came from a different family. The total number of persons in the 7 affected families was 32. One incubation period later, 5 family members of the 7 infected children also developed hepatitis A."[11(p. 89)] By applying the formula shown in Exhibit 12–1 to these data, we obtain the following information:

Numerator = 5 (number of cases of hepatitis A among family contacts with hepatitis)

Denominator = 25 = 32 − 7 (total number of family members − children already infected)

Note: In this example, no subtraction is necessary in calculating the numerator because the initial cases have already been removed from the number of new cases in the group; the problem specified that five family members developed hepatitis one incubation period later.

For diseases such as measles, which confer prolonged immunity, the index cases (and coprimaries) are excluded from the denominator.[12] If means are available to determine immune status, any other immune persons also would be excluded from the denominator (as implied by the definition).[11] In addition to assessing the infectivity of an infectious disease agent, the secondary attack rate may be used to evaluate the efficacy of a prophylactic agent (e.g., a vaccine or gamma globulin). It also may be used to trace the secondary spread of a disease of unknown etiology to determine whether there is a transmissible agent.[13]

Case Fatality Rate

The CFR is different from the mortality rate, or death rate, for a disease. We have already discussed the crude death rate (refer to Chapter 3), which is defined as the number of deaths that occur in a population of interest during a time period. The CFR refers to a proportion formed by the number of deaths caused by a disease among those who have the disease during a time interval (Exhibit 12–2). It provides an index of the deadliness of a particular disease within a specific population.

Let us compare the kinds of information yielded by the death rate and the CFR. Recent epidemiologic surveillance demonstrates that mortality from human rabies is very uncommon in the United States. The fact that rabies is uncommon in humans may be attributed to its confinement to wildlife (epizootic rabies) and to postexposure prophylaxis (passive immunization and vaccines) among those who have been potentially exposed to rabies. Therefore, the cause-specific death rate for any given recent year due to rabies would be low. The

---

EXHIBIT 12–2

Case Fatality Rate (CFR)

$$\text{CFR (\%)} = \frac{\text{Number of deaths due to disease “X”}}{\text{Number of cases of disease “X”}} \times \frac{100 \text{ during a}}{\text{time period}}$$

Note that the numerator and denominator refer to the same time period.

Sample calculation: Assume that an outbreak of plague occurs in an Asian country during the month of January. Health authorities record 98 cases of the disease, all of whom are untreated. Among these, 60 deaths are reported.

$$\text{CFR} = (60/98) \times 100 = 61.2\%$$

Examples of diseases with a high CFR are rabies, untreated bubonic plague, and acquired immune deficiency syndrome (AIDS). ■

reason is that the CFR for this condition has a small numerator and uses the to-tal population as the denominator. The cause-specific mortality rate due to rabies therefore would be a small number. In contrast, the CFR for rabies would be high. The CFR reflects the fatal outcome of disease, which is affected by efficacy of treatment. Among the cases of human rabies that may occur as a result of fail-ure to receive postexposure prophylaxis, mortality remains almost invariably cer-tain, as has been historically true.

Procedures Used in the Investigation of Infectious Disease Outbreaks

These include many of the techniques developed by John Snow[14]: mapping and tabulation of cases, identification of agents, and clinical observation. The investi-gation of an outbreak can be logically divided into five basic steps:

1. *Define the problem.* It is important to determine from the outset whether the outbreak or epidemic is real. For example, suppose a restaurant pa-tron claimed that a gastrointestinal illness she developed was caused by the food she ate in the restaurant. The epidemiologist would need to ver-ify that this was a case of foodborne illness and not a sporadic case of stomach upset. Other cases of the same illness reported to the health de-partment would increase the index of suspicion that the illness originated at the restaurant.

2. *Appraise existing data.* This step includes evaluation of known distribu-tions of cases with respect to person, place, and time. Examples of activi-ties performed at this stage include case identification, making clinical observations, and generation of tables and spot maps.

   - *Case identification.* This step includes tracking down all cases of dis-ease potentially involved in the outbreak, for instance, in a mass oc-currence of foodborne illness. Examples of foodborne illnesses include staphylococcal food poisoning and trichinosis. For communicable dis-eases, such as TB, contacts of cases need to be identified.

   - *Clinical observations.* The epidemiologist records the number, types, and patterns of symptoms associated with the disease (e.g., whether the symptoms are primarily gastrointestinal, respiratory, or febrile). Additional clinical information may come from stool samples, cul-tures, or antibody assays.

   - *Tabulation and spot maps.* Cases of disease may be plotted on a map to show geographic clustering (as in an outbreak of TB in a high school). Cases may be tabulated by date or time of onset of symptoms, by demographic characteristics (i.e., age, sex, and race), or by risk categories (e.g., intravenous drug use or occupational exposure). This method is similar to Snow's mapping of cholera cases in the Broad Street district of London in the mid-1800s.[14] It remains an important epidemiologic technique. Graphing cases according to time of onset helps determine the modal incubation period or other aspects of the outbreak.

- *Identification of responsible agent.* The epidemiologist may be able to determine the agent or other factors responsible for the disease outbreak by estimating the incubation period, by reviewing the specific symptoms, and by noting evidence from cultures and other laboratory tests. In some outbreaks of foodborne illness, it may be possible to link an etiologic agent to cultures of food specimens and stool samples.

3. *Formulate a hypothesis.* What are the possible sources of infection? What is the likely agent? What is the most likely method of spread? What would be the best approach for control of the outbreak?

4. *Test the hypothesis.* Collect the data that are needed to confirm or refute your initial suspicions. At this stage it is important to continue to search for additional cases, evaluate alternative sources of data, and begin laboratory investigations to identify the causative agent.

5. *Draw conclusions and formulate practical applications.* Based on the results of your investigation, it is likely that programs, policies, or procedures will need to be implemented to facilitate long-term surveillance and ultimate prevention of the recurrence of similar outbreaks.

Epidemiologically Significant Infectious Diseases in the Community

The following discussion illustrates major outbreaks of infectious diseases and demonstrates how the foregoing methods are utilized. A partial list of epidemiologically significant infectious diseases is shown in Figure 12–2. These include the broad categories of foodborne, waterborne, vaccine preventable, sexually transmitted, person to person, arthropod-borne, zoonotic, and fungal diseases.

Foodborne Illness in the Community

Table 12–5 provides examples of agents and diseases that are associated with food contamination, which is one of the most common infectious disease

Table 12-5   Partial List of Infectious Agents That Cause Foodborne Illness

Disease/Agent	Incubation Period and Syndrome	Mode of Transmission
Classic botulism/ Clostridium botulinum	12–36 hours, classic syndrome compatible with botulism	Contaminated food containing toxins (e.g., home-canned foods)
Salmonellosis/various species of Salmonella (e.g., S. typhimurium and S. enteritidis)	12–36 hours, gastrointestinal syndrome	Contaminated food that contains Salmonella organisms (e.g., undercooked chicken, eggs, meat; raw milk)
Staphylococcal food poisoning/ Staphylococcus aureus (see Fig. 12-6)	1–7 hours, gastrointestinal syndrome; majority of cases with vomiting	Contaminated food that contains staphylococcal enterotoxin
Cholera/Vibrio cholerae	2–3 days, profuse watery diarrhea (painless)	Contaminated water that contains infected feces or vomitus; also contaminated food
Clostridium perfringens food poisoning	6–24 hours, diarrhea	Heavily contaminated food (e.g., meats and gravies inadequately heated or stored at temperatures that permit multiplication of bacteria)
Campylobacter enteritis/ Campylobacter jejuni	2–5 days, diarrhea, abdominal pain, malaise, fever	Undercooked chicken or pork, contaminated food and water, raw milk

Source: Data are from Heymann DL. *Control of Communicable Diseases Manual,* 18th ed. Washington, DC: American Public Health Association; 2004.

problems in the community. Among the agents of foodborne illness noted in Table 12–5 is *Staphylococcus aureus.* Figure 12–6 illustrates a mass episode of foodborne illness that was transmitted from *Staphylococcus*-infected lesions to passengers on an international flight. There were 144 cases of illness among 343 passengers. Storage of the food at improper temperatures contributed to development of the *Staphylococcus* toxin. Another foodborne illness is trichinosis (Exhibit 12–3). Trichinosis is most commonly associated with consumption of pork products that have not been adequately cooked.

Water- and Foodborne Diseases

Diseases associated with food or water include amebiasis, cholera, giardiasis, legionellosis, and schistosomiasis. The following example describes the transmission of schistosomiasis in Africa along the Nile River. Transmission of schistosomiasis requires *Biomphalaria glabrata,* the intermediate snail host for

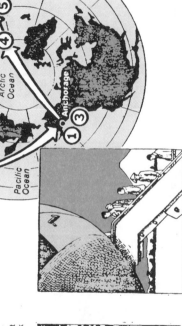

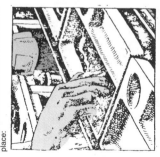

The classic pattern of cause and effect in an outbreak of mass illness is often postulated but not proven. . . the actual sequence involved in food poisoning on an international jet flight was traced by epidemiologists, and their findings fit the textbook pattern. Here is what took place:

1. On the weekend of Feb. 1, a cook in Alaska preparing ham and omelet breakfasts for International Inflight Catering has blisters on two fingers. The blisters are infected with staphylococcus, a common contagious bacteria. The cook handles at least 205 portions of ham, which are kept at room temperature for 6 hours during preparation of the food trays.

2. The 543 passengers board a Japan Air Lines Jumbo jet in Tokyo. While the plane flies to its scheduled refueling stop in Anchorage, the contaminated food trays are stored overnight at 50 degrees. Staph multiply at temperatures over 40; as they multiply, they produce a toxin which is a common cause of food poisoning.

FIGURE 12–6 Textbook case of foodborne illness. *Source: The New York Times,* February 16, 1975, p. 7. Drawings by Oliver Williams. Copyright © 1975 The New York Times Company. Reprinted by permission.

5. The sick; 144 of them disembark at Copenhagen the morning of February 3. The rest, 51 of whom later become ill, go on to Paris.

The pattern of contagion was reconstructed through laboratory analysis that matched bacterial samples from the cook's blisters, uneaten tainted food, and the victims' vomit and stool. Dr. Mickey S. Eisenberg, the U.S. Public Health Service officer in Anchorage who had pinpointed the probable source of infection, completed the picture by comparing passenger interviews with the galley plan.

4. Six to seven hours later, the passenger breakfasts are heated in 300-degree ovens for 15 minutes, treatment which cannot inactivate the toxin. The passengers are served. For the crew it is dinner time and only one stewardess takes a ham and omelet tray. As the plane approaches Copenhagen, those who ate contaminated food begin to experience staph food-poisoning symptoms: nausea, vomiting, cramps, and diarrhea.

3. Food trays are loaded on the 747 at Anchorage. The trays have been labeled for distribution on the plane: The contaminated trays go to Galley 1, which serves 40 first class seats, and Galley 2, which serves 93 seats in the forward portion of the coach cabin; 72 of them go to Galleys 3 and 4 to the rear. A fresh crew boards, and the plane takes off for Copenhagen, the next refueling stop on its polar route to Paris.

FIGURE 12–6 *continued*

EXHIBIT 12–3

Trichinosis Associated with Meat from an Alaskan Grizzly Bear

Eight cases of trichinosis reported from Barrow, Alaska, were associated with a dinner on December 20, 1980. The 12 persons who attended were served a meal that included maktak (whale blubber), ugruk (bearded-seal meat, dried and stored in seal oil), fresh raw whitefish and grayling, and quaq (raw frozen meat), thought by the participants to be caribou but later discovered to have been grizzly bear.

Five men and three women, ranging in age from 32 to 76 years, became ill 2 to 16 days after the meal (mean, 8.6 days). All eight reported eating quaq; the four who denied doing so remained well, a statistically significant difference. Quaq was the only meat eaten by all the persons who became ill. Thirty other family members who were not present at the dinner also remained well, which again is a statistically significant difference. Signs and symptoms of illness included edema (100%), fatigue (100%), myalgia (87.5%), rash (87.5%), fever (87.5%), chills (75%), periorbital edema (62.5%), headache (50%), visual disturbance (37.5%), diarrhea (37.5%), abdominal cramps (25%), nausea (25%), and vomiting (25%). None of the ill persons had notable pulmonary, neurologic, or cardiac complications. Five were hospitalized. Five received steroids, and two received anthelmintic therapy.

The grizzly bear from which the meat came had been shot the previous autumn at the family's summer camp, 140 miles inland from Barrow. At that time, parts had been cooked thoroughly and consumed without adverse effects. The hindquarters were included in a large cache of moose and caribou meat that was returned to Barrow and stored frozen in the family's cold cellar. None of the bear meat had been eaten in Barrow before the dinner on December 20, and none had been given away. The remains of the hindquarter eaten at the dinner were fed to dogs; the other hindquarter remained in cold storage. A sample taken from the digestive tract of one of the patients contained 70 *Trichinella* larvae per gram of meat. ■

Source: Adapted from Centers for Disease Control and Prevention. Trichinosis associated with meat from a grizzly bear—Alaska. *MMWR.* Vol 30, pp. 115–116, March 20, 1981.

Schistosoma mansoni, the species that is the major cause of schistosomiasis in Africa. The life cycle of schistosomes entails a complex cycle involving alternate human and snail hosts. According to the U.S. Department of Health and Human Services:

> Upon reaching fresh water, parasite eggs, voided in the urine and feces, hatch immediately into larvae called miracidia, which swim about until they find a suitable snail host. After penetrating the snail, miracidia develop into another larval form called cercariae. The cercariae are the forms capable of infecting [humans]. They do this after emerging from the snail host, burrowing through the skin of persons exposed to the contaminated water. Once inside the body, the cercariae develop into adult worms.[15(p. 13)]

The Nile River is used for a wide variety of common activities, including sewage disposal, personal hygiene, and recreation. Deposition of human wastes into the river water causes contamination by the agent. Those who come into contact with the water are at increased risk of exposure to the cercariae. After the building of the Aswan Dam, there was an increase in rates of schistosomiasis, attributable to human intervention in the life cycle of the schistosome. Figure 12–7 illustrates the life cycle of *Schistosoma mansoni.*

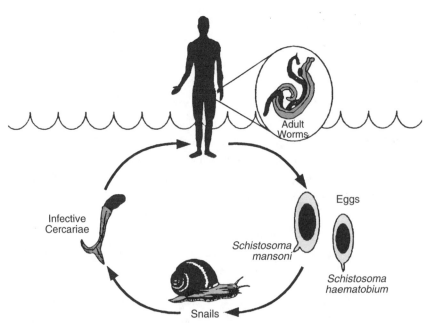

FIGURE 12–7　Life cycle of *Schistosoma mansoni. Source:* Adapted from Centers for Disease Control and Prevention. Schistosomiasis in U.S. Peace Corps Volunteers—Malawi, 1992. *MMWR.* Vol 42, p. 568, July 30, 1993.

Cholera is another example of a water- or foodborne disease. It is character-ized as an acute enteric disease with sudden onset, occasional vomiting, rapid de-hydration, acidosis, and circulatory collapse.[7] Caused by the bacterial agent *Vibrio cholerae*, it still occurs in many parts of the developing world. In the early 1990s, epidemic cholera continued to spread throughout Central and South America. The Centers for Disease Control and Prevention (CDC) tallied more than 300,000 cholera cases and more than 200 deaths from cholera-related causes in 1992. In that same year, 102 cholera cases were reported in the United States.[16] Presently, cholera is an infrequent condition in the United States, with 2 to 9 cases reported during each year between 2002 and 2006 and 7 cases re-ported in 2007.[17] Figure 12–8 illustrates the spread of cholera from South

FIGURE 12–8   Spread of epidemic cholera in Latin America from 1991 to 1992. *Source:* Adapted from Centers for Disease Control and Prevention. Update: Cholera—Western Hemisphere, 1992. *MMWR.* Vol 42, p. 89, February 12, 1993.

America to Central America and Mexico during the epidemics of 1991 and 1992. Between 2000 and 2006, outbreaks of cholera were reported in Africa, e.g., Sudan, Angola, Nigeria, Senegal, and South Africa.[18] An outbreak during August 2007 affected 30,000 people in Kirkuk, Iraq.[19]

A third example of a water- or foodborne disease agent is *Entamoeba histolytica*, a fairly common parasitic organism associated with amebiasis, which in many cases manifests as intestinal disease. The following excerpt from a report by the Centers for Disease Control and Prevention demonstrates the transmission of *E. histolytica* through colonic irrigation:

> The Colorado State Department of Health has reported an outbreak of amebiasis that occurred in the period December 1977–November 1980 and was associated with a chiropractic clinic. All of the cases had received colonic irrigation—a series of enemas performed by machine to "wash out" the colon—a practice that has been gaining popularity recently among some chiropractors, naturopaths, and nutritional counselors. Thirteen cases were confirmed by biopsy review or serologic tests. Seven cases were fatal.[20(p. 101)]

Stool cultures, blood tests, and biopsy studies strongly suggested amoebas as the etiologic agent. Specimens from the colonic irrigation machine were heavily contaminated with fecal bacteria.

Sexually Transmitted Diseases

A major public health problem from this category is the AIDS epidemic, which has had major consequences for the economic activities and health resources of many nations. According to the CDC, "The greatest impact of the epidemic is among men who have sex with men (MSM) and among racial/ethnic minorities, with increases in the number of cases among women and of cases attributed to heterosexual transmission. The number of persons living with AIDS has increased as deaths have declined."[21(p. 430)] In addition, the CDC notes that "As of December 31, 2000, 774,467 persons had been reported with AIDS in the United States; 448,060 of these had died; 3,542 persons had unknown vital status. The number of persons living with AIDS (322,865) is the highest ever reported. Of these, 79% were men, 61% were black or Hispanic, and 41% were infected through male-to-male sex."[21(p. 430)] The CDC indicated that "Male-to-male sex has been the most common mode of exposure among persons reported with AIDS (46%), followed by injection drug use (25%) and heterosexual contact (11%). The incidence of AIDS increased rapidly in all three of these risk categories through the mid-1990s; however, since 1996, declines in new AIDS cases have been higher among MSM and injection drug users than among persons exposed through heterosexual contact. . . ."[21(p. 430)] The CDC reported that, "The estimated number of HIV/AIDS cases in the 33 states with confidential name-based HIV infection reporting decreased each year from 2001 through 2004 and then increased in 2005. . . . In 2005, the estimated rate of HIV/AIDS cases in the 33 states was 19.8 per 100,000 population. . . ."[22(p. 6)]

The human immunodeficiency virus (HIV) epidemic is particularly acute from a worldwide perspective. For example, approximately 24.7 million HIV-infected adults and children were estimated to be living in the Sub-Saharan region of Africa. Other high prevalence regions included South/Southeast Asia, 7.8 million persons; and Eastern Europe/Central Asia and Latin America, each reporting 1.7 million cases.[23] (Figure 12–9).

Vaccine-Preventable Diseases

In the United States, healthcare providers administer routine vaccinations to children aged 0 to 6 years for the prevention of several diseases: diphtheria, pertussis, tetanus, *Haemophilus influenzae* type b infections, hepatitis A, hepatitis B,

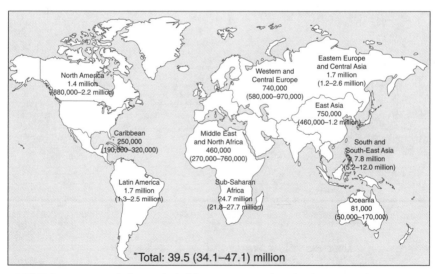

FIGURE 12–9 Adults and children estimated to be living with HIV in 2006. *Source:* From World Health Organization, AIDS epidemic update, Dec. 6, p. 64. Available at: http://www.unaids.org. Accessed November 11, 2007. Reproduced with kind permission from UNAIDS (2006).

measles, mumps, rubella, paralytic poliomyelitis, influenza, meningococcal meningitis, chickenpox, pneumococcal disease, and rotaviral enteritis. According to data reported by the CDC for 2006,[17] the following are the reported numbers of cases of several vaccine-preventable conditions that reached very low frequency:

- congenital rubella syndrome, 1
- rubella, 11
- diphtheria, 0
- paralytic poliomyelitis, 0

In 1997, there were 138 measles cases. This number represented a dramatic drop after a major resurgence of measles occurred during the period 1989 to 1990. Subsequently, the reported numbers of cases declined. The respective numbers were 27,786 (1990); 9,643 (1991); and 2,231 (1992).[24] The measles rate continued to decline thereafter to 55 cases (2006).[17] Figure 12–10 illustrates the number of reported cases of measles from 1970 to 2005.

Formerly, measles outbreaks occurred in institutional settings, such as universities or colleges and other places where susceptible persons congregated.

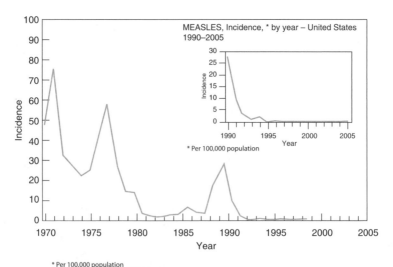

* Per 100,000 population

Measles incidence remains at less than one case per 1 million population. Measles vaccine was licensed in 1963.

FIGURE 12–10   Measles. Incidence (per 100,000 population), by year— United States, 1970–2005. *Source:* From Centers for Disease Control and Prevention. Summary of Notifiable Diseases—United States, 2005. *MMWR.* Vol 54, p. 60, March 30, 2007.

Nowadays, measles outbreaks are unlikely to occur in the United States because most people have been immunized. The epidemiology of measles supports the conclusion that endemic transmission of measles has been eliminated in the United States. Sporadic cases that have occurred in recent years were imported from foreign countries. Because 100% coverage of U.S. residents might never be achieved, accurate surveillance and rapid response to outbreaks are essential to prevention of widespread transmission of imported measles. Public health practitioners will need to continue advocating for high levels of immunization. Exhibit 12–4, which typifies measles outbreaks that can occur in contemporary times, describes an import-associated measles outbreak in Indiana during 2005.

EXHIBIT 12–4

Import-Associated Measles Outbreak— Indiana, May–June 2005

On May 29, 2005, the Indiana State Department of Health (ISDH) was notified of suspected measles in a female Indiana resident aged 6 years who was hospitalized in Cincinnati, Ohio, where she had been visiting relatives. Serologic analyses performed by the Ohio State Department of Health Laboratory and a private reference laboratory confirmed the diagnosis of measles. The hospital in Cincinnati and the girl's parents told ISDH she had been at a church gathering in northwestern Indiana on May 15 where a fellow attendee had been ill. This fellow attendee was an adolescent girl aged 17 years, an Indiana resident who had not been vaccinated for measles and who had worked during May 4–14 as a missionary in an orphanage and hospital in Bucharest, Romania, where a large measles outbreak was subsequently reported. The teen had returned to the United States with prodromal fever, cough, conjunctivitis, and coryza, traveling on international and domestic commercial airliners on May 14. The next day the teen attended the church gathering along with others who had not been vaccinated because of nonmedical exemptions. Family members recalled that the teen had a rash on May 16; measles was diagnosed retrospectively, and the teen was identified as the index patient. . . . [An outbreak of 34 cases ensued.] Among

continues

EXHIBIT 12–4 *continued*

the measles patients, 33 were residents of Indiana and one resided in Illinois. Patients ranged in age from 9 months to 49 years (median age: 12 years); [measles] vaccination . . . was documented for two (6%) persons, one who had received 1 dose, and one who had received 2 doses. . . . [State and local health departments introduced control measures that included voluntary isolation and quarantine of patients, tracking exposed contacts, and immunizing susceptible contacts.] ■

Source: Modified from Centers for Disease Control and Prevention. Import-Associated Measles Outbreak—Indiana, May–June 2005, *MMWR.* Vol 54, No 42, pp. 1073–1074, 2005.

Diseases Spread by Person-to-Person Contact

TB, a significant cause of morbidity and mortality throughout the world, was uncommon in many developed countries, including the United States, until the late 1980s, when it began to increase in frequency. Reasons for the resurgence of TB include the increasing prevalence of HIV infection, the increase in the homeless population, and the importation of cases from endemic areas. As an illustration of current trends in the occurrence of TB, Exhibit 12–5 shows data from migrant farm workers and the homeless population, two high-risk groups. From

EXHIBIT 12–5

Tuberculosis Among Migrant Farm Workers and the Homeless Population

Farm workers are approximately six times more likely to develop TB than the general population of employed adults.

. . . The following services, listed by priority, that should be available for migrant and seasonal farm workers and their family members are: a) detection and diagnosis of those with current symptoms of active TB; b) appropriate treatment and monitoring for those who have

continues

EXHIBIT 12–5 *continued*

current disease; c) contact investigation and appropriate preventive therapy for those exposed to infectious persons; d) screening and appropriate preventive therapy for asymptomatically infected workers who may be immunosuppressed, such as those with HIV infection; e) screening and appropriate preventive therapy for children of migrant and seasonal farm workers; and f) widespread tuberculin test screening for workers and families with preventive therapy prescribed, as appropriate. Healthcare providers should immediately perform appropriate diagnostic studies for persons with a productive, prolonged cough, or other symptoms suggestive of TB. Health departments should be immediately notified when TB is suspected or diagnosed to enable examination of contacts and initiation of other health department diagnostic, preventive, or patient management services.

Homeless persons suffer disproportionately from a variety of health problems, including TB. Although there is no generally agreed upon definition of homelessness, the homeless can be defined, on a general level, as those who do not have customary and regular access to a conventional dwelling or residence. . . . Since 1984, three outbreaks of TB in shelters for the homeless have been reported to CDC . . . , and recent investigations have shown a prevalence of 1.6% to 6.8% for clinically active TB among selected homeless populations. . . . These prevalence rates are 150 to 300 times higher than the nationwide prevalence rate. The prevalence of asymptomatic TB infection among the homeless has been reported to be as high as 22% to 50% . . . , thus indicating that a large reservoir of infection may exist from which future cases will emerge unless large-scale preventive measures are undertaken. ■

Source: Data from Prevention and control of tuberculosis in migrant farm workers recommendations of the Advisory Council for the Elimination of Tuberculosis. *MMWR.* Vol 41 (RR10), 1992; and, Perspectives in disease prevention and health promotion tuberculosis control among homeless populations. *MMWR.* Vol 36, No 17, pp. 257–260, 1987, Centers for Disease Control and Prevention.

1984 to 1992, there was an upward trend in the number of reported TB cases from 22,201 to 26,673. For this time period, 51,700 excess cases were reported, according to statistical models of expected cases in comparison to observed cases

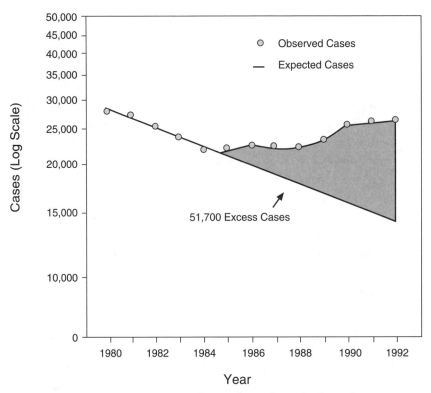

FIGURE 12–11 Expected and observed number of tuberculosis cases in the United States during 1980 to 1992. *Source:* Reprinted from Centers for Disease Control and Prevention. Tuberculosis morbidity—United States, 1992. *MMWR.* Vol 42, p. 696, September 17, 1993.

(Figure 12–11). The number of cases increased in all racial/ethnic groups except non-Hispanic whites and Native Americans. All age groups except for the over-65 age group showed increases, with the largest increase occurring among the 25- to 44-year age group.[25] Between 1995 and 2005, TB incidence in most racial/ethnic groups tended to decline (e.g., to 10.9 per 100,000 for non-Hispanic blacks and 1.3 per 100,000 for non-Hispanic whites). (For more information see Chapter 4.) In 2007, a suspected case of extensively drug-resistant tuberculosis (XDR TB) commanded media attention (refer to the case study).

Viral hepatitis includes several forms: Hepatitis A and hepatitis B are caused by the hepatitis A virus (HAV) and the hepatitis B virus (HBV), respectively.

Hepatitis C (caused by the hepatitis C virus; HCV) is discussed in Exhibit 12–6. The incidence of hepatitis A and hepatitis B generally has been declining since the late 1980s. One of the reasons for reductions in the incidence of HAV infections is the vaccination of children in states that have high rates of such infections. Reduction in the incidence of HBV infections has been linked to routine vaccination of infants.[26]

What are the modes of transmission of hepatitis A and B? Hepatitis A is spread by fecal-oral means. Hepatitis B can be spread by adults who engage in risky sexual practices; hence, HBV infection remains more common in this subpopulation than in other groups. Among other means for spread of HBV are contacts with

Case Study
Extensively Drug-Resistant Tuberculosis (XDR TB)

On May 12, 2007, a suspected XDR TB patient traveled to Europe for his honeymoon. The traveler boarded a commercial flight, Air France number 385, to Paris. His itinerary took him to several European countries. On May 24, he returned to Canada on Czech Air flight number 410 from Prague, Czech Republic. During his voyage, the CDC issued an advisory that warned of the traveler's infection with XDR TB. He returned to the United States from Canada via automobile without being detained by U.S. officials at the border. Upon arrival in the United States, he was hospitalized in a respiratory isolation unit for evaluation.

The form of TB known as XDR TB resists treatment with first-line drugs (e.g., isoniazid) and second-line drugs. Fellow passengers aboard flight 385 and other flights the patient took, as well as other persons who came into contact with the patient during his 14-day trip, potentially were exposed to XDR TB. (Later the traveler's diagnosis was downgraded to multidrug-resistant TB: MDR TB). Refer to Figure 12–12 for a timetable of events. ▣

Source: Data from Centers for Disease Control and Prevention, Health Alert Update. Corrected: Investigation of U.S. traveler with extensively drug-resistant tuberculosis (XDR TB). Available at http://ww2a.cdc.gov/HAN/ArchiveSys/ViewMsgV.asp?AlertNum=00262. Accessed June 21, 2007; and from Centers for Disease Control and Prevention, Extensively drug-resistant tuberculosis–United States, 1993–2006, *MMWR.* Vol 56, No 11, pp. 250–253, 2007.

INTERIM* TIMETABLE

ACTIONS to PROTECT PUBLIC HEALTH: XDR TB CASE

TESTING

LOCATE XDR TB PATIENT

Timeline dates: Jan '07 | 3/8 | 3/26 | 4/10 | 4/25 | 4/27 | 4/30 | 5/4 | 5/9 | 5/10 | 5/11 | 5/12

Jan '07 Patient's chest X-Ray and CT[6] scan are abnormal

Jan '07 Sputum smear negative for TB

3/8 Diagnostic bronchoscopy

3/26 Specimen culture positive for M.TB[5] at hospital lab

3/26 Prescribed 1st line, 4 drug TB therapy for self administration

4/10 Specimen confirmed for M.TB[5] at hospital lab

4/10 GA PHL[1] receives isolate for M.TB[5] susceptibility testing and reincubation

4/25 Patient reports to the Fulton Co. TB Clinic

4/25 Patient advises clinic physician of overseas travel (not itinerary)

4/25 Physician asks for expedited susceptibility testing of isolate culture

4/26 GA PHL[1] finds sufficient growth to begin susceptibility testing

4/27 CDC receives patient sample for susceptibility testing

4/30 GA PHL[1] preliminary susceptibility test results indicate MDR[7] TB

5/4 GA PHL[1] final susceptibility test results indicate MDR[7] TB

5/9 GA PHL[1] repeated susceptibility test results indicate MDR[7] TB

5/10 Family meeting held at PMD[2] office with Fulton Co. TB clinic represented.

5/10 Fulton Co. HD[3] begins review of legal remedies to restrict patient movement

5/10–5/11 GA DPH[4] asks CDC for options that could be used to restrict travel in a person with untreated MDR[7]TB. CDC responds with options.

5/11–5/12 Fulton Co. HD[3] attempts to hand deliver written advisory to patient, Patient cannot be located.

5/11 Patient changes flight departure from 5/14 to 5/12 (unknown to health authorities)

5/12 Patient departs U.S. on Air France #385 unknown to health authorities)

*6/19/07, Subject to Updates
All dates reflect EDT

[1]PHL = Public Health Laboratory
[2]PMD = Private Doctor
[3]HD = Health Department
[4]DPH = Division of Public Health
[5]M.TB = Mycobacterium tuberculosis
[6]CT = Computed Tomography (CAT scan)
[7]MDR = Multidrug Resistant

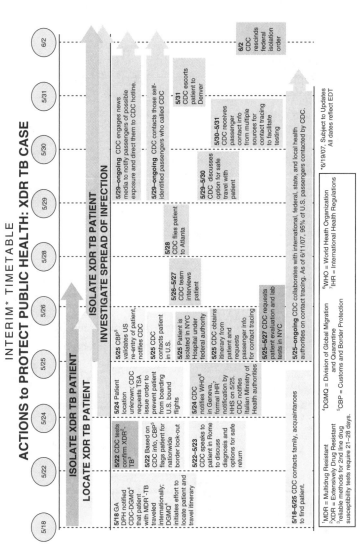

FIGURE 12–12 Actions to protect public health: XDR TB case. *Source:* Data from Centers for Disease Control and Prevention, Extensively drug-resistant tuberculosis, Interim timeline—Actions to protect public health: Investigation of U.S. traveler with XDR TB—June 19, 2007. Available at: http://www.emergency.cdc.gov/coca/updates/2007/2007jun18.asp. Accessed January 19, 2008.

EXHIBIT 12–6

Hepatitis C Fact Sheet

Clinical features

- 80% of infections asymptomatic
- Jaundice
- Fatigue
- Abdominal pain
- Loss of appetite
- Nausea
- Dark urine

Etiologic agent

- Hepatitis C virus (HCV)

Incidence in the United States

- From 240,000 in the 1980s to about 26,000 in 2004

Sequelae

- Chronic infection: 55%–85% of infected persons
- Chronic liver disease: 70% of chronically infected persons
- Deaths from chronic liver disease: 1%–5%
- Leading indication for liver transplantation

Prevalence

- Estimated 4.1 million (1.6%) Americans have been infected with HCV, of whom 3.2 million are chronically infected.

Transmission

- Primarily bloodborne; also sexual and perinatal

Recommendations for testing based on risk for HCV infection

Persons	Risk of Infection	Testing Recommended?
Injecting drug users	High	Yes
Recipients of clotting factors made before 1987	High	Yes
Hemodialysis patients	Intermediate	Yes
Recipients of blood and/or solid organs before 1992	Intermediate	Yes
People with undiagnosed liver problems	Intermediate	Yes
Infants born to infected mothers	Intermediate	After 12–18 months old
Healthcare/public safety workers	Low	Only after known exposure
People having sex with multiple partners	Low	No
People having sex with an infected steady partner	Low	No

continues

EXHIBIT 12–6 *continued*

Trends

- Transfusion-associated cases occurred prior to blood donor screening; now very rare
- Most infections due to illegal injection drug use

Prevention

- Screening of blood/organ/tissue donors
- Counseling to reduce/modify high-risk practices

Source: Adapted from Centers for Disease Control and Prevention, Hepatitis C Fact Sheet. Last reviewed December 8, 2006. Available at: http://www.cdc.gov/ncidod/diseases/hepatitis/c/fact.htm. Accessed November 10, 2007.

blood and blood products, such as through accidental needle sticks. Refer to Figure 12–13 for trends in viral hepatitis incidence in the United States.

Zoonotic Diseases

Q fever, the agent for which is *Coxiella burnetii*, is an example of a zoonosis, a disease that, under natural conditions, can be spread from vertebrate animals to

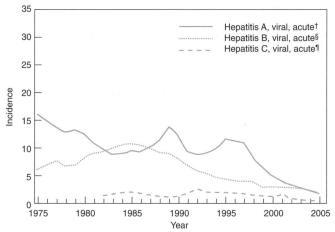

* Per 100,000 population.
† Hepatitis A vaccine was first licensed in 1995.
§ Hepatitis B vaccine was first licensed in June 1982.
¶ An anti-hepatitis C virus (HCV) antibody test first became available in May 1990.

FIGURE 12–13 Incidence of viral hepatitis* by year in the United States during 1975 to 2005. *Source:* From Centers for Disease Control and Prevention, Summary of notifiable diseases—United States, 2005, *MMWR.* Vol 54, No 53, p. 57, 2007.

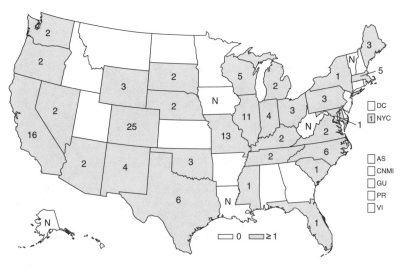

N = not notifiable in jurisdiction.

Q fever became nationally notifiable in 1999. To capture as many cases of Q fever as possible, the Q fever case definition is intentionally broad. However, identification and reporting of Q fever remains incomplete, and the numbers of cases reported might not represent the overall distribution or regional incidence of disease.

FIGURE 12–14 Number of reported cases of Q fever in the United States and U.S. territories (2005). *Source:* From Centers for Disease Control and Prevention, Summary of notifiable diseases—United States, 2005. *MMWR.* Vol 54, No 53, p. 63, 2007.

humans (Figure 12–14). Zoonotic diseases may be either enzootic (similar to endemic in human diseases) or epizootic (similar to epidemic in human diseases).[7] The reservoir for the agent in Q fever is infected livestock (cattle, sheep, and goats). The spectrum of infection in humans ranges from mild to severe, debilitating illness with symptoms similar to those of influenza or pneumonia. Those at high risk for infection include workers and others who come into contact with infected livestock: veterinarians, farmers, agricultural employees, and laboratory personnel. For example, Q fever occurred among laboratory personnel who used sheep in their research at a medical center in San Francisco, California. A more ordinary source of transmission is infected raw milk.

Mycoses

Coccidioidomycosis (San Joaquin Valley fever) often manifests as a lung disease and is caused by a fungus, *Coccidioides immitis*. The agent is endemic to the San Joaquin Valley in California and to the lower Sonoran life zone, which covers parts of California, Arizona, Texas, and Mexico. Cases of infection have been associated with those occupations or activities that bring susceptible persons in contact with contaminated soil (e.g., construction, archeology, and dirt bike riding). Merely driving through an endemic area may result in infection. The following excerpt describes an epidemic that occurred after exposure to a severe dust storm at a naval air station in Lemoore, California:

> Eighteen new cases of symptomatic valley fever were diagnosed at the Naval Hospital, Lemoore . . . following a severe natural dust storm that occurred from December 20 to 22, 1977. This storm arose from the southeast near Bakersfield, California, an area of high endemicity. The storm lasted approximately 48 hours. Visibility during the storm decreased to approximately 0.25 mile. The wind velocity rose to 34 mph. The dust was ubiquitous. It seeped through windows, depositing a layer of soot on car seats and household furniture, making it virtually impossible to avoid exposure to the dust.[27(p. 566)]

Williams et al.[27] concluded that a temporal relationship existed between the dust storm and the marked increase in the incidence of symptomatic San Joaquin Valley fever.

In 1991, an outbreak of coccidioidomycosis (1,208 cases) was reported in California. The majority of cases (80%) occurred in Kern County, where coccidioidomycosis is endemic.[28] The numbers of reported cases of coccidioidomycosis in the United States for year 2005 are shown in Figure 12–15. California and Arizona reported the largest numbers of cases; the frequency of reported U.S. cases of coccidioidomycosis increased during 2005.

Arthropod-Borne Diseases

Arthropod-borne diseases include arboviral diseases. These are a diverse group of diseases that involve transmission of arboviruses between vertebrate hosts (e.g., from animal to animal or from animal to human) by blood-feeding arthropod vectors.[9] Examples of these vectors are sand flies, ticks, and mosquitoes, the last of which are responsible for transmission of the encephalitis virus. During 2006, the following types and numbers of cases of encephalitis were reported: St. Louis encephalitis, 10 reported cases; California serogroup, 67 reported cases; Eastern equine encephalitis, 8 reported cases, and Western equine encephalitis, 0 reported cases.[17] Enzootic diseases are those that afflict animals in a particular locality. Viral isolates or antigens of arboviruses may be found in wild birds, sentinel birds, and captured mosquitoes; epizootic cases have been documented in horses.[29]

Lyme disease, a second example of a vector-borne illness, is transmitted by ticks. Cases, which are distributed across the United States, showed a steady increase from 1982 to 1991, during which time period 40,195 cases were re-

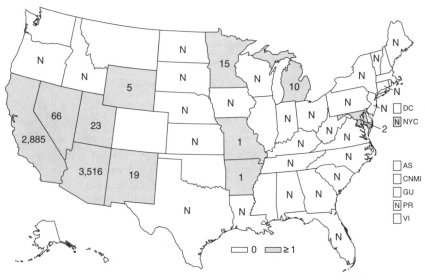

N = not notifiable in jurisdiction.

*In the United States, coccidioidomycosis is endemic in the southwestern states. However, cases have been reported in other states, typically among travelers returning from areas in which the disease is endemic.

FIGURE 12–15   Coccidioidomycosis. Number of reported cases— United States* and U.S. territories, 2005. *Source:* From Centers for Disease Control and Prevention. Summary of notifiable diseases—United States, 2005. *MMWR.* Vol 54, p. 45, March 30, 2007.

News Headline:
Chikungunya Virus (CHIKV) Spreading

CHIKV virus causes chikungunya fever, which can be a disabling illness that produces crippling symptoms such as headache, nausea, and joint pain. Named for the Swahili word for "that which bends up," the disease is carried to humans by infected mosquitoes. Because of recent mutations in the virus that enable it to infect new species of mosquitoes, CHIKV has the potential to spread beyond Africa and Asia to Europe and North America.

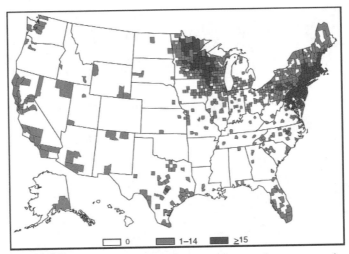

A rash that might be confused with the erythema migrans of early Lyme disease can occur after the bite of the Lone Star tick (*Amblyomma americanum*). These ticks, which do not transmit the Lyme disease bacterium, are common human-biting ticks in the southern and southeastern United States.

FIGURE 12–16 Number of reported cases of Lyme disease, by county in the United States (2005). *Source:* From Centers for Disease Control and Prevention, Summary of notifiable diseases—United States, 2005, *MMWR.* Vol 54, No 53, p. 59, 2007.

ported. In 1992, a total of 9,677 cases were reported, representing an incidence rate of 3.9 per 100,000 population.[30] Figure 12–16 shows a map of the distribution of cases during 2005, with cases heavily concentrated in New England and the upper Midwest.

Emerging Infections

The emergence of seemingly new infections presents a challenge to epidemiologists worldwide. When a young man and his fiancée appeared in an emergency room in New Mexico with fever and acute respiratory distress, a whole chain of events began, which eventually led to the definition of U.S. hantaviral syndrome.[31] This syndrome, identified initially in the Four Corners region of the United States, claimed 20 lives out of 36 patients: a greater than 50% case fatality rate. Subsequently it has been identified in California and other states. Hantavirus infection had been described previously in other parts of the world, but appeared suddenly in a slightly altered form in several locations in the United States.

Escherichia coli: An Emerging Foodborne Pathogen

E. coli foodborne illness outbreaks have received dramatic and continuing attention in the media. Two outbreaks were associated with the same fast food restaurant chain in 1982. A multistate outbreak in the western United States produced 700 cases of illness and four deaths in 1993.[32] The pathogen responsible for the vast majority of cases of illness that present as severe bloody diarrhea (hemolytic uremic syndrome) is called *E. coli* O157:H7. This organism is regarded as an emerging pathogen because of the occurrence of major foodborne illness outbreaks that have been distributed over a wide geographic area. Such large-scale outbreaks were not generally recognized before the early 1980s. Although other foods have been associated with *E. coli* O157:H7, the vehicle implicated most frequently in foodborne illness outbreaks is ground beef. When hamburgers made with contaminated ground beef are eaten rare or are inadequately cooked, infections may occur. Refer to Chapter 1 for a description of an *E. coli* O157:H7 outbreak associated with raw spinach.

"Emerging infections are those that erupt suddenly, like the U.S. hantaviral pulmonary syndrome, or that suddenly increase in incidence or geographic scope. Recent examples range from Lyme Disease to AIDS."[31(p. 85)] Also included in this category is foodborne illness caused by *E. coli*. Many emerging infections are not caused by sudden mutations in a pathogen; instead they appear when an existing pathogen gains access to new host populations. Changes in climate, human activities such as farming or reforestation, technologic changes such as air travel and organ transplantation, and demographic changes such as migration to cities may all contribute to the emergence of seemingly new and deadly infections. Table 12–6 shows a summary of examples of emerging infections. One of these infections is caused by the HCV (Exhibit 12–6), for which a routine vaccination is not presently available. Another example is West Nile virus infection (refer to case study shown in box).

Table 12-6   Examples of Emerging Infections

Pathogen	Disease	Distribution	Natural Host	Transmission	Notable Factors in Emergence
Bunyaviridae/ (Hantaviruses)	Hemorrhagic fever	Asia	Rodents	Inhalation of infected excreta	Contact with rodent host during rice harvest, dissemination by ship-borne infected rats
	Respiratory distress syndrome	U.S., probably Europe and South America	Rodents	Inhalation of infected excreta	Ecologic changes causing increased contact with rodents
Cryptosporidium	Cryptosporidiosis	Probably worldwide	?Ungulates*	Ingestion of contaminated water	Faulty water purification
Filoviridae (Ebola, Marburg)	Hemorrhagic fever	Africa	Unknown	Contact with unknown host, nosocomial (infected needles)	Unknown (in Europe and U.S., importation of monkeys)
Group A streptococci	Necrotizing fasciitis; other invasive infections	Probably worldwide	?Humans	Inhalation (classic strep), wound infection; skin contamination	Unknown, possibly new strain or strain not recently prevalent
Hepatitis C virus	Hepatitis	Worldwide	?Humans	Contaminated IV needles, transfusions, organ transplantation, probably sexual	Transfusions
Lassa virus	Lassa fever	West Africa	Rodents	Contact with infected secretions (of natural host or infected persons)	Urbanization
Vibrio cholerae	Cholera	Asia; recently reintroduced to South America, Africa	?Zooplankton	Ingestion of infected human excreta in food or water	Transoceanic shipping, lapsed public health measures, travel

*Hoofed mammals such as sheep, goats, and reindeer.

Source: Reproduced with permission, SS Morse. Patterns and predictability in emerging infections. *Hospital Practice,* 1996, 31(4), p. 85. © 1996 The McGraw-Hill Companies, Inc.

Case Study: West Nile Virus

West Nile virus (WNV) is a potentially serious mosquito-borne illness that in most cases (about 80% of people) does not produce symptoms. The incubation period is approximately 3 to 14 days after the bite of an infected mosquito. Evidence suggests that a minority of infected persons (up to 20%) will develop a mild illness with fever, headache, body aches, and sometimes skin rash and swollen glands. Infection infrequently (1 in 150 cases) results in severe illness; symptoms include high fever, coma, and paralysis. A small number of cases have been fatal; of the 3,359 cases as of November 27, 2007, there were 98 deaths. The principal transmission cycle of WNV involves several species of mosquitos and various species of birds.

WNV first was recognized in 1999 as the cause of severe and fatal human illness in metropolitan New York City. WNV is commonly found in Africa, West and Central Asia, and the Middle East. It is not known how the virus first was introduced into the United States, but since the initial appearance it has spread rapidly, with human, avian, animal, or mosquito WNV activity reported in all U.S. states except Hawaii, Alaska, and Oregon. ■

Source: Adapted from Centers for Disease Control and Prevention. West Nile Virus. Modified November 27, 2007. Available at: http://www.cdc.gov/ncidod/dvbid/westnile. Accessed December 8, 2007.

Conclusion

Infectious disease epidemiology has developed a body of methods for investigating and controlling infectious diseases in the community. The reservoir for infectious diseases may consist of humans, animals, arthropods, or the physical environment. Transmission of disease may be direct (person to person) or indirect. Noteworthy terms used to describe infectious disease outbreaks include attack rate, secondary attack rate, and case fatality rate. Agents for infectious disease encompass a broad range of microbial agents, from bacteria to viruses to protozoa. Infectious diseases remain major causes of morbidity and mortality. Examples of significant problems include foodborne illness, vaccine-preventable diseases such as measles, diseases spread from person to person such as TB, and sexually transmitted diseases, notably AIDS.

Study Questions and Exercises

1. Define and give the formulas for attack rate, secondary attack rate, and CFR.

2. A flu outbreak occurred in a military barracks that housed 20 soldiers. Case A began on October 1 and case B was diagnosed on October 2. After approximately 10 days, 12 additional cases occurred during approximately a one-week time span. Military epidemiologists believed that this second group of cases represented the same generation of cases, and was in the second incubation period after the occurrence of cases A and B; none of the 20 soldiers was known to be immune. Calculate the secondary attack rate using the foregoing data.

3. Explain the etiology of TB, measles, and rabies by applying the epidemiologic triangle (Figure 12–1).

4. Give one example of each type of prevention—primary, secondary, and tertiary—for foodborne salmonellosis, malaria, and AIDS. To answer this question, you will need to review the chapters where the three types of prevention are discussed and apply the methods to a new situation.

5. What is the epidemiologic importance of an inapparent infection?

6. Name two examples of a disease spread from person to person, and suggest methods for the control of such a disease in the community.

7. When is isolation for an infectious disease not likely to be an effective means of control of the disease in the community?

8. Discuss host responses to infectious disease agents. Be sure to include herd immunity as a community health concept.

9. Discuss the following statement: High cooking temperature will sanitize food even after it has been stored improperly (e.g., at room temperature for 6 hours); one can be certain that there will be no remaining hazard to human health and that all the pathogenic material has been destroyed. (Refer to Figure 12–6, the illness outbreak on a 747 jetliner.)

10. A local health department epidemiologist investigated an outbreak of gastrointestinal illness thought to be associated with a college cafeteria. There were many complaints about the quality of the cafeteria's offerings, and it appeared that the students' worst expectations were confirmed when several students visited the college's infirmary during the middle of the night and the following day complaining of nausea, diarrhea, fever, vomiting, and cramps. The health department's investigation revealed that 24 students had eaten in the cafeteria immediately before the outbreak. The times between eating in the cafeteria and the development of

active symptoms ranged from 20 to 36 hours. A list of foods eaten, the number of persons eating the foods, and tabulations of illness are presented in Appendix 12. Fill in the attack rates where indicated. On the basis of your calculations, answer the following questions:

a. What food or foods would you suspect caused the problem?

b. Based on the description of the clinical symptoms and the list of infectious disease agents presented in Table 12–5, which agent(s) do you think was (were) responsible?

11. Sharpen your skills in interpreting charts. Figure 12–17 is a chart that shows data on rabies for 1975 through 2005. The X-axis (abscissa) is the horizontal axis. The Y-axis (ordinate) is the vertical axis.

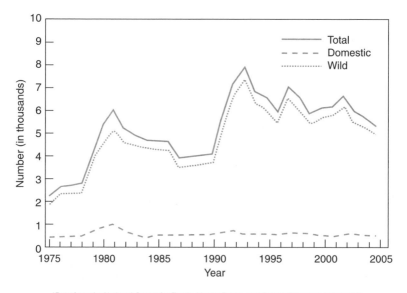

*Data from the National Center for Zootic, Vector-Borne, and Enteric Diseases (proposed).

Periods of resurgence and decline of rabies incidence are primarily the result of cyclic reemergence. As populations are decimated by epizootics, numbers of reported cases decline until populations again reach levels to support epizootic transmission of disease. Recent declines in the number of reported cases among terrestrial reservoir species (raccoons, skunks, and foxes) have been offset by increases in testing and the subsequent detection of rabid bats. In addition, interventions such as the oral vaccination of wildlife species might contribute to the decreasing trend in recent years.

FIGURE 12–17   Number of reported cases of rabies among wild and domestic animals,* by year, in the United States and Puerto Rico from 1975 to 2005. *Source:* From Centers for Disease Control and Prevention, Summary of notifiable diseases—United States, 2005. *MMWR.* Vol 54, No 53, p. 63, 2007.

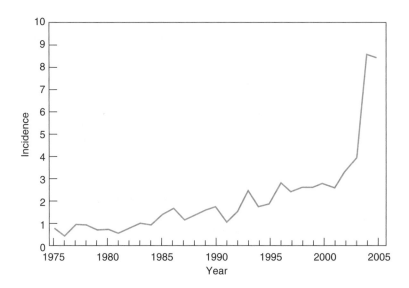

* Per 100,000 population.

In 2005, incidence of reported pertussis remained stable after doubling during 2003–2004.
Increased availability of sensitive diagnostic tests and improved case recognition and reporting
account for an unknown fraction of this increase.

FIGURE 12–18   Incidence of pertussis,* by year, in the United States
from 1975 to 2005. *Source:* Modified from Centers for Disease Control
and Prevention, Summary of notifiable diseases—United States, 2005.
MMWR. Vol 54, No 53, p. 62, 2007.

a. What are the labels of the X and Y axes?
b. Describe the overall trends reflected in the chart.
c. Why does the line for domestic animals diverge from that of wild
   animals?
d. What type of disease is rabies?

12. Figure 12–18 is a chart that presents data on the incidence of pertussis
    (whooping cough) for 1975 through 2005.
    a. What are the labels of the X and Y axes?
    b. Describe the overall trends reflected in the chart.

References

1. Miniño AM, Heron MP, Murphy SL, Kochankek KD. Deaths: Final Data for 2004.
   National Vital Statistics Reports; 2007;55(19). Hyattsville, MD: National Center for
   Health Statistics.

2. World Health Organization. Infectious Diseases Report, Chapter 1. Infectious diseases are the biggest killer of the young. Available at: http://www.who.int/infectious-disease-report/pages/ch1text.html. Accessed December 3, 2007.

3. Klevens RM, Edwards JR, Richards CL Jr., et al. Estimating health care-associated infections and deaths in U.S. hospitals, 2002. *Public Health Rep*. 2007;122:160–166.

4. Yoder JS, Beach MJ. Giardiasis surveillance—United States, 2003–2005. *MMWR. Surveillance Summaries*. 2007;56(SS-7):11–18.

5. Mausner JS, Kramer S. *Mausner & Bahn Epidemiology—An Introductory Text*, 2nd ed. Philadelphia, PA: Saunders; 1985.

6. Centers for Disease Control and Prevention. WHO Collaborating Center for the Mycoses. Available at: http://www.cdc.gov/Ncidod/dbmd/mdb/index.htm. Accessed December 9, 2007.

7. Heymann DL, ed. *Control of Communicable Diseases Manual*, 18th ed. Washington, DC: American Public Health Association; 2004.

8. Centers for Disease Control and Prevention. Vaccines and Immunizations: Immunity Types. Available at: http://www.cdc.gov/vaccines/vac-gen/immunity-types.htm. Accessed December 9, 2007.

9. Last JM, ed. *A Dictionary of Epidemiology*, 4th ed. New York, NY: Oxford University Press; 2001.

10. Hennekens CH, Buring JE. *Epidemiology in Medicine*. Boston, MA: Little, Brown; 1987.

11. Centers for Disease Control and Prevention. *Principles of Epidemiology*, 2nd ed. Atlanta, GA: CDC; 1992. (Reviewed October 1998.)

12. MacMahon B, Pugh TF. *Epidemiology Principles and Methods*. Boston, MA: Little, Brown; 1970.

13. Lilienfeld AM, Lilienfeld DE. *Foundations of Epidemiology*, 2nd ed. New York, NY: Oxford University Press; 1980.

14. Snow J. *Snow on Cholera*. Cambridge, MA: Harvard University Press; 1965.

15. U.S. Department of Health and Human Services. Center supplies etiological agents of schistosomiasis. *Res Resour Rep*. 1981;5:12–13.

16. Centers for Disease Control and Prevention. Update: cholera—Western Hemisphere, 1992. *MMWR*. 1993;42:89–91.

17. Centers for Disease Control and Prevention. Table: Provisional cases of infrequently reported notifiable diseases (<1,000 cases reported during the preceding year)—United States, week ending November 24, 2007 (47th Week). *MMWR*. 2007; 56:1243.

18. World Health Organization. Cholera: Epidemic and Pandemic Alert and Response (EPR). Available at: http://www.who.int/csr/don/archive/disease/cholera/en. Accessed December 6, 2007.

19. World Health Organization. Weekly epidemiological record. Cholera, Iraq—update. 2007;82(41):357–360.

20. Centers for Disease Control and Prevention. Amebiasis associated with colonic irrigation—Colorado. *MMWR*. 1981;30:101–102.

21. Centers for Disease Control and Prevention. HIV and AIDS—United States, 1981–2000. *MMWR*. 2001;50:429–455.

22. Centers for Disease Control and Prevention. HIV/AIDS Surveillance Report, 2005. Vol 17. Rev ed. Atlanta: U.S. Department of Health and Human Services, Centers for Disease Control and Prevention; 2007:1–54.

23. World Health Organization. AIDS epidemic update, Dec 06. Available at: http://www.unaids.org. Accessed November 10, 2007.

24. Centers for Disease Control and Prevention. Measles surveillance—United States, 1991. *MMWR*. 1992;41:1–11.

25. Centers for Disease Control and Prevention. Tuberculosis morbidity—United States, 1992. *MMWR*. 1993;42:696–697, 703–704.

26. Centers for Disease Control and Prevention. Summary of notifiable diseases–United States, 2005. Hepatitis, viral. Incidence, by year—United States, 1975–2005. *MMWR*. 2007;54.

27. Williams PL, Mendez P, Smyth LT. Symptomatic coccidioidomycosis following a severe natural dust storm. *Chest*. 1979;76:566–569.

28. Centers for Disease Control and Prevention. Coccidioidomycosis—United States, 1991–1992. *MMWR*. 1993;42:21–24.

29. Centers for Disease Control and Prevention. Arboviral diseases—United States, 1992. *MMWR*. 1993;42:467–468.

30. Centers for Disease Control and Prevention. Lyme disease—United States, 1991–1992. *MMWR*. 1993;42:345–348.

31. Morse SS. Patterns and predictability in emerging infections. *Hosp Pract*. 1996;31:85–91, 96–101, 104.

32. Armstrong GL, Hollingsworth J, Morris JG. Emerging foodborne pathogens: *Escherichia coli* O157:H7 as a model of entry of a new pathogen into the food supply of the developed world. *Epidemiol Rev*. 1996;18:29–51.

APPENDIX
12

Data from a Foodborne Illness Outbreak in a College Cafeteria

Food Items Served	Number of Persons Who Ate				Number Who Did Not Eat			
	Ill	Not Ill	Total	Attack Rate	Ill	Not Ill	Total	Attack Rate
Three-bean salad	10	3	13		7	4	11	
Beef, rare	17	6	23		0	1	1	
Beef, specified well cooked	3	6	9		5	10	15	
Potato salad	12	6	18		4	2	6	
Macaroni salad	11	5	16		5	3	8	
Tuna salad*	13	1	14		3	7	10	
Cold cuts and cheese plate	10	6	16		5	3	8	
Rolls and butter	13	4	17		4	3	7	

*The tuna salad was prepared from fresh ingredients approximately 1 hour before consumption and stored under refrigeration.

CHAPTER 13

Epidemiologic Aspects of Work and the Environment

LEARNING OBJECTIVES

By the end of this chapter the reader will be able to:

- define the term *environmental epidemiology*
- give examples of environmental agents that are associated with human health effects
- provide examples of study designs used in environmental epidemiology
- state methodologic difficulties with research on environmental health effects
- list some of the terms used to characterize environmental exposure and human responses to exposure
- cite health outcomes studied in relation to environmental agents

CHAPTER OUTLINE

   I. Introduction
  II. Health Effects Associated with Environmental Hazards
 III. Study Designs Used in Environmental Epidemiology
 IV. Toxicologic Concepts Related to Environmental Epidemiology

V. Types of Agents
VI. Environmental Hazards Found in the Work Setting
VII. Noteworthy Community Environmental Health Hazards
VIII. Conclusion
IX. Study Questions and Exercises

Introduction

During the 21st century, adverse human impacts upon the environment have risen to the forefront as pressing concerns for global society. Human activities cause hazards that portend enormous ramifications for society, health, and the economy. The World Health Organization estimates that environmental factors are linked to as much as 24% of the global burden of disease and 23% of all deaths.[1] The causes of environmentally related morbidity and mortality include exposure to toxic chemicals, indoor and outdoor air pollution, dangerous conditions found in the workplace, and land use policies that encourage the survival of microbes and disease vectors.

What is the potential role for epidemiologists in examining linkages between the environment and human health? Through epidemiologic research, it may be possible to control or prevent environmentally associated adverse health outcomes by identifying relevant exposures, demonstrating how the exposures are associated with the outcomes, and suggesting methods for control of exposures and remediation of hazards. Among the more notable of human exposures to environmental hazards are the following:

- chemical agents (from chemical spills, pesticides, and hazardous wastes)
- electromagnetic radiation from high-tension wires
- ionizing radiation from natural and synthetic sources
- heavy metals
- air pollution
- temperature increases from global warming and climate change

Environmental epidemiology is one of the disciplines that have the potential to provide insight into health effects associated with the environment. The term *environmental epidemiology* refers to the study of diseases and conditions (occurring in the population) that are linked to environmental factors. Generally speaking, exposures are involuntary—outside of the control of the exposed individual. Environmental epidemiology applies standard epidemiological methods to the study of health outcomes hypothesized to be associated with the environment. Other closely allied disciplines include toxicology and molecular epidemiology (discussed in Chapter 14).[2]

Health Effects Associated with Environmental Hazards

Health effects (both morbidity and mortality) attributed to environmental exposures encompass a wide range of conditions, including cancer, infertility, reproductive impacts (e.g., congenital malformations and low birth weight), and infectious diseases. In the work environment, ionizing radiation, infectious agents, toxic substances, and drugs may pose unique health risks for pregnant workers and the unborn fetus.[3] Other adverse health outcomes associated with the occupational environment include lung diseases (byssinosis, coal workers' pneumoconiosis, and asbestosis), dermatologic problems, neurotoxicity, coronary heart disease, injuries and trauma, and various psychological conditions (e.g., work absenteeism and stress at work). Researchers have been concerned about the possible link between occupational exposure to carcinogenic agents and certain forms of cancer (e.g., bladder cancer in dye workers and leukemia among workers exposed to benzene). Finally, deaths from malaria are increasing as a result of deforestation and inadequate water management practices.[1]

Study Designs Used in Environmental Epidemiology

Environmental epidemiology employs a wide range of study designs, including both descriptive and analytic approaches. Wegman offered definitions of descriptive and etiologic studies applied to the epidemiology of occupational diseases that apply equally well to the broader category of environmental epidemiology. "Descriptive studies provide information for setting priorities, identifying hazards, and formulating hypotheses for new occupational risk."[4(p. 944)] A historical example is William Farr's work showing that Cornwall metal miners

(1848–1853) had higher mortality from all causes than the general population.[4] "Etiologic studies are planned examinations of causality and the natural history of disease. These studies have required increasingly sophisticated analytic methods as the importance of low-level exposures is explored and greater refinement in exposure-effect relationships is sought."[4(p. 945)] Examples of different study designs that may be employed in environmental epidemiology are introduced below in an effort to present a broad overview of the field.

Retrospective Cohort Studies

In evaluating the health effects of occupational exposures to toxic agents, researchers may study various end points. For example, in some studies self-reported symptom rates are used as a measure of the effects of low-level chemical exposure. Occupational health investigators can design and administer self-report questionnaires inexpensively. Self-reports to questionnaires, however, may not always be reliable, and although they often correlate with clinical diagnoses they also may differ markedly.[5] Physiologic or clinical examinations are other means to evaluate adverse health effects. For example, in a study of respiratory diseases, pulmonary function tests, such as forced expiratory volume, may be an appropriate indicator. While clinical examinations may provide "harder" evidence of health effects than self-reports, they may be expensive or impractical to collect in the case of workers who have left employment. In other studies, mortality is the outcome of interest; research on mortality frequently uses a retrospective cohort study design.[6] Mortality experience in an employment cohort can be compared with the expected mortality in the general population (national, regional, state, or county) by using the standardized mortality ratio (see Chapter 3). One also can contrast the mortality experience of exposed workers with the mortality rate of nonexposed workers in the same industry. For example, production workers might be compared with drivers or office workers. Another option is to identify a second industry or occupation that is comparable in terms of skill level, educational requirements, or geographic location, but in which the exposure of interest is not present.

Use of mortality as a study end point has several advantages, including the fact that it may be relevant to agents that have a subtle effect over a long time period. Although any fatal chronic disease may be investigated, mortality from cancer is often studied as an outcome variable in occupational exposures.

According to Monson, "cancer specifically tends to be a fatal illness; its presence is usually indicated on the death certificate. Also, cancer is a fairly specific disease and is less subject to random misclassification than, say, one of the cardiovascular diseases."[6](p. 106)

Methods for Selection of a Research Population and Collection of Exposure Data

The investigator may select a study population from personnel records maintained by a company. If the records of former and retired workers are retained by the company, a complete data set spanning long time periods may be available. Ideally, every previous and current worker exposed to the factor should be included. Selection bias may occur if some workers are excluded because their records have been purged from the company's database.[6] Data collected from employment records may include:

- personal identifiers to permit record linkage to Social Security Administration files and retrieval of death certificates
- demographic characteristics, length of employment, and work history with the company
- information about potential confounding variables, such as the employee's medical history, smoking habits, lifestyle, and family history of disease

The Healthy Worker Effect

One of the factors that may reduce the validity of exposure data is the healthy worker effect. (Note that the validity of exposure data was discussed in Chapter 10.) Monson states that the healthy worker effect refers to the "observation that employed populations tend to have a lower mortality experience than the general population."[6](p. 114) The healthy worker effect may have an impact on occupational mortality studies in several ways. People whose life expectancy is shortened by disease are less likely to be employed than healthy persons. One consequence of this phenomenon would be a reduced (or attenuated) measure of effect for an exposure that increases morbidity or mortality. That is, because the general population includes both employed and unemployed individuals, the mortality rate of that population may be somewhat elevated compared with a population in which everyone is healthy enough to work. As a result, any excess mortality associated with a given occupational exposure is more difficult to detect when the healthy worker effect is operative. The healthy worker effect is likely to be stronger for nonmalignant causes of mortality, which usually produce worker attrition during an earlier career phase, than for malignant causes of mortality, which typically have longer latency periods and occur later in life. In addition, healthier workers may have greater total exposure to occupational hazards than those who leave the work force at an earlier age because of illness.

Ecologic Study Designs

Studies of the health effects of air pollution have used ecologic analyses to correlate air pollution with health effects. Instead of correlating individual exposure to air pollution with mortality, the researcher measures the association between average exposure to air pollution within a census tract and the average mortality in that census tract. Other types of geographic subdivisions besides census tracts may be used as well. This type of study attempts to demonstrate that mortality is higher in more polluted census tracts than in less polluted census tracts. A major problem of the ecologic technique for the study of air pollution, however, stems from uncontrolled factors. Examples include individual levels of smoking and smoking habits, occupational exposure to respiratory hazards and air pollution, differences in social class and other demographic factors, genetic background, and length of residence in the area.[7] Nonetheless, ecologic studies may open the next generation of investigations. Future studies will probably attempt to measure the relevant potential confounders in more rigorous analytic study designs.

Case-Control Studies

Case-control studies collect information on past exposures to environmental hazards and toxins among persons who have or do not have a health outcome of interest. In comparison with ecologic study designs, case-control studies may provide more complete exposure data, especially when the exposure information is collected from the friends and relatives of cases who died of a particular cause. Nevertheless, some unmeasured exposure variables as well as confounding variables may remain in case-control studies. For example, in studies of health and air pollution, precise quantitation of both air pollution exposure and unobserved confounding factors, including smoking habits and occupational exposure to air pollution, may be difficult to achieve.[7]

Toxicologic Concepts Related to Environmental Epidemiology

The terms *dose-response curve, threshold, latency,* and *synergism,* which are from toxicology, characterize exposure to hazardous agents. For more information about toxicology see *Casarett and Doull's Essentials of Toxicology.*[8]

Dose-Response Curve

A dose-response relationship refers to a type of correlative association between an exposure (e.g., a toxic chemical) and effect (e.g., a biologic outcome such as cell death). A dose-response curve maps this association and is used to assess the effect of exposure to a chemical or toxic substance upon an organism (e.g., an experimental animal). A typical dose-response curve is shown in Figure 13–1. The dose is indicated along the x-axis, and the response is shown along the y-axis. The response could be measured as the percentage of exposed animals showing a particular effect, or it could reflect the effect in an individual subject. The dose-response curve, which has a sigmoid shape, is also a cumulative percentage response curve. At the beginning of the curve, there is a flat portion suggesting that at low levels an increase in dosage produces no effect. This is also known as the subthreshold phase. After the threshold is reached, the curve rises steeply and

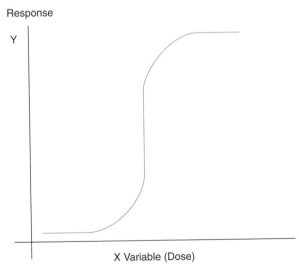

FIGURE 13–1 Illustration of the dose-response curve

then progresses to a linear phase, where an increase in response is proportional to the increase in dose. When the maximal response is reached, the curve flattens out. A dose-response relationship is one of the indicators used to assess a causal effect of a suspected exposure upon a health outcome.

Threshold

The threshold refers to the lowest dose at which a particular response may occur. It is unclear whether exposure (especially long-term exposure) to toxic chemicals at low (subthreshold) levels is sufficient to produce any health response. The effects of low-level exposures within the population are difficult to assess. Nevertheless, some occupational health specialists voice their increasing concerns over the long-term effects of low-level exposures to toxic substances in the workplace.[6] Although some researchers hypothesize that the effects of low-level exposures may be pathologic, other investigators express a point of view known as hormesis—the belief that low-level exposures may induce protective effects for high-level exposures. Hormesis is controversial and some experts believe that it may disregard established science.[9]

Latency

Latency refers to the time period between initial exposure and a measurable response. The latency period can range from a few seconds (in the case of acutely toxic agents) to several decades. For example, mesothelioma (a rare form of cancer) has a latency period as long as 40 years between first exposure to asbestos and subsequent development of the condition. The long latency for many of the health events studied in environmental research makes detection of hazards a methodologically difficult problem. Because multiple exposures (often at low levels) may have occurred during the latency period, the epidemiologist may be unable to sort out which exposures are salient for a disease of interest from those that are not important.

Synergism

Synergism refers to a situation in which the combined effect of several exposures is greater than the sum of the individual effects. The synergistic relationship between asbestos and smoking in causing lung cancer is an example. A classic study of lung cancer risk among asbestos insulation workers was reported by Selikoff and colleagues.[10] A total of 370 workers were studied between 1963 and 1967. The occurrence of lung cancer in this occupational group was seven to eight times greater than that expected for the general white population of the United States. It was apparent that exposure to asbestos was not the entire explanation, however. No lung cancer deaths were observed among the 87 workers who did not smoke, but 24 of 283 workers who smoked died of lung cancer, a 92-fold greater risk than that for workers who did not smoke and were not exposed to asbestos as part of their occupation.

Types of Agents

A partial list of potential disease agents found in the environment (work, home, and external) is shown in Table 13–1. The nature and significance of these agents are discussed below. Although there are thousands of possible agents of environmental disease, the broad categories include toxic chemicals, metals (especially heavy metals, e.g., lead), electric and magnetic radiation, ionizing radiation, allergens and molds, dusts (e.g., silica and coal dust), asbestos, and mechanical and physical energy.

Chemical Agents

Although chemicals are essential to the functioning of modern society, their use raises concerns about their possible short-term and long-term health effects. Human beings are exposed to chemical agents from a variety of sources in the

Table 13–1   Selected List of Environmental Disease Agents

Type of Agent	Examples	Health Effects Studied
Chemical	Pesticides, organochlorides Vinyl chloride Benzene	Cancers Angiosarcoma Leukemia
Heavy metals and metallic compounds	Mercury Lead Cadmium, manganese Arsenic	Minamata disease Neurologic impairment Cancers Cancers
Electric and magnetic radiation	Radiation from high-tension power lines	Leukemia
Ionizing radiation	γ-rays X-rays Radon	Cancers Cancers Lung cancer
Allergens and molds	Animal fur and dander; pollen	Allergic responses
Asbestos	Brake linings Construction materials	Lung cancer, mesothelioma
Dusts	Coal dust Silica	Pneumoconiosis Silicosis
Physical/mechanical energy	Industrial machinery, high ambient temperature	Noise-induced hearing loss, mortality

home and at work. And, as the use of chemicals continues to grow exponentially, possibilities for exposure to them increase. A wide range of potential adverse impacts on human health have been studied in relationship to chemical agents, e.g., acute toxicity, direct skin irritation, pulmonary diseases, and long-term effects such as cancer.

Among the sources of chemical exposure are foods, household cleaning agents, automotive chemicals, paints, and pesticides. Present in our food are chemical additives that increase shelf life, preserve quality, enhance taste and appearance, and increase nutritional value. Among the household products that make use of chemicals are disinfectant soaps, detergents, air fresheners, and many others. Some brands of auto body and engine cleaners and related products contain volatile and corrosive solvents. Many types of paints and solvents produce vapors that are potentially hazardous when inhaled or when these products come into direct contact with the skin. Other sources of chemical exposure at home are construction materials that emit formaldehyde-containing vapors. Finally, several types of pesticides—used routinely to control insects, rodents, and weeds—are highly toxic to human beings and animals.

Pesticides

Pesticides are substances used to control pests; included in this category are insecticides, herbicides, and rodenticides. The four major classes of insecticides are organophosphates, organocarbamates, pyrethroids, and organochlorides (also known as organochlorines), which include dichlorodiphenyltricloroethane (DDT), lindane, and chlordane. Polychlorinated biphenyls and dioxins are also from the organochloride family. Direct exposure to pesticides may follow mishandling, improper disposal, accidents, or spills; indirect pesticide exposure may result from ground water contamination through agricultural use of pesticides.

An example of a pesticide that has aroused the concern of public health officials is the organochloride insecticide DDT, which was used widely after introduction in the 1940s for the control of mosquitoes and other insect vectors. Because of concerns about DDT's toxicity to wildlife and its persistence in the environment, its use was banned in the United States in 1972. DDT has a long half-life (10 to 15 years) in the environment and tends to increase in concentration as a result of biomagnification, a process whereby DDT levels strengthen as pesticide residues move up the food chain from lower to higher organisms. DDT also has the propensity to bind with fat molecules in animals.[11] Consequently, even though application of DDT has been banned, human exposure still may occur via the consumption of contaminated fatty foods derived from animal sources as well as by eating contaminated fish.[12] Although some of the effects (e.g., neurotoxicity and changes in the liver) of acute and long-term occupational exposure to organochlorine pesticides have been observed, the health effects of exposure of the general population to DDT and similar agents have not been established definitively.

Asbestos

Formerly, asbestos was used widely in shipbuilding, automotive brake linings, insulation, and construction, resulting in the widespread contamination of schools, homes, and public buildings. Before the United States curtailed use of asbestos in the 1980s, billions of tons of the substance were added to consumer products and applied to construction sites. Despite a 1991 court action that permitted many uses of the mineral, it is found less commonly in consumer products than it once was.

Classic epidemiologic studies determined that asbestos exposure was associated with asbestosis, malignant mesothelioma, and lung cancer. The research of Selikoff stands out as a pioneering effort to explore the epidemiology of asbestos-related health effects. Selikoff et al.[13] reported unexpectedly high death rates due to cancer of the lung or pleura; mesothelioma; and cancer of the stomach, colon, or rectum among building trade insulation workers who had relatively light exposure to asbestos.

Metallic Compounds

Metallic compounds that pose an environmental hazard include aluminum, arsenic, antimony, beryllium, cadmium, chromium, lead, mercury, nickel, and tin. Three of these—arsenic, mercury, and lead—merit elaboration.

Arsenic

Arsenic in its pure form is a crystalline metalloid, an element with properties that are intermediate between those of a metal and a nonmetal. It is able to combine with other substances, metallic and nonmetallic, and also to form stable organic compounds.[14] A poisonous material that is ubiquitous in nature—in soils and water—arsenic varies in toxicity depending upon its chemical form; it is also the byproduct of refining gold and other metals. Although arsenic formerly was used for medicinal purposes, it is no longer indicated for this use but has commercial applications as a pesticide and wood preservative and in manufacturing processes.[15]

Several massive arsenic poisoning incidents, due to the contamination of food-stuffs with arsenic, have been documented.[14] Arsenic-contaminated beer killed 6,000 people in England in 1900; several thousand people were poisoned in Japan in the mid-twentieth century due to arsenic-contaminated dry milk and soy sauce. Particularly at risk of arsenic exposure are some groups of mining and smelter workers as well as agricultural workers who come into contact with pesticides.

Accumulated evidence suggests that arsenic is a carcinogen. It is a cause of skin and lung cancer, when ingested or inhaled, and has been linked to internal cancers, such as bladder, kidney, and liver cancers.[16] Geographic regions that have high levels of naturally occurring arsenic in the drinking water (e.g., Taiwan and Argentina) also have elevated levels of bladder cancer mortality.[17] A dose-response relationship between exposure to inorganic arsenic in drinking water and bladder cancer has been reported. However, because many of the studies that report this association have used ecologic study designs, additional analytical epidemiologic research would be helpful in clarifying the relationship.

Mercury

A naturally occurring chemical that is highly toxic, mercury has been used medically to treat syphilis, as an agricultural fungicide, and in dental amalgams. Nowadays, consumers are advised to avoid certain species of fish that may contain high levels of mercury; these types of fish include swordfish, canned albacore, and several others. In 1956, an environmental catastrophe occurred in Minamata Bay, Japan, where approximately 3,000 cases of neurologic disease resulted among people who ate fish contaminated with methyl mercury.[18] The neurologic condition, which became known as Minamata disease, was characterized by numbness of the extremities, deafness, poor vision, and drowsiness; the condition was unresponsive to medical intervention and frequently culminated in death. The cause was attributed to discharges of mercury compounds into the bay by a plastics factory. Mercury contamination of local waterways is a legacy of mining operations in some areas, e.g., California.

Lead

Exposure to lead, which was once widely used in paint, motor vehicle fuels, and industrial processes, is associated with grave central nervous system effects (e.g., intellectual impairment and deficits) among children and hypertension and kidney disease among adults.[19] Very high blood lead levels (BLLs), defined as greater than 70 μg/dL of blood, are associated with acute effects (e.g., coma and death).[20] However, even at low levels exposure to lead is thought to be harmful, because the threshold for adverse effects is unknown. Young children are particularly at risk of the harmful effects of lead exposure.

According to *Healthy People 2010,* the national objective of the United States is to eliminate BLLs that exceed 10 μg/dL of blood. Although the percentage of children who have BLLs that exceed this standard has declined steeply during the past two decades, approximately 310,000 children aged one to five years remain at risk for elevated BLLs.[19] BLLs have declined greatly in all groups in recent years but remain highest among non-Hispanic black children in comparison with non-Hispanic white and Mexican-American children. The prevalence in 1999–2002 of elevated BLLs in the population (among persons aged one year or older) was 0.7%. (Refer to Figure 13–2.)

A frequent source of children's exposure to lead is paint. The use of lead-containing paint in residential construction was banned in 1978. Nevertheless, children may come into contact with lead in paint chips and dust from buildings constructed before the ban was introduced. Lead exposure from buildings is of particular concern to children and their families who reside in low-income areas. Some imported toys, jewelry, and lunchboxes for children have been demonstrated to contain possibly dangerous lead levels.

Electric and Magnetic Fields

Electric and magnetic fields are forms of energy known as non-ionizing radiation. Examples of sources of electric and magnetic fields are high-voltage electric lines, microwave ovens, stoves, clocks, electric blankets, toasters, and cellular telephones. Epidemiologic research has found an association between residential proximity to high-tension wires and childhood cancers.[21–24] London et al.[25] conducted a case-control study of leukemia risk among children in Los Angeles as a function of measured magnetic or electric fields and wiring configuration (e.g., overhead electric transmission and distribution facilities). They reported an association for wiring configuration and childhood leukemia risk but not for measured magnetic and electric fields. A second case-control study investigated everyone in Sweden under age 16 years who had lived on property within 300 meters of high-tension power lines during a 25-year period.[26] A total of 142 cancer cases were identified (including 39 leukemia cases and 33 central nervous system tumors) from the Swedish Cancer Registry. Models of historical exposure to

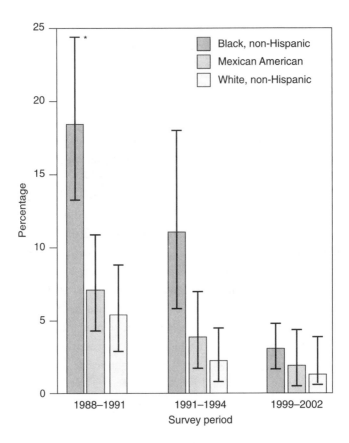

*95% confidence interval.

FIGURE 13–2 Percentage of children aged 1–5 years with blood lead levels ≥10 μg/dL, by race/ethnicity and survey period—National Health and Nutrition Examination Surveys, United States, 1988–1991, 1991–1994, and 1999–2002. *Source:* Centers for Disease Control and Prevention. *MMWR.* 2005, Vol 54, No 20, p. 515.

magnetic fields were used. The estimated relative risk for childhood leukemia increased at higher magnetic field exposure levels. Other research found no significant association between childhood leukemia and power lines.[27] Regarding other carcinogenic effects of exposure to electromagnetic radiation, research conducted in the United States and Norway reported an increased risk of male breast cancer (which is rare) among male electrical workers potentially exposed to electromagnetic fields.[28]

This field of epidemiologic inquiry, which has numerous methodologic challenges, provides a rich opportunity to address an important public policy issue. Among the methodologic issues is the precise measurement of residential and other exposure to electromagnetic radiation.[29] The issues of the association of electromagnetic fields with outcomes such as breast cancer, heart disease, suicide, and depression are controversial. With the expanding use of cellular telephones, some experts have explored the relationship between exposure to radiofrequency fields and cancer, especially brain tumors. Despite concerns about the possible carcinogenic effects of cellular telephone use, one of the major health effects of their use seems to be automobile accidents caused by inattentive drivers who do not pay attention to the road while talking on the telephone.

Ionizing Radiation

Ionizing radiation, a more intense form of energy than non-ionizing radiation, consists of either particle energy (e.g., highly energetic protons, neutrons, and α and β particles) or electromagnetic energy (e.g., γ-rays and X-rays). U.S. radiation sources comprise two main categories: natural radiation, which is responsible for the majority of the annual radiation exposure of the human population, and synthetic radiation. Natural radiation consists of radon, cosmic rays from outer space, and radiation from geologic sources. Synthetic sources are medical X-rays and agents used in nuclear medicine, consumer products, nuclear generators, and nuclear weapons explosions.

Examples of topics in the field of ionizing radiation of interest to epidemiologists are:

- Health effects associated with ionizing radiation from nuclear facilities and disposal of nuclear waste (discussed later in this chapter).
- Long-term consequences of exposure to radiation from nuclear weapons detonated as part of above-ground testing or used during warfare. For example, radiation from atomic bombs dropped in Japan was associated with increases in the risk of breast cancer, especially if exposure occurred between the ages of 10 and 19 years.[30]
- Intentional exposure of the population to ionizing radiation through terrorists' detonation of dirty bombs. In this scenario, terrorists would use conventional explosives to disperse radioactive materials. Emergency response agencies would need to have a protocol in place to deal with such an act. Although the radiation from a terrorist act would be confined to a

limited geographic area, this event would cause panic among the general population.

- Health effects associated with low-level exposures as in the case of patients who receive X-rays and diagnostic nuclear medicine tests. The dose of radiation received from medical tests is generally low and carries more benefits than risks. Nevertheless, the possibility for adverse health effects exists.
- Adverse impacts of occupational exposure to ionizing radiation. Important epidemiologic research questions include the effects of occupational exposure upon pregnant women and health outcomes associated with continuous long-term exposures at low levels.
- Effects of exposure to naturally occurring radiation such as that emitted by radon gas, as noted below.

Radon is an inert gas produced by the decay of radium and uranium, which are found universally in the earth's crust in varying amounts. Environmental radon produces one of the largest sources of human exposure to ionizing radiation. Up to 20% of U.S. lung cancers may be caused by radon despite evidence that cigarette smoking, asbestos exposure, and urban air pollution are the leading causes of lung cancer. Radon gas builds up in the basements of homes located in some regions of the United States. Radon exposure found in these residences is thought to be linked to cancer. Both lifetime risk of lung cancer and years of life lost show a dose-response increase with increasing radon exposure.[31]

Allergens and Molds

Allergens, found in ambient air and elsewhere in the environment, are substances that provoke an allergic reaction in susceptible persons. If susceptible, individuals can demonstrate a great deal of variation in their sensitivity and responses. The allergenic stimulus may consist of fur, pollen, or any of numerous other substances in the environment. Allergic reactions range from dermatitis, asthma, itchy eyes, and other uncomfortable sensations to anaphylactic shock.

Mold proliferates in moist environments and is omnipresent in the environment. In sensitive individuals molds produce health effects such as irritation of the respiratory system; symptoms may include wheezing and coughing. Some persons who have mold allergies may undergo more serious reactions. Patients who are immunocompromised can develop serious lung infections. Although reported in some research, other serious health effects, including memory loss and pulmonary hemorrhage among infants, have not been substantiated.[32]

While employed by a local health department, Robert Friis once investigated a community outbreak of respiratory disease symptoms alleged to be an allergy associated with molds that were growing in a certain housing tract. A visit to the area disclosed a large number of expensive homes that had been constructed with elegant sunken living rooms. After intense rainfall, the sunken areas flooded and remained permanently saturated with water. Molds of four different colors flourished on the nearby walls and carpets and resisted all attempts at elimination. Some of the residents began to complain of increased numbers of colds, respiratory illnesses, and allergic symptoms. The health department's serologic tests and questionnaire studies, however, did not reveal any increase in illness or symptoms above what might usually be expected. Investigators concluded that, in this instance, there was no statistically significant relationship between exposure to molds and lung diseases or other health conditions examined.

The 2005 Hurricanes Katrina and Rita caused severe flooding in the New Orleans area. One of the consequences was widespread mold growth, which created the specter of residents and workers being exposed to high levels of mold in buildings that had been inundated.[33]

Physical and Mechanical Energy

In addition to extremes of temperature, agents of physical and mechanical energy include traumatic forces, noise, and vibration. Traumatic forces are associated with unintentional injuries, as in automobile accidents or accidents in the home and workplace. Among the adverse effects of noise and vibration are hearing loss and musculoskeletal disorders.

Morbidity and mortality from the effects of physical and mechanical energy may be studied epidemiologically. Here is an example of the descriptive epidemiology of unintentional injury: In the United States between 1999 and 2004, unintentional injuries were the leading cause of death within the age group 1 to 44 years. Such injuries caused approximately 625,000 fatalities. The distribution of the respective percentages of deaths was as follows: motor vehicle-traffic injuries (41.0%), poisonings (15.5%), falls (15.0%), and suffocation (5.4%).[34] In view of the significance to society of deaths from unintentional injuries, epidemiologists should accord priority to this topic.

Another type of physical energy is high heat such as that associated with the postulated effects of global warming. One of the outcomes attributed to global warming (the gradual increase in the earth's surface temperature over time) has been extreme climatic conditions and high temperatures, for example, the heat waves observed in recent decades. Exhibit 13–1 reports on high temperature and mortality in the United States. Another example of the impact of high temperatures was the July 1995 episode in Chicago, during which an excess of at least

EXHIBIT 13–1

High Temperature and Mortality in the United States

High temperatures contribute to a significant number of deaths in the United States. When the ambient temperatures increase to high levels, the body may develop cramping, fainting, heat exhaustion, and heat stroke. Those who are most susceptible to heat-induced illness are the elderly, young children, and individuals with certain pre-existing medical conditions. Within the 5-year span of 1999 to 2003, the death certificates of 3,442 (annual mean = 688) persons listed excessive heat as either an underlying or contributing cause of death. Of the 3,442 deaths, excessive heat was listed as an underlying cause for 2,239 (65%), and hyperthermia was noted as a contributing cause for 1,203 (35%). For 681 (57%) of those with hyperthermia as a contributing cause of death, the underlying cause of death was cardiovascular disease. ■

Source: Data from Centers for Disease Control and Prevention. Heat-related deaths—United States, 1999–2003. *MMWR.* Vol 55, No 29, pp. 796–798, July 28, 2006.

700 deaths occurred at the same time as a record-breaking heat wave; most of this excess mortality was classified as heat-related. Semenza et al. conducted a case-control study of risk factors associated with heat-related and cardiovascular mortality.[35] The investigators reported that those at greatest risk of dying from heat-related causes did not have access to air conditioning or were socially isolated. Yet another example was the August 2003 calamity in Europe that caused at least 35,000 deaths.

Environmental Hazards Found in the Work Setting

Monitoring and Surveillance of Exposure to Occupational Hazards

Surveillance programs aid in the prevention of occupational illness. The programs can be used to identify occurrence of illness or injury in the workplace and to monitor trends in illnesses or injuries. The trends may vary by industry, geographic area, and over time, and suggest specific industries to be targeted for further investigation or intervention. Hazard surveillance refers to the characterization of known chemical, physical, and biologic agents in the workplace. If measurements demonstrate that the hazards are present in sufficient quantities to affect health, strategies can be used to reduce exposure of workers to those hazards.[36] Related to hazard surveillance is the concept of the sentinel health event, popularized by Rutstein and colleagues.[37] This concept facilitates the recognition of unhealthful workplaces. Seligman and Frazier stated, "A sentinel health event is a case of unnecessary disease, unnecessary disability, or untimely death whose occurrence is a warning signal that the quality of preventive or medical care may need to be improved."[38(p. 16)]

Biologic Hazards

Hospital employees, sewage workers, and agricultural workers are examples of persons who are potentially exposed to hazards from biologic agents of disease. Physicians and nurses come into direct contact with patients who may be affected by a communicable disease, sewage workers may be exposed to the hazards of disease carried in raw sewage, and agricultural workers are at increased risk of exposure to zoonotic diseases and disease agents contained in the soil. One study showed increased risk of hepatitis B among employees at a major urban hospital center.[39] Sources of infection included possible accidental needle punctures and errors in routine laboratory procedures. The hospital also had a large dialysis center that brought employees into direct contact with blood and blood products. Of great concern is the possible transmission of the human immunodeficiency virus through accidental needle sticks.

Mineral and Organic Dusts

Prolonged and even short-term exposure to dusts in the work environment can pose major health hazards to workers. One of the important contributions of epidemiology to the study of occupational exposure to dusts has been the identification of health risks and measures to control them. Among the notorious examples of occupational diseases resulting from exposure to dusts are black lung disease (also known as coal miners' pneumoconiosis) and silicosis, which occurs among sandblasters and others exposed to silica dust. Another example is the association between exposure to rubber dust and chronic obstructive pulmonary disease (COPD).[40] Rochette[41] found that the standardized mortality ratio for overall mortality was higher among coal miners than among the total U.S. male population. Mortality from nonmalignant respiratory disease, accidents, and stomach cancer also was higher than expected. Milham[42] reported an association between lung cancer and pulmonary emphysema among aluminum workers.

Industrial Chemicals

Exposures to vastly higher concentrations of chemicals may occur among workers than among the general population. Exposure to chemicals in the occupational setting averages 1 to 100 times higher than in the ambient environment.[43] Each year, an estimated 50,000 to 70,000 U.S. workers develop chronic occupational diseases produced by exposure to toxic chemicals in the workplace.[43]

Vapors and fumes represent a significant occupational hazard in many types of work. Given the yearly increase in the numbers of chemical substances and solvents that are utilized in the work environment, fumes and vapors are likely to become an increasing hazard to the health of workers. Various organic solvents, such as benzene and vinyl chloride, may act as carcinogenic agents.

Buffler et al.[44] discussed the relationship between exposure to vinyl chloride and angiosarcoma. In addition to being potential carcinogenic agents, organic solvents may damage internal organs of the body, the liver being especially vulnerable. Vinyl chloride, used in the plastics industry, has been associated with angiosarcoma of the liver and is described also as a carcinogenic substance related to lung and central nervous system tumors.[44] Workers in employment settings who are occupationally exposed to vinyl chloride have experienced the specific hazard of hepatic angiosarcoma. However, research evidence has not supported vinyl chloride as responsible for other cancers or nonmalignant diseases.[45]

Occupational exposure to pesticides such as organophosphates is of great potential concern for up to five million farm workers in the United States. Some of the acute effects of such exposure are nausea, vomiting, and vertigo.[46] Research investigations have suggested that the long-term effects of pesticide exposure include several types of cancer, miscarriages and teratogenic effects, sterility, spontaneous abortions, skin problems, respiratory difficulties, and cognitive deficits. However, a comprehensive literature review concluded that aside from the acute effects of pesticide exposure, clearly delineated long-term health effects have not been identified.[46] Some of the long-term effects may be nonspecific, e.g., fatigue, poor concentration, and dizziness. McCauley et al. argued that challenges to epidemiologic research in examining the association between farm workers' exposure to pesticides and health outcomes ". . . are determination of the population at risk; a valid determination of exposure; verification of diagnosis, symptom, or biological marker of a health effect among the populations being studied; methods to link individual exposure to health effects; and the ability to establish a temporal relationship between the exposure and the health effect. In attempts to study farmworker populations, these tools are often incomplete, dysfunctional, or nonexistent."[46(p. 954)]

Psychosocial Aspects of Employment and Health

Stresses and other psychosocial aspects of the work environment represent an important area of investigation for occupational health epidemiologists. Some of the findings related to this field of inquiry are reported in Chapter 15. Researchers have probed the psychosocial aspects of the job environment in great depth. Examples of research topics include work overload and coronary heart disease, job stresses and absenteeism due to infectious and chronic diseases, shift work and physical and mental health, health effects of physical activity at work, and variations in chronic disease mortality according to occupational status. A representative study reported that stress-related characteristics of work (e.g., overwork, time pressure, and high levels of mental demand) were associated with periodontal health status.[47]

Noteworthy Community Environmental Health Hazards

Not confined to the workplace, environmental hazards also impinge upon the community at large. Such potential hazards include chemicals from industrial sources and toxic waste dumps, air pollution, emissions of ionizing radiation from nuclear power facilities, and degradation of water quality. Examples of two specific community environmental health issues are the sick building syndrome and Gulf War syndrome (see Exhibits 13–2 and 13–3, respectively).

Hazardous Waste Sites

Globally and in the United States, hazardous waste sites represent a potential source of human exposure to toxic chemicals. Outside of the United States, the volume of hazardous wastes is increasing with growing industrialization of less developed regions of the world. Disposal of hi-tech trash has become the burden of developing countries. In the United States, more than 750 million tons of toxic chemical substances had been discarded into as many as 50,000 hazardous

EXHIBIT 13–2

The Sick Building Syndrome (SBS)

SBS has enormous potential for great economic impact from lost workdays, litigation, and workers' compensation claims. It is a condition that has several hypothesized etiologies, one being poor indoor air quality, which may affect health adversely. Indoor air quality became an issue during the 1970s when, in response to an energy crisis, buildings were made more airtight and ventilation rates were reduced.[48] Cases of SBS frequently occur in heavily populated, carpeted, and poorly cleaned buildings.

The term *sick building syndrome* was coined in 1983 at a World Health Organization meeting in Geneva to describe illnesses of office employees that included "dryness of the skin and mucous membranes, mental fatigue, headaches, general pruritis, and airway infections."[49] The prevalence of SBS has not been determined accurately because of the lack of a precise case definition and the absence of specific biologic markers.

Not only is the precise definition of SBS unclear, but it also bears some similarity to three other controversial disorders: multiple chemical sensitivity, chronic fatigue syndrome, and fibrositis. For example, all have fatigue as a component as well as sharing a nonspecific quality. One of the noteworthy features of SBS, in contrast to these other disorders, is temporality of symptoms; they begin when the affected person enters the building and diminish when the person leaves. One study showed that the prevalence of SBS symptoms decreased greatly when employees were exposed to an improved ventilation system.[50]

In addition to poor indoor air quality and inadequate ventilation, other proposed causes of SBS include exposure to volatile organic compounds (e.g., solvents), low humidity, airborne microbial agents—bacterial endotoxins, molds, dust mites—and tobacco smoke and odors.[48] Several psychosocial factors for SBS have been linked to the nature of some work environments: monotonous, authoritarian, and overly demanding.[48] Organizational stress—poor worker cooperation and physical and mental stress—may be an important component of the SBS.[51]

EXHIBIT 13-3

The Gulf War Syndrome (GWS)

Following the conclusion of the 1991 war in the Persian Gulf, veterans began to report symptoms of GWS.[52] As of the late 1990s, nearly 15% of the almost 700,000 U.S. veterans who served in this conflict complained of health conditions that they believed were the result of the war. Some of the veterans' health problems could be accounted for by standard medical or psychiatric diagnoses that were not connected with the war. Nevertheless, for many of the remaining ill veterans, GWS emerged as a common pattern or array of nonspecific, vague symptoms with uncertain etiology.[53]

An influential Presidential Advisory Committee on Gulf War Veterans' Illnesses suggested that GWS might be explained by wartime stress. GWS appeared to bear similarities to the posttraumatic stress disorder that was said to follow other wars. However, some reports have been critical of this explanation.[53]

Among other causes suggested for GWS were chronic fatigue syndrome, fibromyalgia, or exposure to nerve gas, which is known to be a cholinesterase inhibitor.[52] Possible contact with nerve gas might have occurred when U.S. troops destroyed an ammunition dump that was later found to contain traces of mustard gas and the potent nerve agent sarin.[54] A large number of troops were downwind from the dump. Many of the symptoms of GWS would be consistent with neurotoxicity from low-grade nerve gas poisoning, pesticides, or other cholinesterase inhibitors. Exposure to these agents might account for the muscle weakness, sweating, wheezing, and other symptoms that the affected Gulf War veterans reported.

An extensive review of U.S. Gulf War veterans' mortality and utilization of healthcare services noted that many large controlled studies ". . . revealed an increased post-war risk for mental health diagnoses, multi-symptom conditions and musculoskeletal disorders. Again, these data failed to demonstrate that Gulf War veterans suffered from a unique Gulf War-related illness."[55(p. 553)] A thorny issue for epidemiologic research on GWS is that the questions that must be asked are not clearly delineated, nor are the possible exposures involved. ■

waste sites as of the late 1980s.[56] Notorious toxic waste sites in the United States and the dates when they gained public attention include Love Canal, New York (1978); the Valley of the Drums in Kentucky (1967); Times Beach, Missouri (1985); the Stringfellow acid pits in California (1980s), and the Casmalia Waste Disposal Facility in California (1990s). A major public health concern is the potential impact upon human health of waste leachates emitted by disposal sites into community water supplies. Most communities in the United States receive water supplies from underground aquifers and surface water, which are at potential risk of contamination by toxic wastes. One study reported a statistically significant excess of some forms of cancer mortality among residents of counties that contain hazardous waste sites.[56]

Epidemiologic research into the health effects associated with hazardous waste sites confronts several methodologic difficulties. Because hazardous wastes involve a complex mixture of substances, it is difficult not only to sort out which chemicals affect human health, but also to determine how best to measure specific exposures in a valid and reliable manner. Some studies may not control adequately for potentially confounding factors and thus need to be interpreted with caution.[57] Measurement of the long-term effects of continuous exposure is difficult. Some of the research in this field is based upon small study samples, relatively few health events, statistically nonsignificant findings, and inadequate assessment of exposures. A technique for reducing the danger of misinterpretation inherent in a single study is the use of meta-analysis, which allows for the pooling of the results of all available research. In summary, epidemiologists face challenges in quantifying risks associated with hazardous waste sites. Not only is accurate exposure information difficult to obtain, but also the effects of low-level exposures are difficult to demonstrate.[58]

Reported adverse effects of hazardous waste exposure include birth outcomes (low birth weight and occurrence of congenital malformations or other birth defects), neurologic disease, cancer, synergistic effects, illness symptoms, and other adverse health conditions. A study of residents of Love Canal (which is located in upstate New York near Niagara Falls) showed an excess of low birth weights as well as growth retardation for those exposed compared with the general population and an excess of birth defects in residents closest to the site. The rate of respiratory cancer was similar to that for the Niagara Falls area, however.[57] An extensive case-control study of over 9,000 newborns with congenital malformations living in proximity to hazardous waste sites in New York state found a small but statistically significant risk for birth defects.[59] A population-based case-control study that reviewed vital records in Washington state for the years 1987 through 2001 suggested that residence near hazardous waste sites was not associated with fetal deaths, although living in proximity to sites that contained pesticides increased risk of fetal death.[60]

Air Pollution

Not only does air pollution lower our quality of life by obscuring the natural environment and, in some instances, by being malodorous, but it also has been implicated in adverse human health impacts. Many cities in the developed world have made strides in reducing air pollution levels. Unfortunately, severe episodes of air pollution are becoming increasingly common in the rapidly industrializing cities of developing countries. Noteworthy are the high levels in some of the large cities in China, the Middle East, South Asia, and Latin America. For example, air pollution associated with heart attacks exacts a significant toll in Iran; the residents of cities in India breathe excessive amounts of toxic pollutants. Regrettably, air quality standards in many developing countries are nonexistent or poorly enforced. Hazards from polluted air are not confined to the developing world. Several regions of the United States such as the Los Angeles Basin continue to have excessive air pollution levels.

Among the constituents of air pollution (although these vary from one location to another depending upon the types of fuels in use) are sulfur oxides, particles, oxidants (including ozone, carbon monoxide, hydrocarbons, and nitrogen oxides), lead, and some other heavy metals.[61] Indoor air pollution from cigarette smoke, gas stoves, and formaldehyde may pose a risk for respiratory illness.[62] Fine airborne particles can bypass the body's defenses, be inhaled deeply into the respiratory system, enter the circulatory system, and be distributed throughout the body. Another example related to indoor air pollution is the SBS,[63,64] described earlier in this chapter.

Major lethal air pollution episodes include those in Donora, Pennsylvania (1948); London, England (1952); and Meuse Valley in Western Europe (1930). Air pollution levels, which in many urban areas (e.g., Mexico City) are alarmingly high, are related to human mortality. Individuals who have preexisting heart and lung disease may be at particular risk for the fatal or aggravating effects of air pollution. Cigarette smoking and air pollution may act synergistically in aggravation of lung diseases, such as emphysema.[61]

A venerable example of research on air pollution's health effects is that conducted by Henderson et al.[65] Census tracts in Los Angeles were aggregated into 14 study areas that represented homogeneous air pollution profiles. The study reported a correlation between the geographic distribution of lung cancer cases and the general location of emission sources for hydrocarbons.

Other epidemiologic analyses have shown a correlation between increases in total daily mortality and increased air pollution in New York City.[66] Daily mortality also was related to gaseous and particulate air pollution in St. Louis, Missouri, and the counties in eastern Tennessee.[67] Researchers estimated the daily mortality rate associated with inhalable particles, fine particles, and aerosol acidity. The total mortality rate was found to have increased by 16% in St. Louis, Missouri, and by 17% in the eastern Tennessee counties. The data further suggested that the mass concentrations of particles have an association with daily mortality.

Carbon monoxide arises from cigarette smoking, automobile exhaust, and certain types of occupational exposures. An investigation into the possible association between angina pectoris and heavy freeway traffic found no direct association between myocardial infarction and ambient carbon monoxide. It was hypothesized that there was an indirect association between exposure to carbon monoxide in the ambient air and acute myocardial infarction through smoking, which is associated with elevated blood carbon monoxide levels.[68] An analysis of data from European cities demonstrated significant associations of carbon monoxide levels with total mortality and cardiovascular deaths.[69]

The air of one large metropolitan city exposed pedestrians and outdoor workers to carbon monoxide levels that ranged from 10 to 50 ppm; there were even higher levels in poorly ventilated areas of the city.[70] The recommended standard for carbon monoxide in ambient air is a maximum of 40 ppm, not to be exceeded more than once a year. Pedestrians and workers who have heart problems may be at increased risk of aggravation of their condition when exposed to high levels of ambient carbon monoxide in the urban environment.

In addition to all-cause mortality and chronic diseases such as lung cancer and heart disease, another condition linked to air pollution is COPD, which is among the top sources of morbidity and mortality in the United States and the world. A major investigation, the Tucson Epidemiological Study of Airways Obstructive Diseases, has tracked the etiology and natural history of obstructive lung disease.[71] Based on a multistage stratified cluster sample of white households in the Tucson, Arizona, area, the study has generated many important findings, including the effects of passive smoking in children.[72] Another report on the same topic comes from the Renfrew and Paisley (MIDSPAN) Study, a 25-year prospective investigation of 15,411 residents of west central Scotland. Information on respiratory symptoms and function was collected at baseline between 1972 and 1976. A total of 4,064 married couples from the original cohort were re-contacted in 1995. Allowing for subjects lost to follow-up and nonresponse, data were collected in 1996 from 1,477 families and their offspring (1,040 males and 1,298 females). The MIDSPAN study has yielded noteworthy insights into the natural history of COPD including a familial association of cigarette smoking and passive smoking with lowered cardiorespiratory health.[73]

The term *passive smoking*, also known as secondhand or sidestream exposure to cigarette smoke, refers to the involuntary breathing of cigarette smoke by nonsmokers in an environment where there are cigarette smokers present. In restaurants, waiting rooms, international airliners, and other enclosed areas where there are cigarette smokers, nonsmokers may be unwillingly (and, perhaps, unwittingly) exposed to a potential health hazard. The effects of chronic exposure to cigarette smoke in the work environment were examined in a cross-sectional study of 5,210 cigarette smokers and nonsmokers. Nonsmokers who did not work in a smoking environment were compared with nonsmokers who worked in a smoking environment as well as with smokers. Exposure to smoke in the work environment among the nonsmokers was associated with a statistically significant reduction in pulmonary function test measurements in comparison with the nonsmokers in the smoke-free environment.[74]

A 1992 report from the U.S. Environmental Protection Agency (EPA) concluded that environmental tobacco smoke is a human lung carcinogen responsible for approximately 3,000 lung cancer deaths annually among U.S. nonsmokers.[75] Among children, passive smoking is associated with bronchitis, pneumonia, fluid in the middle ear, asthma incidence, and aggravation of existing asthma. A review of data on 53,879 children from 12 cross-sectional studies concluded that parental smoking is related to respiratory symptoms such as wheezing, asthma, bronchitis, and nocturnal cough.[76] The 2006 U.S. Surgeon General's[77] report on the health consequences of involuntary exposure to tobacco concluded that "Secondhand smoke exposure causes disease and premature death in children and adults who do not smoke." In addition, the report noted that "Exposure of adults to secondhand smoke has immediate adverse effects on the cardiovascular system and causes coronary heart disease and lung cancer."

Research on passive smoking presents several methodologic difficulties.[78] Relatively small increases in risk of death from passive smoking are difficult to demonstrate in those situations where exposure assessment has not been well-developed, as in the use of questionnaires to quantify exposure. Studies need to account for long- and short-term variability in exposures to cigarette smoke from many sources (e.g., those at workplaces, restaurants, and entertainment venues). The long latency period between exposure to cigarette smoke and onset of disease contributes to the methodologic difficulties of this field of research. Additional research will require improved methods for assessing exposure to cigarette smoke, such as the use of biologic markers (e.g., cotinine).

Nevertheless, despite the complexity of assessing the relationship between exposure to environmental tobacco smoke and adverse health outcomes, the weight of the evidence supports the view that secondhand cigarette smoke poses health risks to children and adults. This inference is consistent with findings of research conducted in the United States and elsewhere. For example, EPIC is a massive European prospective cohort study of 500,000 participants.[79] A nested case-control study that incorporated information from more than 300,000 persons in the EPIC database demonstrated that exposure to environmental tobacco smoke increased the risk for respiratory diseases and lung cancer. Many countries, states, and localities now restrict cigarette smoking in areas such as the workplace, bars and restaurants, and airliners.

Nuclear Facilities

Nuclear facilities include weapons production plants, test sites, and nuclear power plants. In the United States, nuclear weapons have been produced at Oak Ridge, Tennessee; Hanford, Washington; and Rocky Flats in Denver, Colorado. Epidemiologists have studied the health effects of a nuclear accident at Three Mile Island, Pennsylvania, that occurred on March 26, 1979. One study reported that there was a modest association between postaccident cancer rates and proximity to the power plant. There was a postaccident increase in cancer rates during 1982 and 1983, which subsequently declined. Radiation emissions from the plant did not appear to account for the observed increase in cancer rates, however.[80]

The nuclear power plant accident at Chernobyl, Ukraine, in April 1986 was a major public health disaster that produced massive exposure of European populations to ionizing radiation. Radioactive materials, primarily iodine and cesium, were dispersed over the eastern part of the former Soviet Union, Sweden, Austria, Switzerland, and parts of Germany and northern Italy.[81] Preliminary epidemiologic research investigated the association between cases of childhood cancers (leukemia and lymphoma) and the accident. Although one study found a statistically significant increase in childhood cancers after the mishap, it was unclear whether these cases were linked to radiation from Chernobyl.[81]

Closer to the Chernobyl nuclear facility, however, there were marked increases in thyroid cancer as soon as four to five years after the accident. The Gomel region of Belarus in the former Soviet Union lies immediately to the north of Chernobyl. There was a sharp increase in thyroid cancer cases among children in Gomel from 1 to 2 per year during 1986–1989 to 38 in 1991.[82] These increases in the number of thyroid cancer cases suggested that the carcinogenic effect of radioactive fallout is much greater than previously believed.[83] Hatch et al.[84] concluded that thyroid cancer incidence was elevated among residents of areas contaminated by radiation when exposure occurred during childhood. Adults who resided in these same areas did not experience increased risk of thyroid cancer, leukemia, and other cancers. Workers who were exposed to radiation while cleaning up had increased risk of leukemia.

Another health effect of the Chernobyl accident could be the production of birth defects, such as congenital anomalies. Data from the EUROCAT epidemiologic surveillance of congenital anomalies did not suggest an increase in central nervous system anomalies or Down syndrome in Western Europe approximately five years after the incident.[85]

With the exception of cleanup workers directly exposed to radiation from Chernobyl, increases in incidence of cancers such as leukemia among other persons who resided away from the reactor and in other parts of Europe may be difficult to demonstrate. Currently, no method exists to distinguish between cases of leukemia that resulted from the Chernobyl disaster and cases that might be linked to other sources of ionizing radiation. In addition to radiation from the Chernobyl release, European populations also are exposed to natural background radiation and medical radiation.

In terms of cancer rates and proximity to other nuclear installations, studies with conflicting results have emerged. One study reported an excess of leukemia in a five-town area in Massachusetts in which one of the towns was the site of a commercial nuclear power plant. The excess cases were found mostly in adults and the elderly, but the authors believed that the results from this descriptive study were suggestive and warranted additional, more intensive follow-up investigations.[86] In contrast, no excess of cancer deaths was found among populations near the Rocky Flats nuclear weapons plant in Colorado[87] or the San Onofre nuclear power plant in California.[88] A systematic literature review concluded that, although many studies of the health effects of community exposure to radiation were statistically sound, they did not provide adequate quantitative estimates of radiation dose that could be used to assess dose-response relationships.[89]

There have been many studies of the health effects of above-ground atmospheric testing of nuclear weapons at the Nevada test site in the United States during the period from 1951 to 1958. Among the components of fallout from weapons testing is radioactive iodine, which may become concentrated in the thyroid gland, producing thyroid cancer. An ongoing epidemiologic project is a cohort study of young people who lived in proximity to the test site during infancy and childhood.[90] Three cohorts, similar in demographic and lifestyle characteristics, were selected. Two cohorts were from Washington County, Utah, and Lincoln County, Nevada, both on the west side of the test site, close to the site, and in the pathway of the heaviest fallout. A third cohort (unexposed) was selected from Graham County, far to the south of the test site. At 12 to 15 years and 30 years after the heaviest fallout, there was a slight but nonsignificant increase in rates of thyroid cancer among the two exposure cohorts in comparison with the control cohort. Thus, it was concluded that living near the Nevada test site did not produce a statistically significant increase in thyroid neoplasms.

Drinking Water

Public health experts increasingly have been concerned about possible degradation of the quality of water supplies in the United States due to development of polluting hi-tech industries, urbanization, and population growth. In fact, unavailability of adequate, reliable, and safe water resources is currently an issue for the residents of many countries worldwide, especially those in arid parts of the globe. Approximately one-sixth of the world's population lacks safe drinking water, and many of these who are most vulnerable are children. Sources of ground water contamination include industrial facilities (e.g., chemical plants and nuclear installations), new human habitation, and runoff from growing urbanized areas, all of which threaten the supply of potable water with permanent contamination from pesticides, industrial chemicals and solvents, radioactivity, and pathogenic microorganisms. The roles of environmental epidemiology in water quality include monitoring and control of infectious disease outbreaks and study of the health effects of low levels of toxic agents that may be present in the water supply. The problem of health hazards associated with low water quality is one that requires much additional epidemiologic study.

In the United States, water quality is regulated by the EPA, which sets drinking water standards for more than 80 contaminants that may be implicated in human health.[91] The contaminants are categorized according to whether they are responsible for acute effects (occurring within a few hours or days) or chronic effects (long-term after consumption for many years). Generally, microorganisms are responsible for the former, whereas contaminants that increase risk of chronic effects fall into the following classes: chemicals (pesticides, solvents, and byproducts of the disinfection of water), radionuclides, and minerals (arsenic and lead). Epidemiologic research has examined the relationship between exposure to the foregoing types of contaminants and outcomes such as cancer and disruption of reproductive processes. Much is unknown about the effects of organic compounds, such as pesticides, in water.

In addition to the types of contaminants noted in the preceding paragraph, particles, finely divided solids, may be found in drinking water supplies, especially those not treated by filtration. Although many of these particulate contaminants are not believed to be harmful, asbestos fibers may pose a hazard to health. The evidence regarding the toxicity of waterborne asbestos particles is not conclusive, however.

The use of chlorination and standard drinking water treatments adopted early in the 20th century have led to a decline in the incidence of gastroenteric diseases; implementation of EPA water quality regulations in the late 1980s has led to further reduction in the number of cases of waterborne diseases. In 2001 through 2002, a total of 31 waterborne disease outbreaks were reported in the United States; this number represented a decline of eight cases in comparison with the 1999 through 2000 time period. These 31 outbreaks involved approximately 1,020 persons and were associated with seven deaths.[92]

As noted previously, one type of chemical contaminants of drinking water is disinfection byproducts, which may be associated with adverse health effects. Epidemiologic research has suggested that tap water consumption might endanger pregnant women by causing spontaneous abortions. In response to media reports of epidemiologic research that linked water disinfection to adverse pregnancy outcomes, panicked citizens besieged public health officials with their concerns about the safety of the water supply. A flurry of reports and an acerbic public debate ensued for several weeks (see Exhibit 13–4).

Conclusion

Environmental epidemiology is the study of the impact of the environment on human health in populations. Epidemiologic methods can be used to investigate a wide variety of conditions that are thought to be associated with

EXHIBIT 13–4

Findings That Link Tap Water to Miscarriages Evoke Panic: Los Angeles Area Residents Urged To Show Prudence

"Reacting to a new study that suggests a possible link between drinking tap water and miscarriages by pregnant women in their first trimester, Los Angeles officials said Tuesday that the city's water often contains amounts of the suspect contaminants exceeding the levels that have triggered concern. But the officials advised prudence rather than panic."[93]

During early 1998, the media reported a possible association between use of tap water from public drinking water supplies and increased risk of miscarriages. Physicians were besieged by calls from anxious patients, and some young expectant couples agonized over how they would pay the cost of bottled water.

With increasing industrialization, urbanization, and population growth, some residential water supplies may carry dangerous pollution levels. Industrial solvents and chemicals as well as household pesticides may leach into aquifers or contaminate ground water that is used in tap water. Even when the public water supply is free from these sources of pollution, potentially dangerous chemicals may be released when the chlorine used to sanitize the water and kill microbial agents reacts with organic materials in the water. The resulting end products are known as trihalomethanes. The abbreviation TTHM is used to denote total trihalomethanes.

Epidemiologists Swan and colleagues, affiliated with California's Department of Health Services, published findings on potential reproductive health effects of drinking water use.[94] The investigators noted that TTHMs are found in nearly all U.S. drinking water supplies. TTHMs, which include chemicals such as chloroform, have possible associations with reproductive abnormalities in animal studies. Human exposure to TTHMs may be related to adverse pregnancy outcomes, such as spontaneous abortions.

In their research, Swan et al. addressed the specific issue of whether use of tap water was associated with adverse pregnancy outcomes in humans. The investigators' previous research (based on retrospective studies)

EXHIBIT 13–4 *continued*

reported an association between spontaneous abortion rates and use of tap water in comparison with bottled water among pregnant women in a single California county. In subsequent research (a prospective study), they followed pregnant women who resided in three California regions, two in the north (regions I and II) and one in the south (region III), served by the Kaiser Permanente Medical Care Program. The respective regions were served by one of three types of water: ground water mixed with surface water; primarily surface water; or primarily ground water. A total of 5,342 pregnant women completed interviews during the first trimester of their pregnancy. Information was collected on a range of topics, including medical history, lifestyle and psychosocial factors, and water consumption practices during the week beginning with the last menstrual period and the week before the interview. For example, information regarding use of cold tap water, heated tap water, noncarbonated bottled water, and carbonated water was assessed. Water consumption was quantitated in glasses per day. Finally, pregnancy outcomes were ascertained from various sources that included review of medical and vital records and telephone interviews.

The study demonstrated that spontaneous abortion rates were slightly different from one region to another, ranging from 9.2% to 10.1%. In region I only, consumption of cold tap water was associated with the occurrence of spontaneous abortions. High levels of tap water consumption were even more strongly related to the rate of spontaneous abortions. High consumption levels of bottled water in comparison to tap water seemed to be associated with a reduced rate of spontaneous abortions. Type of water consumption did not alter the risk of spontaneous abortion in the other two regions studied. Further research showed that one type of TTHM (bromodichloromethane) found in cold tap water was associated with spontaneous abortions.[95] ■

the physical environment and the work environment. Suspected health outcomes include morbidity and mortality from cancer, lung disease, birth defects, injuries and trauma, neurologic disease, and dermatologic problems. Many of the traditional study designs are used to conduct epidemiologic research into environmentally associated health problems. Toxicologic concepts also play a central role in this field of research. Suspected agents of environmentally associated disease include toxic chemicals, dusts, metals, and electromagnetic and ionizing radiation. Workers in many occupational settings are at risk of exposure to a wide variety of hazardous agents. Environmental health hazards that may affect the community include toxic waste dumps, air pollution, ionizing radiation from power plants and weapons testing, and polluted drinking water. Increases in the human population and urbanization are certain to perpetuate society's concern about health hazards potentially associated with the environment.

Study Questions and Exercises

1. Define the following terms:
   a. environmental epidemiology
   b. latency
   c. synergism
   d. threshold
   e. dose-response curve
   f. ionizing radiation
   g. hazard surveillance
2. A hypothetical community located near a large military base is suspected of having a toxic chemical present in the ground water. Propose the design of a case-control and a cohort study to examine the impacts on humans of exposures to the toxic chemicals.
3. An ecologic study reports an increase in mortality in census tracts that have high levels of air pollution in comparison with less polluted census tracts. What are some possible alternative explanations for the findings of the study?
4. What is meant by end points in occupational health studies? Discuss the advantages and disadvantages of using each of the following end points: self-reported symptoms, results of clinical examinations, and mortality.
5. How does the "healthy worker effect" influence the interpretation of findings from occupational health research? An epidemiologic researcher finds that mortality for assembly line workers in an automobile factory is slightly higher than the mortality of the general population.

Assume that the healthy worker effect is operative. Would it tend to decrease or increase mortality differences between the workers and the general population?

6. Name the four major classes of pesticides. What are some of the possible hazards associated with the organochloride pesticide DDT?

7. Discuss the possible long-term and short-term effects that farm workers may experience when they are exposed to organophosphate pesticides.

8. List examples of metallic compounds that pose environmental hazards. What are some examples of health effects thought to be associated with arsenic, mercury, and lead?

9. Discuss the possible health effects that have been associated with exposure to electric and magnetic fields and ionizing radiation. What methodologic difficulties exist with respect to investigations of the health effects of these forms of radiation?

10. Examples of environmental hazards found in the work setting include biologic agents, mineral and organic dusts, vapors, and occupational stress. What are possible roles for epidemiologists in designing research studies to investigate and control exposures to these hazards?

11. Identify challenges and opportunities for epidemiology from the following environmental health problems: hazardous waste sites, air pollution, and nuclear electricity generating plants.

12. Name three historically important lethal air pollution episodes. What countries or regions of the world are currently faced with extremely poor air quality?

13. Describe two major adverse health outcomes associated with air pollution. Give your own opinions about what can be done to control air pollution.

14. Define the term *passive smoking*. State why public health officials are concerned about exposure to secondhand tobacco smoke. What is being done to control secondhand tobacco smoke?

15. Describe the 1986 incident in Chernobyl. What health effects have been studied in relation to this event? Have similar events occurred in the United States?

16. Why is the availability of a reliable and safe water source a concern to officials in the United States and the rest of the world? What types of challenges impact the availability of a safe water supply? What is meant by the term *TTHM*, and why is it relevant to water quality?

17. Regarding the various environmental epidemiologic topics covered in this chapter, name three common challenges that relate to exposure assessment.

References

1. Prüss-Üstün A, Corvalán C. *Preventing Disease through Healthy Environments: Towards an Estimate of the Environmental Burden of Disease.* Geneva, Switzerland: World Health Organization; 2006.
2. Friis RH. *Essentials of Environmental Health.* Sudbury, MA: Jones and Bartlett Publishers; 2007.
3. National Institute for Occupational Safety and Health (NIOSH). The Effects of Workplace Hazards on Female Reproductive Health. DHHS (NIOSH) Publication No. 99-104. Cincinnati, OH: NIOSH; 1999.
4. Wegman DH. The potential impact of epidemiology on the prevention of occupational disease. *Am J Public Health.* 1992;82:944–954.
5. Lebowitz MD, Burrows B, Traver GA, et al. Methodological considerations of epidemiological diagnoses in respiratory diseases. *Eur J Epidemiol.* 1985;1:188–192.
6. Monson RR. *Occupational Epidemiology,* 2nd ed. Boca Raton, FL: CRC Press; 1990.
7. Lave LB, Seskin EP. Air pollution and human health. *Science.* 1970;169:723–733.
8. Klaassen CD, Watkins JB III, eds. *Casarett and Doull's Essentials of Toxicology.* New York, NY: The McGraw-Hill Companies, Inc.; 2003.
9. Thayer KA, Melnick R, Burns K, et al. Fundamental flaws of hormesis for public health decisions. *Environ Health Perspect.* 2005;113:1271–1276.
10. Selikoff IJ, Cuyler HE, Chung J. Asbestos exposure, smoking, and neoplasia. *JAMA.* 1968;204:106–112.
11. The Breast Cancer Fund. Chemical Fact Sheets: Organochlorine Pesticides. Available at: http://www.breastcancerfund.org/site/pp.asp?c=kwKXLdPaE&b=84567. Accessed December 23, 2007.
12. Centers for Disease Control and Prevention. Spotlight on Organochlorine Pesticides. CDC's *Third National Report on Human Exposure to Environmental Chemicals.* Atlanta, GA: CDC, 2005. Available at: http://www.cdc.gov/exposurereport/pdf/factsheet_organochlorine.pdf. Accessed December 24, 2007.
13. Selikoff IJ, Chung J, Hammond EC. Asbestosis exposure and neoplasia. *JAMA.* 1964;188:142–146.
14. Peters GR, McCurdy RF, Hindmarsh JT. Environmental aspects of arsenic toxicity. *Crit Rev Clin Lab Sci.* 1996;33:457–493.
15. Jager JW, Ostrosky-Wegman P. Arsenic: a paradoxical human carcinogen. *Mutat Res.* 1997;386:181–184.
16. Cantor KP. Arsenic in drinking water: how much is too much? *Epidemiology.* 1996;7:113–115.
17. Hopenhayn-Rich C, Biggs ML, Fuchs A, Bergoglio R, Tello EE, Nicolli-Smith AH. Bladder cancer mortality associated with arsenic in drinking water in Argentina. *Epidemiology.* 1996;7:117–124.
18. Powell PP. Minamata disease: a story of mercury's malevolence. *South Med J.* 1991; 84:1352–1358.

19. Centers for Disease Control and Prevention. Blood lead levels—United States, 1999–2002. *MMWR*. 2005;54(20):513–516.

20. Centers for Disease Control and Prevention. Surveillance for elevated blood lead levels among children—United States, 1997–2001. *MMWR Surveill Summ*. 2003; 52(No. SS-10):1–8.

21. Draper G, Vincent T, Kroll ME, Swanson J. Childhood cancer in relation to distance from high voltage power lines in England and Wales: a case-control study. *Br Med J*. 2005;330:1290–1293.

22. Wertheimer N, Leeper E. Electrical wiring configurations and childhood cancer. *Am J Epidemiol*. 1979;109:273–284.

23. Tomenius L. 50-Hz electromagnetic environment and the incidence of childhood tumors in Stockholm County. *Bioelectromagnetics*. 1986;7:191–207.

24. Savitz DA, Wachtel H, Barnes FA, et al. Case-control study of childhood cancer and exposure to 60-Hz magnetic fields. *Am J Epidemiol*. 1988;128:21–38.

25. London SJ, Thomas DC, Bowman JD, et al. Exposure to residential electrical and magnetic fields and risk of childhood leukemia. *Am J Epidemiol*. 1991;134:923–937.

26. Feychting M, Ahlbom A. Magnetic fields and cancer in children residing near Swedish high-voltage power lines. *Am J Epidemiol*. 1993;138:467–481.

27. Fulton JP, Cobb S, Preble L, et al. Electrical wiring configurations and childhood leukemia in Rhode Island. *Am J Epidemiol*. 1980;111:292–296.

28. Thomas DB. Breast cancer in men. *Epidemiol Rev*. 1993;15:220–231.

29. Ahlbom A, Cardis E, Green A, et al. Review of the epidemiologic literature on EMF and health. *Environ Health Perspect*. 2001;109 (Suppl 6):911–933.

30. Tokunaga M, Norman JE, Asano M, et al. Malignant breast tumors among atomic bomb survivors, Hiroshima and Nagasaki, 1950–1974. *J Natl Cancer Inst*. 1979; 62:1347–1359.

31. Vonstille WT. Radon and cancer. *J Environ Health*. 1990;53:25–27.

32. Centers for Disease Control and Prevention. Mold: Facts About Mold and Dampness. Available at: http://www.cdc.gov/mold/dampness_facts.htm. Accessed December 24, 2007.

33. Centers for Disease Control and Prevention. Health concerns associated with mold in water-damaged homes after Hurricanes Katrina and Rita—New Orleans area, Louisiana, October 2005. *MMWR*. 2006;55(2):41–44.

34. Centers for Disease Control and Prevention. State-specific unintentional-injury deaths—United States, 1999-2004. *MMWR*. 2007;56(43):1137–1140.

35. Semenza JC, Rubin CH, Falter KH, et al. Heat-related death during the July 1995 heat wave in Chicago. *N Engl J Med*. 1996;335:84–90.

36. Baker EL, Matte TP. Surveillance of occupational illness and injury. In: Halperin W, Baker EL Jr, Monson RR, eds. *Public Health Surveillance*. New York, NY: Van Nostrand Reinhold; 1992.

37. Rutstein DD, Mullan RJ, Frazier TM, et al. Sentinel health events (occupational): a basis for physician recognition and public health surveillance. *Am J Public Health*. 1983;73:1054–1062.

38. Seligman PJ, Frazier TM. Surveillance: the sentinel health event approach. In: Halperin W, Baker EL Jr, Monson RR, eds. *Public Health Surveillance*. New York, NY: Van Nostrand Reinhold; 1992:16–25.

39. Schneider WJ. Hepatitis B: an occupational hazard of health care facilities. *J Occup Med*. 1979;21:807–810.

40. Lednar WM, Tyroler HA, McMichael AJ, Shy CM. The occupational determinants of chronic disabling pulmonary disease in rubber workers. *J Occup Med.* 1977; 19:263–268.

41. Rochette HE. Cause specific mortality of coal miners. *J Occup Med.* 1977; 19:795–801.

42. Milham S. Mortality in aluminum reduction plant workers. *J Occup Med.* 1979; 21:475–480.

43. Landrigan PJ. Commentary: environmental disease—a preventable epidemic. *Am J Public Health.* 1992;82:941–943.

44. Buffler PA, Wood S, Eifler C, et al. Mortality experience of workers in a vinyl chloride monomer production plant. *J Occup Med.* 1979;21:195–203.

45. Doll R. Effects of exposure to vinyl chloride: an assessment of the evidence. *Scand J Work Environ Health.* 1988;14:61–78.

46. McCauley LA, Anger WK, Keifer M, et al. Studying health outcomes in farmworker populations exposed to pesticides. *Environ Health Perspect.* 2006;114:953–960.

47. Marcenes WS, Sheiham A. The relationship between work stress and oral health status. *Soc Sci Med.* 1992;35:1511–1520.

48. Horvath EP. Building-related illness and sick building syndrome: from the specific to the vague. *Cleve Clin J Med.* 1997;64:303–309.

49. Bardana EJ. Sick building syndrome—a wolf in sheep's clothing. *Ann Allergy Asthma Immunol.* 1997;79:283–293.

50. Bourbeau J, Brisson C, Allaire S. Prevalence of the sick building syndrome symptoms in office workers before and six months and three years after being exposed to a building with an improved ventilation system. *Occup Environ Med.* 1997;54:49–53.

51. Ooi P, Goh K. Sick building syndrome: an emerging stress-related disorder. *Int J Epidemiol.* 1997;26:1243–1249.

52. Roberts J. New U.S. theory on Gulf War syndrome. *Br Med J.* 1996;312:1058.

53. Haley RW. Is Gulf War syndrome due to stress?: the evidence reexamined. *Am J Epidemiol.* 1997;146:695–703.

54. Roberts J. US responds to new suggestion of Gulf War syndrome. (News) *Br Med J.* 1996;312:1629.

55. Gray GC, Kang HK. Healthcare utilization and mortality among veterans of the Gulf War. *Phil Trans R Soc B.* 2006;361:553–569.

56. Griffith J, Riggan WB. Cancer mortality in U.S. counties with hazardous waste sites and ground water pollution. *Arch Environ Health.* 1989;44:69–74.

57. Najem GR, Cappadona JL. Health effects of hazardous chemical waste disposal sites in New Jersey and in the United States: a review. *Am J Prev Med.* 1991;7:352–362.

58. Vrijheid M. Health effects of residence near hazardous waste landfill sites: a review of epidemiologic literature. *Environ Health Perspect.* 2000;108(Suppl 1):101–112.

59. Geschwind SA, Stolwijk JAJ, Bracken M, et al. Risk of congenital malformations associated with proximity to hazardous waste sites. *Am J Epidemiol.* 1992;135: 1197–1207.

60. Mueller BA, Kuehn CM, Shapiro-Mendoza CK, Tomashek KM. Fetal deaths and proximity to hazardous waste sites in Washington state. *Environ Health Perspect.* 2007;115:776–780.

61. Mitchell RS, Judson FN, Moulding TS, et al. Health effects of urban air pollution. *JAMA.* 1979;242:1163–1168.

62. Lebowitz MD, Holberg CJ, Boyer B, Hayes C. Respiratory symptoms and peak flow associated with indoor and outdoor air pollutants in the southwest. *J Air Pollut Control Assoc.* 1985;35:1154–1158.

63. Jaakkola JJK, Tuomaala P, Seppänen O. Air recirculation and sick building syndrome: a blinded crossover trial. *Am J Public Health.* 1994;84:422–428.

64. Mendell MJ, Fine L. Building ventilation and symptoms—where do we go from here? *Am J Public Health.* 1994;84:346–348.

65. Henderson BE, Gordon RJ, Menck H, et al. Lung cancer and air pollution in south-central Los Angeles County. *Am J Epidemiol.* 1975;101:477–488.

66. Schimmel H, Greenberg L. A study of the relation of pollution to mortality: New York City, 1963–1968. *J Air Pollut Control Assoc.* 1972;22:607–616.

67. Dockery DW, Schwartz J, Spengler JD. Air pollution and daily mortality: associations with particulates and acid aerosols. *Environ Res.* 1992;59:362–373.

68. Kuller LH, Radford EP, Swift DP, et al. Carbon monoxide and heart attacks. *Arch Environ Health.* 1975;30:477–482.

69. Samoli E, Touloumi G, Schwartz J, et al. Short-term effects of carbon monoxide on mortality: an analysis within the APHEA Project. *Environ Health Perspect.* 2007; 115:1578–1583.

70. Wright GR, Jewizyk S, Onrot J, et al. Carbon monoxide in the urban atmosphere. *Arch Environ Health.* 1975;30:123–129.

71. Lebowitz MD, Holberg CJ, Knudson RJ, Burrows B. Longitudinal study of pulmonary function development in childhood, adolescence, and early adulthood. *Am Rev Respir Dis.* 1987;136:69–75.

72. Lebowitz MD. The relationship of socio-economic factors to the prevalence of obstructive lung diseases and other chronic conditions. *J Chronic Dis.* 1977;30: 599–611.

73. Mannino DM, Watt G, Hole D, et al. The natural history of chronic obstructive pulmonary disease. *Eur Respir J.* 2006;27:627–643.

74. White JR, Froeb HF. Small-airways dysfunction in nonsmokers chronically exposed to tobacco smoke. *N Engl J Med.* 1980;302:720–723.

75. US Environmental Protection Agency (EPA). *Respiratory Health Effects of Passive Smoking: Lung Cancer and Other Disorders.* EPA publication 600/6-90/006F. Washington, DC: EPA; 1992.

76. Pattenden S, Antova T, Neuberger M, et al. Parental smoking and children's respiratory health: independent effects of prenatal and postnatal exposure. *Tob Control.* 2006;15:294–301.

77. U.S. Department of Health and Human Services. *The Health Consequences of Involuntary Exposure to Tobacco Smoke: A Report of the Surgeon General.* 6 Major Conclusions of the Surgeon General Report. U.S. Department of Health and Human Services, Centers for Disease Control and Prevention, National Center for Chronic Disease Prevention and Health Promotion, Office on Smoking and Health, 2006. Available at: http://www.surgeongeneral.gov/library/secondhandsmoke/factsheets/factsheet6.html. Accessed December 26, 2007.

78. Boyle P. The hazards of passive—and active—smoking. *N Engl J Med.* 1993; 328:1708–1709.

79. Vineis P, Airoldi L, Veglia F, et al. Environmental tobacco smoke and risk of respiratory cancer and chronic obstructive pulmonary disease in former smokers and never smokers in the EPIC prospective study. *Br Med J.* 2005;330:277–280.

80. Hatch M, Wallenstein S, Beyea J, et al. Cancer rates after the Three Mile Island nuclear accident and proximity of residence to the plant. *Am J Public Health.* 1991; 81:719–724.

81. Vanchieri C. Chernobyl has no early effect on childhood leukemia. (News) *J Natl Cancer Inst.* 1992;84:1616.

82. Kazakov VS, Demidchik EP, Astakhova LN. Thyroid cancer after Chernobyl. (Letter) *Nature.* 1992;359:21.

83. Beaverstock K, Egloff B, Pinchera A, Ruchti C, Williams D. Thyroid cancer after Chernobyl. (Letter) *Nature.* 1992;359:21–22.

84. Hatch M, Ron E, Bouville A, et al. The Chernobyl disaster: cancer following the accident at the Chernobyl nuclear power plant. *Epidemiol Rev.* 2005;27:56–66.

85. Dolk H, Lechat MF. Health surveillance in Europe: lessons from EUROCAT and Chernobyl. *Int J Epidemiol.* 1993;22:363–368.

86. Clapp R, Cobb S, Chan C, Walker B. Leukemia near Massachusetts nuclear power plant. (Letter) *Lancet.* 1987;2:1324–1325.

87. Johnson CJ. Cancer incidence in an area contaminated with radionuclides near a nuclear installation. *Ambio.* 1981;10:176–182.

88. Enstrom JE. Cancer mortality patterns around the San Onofre nuclear power plant, 1960–1978. *Am J Public Health.* 1983;73:83–91.

89. Shleien B, Ruttenber AJ, Sage M. Epidemiologic studies of cancer in populations near nuclear facilities. *Health Phys.* 1991;61:699–713.

90. Rallison ML, Lotz TM, Bishop M, et al. Cohort study of thyroid disease near the Nevada test site: a preliminary report. *Health Phys.* 1990;59:739–746.

91. United States Environmental Protection Agency. *Drinking Water and Health: What You Need to Know!.* EPA 816-K-99-001. Washington, DC: Office of Water; 1999.

92. Blackburn BG, Craun GF, Yoder JS, et al. Surveillance for waterborne-disease outbreaks associated with drinking water—United States, 2001–2002. *MMWR Surveill Summ.* 2004;53(No. SS-8):23–39.

93. Newton J, Maugh TH II. Water officials suggest prudence, not panic. *Los Angeles Times.* February 11, 1998, p. 1.

94. Swan SH, Waller K, Hopkins B, et al. A prospective study of spontaneous abortion. Relation to amount and source of drinking water consumed in early pregnancy. *Epidemiology.* 1998;2:126–133.

95. Waller K, Swan SH, DeLorenze G, Hopkins B. Trihalomethanes in drinking water and spontaneous abortion. *Epidemiology.* 1998;9:134–140.

CHAPTER 14

Molecular and Genetic Epidemiology

LEARNING OBJECTIVES

By the end of this chapter the reader will be able to:

- state the fundamental differences between molecular and genetic epidemiology
- describe the basic principles of inheritance and sources of genetic variation
- identify at least three reasons for the familial aggregation of a given disease
- define epidemiologic approaches for the identification of genetic components to disease
- explain the basic principles of segregation and linkage analysis
- state research applications of molecular and/or genetic epidemiology in infectious diseases, cancer, and other chronic diseases

CHAPTER OUTLINE

I. Introduction
II. Definitions and Distinctions: Molecular Versus Genetic Epidemiology
III. Epidemiologic Evidence for Genetic Factors
IV. Causes of Familial Aggregation
V. Shared Family Environment and Familial Aggregation

VI. Gene Mapping: Segregation and Linkage Analysis
VII. Genome-Wide Association Studies (GWAS)
VIII. Linkage Disequilibrium Revisited: Haplotypes
IX. Application of Genes in Epidemiologic Designs
X. Genetics and Public Health
XI. Conclusion
XII. Study Questions and Exercises

Introduction

Mapping of the human genome and the subsequent advances in molecular biology forever changed epidemiologic research on disease etiology. (Refer to Figure 14–1 for a photograph of the deoxyribonucleic acid [DNA] helix.) Gone are the days when measurements of exposure are limited to simple interview data, mailed questionnaires, inspection of secondary data, and surrogate measures of the primary exposure of interest. The value of descriptive epidemiology and disease monitoring and surveillance remain important applications of epidemiology. However, modern epidemiologists find themselves armed with several new strategies to assess precursors of disease, identify biologic markers of exposure, and search for the biologic bases for responses. The wide differential in human responses to the same environmental exposure is an intriguing issue for epidemiology that may be explored by using these advanced techniques.

The traditional epidemiologic approach—characterized by examination of the distribution of health conditions in populations and discerning risk factors for them—has proved useful for generating hypotheses and unraveling disease etiologies. However, suppose that it were possible to go beyond these methods and look inside the "black box" of disease processes. If this black box were to become transparent, epidemiologists would be able to change the definition of risk factors or clarify their location in a causal model.[1]

This chapter presents an overview of this rapidly growing area of epidemiology. For readers without a strong background in biology, we begin with a review of basic principles of human genetics (Exhibit 14–1). This review is followed by definitions of the terms *genetic epidemiology* and *molecular epidemiology* and an attempt to distinguish one from the other. We then present several epidemiologic

FIGURE 14–1   Model of the DNA helix. *Source:* Photodisc.

approaches to identify genetic components of disease, provide an overview of the strategies that geneticists use to identify genes in studies of families, and present a description of the latest trend: genome-wide association studies (GWAS). The chapter provides examples of this exciting new frontier, and concludes with an overview of how the field of genetics has and will continue to influence the practice of public health.

Definitions and Distinctions: Molecular Versus Genetic Epidemiology

It is becoming increasingly fashionable to be a hyphen-epidemiologist. That is, rarely is it sufficient to describe oneself as a "simple country epidemiologist" anymore. Many folks in the field add some sort of modifier to their title, for example, pharmaco-epidemiologist, behavioral-epidemiologist, or neuro-epidemiologist. To this partial list we must add molecular-epidemiologist and

EXHIBIT 14–1

Basic Principles of Human Genetics

Readers with a prior background in molecular biology and genetics (MBG) may be tempted to skip this section. It is primarily intended to be a refresher for readers who have some familiarity with MBG or who have been away from the topic. However, we include some discoveries about the nature of the genetic code with which you may not be familiar. For readers with limited grounding in MBG, this brief review may be insufficient. You are encouraged to pursue additional details in one of several fine textbooks on human genetics. In order of simplest to most complex, we recommend the following texts:

Mange EJ, Mange AP. *Basic Human Genetics,* 2nd ed. Sunderland, MA: Sinauer Associates, Inc; 1999.

Vogel F, Motulsky AG. *Human Genetics: Problems and Approaches*, 3rd ed. Heidelberg, Germany: Springer; 1996.

Singer M, Berg P. *Genes & Genomes: A Changing Perspective*. Mill Valley, CA: University Science Books; 1991.

The Genetic Code

The genetic code is the blueprint of instructions to make our body. These instructions, coded in the form of DNA, are passed on from parents to their children at the time of conception and are recorded using a very simple "alphabet" of only four "letters:" A, C, G, and T. These represent four different nucleic acids—adenine, cytosine, guanine, and thymine—that are used to spell "words," called *codons*. Each codon ("word") contains only three "letters" and represents the codes to construct amino acids.

Although the genetic alphabet contains only four letters (deoxyribonucleic acids), they can be combined to code for 64 different codons (amino acids). However, the human body is composed of only 20 amino acids, some of which can be encoded in more than one way. This possibility means that our genetic code is *degenerate,* meaning that most amino acids can be specified in several ways. The only exceptions to coding in several ways are methionine (TAC) and the least frequent amino acid, tryptophan (ACC), which are encoded in one unique way. In fact, nine amino acids can be coded in two different ways, one can be coded three different ways,

continues

EXHIBIT 14–1 *continued*

five can be coded four different ways, and three can be coded with six different codons. Three codons do not code for an amino acid, but rather signal the end of the gene (ACT, ATT, ATC).

The amino acids ("words") are strung together in long sequences to form "sentences." These sentences are the complete instructions to make a specific protein in a part of our body—such as skin, hair, red blood cells, bone, nerve spindles—or the enzymes, hormones, and growth factors that regulate our body and make us what we are. A *gene* is the genetic code corresponding to one "sentence."

Physical Arrangement of DNA

Although the coded instructions for making our body are contained in linear sequences of DNA (representing roughly 3 billion bases), these sequences are not one long garbled string of genes. Rather, the units of DNA themselves are organized onto chromosomes. Each human should have 23 pairs of chromosomes: one pair to determine sex and 22 pairs of *autosomes*. Each chromosome differs in size and is numbered from 1 to 22. Women have two X chromosomes (one from the mother and one from the father) and men have one X from their mother and a Y chromosome from their father. Transmission of chromosomes from parents to offspring occurs through the formation of gametes during a process called *meiosis*. For men, meiosis is the production of sperm, and occurs throughout life. For women, meiosis leads to the production of oocytes, or eggs. As opposed to men, women are born with their full complement of oocytes, but only one or two are allowed to mature each month during their years of reproductive potential. Normal sperm and oocytes contain only one copy of each chromosome, so at the time of conception a full complement of 23 pairs of chromosomes is formed.

From DNA to Protein

There are several important things to know about the human genome. The first point is that not all DNA contained in our cells is transcribed into protein. Second, within a region of DNA on a particular chromosome that codes for a gene, only certain segments are *transcribed*—the process by

continues

EXHIBIT 14–1 *continued*

which DNA is copied into RNA (ribonucleic acid)—and *translated*—the process by which RNA is read and proteins are assembled. That is, the sequence of nucleic acids that determine the order and length of amino acids needed to build a certain protein is not necessarily a straight run. Certain stretches of DNA will be copied (called *exons* or *expressed sequences*) and other stretches of DNA will be essentially ignored (called *introns* or *intervening sequences*). As an extreme example, the gene that codes for clotting factor VIII (and is mutated in persons with hemophilia) has 26 exons that code for about 2,000 amino acids. However, these codes represent only about 4% of the total length of the gene! The final, and most important, point is that individuals differ from one another in terms of their DNA. Although all humans can be thought of as having essentially the same number of genes, they clearly do not have identical sequences of DNA. Several recent discoveries have revealed that the genome is far more complex. For example, the amount of DNA individuals carry is not identical, with the difference in genomic size between two individuals being as large as 9 million base pairs.[2]

Genetic Variation

How is DNA different from one person to another? Although the complete story is beyond the scope of this chapter, suffice it to say that changes can occur in a wide variety of ways. A *mutation* is defined as a change in DNA that may adversely affect the host. One category of mutations, known as *frameshift mutations*, is the result of deletions or insertions of one or more DNA bases. These mutations not only alter the codon in which they occur, but also may shift the *reading frame* of all successive three-letter words.

Another type of mutation is one that changes the chemical structure of one nucleic acid to that of another. Because most amino acids can be formed from more than one combination of nucleic acids, sometimes mutations can be "silent" and not result in a change in amino acid. For example, a mutation from AAA to AAG would still lead to the incorporation of phenylalanine. Thus, although the sequence of DNA has changed, the amino acid sequence of the transcribed protein has not. Alternatively, the alteration of a single codon can have a profound effect. For example, a

continues

EXHIBIT 14–1 *continued*

mutation of T to A in the middle base of the sixth codon for the b chain of hemoglobin changes the amino acid from glutamine to valine. The result is a change in the shape of hemoglobin from smooth and rounded to distorted, and ultimately a disease known as sickle-cell anemia.

Mutations also can occur within *introns*, the noncoding regions of DNA, which would be expected to have little effect on the protein product of that gene. Recent evidence suggests that even mutations in introns can sometimes have a profound effect on the protein product of a gene. The most serious, and easiest to recognize, mutations are ones in which a mutation in a nucleic acid produces an inadvertent *"stop" codon* that signals the end of transcription before the full-length gene product can be transcribed. The result is a protein that is shorter than normal, or truncated, with a corresponding effect on its function or integrity.

Alterations can be much larger in scale than a single base pair. Recent studies show that alterations may be as large as one thousand to several thousand base pairs.[3,4] The concept of "copy number variations" (CNVs) also has been established recently. The concept CNV refers to a situation in which the number of copies of a gene differs between individuals.[1] Interestingly, many of these CNVs have been identified in human genes that reflect senses (smell, hearing, taste, and sight) and disease susceptibility. It has been hypothesized that several thousand of these CNVs occur; their presence raises important questions about their public health significance.

Review of Genetic Terminology

Having finished this brief review of DNA and genetic variation, we present a few more definitions. The basic unit of heredity is a *gene*, the particular segment of a DNA molecule on a chromosome that determines the nature of an inherited trait. An *allele* is one of two or more alternative forms of a gene that occurs at the same *locus*. Of course, we have not yet defined a locus, either. It is the site or location on a chromosome occupied by a gene (i.e., a particular set of alleles). The *genotype* of an individual refers to his or her genetic constitution, often stated in reference to a specific trait or at a particular locus. The *phenotype* is the realized expression of the genotype, or the observable physical appearance or functional expression of a gene. An

continues

EXHIBIT 14–1 *continued*

important situation in which genetics intersects with epidemiology happens when a genotype is modified (or interacts with environment) to affect a phenotype (disease). Another important term is *Mendelian inheritance* (named for its discoverer, the 19th century Austrian monk, Gregor Mendel), which denotes the transmission of a disease or trait from parents to offspring according to simple laws of inheritance. ■

genetic-epidemiologist, terms that many people use interchangeably. We describe in which respects these two fields overlap, how they differ, and how recent technological advances in a type of genotyping called high throughput genotyping are reuniting molecular and genetic epidemiology. (Throughput refers to the amount of work that can be performed in a given period of time.)

Genetic Epidemiology

The field of *genetic epidemiology* is devoted to the identification of inherited factors that influence disease, and how variation in the genetic material interacts with environmental factors to increase (or decrease) risk of disease. A popular textbook on the subject defines it as a "discipline that seeks to unravel the role of genetic factors and their interactions with environmental factors in the etiology of diseases, using family and population study approaches."[5] An important premise of the field is that a better understanding of the genetic etiology of disease can facilitate early detection in high-risk subjects and the design of more effective intervention strategies.[6] The unifying theme of genetic epidemiology is the focus on genes and evidence for genetic influences.

Genetic epidemiology can be thought of as a collection of methodologies designed to answer four questions:

1. Does the disease of interest cluster in families?
2. Is the clustering a reflection of shared lifestyle, common environment, or similar risk factor profiles?
3. Is the pattern of disease (or risk factor for a disease) within families consistent with the expectations under Mendelian transmission of a major gene?
4. Where is the chromosomal location of the putative gene?

Note that to answer questions two through four, families (or at least pairs of relatives) are required. This approach is quite different from traditional epidemiology, which assumes that the subjects under study are independent. When study subjects share genetic factors, by definition they are no longer independent. Lack of independence necessitates special rules in selection of subjects and analytic approaches. These methods capitalize on the situation to improve our understanding of disease etiology.

The epidemiologic approach to identify genetic factors that influence disease does not require prior knowledge about the pathophysiologic process that underlies the inherited susceptibility. Rather, given that the clustering of a disease in families is not due to shared environment, and is consistent with Mendelian transmission of a major gene, the goal is to identify regions of DNA that cosegregate (are inherited in the same pattern) with the disease of interest. Once the chromosomal region is narrowly defined, the torch is passed to molecular geneticists to identify the appropriate gene using highly specialized techniques. This approach, called *positional cloning* or *physical mapping*, contrasts with a more traditional laboratory approach called *functional cloning* or *functional mapping*. The latter does not require epidemiology or families and is based instead on identification of proteins that are involved in a disease process. Once a protein has been identified, scientists can determine its amino acid sequence. Working backward, the researcher is able to decipher the DNA code for the sequence of amino acids. Finally, the investigator finds where this DNA sequence occurs in the human genome. Note that physical mapping works well only when the genetic influence on disease is great enough that there will be a Mendelian pattern of disease in the family. These contrasts in approaches are depicted in Figure 14–2, adapted from a review on the subject by Dr. Francis Collins.[7]

Molecular Epidemiology

Basically, a greater precision in estimating exposure–disease associations can be made by using molecular biology to improve the measurement of exposures and disease. The term *molecular epidemiology* has been attributed to researchers Perera and Weinstein. Molecular epidemiology has the possibility of providing early warnings for disease by flagging preclinical effects of exposure.[8] The field is much broader than genetic epidemiology and includes a wide variety of biologic measures of exposure and disease. As it relates to her research on the causes of cancer, Perera noted that molecular epidemiology combines "advances in the molecular biology and molecular genetics of cancer with epidemiology to understand the molecular dose of specific agents, their preclinical effects, and the biologic factors that modulate susceptibility to their exposure."[9(p. 233)] Many

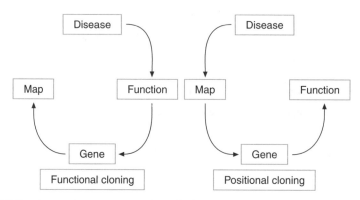

FIGURE 14–2   Strategies to identify human genes. *Source:* Adapted from Collins FS, Positional Cloning Moves from Perditional to Traditional, as published in *Nature Genetics,* Vol 9, pp. 347–350, 1995.

definitions of molecular epidemiology include the concept of biomarkers.[10] Consider the following examples:

- Rather than rely on individual recall of a usual diet to classify individuals according to intake of fruits and vegetables, assess serum levels of micronutrients to obtain more precise measurements of intake of fruits and vegetables.
- Rather than conduct a clinical trial with colon cancer as the end point, use an intermediate marker (an accepted precursor lesion: the adenomatous polyp).
- Rather than treat all cases of breast cancer as the same disease, use tumor markers to identify potentially more heterogeneous subsets.
- In trying to identify whether clusters of cases of infectious disease are from a common source, characterize the agents according to their DNA fingerprint.

From these examples, the reader should notice that the markers (exposures) are based on biologic specimens (e.g., blood, tissue, urine, and sputum) rather than questionnaire or medical records data. As stated earlier, the terms molecular epidemiology and genetic epidemiology are sometimes used interchangeably. One reason for this confusion is that another common application of molecular epidemiology is the use of inherited variation in DNA (as opposed to acquired variation—mutations—in our DNA) to classify subjects. Thus, when genes are involved, there is an overlap between molecular and genetic epidemiology. One distinction between the two is that molecular epidemiology does not involve studies of biologically related individuals. Another distinction is that most molecular epidemiologic studies are conducted to evaluate the significance of variation in genes that would not necessarily manifest as Mendelian patterns of disease in a family. As molecular biologists and molecular geneticists work to unravel disease processes, they discover various proteins that are involved. Genes determine these proteins; if individuals differ from one another in the genetic sequence of a protein that is functionally involved in the disease process, then evaluation of this genetic variation in epidemiologic studies could yield important insights into disease etiology. Molecular epidemiology evaluates the association of variation in *known* genes with risk of disease, whereas genetic epidemiology includes the identification of *unknown* genes that influence risk of disease.

Molecular Versus Genetic Epidemiology

Genetic epidemiology: concerned with inherited factors that influence risk of disease

Molecular epidemiology: uses molecular markers (in addition to genes) to establish exposure–disease associations

---

Epidemiologic Evidence for Genetic Factors

If a disease has a genetic component, at the very least one might expect to observe the occurrence of the same disease among close family members, the rationale being that, because close relatives of a case have a certain probability of sharing the same gene that influences risk of disease, there should be an excess occurrence of disease in that family. From an etiologic perspective, measurement and evaluation of family history as a risk factor may shed light on the contribution of "familial" factors on the pathogenesis of the outcome of interest. A simple definition of a positive family history is the occurrence of the same disease or trait within a family. A more precise definition would include the specific types of relatives that will be considered, for example first-degree relatives (parents, siblings, and offspring) or second-degree relatives (grandparents, aunts and uncles, nieces and nephews, grandchildren).

Several epidemiologic designs might be employed to evaluate the association of family history with disease. A cross-sectional survey of a representative sample of the population could assess the frequency of respondents with a positive history. However, if the frequency of the disease of interest was rare, this method would not be very efficient. A more common strategy is to conduct a case-control study and compare the frequency of family history in both groups. If there was a genetic component to the disease, one would expect the odds of a positive family history of the disease to be greater among the cases than among the controls.

As with any case-control study, recall bias is always a potential problem with family studies. *Family recall bias* is the special situation where cases are more likely to be informed about their family history than are controls.[11] It is not difficult to imagine that, as a consequence of having the disease, one learns much greater detail about affected family members than had been known prior to disease onset. An approach to overcome family recall bias is to perform a cohort study in which assessment of family history occurs at baseline, prior to the onset of disease. The cohort is then followed prospectively for the development of the outcome under investigation. A disadvantage, of course, is that the length of the follow-up period could be extensive before sufficient cases accrue for meaningful analysis. In addition, family history is not a static characteristic, but a dynamic risk factor that can change with time as unaffected relatives develop the outcome under investigation. Assessment of family history at a single point in time cannot capture such changes.

Causes of Familial Aggregation

Although demonstration that a disease or trait clusters in families is certainly acceptable evidence that genetics may be important, several alternative explanations must be considered. The explanations include the operation of chance and the influence of environmental factors. Zhao and colleagues have presented the case that the series of inquiries that characterize genetic epidemiology can be considered as part of a sequence of studies, built upon a common epidemiologic framework.[12]

Bad Luck

The first of the explanations for the familial aggregation of disease is simply chance. Given that there is a finite probability for the development of a particular disease or adverse health phenomenon, even in the absence of any genetic contribution at all, the disease may afflict several members of the same family. This occurrence is especially prevalent for the common diseases of major public health importance, such as obesity, mental illness, heart disease, and cancer. For example, an early study of the aggregation of cancer used cancer mortality rates for the adult British population to show that half of all families with more than five adults would have at least one case of cancer by chance alone.[13]

Two other factors—not necessarily a simple reflection of "bad luck"—would affect the likelihood that someone reports a positive family history: age and family size. Although every person has at least two first-degree biologic relatives (our parents), the person's numbers of siblings, aunts, uncles, cousins, and children are clearly random variables. For example, someone who has 15 close relatives at risk for a common chronic disease is more likely to have a relative with the disease than a person with only two relatives at risk. Similarly, because age is the single most important risk factor for many diseases of public health importance, an older person (with older relatives) is more likely than a younger person (with corresponding younger relatives) to have a family history for nongenetic reasons. Consequently, adjustment for age and family size in the analysis is encouraged when one is trying to assess the association of family history with risk of a particular disease.

Bad Environment

Epidemiologists historically have devoted their energies and attention to the identification of nongenetic risk factors for disease. As illustrated throughout the earlier chapters of this book, history is replete with many success stories. This information on exposure-disease relationships must be considered as explanation for any observed clustering of disease in families. For example, although roughly 95% of all lung cancer cases are current or former smokers, fewer than 20% of heavy smokers ever develop the disease.[14] This observation has caused some to hypothesize that host factors might influence response to environmental agents (tobacco). A complicating factor in the study of a disease with such a strong environmental risk factor is the extent to which family members also smoke cigarettes. Twin studies conducted in the 1930s provided strong evidence that smoking habits clustered in families.[15] Therefore, if family members of cases were more likely to smoke than family members of controls, a greater proportion of cases would be expected to report a positive family history of lung cancer. In this situation, however, clustering of cases in families could be due to shared lifestyle, rather than shared genes.

We know that diet relates to disease risk in a variety of ways: high-fat diets, particularly those high in saturated fat, are associated with coronary heart disease and cancer. Diets low in complex carbohydrates and fruits and vegetables are associated with diabetes and cancer. Several studies suggest the familial nature of dietary intake patterns.[16,17] To the extent that family members share dietary habits that increase risk for a given disease, familial clustering of disease may occur. Similarly, behaviors and personality traits, such as exercise habits, alcohol intake, and use of sunscreen, may be learned within a family and indirectly relate to clustering of disease. Some of these behavioral factors in disease are discussed in Chapter 15.

Many risk factors shared by family members are a reflection of shared environment, such as water supply, radon from the soil, air quality, pesticides, lead paints, and even occupation. A case report of a family with four members with mesothelioma, a rare cancer of the lining of the peritoneal cavity, was traced back to a common occupational exposure to asbestos.[18] Infectious diseases also may be included in this category, and there are a number of published examples in which familial clustering of hepatitis or tuberculosis occurs from common exposures.

Shared Family Environment and Familial Aggregation

A difficulty in the interpretation of "family history" data is the inability to determine the influence of nongenetic risk factors on any observed familial clustering. From an etiologic perspective, measurement and evaluation of risk factors are necessary in order to answer the question, "Is the observed clustering due to (shared) environmental factors?" A *family study* can be defined as one in which data on phenotype and risk factors are measured on individual family members.

Design of Case-Control Family Studies

As with all epidemiologic studies, several issues must be considered regarding selection of case and control families. In genetic jargon, a *proband* is the individual in a family who brings a disease of interest to the attention of the investigator. In a case family, the proband is likely to be a person affected with the disease (although one can select families on the basis of an unusual family history among healthy study participants). The proband in a control family is the subject matched to the case. The definition of family also must be clearly stated: three-generation families (or more) are most valuable for elucidation of genetic mechanisms, but this comes at the expense of less complete data and greater difficulty validating medical histories. For diseases with late ages at onset, parents might be deceased and offspring will not be informative, owing to their youth. Therefore, some study designs include only siblings of probands as families.

As opposed to most types of epidemiologic study designs, two steps (rather than only one) are required to establish the sampling frame for a case-control family study:

- Step 1: Ascertainment of cases (probands) and controls
- Step 2: Enumeration of the relatives of the probands and controls

---

The ascertainment considerations might include:

1. Where will probands be drawn from? A random sample of the population might be considered for a common condition (high prevalence), but is inefficient for rare diseases. If the researcher is fortunate, there might be a disease registry that contains all incident cases in a defined geographic region. In many situations, one is restricted to ascertainment of probands from hospitals and clinics, which raises questions about the representativeness of the probands if only specialized facilities are canvassed. Probands may be identified also through death certificates,[19] although this selection method would complicate the collection of biologic samples from the index case (unless there were stored samples collected previously).

2. Does the disease or trait require medical attention? It is not difficult to envision a number of important public health problems that may have a significant genetic component (e.g., alcohol or drug abuse), but the condition either does not require medical attention or required medical care is not sought. In those situations, it is virtually impossible to determine whether all eligible probands have been identified.

3. Is the prevalence of the disease known? When the incidence or prevalence of the condition under study is known, one has a much greater likelihood of evaluating whether or not the sampling frame of probands includes all eligible cases with the disease or condition.

The purpose of control families derives from the need to be able to evaluate whether familial clustering among cases is greater than can be expected. This consideration is especially important when there are no population-based rates to calculate the expected number of disease events in case families. Control families also are needed to be able to rule out common familial (measured) exposure as an explanation for any observed familial aggregation. Control families must be as similar as possible to the case families for all other (unmeasured) environmental exposures in order to determine properly whether or not a disease or trait truly has a genetic component (Exhibit 14–2).

EXHIBIT 14–2

Family Study of Lung Cancer Risk in Southern Louisiana

Carcinoma of the lung has been traditionally cited as an example of a malignancy solely determined by the environment.[20] Indeed, the risks associated with cigarette smoking are well documented. Numerous studies also have found that lung cancer cases are significantly more likely than controls to report a positive family history of the disease.[16] Before concluding that lung cancer clusters in families as a result of a genetic predisposition, it is important to control for the fact that smoking itself "runs in families."[21] Southern Louisiana has some of the highest lung cancer mortality rates in the country.[22] Epidemiologic studies designed to identify the basis for these high rates were unable to attribute the excess rates to high prevalence of tobacco exposure or industrial exposures, such as those that occur in shipbuilding,[23] oil refining,[24] and sugarcane farming.[25]

To investigate the hypothesis that a genetic predisposition was operative, Ooi and colleagues conducted a case-control family study.[19] Probands were deceased lung cancer patients identified from a listing of all deaths attributed to lung cancer in a 10-parish (county) area over a four-year period (1976–1979). A total of 440 case probands were identified. Control probands were identified as the spouse of the case (if he or she had ever been married), as listed on the death certificate. Telephone interviews were conducted to construct pedigrees of parents, siblings, offspring, and half-siblings of the cases and controls. Interviews also collected data on cancer history, current age (or age at death), age at onset for affected persons, smoking histories, and occupational exposures. Participation rates were equivalent for case and control families (76%).

continues

EXHIBIT 14–2 *continued*

The study reported that cases were 2.4 times more likely than controls to have a first-degree relative with lung cancer. After excluding the probands and spouses, statistical models were fitted to predict the risk of lung cancer in relatives. The models adjusted for age, sex, pack-years of cigarette smoking, occupational/industrial exposures, and a variable to reflect whether or not a study participant shared genes with the lung cancer proband (i.e., was a case relative or a control relative). After adjusting for the established risk factors for lung cancer, relationship to a lung cancer proband remained a significant predictor of risk (odds ratio [OR] = 2.4). Risk was especially elevated for parents (OR = 4.4) and nonsmoking sisters of the probands (OR = 4.6). Further analysis of the data suggested that susceptibility to cancer included sites besides the lung, notably other smoking-associated cancers.[26] ■

Control families can be identified from several possible sources. One would be the same disease registry, clinic, or hospital from which the probands were drawn, but with sampling based on a different disease. Another choice is random selection from the general population (e.g., neighborhood controls). Relatives of the proband's spouse have been used as controls since the beginning of the twentieth century. This clever approach "matches" families on unmeasured lifestyle, economic status, education, and even religious influences, because likes tend to marry likes.[27]

Although the primary focus of this section has been on the selection of families through a proband with a disease of interest, other strategies may be considered. For example, a random sample of families from a cross-sectional study might be considered if one is interested in the genetic epidemiology of a common biologic trait or process, such as steroid hormone levels or eating behaviors.

Gene Mapping: Segregation and Linkage Analysis

Historically, when the number of genetic markers available were few and expensive to type, compelling evidence of a possible genetic link to a disease or condition was required to justify the efforts to map complex diseases. In particular, the disease or trait had to be shown to cluster in families and not be accounted for by shared nongenetic risk factors before a hypothesis of familial aggregation of an underlying genetic influence could be made. As we explain later in the chapter, the current ease and cost efficiency of genetic mapping is revolutionizing the field. Nevertheless, in this section we present the traditional approach that is still commonly used for rare genetic traits or syndromes for which nongenetic influences are less evident.

For studies of genetic transmission, families or pairs of related individuals are required. Ideally, one would want a population-based sample of families ascertained through probands diagnosed in a defined geographic area over a specific time period. If one had conducted a case-control family study to rule out shared environment as the cause of familial aggregation, then the case families from that investigation could be subjected to further analysis. *Segregation analysis* is an approach to determine, from a sample of families, whether a particular disease or trait is inherited in Mendelian fashion. By Mendelian, we mean the situation in which the mode of transmission of a disease or trait from parents to offspring is consistent with simple laws of inheritance (Figure 14–3).

Modes of Inheritance

The mode of inheritance refers to the association between the number of mutated alleles at a locus and a given phenotype (disease or trait) and whether or not the locus is situated on one of the 22 autosomes or on a sex chromosome. Consider the simple situation in which there are only two possible alleles at a locus, B and b. Furthermore, suppose that allele B is associated with disease. Because humans have two alleles at a locus, the three possible genotypes are therefore BB, Bb, or bb. An individual's genotype is determined by the genotypes of his or her parents and the particular two alleles that were passed on at meiosis. According to the principles of Mendelian inheritance, the alleles transmitted from parents to offspring are randomly determined. Consequently, a parent whose genotype is Bb will transmit, on average, the B allele 50% of the time and the b allele the other 50%. Parents who are either BB or bb are capable of transmitting only the B and b alleles, respectively. Another way of stating Mendelian transmission is in terms of the probability that the deleterious gene is passed from a parent to child. The expectations that BB, Bb, and bb parents transmit a B allele are 1.0, 0.5, and 0.0, respectively.

Some diseases are referred to as autosomal dominant or recessive. The term *autosomal dominant* refers to the situation in which only a single copy of an al-

FIGURE 14-3   Gregor Mendel. *Source:* From National Institutes of Health, Deciphering the Genetic Code. Available at: http://history.nih.gov/exhibits/ nirenberg/popup_htm/01_mendel.htm. Accessed November 14, 2007.

tered gene located on a non-sex chromosome is sufficient to cause an increased risk of disease. In these situations, one typically expects to see an affected parent and, on average, half of his or her offspring affected with the same disease or condition. *Autosomal recessive* diseases denote those for which two copies of an altered gene are required to increase risk of disease. Carriers, individuals who have only one copy of the altered gene (heterozygotes), are typically not thought to be at increased risk of the disease. Matings of two carriers will produce, on average, affected children one-fourth of the time.

Traits are said to be genetically additive or codominant when heterozygotes have a phenotype that is distinguishable from the two homozygous states. Codominance may occur for both quantitative and qualitative traits. Codominance is easy to imagine for a quantitative trait—such as blood pressure or enzyme activity—that facilitates categorizing individuals into one of three levels (say high, medium, or low enzyme activity). For a qualitative trait (e.g., presence or absence of a type of cancer), the effect may be on the age at onset of disease. Homozygous carriers would have an earlier mean age at onset than heterozygotes, who in turn have an earlier mean age at onset than noncarriers of an altered allele. Although disease-predisposing genes may be carried on the X or the Y chromosome, there are very few known examples of the latter. X-linked traits are passed from women to sons or daughters, but from men only to daughters (because fathers pass their Y chromosome to sons). X-linked recessive traits affect men much more frequently than women, because men need only have the gene on their one X chromosome mutated to be in the recessive state at that locus.

Determining the Mode of Inheritance

Elucidation of the potential mode of inheritance of susceptibility to a complex disease is determined by comparing how well different hypotheses (genetic and nongenetic) fit the observed pattern of disease in a collection of families.[28] Known as *segregation analysis,* a variety of computer software programs are available to perform this analysis (e.g., some acronyms are SAGE, PAP, and POINTER). Coverage of these various options is beyond the scope of this chapter, as is the mathematical underpinnings showing how the various hypotheses are constructed. The concept, however, is basically as follows. In the traditional realm of science, hypotheses are generated and data are collected and analyzed to accept or refute the hypothesis. With segregation analysis, the outcome of the experiment (random mating and assortment of genes from parents to offspring) has already occurred (individuals who inherit the deleterious gene have an increased risk for disease). Thus, one is essentially asking the question, "Given the pattern of disease in these families, what is the likelihood that the underlying cause was transmission of an altered allele in a Mendelian fashion?" Models representing possible modes of transmission (genetic and nongenetic) are fit to the data. The goodness-of-fit is compared for the various models to determine which one is the most likely explanation for the observed pattern of disease.

Exhibit 14–3 describes the findings of a segregation analysis of breast cancer.

LOD Score Linkage Analysis

The results of the Claus et al.[29] analysis (Exhibit 14–3) provided strong evidence, but not definitive proof, for the existence of a gene that influenced risk of breast cancer. Linkage analysis is an attempt to identify a DNA marker that cosegregates with the disease of interest and is considered strong evidence for the existence of a gene.[28] The basis for linkage analysis is the simple concept that there are exceptions to Mendel's law of independent assortment of traits.

EXHIBIT 14–3

Genetic Epidemiology of Early-Onset Breast Cancer in the CASH Study

The Cancer and Steroid Hormone (CASH) study is a multicenter, population-based case-control study conducted by the Centers for Disease Control and Prevention. Researchers studied a total of 4,730 histologically confirmed cases of breast cancer among patients (aged 20–54 years) and 4,688 controls. Initial analyses confirmed that cases were significantly more likely than controls to have a family history of the disease, especially the earlier the age at onset.[30] Segregation analysis of the case families provided evidence that the pattern of breast cancer was consistent with Mendelian dominant transmission of a rare allele (carrier frequency of 3 women per 1,000) associated with increased breast cancer risk.[29] The proportion of cases predicted to carry the allele was highest (36%) among women aged 20 to 29 years but decreased to only 1% of cases aged 80 or older. The cumulative lifetime risk among carriers was predicted by the model parameters to be high: approximately 92%. For noncarriers the predicted lifetime risk was roughly 10%, essentially the same as the lifetime risk for the general population. ◼

Specifically, genes that are in close physical proximity to each other on the same chromosome tend to be *linked* (i.e., inherited together). Two genes on different chromosomes are unlinked and will be inherited together roughly 50% of the time. It is important to emphasize that two genes on the same chromosome will be linked only if they are close together on the chromosome. That is because during meiosis (the formation of gametes), homologous pairs of chromosomes can undergo *recombination* through "crossing over" of the DNA strands. Although earlier in the chapter we said that parents assort half of their chromosomes to their offspring, the shifting of genetic material across homologous chromosomes often modifies the chromosomes. If genes are far apart on the same chromosome, there is a high probability that a crossover event will occur, and the genes will end up on different chromosomes. Genes that are close together on the same chromosome have a much lower probability of being separated during meiosis by a recombination (crossover) event. Therefore, the probability of a recombination event is a function of the distance between two loci. In a given number of meioses, the proportion that yields a recombinant chromosome is defined as the *recombination fraction* (θ). If the number of recombinants between two loci is estimated through analysis to be quite small (or zero), then the two loci are "linked" and the physical location of the disease-causing gene possibly has been identified. In linkage analysis between two loci, the question of whether they are linked is answered by comparing the value of the observed recombination fraction to the expected recombination fraction (under no linkage) of 0.5. Evidence for linkage is expressed as a ratio of the likelihood of the data under linkage at some specified recombination fraction to the likelihood of the data under a recombination fraction of 0.5. The results are typically expressed as a LOD (logarithm of the odds) score, which stands for the logarithm of the odds of linkage. A LOD score of 3.0 is equivalent to a *P* value of 10^3, or 1,000 to 1; this evidence is commonly accepted for significant linkage.

Earlier in the chapter we described ways in which specific genetic alterations can occur. Note that all of these were presented in reference to a specific gene. However, variation in DNA also occurs in noncoding regions of the genome. Regardless of whether they occur in coding or noncoding regions of DNA, base pair sequences that are highly *polymorphic* (i.e., that vary greatly from individual to individual) can be used to help characterize individuals as unique at a particular locus and thus can be tracked within families. Highly polymorphic, closely spaced markers that cover each of the human chromosomes thus facilitate linkage analysis. Exhibit 14–4 presents an example of a linkage study.

Samples of families selected for linkage analysis are usually highly biased. Although they may be a subset of case families initially ascertained as part of a population-based case-control study, not all of the case families will be informative for linkage analysis. That is, only families with multiply affected individuals are useful for attempts to identify genetic markers that cosegregate with disease, thus revealing the chromosomal location of the disease locus, which is the ultimate goal of the study. For many diseases, evidence suggests that if two forms of the disease exist, one genetic and the other not, the genetic form of the disease will tend to have an earlier age at onset. Accordingly, preference is often given to those families with multiple cases of disease, especially when those affected have an age at onset earlier than the general population average. Finally, it is imperative that the affected individuals be living, available, and interested in participating in the research study. Linkage analysis is particularly susceptible to misclassification errors, so it is critical to validate all disease end points of interest and check the pedigrees for nonpaternity. If one is trying to track markers from parents to offspring, then it makes no sense to compare the transmission

EXHIBIT 14–4

Linkage Analysis of Early-Onset Breast Cancer

One of the most exciting success stories in genetic epidemiologic research was the identification of two genes—*BRCA1* and *BRCA2*—through linkage analysis and positional cloning. Mary-Claire King and colleagues were the first to report that autosomal dominant susceptibility to breast cancer was due to a gene located on a region of the long arm of chromosome 17.[31] This finding was based on 23 families: 7 with an average age at onset younger than 45 years, and 16 families in which average age at onset was older than 45 years. Two of the early-onset families also included women with ovarian cancer. Thus, they also were considered to be part of the phenotype in the analysis. Further analysis with more markers in the 17q12-17q21 region revealed that significant evidence for linkage was limited to the seven early-onset families.[32] The markers used were dinucleotide repeat polymorphisms: anonymous sequences of variable length repeats of DNA $(CA)_n$. The most informative marker (D17S579) included 12 alleles of size 111 to 133 base pairs. The initial report was soon confirmed,[33] and an international consortium was formed to pool results and clone the gene. After a furious competition, others reported the successful identification of the *BRCA1* gene on chromosome 17.[34] Because this locus appeared to account for roughly half of the families included in the linkage consortium, work continued to identify a second locus. Roughly a year later, a second gene (*BRCA2*) was identified on chromosome 13 by restricting analysis to families that included male and female breast cancer.[35]

Identification of these two genes has only been the beginning for genetic epidemiologic investigations. Considerable work has been done since their discovery to characterize the sites and types of mutations, the complete phenotype (cancers other than breast and ovarian), ethnic variation in allele frequency, and ethical and psychosocial issues related to genetic testing. Subsequent research has implicated these two genes in repair of DNA damage.[36] Data have begun to emerge on the effectiveness of surgical and other prevention strategies.[37]

of alleles when one of the parents (usually the father) is not really biologically related.

It is important to understand that the phenomenon of genetic linkage is a function of the *distance* between the disease locus and the marker locus. It is not necessarily an association of a *specific allele* at the marker locus with disease. For example, in Exhibit 14–4, suppose that the marker locus (Mfd188) that was found to be most closely linked to the BRCA1 locus had four alleles: a, b, c, and d. The premise is that Mfd188 is close to the disease locus but is not the disease locus. This premise means that the breast cancer locus will cosegregate with allele a in some families. However, in other families, the relevant marker may be allele b, or c, or d. As a result, *within* a family there will be cosegregation of a particular allele at the marker locus with the disease locus. *Across* families, any one of the four alleles at the marker locus may cosegregate with the *BRCA1* mutation. The only time one would expect to see the same marker associated with disease risk across families is when the marker is within the disease-causing gene itself and is closely linked to the actual mutation in the gene. This situation, in which a specific allele at the marker locus is strongly associated with the mutant allele, is known as *linkage disequilibrium*. The importance of this phenomenon will become increasingly clear in the later section on GWAS.

Nonparametric Linkage Analysis

Historically, linkage analysis has required knowledge about the mode of inheritance of the disease. Thus, a formal segregation analysis would be done to see if the pattern of disease in the family (or collection of families) was consistent with Mendelian transmission. In addition, segregation analysis provided estimates of important parameters that are essential for linkage analysis, such as the frequency of the disease-associated allele in the population and the age-specific penetrance of the gene. Although all of these parameters can theoretically be estimated through formal segregation analysis, it can be extremely difficult to ascertain the true genetic model for a common disease with both genetic and environmental influences (considered a "complex trait" in genetic terms). Consequently, methods have been developed that do not require specification of the parameters of the underlying genetic model (hence the term *nonparametric*). Initially, they were based on sibling pairs[38,39] but now have been extended to include additional (and more distant) relatives.[40]

One of the great attractions of sib-pair approaches is their simplicity. Although siblings will share an average of 50% of their genes *identical by descent (IBD),* at any given locus two siblings may share 0, 1, or 2 alleles in common.

IBD means that the allele comes from the same parent. If an allele is very common in the population, siblings might share the same allele but have the allele transmitted from different parents. Such alleles that are the same but come from different parents are said to be *identical by state*. This complexity underscores the importance of highly polymorphic markers. For a qualitative trait (presence or absence of a given disease), under the hypothesis of a genetic influence, one would expect affected sibs to share more alleles IBD than under random Mendelian segregation. Similarly, for a quantitative trait, one would expect that siblings with similar trait values would share more alleles IBD than siblings with dissimilar trait values.

A limitation of sib-pair analysis occurs in the following situations: one cannot unambiguously determine the number of alleles shared IBD. This ambiguity is especially an issue when the marker locus is not highly polymorphic. When there are few alleles at a marker locus, the probability increases that alleles are identical by state rather than IBD. The uncertainty can be resolved if parents are available for genotyping at the locus, but only if the parent is heterozygous at that locus and the nonshared alleles are different. Kruglyak and Lander have developed analysis methods for sibling pairs that utilize multiple loci, thus improving the power and efficiency of gene mapping efforts.[41] The method works for both qualitative and quantitative traits and has been implemented in a new computer package known as MAPMAKER/SIBS, but several others are available, such as SIBLINK, SPLAT, GASP, and SOLAR.

Genome-Wide Association Studies (GWAS)

As mentioned in the introduction to this chapter, the distinction between molecular epidemiology (which does not require related individuals) and genetic epidemiology (which does) has become irrevocably blurred because of two important developments. The first is the International HapMap Project, which is described in more detail below. The second is radical advances in genotyping capability that have enabled the cost per genotyping on some chip-based platforms to fall to $0.001 per single nucleotide polymorphism (SNP). SNPs denote minor variations in our genome; although many SNPs do not cause any alteration in cell functions, other SNPs increase vulnerability to disease (Figure 14–4). These developments have had a profound impact on the epidemiologic community, creating greater pressure for team science (large consortia to pool data and biologic samples across studies) and stretching the capabilities to manage, store, and analyze data. (Refer to Exhibit 14–5 for GWAS on breast cancer.)

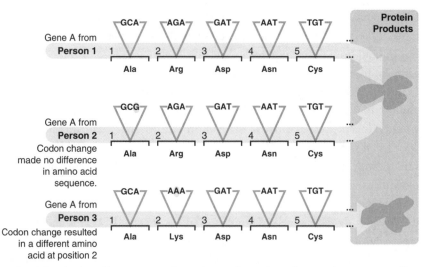

FIGURE 14–4   Illustration of single nucleotide polymorphisms—small variations in the genome. *Source:* From U.S. Department of Energy, Office of Science, Joint Genome Institute. Available at: http://www.jgi.doe.gov/education/genomics_3.html. Accessed November 14, 2007. ©2006 The Regents of the University of California. ("The public may copy and use this information without charge, provided that this Notice and any statement of authorship are reproduced on all copies.")

Genome-Wide Association Studies of Breast Cancer

Throughout this chapter, we have used examples from the breast cancer literature to illustrate the various genetic epidemiologic study designs. The traditional approach resulted in the identification of several major genes (i.e., *BRCA1*, *BRCA2*, and *p53*), but there was a general appreciation that more genes remained to be discovered. Recently, investigators reported three GWAS that offer proof-of-principle of the merit of the segregation/linkage approach.

Easton and colleagues[48] used a three-stage design. They began by genotyping 408 breast cancer cases with a strong family history of the disease

continues

EXHIBIT 14–5 *continued*

and 400 cancer-free controls on a panel of 227,876 SNPs. The second stage involved 12,711 SNPs typed on 3,990 cases and 3,916 controls. After statistical analysis, the top 30 SNPs were then typed in 22 additional case-control studies representing 21,860 cases of invasive breast cancer, 988 cases with carcinoma in situ, and 22,578 controls. Six SNPs were significant at $P \leq .00001$ in the same direction as the first two stages: 5 of the 6 SNPs were in genes or LD (linkage disequilibrium) blocks containing genes: *FGFR2*, *TNRC9* (2 SNPs), *MAP3K1*, and *LSP1*. None of these loci had been reported previously as breast cancer risk factors. The risk SNP in the most strongly associated gene, *FGFR2*, is common in the population (estimated frequency of 0.38), and although associated with a modest increase in risk for breast cancer (OR = 1.63; 96% confidence interval [CI] = 1.53–1.72), the population attributable risks are significant.

The findings implicating *FGFR2* were replicated in a report published by Hunter and colleagues[49] one month after Easton et al.'s study.[48] The study by Hunter et al. began with 1,183 postmenopausal breast cancer cases and 1,185 individually matched controls from the Nurses Health Study typed for 528,173 SNPs. The researchers then genotyped an additional 1,776 cases and 2,072 controls nested within three other prospective cohort studies: NHS-2, PLCO, and the American Cancer Society Cancer Prevention Study II. The SNP in *FGFR2* most strongly associated with risk in the initial scan maintained a highly significant result when pooled across all four studies ($P = 4.2 \times 10^{-10}$). Interestingly, the result was obtained using a different SNP than was typed in the study by Easton et al.

The third GWAS study was reported by Stacey et al.[50] They genotyped approximately 300,000 SNPs among 1,600 breast cancer cases and 11,563 controls from Iceland. Selected SNPs were then typed in five replication sample sets from Sweden, Spain, and Holland as well as European Americans from the Multi-Ethnic Cohort Study. The strongest findings identified a region of chromosome 2q35, but the SNP was not within a gene and no genes were located within the identified haplotype block. However, the results did implicate *TNRC9*, which was also identified in the study by Easton et al.

continues

EXHIBIT 14–5 *continued*

These recent reports have sent scientists in new directions to identify the relevant genes and alterations. As exciting as these developments have proven to be, many researchers are predicting that the lifespan of GWAS was probably going to be short, owing to the imminent promise of the ability to sequence the entire genome. ■

Linkage Disequilibrium Revisited: Haplotypes

In the section on genetic linkage, we emphasized that DNA markers that are close together are often inherited together, because crossover events between homologous chromosomes are rare. This phenomenon is used to localize (map) disease susceptibility genes to chromosomal regions. It has been increasingly recognized that the human genome is highly variable in the frequency with which such crossover events are observed within and among loci and populations (for more detail the reader is referred to several reviews.[42–44] Moreover, when a new mutation arises, this happens on the background of a particular chromosome, and several DNA markers nearby will continue to be inherited with it for many generations. This combination of DNA markers along the chromosome is referred to as a *haplotype*. A landmark study by Gabriel and colleagues[45] examined genetic markers across 51 autosomal regions in DNA samples from Africa, Europe, and Asia. Their analysis of these markers provided compelling evidence of sizable regions of the genome where there is little historical evidence for recombination. They termed these regions "*haplotype blocks*" and noted the particular effect the regions could have on studies to identify susceptibility genes across the genome. In particular, the identification of SNPs that "*tag*" a region means, essentially, that you would be capturing the genotypes at other loci within that block that were co-inherited with the block. Thus, one could scan across the entire genome with far fewer genetic markers than would be required in the absence of haplotype blocks (which has been estimated to be around 10 million SNPs).

The International HapMap Project

This ambitious project began officially at a meeting held from October 27 to 29 in 2002. A collaboration among scientists and funding agencies in Japan, the

United Kingdom, Canada, China, Nigeria, and the United States, their goal was to develop a haplotype map of the human genome and generate 200,000 to perhaps a million SNPs that would "tag" (represent) the most common haplotypes in all human populations. When completed, this public catalog will allow researchers to determine chromosomal similarities and differences worldwide as well as to seek for genetic connections between human diseases and responses to pharmaceuticals.

DNA samples came from 270 individuals from the Yoruba people in Ibadan, Nigeria (30 trios of two parents and a child), Japanese (45 unrelated individuals), Han Chinese from Beijing (45 unrelated individuals) as well as 30 parent-child trios collected by the Centre d'Etude du Polymorphisme Humain (CEPH). The CEPH families are residents of the United States with Northern and Western European ancestry. The goal was to generate a map of 600,000 SNPs evenly spaced across the genome, such that there is one SNP for every 5,000 bases. The data are publicly available, and updates are released in regular intervals (see the project Web site at: http://www.hapmap.org). The Web site is logically organized into three main sections: 1) an overview of the project (including more details on the background, ethical issues, protocols, and publications arising from the project); 2) a data section that includes downloads of the data and interactive access; and (3) useful Internet links. The reader can download and read a tutorial that provides very helpful instructions on using this resource.

Application and Implications of the HapMap Project

The epidemiologic approach to the application of genetics to human disease is best described as one based on *candidate genes*. This approach requires some understanding of the biology of the disease (at least enough to identify proteins that are likely to be involved), and information that the genes encoding the proteins are polymorphic. The latter requirement is no longer an issue because the National Center for Biotechnology Information (NCBI; available at: http://www.ncbi.nlm.nih.gov/) maintains an up-to-date database of SNPs that have been identified across 43 organisms (including *Homo sapiens*). As of December 2007, Build 127 held 11.8 million reported SNPs in humans, of which over 5.6 million have been validated. The downside, of course, is incomplete knowledge of a disease and, thus, important genes may be entirely missed. Genome-wide approaches can be considered unbiased to any prior information about the disease or trait, making these approaches complementary to the candidate gene (or candidate pathway) approach.

There are several important issues to consider in genomewide studies. The efficiency of this design is informed by power (true positives), sample size, false positives, and cost. It is also recognized that variants that contribute to common diseases are likely to have small relative risks; consequently, large sample sizes are required. Although the cost per genotype may be low, the cost per chip (and therefore per study subject) is still hundreds of dollars. This high expense and need for large samples have led to methodologic research on multi-stage designs (e.g., Boddeker and Ziegler[46]), whereby at the first phase a subset of subjects are genotyped for the full genome-wide panel of SNPs, and a subsequent phase is conducted in which fewer SNPs (including the most interesting markers identified in the first phase) are typed in a larger sample. This larger sample may be an independent sample set or one in which subjects from the first phase are carried forward and included. Given the large number of SNPs (anywhere from 300,000 to 1,000,000 per subject), due caution must be exercised regarding the appropriate level of statistical significance. Consider, for example, that a study that types subjects on 550,000 SNPs would be expected to yield 27,500 P-values less than 0.05. Thus, methods are being developed that seek to control the false discovery rate caused by large sample sizes.[47]

Application of Genes in Epidemiologic Designs

The previous sections of this chapter outlined how genetic epidemiologists determine whether a disease has a genetic component, and how they contribute to efforts (primarily by geneticists) to map genes through segregation and linkage analysis. The primary utility of epidemiology will be realized *after* the etiologically important genes are identified. According to Friend, "As we enter this post-genomic era, we should expect more and more emphasis on something that could not previously be studied: the gene-gene and gene-environmental interactions that we have always suspected would end up being important."[51(p. 17)] The next section begins with a brief review of the recent accomplishments of the Human Genome Project and concludes with a series of examples of the types of epidemiologic studies that can be conducted with knowledge of genetics. Figure 14–5 symbolizes the far-reaching impact of the Human Genome Project.

The mapping of the human genome[52,53] has been heralded as the signal accomplishment that will transform our understanding of biology and the practice of medicine. Collins has enumerated several of the potential medical implica-

FIGURE 14–5   Influence of the Human Genome Project. *Source:* U.S. Department of Energy Human Genome Program. Available at: http://genomics.energy.gov/gallery/basic_genomics/detail.np/detail=30.html. Accessed January 24, 2008.

tions this mapping may enable, including improved diagnosis, prognosis, and treatment of disease.[54] Without question, increased knowledge of genetics and the incredible advances in technology also will have a profound impact on the field of epidemiology. First, the complete sequence of the 3.3 billion nucleotides comprising the genome is available over the Internet (http://genome.ucsc.edu/). This includes the location and nearly complete sequence of the 26,000 to 31,000 protein-encoding genes.[55] As of March 2006, the NCBI Build 36.1 reference sequence is considered to be "finished," a technical term indicating that the sequence is highly accurate (with fewer than one error per 10,000 bases) and highly contiguous (with the only remaining gaps corresponding to regions whose sequence cannot be reliably resolved with current technology). Although the full benefit of this milestone will not be realized for years, the initial discovery revealed some startling facts:

- Less than 5% of the genome appears to code for actual genes.
- The size of the human genome is only slightly larger than that of some plants.

- Certain sequences of DNA appear to be highly conserved (highly invariant) across species (yeast, worms, fruit flies, mice, etc.). These sequences are thought to be highly important.
- Human DNA is highly polymorphic, meaning that it has many forms. Aside from monozygotic twins, we are virtually unique in our DNA sequence.

Applications of Molecular Epidemiology to the Study of Infectious Diseases

Use of molecular techniques in infectious disease epidemiology is continuing to grow. Maslow et al.[56] noted the types of questions that infectious disease epidemiologists might want to answer, questions that can best be answered through applications of molecular epidemiology, rather than traditional epidemiology:

- Several patients on a surgical ward develop postoperative pneumonia that is caused by the same organism, *Klebsiella pneumoniae*. Does this occurrence represent an outbreak?
- Does a patient who returns to a clinic with a second infection for *Escherichia coli* suffer from a new infection or a relapse caused by the original organism?
- A patient who has a prosthetic cardiac device is found to have blood cultures that are infected with *Staphylococcus epidermidis*. Is the infection caused by a single strain or by multiple contaminants?

By using methods derived from immunology, biochemistry, and genetics, it is possible to determine whether a bacterial disease (from the same organism) is caused by multiple bacterial isolates or by identical isolates. (This issue relates to all of the foregoing questions.) To illustrate, Hlady et al. described the use of molecular epidemiologic techniques to identify the source of an outbreak of Legionnaires' disease.[57] They conducted a case-control study of five infected patients who attended conventions at a hotel in Orlando, Florida. Nearly all conventioneers were probably exposed at least briefly to a decorative fountain in the hotel, ultimately determined to be the source of the infections. Statistical techniques could not identify an association between the disease and the fountain due to the small number of cases and the fact that many control subjects also had been near the fountain. However, it was possible to confirm an association between exposure to the fountain and *Legionella* by using two techniques, monoclonal antibody subtyping and pulsed-field gel electrophoresis, which are molecular biologic strategies that can assess if the cases were affected by identical bacterial strains.

Blanc et al. illustrated how the use of molecular markers helped to control an epidemic of *Pseudomonas aeruginosa*.[58] An outbreak of infections due to this organism was linked to contaminated bronchoscopes. Two clones of the organism were apparently identified in the outbreak, an epidemic and a nonepidemic form. When manual disinfection of the endoscopes was reintroduced, the incidence of the epidemic form declined but the incidence of the nonepidemic form did not. Investigators used a form of molecular typing known as ribotyping to distinguish between the sporadic and epidemic cases.

Applications of Molecular Epidemiology in Occupational and Environmental Epidemiologic Research

Use of biomarkers helps enlarge our understanding of the etiology and prevention of occupationally related health problems.[59] Of particular interest would be longitudinal studies in which the predictive value of biomarkers for disease is established.[9] Cohorts of workers who have been exposed to hazardous materials, such as benzene or asbestos, could be followed prospectively. Other groups that have had environmental exposures to hazardous wastes or toxic chemicals could be studied also in a similar prospective manner. Clearly, the marriage of detailed exposure records with stored biological specimens (e.g., DNA) can be used for historical cohort designs, too.

The application of techniques from molecular epidemiology to the study of occupational and environmental health problems could yield several important dividends[60]:

- improvements in the classification of exposures
- more accurate definition of risk groups through the use of susceptibility markers
- increased specificity in the classification of disease
- greater understanding of etiologic mechanisms for disease

Groopman et al.[10] pointed out that epidemiologists are concerned with the potential associations between exposure variables and health effects. Before the advent of molecular epidemiology, it was not feasible to quantify accurately the relationships among exposure, dose, and health outcomes. Molecular biomarkers may be used to denote exposures, outcomes, or vulnerability to disease because they are more sensitive indicators than other measures of exposure.

An example of the use of a biomarker in environmental health studies is the *p53* gene in liver tumors.[61] The *p53* gene is thought to suppress tumor formation. Researchers in China examined the association between mutations in the gene and exposure to the hepatitis B virus and aflatoxin. They found that half of a small sample of liver cancer patients indeed had mutations in this gene. This research and related studies suggest that hazardous exposures may induce genetic changes that in turn are linked to cancer or other diseases.

Applications of Molecular Epidemiology to the Study of Cancer

The complex nature of cancer makes it an ideal target for the use of molecular biology and molecular genetics to improve our understanding of disease etiology. Consider this brief list of possibilities:

- Rather than rely on diet recall to assess fat intake, use biopsy of human tissue to determine the fatty acid composition.
- Rather than consider cancer a simple dichotomy, use understanding of the pathologic changes from normal to malignant cells to study early stages of disease.
- Rather than use cancer recurrence (or incidence) in studies of prevention, utilize precursor lesions, such as adenomatous polyps of the colon.
- Rather than consider cancer at a particular site a single disease, use expression of tumor markers (cell proliferation, oncogenes, tumor suppressor genes, hormone receptors, etc.) as evidence of distinct etiologic pathways. Use tumor markers to elucidate mechanisms of exposure (e.g., radon and alterations in the *p53* tumor suppressor gene).

As a brief example of molecular epidemiologic approaches to the study of cancer, consider the work by Taylor and colleagues at the National Institute of Environmental Health Sciences.[62] Previous studies of leukemia had found only weak associations of occupational and chemical exposures with risk of the disease. Taylor et al. hypothesized that, because acute myeloid leukemia (AML) appears to be a heterogeneous disease at the molecular and cytogenetic level, certain environmental exposures might be linked to a specific molecular subtype. The net effect would be a strong association between an exposure with a particular subtype and a weak association with the remainder. Animal studies suggested that mutations in the *ras* family of proto-oncogenes are a frequent early event in chemically induced tumors. (The term *ras* protein refers to a protein that is associated with cell multiplication and differentiation; proto-oncogenes promote normal cell growth and division.) Moreover, *ras* mutations were known to occur in 15% to 30% of patients with AML.

Taylor et al. conducted a case-control study of 62 cases and 630 controls.[62] This study revealed that cases with mutations in *H-ras*, *K-ras-2*, or *N-ras* were 6.8 times more likely to have worked at least five years in high-risk occupations than *ras*-negative cases, and nine times more likely to have breathed chemical vapors on the job. When compared with the control group, the associations with occupational exposures were observed only among the subset of cases with *ras* mutations in their bone marrow cells. This landmark study was one of the first to demonstrate that disease etiology may be better understood if epidemiologic measures of exposure are integrated with molecular assays of the genetic defects responsible for cancer initiation and promotion.

Molecular and Genetic Epidemiology of Alzheimer's Disease

Alzheimer's disease (AD) is a neurodegenerative disorder characterized by the presence of senile plaques, neurofibrillary tangles, and congophilic angiopathy in the brain at the time of death. In approximately 50% of families, the disease is inherited in an autosomal dominant manner.[63] However, AD is quite complex and probably genetically heterogeneous: linkage studies have implicated regions on chromosome 21,[64] chromosome 19,[65] and chromosome 14.[66] Evidence suggests that the relevant gene on chromosome 19 is the one that codes for apolipoprotein E (Apo E). Apo E is a constituent of plasma lipoproteins that participates in the transport of cholesterol and specific lipids. It is involved in degeneration and regeneration of nervous tissue and is found in high concentration in brain and cerebrospinal fluid. The fact that it is genetically highly polymorphic makes it a suitable candidate gene for AD. The three common alleles have been examined in a number of case-control studies. As one example, consider the work of Tsai et al.[67] These researchers identified 77 patients with late-onset AD from the Mayo Clinic Alzheimer's Disease Patient Registry (operated by the Division of Community Internal Medicine). For each case, the next age- and sex-matched, cognitively normal person presenting to the same Division was recruited as a control. All subjects received a general medical examination, comprehensive neurologic examination, and rigorous neuropsychologic evaluation. A small sample of blood was drawn as a source of DNA. Consistent with earlier studies, the investigators found that the frequency of the e4 allele was significantly higher among cases than controls (0.351 vs. 0.130,

$P < 0.0001$). Cases were 4.6 times more likely to carry at least one copy of the e4 allele than controls (CI: 1.9–12.3). Moreover, carriers were found to have significantly earlier age at onset than noncarriers. Thus, the Apo E-e4 allele appears to be an important genetic susceptibility risk factor for AD in the general population.

Molecular and Genetic Epidemiology of Psychiatric Disorders

We noted earlier in this chapter that genetic epidemiology (in comparison with molecular epidemiology) is more concerned with the inherited basis for health outcomes. A field known as *psychiatric genetic epidemiology* takes several approaches to uncover the role of inheritance and environmental factors in disorders. The identification of familial aggregations of psychiatric disorders among close family members provides evidence for a possible genetic component.[68] Additional support comes from studies that find a greater concordance of psychiatric illness among monozygotic (identical) than dizygotic (fraternal) twins. A more recent development has been to identify genetic markers for disorders through studies of pedigrees and sibling pairs.

Psychiatric disorders appear to result from complex mechanisms that are influenced by genes, but few present in simple Mendelian fashion. Therefore, elucidation of the genetic component is complicated by the fact that such disorders are likely heterogeneous (different genetic basis in different families), polygenic (multiple genes may influence the trait), and multifactorial (genes and environment matter). In recent years, a number of studies have reported linkage in psychiatric disorders, but with few findings replicated. For example, a type of affective disorder, bipolar disorder (BPAD; also known as manic-depression), appears to have an inherited basis but the mode of inheritance is not well defined. Susceptibility to manic-depressive illness has been linked to the tyrosine hydroxylase locus within the chromosome 11p15 region using both parametric and nonparametric approaches.[69] BPAD has been linked to chromosome 18q and chromosome 21, but the regions remain poorly defined.[70] The disease has been associated also with the dopamine transporter gene locus on chromosome 5.[71] A Genetic Analysis Workshop (GAW10) convened 25 groups to analyze five distributed published data sets containing chromosome 5 and chromosome 18 markers. Results were suggestive, but not definitive, for linkage to a bipolar susceptibility locus on chromosome 18; evidence for chromosome 5 was minimal.[72]

By further clarifying the genetic component for these conditions, it may be possible to further specify high-risk groups and to clarify the environmental risk factors for BPAD and other affective disorders. Nevertheless, progress in this field of research is impeded by the fact that the brain is a very complex organ and that several genes may be implicated in the inheritance of mental disorders.

Genetics and Public Health

Although few will question the importance of new discoveries in the basic sciences, their true value lies in their ultimate translational potential in improved health. To a certain extent, the benefit of knowledge gleaned from the revolution in molecular genetics and the mapping of the human genome has not been realized. However, the potential has been recognized and is considerable given the role of genes in the etiology of many common diseases.[73] Khoury commented that it is up to public health professionals to harness the utility of genetic information and technology for disease prevention.[74] Khoury grouped the range of activities into three categories:

1. Assessment of the impact of genes and their interactions with modifiable disease risk factors on the health status of the population.
2. Development of policies as to when and how genetic tests are to be applied in disease prevention programs.
3. Assurance that the public health genetic programs developed are effective and of the highest quality.

Potential applications include, at a minimum, the following areas: screening for genetic susceptibility, early detection of disease, more appropriate targeting of high-risk population subgroups for interventions, more tailored prevention approaches that recognize underlying differences in host susceptibility, and new therapies and treatments for disease. In an effort to demonstrate this potential, we will give examples related to a common theme: colorectal cancer.

Colorectal cancer is the third most common cause of cancer death in the United States; men statistically are more vulnerable than women after age 50.[75] There were an estimated 154,000 cases of colorectal cancer in the United States in 2007, with 52,180 deaths.[76] Colon cancer is a part of several well-defined cancer-predisposing syndromes: familial adenomatous polyposis (FAP), Lynch syndrome I, and Lynch syndrome II.[77] FAP is caused by inherited mutations in the *APC* gene. The cancer family syndromes defined by Lynch are caused by mutations in one of five other genes (*MLH1, MSH2, PMS1, PMS2,* and *PMS6*). It has been estimated that roughly 10% of all colorectal cancers in this country are due to mutations in one of these five genes associated with autosomal dominant susceptibility to cancer.

Screening for Colorectal Cancer

Colon cancer is a preventable disease because it has an easily identifiable precursor lesion, the adenomatous polyp. Through regular sigmoidoscopy and colonoscopy, these early lesions can be detected and removed before they become cancerous. Sigmoidoscopy is effective only for polyps that arise in the distal colon and is therefore not a perfect screening tool. Although colonoscopy enables inspection of the entire colon, it is too expensive to be used as a routine screening modality and presents some inherent risks (e.g., perforation of the colon occurs in rare instances). However, the expense and the risk are not excessive for high-risk populations, where the prevalence of disease justifies the procedure. In 2002, new guidelines were released that defined appropriate screening modalities for colorectal cancer based on age and family history of the disease. Because susceptibility is transmitted in an autosomal dominant fashion, on average only 50% of the offspring of affected individuals will inherit the susceptibility gene. If genetic analysis for mutations in the known colorectal cancer genes were included as part of the risk assessment, then the intense screening regimen would be required to be applied only to gene carriers within a given high-risk family. Family members without the inherited mutation would require only the screening intervals suggested for the general population. Thus, resources are targeted to those truly at greatest risk, and unnecessary screening (and risk) can be avoided.

An alternative approach for screening makes use of the following observation: genes that influence inherited susceptibility in a minority of the population are the same genes targeted for acquired mutations in the general population. Colonic epithelial cells that acquire these mutations are occasionally shed into the lumen of the colon and excreted in the feces. Ahlquist and colleagues at the Mayo Clinic developed an assay to extract DNA from stool. Using a panel of markers, they were able to identify correctly 91% of the samples as being derived from cancer cases, 82% of the samples as being derived from patients with precursor lesions (adenomatous polyps), and 93% of the samples as being derived from cancer-free controls.[78] Thus, knowledge of genetics also can benefit the screening of average-risk populations.

Interventions for High-Risk Populations

The public health approach posits that shifts in the population distribution of risk factors will lead to substantial changes in disease frequency. Although these shifts should continue to be the goal to which we in public health aspire, the current reality is that there are too many risk factors, too many worthy interventions, not enough intervention professionals, and not enough financial resources to apply this model routinely. A useful adjunct to the population approach is to focus energies on particular high-risk subgroups for interventions. Consider our example of colorectal cancer screening. Once carriers of a deleterious mutation are identified, several options for disease prevention can be considered. One would simply be to perform closer surveillance and remove any polyps as they occur. For patients with mutations in the *APC* gene, the colon can literally be carpeted with thousands of polyps. The solution for these patients is removal of the colon before cancer can occur. For subjects who inherit mutations in one of the other susceptibility genes, a viable option may be chemoprevention. Sulindac has been found to reduce the occurrence of polyps in high-risk individuals.[79] Note the case of persons who have a family history of colon cancer and who do not have a genetic mutation in one of the syndromic genes. They may have a family history because of either undesirable lifestyle (physical inactivity, diets low in fruits and vegetables or high in red meat) or a polymorphism in a gene with a more moderate effect on risk. Such individuals would still be candidates for interventions, particularly for diet and exercise changes.

Tailored Interventions

Many epidemiologists traditionally have ignored the possibility that individuals respond differently to the challenges in the environment. Genetic epidemiology is predicated upon the notion first stated by Galen in 200 AD: "But remember throughout that no cause is efficient without a predisposition of the body itself. Otherwise, external causes which affect one would affect all." Indications that individuals differ in response to an intervention have been around for decades. For example, Garrod, the founder of human biochemical genetics, and Haldane, the great British geneticist, had both suggested that biochemical individuality might explain unusual reactions to drugs and foods. We now know that the enzymes involved in these responses are genetically determined, and many are polymorphic. Indeed, this area (known as *pharmacogenetics*) is seeing a resurgence as pharmaceutical companies race to determine ways to tailor prescriptions and doses to patients for therapeutic (and ultimately chemopreventive) purposes.

Continuing with our example of colorectal cancer, the epidemiology suggests several dietary strategies for risk reduction. For example, diets rich in fruits, vegetables, fiber, and calcium are associated with lower risk for the disease.[80,81] Conversely, diets high in meat and fat are positively related to risk.[80,82] It is tempting to speculate that dietary associations observed at the population level would translate to effective risk-reduction strategies for individuals at high risk for familial or genetic reasons. However, if the biology is different for hereditary and nonhereditary colorectal cancer, then such an approach may not be prudent.[83] For example, a clinical trial of calcium among 30 members of families with hereditary nonpolyposis colorectal cancer found no significant effect of calcium on cell proliferation in the colon.[84] Sellers et al., utilizing the Iowa Women's Health Study cohort, observed that high intakes of calcium were associated with 50% decreased risk of colon cancer (95% CI, 0.3–0.7) among women without, but not with (relative risk, 1.2; CI, 0.6-2.2), a family history of the disease.[85] In addition, high total intakes of vitamin E had been previously associated with lower risk in this cohort.[86] High total vitamin E intakes were observed to decrease risk of colon cancer by 33% among women without a family history (upper vs. lower tertile), but only a nonstatistically significant 10% among the family history-positive subset. These results suggest that care should be exercised before implementing a risk reduction intervention among subjects at elevated risk for disease based on their family history.

Conclusion

This chapter covered the topics of genetic and molecular epidemiology. These fields are truly on the cutting edge of epidemiology as a result of their promise to provide insights into the "black box" of disease etiology. We reviewed concepts and applications of the field in diverse areas from infectious diseases to occupational health to the epidemiology of cancer and other chronic diseases. Progress in the field will require training a new generation of scientists with requisite skills, as well as greater collaboration and interdisciplinary work among scientists with laboratory skills and those versed in genetics who have training in analytic epidemiology.[59,60] Scientific discoveries utilizing these methods will not only improve our understanding of disease etiology, but may lead to better and more tailored approaches to screening for disease, and primary and secondary prevention.

Study Questions and Exercises

1. Consider a disease with two alleles, B and b. List all of the mating types that could produce a heterozygous child.
2. For the situation described in problem 1, which mating type gives the highest proportion of heterozygous offspring?

3. It is impossible for you to have received a sex chromosome from one of your four grandparents. Which grandparent could not have transmitted, via your parents, a sex chromosome to you? Answer as if you were (a) male and (b) female.

4. A case-control study of multiple sclerosis (MS) was conducted in which family history of MS was collected on all first-and second-degree relatives. Among the 500 cases, 16 reported an affected relative. Among the 500 age-and sex-matched controls, 8 reported an affected relative. Do these data suggest a familial component to MS?

5. For a disease with an adult age at onset, what is the rationale for matching cases and controls on age when one is most interested in family history of the disease?

6. You are interested in determining whether or not there is a genetic predisposition to lung cancer. Provide at least five reasons why lung cancer might cluster in a family for nongenetic reasons.

7. A published segregation analysis of asthma shows that all Mendelian patterns of inheritance do not provide a good fit to the data compared with the general model. Does this rule out the possibility that genes influence risk of asthma?

References

1. McMichael AJ. Invited commentary—molecular epidemiology: new pathway or new traveling companion? *Am J Epidemiol.* 1994;140:1–11.
2. Wong KK, deLeeuw RJ, Dosanjh NS, et al. A comprehensive analysis of common copy-number variations in the human genome. *Am J Hum Genet.* 2007;80:91–104.
3. Conrad DE, Andrews TD, Carter NP, Hurles ME, Pritchard JK. A high-resolution survey of deletion polymorphism in the human genome. *Nat Genet.* 2006;38:75–81.
4. Iafrate AJ, Feuk L, Rivera MN, et al. Detection of large-scale variation in the human genome. *Nat Genet.* 2004;36:949–951.
5. Khoury MJ, Beaty TH, Cohen BH. *Fundamentals of Genetic Epidemiology.* New York, NY: Oxford University Press; 1993.
6. Ellsworth DL, Hallman DM, Boerwinkle E. Impact of the human genome project on epidemiologic research. *Epidemiol Rev.* 1997;19:3–13.
7. Collins FS. Positional cloning moves from perditional to traditional. *Nat Genet.* 1995;9:347–350.
8. Perera FP. Molecular epidemiology: insights into cancer susceptibility, risk assessment, and prevention. *J Natl Cancer Inst.* 1996;88:496–509.
9. Perera FP. Molecular epidemiology and prevention of cancer. *Environ Health Perspect.* 1995;103(suppl 8):233–236.
10. Groopman JD, Kensler TW, Links J. Molecular epidemiology and human risk monitoring. *Toxicol Lett.* 1995;82–83:763–769.

11. Love RR, Evans AM, Josten DM. The accuracy of patient reports of a family history of cancer. *J Chronic Dis.* 1985;38:289–293.

12. Zhao LP, Hsu L, Davidov O, Potter J, Elston RC, Prentice RL. Population-based family study designs: an interdisciplinary research framework for genetic epidemiology. *Genet Epidemiol.* 1997;14:365–388.

13. Schneider NR. Familial aggregation of cancer. In: Chaganti RSK, German J, eds. *Genetics in Clinical Oncology.* New York, NY: Oxford University Press; 1985: 133–145.

14. Mattson ME, Pollack ES, Cullen JW. What are the odds that smoking will kill you? *Am J Public Health.* 1987;77:425–431.

15. Fisher RA. Lung cancer and cigarettes? *Nature.* 1958;182:108.

16. Sellers TA. Familial predisposition to lung cancer. In: Eeles R, Easton D, Ponder B, Horwich A, eds. *Genetic Predisposition to Cancer.* London, UK: Chapman & Hall Medical; 1996:344–354.

17. Vachon CM, Sellers TA, Kushi LH, Folsom AR. Familial correlation of dietary intakes among postmenopausal women. *Genet Epidemiol.* 1998;15:553–563.

18. Krousel T, Garcas N, Rothschild H. Familial clustering of mesothelioma: a report on three affected persons in one family. *Am J Prev Med.* 1986;2:186–188.

19. Ooi WL, Elston RC, Chen VW, et al. Increased familial risk for lung cancer. *J Natl Cancer Inst.* 1986;76:217–222.

20. Doll R, Peto R. *The Causes of Cancer.* New York, NY: Oxford University Press; 1981.

21. Tokuhata GE. Familial factors in human lung cancer and smoking. *Am J Public Health.* 1964;54:24–32.

22. Rothschild HR, Voors AW, Weed SG, et al. Trends in respiratory system cancer mortality in Louisiana: geographic distribution in 1950–1969 and 1967–1976 compared. *Am J Public Health.* 1979;69:380–381.

23. Blot WH, Harrington JM, Toledo A, et al. Lung cancer after employment in shipyards during World War II. *N Engl J Med.* 1978;229:620–624.

24. Gottlieb MS, Pickle LW, Blot WJ, et al. Lung cancer in Louisiana: death certificate analysis. *J Natl Cancer Inst.* 1976;57:3–7.

25. Mulvey JJ, Rothschild H. Sugarcane farming—is there a link with cancer? *Ecol Dis.* 1983;2:267–270.

26. Sellers TA, Ooi WL, Elston RC, et al. Familial risk of non-lung cancer among relatives of lung cancer patients. *Am J Epidemiol.* 1987;126:237–246.

27. Vandenberg SG. Assortative mating, or who marries whom? *Behav Genet.* 1972;2:127–157.

28. Elston RC. Segregation analysis. *Adv Hum Genet.* 1981;11:63–120.

29. Claus EB, Risch N, Thompson WD. Genetic analysis of breast cancer in the cancer and steroid hormone study. *Am J Hum Genet.* 1991;48:232–242.

30. Claus EB, Risch N, Thompson WD. Age of onset as an indicator of familial risk of breast cancer. *Am J Epidemiol.* 1990;131:961–972.

31. Hall JM, Lee MK, Morrow J, et al. Linkage of early-onset familial breast cancer to chromosome 17q21. *Science.* 1990;250:1684–1689.

32. Hall JM, Friedman L, Guenther C, et al. Closing in on a breast cancer gene on chromosome 17q. *Am J Hum Genet.* 1992;50:1235–1242.

33. Narod SA, Feunteun J, Lynch HT, et al. Familial breast-ovarian cancer locus on chromosome 17q12-q23. *Lancet.* 1991;338:82–83.

34. Miki Y, Swensen J, Shattuck-Eidens D, et al. A strong candidate for the breast and ovarian cancer susceptibility gene BRCA1. *Science.* 1994;266:66–71.

35. Wooster R, Bignell G, Lancaster J, et al. Identification of the breast cancer suscepti-bility gene BRCA2. *Nature.* 1995;378:789–792.

36. Reliene R, Bishop AJ, Schiestl RH. Involvement of homologous recombination in carcinogenesis. *Adv Genet.* 2007;58:67–87.

37. Bermejo-Pérez MJ, Márquez-Calderón S, Llanos-Méndez A. Effectiveness of preven-tive interventions in *BRCA1/2* gene mutation carriers: a systematic review. *Int J Cancer.* 2007;121:225–231.

38. Penrose GS. Genetic linkage in graded human characters. *Ann Eugenics.* 1938:8: 223–237.

39. Haseman JK, Elston RC. The investigation of linkage between a quantitative trait and a marker locus. *Behav Genet.* 1972;2:3–19.

40. Weeks DE, Lange K. The affected-pedigree-member method of linkage analysis. *Am J Hum Genet.* 1988;42:315–326.

41. Kruglyak L, Lander ES. Complete multipoint sib-pair analysis of qualitative and quantitative traits. *Am J Hum Genet.* 1995;57:439–454.

42. Pritchard JK, Przeworski M. Linkage disequilibrium in humans: models and data. *Am J Hum Genet.* 2001;69:1–14.

43. Jorde LB. Linkage disequilibrium and the search for complex disease genes. *Genome Res.* 2000;10:1435–1444.

44. Boehnke M. A look at linkage disequilibrium. *Nat Genet.* 2000;25:246–247.

45. Gabriel SB, Schaffner SF, Nguyen H, et al. The structure of haplotype blocks in the human genome. *Science.* 2002;296:2225–2229.

46. Boddeker IR, Ziegler A. Sequential designs for genetic epidemiologic linkage or asso-ciation studies. *Biomed J.* 2001;43:501–525.

47. Kuchiba A, Tanaka NY, Ohashi Y. Optimum two-stage designs in case-control associ-ation studies using false discovery rate. *J Hum Genet.* 2006;51:1046–1054.

48. Easton DF, Pooley KA, Dunning AM, et al. Genome-wide association study identi-fies novel breast cancer susceptibility loci. *Nature.* 2007;447:1087–1093.

49. Hunter DJ, Kraft P, Jacobs KB, et al. A genome-wide association study identifies alleles in FGFR2 associated with risk of sporadic postmenopausal breast cancer. *Nat Genet.* 2007;39:870–874.

50. Stacey SN, Manolescu A, Sulem P, et al. Common variants on chromosomes 2q35 and 16q12 confer susceptibility to estrogen receptor-positive breast cancer. *Nat Genet.* 2007;39:865–869.

51. Friend SH. Breast cancer susceptibility testing: realities in the post-genomic era. *Nat Genet.* 1996;13:16–17.

52. The International Human Genome Mapping Consortium. A physical map of the hu-man genome. *Nature.* 2001;409:934–941.

53. Venter JC, Adams MD, Myers EW, et al. The sequence of the human genome. *Science.* 2001;291:1304–1351.

54. Collins FS. Genetics: An explosion of knowledge is transforming clinical practice. *Geriatrics.* 1999;54:41–47.

55. Baltimore D. Our genome unveiled. *Nature.* 2001;409:814–816.

56. Maslow JN, Mulligan ME, Arbeit R. Molecular epidemiology: application of con-temporary techniques to the typing of microorganisms. *Clin Infect Dis.* 1993; 17:153–164.

57. Hlady WG, Mullen R, Hopkins R, Mintz C, Shelton B, Daikos G. Outbreak of Legionnaires' disease linked to a decorative fountain by molecular epidemiology. *Am J Epidemiol.* 1993;138:555–562.

58. Blanc DS, Parret T, Janin B, Raselli P, Francioli P. Nosocomial infections and pseudoinfections from contaminated bronchoscopes: two-year follow-up using molecular markers. *Infec Control Hosp Epidemiol.* 1997;18:134–136.

59. Schulte PA. Use of biological markers in occupational health research and practice. *J Toxicol Environ Health.* 1993;40:359–366.

60 Soderkvist P, Axelson O. On the use of molecular biology data in occupational and environmental epidemiology. *J Occup Environ Med.* 1995;37:84–90.

61. Bang KM. Applications of occupational epidemiology. *Occup Med.* 1996;11: 381–391.

62. Taylor JA, Sandler DP, Bloomfield CD, et al. Ras oncogene activation and occupational exposures in acute myeloid leukemia. *J Natl Cancer Inst.* 1992;84:1626–1632.

63. Van Duijn CM, Clayton D, Chandra V, et al. Familial aggregation of Alzheimer's disease and related disorders: a collaborative re-analysis of case-control studies. *Int J Epidemiol.* 1991;20(suppl 2):S13–S20.

64. Goate A, Chartier-Harlin M-C, Mullan M, et al. Segregation of a missense in the amyloid precursor protein gene with familial Alzheimer's disease. *Nature.* 1991; 349:704–706.

65. Pericak-Vance MA, Bebout JL, Gaskell PC, et al. Linkage studies in familial Alzheimer disease: evidence for chromosome 19 linkage. *Am J Hum Genet.* 1991; 48:1034–1050.

66. Schellenberg GD, Bird TD, Wijsman EM, et al. Genetic linkage evidence for a familial Alzheimer's disease locus on chromosome 14. *Science.* 1992;258:668–671.

67. Tsai M-S, Tangalos EG, Petersen RC, et al. Apolipoprotein E: risk factor for Alzheimer disease. *Am J Hum Genet.* 1994;54:643–649.

68. Kendler KS. The genetic epidemiology of psychiatric disorders: a current perspective. *Soc Psychiatry Psychiatr Epidemiol.* 1997;32:5–11.

69. Malafosse A, Leboyer M, d'Amato T, et al. Manic depressive illness and tyrosine hydroxylase gene: linkage heterogeneity and association. *Neurobiol Dis.* 1997; 4:337–349.

70. McMahon FJ, Hopkins PJ, Xu J, et al. Linkage analysis of bipolar affective disorder to chromosome 18 markers in a new pedigree series. *Am J Hum Genet.* 1997; 61:1397–1404.

71. Waldman ID, Robinson BF, Feigon SA. Linkage disequilibrium between the dopamine transporter gene (DAT1) and bipolar disorder: extending the transmission disequilibrium test (TDT) to examine genetic heterogeneity. *Genet Epidemiol.* 1997;14:699–704.

72. Rice J. Genetic analysis of bipolar disorder: summary of GAW10. *Genet Epidemiol.* 1997;14:549–561.

73. King RA, Rotter JI, Motulsky AG. *The Genetic Basis of Common Diseases.* New York, NY: Oxford University Press; 1992.

74. Khoury MJ. From genes to public health: the applications of genetic technology in disease prevention. *Am J Public Health.* 1996;86:1717–1722.

75. Schottenfeld D, Winawer SJ. Cancer of the large intestine. In: Schottenfeld D, Fraumeni JF, eds. *Cancer Epidemiology and Prevention,* 2nd ed. New York, NY: Oxford University Press; 1996:813–840.

76. National Cancer Institute. Colon and Rectal Cancer. Available at http://www .cancer.gov/cancertopics/types/colon-and-rectal. Accessed January 26, 2008.

77. Potter JD, Sellers TA, Rich SS. Colorectal cancer. In: Ponder BAJ, Waring MJ, eds. *Cancer Biology and Medicine* (Vol 4): *The Genetics of Cancer*. Amsterdam, Netherlands: Kluwer Academic Publishers; 1995:45–65.

78. Ahlquist DA, Skoletsky JE, Boynton KA, et al. Colorectal cancer screening by detection of altered human DNA in stool: feasibility of a multitarget assay panel. *Gastroenterology*. 2000;119:1219–1227.

79. Waddell WR, Loughry RW. Sulindac for polyposis of the colon. *J Surg Oncol*. 1983;24:83–87.

80. Potter JD, Slattery ML, Bostick RM, Gapstur SM. Colon cancer: a review of the epidemiology. *Epidemiol Rev*. 1993;15:499–545.

81. Bostick RM, Potter JD, Sellers TA, et al. Relation of calcium, vitamin D, and dairy food intake to incidence of colon cancer among older women: the Iowa Women's Health Study. *Am J Epidemiol*. 1993;127:1302–1317.

82. Willett WC, Stampfer MJ, Colditz GA, et al. Relation of meat, fat, and fiber intake to the risk of colon cancer in a prospective study among women. *N Engl J Med*. 1990;323:1664–1672.

83. Alberts DS, Lipkin M, Levin B. Genetic screening for colorectal cancer and intervention. *Int J Cancer*. 1996;69:62–63.

84. Cats A, Kleibeuker JH, van der Meer R, et al. Randomized, double-blinded, placebo-controlled intervention study with supplemental calcium in families with hereditary nonpolyposis colorectal cancer. *J Natl Cancer Inst*. 1995;87:598–603.

85. Sellers TA, Bazyk AE, Bostick RM, et al. Diet and risk of colon cancer in a large prospective study of older women: an analysis stratified on family history. *Cancer Causes Control*. 1998;9:357–367.

86. Bostick RM, Potter JD, McKenzie DR, et al. Reduced risk of colon cancer with high intake of vitamin E: the Iowa Women's Health Study. *Cancer Res*. 1993;53:4230–4237.

Psychologic, Behavioral, and Social Epidemiology

LEARNING OBJECTIVES

By the end of this chapter the reader will be able to:

- define the terms *social epidemiology, behavioral epidemiology,* and *psychosocial epidemiology*
- state the role of psychologic, behavioral, and social factors in health and disease
- discuss the stress concept as a hypothesized determinant of disease
- define status discrepancy, person-environment fit, and stressful life events
- discuss moderators of the stress-illness relationship
- state outcomes of exposure to stress

CHAPTER OUTLINE

I. Introduction
II. Research Designs Used in Psychologic, Behavioral, and Social Epidemiology
III. The Social Context of Health
IV. Independent Variables
V. Moderating Factors in the Stress-Illness Relationship

VI.   Outcome Variables: Physical Health, Mental
        Health, Affective States
VII. Conclusion
VIII. Study Questions and Exercises

Introduction

In his discussion of grief (Exhibit 15–1), Engel[1] questioned the adequacy of the medical model in explaining certain types of health problems. He suggested a new category of variables—psychologic factors—that are not usually discussed in the agent, host, and environment model (Figure 12–1). This chapter covers the role of psychologic factors as well as social and behavioral factors as determinants of health. These factors, which have inspired a rich tradition of epidemiologic research, encompass determinants of health and illness that are enmeshed in the social fabric, are part of the psychologic constitution of the person, and may involve a complex interaction of the person and environment. The determinants are not single agents, such as specific bacteria or other biologic determinants of disease, nor are they demographic variables, such as age or sex. Rather, they incorporate social and personality factors, cultural influences upon individual behavior, stress, and related psychosocial factors, all of which are multifactorial.

Three specializations embody the foregoing types of variables: social epidemiology, behavioral epidemiology, and psychosocial epidemiology. Syme noted that the field of social epidemiology is concerned with the influence of a person's position in the social structure upon the development of disease.[2] A broader conception of the field defines it as ". . . the branch of epidemiology that studies the social distribution and social determinants of states of health." The field ". . . aim[s] to identify socioenvironmental exposures that may be related to a broad range of physical and mental health outcomes." The types of exposures include ". . . social phenomena such as socioeconomic stratification, social networks and support, discrimination, work demands, and control . . ."[3(p. 6)]

Behavioral epidemiology studies the role of behavioral factors in health. Examples of behavioral factors are tobacco use, physical activity, risky sexual behavior, and consumption of unhealthful foods. Closely related to the field of behavioral epidemiology is behavioral medicine, which emphasizes the application

EXHIBIT 15–1

When Is Grief a Disease?

"To enhance our understanding of how it is that 'problems of living' are experienced as illness by some and not by others, it might be helpful to consider grief as a paradigm of such a borderline condition. For while grief has never been considered in a medical framework, a significant number of grieving people do consult doctors because of disturbing symptoms, which they do not necessarily relate to grief. Fifteen years ago I addressed this question in a paper entitled, 'Is grief a disease? A challenge for medical research.' Its aim too was to raise questions about the adequacy of the biomedical model. A better title might have been, 'When is grief a disease?', just as one might ask when schizophrenia or when diabetes is a disease. For while there are some obvious analogies between grief and disease, there are also some important differences . . . Grief clearly exemplifies a situation in which psychological factors are primary; no preexisting chemical or physiological defects or agents need be invoked. Yet as with classic diseases, ordinary grief constitutes a discrete syndrome with a relatively predictable symptomatology which includes, incidentally, both bodily and psychological disturbances. It displays the autonomy typical of disease; that is, it runs its course despite the sufferer's efforts or wish to bring it to a close. A consistent etiologic factor can be identified, namely, a significant loss. On the other hand, neither the sufferer nor society has ever dealt with ordinary grief as an illness even though such expressions as 'sick with grief' would indicate some connection in people's minds. And while every culture makes provisions for the mourner, these have generally been regarded more as the responsibility of religion than of medicine." ■

Source: Reprinted from Engel GL, The Need for a New Medical Model: A Challenge for Biomedicine. *Science*, Vol 196, p. 133, American Association for the Advancement of Science, © 1977.

---

of behavioral factors to specific clinical interventions, as in the case of biobehavioral approaches to the management of high blood pressure. Biobehavioral approaches include nonpharmacologic treatment methods, e.g., exercise, maintenance of desirable weight, changes in diet, and meditation.[4]

In comparison with social epidemiology and behavioral epidemiology, the term psychosocial epidemiology is somewhat more broadly conceptualized to include psychological, behavioral, and social factors. These variables are relevant to mental health states, including grief and depression; to physical health states, such as the chronic diseases; and to the etiology of infectious diseases, such as increased susceptibility to the common cold virus, herpes virus, and other agents. The conditions that presently compel the attention of psychosocial epidemiologic researchers, however, are the chronic, degenerative diseases: hypertension, coronary heart disease (CHD), arthritis, certain varieties of cancer, and diabetes, to name a few examples. Heart disease, cancer, and stroke are the leading causes of mortality in developed countries (and also to a significant extent in less developed countries) and, accordingly, the psychosocial aspects of these conditions should receive high priority within public health agencies and among researchers.

Public health, epidemiology, and the medical sciences have borrowed with increasing frequency from the theoretical and conceptual bases of the behavioral sciences for etiologic models of disease. The behavioral sciences hold potential for the development of explanatory frameworks and for expanding knowledge of conditions of unknown etiology. Sociology contributes an interweaving of social conditions as they affect disease processes. Psychology is concerned with the study of personal behavior, which is an important aspect of health outcomes. In comparison with the first part of the 20th century, the latter part of that century and the beginning of the 21st century have seen the elaboration of psychologic and social models as the etiologic bases of the chronic, noninfectious diseases as well as some of the infectious diseases.

In order to synthesize and integrate some of the findings of the psychosocial literature, we have developed the model that is presented in Figure 15–1. The chart groups some of the components of this literature under a theoretical framework that consists of the major categories of independent, moderating, and dependent variables. We have organized the remainder of this chapter according to these categories. *Independent variables* (also referred to as exposure or risk factor variables) are defined as hypothesized causal factors in a theoretical model. *Moderating (intervening) variables* are intermediate in the causal process between an independent variable (risk or exposure) and outcome. A *dependent variable* is a variable in a theoretical model that is affected or influenced by an independent variable.

The field of psychosocial epidemiology covers a vast body of literature; hence, the review that follows is not exhaustive, but rather surveys some of the major issues and applications in this area of epidemiology. The list of topics includes the concepts of stress and stressful life events; personality factors, culture, personal

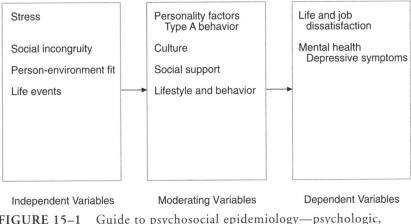

Stress	Personality factors Type A behavior	Life and job dissatisfaction
Social incongruity	Culture	Mental health Depressive symptoms
Person-environment fit	Social support	
Life events →	Lifestyle and behavior →	
Independent Variables	Moderating Variables	Dependent Variables

FIGURE 15–1   Guide to psychosocial epidemiology—psychologic, behavioral, and social (examples of variables studied)

behavior, and social support; and mental and physical health status (linked to psychologic, social, and behavioral factors). For the sake of clarity and to highlight some of the traditional concerns of psychosocial epidemiology, the foregoing psychologic and social dimensions are treated as discrete categories. In reality, they are overlapping dimensions; for example, personal behavior is a function of sociocultural influences that also are related to stress.

Writings about psychologic and social processes in disease often include the variables of socioeconomic status, ethnicity, religion, and familial characteristics. Because these are primarily demographic variables, they were covered earlier in Chapter 4. The objective of the present chapter is to consider those psychosocial variables that are compatible with a theoretical framework for explaining illness etiology, that is, independent or intervening variables in the causality of disease.

Typically, psychosocial epidemiologic studies involve diseases that have multiple independent risk factors or that involve interaction of risk factors (i.e., social, psychologic, and biochemical). For example, in the case of CHD the risk factors hypertension, blood lipids, smoking, diet, and lifestyle operate jointly to increase the risk of disease. This statement is an oversimplification, however, because behavioral and psychologic factors may be related indirectly to CHD by activating certain biochemical processes that, in turn, may be related directly to elevated status on risk factors for CHD. Another characteristic of etiologic models developed thus far for CHD and other chronic diseases is that the set of known risk factors does not explain 100% of the variance in the phenomenon under study. That is, the risk factor variables do not form a perfect causal explanation for

CHD; many unexplained causes for CHD other than those known to science remain. In addition, a small percentage of individuals who are at high risk on all the known causal factors never develop an overt case of the disease and may go on to outlive the low-risk individuals.

Research Designs Used in Psychologic, Behavioral, and Social Epidemiology

This field of investigation has employed many of the standard epidemiologic designs, e.g., case-control, cohort, cross-sectional, and experimental designs. The role of stress in health outcomes is one of the major concerns of psychosocial epidemiology. Some of the earlier research studies on this topic used cross-sectional investigations of captive and readily available populations (e.g., work-related groups of white male professionals). At present the research community acknowledges the importance of including diverse study populations in epidemiologic investigations. Cross-sectional studies of psychosocial factors in health are attractive because of the relative ease of such research. Cross-sectional designs, however, may not be adequate to detect the subtle effects associated with psychosocial factors, especially the issues of temporality of cause and effect and the influence of confounding variables.

Also needed are more longitudinal, prospective studies of the role of psychosocial factors in health as well as studies of women and minority groups, although much progress has been made in developing these types of studies in recent years. Among the many excellent initiatives in this area is the work of investigators in Germany.[5] Researchers, conducting the Early Developmental Stages of Psychopathology study (EDSP), began data collection in 1994–95. The EDSP was a prospective study of adolescents and young adults who resided in the city of Munich, Germany. A total of 3,021 adolescents and young adults aged 14 through 24 years were included at baseline. Subjects were followed up on average after a 42-month interval. This project has made possible the study of the incidence of various mental disorders, including the general anxiety syndrome and depression.[6,7]

A unique challenge of psychosocial studies is to obtain valid and reliable operationalization of measures. The process of *operationalization* refers to the methods used to translate some of the concepts employed in psychosocial epidemiology into actual measurements. For example, much controversy surrounds the development of measures of stress, epidemiologically useful measures of mental health, and measures of social support. In addition, as part of the process of improving measures used, epidemiologists need to develop well-delineated conceptual models of psychosocial processes.

The Social Context of Health

Interest in the role of the social environment in health has flourished in the last three decades, perhaps because epidemiologists have recognized that the social environment may contribute to the regulation of psychosocial influences upon health. In Chapter 12, we defined the social environment as the totality of the behavioral, personality, attitudinal, and cultural characteristics of a group of people. The social environment provides the context in which psychosocial factors operate. From the population perspective, we find that the social environment impacts the health of residents of both the less developed and more developed worlds.[8] In the former geographic areas, life expectancy is reduced in comparison with the developed world due to the impact of poverty, with its attendant malnutrition and infectious diseases. Overcrowding, poor living conditions, and lack of preventive health care foster the spread of infectious diseases. In the latter areas, the social environment is also an influential component of the major causes of morbidity and mortality through the impact of noninfectious conditions, which are the leading causes of death in the developed world. Lifestyle factors—smoking, diet, insufficient exercise, and use of illegal substances—undoubtedly play a role in the etiology of many of these conditions. A noteworthy example is the reduced life expectancy in the countries of central and Eastern Europe and the former Soviet Union in comparison to the European Union countries. Some authorities have suggested that one of the contributing factors to this reduction in life expectancy is excessive alcohol consumption, although the influence of alcoholism on life expectancy is by no means clear-cut.[8]

In order to compare accurately among nations the contributions of disease to morbidity and mortality, work has proceeded on the development of measures that could be used in all countries. The Global Burden of Disease Study attempts to quantify and provide an epidemiologic assessment of the worldwide consequences of disease by using a measure known as the disability-adjusted life year (DALY) to assist in comparisons across countries.[9] The DALY is a statistical measure applied to populations that combines information on mortality with information on morbidity for specific causes. The advantage of DALYs is that they provide a standard epidemiologic unit for comparative purposes. According to Murray and Lopez, "The ten leading specific causes of global DALYs are, in descending order, lower respiratory infections, diarrhoeal diseases, perinatal disorders, unipolar major depression, ischaemic heart disease, cerebrovascular disease, tuberculosis, measles, road-traffic accidents, and congenital anomalies. [A total of] 15.9% of DALYs worldwide are attributable to childhood malnutrition and 6.8% to poor water, and sanitation and personal and domestic hygiene."[9(p. 1436)] The social environment contributes to many of these DALYs via a range of pathways including unsanitary living conditions associated with crowding; discrimination and social exclusion; low status on the social hierarchy; social isolation; and adverse lifestyle choices. In addition to the social environment, we will now consider how the major categories of psychosocial variables listed in Figure 15–1 affect health outcomes.

Independent Variables

Examples of independent variables covered in psychosocial epidemiologic research include general concepts of stress, social incongruity theory, person-environment fit, and stressful life events.

General Concepts of Stress

Stress as an independent, antecedent variable to health and illness represents an intriguing notion because it seems to support common-sense explanations for the cause of some mental disorders, sudden death due to heart attacks, and other chronic conditions. Regardless, the scientific evidence for stress as an etiologic agent of disease is contradictory. A review of the numerous writings on stress leads one to conclude that the concept has more than one meaning and that some of the meanings tend to be vague or inconsistent. The concept of stress has a venerable historical background in the field of medicine and in other disciplines, but is often regarded with scientific skepticism. There do seem to be several supportive findings in stress research, however. For instance, Wolf[10] cited the classic work of Walter Canon, who studied changes in gastrointestinal function that accompanied stressful events, such as pain, hunger, and major emotion. Selye[11] specified in detail the stages of reaction to stress through the concept of the general adaptation syndrome. Selye conceived of stress as a change in the environment of the organism and proposed that the organism's response consisted of three stages: alarm reaction, stage of resistance, and stage of exhaustion. Activation of the general adaptation syndrome, associated with corticoid secretion, may produce somatic disease (e.g., mineralocorticoid hypertension and cardiac necroses).[12]

> # Selye's Concept of the General Adaptation Syndrome
>
> 1. Alarm reaction: physiologic responses associated with preparation to deal with stress that lead the animal or person to fight or escape from the stressor.
> 2. Stage of resistance: return of physiologic responses to normal and resistance to further stressful stimuli.
> 3. Stage of exhaustion: failure of the organism to adapt to overwhelming stresses. "Adaptation energy" becomes exhausted, and, in the case of humans, severe bodily disease and death may result.

Crider[13] proposed that adverse environmental events produce stress. Three examples of adverse events that may produce stress are noxious stimuli, removal of a reinforcement, and a conflict situation. An example of presentation or threat of presentation of a noxious or biologically damaging stimulus is electric shock experimentation. The early executive monkey experiments demonstrated that physiologic arousal linked to behavioral responses to remove the threat of electric shock was associated with gastric ulcer in monkeys.[13] Removal of a positively reinforcing stimulus includes removal of rewards, such as those associated with good behavior. There may be an association between removal of positive reinforcers and impaired mental health and other illnesses. Finally, a conflict situation is one that generates two or more incompatible responses in the same individual. Examples are attitude conflicts, role conflicts, and conformity conflicts, the last of which was associated with changes in lipid metabolism in one experiment.[13]

Social Incongruity Theory (Status Discrepancy Models)

Investigators have hypothesized that either social mobility or status incongruity may be associated with morbidity. General themes of research have included changes in residence from one country or culture to another, changes in residence from a rural to an urban area, upward intragenerational mobility, and discrepancy between husband and wife in social and educational status.

Cobb et al.[14] found that discrepancy between parents in social status (e.g., a high-status mother married to a low-status father) was associated with arthritis in the married daughter. Shekelle and colleagues[15] noted that risk of new coronary disease among men in a prospective study was associated with discrepancy between their social class at the time of the study and either their own or their wives' social class in childhood.

Syme and coworkers,[16] in research using urban male subjects from the California Health Survey, reported that cultural mobility was associated with CHD. Cultural mobility was defined as moving from one social setting to another or remaining stable within a given social setting while the setting itself undergoes change. In a case-control study, Syme et al. operationalized cultural mobility as cultural discontinuity and occupational mobility. Among male progeny of foreign-born fathers, sons who had college-level education had observed to expected (O/E) CHD ratios that were five times higher than those of sons who had completed only grade school or high school. Among college educated men, sons of foreign-born fathers had O/E CHD ratios that were more than two times higher than those of sons of native-born fathers. Regarding occupational mobility, men who held three or more different jobs for brief time periods during their lifetimes had O/E CHD ratios that were four times as high as the ratios of those who held only one or two jobs. Thus, in an urban setting, Syme et al. replicated findings regarding cultural mobility and increased CHD risk observed previously in rural areas.[16]

The Person-Environment Fit Model

Originally formulated to conceptualize various aspects of mental health, such as adjustment and coping, the person-environment fit model is applicable also to the etiology of physiologic illness.[17] Person-environment fit is one aspect of a larger system of variables that relate to health or illness outcome. French et al. stated that person-environment fit "conceives of *adjustment* as the goodness of fit between the characteristics of the person and the properties of [his or her] environment."[18(p. 316)] The model further distinguishes between the objective environment, which exists independent of the person's perceptions, and the subjective environment, or the environment that is perceived by the person. Corresponding distinctions are made for the person: the objective person and the subjective person (self-concept). Lack of adjustment (poor person-environment fit) occurs when there are discrepancies between demands and supplies. The result contributes to a stressful state that may culminate in illness. An example of lack of adjustment would be an overloaded executive who has far too many work responsibilities than he or she feels capable of handling; as a result, he or she is more prone than a well-adjusted executive to heart attacks, other chronic diseases, or other health problems.

The person-environment fit model portrays a web of variables that incorporates precursors of illness (e.g., lack of adjustment), mediating factors, and specific illnesses, such as CHD, arthritis, or some of the infectious diseases. Some of the variables are hypothesized to be directly related to a given outcome, others are considered intervening variables, and still others operate interactively in predicting illness. No single factor is a sufficient cause of a particular disease. The model suggests interconnection among mental health factors, physical health status, and psychologic factors that predispose to illness, precipitate illness, and determine recovery rates.[17]

The model specifies two dimensions of the person and, similarly, two dimensions of the environment that are incorporated in the quantification of stress. Person characteristics are needs and abilities, and environmental characteristics are supplies and demands. One variety of stress may result from lack of fit between the needs of the person and supplies in the environment. For example, one may consider person-environment fit in the area of affiliation. If a person who has a high affiliation need becomes a night guard, the person will experience stress with respect to the affiliation motive. Stress also may result from discrepancy between the abilities of the individual and demands emanating from the environment. Examples of this type of stress are particularly relevant to the study of occupational stress. For example, the piece worker who is required to produce 50 widgets per hour will be under stress if that individual has the ability to produce only 25 widgets.

The model theorizes that the relationship between lack of person-environment fit and stress is curvilinear. When a person's needs are exactly supplied, stress is at a minimum. Stress may result under either of the following two conditions, however: oversupply or undersupply of gratifications. Returning to the example of need for affiliation, the husband or wife who desires to affiliate with a spouse for two hours a day will experience stress if the spouse shows affiliative behavior for one hour or less or, at the other extreme, for three hours or more.

Empirical studies that employed the model and were conducted in occupational environments in which the major outcome was job dissatisfaction demonstrated that poor person-environment fit correlated significantly with job dissatisfaction.[17] An experimental study found that subjects who were faced with work overload demonstrated increases in serum cholesterol.[19]

Stressful Life Events

This vein of theory and research postulates that there is a relationship between the happenings in one's life and the development of illness. Two crucial issues of life events research are, first, to determine which attributes distinguish more stressful from less stressful life events and, second, to refine the knowledge base regarding the pathologic effects of stressful life events.

Holmes and Rahe[20] developed the Social Readjustment Rating Scale, which comprised 43 life event items. Research suggested that the items should be rank ordered in terms of importance to the individual; for example, the death of a spouse was found to be most stressful and was given the highest weight, 100 points; pregnancy was given a weight of 40; and minor violations of the law were given a weight of 11. The more severe the life change event and the higher the frequency of the event, the greater the chance that severe disease will occur. The following are the 10 leading life change events that Holmes and Rahe formulated during the late 1960s[20]:

1. death of a spouse
2. divorce
3. marital separation
4. jail term
5. death of a close family member
6. personal injury or illness
7. marriage
8. being fired from a job
9. marital reconciliation
10. retirement

Holmes and Masuda[21] reported that the greater the magnitude of life event as measured by the scale, the greater the probability that it would be associated with disease. In addition, there was an association between the magnitude of life change and the seriousness of illness. These investigators suggested that life stresses lower the resistance to disease and that the greater the stress or stresses in the person's life, the more severe the illness that may develop.

Langner and Michael[22] studied the association of life stresses with risk of mental disorders among a representative population of 1,660 residents of mid-town Manhattan in New York City. Subjects were administered a carefully designed interview that contained items about childhood and adult stress factors, psychiatric status, and other hypothesized risk factors for mental disorders. Examples of items were poor physical health as an adult or quarrels between parents during childhood. It was found that the greater the number of negative life factors, the greater the mental health risk.

Hinkle[23] reported on the frequency of disabling illness for a 20-year period that occurred among a group of career telephone operators who had been employed steadily in semiskilled occupations and among a group of blue-collar workers who worked for a similar division of the same company. Some employees had a much greater risk than others of becoming disabled, and, among those who had the greatest risk, there was also a greater likelihood of recurrent illnesses and more severe disability. Susceptibility to illness seemed to exacerbate the effect of stresses in the life of the individual. Among those who were not susceptible to illness, stressful life events did not seem to produce a decrement in health. There was also a tendency for the workers who were most frequently ill to be those who had occupations that seemed to be out of line with their educational and social backgrounds. For example, female telephone operators from blue-collar backgrounds were likely to be well adjusted and healthy, but college-educated women with the same job title expressed job dissatisfaction and were also more likely to experience frequent illness.

Characteristics of life events that are most salient as stressors include desirability of an event, control, and required readjustment.[24] Methodologic problems in life events research include subjects' recall ability, memory biases, reliability of measurement, and possible interconnectedness among life events.

The Stress Process Model

Pearlin[25] proposed the stress process model as an organizing and orienting framework for the diverse themes of stress research. The model would be heuristic by guiding researchers toward potentially useful lines of research, highlighting needed data for research, and aiding in the interpretation of results.

One of the important features of the model is that it emphasizes the interrelatedness of factors that play a role in the individual's health and well-being. Some of the factors include the contexts of persons' lives, their social statuses, their exposure to stress, the resources that they have available to deal with stressors, and the outcomes of stress exposure, both somatic and mental. The model is particularly intriguing because it specifies that stress is a process that occurs over a course of time. Events chain from one to another with interconnectedness among factors. As an example, Pearlin cited the role of social and economic status in the stress process. Those who are at the lower end of the economic hierarchy may face a life of fear and uncertainty or may lack economic resources. These circumstances, in turn, may be exacerbated by the individual's neighborhood context should it be unsafe, deteriorated, or unstable. Some of the problems that arise from a stressful neighborhood context, such as lack of access to needed services, are known as daily hassles.

In addition to the individual's social status and neighborhood context, the stress process model incorporates life events (defined earlier) and chronic or repeated strains. Examples of strains include life-course issues, for example, the need for spouses or children to assume long-term caregiving roles for elderly loved ones or parents. Finally, the model specifies moderating resources, such as coping and social support (covered later in this chapter), and stress outcomes, such as mental disorders (also covered later in the chapter). The epidemiologic features of depression and depressive symptoms indicate that these disorders are unequally distributed according to socioeconomic status, gender, marital status, and age. Turner and Lloyd provided empirical support for the stress process model with respect to the association of socioeconomic status with depressive symptoms.[26]

Moderating Factors in the Stress-Illness Relationship

Previously, we defined moderating (intervening) variables as those that are intermediate in the causal process between risk factors and outcomes. Examples of moderating variables are the type A behavior pattern, personal behaviors and lifestyle, and supportive interpersonal relationships. Personality variables also may have a moderating effect upon health outcomes by affecting how individuals respond to and cope with stress. For example, personality hardiness has been posited as a resistance resource that moderates the relationship between stressful life events and illness outcomes. Kobasa et al. wrote that "hardiness is considered a personality style consisting of the interrelated orientations of commitment (vs. alienation), control (vs. powerlessness), and challenge (vs. threat). Persons high in commitment find it easy to involve themselves actively in whatever they are doing, being generally curious about and interested in activities, things, and people . . . Persons high in control believe and act as if they can influence the events taking place around them through what they imagine, say, and do . . . Challenge involves the expectation that life will change and that the changes will be a stimulus to personal development."[27(p. 525)] Kobasa et al. reported that hardiness was the most important of resistance resources studied—including social support and exercise—in predicting the probability of illness among male business executives.

Type A (Coronary-Prone) Behavior Pattern

The type A behavior pattern has been found to be associated with CHD in prospective, cross-sectional, and retrospective studies. Researchers have focused upon clinical assessment of the behavior pattern through interview techniques and the development of a self-administered questionnaire measure. Rosenman and colleagues,[28] who pioneered work in the concept of the type A behavior pattern, characterized type A as including the traits of aggressiveness, ambition, drive, competitiveness, and time urgency. Jenkins subsequently enlarged the coronary-prone behavior pattern, which he conceptualized as an "overt behavioral syndrome or style of living . . . to include restlessness, hyperalertness, and explosiveness of speech."[29(p. 255)]

Interview Measure of Type A

Rosenman et al.[30] measured the type A syndrome by means of a structured clinical interview that was administered to a sample of 3,524 men, aged 39 to 59 years. Known as the Western Collaborative Group Study, the research prospectively followed the incidence of CHD among men in various occupations, beginning in 1960. Interview questions were designed to measure the several dimensions of the type A personality outlined above: drive, ambition, competitiveness, aggressiveness, hostility, and a sense of time urgency; motor and speech characteristics also were noted. The investigators, sometimes in collaboration with other researchers, have published numerous reports that contain data supportive of a significant and positive relationship between the type A personality and increased frequency of CHD.

Self-Administered Measure of Type A

To measure the type A behavior pattern objectively, several researchers reported the development of a self-administered checklist. Purported advantages of a checklist measure over a structured interview are greater standardization of research procedures in replication studies, ease of administration, and elimination of possible interviewer biases. Bortner[31] reported the development of a short rating scale (14 items) for the behavior pattern. The measure discriminated significantly between two groups of male workers who previously had been classified as behavior pattern A or B by the interview measure. (Type B refers to those people who do not have the type A pattern.) Jenkins[29] developed a self-administered, machine-scored test known as the Jenkins Activity Scale to measure the type A personality.

Social Support

Social support is defined as supportive relationships that arise from friends, family members, and others. Cobb[32] suggested that social support may moderate the effects of stress. Although the term *social support* refers to perceived emotional support that one receives from social relationships, the term *social network ties* is a quantitative concept that refers to the number (and, in some cases, the pattern) of ties that one has with other people or organizations. Social support systems operate as mediators that serve as buffers against stress.[33] Research has focused on the stress-buffering effects of social network ties and social support. For example, it has been hypothesized that social support may enhance immune status. Cancer patients' spouses, who would be presumed to have severe, chronic life stresses, demonstrated an association between social support and immune status; those who had higher levels of perceived social support tended to have better indexes of immune function.[34]

Social networks refer to the structure of people's social attachments[35] and are considered mediators because they help explain differences in the individual's ability to respond to stressors. The buffering model states that one of the functions of social network ties is to lessen the adverse psychologic consequences of stress.[36] The underlying assumption is that support and resources provided by social network ties may act as a buffer against the potentially harmful effects (e.g., depression) of stressful life events.[37] Conversely, lack of family social support and close affectional ties contributes to vulnerability, onset, and severity of psychologic stress.[38] Variations in the effects of support are thought to be related to the source of support.[39] For example, support from spouses or friends may be more important than support derived from other network ties.

Supportive relationships may be deduced from social networks, including ties with family and friends and memberships in formal and informal organizations. Marital status has been found to be salient in the social support process; married older adults have more contact with family members than with friends and receive more emotional support than unmarried older adults.[40] In addition, social contact, received emotional support, and anticipated support are interrelated. Increased social contact is associated with increased emotional support and perceptions of support availability.[39] The specificity hypothesis postulates that interpersonal relationships provide a stress-buffering effect when there is concordance between coping requirements demanded by a particular stressor and specific types of support provided.[41]

Personal Behavior, Lifestyle, and Health

In this section, we include characteristics such as personal risk taking, smoking, alcohol consumption, choice of diet, and exercise levels. Breslow[42] summarized the results from the Human Population Laboratory in Alameda County, California, where investigators observed a positive association between seven healthful habits and physical health status and longevity. The seven habits were moderate food intake, eating regularly, eating breakfast, not smoking cigarettes, moderate or no use of alcohol, moderate exercise, and seven to eight hours of sleep daily. There was a direct correlation between the number of healthful habits followed and good health status and reduced mortality.

Behavior and lifestyle are related to a number of diseases that are of major importance to modern Western civilization. Burkitt[43] believed that these include noninfectious diseases of the large bowel, venous disorders, and obesity. Appendicitis, diverticular diseases, cancer of the large bowel, pulmonary embolism, gallbladder disease, ischemic heart disease, and diabetes are relatively common diseases in the United States and Britain. Burkitt stated that these same conditions are uncommon in developing countries and were rare a century ago in Western nations. Suchman[44] referred to the chronic, degenerative diseases as way-of-life diseases because of their closer relationship to human behavior than to any bacteriologic or infectious agent.

Personal behavior was related to accidents, the fifth major cause of death in 2003 in the United States.[45] Mortality and morbidity from accidents are largely, if not completely, preventable. Although accidents might appear to be unpredicted, unexpected events, epidemiologic data suggest, contrary to this notion, that accidental injuries and death are not randomly distributed. Rather, accidents tend to be more common among individuals with certain identifiable host characteristics, such as sex, age, choice of occupation, and safety practices, which are influenced by attitudinal and behavioral variables in relation to risk taking.[44]

Personal behavior is intimately connected with personal health status. Health-relevant behavior is a function of both psychologic and contemporary sociocultural influences. For example, there is great variety in the amount of personal risk that one may want to assume in the conduct of daily existence, from minimal risk to such high-risk activities as motorcycle riding, sky diving, and hang gliding, which place one at direct risk of accidental death and injury. Sexual behavior, dietary practices, smoking, alcohol consumption, method of infant feeding, and choice of occupation are all components of personal behavior that affect health and are governed by personality constitution, cultural influences, and the prevailing social climate. Personal behavior is of such importance that the U.S. National Center for Chronic Disease Prevention and Health Promotion established a behavioral risk factor surveillance program. The purpose of this program was to modify behavioral risk factors to accomplish national health objectives for the year 2000. The objective areas for the behavioral risk factor surveillance program included obesity, lack of physical activity, smoking, safety belt use, and medical screening for breast and cervical cancer and elevated blood cholesterol. The surveillance program was a state-based, random-digit dialing telephone survey.[46]

Healthy People 2000 established a framework in the United States for national health promotion and disease prevention objectives.[47] Several of these objectives relate to health promotion through encouragement of a desirable lifestyle. A more recent document, *Healthy People 2010*, builds on earlier initiatives such as *Healthy People 2000*. The newer document states two major goals and 28 focus areas for improvement of health. Note that many areas, such as fitness, nutrition, substance abuse, and tobacco use, are related to lifestyle. The topics acknowledge the awareness of the U.S. Department of Health and Human Services regarding the significant function that lifestyle plays in health (see Exhibit 15–2).

EXHIBIT 15–2

What is *Healthy People 2010?*

Healthy People 2010 is a comprehensive set of disease prevention and health promotion objectives for the Nation to achieve over the first decade of the new century. Created by scientists both inside and outside of Government, it identifies a wide range of public health priorities and specific, measurable objectives.

Overarching Goals:

1. Increase quality and years of healthy life
2. Eliminate health disparities

Focus Areas

1. Access to Quality Health Services
2. Arthritis, Osteoporosis, and Chronic Back Conditions
3. Cancer
4. Chronic Kidney Disease
5. Diabetes
6. Disability and Secondary Conditions
7. Educational and Community-Based Programs
8. Environmental Health
9. Family Planning
10. Food Safety
11. Health Communication
12. Heart Disease and Stroke

continues

EXHIBIT 15–2 *continued*

13. HIV
14. Immunization and Infectious Diseases
15. Injury and Violence Prevention
16. Maternal, Infant, and Child Health
17. Medical Product Safety
18. Mental Health and Mental Disorders
19. Nutrition and Overweight
20. Occupational Safety and Health
21. Oral Health
22. Physical Activity and Fitness
23. Public Health Infrastructure
24. Respiratory Diseases
25. Sexually Transmitted Diseases
26. Substance Abuse
27. Tobacco Use
28. Vision and Hearing

Source: Modified from *Healthy People 2010* Fact Sheet, Office of Disease Prevention and Health Promotion, U.S. Department of Health and Human Services. Available at: http://www.healthypeople.gov/About/hpfact.htm. Accessed December 27, 2007.

Smoking and Health

Three major reports by the U.S. Surgeon General—the 1964 report discussed in Chapter 2, the 1979 report,[48] and the 2004 report[49]—summarized conclusions regarding the relationship between smoking and various adverse health consequences. Epidemiologic research suggests that smoking is a significant cause of excess mortality and morbidity. For example:

- Current cigarette smokers in comparison with nonsmokers have an overall 70% excess mortality regardless of amount of smoking.
- Mortality from smoking increases with the quantity of cigarettes smoked; mortality is increased by duration of smoking, starting at earlier ages, and amount of smoke inhaled.
- Associations have been observed between smoking and morbidity from cardiovascular diseases; cancer of the lung, larynx, mouth, bladder, and pancreas; and non-neoplastic bronchopulmonary diseases.

- There are interactive and synergistic effects of smoking and occupational exposures to asbestos, chromium, nickel, and other potentially toxic or carcinogenic materials.
- Smoking is a direct cause of reduction in birth weight and increased prenatal mortality; nicotine is found in the breast milk of mothers who smoke.

With respect to the behavioral aspects of smoking, the 1979 Surgeon General's report concluded that the reason why the smoking habit is so widespread and difficult to break is largely unknown: "It is no exaggeration to say that smoking is the prototypical substance abuse dependency and that improved knowledge of this process holds great promise for the prevention of risk. Establishment and maintenance of the smoking habit are, obviously, prerequisite to the risk, and cessation of smoking can eliminate or greatly reduce the health threat."[48(pp. 1–32)] Since the 1979 report, much additional information has been acquired regarding the nature of nicotine addiction. The Surgeon General's 2004 report identified ". . . a substantial number of diseases found to be caused by smoking that were not previously causally associated with smoking: cancers of the stomach, uterine cervix, pancreas, and kidney; acute myeloid leukemia; pneumonia; abdominal aortic aneurysm; cataract; and periodontitis."[49(p. 1)]

Alcohol Consumption

Excessive alcohol consumption is a risk factor for specific diseases (e.g., various cancers, liver cirrhosis, and gastric disorders); increases the likelihood of involvement in motor vehicle accidents and other unintentional injuries; and is associated with deterioration of the social environment (e.g., interpersonal violence, family strife, and lessened job performance). In 2004, The World Health Organization (WHO) reported that approximately 2 billion people in the world partake of alcoholic beverages and that almost 80 million individuals have diagnosable alcohol use disorders. WHO highlighted the negative implications of excessive alcohol consumption for people's health and the functioning of society.[50]

In the United States, over-consumption of alcohol was recorded as the third leading preventable cause of death in 2001 and accounted for more than 75,000 deaths and 2.3 million years of potential life lost (YPLL).[51] (The term YPLL is defined in Chapter 7.) That number is about half the total YPLL from smoking in 1999, the most recent year for which comparative data were available. Slightly more than 40,000 deaths were from alcohol-related injuries attributed to binge drinking. (Refer to Table 15–1.)

For the population sub-group aged 12 to 20 years, excessive alcohol consumption was a factor in the three leading causes of death—unintentional injury,

Table 15-1 Selected Number of Deaths (Total Number of Male + Female Deaths > 1,000) and Years of Potential Life Lost (YPLL) Attributable to the Harmful Effects of Excessive Alcohol Use, by Cause and Sex—United States, 2001

	Deaths			YPLL		
Cause	Male	Female	Total	Male	Female	Total
Chronic conditions						
Alcohol abuse	1,804	517	**2,321**	50,375	16,433	**66,808**
Alcohol dependence syndrome	2,770	750	**3,520**	71,782	22,017	**93,799**
Alcoholic liver disease	8,927	3,274	**12,201**	221,369	94,952	**316,321**
Hypertension	632	552	**1,184**	9,458	6,460	**15,918**
Liver cirrhosis, unspecified	3,917	2,802	**6,719**	80,616	54,528	**135,144**
Stroke, hemorrhagic	1,399	290	**1,690**	22,476	4,592	**27,068**
Total	**24,448**	**10,385**	**34,833**	**548,386**	**239,619**	**788,005**
Acute conditions						
Fall injuries	2,560	2,206	**4,766**	41,627	24,288	**65,914**
Fire injuries	702	465	**1,167**	18,991	11,729	**30,720**
Homicide	5,963	1,692	**7,655**	262,379	71,543	**333,922**
Motor-vehicle—traffic injuries	10,674	3,000	**13,674**	442,943	136,558	**579,501**
Poisoning (not alcohol)	2,782	1,182	**3,964**	103,917	45,127	**149,043**
Suicide	5,617	1,352	**6,969**	186,568	49,297	**235,865**
Total	**30,399**	**10,534**	**40,933**	**1,131,028**	**360,289**	**1,491,317**
Total	**54,847**	**20,918**	**75,766**	**1,679,414**	**599,908**	**2,279,322**

Note: Numbers do not add up to column subtotals because categories with small frequencies have been omitted.

Source: Modified from Centers for Disease Control and Prevention, Alcohol-attributable deaths and years of potential life lost—United States, 2001. *MMWR.* Vol 53, p. 869, 2004.

homicide, and suicide.[52] Promotion of alcohol use by alcoholic beverage manufacturers in advertisements placed in magazines that have a 15% to 30% youth readership has remained a common practice.

Pregnant women's alcohol consumption is related to the fetal alcohol syndrome (FAS), which is characterized by postnatal growth deficiency, mental retardation, and various physical abnormalities.[53] According to Streissguth,[53] FAS presents as a set of specific characteristics: small stature, small head, small eyes, flattened nasal bridge, and a thin, narrow upper lip. In addition to FAS, there is an association between low to moderate intake of alcohol during pregnancy and low birth weight. The sequelae of FAS last a lifetime, even though the effects may range from mild to severe.[54] As a result of pervasive alcohol consumption among women of childbearing age (more than 50%), there is a high likelihood of exposure to alcohol during pregnancy. Additional health education programs are needed to inform women of childbearing age about FAS and other hazards of alcohol consumption during pregnancy.

Dietary Practices

Choice of habitual diet affects the development of chronic diseases and is an aspect of personal behavior that is related to sociocultural influences. Burkitt[43] noted the association between the consumption of refined carbohydrate foods and obesity and diabetes. He suggested that lack of fiber in the food of Western diets is related to diseases of the bowel, such as colon cancer and diverticular disease.

The diet-heart hypothesis suggests that a diet high in saturated fats and cholesterol is linked to high blood lipids, which are in turn associated with arteriosclerosis and heart disease. More recent evidence has shown that low levels of high-density lipoproteins and high levels of low-density lipoproteins in the blood are associated with heart disease. Diets that maintain a high ratio of polyunsaturated to saturated fat lower risk of CHD, a phenomenon supported by findings from studies of California Seventh-Day Adventists (see Chapter 4). About half the membership consumes a non-meat, lacto-ovovegetarian diet. Adult members have CHD mortality rates that are about 30% of the rate for an equivalent age group within the total California population.

Dietary practices such as consumption of fats, fruits, and vegetables are hypothesized to be related to cancer incidence. Consumption of animal fats, a high-meat diet, and vegetables has been studied in relationship to colon cancer.[55] The linkage between low blood cholesterol and risk of developing cancer also has been investigated. Dietary fat may play a role in mediating the relationship between blood cholesterol and cancer.[56] Among residents of Shanghai, China, a case-control study determined that consumption of fruits, certain dark green/yellow vegetables, and garlic was a protective factor for laryngeal cancer, whereas intake of salt-preserved meat and fish increased risk.[57] Another factor studied in relation to cancer is β-carotene, for which investigators hypothesize a protective role. Low serum β-carotene may be associated with cancers of the lung, stomach, cervix, esophagus, small intestine, and uterus.[58]

Coffee and tea consumption as factors in morbidity and mortality from CHD and other chronic diseases has been studied extensively. Although the findings are conflicting for the association of coffee drinking with cardiovascular disease, there does appear to be an indirect connection through association with adverse lifestyle factors. An Austrian study reported that coffee drinking was related to lifestyle factors—smoking, drinking, eating, and lack of physical activity—that could increase risk of cardiovascular disease.[59] The reverse of this association was found between tea drinking and lifestyle factors.

One of the crucial diet-related issues in the United States is obesity (often referred to as a modern epidemic), given the association of overweight and obesity with diabetes and CHD risk factors. The rising obesity rates in the United States have become a dominant concern of public health practitioners, who are encouraging increased consumption of fruits and vegetables. Currently, only about one-third of the population consumes fruit two or more times per day and vegetables three or more times per day. Although school cafeterias, fast food restaurants, and grocery chains are increasing the availability of low-fat and healthful food choices, many individuals prefer high-fat foods and large portion sizes. Some localities (e.g., New York City) have banned the use of trans fats (made by hydrogenating oils) in foods sold in restaurants; trans fats increase the risk of CHD.

Sedentary Lifestyle

Sedentary Western existence, with its use of labor-saving devices and reduced level of physical activity, is identified as a risk factor for CHD and other conditions. As reviewed earlier in Chapter 7, Morris et al.[60] examined the leisure time activities of 17,000 male executive-grade British civil servant office workers aged 40 to 64 years. Workers who participated in vigorous active recreations, such as swimming and heavy gardening, had about one-third the incidence of CHD as the less active workers. Light exercise that did not have a training effect on the cardiovascular system did not reduce the incidence of heart disease. The results were interpreted as demonstrating that vigorous exercise promotes cardiovascular health.

Paffenbarger et al.[61] corroborated these results in a study of about 17,000 Harvard male alumni aged 35 to 74 (refer to Chapter 7). Risk of first heart attack was inversely related to involvement in vigorous physical exercise (e.g., stair climbing, walking, and strenuous athletics). Those who were college athletes and discontinued exercise during later life were at greater risk of heart attack than adults who began exercising at a later age.

Streja and Mymin[62] designed an exercise program to determine whether there is a relationship between exercise and cholesterol level among sedentary persons. They observed that low levels of high-density lipoprotein cholesterol (HDL-C, the so-called good cholesterol) have been shown to precede arteriosclerosis and that athletes in comparison with control subjects have high levels of HDL-C. In an exercise program that consisted of walking and slow jogging, a small sample of middle-aged men with coronary artery disease had increased levels of HDL-C. The results of the study suggest that exercise programs may retard the development of arteriosclerosis.

Many epidemiologic investigations have followed the early work of Morris et al. on the role of physical activity in health. These later studies have incorporated diverse populations in terms of sex, ethnicity, age, social composition, and geographic location. In their follow-up study, Paffenbarger et al. concluded that, "These studies have extended and amplified those by the Morris group, thereby helping to solidify the cause-and-effect evidence that exercise protects against heart disease and averts premature mortality."[63(p. 1184)] Not only does exercise benefit the general population, but it also promotes physical functioning in subgroups of the population, for example, persons with disabilities[64] and the elderly.[65]

Sociocultural Influences on Health

One of the concerns of contemporary epidemiologic research is the role of social and cultural factors in health. Epidemiologic research has produced a voluminous literature regarding the effects of social, cultural, and psychosocial factors in the etiology of disease.[66] Culture may be defined as the set of values to which a group of people subscribes, as the way of life of a group of people, or as the totality of what is learned and shared through interaction of the members of a society. Specific behaviors associated with a particular culture have implications for the health of the individual. In support of this notion, Susser et al. wrote, "Habits that affect health, in childbearing and midwifery, in nutrition and in daily living, are not merely the negative result of ignorance among people who know no better. They are often an intrinsic element in a way of life, customs that have positive value and symbolic significance."[67(pp. 152–153)]

One explanation for the role that cultural factors play in health is that they may mediate the amount of stress to which the individual is exposed. Matsumoto[68] observed that Japan historically has had one of the lowest rates of CHD in the world and that the United States has had one of the highest. He hypothesized:

> The etiology of coronary heart disease is multiple and complex, but in urban-industrial Japan, the in-group work community of the individual, with its institutional stress-reducing strategies, plays an important role in decreasing the frequency of the disease. . . . Deleterious circumstances of life need not be expressed in malfunctioning of the physiologic or psychologic systems if a meaningful social group is available through which the individual can derive emotional support and understanding.[68(p. 14)]

Marmot and colleagues[69] studied a large population of men of Japanese ancestry: 2,141 men who were being followed by the Atomic Bomb Casualty Commission in Hiroshima and Nagasaki, Japan; 8,006 men in Honolulu; and 1,844 men in the San Francisco Bay area. Japanese who lived in California had a higher prevalence of CHD and its manifestations than those who resided in

Hawaii or Japan. The Hawaiian Japanese tended to have higher CHD rates than residents of Japan. The investigators speculated that differences in prevalence of CHD may have been due to differences in the way of life in Japan and the United States. For example, there are major variations between the two countries in diet, occupation, and the social and cultural milieu.

Studies have pursued the role of sociocultural factors in mental retardation. Mercer[70] suggested that excessively large numbers of individuals from minority backgrounds were being labeled by the public schools as mentally retarded because available standardized tests of intelligence did not adequately take into account the background of the students. The dimensions that are measured on IQ and other tests are taken from the white, middle-class society and do not constitute a culture-free measure.

Both utilization of health services and, in fact, the very definition of illness are related to cultural background and show variation from person to person. According to Mechanic, illness refers to objective symptoms, whereas illness behavior "refers to the varying perceptions, thoughts, feelings, and acts affecting the personal and social meaning of symptoms, illness, disabilities and their consequences. . . . [Some people will] make light of symptoms and impairments. Others magnify even minimal problems, allowing them to affect their life adjustments substantially."[71(p. 79)] It is possible that those who seek medical care readily may, over the long run, experience increased life expectancy through early identification of potentially life-threatening illness.

In citing differences in preference for type of medical services by cultural group membership, Mechanic[72] stated that some Mexican Americans might prefer folk medicine and family care. Whites, however, would show a predilection for modern medical services in a technologically advanced medical center. Elsewhere, Mechanic wrote, "Illness perception and response may be socially learned patterns developed early in life as a result of exposure to particular cultural styles, ethnic values, or sex role socialization."[71(p. 79)]

Social and cultural factors are related to the successful control of communicable diseases; a notable example is control of tuberculosis among immigrants to the United States from Mexico. People of Mexican descent with tuberculosis showed delayed response in seeking medical attention. These delays were attributed to diagnosis by a layperson of the symptoms of the folk illness *susto*, a condition not considered susceptible to the ministrations of physicians. Among undocumented Mexican workers residing in Orange County, California, the average delay between acknowledgment of tuberculosis symptoms and the presentation of a complaint to a physician was 8.5 months.[73]

Outcome Variables: Physical Health, Mental Health, Affective States

Psychosocial epidemiologic research covers both physical and mental health outcomes. Examples of physical health outcomes that are studied within a psychosocial framework include specific chronic diseases (e.g., CHD). Those related to psychologic status embrace affective states, life and job dissatisfaction, and depressive symptoms. We also point out that the physical and mental dimensions of health have been shown to overlap. There is evidence that psychiatric and physical disorders are risk factors for each other.[74]

Life and Job Dissatisfaction

According to Jenkins, "The hypothesis that life dissatisfaction is a risk factor for coronary disease is a promising one and deserves careful examination in prospective studies."[29(p. 254)] One aspect of life dissatisfaction that is increasingly shown to be related to coronary disease is job dissatisfaction. Empirical findings suggest that life and job dissatisfaction are directly related to morbidity and mortality from CHD. An ecologic analysis by Sales and House[75] reported strong negative correlations between job satisfaction and coronary disease death rates for white-collar and blue-collar workers when the effects of social class were controlled. In a study of identical twins, Liljefors and Rahe[76] similarly reported a strong association between various life dissatisfactions, including job dissatisfactions, and heart disease. Other studies have implicated various themes of job dissatisfaction in coronary disease. Tedious work, feeling ill at ease at work, lack of recognition, difficulties with coworkers, demotion, and prolonged emotional strain associated with work overload have all been shown to be related to coronary disease.

Several investigators have focused upon extrinsic-intrinsic motivation (motivation for power and money as opposed to motivation for the internal qualities of an occupation) as a job-related motivational dimension that may be associated with CHD. Using a sample from the University of Michigan Tecumseh Study, House[77] found that the association between extrinsic-intrinsic motivation and risk of CHD was conditioned by occupational status. Among white-collar workers, extrinsic motivation was positively related to risk of CHD; the relationship between intrinsic motivation and risk of CHD was negative. The reverse associations were found for blue-collar workers.

Mental Health and Stressors

Epidemiologic research has examined various mental health outcomes, such as psychologic disorders (e.g., posttraumatic stress disorder [PTSD] and major depression) and affective states, as outcomes of the stress-illness paradigm. PTSD is an example of a mental disorder that is associated with exposure to extremely traumatic events. PTSD victims tend to reexperience the traumatic event—whether a natural disaster, war, rape, or other trauma—and may progress in some instances to persisting psychopathology. PTSD is a potentially noteworthy disorder for epidemiologic research because it often stems from a massive trauma that has been experienced by an entire population.[78] Examples include the 1994 Northridge earthquake in southern California, the 2001 terrorist attack on the World Trade Center in New York, and the 2005 flooding of New Orleans caused by Hurricanes Katrina and Rita. Still another example is the frequent occurrence of PTSD among returning war veterans, most recently those stationed in Iraq. Not only do individuals who experience a natural disaster, such as an earthquake, vary in the severity of their responses, but there also appears to be a dose-response relationship between proximity to the traumatic event and degree of mental impairment.

Let us now turn to a unique problem for mental health epidemiology. Of particular interest to epidemiologists has been the development of an easily administered instrument to assess the prevalence of mental disorders in population surveys. Prior to the development of such a measure, some epidemiologic investigations relied on individual clinical ratings, hospital admission rates, or other utilization data to determine rates of conditions such as depression. Langner's 22-item Index of Psychophysiologic Disorder represented one of the first efforts to design an epidemiologic measure of psychiatric impairment.[79] A later instrument is the Center for Epidemiologic Studies depression (CES-D) scale, a brief, 20-item self-report depression symptom scale.[80,81] Possible scores on the CES-D scale range from a minimum of 0 to a maximum of 60. Research studies have found it to be as reliable, sensitive, and valid a measure of depressive symptoms and change in depressive symptoms as clinical interview ratings. The instrument permits differentiation between acute depressives and recovered depressives as well as between depressives and other diagnostic groups.[82] The measure has been validated in predominantly urban populations[83–85] and more recently in rural populations.[86] Sample items are self-reported feelings of depression, fearfulness, loneliness, and sadness. Subjects indicate the frequency with which these symptoms have occurred during the past week (range, 0 to 5–7 days; range of item scores, 0–3). A total CES-D score of 16 or greater has been defined in literature reports as the criterion for a case of depression.[82]

Several major surveys have examined the prevalence of self-reported symptoms of depression as assessed by the CES-D scale. The prevalence of depression in a representative sample of adults in Los Angeles County was 19%.[87] Rates of depression were higher among women than men (23.5% vs. 12.9%). Depressed persons reported more physical illnesses than the nondepressed. Using data from the Hispanic Health and Nutrition Examination Survey, other investigators reported a caseness (i.e., CES-D score of 16 or greater) rate for high levels of depressive symptoms of 13.3%; female sex, low educational achievement, low income, birth in the United States, and white-oriented acculturation of the Hispanic sample were associated with depressive symptoms.[88]

The National Institute of Mental Health Epidemiological Catchment Area Program was a comprehensive collaborative effort by scientists to gather data on the prevalence of mental disorders in the United States. The disorders studied were the major psychiatric illnesses classified in the third edition of the *Diagnostic and Statistical Manual* (a manual for the classification of mental disorders). The study was unprecedented in its scope, covering 17,000 residents of five community sites across the United States.[89]

Premorbid Psychologic Factors and Cancer

Fox[90] compiled a comprehensive literature review and evaluation of studies of premorbid psychologic and personality factors associated with cancer. Possible deficiencies of the prospective and retrospective studies done in this field through 1977 include small sample sizes, inappropriate use of statistical tests, methodologic flaws, and possible alternative interpretations. One group of prospective studies suggested that cancer patients show lack of warm relationships with their parents and pathologic responses to the Rorschach test (a personality test that uses ink-blot designs to evoke associations). Other studies mentioned in Fox's review suggested that women who were later found to have breast cancer deliberately repress and fail to express anger. Still another investigation reported that lung cancer patients had higher-than-average scores on the lie scale of the Minnesota Multiphasic Personality Inventory, but the interpretation of this finding has been challenged.

Deficiencies of research notwithstanding, Fox[90] summarized two major personality types at increased risk of cancer. He portrayed the first type as yielding, compliant, and eager to please. Among the first personality type, activation of hormonal mechanisms might be associated with repression of feelings. Repressed emotion might alter immune system responses to carcinogenic agents, thereby increasing incidence of cancer in individuals with this personality type. The second type consisted of extroverted, non-neurotic individuals who tend toward heaviness. He predicted that male or female extroverts, as a result of physical lifestyle (sometimes involving excessive eating, drinking, and smoking), would have higher rates than others of colorectal, breast, lung, prostate, esophageal, and cervical cancer. The primary etiologic mechanism would be the indirect linkage between personality and cancer through lifestyle factors.

A subsequent review of the associations among psychologic variables (e.g., stress, bereavement, depressed mood, mental illness, suppressed emotions, helplessness and hopelessness, and social support) and various cancer outcomes, including mortality or course of the disease, appeared approximately two decades later.[91] It was concluded that the literature remains contradictory, marked by both positive findings and the absence of associations; however, the evidence against the relationship between psychologic factors and cancer outcomes is most notable for stress, depressed mood, psychosis, and bereavement.

Effects of Major Diseases on Personality

Not only might one conceive of personality characteristics as a cause of diseases, but one might look also at the reverse side of the coin and examine the effect of disease upon personality. Affliction with a chronic illness may become a substantial stress factor for the person and for members of his or her immediate social environment. A severe drinking problem, substance abuse, or a heart attack may induce personality changes in the afflicted individual and may affect other persons, including one's children, spouse, and coworkers. A number of personality effects accompany severe illness; for example, wives of heart attack victims experience depression, fear, anxiety, and guilt.[92] Wives have increasing anxiety about the future and guilt feelings about being a possible cause of the attack. Additionally, the victim may experience increased feelings of depression, anxiety, guilt, and hopelessness. One implication for epidemiologic research is that studies should carefully separate out the direction of causality. Did the personality characteristic cause the disease, or did the disease cause the personality characteristic?

Personality and Smoking

An issue that has commanded the attention of epidemiologic researchers and others concerns the extent to which smoking behavior is determined by personality factors. The Surgeon General's Report of 1979[49] indicated that personality factors that may be related to smoking behavior are extroversion, neuroticism, antisocial tendencies, and the belief that one is externally controlled (i.e., that fate, luck, or other factors beyond one's control will bring one rewards). Smokers show a greater willingness than nonsmokers to take risks and are more impulsive, more likely to divorce and change jobs, more interested in sex, and more likely to consume tea, coffee, and alcohol.

Research conducted subsequently to the Surgeon General's Report also suggested that cigarette smokers may possess distinctive personality characteristics in comparison with nonsmokers, for example, with respect to risk behaviors.[93] A major review of the epidemiology of tobacco use concluded that some studies have linked cigarette smoking to several types of psychiatric disorders.[93] Associations between depressive states and smoking, anxiety disorders and smoking, and schizophrenia and smoking have been reported by several investigators. For example, Acton et al.[94] examined smoking status and diagnosis among patients hospitalized for psychiatric disorders. Among never smokers, rates of currently diagnosed major depressive disorder were lower than among patients who were ever smokers.

Habitual Mental Outlook and Health Status

One's prevailing attitudes toward life and one's mental health status have been probed with respect to their association with physical health status and longevity. A major study of male mental health followed up 204 men biennially over a period of four decades, beginning at adolescence.[95] Information regarding the mental health status as well as the physical health status of the subjects was routinely collected during the study. Among the 59 men with the best mental health between the ages of 21 and 46, only 2 developed chronic illness or died by age 53. Among 46 men with the worst mental health levels, 18 developed chronic illnesses or died. The association between mental and physical health remained statistically significant when the variables of alcohol and tobacco consumption, obesity, and longevity of relatives were controlled.

The foregoing research addressed the possible role of mental health and adult adjustment in men's physical health. Aspects of mental health potentially associated with physical health include habitual mental outlook, such as optimism. The self-reported health of midlife women has been shown to be positively related to optimism.[96] However, the positive association between cheerfulness—one aspect of habitual mental outlook—and health (specifically longevity) has been contradicted by a study of subjects from Terman's seven-decade longitudinal investigation of highly intelligent children.[97] While the findings suggested that conscientiousness in childhood was associated with survival in middle to old age, cheerfulness—characterized by optimism and sense of humor—was inversely related to longevity.

In conclusion, while research into the association between characteristics of habitual mental outlook (mental health, adult adjustment, cheerfulness, optimism, and sense of humor) and health status (self-reported physical health, chronic disease, and longevity) has evolved and produced some intriguing hypotheses and findings, further work is needed because of inconsistent results. For example, there is a possible need to reconceptualize the health relevance of variables such as cheerfulness.[97] The role of habitual mental outlook in health may be elucidated further by prospective studies that refine measurement techniques and clarify the theoretical pathways through which this factor may operate.

Conclusion

The field of social epidemiology is concerned with the influence of a person's position in the social structure upon the development of disease. Behavioral epidemiology studies the role in health of factors such as tobacco use, physical activity, and risky sexual behavior. The term psychosocial epidemiology has been more broadly conceptualized to include social, behavioral, and psychologic factors. This field of investigation has used case-control, cohort, cross-sectional, and experimental designs to research a wide variety of health outcomes.

This chapter first examined the independent variables of stress, status incongruity, person-environment fit, and stressful life events. Stress as an independent, antecedent variable to health and illness represents an intriguing notion because it seems to fit in with commonsense explanations for the cause of some mental disorders and chronic physical illnesses, yet documentation of stress as an etiologic agent of disease is inconsistent. Investigators have hypothesized that either social mobility or status incongruity may be associated with morbidity and mortality. Person-environment fit, originally formulated to conceptualize various aspects of mental health such as adjustment and coping, is another example of a social and psychologic precursor to the etiology of physiologic illness. A fourth example of an independent variable is the concept of stressful life events. The central postulate of life events research is that there is a relationship between the happenings in one's life and the development of illness.

Examples of moderating (intervening) variables in psychosocial epidemiologic research are the type A behavior pattern, personal behaviors and lifestyle, supportive interpersonal relationships, and social and cultural influences. Outcome variables include affective states, life and job dissatisfaction, chronic disease, and depressive symptoms. The increasing number of psychosocial epidemiologic research studies point to the need for well-delineated conceptual models, which at present have not been implemented satisfactorily.[98] Also needed is the development of strong, research-based intervention programs.[99]

Study Questions and Exercises

1. Define the following:
   a. stress
   b. general adaptation syndrome
   c. social incongruity
   d. person-environment fit
   e. life events
   f. type A behavior pattern
   g. social support
   h. lifestyle
   i. depressive symptoms
   j. stress process model
2. Propose a model for the relationship between stress and illness. Be sure to choose a specific outcome and include moderating factors. How will your model operationalize stress? Draw a diagram of all major relationships among the variables.
3. How do one's culture and environment relate to health? In answering this question, consider the cultural dynamics of a Western and non-Western country. Identify an immigrant group in your community and discuss how this group's health-related practices differ from those of the larger community.
4. Give examples of two personality traits that may modify the relationship between stress and disease. Can you give your own examples of personality traits that are not mentioned in the chapter?
5. What is the role of stressful life events as an influence upon disease? To what extent are each of the 10 leading life events identified during the 1960s relevant to the 21st century? Can you identify other life events that might be more salient to contemporary society?

6. Describe the association between social incongruity and chronic disease. What types of study populations would be appropriate to an epidemiologic investigation of the health effects of social incongruity?

7. How is person-environment fit relevant to studies of occupational health and job-related stress? What type of person would adjust well to an authoritarian work environment, and what type to an unstructured environment? What is meant by a curvilinear relationship between person-environment fit and stress?

8. Give examples of how the following lifestyle variables affect health:
   a. alcohol and smoking
   b. exercise
   c. risk taking

9. Stress has been hypothesized to be associated with human illness. Apply the concepts and criteria presented in Chapter 2 to argue for and against a causal association between stress and CHD.

10. To what extent are health outcome variables distinct or overlapping? For example, discuss the possibility that impaired mental health may be a risk factor for impaired physical health and vice versa. What types of epidemiologic study designs might be able to disentangle the time sequencing of overlapping mental disorders and impaired physical health?

11. Capstone exercise: This exercise is included here because it requires skills developed in the previous chapters of the text. Select a data-based article from the *American Journal of Public Health*, the *American Journal of Epidemiology*, or other public health journal of your choice. Refer to Appendix A (Guide to the Critical Appraisal of an Epidemiologic/Public Health Research Article). Using the criteria shown in the Appendix, write a brief critique of the article. In addition to discussing the criteria suggested in the appendix, mention what improvements, if any, you would make in the article.

References

1. Engel G. The need for a new medical model: a challenge for biomedicine. *Science*. 1977;196:129–136.
2. Syme SL. Behavioral factors associated with the etiology of physical disease: a social epidemiological approach. *Am J Public Health*. 1974;64:1043–1045.
3. Berkman LF, Kawachi I. A historical framework for social epidemiology. In: Berkman LF, Kawachi I, eds. *Social Epidemiology*. New York, NY: Oxford University Press; 2000.

4. Blumenthal JA, Sherwood A, Gullette EC, et al. Biobehavioral approaches to the treatment of essential hypertension. *J Consult Clin Psychol.* 2002;70:569–589.

5. Wittchen HU, Perkonigg A, Lachner G, Nelson CB. Early developmental stages of psychopathology study (EDSP): objectives and design. *Eur Addict Res.* 1998;4:18–27.

6. Lieb R, Zimmermann P, Friis RH, et al. The natural course of DSM-IV somatoform disorders and syndromes among adolescents and young adults: a prospective-longitudinal community study. *Eur Psychiatry.* 2002;17:321–331.

7. Friis RH, Wittchen HU, Pfister H, Lieb R. Life events and changes in the course of depression in young adults. *Eur Psychiatry.* 2002;17:241–253.

8. Marmot M. Introduction. In: Marmot M, Wilkinson RG, eds. *Social Determinants of Health.* New York, NY: Oxford University Press; 1999:1–16.

9. Murray CJ, Lopez AD. Global mortality, disability, and the contribution of risk factors: global burden of disease study. *Lancet.* 1997;349:1436–1442.

10. Wolf S. Psychosocial influences in gastrointestinal function. In: Levi L, ed. *Society, Stress, and Disease.* London, UK: Oxford University Press; 1971:362–366.

11. Selye H. *The Stress of Life.* New York, NY: McGraw Hill; 1956.

12. Selye H. The evolution of the stress concept—stress and cardiovascular disease. In: Levi L, ed. *Society, Stress, and Disease.* London, UK: Oxford University Press; 1971:299–311.

13. Crider A. Experimental studies of conflict-produced stress. In: Levine S, Scotch NA, eds. *Social Stress.* Chicago, IL: Aldine; 1970:156–188.

14. Cobb S, Schull WJ, Harburg F, et al. The intrafamiliar transmission of rheumatoid arthritis—VIII: summary of findings. *J Chronic Dis.* 1969;22:295–296.

15. Shekelle RB, Ostfeld AM, Paul O. Social status and incidence of coronary heart disease. *J Chronic Dis.* 1969;22:381–394.

16. Syme SL, Borhani NO, Buechley RW. Cultural mobility and coronary heart disease in an urban area. *Am J Epidemiol.* 1966;82:334–346.

17. Caplan RD, Cobb S, French JRP Jr, et al. *Job Demands and Worker Health.* Department of Health, Education and Welfare Publication (NIOSH) 75–160. Washington, DC: Department of Health, Education and Welfare; 1975.

18. French JRP Jr, Rodgers W, Cobb S. Adjustment as person-environment fit. In: Coelho GV, Hamburg DA, Adams JE, eds. *Coping and Adaptation.* New York, NY: Basic Books; 1974:316–333.

19. Sales SM. *Differences Among Individuals in Affective, Behavioral, Biochemical, and Psychological Responses to Variations in Workload.* Thesis. Ann Arbor, MI: University of Michigan; 1969.

20. Holmes T, Rahe R. The social readjustment rating scale. *J Psychosom Res.* 1967;11:213–218.

21. Holmes TH, Masuda M. Life change and illness susceptibility. In: Dohrenwend BS, Dohrenwend BP, eds. *Stressful Life Events: Their Nature and Effects.* New York, NY: Wiley; 1974:45–72.

22. Langner TS, Michael ST. *Life Stress and Mental Health.* New York, NY: Free Press; 1963.

23. Hinkle LE Jr. The effect of exposure to culture change, social change, and changes in interpersonal relationships on health. In: Dohrenwend BS, Dohrenwend BP, eds. *Stressful Life Events: Their Nature and Effects.* New York, NY: Wiley; 1974:9–44.

24. Pilkonis PA, Imber SD, Rubinshy P. Dimensions of life stress in psychiatric patients. *J Hum Stress.* 1985;11:5–10.

25. Pearlin LI. The stress process revisited: reflections on concepts and their interrelationships. In: Aneshensel CA, Phelan JC, eds. *Handbook of the Sociology of Mental Health*. New York, NY: Plenum Publishing Corp; 1999: Chapter 19.

26. Turner RJ, Lloyd DA. The stress process and the social distribution of depression. *J Health Soc Behav*. 1999;40:374–404.

27. Kobasa SCO, Maddi SR, Puccetti MC, Zola MA. Effectiveness of hardiness, exercise and social support as resources against illness. *J Psychosom Res*. 1985;29:525–533.

28. Rosenman RH, Friedman M, Straus R, et al. Coronary heart disease in the Western Collaborative Group Study: a follow-up experience of two years. *JAMA*. 1966; 195:86–92.

29. Jenkins CD. Psychologic and social precursors of coronary disease. *N Engl J Med*. 1971;284:244–255; 307–317.

30. Rosenman RH, Friedman M, Straus R, et al. A predictive study of coronary heart disease: the Western Collaborative Group Study. *JAMA*. 1964;189:113–120.

31. Bortner RW. A short rating scale as a potential measure of pattern A behavior. *J Chronic Dis*. 1969;22:87–91.

32. Cobb S. Social support as a moderator of stress. *Psychosom Med*. 1976;38:300–314.

33. Rabkin JG, Struening EL. Life events, stress, and illness. *Science*. 1976;194: 1013–1020.

34. Baron RS, Cutrona CE, Hicklin D, et al. Social support and immune function among spouses of cancer patients. *J Pers Soc Psychol*. 1990;59:344–352.

35. Pearlin LI. The sociological study of stress. *J Health Soc Behav*. 1989;30:241–256.

36. Aneshensel CS, Stone JD. Stress and depression: a test of the buffering model of social support. *Arch Gen Psychiatry*. 1982;39:1392–1396.

37. Lin N, Woefel MW, Light SC. The buffering effect of social support subsequent to an important life event. *J Health Soc Behav*. 1985;26:247–263.

38. Mitchell RE, Cronkite RC, Moos RH. Stress, coping, and depression among married couples. *J Abnorm Psychol*. 1983;92:433–447.

39. Dean A, Kolody B, Wood P. Effects of social support from various sources on depression in elderly persons. *J Health Soc Behav*. 1990;31:148–161.

40. Krause N, Liang J, Keith V. Personality, social support, and psychological distress in later life. *Psychol Aging*. 1990;5:315–326.

41. Tetzloff CE, Barrera M Jr. Divorcing mothers and social support: testing the specificity of buffering effects. *Am J Community Psychol*. 1987;15:419–434.

42. Breslow L. Prospects for improving health through reducing risk factors. *Prev Med*. 1978;7:449–458.

43. Burkitt DP. Some diseases characteristic of modern Western civilization. In: Logan MH, Hunt EE Jr, eds. *Health and the Human Condition: Perspectives on Medical Anthropology*. North Scituate, MA: Duxbury; 1978:137–147.

44. Suchman EA. Health attitudes and behavior. *Arch Environ Health*. 1970;20:105–110.

45. Heron MP, Smith BL. Deaths: Leading Causes for 2003. *National Vital Stat Rep*. 2007;55(10);1–92.

46. Siegel PZ, Frazier EL, Mariolis P, et al. Behavioral risk factor surveillance, 1991: monitoring progress toward the nation's year 2000 health objectives. *MMWR*. 1993;42(SS-4):1–21.

47. US Department of Health and Human Services, Public Health Service. *Healthy People 2000*. DHHS Publication No. (PHS) 91-50213. Washington, DC; 1991.

48. U.S. Department of Health, Education and Welfare, Public Health Service. *Smoking and Health, a Report of the Surgeon General*. Department of Health, Education and

Welfare publication 79-50066. Washington, DC: Department of Health, Education and Welfare; 1979.

49. U.S. Department of Health and Human Services. *The Health Consequences of Smoking: A Report of the Surgeon General.* Atlanta, GA: U.S. Department of Health and Human Services, Centers for Disease Control and Prevention, National Center for Chronic Disease Prevention and Health Promotion. Office on Smoking and Health; 2004.

50. World Health Organization. *Global Status Report on Alcohol 2004.* Geneva, Switzerland: World Health Organization, Department of Mental Health and Substance Abuse; 2004.

51. Centers for Disease Control and Prevention. Alcohol-attributable deaths and years of potential life lost—United States, 2001. *MMWR.* 2004;53:866–870.

52. Centers for Disease Control and Prevention. Youth exposure to alcohol advertising in magazines—United States, 2001–2005. *MMWR.* 2007;56:763–767.

53. Streissguth AP. Fetal alcohol syndrome: an epidemiologic perspective. *Am J Epidemiol.* 1978;107:467–478.

54. Centers for Disease Control and Prevention. Guidelines for identifying and referring persons with fetal alcohol syndrome. *MMWR.* 2005;54:1–10.

55. Graham S, Mettlin C. Diet and colon cancer. *Am J Epidemiol.* 1979;109:1–20.

56. Kritchevsky SB. Dietary lipids and the low blood cholesterol-cancer association. *Am J Epidemiol.* 1992;135:509–520.

57. Zheng W, Blot W, Shu X, et al. Diet and other risk factors for laryngeal cancer in Shanghai, China. *Am J Epidemiol.* 1992;136:178–191.

58. Smith AH, Waller KD. Serum β-carotene in persons with cancer and their immediate families. *Am J Epidemiol.* 1991;133:661–671.

59. Schwartz B, Bischof H-P, Kunze M. Coffee, tea, and lifestyle. *Prev Med.* 1994; 23:377–384.

60. Morris JN, Chave SPW, Adam C, et al. Vigorous exercise in leisure-time and the incidence of coronary heart-disease. *Lancet.* 1973;1:333–339.

61. Paffenbarger RS Jr, Wing AL, Hyde RT. Physical activity as an index of heart attack risk in college alumni. *Am J Epidemiol.* 1978;108:161–175.

62. Streja D, Mymin D. Moderate exercise and high-density lipoprotein-cholesterol. *JAMA.* 1979;242:2190–2192.

63. Paffenbarger RS, Blair SN, Lee I-M. A history of physical activity, cardiovascular health, and longevity: the scientific contributions of Jeremy N. Morris, DSc, DPH, FRCP. *Int J Epidemiol.* 2001;30:1184–1192.

64. Cooper RA, Quatrano LA. Research on physical activity and health among people with disabilities: a consensus statement. *J Rehabil Res Dev.* 1999;36:142–154.

65. Friis RH, Nomura WL, Ma CX, et al. Socioepidemiologic and health-related correlates of walking for exercise among the elderly: results from the Longitudinal Study of Aging. *J Aging Phys Act.* 2003;11:54–65.

66. Fabrega H, Van Egeren L. A behavioral framework for the study of human disease. *Ann Intern Med.* 1976;84:200–208.

67. Susser MW, Watson W, Hopper K. *Sociology in Medicine,* 3rd ed. New York, NY: Oxford University Press; 1985.

68. Matsumoto YS. Social stress and coronary heart disease in Japan: a hypothesis. *Milbank Mem Fund Q.* 1970;48:9–36.

69. Marmot MG, Syme SL, Kagan A, et al. Epidemiologic studies of coronary heart disease and stroke in Japanese men living in Japan, Hawaii and California: prevalence of coronary and hypertensive heart disease and associated risk factors. *Am J Epidemiol.* 1975;102:514–525.

70. Mercer JR. Sociocultural factors in educational labeling. In: Begab MJ, Richardson SA, eds. *The Mentally Retarded and Society: A Social Science Perspective.* Baltimore, MD: University Park Press; 1975:141–157.

71. Mechanic D. Illness behavior, social adaptation, and the management of illness. *J Nerv Ment Dis.* 1977;165:79–87.

72. Mechanic D. Social psychologic factors affecting the presentation of bodily complaints. *N Engl J Med.* 1972;286:1132–1139.

73. Rubel AJ, Garro LC. Social and cultural factors in the successful control of tuberculosis. *Public Health Rep.* 1992;107:626–634.

74. Dohrenwend BP. A psychosocial perspective on the past and future of psychiatric epidemiology. *Am J Epidemiol.* 1998;147:222–231.

75. Sales SM, House J. Job dissatisfaction as a possible risk factor in coronary heart disease. *J Chronic Dis.* 1971;23:861–873.

76. Liljefors I, Rahe RH. An identical twin study of psychosocial factors in coronary heart disease in Sweden. *Psychosom Med.* 1970;32:523–542.

77. House JS. *The Relationship of Intrinsic and Extrinsic Work Motivations to Occupational Stress and Coronary Heart Disease Risk.* Thesis. Ann Arbor, MI: University of Michigan; 1972.

78. Friis RH, Lee JA. *Natural disasters and posttraumatic stress disorder: an epidemiologic approach.* Paper presented at the Seventh International Conference on Social Stress Research, Budapest, Hungary, May 26–29, 1998.

79. Langner TS. A twenty-two item screening score of psychiatric symptoms indicating impairment. *J Health Hum Behav.* 1962;3:267–269.

80. Markush RE, Favero RV. Epidemiologic assessment of stressful life events, depressed mood, and psychophysiological symptoms: a preliminary report. In: Dohrenwend BS, Dohrenwend BP, eds. *Stressful Life Events: Their Nature and Effects.* New York, NY: Wiley; 1974:171–190.

81. Radloff LS. The CES-D scale: a self-report depression scale for research in the general population. *Appl Psychol Meas.* 1977;1:385–401.

82. Weissman MM, Sholomskas D, Pottenger M, et al. Assessing depressive symptoms in five psychiatric populations: a validation study. *Am J Epidemiol.* 1977;106:203–214.

83. Comstock GW, Helsing KJ. Symptoms of depression in two communities. *Psychol Med.* 1976;6:551–563.

84. Craig TJ, Van Natta PA. Presence and persistence of depression symptoms in patient and community populations. *Am J Psychiatry.* 1976;133:1426–1429.

85. Frerichs RR, Aneshensel CS, Clark VA. Prevalence of depression in Los Angeles County. *Am J Epidemiol.* 1981;113:691–699.

86. Husaini BA, Neff JA, Harrington JB, et al. Depression in rural communities: validating the CES-D scale. *J Community Psychol.* 1980;8:20–27.

87. Frerichs RR, Aneshensel CS, Yokopenic PN, Clark VA. Public health and depression: an epidemiologic survey. *Prev Med.* 1982;11:639–646.

88. Moscicki EK, Locke BZ, Rae DS, Boyd JH. Depressive symptoms among Mexican Americans: the Hispanic Health and Nutrition Examination Survey. *Am J Epidemiol.* 1989;130:348–360.

89. Freedman DX. Psychiatric epidemiology counts. *Arch Gen Psychiatry*. 1984;41:931–933.
90. Fox BH. Premorbid psychological factors as related to cancer incidence. *J Behav Med*. 1978;1:45–133.
91. Fox BH. The role of psychological factors in cancer incidence and prognosis. *Oncology*. 1995;9:245–253.
92. Croog SH, Fitzgerald EF. Subjective stress and serious illness of a spouse: wives of heart patients. *J Health Soc Behav*. 1978;19:166–178.
93. Giovino GA, Henningfield JE, Tornar SL, et al. Epidemiology of tobacco use and dependence. *Epidemiol Rev*. 1995;17:48–65.
94. Acton GS, Prochaska JJ, Kaplan AS, et al. Depression and stages of change for smoking in psychiatric outpatients. *Addict Behav*. 2001;26:621–631.
95. Vaillant GE. Natural history of male psychologic health: effects of mental health on physical health. *N Engl J Med*. 1979;301:1249–1254.
96. Thomas SP. Psychosocial correlates of women's health in middle adulthood. *Issues Mental Health Nurs*. 1995;16:285–314.
97. Friedman HS, Tucker JS, Tomlinson-Keasey C, et al. Does childhood personality predict longevity? *J Pers Soc Psychol*. 1993;65:176–185.
98. Martikainen P, Bartley M, Lahelma E. Psychosocial determinants of health in social epidemiology. *Int J Epidemiol*. 2002;31:1091–1093.
99. Syme SL. Historical perspective: the social determinants of disease—some roots of the movement. *Epidemiol Perspect Innov*. 2005;2(1):2.

CHAPTER 16

Epidemiology as a Profession

LEARNING OBJECTIVES

By the end of this chapter the reader will be able to:

- describe five areas of specialization within epidemiology
- describe four career roles for epidemiologists
- name three resources for education and employment in epidemiology
- name three epidemiology associations and three journals that publish articles on epidemiology
- list four competencies required in the field of epidemiology
- state five ethical issues that pertain to the practice of epidemiology

CHAPTER OUTLINE

I. Introduction
II. Specializations Within Epidemiology
III. Career Roles for Epidemiologists
IV. Epidemiology Associations and Journals
V. Competencies Required of Epidemiologists
VI. Resources for Education and Employment
VII. Professional Ethics in Epidemiology
VIII. Conclusion
IX. Study Questions and Exercises

Introduction

This chapter was written in response to the many questions received from students about career opportunities in epidemiology. As noted previously in the introduction to this text, epidemiology is an exciting and rewarding field. It is unusual for a day to pass without media reports about health-related studies based on the epidemiologic method. To illustrate, headlines have announced findings about obesity and consumption of diet sodas, obesity and choice of friends, the association between contaminants in imported foods and potential adverse health effects, and hazards from lead in toys. Moreover, the authors have provided many examples of epidemiology applied to public health practice throughout this book. We hope that we have been able to share our enthusiasm sufficiently to interest the reader in a possible career in this growing field.

What types of work does an epidemiologist perform? What are sources of career information about the field? What are the professional and ethical obligations of epidemiologists? For those interested in embarking on a career in epidemiology, this chapter will provide resources such as examples of specializations, possible career roles, contacts for employment, epidemiology journals and organizations, and professional and ethical issues. For a quick introduction to ongoing issues and professional concerns of the field, we recommend *The Epidemiology Monitor* (http://www.epimonitor.net), a monthly newsletter that is always an interesting read. A typical issue of *The Epidemiology Monitor* lists more than 150 employment opportunities in national and international locations (Figure 16–1).

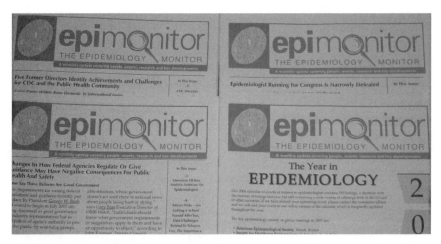

FIGURE 16–1 *The Epidemiology Monitor. Source:* With permission from *The Epidemiology Monitor.*

Specializations Within Epidemiology

Table 16–1 lists more than 30 specializations in epidemiology, ranging from the epidemiology of aging to chronic disease epidemiology, infectious disease epidemiology, and women's health epidemiology. Given the expanding number of specializations within the field, the information provided in the table is not exhaustive.

Several of the specializations were covered previously in Chapter 1 as well as other chapters. Here are some more detailed statements regarding several of the examples shown in the table and not covered elsewhere:

- *Reproductive epidemiology:* "... Covers a wide range of topics from the development, adult capacity, and senescence of the reproductive systems, to conception and pregnancy, to delivery and health of the offspring."[1(p. 585)]
- *Nutrition epidemiology:* "... Uses epidemiologic approaches to determine relations between dietary factors and the occurrence of specific diseases."[2(p. 623)] An illustration of a field project in nutrition is shown in Figure 16–2.

Table 16–1 Specializations Within Epidemiology

Epidemiology of Aging	Parasitology
Assessment of Health Care Epidemiology	Surveillance
Behavioral Epidemiology	Vector-borne
Biostatistics and Epidemiologic Methods	Virology
Disease Informatics	Zoonoses
Meta-Analysis	Injury Epidemiology
Birth Defects Epidemiology	Neuroepidemiology
Chronic Disease Epidemiology	Nutrition Epidemiology
Coronary Heart Disease	Occupational Epidemiology
Diabetes	Oral/dental Epidemiology
Obesity	Pediatric Epidemiology
Clinical Epidemiology	Pharmacoepidemiology
Primary Care Epidemiology	Psychiatric Epidemiology
Environmental Health Epidemiology	Psychologic Epidemiology
Epidemiology of Cancer	Renal Epidemiology
Epidemiology of Urban Health	Reproductive Epidemiology
Field Epidemiology/Public Health Practice	Screening Epidemiology
Epidemiology	Social Epidemiology
Genetic and Molecular Epidemiology	Spatial Epidemiology
Health and Policy Administration	Sport Epidemiology
Epidemiology	Substance Abuse Epidemiology
Health Services Research Epidemiology	Veterinary Epidemiology
Life Course Epidemiology	Women's Health Epidemiology
Infectious Disease Epidemiology	Perinatal
Infection Control and Hospital	Pregnancy
Epidemiology	

FIGURE 16–2 A "weight and height measurement team" in place to assess the nutritional status of Biafran war refugees. *Source:* CDC Public Health Image Library, ID# 7115. Available at: http://phil.cdc.gov/phil/home.asp. Accessed November 16, 2007.

- *Health services research epidemiology:* Applies the methods of epidemiology to the assessment of needs for health services and the evaluation of the quality of health services. This application was discussed in Chapter 2.
- *Neuroepidemiology:* Epidemiologic approaches are applied to investigate the prevalence and risk factors for neurological diseases such as Alzheimer's disease, Parkinson's disease, and multiple sclerosis.
- *Injury epidemiology:* The methods of epidemiology are used to investigate the incidence, prevalence, and risk factors for accidental injury and death; types of accidents include motor vehicle accidents and workplace accidental injuries as well as many other types of accidents.
- *Coronary heart disease epidemiology:* Focuses on ". . . the determinants, distribution, and sequelae of coronary heart disease (CHD) in populations . . ."[3(p. 7)]
- *Pharmacoepidemiology:* This field examines drug utilization and associated effects among the population. Examples are the appropriate and inappropriate use of drugs as well as clinical outcomes linked to drugs.

- *Oral epidemiology/dental epidemiology:* Studies population-based outcomes related to dental health. Concerns of the field are effects of fluoride consumption, oral cancer, dental caries, and tooth loss.
- *Renal epidemiology:* Examines the distribution and determinants of renal (kidney) diseases and abnormality in populations. Renal diseases include end-stage kidney failure, kidney stones, and hematuria.
- *Veterinary epidemiology:* Studies the occurrence of diseases in animal populations. Information acquired from veterinary epidemiology studies can be used to promote the productivity and welfare of animal populations.

Career Roles for Epidemiologists

The field of epidemiology provides numerous potential career roles in teaching, research, and applied settings. Private industry, government, universities, research organizations, hospitals, and nonprofit organizations are among the employers of epidemiologists. The following list (not exhaustive) contains a few of the many occupations found within epidemiology:

- academic workers, including college professors
- research workers
- public health nurse epidemiologists
- biostatisticians who focus on epidemiology
- healthcare planners
- pharmaceutical and biotech industry researchers
- epidemiology surveillance workers (Figure 16–3)

Epidemiologists who work in local health departments investigate local outbreaks of disease such as foodborne illnesses, vector-borne diseases, and communicable diseases in schools. They provide assistance to local hospitals and other healthcare providers regarding control of infectious diseases. They also participate in local initiatives for prevention and control of chronic diseases.

In the United States, depending on the size of the state, epidemiologists contribute to statewide initiatives to monitor and control infectious and chronic diseases. Also, they play a role in implementing health-related mandates issued by the executive and legislative branches of state government. In larger states, epidemiologists may hold staff and research positions in specialized health-related programs such as those devoted to air pollution control and environmental health impacts of toxic wastes.

FIGURE 16-3 A CDC field researcher is shown detaching a collection bag from a CDC light trap, which has captured numerous mosquitoes. *Source:* CDC Public Health Image Library, ID# 5600. Available at: http://phil.cdc.gov/phil/home.asp. Accessed November 16, 2007.

Nationally, numerous U.S. government agencies employ epidemiologists in administrative and research positions. Two examples are the Centers for Disease Control and Prevention (CDC) and the National Institute of Occupational Safety and Health (NIOSH).

Centers for Disease Control and Prevention

At the CDC in Atlanta, Georgia, epidemiologists are involved in program administration, basic research, and "shoe leather" activities for the control and prevention of infectious and chronic diseases. Much information from the CDC has been reported elsewhere in this text. An important educational and public health practice arm of the CDC is the Epidemic Intelligence Service, established in 1951 to warn against the use of biological warfare (Figure 16-4).

National Institute of Occupational Safety and Health

Headquartered in Washington, D.C, NIOSH is a branch of the CDC located in the U.S. Department of Health and Human Services. NIOSH was ". . . es-

FIGURE 16–4 The Epidemic Intelligence Service (EIS) graduating class of 2004. *Source:* CDC Public Health Image Library, ID# 7284. Available at: http://phil.cdc.gov/phil/home.asp. Accessed November 16, 2007.

tablished to help assure 'safe and healthful working conditions for working men and women by providing research, information, education, and training in the field of occupational safety and health.'"[4(p. 1)] As stated in the agency's Web site,

> NIOSH epidemiologists may effect occupational changes globally by identifying and monitoring diseases and injuries in the workplace. They plan, develop, and direct their own research projects within broad parameters set by the mission and priorities of NIOSH. Past epidemiologic studies have examined reproductive hazards to women who use video display terminals, morbidity and mortality among automobile pattern makers, electrocution hazards to utility linemen, and fall hazards to construction workers. NIOSH epidemiologists often work in collaboration with their counterparts around the world; for example, they have conducted joint epidemiologic studies on common occupational hazards such as asbestos, benzene, and formaldehyde. These studies have advanced the safety and health of the American worker and of workers everywhere.[5]

Epidemiology Associations and Journals

A list of professional associations related to epidemiology is presented in Table 16–2. Also provided in the text is a list of journals that publish epidemiologic studies. Contact information for both associations and journals is shown. The lists are not exhaustive but provide a launching point for your further investigation. For example, The Society for Epidemiologic Research, one of the lead organizations for epidemiologists, publishes the *American Journal of Epidemiology.*

Professional Associations

The following paragraphs describe in more detail some of the associations listed in Table 16–2. The quoted material is reproduced verbatim from the organizations' Web sites.

American Academy of Pediatrics, Section on Epidemiology: ". . . Founded in 1988, [the AAP] is dedicated to educating the general pediatrician and pediatric subspecialist on the basic principles of epidemiology and its relation to pediatrics and its various disciplines. The section consults to the AAP Board of Directors and works with various AAP committees, sections and task forces to provide methodological support and expertise in epidemiology and evidence-based medicine." (Web site: http://www.aap.org/sections/epidemiology/default.cfm)

Table 16–2   Domestic and International Organizations in Epidemiology

Organization	URL
American Academy of Pediatrics, Section on Epidemiology	http://www.aap.org/sections/epidemiology/default.cfm
American College of Epidemiology	http://www.acepidemiology2.org/
American Public Health Association, Epidemiology Section	http://www.apha.org/membergroups/sections/aphasections/epidemiology/
American Statistical Association, Section on Statistics on Epidemiology	www.amstat.orgsections/epi/SIE_Home.htm
Association for Professionals in Infection Control and Epidemiology	http://www.apic.org//AM/Template.cfm?Section=Home
Association of Public Health Epidemiologists in Ontario	http://www.apheo.on.ca/
Australian Epidemiological Association	aea@iceaustralia.com
Council of State and Territorial Epidemiologists	http://www.cste.org/
European Epidemiology Federation	http://www.dundee.ac.uk/iea/Europe.htm
International Epidemiological Association	http://www.dundee.ac.uk/iea/
International Genetic Epidemiology Society	http://www.genepi.org/
International Society for Pharmacoepidemiology	http://www.pharmacoepi.org/
International Society for Environmental Epidemiology	http://www.iseepi.org/
Society for Epidemiologic Research	http://www.epiresearch.org/
Society for Pediatric and Perinatal Epidemiologic Research	http://www.sper.org/
The Canadian Society for Epidemiology and Biostatistics	http://www.cseb.ca/
The Danish Epidemiologic Society	http://www.dansk-epidemiologisk-selskab.dk/
The Hong Kong Epidemiological Association	http://www.epidemiology.org.hk/
The Society for Clinical Trials	http://www.sctweb.org/
The Society for Healthcare Epidemiology in America	http://www.shea-online.org/

American College of Epidemiology (ACE): ". . . Incorporated in 1979 to develop criteria for professional recognition of epidemiologists and to address their professional concerns . . . ACE serves the interests of its members through sponsorship of scientific meetings, publications, and educational activities, recognizing outstanding contributions to the field and advocating for issues pertinent to epidemiology." (Web site: http://www.acepidemiology2.org/)

American Public Health Association: "The mission of the Epidemiology section is to foster epidemiologic research and science-based public health practice and serve as a conduit between the epidemiologic research community and users of scientific information for the development, implementation, and evaluation of policies affecting the public's health." (Web site: http://www.apha.org)

International Epidemiological Association: "The International Corresponding Club, as the IEA was first called, was started in 1954 by John Pemberton of Great Britain and Harold N Willard of the United States with the advice and help of the late Robert Cruickshank. They had found, as traveling Research Fellows each in the other's country, that they were handicapped by not being sufficiently well informed about the research and teaching in the field of social and preventive medicine in the various medical schools and research institutes." (Web site: http://www.dundee.ac.uk/iea/)

Society for Epidemiologic Research: ". . . established in 1968 as a forum for sharing the latest in epidemiologic research. The SER is committed to keeping epidemiologists at the vanguard of scientific developments." (Web site: http://www.epiresearch.org/)

Epidemiology Journals

Numerous scientific journals publish epidemiologic research. However, the following journals are keyed specifically to epidemiologic research. The quoted descriptions are reproduced verbatim from the journals' Web sites.

American Journal of Epidemiology: ". . . the premier epidemiological journal devoted to the publication of empirical research findings, methodological developments in the field of epidemiological research and opinion pieces. It is aimed at both fellow epidemiologists and those who use epidemiological data, including public health workers and clinicians." (Web site: http://aje.oxfordjournals.org/; Figure 16–5)

American Journal of Public Health: ". . . is dedicated to original work in research, research methods, and program evaluation in the field of public health. This prestigious journal also regularly publishes authoritative editorials and commentaries

FIGURE 16–5 *American Journal of Epidemiology. Source:* With permission of Oxford University Press.

and serves as a forum for the analysis of health policy. The stated mission of the Journal is 'to advance public health research, policy, practice, and education.'" Web site: (http://www.ajph.org/?CFID=436612&CFTOKEN=27875102)

Epidemiology: ". . . is a peer-reviewed scientific journal that publishes original research on the full spectrum of epidemiologic topics. Journal content ranges from cancer, heart disease and other chronic illnesses to reproductive, environmental, psychosocial, infectious-disease and genetic epidemiology. The journal places special emphasis on theory and methodology, and welcomes commentaries that explore fundamental assumptions or offer provocative dissent." (Web site: http://www.jstor.org/journals/10443983.html)

Epidemiology and Infection: ". . . publishes original reports and reviews on all aspects of infection in humans and animals. Particular emphasis is given to the epidemiology, prevention and control of infectious diseases. The field covered is broad and includes the zoonoses, tropical infections, food hygiene, vaccine studies, statistics and the clinical, social and public-health aspects of infectious disease." (Web site: http://www.jstor.org/journals/09502688.html)

International Journal of Epidemiology: ". . . an essential requirement for anyone who needs to keep up to date with epidemiological advances and new developments throughout the world. It encourages communication among those engaged in the research, teaching, and application of epidemiology of both communicable and non-communicable disease, including research into health services and medical care." (Web site: http://ije.oxfordjournals.org/archive/)

Cancer Epidemiology, Biomarkers & Prevention: Published by the American Association for Cancer Research, ". . . publishes original, peer-reviewed research on cancer causation, mechanisms of carcinogenesis, prevention, and survivorship. Topics include descriptive, analytical, biochemical, and molecular epidemiology; the use of biomarkers to study the neoplastic and preneoplastic processes in humans; chemoprevention and other types of prevention trials; and the role of behavioral factors in cancer etiology and prevention." Many of these areas are based on epidemiologic methods. (Web site: http://cebp.aacrjournals.org/)

Competencies Required of Epidemiologists

Competencies refer to skills that a professional should acquire in order to perform effectively. Competency levels vary according to the degree acquired—bachelor's, master's, doctoral, or postdoctoral—with more advanced degree holders trained to perform more complex tasks and assume greater independence and responsibility. For example, candidates with a doctoral degree should be able to perform advanced epidemiologic research. Figure 16–6 shows a research worker engaged in laboratory research.

Master of Public Health (MPH) degree candidates are capable of performing a wide range of tasks in the work environment. The Association of Schools of Public Health has developed the following list of competencies in epidemiology to be achieved by MPH degree candidates in public health[6]:

1. Identify key sources of data for epidemiologic purposes.
2. Identify the principles and limitations of public health screening programs.
3. Describe a public health problem in terms of magnitude, person, time, and place.
4. Explain the importance of epidemiology for informing scientific, ethical, economic, and political discussion of health issues.
5. Comprehend basic ethical and legal principles pertaining to the collection, maintenance, use, and dissemination of epidemiologic data.
6. Apply the basic terminology and definitions of epidemiology.
7. Calculate basic epidemiology measures.
8. Communicate epidemiologic information to lay and professional audiences.

FIGURE 16–6   Here a laboratory technician is using a dissecting type of microscope to view a *Legionella pneumophilia* culture specimen. *Source:* CDC Public Health Image Library, ID# 4105. Available at: http://phil.cdc.gov/phil/home.asp. Accessed November 16, 2007.

9. Draw appropriate inferences from epidemiologic data.
10. Evaluate the strengths and limitations of epidemiologic reports.

Resources for Education and Employment

Continuing Education Degree Programs

Education in epidemiology can be obtained via special summer session programs and online programs, such as those offered by Johns Hopkins University and the University of Michigan, Ann Arbor. Examples of summer programs are:

- Graduate Summer Session in Epidemiology: "The summer program at the University of Michigan, School of Public Health, offers instruction in the principles, methods and applications of epidemiology." (Web site: http://www.sph.umich.edu/epid/GSS/)

- Graduate Summer Institute of Epidemiology and Biostatistics: Johns Hopkins Bloomberg School of Public Health ". . . offer courses on modern epidemiologic and biostatistic methods . . . infectious diseases and cancer; the use of epidemiologic methods in evidence-based decision-making; risk sciences and public policy; the management of epidemiologic studies; the teaching of epidemiology; and tobacco-control strategies." (Web site: http://www.jhsph.edu/dept/EPI/Degree_Programs/Summer_Institute/index.html)
- Summer Session for Public Health Studies–Harvard University, School of Public Health ". . . offers courses for academic credit in the following concentrations: biostatistics, environmental health, epidemiology . . ." (Web site: http://www.hsph.harvard.edu/academics/public-health-studies/)

Colleges and universities in the United States and abroad offer master's and doctoral degree programs in epidemiology. Consult the website of the Council on Education for Public Health (CEPH) for a current list of accredited schools of public health and graduate public health programs in the United States (Web site: http://www.ceph.org).

Employment

For information on positions in your local area or at the state level, research the Internet for health departments, hospitals, pharmaceutical firms, and biotech companies. Plan to attend the annual meetings of the Society for Epidemiologic Research and the American Public Health Association for on-site job listings and contacts. Refer to the following Web sites to obtain national listings of employment opportunities for epidemiologists:

- APHA Public Health Career Mart: http://www.apha.org/about/careers/
- APIC Career Center: http://www.apic.org/scriptcontent/custom/careers/autologin.cfm?section=job_bank2
- Epimonitor.net Job Bank: http://www.epimonitor.net/Epidemiology Monitor/JobBank/Index.asp
- Centers for Disease Control and Prevention: http://www.cdc.gov/employment/findcareer.htm
- Council of State and Territorial Epidemiologists Employment Listings: http://www.cste.org/employment/employment_listings2.asp
- National Institutes of Health: http://www.jobs.nih.gov/
- World Health Organization: http://www.who.int/employment/en/

Professional Ethics in Epidemiology

The ACE has developed a framework for ethical principles in epidemiology. Some of these guidelines are reprinted in Exhibit 16–1. Examples of ethical guidelines include the obligation to submit research proposals to ethics committees for review, avoidance of conflicts of interest and partiality, and respecting cultural diversity.

EXHIBIT 16–1

Ethics Guidelines for Epidemiologists

Part I. Core Values, Duties, and Virtues in Epidemiology

1.1. Definition and Discussion of Core Values

Like other scientists, epidemiologists uphold values of free inquiry and the pursuit of knowledge. The goal of science, after all, is to explain and to predict natural phenomena. Epidemiologists not only pursue knowledge about the distribution and determinants of health and disease in populations, but also uphold the value of improving the public's health through the application of scientific knowledge.

These core values underlie the mission and purpose of epidemiology. Here we are concerned with core values that are internal to the profession of epidemiology. As such, they are more restricted in scope than general ethical principles such as beneficence (which relates to the balancing of risks and benefits and the promotion of the common welfare). On the other hand, core values in epidemiology are more general (and more basic) than ethical rules and norms within the profession such as the need to obtain the informed consent of research participants. [Here and elsewhere in this document the term *research participants* is used instead of *human subjects,* which is sometimes regarded as paternalistic; nevertheless, the term *participants* may incorrectly imply that there has been valid consent to participate, which is not always feasible in epidemiologic studies.]

continues

EXHIBIT 16-1 *continued*

Part II. Ethics Guidelines

This section provides a concise set of ethics guidelines for epidemiologists. [Part III, which provides further detail, is not included in this Exhibit.]

2.1. The Professional Role of Epidemiologists

The profession of epidemiology has as its primary roles the design and conduct of scientific research and the public health application of scientific knowledge. This includes the reporting of results to the scientific community, to research participants, and to society; and the maintenance, enhancement, and promotion of health in communities. Other professional roles in epidemiology include teaching, consulting, and administration.

2.2. Minimizing Risks and Protecting the Welfare of Research Participants

Epidemiologists have ethical and professional obligations to minimize risks and to avoid causing harm to research participants and to society. The risks of nonresearch public health practice activities also should be minimized.

2.3. Providing Benefits

Epidemiologists should ensure that the potential benefits of studies to research participants and to society are maximized by, for example, communicating results in a timely fashion. Steps also should be taken to maximize the potential benefits of public health practice activities.

2.4. Ensuring an Equitable Distribution of Risks and Benefits

Epidemiologists should ensure that the potential benefits and burdens of epidemiologic research and public health practice activities are distributed in an equitable fashion.

continues

EXHIBIT 16–1 *continued*

2.5. Protecting Confidentiality and Privacy

Epidemiologists should take appropriate measures to protect the privacy of individuals and to keep confidential all information about individual research participants during and after a study. This duty also applies to personal information about individuals in public health practice activities.

2.6. Obtaining the Informed Consent of Participants

Epidemiologists should obtain the prior informed consent of research participants (with exceptions noted below in Section 2.6.3), in part by disclosing those facts and any information that patients or other individuals usually consider important in deciding whether or not to participate in the research.

2.6.1. Elements of informed consent

Information should be provided about the purposes of the study, the sponsors, the investigators, the scientific methods and procedures, any anticipated risks and benefits, any anticipated inconveniences or discomfort, and the individual's right to refuse participation or to withdraw from the research at any time without repercussions.

2.6.2. Avoidance of manipulation or coercion

Research participants must voluntarily consent to the research without coercion, manipulation, or undue incentives for participation.

2.6.3. Conditions under which informed consent requirements may be waived

Requirements to obtain the informed consent of research participants may be waived in certain circumstances, such as when it is not feasible to obtain the informed consent of research participants, in some studies involving the linkage of large databases routinely collected for other purposes, and in studies involving only minimal risks. In such circumstances, research participants generally need protection in other ways, such as through

continues

EXHIBIT 16–1 *continued*

confidentiality safeguards and appropriate review by an independent research ethics committee (often referred to as institutional review boards in
the United States or as ethics review boards in Canada). Informed consent
requirements may also be waived when epidemiologists investigate disease
outbreaks, evaluate programs, and conduct routine disease surveillance as
part of public health practice activities.

2.7. Submitting Proposed Studies for Ethical Review

Epidemiologists should submit research protocols for review by an independent ethics committee. An exception may be justified when epidemiologists investigate outbreaks of acute communicable diseases, evaluate
programs, and conduct routine disease surveillance as part of public
health practice activities.

2.8. Maintaining Public Trust

To promote and preserve public trust, epidemiologists should adhere to
the highest ethical and scientific standards and follow relevant laws and
regulations concerning the conduct of these activities, including the protection of human research participants and confidentiality protections.

2.8.1. Adhering to the highest scientific standards
Adhering to the highest scientific standards includes choosing an appropriate study design for the scientific hypothesis or question to be answered; writing a clear and complete protocol for the study; using proper
procedures for the collection, transmission, storage, and analysis of data;
making appropriate interpretations from the data analyses; and writing up
and disseminating the results of the study in a manner consistent with accepted procedures for scientific publication.

2.8.2. Involving community representatives in research
To the extent possible and whenever appropriate, epidemiologists also
should involve community representatives in the planning and conduct of
the research such as through community advisory boards.

continues

EXHIBIT 16–1 *continued*

2.9. Avoiding Conflicts of Interest and Partiality

Epidemiologists should avoid conflicts of interest and be objective. They should maintain honesty and impartiality in the design, conduct, interpretation, and reporting of research.

2.10. Communicating Ethical Requirements to Colleagues, Employers, and Sponsors and Confronting Unacceptable Conduct

Epidemiologists, as professionals, should communicate to their students, peers, employers, and sponsors the ethical requirements of scientific research and its application in professional practice.

2.10.1. Communicating ethical requirements

Epidemiologists should provide training and education in ethics to students of the discipline as well as to practicing scientists. They should demonstrate appropriate ethical conduct to colleagues and students by example.

2.10.2. Confronting unacceptable conduct

Epidemiologists should confront unacceptable conduct such as scientific misconduct, even though confronting it can be difficult in practice. Steps should be taken to provide protections for persons who confront or allege unacceptable conduct. The rights of the accused to due process should also be respected.

2.11. Obligations to Communities

Epidemiologists should meet their obligations to communities by undertaking public health research and practice activities that address health problems including questions concerning the utilization of health care resources, and by reporting results in an appropriate fashion.

continues

EXHIBIT 16–1 *continued*

2.11.1. Reporting results

All research findings and other information important to public health should be communicated in a timely, understandable, and responsible manner so that the widest possible community stands to benefit. [In addition, studies that report null results should be published in order to help the scientific community discontinue investigations that do not have merit.]

2.11.2. Public health advocacy

In confronting public health problems, epidemiologists sometimes act as advocates on behalf of members of affected communities. Advocacy should not impair scientific objectivity.

2.11.3. Respecting cultural diversity

Epidemiologists should respect cultural diversity in carrying out research and practice activities and in communicating with community members. ■

Source: Adapted from American College of Epidemiology, Ethics Guidelines. This article was published in *Annals of Epidemiology*, Vol 10, No 8, 2000, pp. 487–497, "Ethics guidelines", Copyright Elsevier, 2000. Available at: http://www.acepidemiology2.org/policystmts/ EthicsGuide.asp. Accessed November 16, 2007.

Conclusion

This chapter provided an introduction to the profession of epidemiology. Because epidemiology is an interdisciplinary field, personnel come from a wide variety of backgrounds. Some epidemiologists may have augmented their previous education and experience in a different field with specialized training in epidemiology; others may have received beginning and/or advanced degrees exclusively in epidemiology. Among the societal trends that reinforce the demand for well-trained epidemiologists are the impact of bioterrorism and the emergence and re-emergence of infectious diseases. Another trend relates to the impacts of demographic changes in the population due to immigration, population growth, and maturation of the "Baby Boom" generation. These demographic changes have resulted in increases in the occurrence of chronic conditions such as diabetes and obesity. Epidemiologists will be needed to conduct research on these and other chronic conditions. Adverse environmental conditions such as global warming will add to the demand for epidemiologic researchers. In view of these trends, epidemiology will continue to be an exciting field well into the foreseeable future.

Study Questions and Exercises

1. Define the following terms:
   a. Pharmacoepidemiology
   b. Neuroepidemiology
   c. Oral/dental epidemiology
   d. Renal epidemiology
   e. Veterinary epidemiology
2. Conduct a search of the Web sites of your local and state health departments regarding activities in epidemiology. Then log on to the Web sites for the following national and international agencies. Describe how an epidemiologist might contribute to the following employment settings:
   a. A local health department
   b. A state government health agency, such as a state department of health services
   c. A federal health agency; examples include:
      i. Centers for Disease Control and Prevention
      ii. Environmental Protection Agency
      iii. National Institute of Occupational Safety and Health
      iv. The Agency for Toxic Substances and Disease Registry
      v. Food and Drug Administration
   d. An international agency
      i. World Health Organization
      ii. Pan American Health Organization
      iii. The European Union Health Organization
3. An epidemiologist has been awarded a large grant to conduct a cohort study on the health of a minority population. What ethical issues might arise in carrying out this research project?
4. Describe how the employment responsibilities might differ among individuals trained at the bachelor's, master's, and doctoral levels.
5. How do the employment roles of epidemiologists differ from those of other public health professionals? An example of an area in which an

epidemiologist might specialize is in the design of research studies. How would the epidemiologist's contributions to a research study be different from those of other public health professionals?

6. Refer to the resources provided for finding employment opportunities in epidemiology. Access an active Web address and identify five current employment openings in the field. Describe what these opportunities involve.

7. Invite an epidemiologist (perhaps a graduate of your program) to your class and request that the individual describe his or her job responsibilities.

8. Arrange a field visit to a health-related agency that is located in your community. An example might be a public health department, nonprofit health-related organization, or research institute. Find out about how epidemiologists contribute to these settings.

References

1. Weinberg CR, Wilcox AJ. Reproductive epidemiology. In: Rothman KJ, Greenland S, eds. *Modern Epidemiology*, 2nd ed. Philadelphia, PA: Lippincott Williams & Wilkins; 1998:585–608.

2. Willett WC. Nutritional epidemiology. In: Rothman KJ, Greenland S, eds. *Modern Epidemiology*, 2nd ed. Philadelphia, PA: Lippincott Williams & Wilkins; 1998:623–642.

3. Tyroler HA. Coronary heart disease epidemiology in the 21st century. *Epidemiol Rev.* 2000;22:7–13.

4. Centers for Disease Control and Prevention. *National Institute for Occupational Safety and Health (NIOSH). Fact Sheet.* Available at: http://www.cdc.gov/niosh/pdfs/2003-116.pdf. Accessed November 16, 2007.

5. Centers for Disease Control and Prevention. National Institute for Occupational Safety and Health (NIOSH). NIOSH Epidemiologist Occupation, GS-0601. Available at: http://www.cdc.gov/niosh/employ/0601.html. Accessed November 16, 2007.

6. Association of Schools of Public Health, Education Committee. *Master's Degree in Public Health Core Competency Development Project*, Version 2.3. Washington, DC: Association of Schools of Public Health; August 11, 2006. Information available at: http://www.asph.org/. Accessed November 16, 2007.

Guide to the Critical Appraisal of an Epidemiologic/Public Health Research Article

For a review of the terms used in this guide, refer to the relevant chapters in the text.

The ability to read an empirical research report and critique its strengths and weaknesses is a desirable skill for epidemiology students to master. When you analyze a published article carefully, you will observe that all research reports contain strengths and weaknesses. The perfect epidemiologic research study has not yet been designed! Despite this assertion, a well-written article effectively communicates the purpose of the research study. It contains sufficient information so that the reader may assess the internal and external validity of the study design, that is, the degree of confidence that the reader can place in the findings that are reported. Many articles, such as those published in the *American Journal of Public Health,* are divided into sections (e.g., introduction, methods, results, and conclusion). Here is a list of criteria to consider when reading an empirical journal article (organized according to the sections contained in a typical empirical research report):

1. Introduction

   The introduction provides a review of the relevant literature and sets the stage for the research study. From the introduction, the reader should be able to infer the:

   - problem studied
   - specific aims of the study
   - research question(s) and/or hypotheses
   - variables included in the study

   The report should communicate clearly the problem being investigated. If the investigator has not stated the objectives of the investigation explicitly, the reader is left uncertain about the purpose of the study. The introduction also may provide an opportunity for the author to introduce variables measured as part of a theoretical framework. In addition to ascertaining the purpose of the research, the astute reader should try to determine the study's principal outcome variable(s)—dependent variables. The next step is to identify exposure, risk factor, or independent variables. Further, it should be possible to assess whether the researchers used intervening (moderating) and control variables.

2. Methods

   The methods section introduces the type of study design, that is, case-control, cohort, intervention, ecologic, or other design. Based upon the type of design specified, it should be apparent to the reader whether a cross-sectional, prospective, or retrospective time frame was used and whether the study was observational or experimental. In addition, the investigator should specify the unit of analysis: individual or group. Depending upon the study design, the investigator should state the number of observations made, that is, a single observation or multiple observations.

   a. Study Sample

      This section presents the method for selecting the subjects. Possible sample designs include, but are not limited to:

      - probability-based sample (simple random sample; stratified random sample)
      - systematic sample of available clinic patients (known as a grab-bag sample)
      - sample of medical records from a healthcare setting

The choice of a study sample forms a crucial aspect of external validity (generalizability) of the study's findings; the reader needs to know the group or groups to which the study's findings apply. These groups comprise the target population to whom the study's results can be generalized. Most researchers intend that the results of their research can be applied to populations other than the specific group from which their sample was selected. Sometimes the target population of the research may not be specified explicitly, leaving to the reader the task of divining the exact nature of the groups to which the findings might apply.

Information should be provided regarding the nature of control or comparison groups; the method of assignment of subjects to study conditions affects the internal validity of the study (as in the control of possible systematic group differences among study conditions). The reader should note whether single or double blinding has been used, especially in clinical trials. How many subjects are chosen is especially crucial to population research; the number of subjects affects statistical power (ability to detect a statistically significant difference) and also must be sufficient for diseases and conditions that have low prevalence in the population. Inappropriate sampling designs may introduce errors and bias into the study. One type of bias is selection bias, which arises from nonrandom assignment of subjects into the study. Other sampling issues include subject attrition (an important feature of sampling that could affect cohort studies and longitudinal studies adversely), which is measured by:

- Refusal rates (the number of selected subjects who refused to participate)
- Follow-up rates
- Drop-out rates

b. Measures (Instruments)

This section provides information on how the study's investigators operationalized the variables used in the study. The term *operationalization* refers to the schema for creation of actual numerical measurements that correspond to the concepts used in the study. For example, the article may discuss how outcome, exposure, and moderating variables were measured. Studies that investigate diseases, (e.g., diabetes, hypertension, or depression) must provide very clear "rule-in" and "rule-out" criteria for making these diagnoses. Other examples of measures that one might find in a study include:

- Physiological measures, e.g., blood pressure, height, weight
- Blood chemistry, e.g., serum cholesterol, hemoglobin, glucose
- Control (demographic) variables, e.g., age, sex, race, socioeconomic status
- Attitudinal surveys/questionnaire measures/clinical assessments, e.g., measures of depressive symptoms, anxiety, type A personality, perceived social support
- Outcome measures (e.g., death, recovery, response to a medication)
- Exposure variables (e.g., medications used, use of toxic chemicals, type of employment

The author should present information on the reliability and validity of measures used, particularly in the case of newly developed measures and measures of psychosocial variables. This information might come from previous reports of research with the measures and from the author's own reliability data.

c. Data Analysis

In this section, the investigator presents information regarding how the association between independent (exposure) and outcome variables was assessed, along with methods to control for potential confounding factors. Some authors cite the statistical software package used (e.g., SAS, SPSS, Epi Info). The report also should mention statistics used (e.g., chi square, t-test, or other appropriate statistic), depending upon the problem investigated. An important issue for data analysis is the use of appropriate statistical techniques. Some data analysis methods (e.g., multiple regression analysis) demand a large number of cases; yet, occasionally reports of research with small sample sizes will show the inappropriate use of multiple regression analysis and other multivariate techniques. Some studies may not test specific hypotheses related to exposure-outcome associations, but instead present descriptive analyses of results (e.g., counts and percents of the number of cases in various categories). While the issue of data analysis can be quite complex, the reader should try to develop a familiarity with some of the common statistical procedures used by referring to a statistics text.

3. Results

This section should refer back to the original issue addressed in the introduction (e.g., research question or hypothesis) and then discuss how the findings either do or do not answer the research question(s) posed in the introduction.

4. Discussion

The discussion places the findings in the context of previous research and an existing theoretical framework. In this section, the study's author may present weaknesses and limitations of the research. At this point, the reader should form an opinion regarding the extent to which the findings and conclusions follow from the design of the research study.

5. Conclusions

The conclusions section should provide a concise review of the main points covered in the paper. Public health or clinical implications of the findings and directions for future research may be disclosed. After reviewing the entire article, the reader should reflect on how the research and its presentation might be improved. The reader also should consider the strengths and weaknesses of the article.

Answers to Selected Study Questions

Chapter 2

Question 3. Professor Morris's list of uses of epidemiology is probably exhaustive.

Question 9.
a. The death rate dropped to 841.9 in 2003. The percentage change in death rate was $(1,719.1 - 841.9)/1,719.1 = 877.2/1,719.1 = (0.5103 \times 100) = 51.0\%$

Chapter 3

Question 2. Age-specific death rates for malignant neoplasms of trachea, bronchus and lung:

Ages 25–34 $154/39,872,598 \times 100,000 = 0.4$
Ages 35–44 $2,478/44,370,594 \times 100,000 = 5.6$
Ages 45–54 $12,374/40,804,599 \times 100,000 = 30.3$
Ages 55–64 $30,956/27,899,736 \times 100,000 = 111.0$
Ages 65–74 $49,386/18,337,044 \times 100,000 = 269.3$
Inferences: Rate increases with age.

Question 3. Age-specific death rates:

Ages 20–24 $19,973/20,727,694 \times 100,000 = 96.4$
Ages 25–34 $41,300/39,872,598 \times 100,000 = 103.6$
Ages 35–44 $89,461/44,370,594 \times 100,000 = 201.6$

Age- and sex-specific death rates:

Males aged 20–24	$14,964/10,663,922 \times 100,000 = 140.3$
Males aged 25–34	$28,602/20,222,486 \times 100,000 = 141.4$
Males aged 35–44	$56,435/22,133,659 \times 100,000 = 255.0$
Females aged 20–24	$5,009/10,063,772 \times 100,000 = 49.8$
Females aged 25–34	$12,698/19,650,112 \times 100,000 = 64.6$
Females aged 35–44	$33,026/22,236,935 \times 100,000 = 148.5$

Question 4.

a. Calculate the crude death rates:

Crude death rate	$2,448,288/290,810,789 \times 100,000 = 841.9$
Death rate, males	$1,201,964/143,037,290 \times 100,000 = 840.3$
Death rate, females	$1,246,324/147,773,499 \times 100,000 = 843.4$

Due to accidents:

Total	$109,277/290,810,789 \times 100,000 = 37.6$
Males	$70,532/143,037,290 \times 100,000 = 49.3$
Females	$38,745/147,773,499 \times 100,000 = 26.2$

Due to malignant neoplasms:

Total	$556,902/290,810,789 \times 100,000 = 191.5$
Males	$287,990/143,037,290 \times 100,000 = 201.3$
Females	$268,912/147,773,499 \times 100,000 = 182.0$

Due to Alzheimer's disease:

Total	$63,457/290,810,789 \times 100,000 = 21.8$
Males	$18,335/143,037,290 \times 100,000 = 12.8$
Females	$45,122/147,773,499 \times 100,000 = 30.5$

b. Proportional mortality ratios (PMRs):

PMR for accidents:

Total	$109,277/2,448,288 \times 100 = 4.5$
Males	$70,532/1,201,964 \times 100 = 5.9$
Females	$38,745/1,246,324 \times 100 = 3.1$

PMR for malignant neoplasms:

Total	$556,902/2,448,288 \times 100 = 22.7$
Males	$287,990/1,201,964 \times 100 = 24.0$
Females	$268,912/1,246,324 \times 100 = 21.6$

PMR for Alzheimer's disease:

Total	$63,457/2,448,288 \times 100 = 2.6$
Males	$18,335/1,201,964 \times 100 = 1.5$
Females	$45,122/1,246,324 \times 100 = 3.6$

c. Maternal mortality rate
$495/4,089,950 \times 100,000 = 12.1$ per 100,000 live births

d. Infant mortality rate
$28,025/4,089,950 \times 1,000 = 6.9$ per 1,000 live births

e. Crude birth rate
$4,089,950/290,810,789 \times 1,000 = 14.1$ per 1,000 population

f. General fertility rate
$4,089,950/61,910,608 \times 1,000 = 66.1$ per 1,000 women aged 15–44

Question 5. The prevalence of HIV is 137.0 per 100,000 population.
The incidence of HIV is 24.1 per 100,000 population.

Question 8.
a. 1.3 to 1.0 (sex ratio, male to female regular drinkers)
b. 42.8% (proportion of regular drinkers who are women)
c. 565.2 per 1,000 (men only); 393.2 per 1,000 (women only); 476.1 per 1,000 (total population)

Question 10. These data are prevalence data from which it is not possible to infer risk.

Question 11. 20%

Chapter 5

Question 8.
SURVEY
Advantages
- More control over the quality of the data
- More in-depth data can be collected on each case than is usually possible with surveillance

- Can identify spectrum of childhood injuries, including those that do not warrant medical care
- More accurate assessment of true incidence and prevalence

Disadvantages

- More costly to perform since survey requires development of *de novo* data collection system and hiring of interviewers who require training and supervision
- Represents only single point in time ("snapshot"); may miss seasonal trends; misses rare diseases; misses rapidly fatal diseases
- Tells little if anything about changes over time in incidence or prevalence of a behavior or outcome
- Recall bias more likely to affect results because data are collected retrospectively (surveillance is usually prospective)

SURVEILLANCE

Advantages

- Cheaper (for the health department)
- Can often use existing systems and health personnel for data collection
- Allows monitoring of trends over time
- Ongoing data collection may allow collection of an adequate number of cases to study those at risk. With surveys, an event may be too infrequent to gather enough cases for study; with surveillance, the observation period can be extended until sufficient numbers of cases are collected.

Disadvantages

- May not provide a representative picture of the incidence or prevalence unless care is taken in selecting reporting sites and ensuring complete reporting
- Data that can be collected are limited by the skill, time, and good will of the data collectors, who usually have other responsibilities.
- Quality control may be a major problem in data collection.
- The quality of data may vary between collection sites.

Question 9.
1. Change in surveillance system/policy of reporting
2. Change in case definition
3. Improved diagnosis
   - New laboratory test

- Increased physician awareness of the syndrome, new physician in town, etc.
- Increase in publicity/public awareness may have prompted individuals or parents to seek medical attention for compatible illness

4. Increase in reporting (i.e., improved awareness of requirement to report)
5. Batch reporting (unlikely in this scenario)
6. True increase in incidence

Question 10.
No right answer, but one sequence might be as follows:

Table 1: Number of reported cases this week, disease by county
Table 2: Number of reported cases, disease by week (going back 6–8 weeks for comparison)
Table 3: Number of reported cases for past 4 weeks, disease by year (going back 5 years for comparison)

Table 1 addresses disease occurrence by place. Tables 2 and 3 address disease occurrence by time. Together, these tables should give an indication of whether an unusual cluster or pattern of disease is occurring. If such a pattern is detected, person characteristics may then be explored.

Question 11.
Many state health department newsletters do not go to "all who need to know." Even among those who receive the newsletter, some do not read it at all; many others skim the articles and ignore the tables altogether. In addition, depending on the timing of the laboratory report and publication deadlines, the information may be delayed by up to several weeks.

This information is important for all who may be affected, and for all who may be able to take preventive measures, including:

- Other public health agencies, e.g., neighboring local health departments, animal control staff, etc.
- Healthcare providers
- Veterinarians
- The public (inform by issuing press release to the media)

Source: (Answers to Questions 8–11): Reprinted from Centers for Disease Control and Prevention. *Principles of Epidemiology,* 2nd ed. Atlanta, GA: CDC; 1998:337–338.

Chapter 6

Question 7.

$$OR = \frac{(37)(121)}{(68)(24)} = 2.74$$

Question 8.

$$OR = \frac{(105)(137)}{(463)(84)} = 0.37 \text{ (a protective effect)}$$

Note: A = 189 − 105
      B = 600 − 137

Question 9.

$$OR = \frac{(37)(752)}{(48)(362)} = 1.60$$

Note: C = 399 − 37
      D = 800 − 48

Chapter 7

Question 5.
Relative risk of anxiety: $(500/10,000)/(200/20,000) = 0.05/0.01 = 5$

Question 8. A cohort study would probably not be necessary given the strong association.

Chapter 8

Question 8. d

Question 9. a (case-control)
            b (prospective cohort)
            c (clinical trial)
            d (retrospective cohort)
            e (prospective cohort)

f (clinical trial)

g (cross-sectional)

Chapter 9

Question 1. $(1.2 - 1)/1.2 = 0.167$

$(1.8 - 1)/1.8 = 0.444$

$(3.0 - 1)/3.0 = 0.667$

$(15.0 - 1)/15.0 = 0.933$

Question 2. c

Question 3. RR (lung cancer) = $(71/100,000)/(7/100,000) = 10.1$

Question 4. RR (coronary thrombosis) = $(599/100,000)/(422/100,000) = 1.4$

Question 5. Etiologic fraction (lung cancer) = $[(71/100,000 - (7/100,000)]/(71/100,000) = 0.90$

Question 6. Etiologic fraction (coronary) = $[(599/100,000) - (422/100,000)]/(599/100,000) = 0.30$

Question 7. Population etiologic fraction (lung cancer) = $[0.55(10.1 - 1)]/[0.55(10.1 - 1) + 1] = (5.005/6.005) \times 100 = 83\%$

Question 8. Population etiologic fraction (coronary) = $[0.55 (1.4 - 1)]/[0.55(1.4 - 1) + 1] = (0.22/1.22) \times 100 = 18.0\%$

Question 9. a. False

b. True. RR for lung cancer is 10.1 vs. 1.4 for coronary thrombosis; and EF for lung cancer is 90% vs. 30% for coronary thrombosis.

c. False

d. False

e. False

Question 10.

a. RR = $(500/10,000)/(200/20,000) = 0.05/0.01 = 5$

b. Risk difference = $0.05 - 0.01 = 0.04$

c. Etiologic fraction = $[(0.05 - 0.01)/(0.05)] \times 100 = 80\%$

d. Population etiologic fraction = 0.33(5 − 1)/0.33(5 − 1) + 1 = 1.32/2.32 × 100 = 56.9%

Chapter 10

Question 1. Yes. Because one-third of the subjects were lost to follow-up, a selection bias is suspected. We do not know why the 20 people died. If they died of the disease in question, the incidence rate would probably be higher than 8%.

Question 2. Stratify the cases and controls.

Question 3. Device B gives greater validity because the two measurements are closer to the actual number of cells to be counted. Device A has greater reliability because its two measurements are closer together than those of Device B.

Question 4. Yes. Smoking is strongly associated with disease (lung cancer) and is likely to be associated with diet. Therefore, smoking should be controlled for in either the study design or data analysis.

Question 5. Yes. The rate among the self-referred group was much higher than the rate the investigator found among members, leading to a potentially elevated RR. The self-referred group may represent a subset of people with special circumstances, because they were not included in the first military group (i.e., discharged, different duty assignment, etc.). They volunteered for the study, so it is possible they suspected their exposure or had a particular interest in the outcome of the study.

Question 6. There is no validity to the scale, except for subjects who actually weigh 30 kg! However, the scale has high reliability because it gives consistent readings.

Question 7. b

Question 8. e

Question 9. d

Question 10. c

Chapter 11

Question 6. Sensitivity = 50%
Specificity = 25%
Predictive value (+) = 25%
Predictive value (−) = 50%

Question 7. Sensitivity = 69%
Specificity = 97%

Question 8. Predictive value (+) = 90%
Predictive value (−) = 90%

Question 9. Accuracy = 83%

Question 10.a. Predictive value of a positive test = 63.0%
Predictive value of a negative test = 98.8%

Chapter 12

Question 2. Secondary attack rate = $[(14 − 2)/(20 − 2)] \times 100 =$
$12/18 \times 100 = 66.7\%$

Question 10.a. Based on the difference in attack rates between those persons who ate and did not eat the food items served, the rare beef was the food most likely to be responsible for the outbreak. The attack rate among those who ate rare beef was $17/23 \times 100 = 74\%$. The attack rate among those who did not eat rare beef was $0/1 \times 100 = 0\%$. The difference in attack rates was $74\% − 0\% = 74\%$. When all of the differences in attack rates between those persons who ate and did not eat the food items served are calculated by using procedures similar to those for the rare beef calculations, one can determine that 74% is the greatest difference.

Chapter 14

Question 1. Bb × BB, Bb × Bb, Bb × bb, BB × bb.

Question 2. BB × bb = 100% heterozygotes.

Question 3. A female receives no sex chromosome from her father's father, whereas a male receives no sex chromosome from his father's mother.

Question 4. This result corresponds to an odds ratio of about 2. Therefore, the data provide minimal evidence for a familial component.

Question 5. This procedure provides an indirect match on the age of the relatives.

Question 6. Smoking, occupation, radon exposure, secondhand smoke, diet, and age.

Question 7. No. Aside from possible biases in selection of the families, and errors in the analysis, another possibility may be that any genetic influence on the disease is insufficient to manifest in a Mendelian pattern of disease (low penetrance).

Glossary

Acculturation   Modifications that individuals or groups undergo when they come into contact with another culture.

Acculturation hypothesis   Proposes that as immigrants become acculturated to a host country, their health profiles tend to converge with that of the native-born population.

Adjusted rate   Rate of morbidity or mortality in a population in which statistical procedures have been applied to permit fair comparisons across populations by removing the effect of differences in the composition of various populations; an example is age adjustment.

Agent   In the epidemiologic triangle, the cause of a disease; in infectious diseases, often the agent is a microbe such as a virus or bacterium.

Age-specific rate   Frequency of a disease in a particular age stratum divided by the total number of persons within that age stratum during a time period.

Allele   One of two or more alternative forms of a gene that occurs at the same locus (site or location on a chromosome occupied by a gene, which comprises a particular set of alleles).

Analytic study   A type of research design concerned with the determinants of disease and the reasons for relatively high or low frequency of disease in specific population subgroups. Analytic studies identify causes of the problem, test specific etiologic hypotheses, generate new etiologic hypotheses, and suggest mechanisms of causation; they also may include case-control studies, cohort studies, and some types of ecologic studies.

Antigenicity   Ability of an agent to induce antibody production in the host.

Attack rate   An alternative form of the incidence rate that is used when the nature of a disease or condition is such that a population is observed for a short time period. The attack rate is calculated by the formula ill/(ill + well) × 100 (during a time period). The attack rate is not a true rate because the time dimension is often uncertain.

Attributable risk   A measure of risk difference. In a cohort study, refers to the difference between the incidence rate of a disease in the exposed group and the incidence rate in the nonexposed group.

Autosomal dominant   A situation in which only a single copy of an altered gene located on a non-sex chromosome is sufficient to cause an increased risk of disease.

Autosomal recessive   Denotes those diseases for which two copies of an altered gene are required to increase risk of disease.

Availability of the data   Refers to the investigator's access to data (e.g., patient records and databases in which personally identifying information has been removed).

Bias (also, systematic errors)   Refers to deviations of results, or inferences, from the truth.

Blinding (also, masking)   An aspect of study design wherein the subject is not aware of his/her group assignment of placebo or treatment; seeks to alleviate bias in study results.

Case clustering   An unusual aggregation of health events grouped together in space or time.

Case fatality rate   Number of deaths caused by a disease among those who have the disease during a time period.

Case-control study   A study that compares individuals who have a disease with individuals who do not have the disease in order to examine differences in exposures or risk factors for the disease.

Cause   Act, event, or state of nature that initiates/permits, alone or in conjunction with other causes, a sequence of events resulting in an effect.

Cause-specific rate   Measure that refers to mortality (or frequency of a given disease) divided by the population size at the midpoint of a time period times a multiplier.

Choropleth map   A map that represents disease rates (or other numerical data) for a group of regions by different degrees of shading.

Classification   Method of arranging disease entities into categories that share similar features, allowing for statistical compilation.

Clinical trial   A carefully designed and executed investigation of the effects of a treatment or technology that uses randomization, blinding of subjects to study conditions, and manipulation of the study factor.

Codon   A set of three of four amino acids that can combine in different orders to code for 64 different amino acids, which when strung together into a long sequence comprise the genetic code of DNA or RNA.

Cohort   A group of individuals who share an exposure in common and who are followed over time; an example is an age cohort.

Cohort effect   Consequence of long-term secular trends in exposure within a specific cohort.

Cohort life table   A table that presents mortality statistics of all persons born during a particular year.

Cohort study (also, prospective or longitudinal study)   A type of study that collects data and follows a group of subjects who have received a specific exposure. The incidence of a specific disease or other outcome of interest is tracked over time. The incidence in the exposed group is compared with the incidence in groups that are not exposed, have different levels of exposure, or have different types of exposures.

Colonization   Situation wherein an infectious agent may multiply on the surface of the body without invoking a tissue or immune response.

Community intervention   An intervention designed for the purpose of educational and behavioral changes at the population level.

Concurrent validity   A type of measurement obtained by correlating a measure with an alternative measure of the same phenomenon taken at the same point in time (see Validity).

Confidence interval   A computed interval of values that, with a given probability, is said to contain the true value of the population parameter; a measure of uncertainty about a parameter estimate. An example is the confidence interval about a relative risk measure.

Confounding   Masking of an association between an exposure and an outcome because of the influence of a third variable that was not considered in the study design or analysis.

Construct validity   Degree to which a measurement agrees with the theoretical concept being investigated.

Content validity (also, rational or logical validity) Degree to which a measure covers the range of meanings included within the concept.

Continuous variable A type of variable that can have an infinite number of values within a specified range (e.g., blood pressure measurements).

Count Total number of cases of a disease or other health phenomenon being studied.

Criterion-referenced validity Type of validity found by correlating a measure with an external criterion of the entity being assessed to determine the accuracy of the data (can include predictive and concurrent validity).

Crossover design Any change of treatment for a patient in a clinical trial that involves a switch of study treatments.

Cross-sectional study (also, prevalence study) A type of descriptive study (e.g., a population survey) designed to estimate the prevalence of a disease or exposure.

Crude birth rate Number of live births during a specified period of time per the resident population during the midpoint of the time period (expressed as rate per 1,000).

Crude rate A summary rate based on the actual number of events in a population over a given time period. An example is the crude death rate, which approximates the proportion of the population that dies during a time period of interest.

Cumulative incidence (cumulative incidence rate) Number or proportion of a population (or group of people) who become diseased or develop a condition being studied during a stated period of time; used to calculate risk.

Cyclic fluctuation An increase or decrease in the frequency of a disease or health condition in a population over a period of years or within each year.

Demographic transition Historical shift from high birth and death rates found in agrarian societies to much lower birth and death rates found in developed countries.

Dependent variable A factor in a theoretical model that is affected or influenced by an independent variable.

Descriptive epidemiology Epidemiologic studies that are concerned with characterizing the amount and distribution of health and disease within a population.

Descriptive study   A type of study designed to portray the health characteristics of a population with respect to person, place, and time. Such studies are utilized to estimate disease frequency and time trends, and include case reports, case series, and cross-sectional surveys.

Determinant   A factor or event that is capable of bringing about a change in the health status of a population.

Direct transmission   Spread of infection through person-to-person contact.

Disability-adjusted life years (DALY)   A measure that adds the time a person has a disability to the time lost to early death; thus, one DALY indicates one year of life lost to the combination of disability and early mortality.

Disappearing disorder   Type of disease or illness that was formerly a common source of morbidity and mortality and that has nearly disappeared in epidemic form.

Dose-response curve   Graphical representation of the relationship between changes in the size of a dose or exposure and changes in response. This curve generally has an "S" shape.

Double-blind design   Feature of a clinical trial in which neither the subject nor the experimenter is aware of the subject's group assignment in relation to control or treatment status.

Ecologic comparison study   Type of research design that assesses the correlation (association) between exposure rates and disease rates among different groups or populations over the same time period. The unit of analysis is the group.

Ecologic fallacy   A misleading conclusion about the relationship between a factor and an outcome that occurs when the observed association obtained between study variables at the group level does not necessarily hold true at the individual level.

Ecologic trend study   Type of study that examines the correlation of changes in exposure and changes in disease over time within the same community, country, or other aggregate unit.

Emerging infection   An abrupt increase in the incidence or geographic scope of a seemingly new infectious disease (e.g., hantaviral pulmonary syndrome found in the Southwestern United States).

Endemic   A disease or infectious agent that is habitually present in a community, geographic area, or population group. Often an endemic disease maintains a low but continuous incidence.

Environment   Domain in which the disease-causing agent may exist, survive, or originate.

Environmental epidemiology   The study of diseases and conditions (occurring in the population) that are linked to environmental factors.

Epidemic   Occurrence of a disease clearly in excess of normal expectancy.

Epidemiologic transition   A shift in the pattern of morbidity and mortality from causes related primarily to infectious and communicable diseases to causes associated with chronic, degenerative diseases; is accompanied by demographic transition.

Epidemiology   Study of the distribution and determinants of health and disease, morbidity, injuries, disability, and mortality in populations.

Etiologic fraction   Proportion of the rate of disease in an exposed group that is due to the exposure.

Experimental study   Research design in which the investigator manipulates the study factor and randomly assigns subjects to exposed and nonexposed conditions.

External validity   Measure of the generalizability of the findings from the study population to the target population.

Family recall bias   A type of bias that occurs when cases are more likely to remember the details of their family history than are controls (see Bias).

Family study   A type of research design in which data on phenotype and risk factors are measured in individual family members.

Fertility rate (see General fertility rate)

Fetal death rate   Number of fetal deaths after 20 weeks or more gestation divided by the number of live births plus fetal deaths after 20 weeks or more gestation during a year (expressed as rate per 1,000 live births plus fetal deaths).

Fetal death ratio   Number of fetal deaths after a gestation of 20 weeks or more divided by the number of live births during a year (expressed as rate per 1,000 live births).

Functional cloning (also, functional mapping)   After the proteins involved with a disease process are identified, a geneticist can determine their amino acid sequence and decipher the DNA code for that sequence; then the geneticist can search for where the sequence occurs in the human genome.

Gene   A particular segment of a DNA molecule on a chromosome that determines the nature of an inherited trait in an individual.

General fertility rate   Number of live births reported in an area during a given time interval divided by the number of women aged 15 to 44 years in that area (expressed as rate per 1,000 women aged 15 to 44).

Generation time   An interval of time between lodgment of an infectious agent in a host and the maximal communicability of the host.

Genetic epidemiology   Field of epidemiology concerned with inherited factors that influence risk of disease.

Genotype   In an individual, refers to his or her genetic constitution, often stated in reference to a specific trait or at a particular locus.

Healthy migrant effect   In studies of migration and health, a bias that results from the migration of younger, healthier persons in comparison with those who remain at home (see Bias).

Healthy worker effect   Error linked to the observation that employed persons tend to have lower mortality rates than the general population; stems from the fact that good health is necessary for obtaining and maintaining employment (see Bias).

Herd immunity   Resistance of an entire community to an infectious disease due to the immunity of a large proportion of individuals in that community to the disease.

Host   Person (or animal) who (that) has a lodgment of an infectious disease agent under natural conditions.

Hypothesis   Supposition tested by collecting facts that lead to its acceptance or rejection.

Identical by descent (IBD)   In siblings, an allele that comes from the same parent.

Identical by state   Alleles that are the same in siblings but come from different parents.

Infestation   Presence of a living infectious agent on the body's exterior surface, causing a local tissue or immune response.

Immunogenicity   The ability of an infection to produce specific immunity (protection against a disease).

Inapparent infection   A type of infection that shows no clinical or obvious symptoms.

Incidence density   Number of new cases of disease during a time period divided by the total person-time of observation; used to calculate incidence when subjects have been observed for varying periods of time.

Incidence rate   (Number of new cases of a disease—or other condition—in a population divided by the total population at risk over a time period) times a multiplier (e.g., 100,000).

Incubation period   Time interval between exposure to an infectious agent and the appearance of the first signs or symptoms of disease.

Independent variable (also, exposure or risk factor variable)   Hypothesized causal factor in a theoretical model.

Index case   In an epidemiologic investigation of a disease outbreak, the first case of disease to come to the attention of authorities (e.g., the initial case of Ebola virus).

Infant mortality rate   Number of infant deaths among infants aged 0 to 365 days during a year divided by the number of live births during the same year (expressed as the rate per 1,000 live births).

Infectivity   Capacity of an agent to enter and multiply in a susceptible host and thus produce infection or disease.

Information bias   Measurement error in assessment of exposure and/or disease; types include recall bias and interviewer bias (see Bias).

Internal validity   Measures the extent to which differences in an outcome between or among groups in a study can be attributed to the hypothesized effects of an exposure, an intervention, or other causal factor being investigated. A study is said to have internal validity when there have been proper selection of study groups and a lack of error in measurement (see Validity).

Intervention study   A type of research design that tests the efficacy of a preventive or therapeutic measure. Intervention studies include controlled clinical trials and community interventions.

Intron   Noncoding region of DNA.

Late fetal death rate   Number of fetal deaths after 28 weeks or more gestation divided by the number of live births plus fetal deaths after 28 weeks or more gestation during a year (expressed as rate per 1,000 live births plus late fetal deaths).

Latency   Time period between initial exposure to an agent and development of a measurable response. The latency period can range from a few seconds (in the case of acutely toxic agents) to several decades (in the case of some forms of cancer).

Lead time bias   Erroneous perception that a screening-detected case of disease has a longer survival than an unscreened case of the same disease simply because the screened case was identified earlier in its natural history than was the un-screened case (see Bias).

Length bias   Error resulting from the fact that some cases of disease (particularly tumors) detected by screening programs tend to progress more slowly than those detected by clinical manifestations (see Bias).

Life expectancy   Number of years that a person is expected to live, at any particular year.

Linkage disequilibrium   When a specific allele at a marker locus is strongly associated with a mutant allele.

Linked   Genes that are in close physical proximity to each other on the same chromosome.

Mass screening (also, population screening)   A type of screening that collects data on total population groups, regardless of any a priori information as to whether the individuals are members of a high-risk subset of the population.

Maternal mortality rate   (Number of maternal deaths ascribed to childbirth divided by the number of live births) times 100,000 live births during a year.

Mendelian inheritance   Named for the 19th century Austrian monk, Gregor Mendel, denotes the transmission of a disease or trait from parents to offspring according to simple laws of inheritance.

Metropolitan statistical areas (MSAs)   Formerly known as standard metropolitan statistical areas (SMSAs), geographic areas of the United States established by the Bureau of the Census to provide a distinction between metropolitan and nonmetropolitan areas by type of residence, industrial concentration, and population concentration.

Moderating variable (also, intervening variable) Third variable (effect modifier) that is intermediate in the causal process between exposure factor (independent variable) and outcome (dependent variable); modifies the effect of the exposure upon disease status.

Molecular epidemiology Field of epidemiology that uses biomarkers to establish exposure–disease associations. Examples of biomarkers are serum levels of micronutrients and DNA fingerprints.

Morbidity Occurrence of an illness or illnesses in a population.

Mortality Occurrence of death in a population.

Mortality difference Measure of the difference between an exposed and nonexposed population in the frequency of death (see Risk difference).

Multiphasic screening Use of two or more screening tests simultaneously among large groups of people.

Multiple causality (multicausality or multifactorial etiology) A portrayal of causality wherein several individual, community, and environmental factors may interact to cause a particular disease or condition.

Mutation A change in DNA that may adversely affect an organism.

Nativity Place of origin (e.g., native-born or foreign-born) of the individual or his or her relatives.

Natural experiment A type of research design in which the experimenter does not control the manipulation of a study factor(s). The manipulation of the study factor occurs as a result of natural phenomena or policies that impact health, an example being laws that control smoking in public places.

Nature of the data Refers to the source of the data (e.g., vital statistics, physician's records, case registries, etc.).

Neonatal mortality rate Number of infant deaths under 28 days of age divided by the number of live births during a year.

Nested case-control study A type of research design wherein both cases and controls come from the population of a cohort study (see case-control study and cohort study).

Nomenclature A highly specific set of terms for describing and recording clinical or pathologic diagnoses to classify ill persons into groups.

Null hypothesis   A hypothesis of no difference in a population parameter among the groups being compared.

Observational study   A type of research design in which the investigator does not manipulate the study factor or use random assignment of subjects. There is careful measurement of the patterns of exposure and disease in a population in order to draw inferences about the distribution and etiology of diseases. Observational studies include cross-sectional, case-control, and cohort studies.

Odds ratio   Measure of association between frequency of exposure and frequency of outcome used in case-control studies. The formula is (AD)/(BC), where A is the number of subjects who have the disease and have been exposed, B is the number who do not have the disease and have been exposed, C is the number who have the disease and have not been exposed, and D is the number who do not have the disease and have not been exposed.

Operationalization   Methods used to translate concepts used in research into actual measurements.

Operations research   A type of study of the placement of health services in a community and the optimum utilization of such services.

Pandemic   An epidemic that spans a wide geographic area. A worldwide influenza outbreak is an example of a pandemic.

Passive smoking (also, secondhand or sidestream exposure to cigarette smoke)   Refers to the involuntary breathing of cigarette smoke by nonsmokers in an environment where cigarette smokers are present.

Pathogenesis   Process and mechanism of interaction of disease agent(s) with a host in causing disease.

Pathogenicity   Capacity of an agent to cause disease in an infected host.

Perinatal mortality rate   Number of late fetal deaths after 28 weeks or more gestation plus infant deaths within 7 days of birth divided by the number of live births plus the number of late fetal deaths during a year (expressed as rate per 1,000 live births and fetal deaths).

Perinatal mortality ratio   Number of late fetal deaths after 28 weeks or more gestation plus infant deaths within 7 days of birth divided by the number of live births during a year (expressed as rate per 1,000 live births).

Period prevalence   Number of cases of illness during a time period divided by the average size of the population.

Periodic life table   A type of statistical table that provides an overview of the present mortality experience of a population and shows projections of future mortality experience.

Persisting disorder   A type of illness or disease that remains common because an effective method of prevention or cure has not yet been discovered.

Point epidemic   Response of a group of people circumscribed in place to a common source of infection, contamination, or other etiologic factor to which they were exposed almost simultaneously.

Point prevalence   Number of cases of illness in a group or population at a point in time divided by the total number of persons in that group or population.

Polymorphic traits   Traits that vary greatly from individual to individual.

Population-based cohort study   A type of cohort study that includes either an entire population or a representative sample of the population (see Cohort study).

Population etiologic fraction (attributable fraction in the population) Proportion of the rate of disease in the population that is due to an exposure. It is calculated as the population risk difference ($I_p - I_{ne}$) divided by the rate of disease in the population (I_p).

Population risk difference   Difference between the incidence rate (risk) of disease in the nonexposed segment of the population (I_{ne}) and the overall incidence rate (I_p): ($I_p - I_{ne}$). It measures the benefit to the population derived by modifying a risk factor.

Positional cloning (also, physical mapping)   Method for geneticists to identify a gene responsible for a disease from a chromosomal region of DNA.

Postneonatal mortality rate   Number of infant deaths from 28 days to 365 days after birth divided by the number of live births minus neonatal deaths during a year (expressed as rate per 1,000 live births).

Predictive validity   Ability of a measure to forecast some attribute or characteristic in the future.

Predictive value (positive and negative)   (+) Proportion of individuals who are screened positive by a test and actually have the disease. (−) Proportion of individuals who are screened negative by a test and actually do not have the disease.

Prepathogenesis   Period of time that precedes the interaction between an agent of disease and the host.

Prevalence   Number of existing cases of a disease or health condition in a population at some designated time.

Prevalence difference   Measure that computes the difference in prevalence between an exposed and nonexposed population (see Risk difference).

Primary prevention   Activities designed to reduce the occurrence of disease that occur during the period of prepathogenesis (i.e., before an agent interacts with a host).

Primordial prevention   Actions and measures that inhibit the emergence and establishment of factors such as environmental, economic, social and behavioral conditions, and cultural patterns of living known to increase the risk of disease.

Probability sample   Type of sample in which every element in the population has a nonzero probability of being included in the sample (e.g., simple random sample).

Proband   Individual in a family who brings a disease to the attention of the investigator. In a case family, the proband is likely to be the person who is affected with the disease of interest.

Prophylactic trial   A type of clinical trial designed to evaluate the effectiveness of a treatment or substance used to prevent disease. Examples are clinical trials to test vaccines and vitamin supplements.

Proportion   Fraction in which the numerator is a part of the denominator.

Proportional mortality ratio (PMR)   Number of deaths within a population due to a specific disease or cause divided by the total number of deaths in the population during a time period such as a year.

Prospective cohort study   A type of cohort study design that collects data on exposure at the initiation (baseline) of a study and follows the population in order to observe the occurrence of health outcomes at some time in the future.

Protective factor   A circumstance or substance that provides a beneficial environment and makes a positive contribution to health.

Psychosocial epidemiology   Field of epidemiology that examines the role of psychological, behavioral, and social factors in health.

P **value**   An assessment that indicates the probability that the observed findings of a study could have occurred by chance alone.

Quasi-experimental study   Type of research design in which the investigator manipulates the study factor but does not assign subjects randomly to the exposed and nonexposed groups.

Random errors   Errors that reflect fluctuations around a true value of a parameter (such as a rate or a relative risk) because of sampling variability.

Randomization   A process whereby chance determines the subjects' likelihood of assignment to either an intervention group or a control group. Each subject has an equal probability of being assigned to either group.

Rate   A ratio that consists of a numerator and denominator in which time forms part of the denominator. Example: The crude death rate refers to the number of deaths in a given year divided by the size of the reference population (during the midpoint of the year) (expressed as rate per 100,000).

Rate difference   Measure of the difference between two rates (for example, incidence rates) between exposed and nonexposed populations (see Risk difference).

Ratio   A fraction in which there is not necessarily any specified relationship between the numerator and denominator.

Record linkage   System of joining data from two or more sources.

Reference population   Group from which cases of a disease (or health-related phenomenon under study) have been taken; also refers to the group to which the results of a study may be generalized.

Registry   Centralized database for collection of information about a disease.

Relative risk   Ratio of the risk of disease or death among the exposed to the risk among the unexposed. The formula used is Relative risk = (Incidence rate in the exposed/Incidence rate in the nonexposed).

Reliability (also, precision)   Ability of a measuring instrument to give consistent results on repeated trials.

Reportable disease statistics   Statistics derived from diseases that physicians and other healthcare providers must report to government agencies according to legal statute. Such diseases are called reportable diseases.

Representativeness (also, external validity)   Refers to the generalizability of the findings of an epidemiologic study to the population.

Residual disorder   An illness or disease for which the key contributing factors are known but specific methods of control have not been effectively implemented.

Resistance   Ability of an agent to survive adverse environmental conditions.

Retrospective cohort study   Type of cohort study that uses historical data to determine exposure level at some time in the past; subsequently, follow-up measurements of occurrence(s) of disease between baseline and the present are taken.

Risk difference (also, attributable risk)   Difference between the incidence rate of disease in the exposed group (I_e) and the incidence rate of disease in the nonexposed group (I_{ne}): risk difference $= I_e - I_{ne}$.

Risk factor   An exposure that is associated with a disease, morbidity, mortality, or adverse health outcome.

Sampling error   As a result of sampling methods, the misrepresentation of the sample selected for a study in relation to the target population.

Screening   Presumptive identification of unrecognized disease or defects by the application of tests, examinations, or other procedures that can be applied rapidly.

Secondary attack rate   Measure of the spread of a disease within a household or similar circumscribed unit. It is calculated by the formula [number of new cases in a group − initial case(s)] / [number of susceptible persons in the group − initial case(s)] × 100.

Secondary prevention   Intervention designed to reduce the progress of a disease after the agent interacts with the host; occurs during the period of pathogenesis.

Secular trends   Gradual changes in disease frequency over long time periods.

Segregation analysis   When the outcome of an experiment (random mating and assortment of genes from parents to offspring) is known, models representing possible modes of transmission (genetic and nongenetic) are fit to the data.

Selection bias   Error that occurs when the relationship between exposure and disease is different for those who participate in a study versus those who would be theoretically eligible for the study but do not participate (see Bias).

Selective factor A circumstance that results in the choice of persons for a group because of their health status or other characteristic.

Selective screening (also, targeted screening) A type of presumptive identification of unrecognized disease or defects applied to subsets of the population at high risk for disease or certain conditions as the result of family history, age, or environmental exposures (see Screening).

Sensitivity Ability of a test to identify correctly all screened individuals who actually have the disease being screened for.

Significance level Chance of rejecting the null hypothesis when, in fact, it is true.

Social network Structure of people's social attachments; helps to explain differences in the individual's ability to respond to stressors.

Social support Perceived emotional support that one receives from family members, friends, and others; mediates against stress.

Spatial clustering Concentration of cases of a disease in a particular geographic area.

Specific rate Statistic that refers to a particular subgroup of the population defined in terms of race, age, or sex; also may refer to the entire population but is specific for some single cause of death or illness, as in a cause-specific rate.

Specificity Ability of a test to identify nondiseased individuals who actually do not have a disease.

Standard metropolitan statistical areas (SMSAs) Standard areas of the United States established by the U.S. Bureau of the Census to make regional comparisons in disease rates and also to make urban/rural comparisons (see also Metropolitan statistical areas (MSAs).

Standardized mortality ratio (SMR) Number of observed deaths divided by the number of expected deaths during a time period. The analogous term for morbidity is the standardized morbidity ratio.

Stratum A homogeneous population subgroup, such as that characterized by a narrow age range, e.g., a five-year age group.

Surveillance Systematic collection, analysis, interpretation, dissemination, and consolidation of data pertaining to the occurrence of a specific disease.

Synergism   Situation in which the combined effect of several exposures is greater than the sum of the individual effects.

Team science   Uses large consortia of scientists to pool data and biological samples across studies.

Temporal clustering   Association between common exposure to an etiologic agent at the same time and the development of morbidity or mortality in a group or population.

Temporality   Timing of information about cause and effect; whether the information about cause and effect was assembled at the same time point or whether information about the cause was garnered before or after the information about the effect.

Tertiary prevention   Intervention that takes place during late pathogenesis and is designed to reduce the limitations of disability from disease.

Therapeutic trial   A type of study designed to evaluate the effectiveness of a treatment in bringing about an improvement in the patient's health. An example is a trial that evaluates new curative drugs or a new surgical procedure.

Threshold   Lowest dose (often of a toxic substance) at which a particular response may occur.

Toxigenicity   Capacity of an agent to produce a toxin or poison.

Vaccination   Procedure in which a vaccine (a preparation that contains a killed or weakened pathogen) is introduced into the body to invoke an immune response against a disease-causing microbe such as a virus or bacterium. Also called inoculation, immunization.

Validity (also, accuracy)   Ability of a measuring instrument to give a true measure (how well the instrument measures what it purports to measure).

Virulence   Severity of the clinical manifestations of a disease.

Vital statistics   Mortality and birth statistics maintained by government agencies.

Years of potential life lost (YPLL)   A type of statistical measure that takes into account the effect of premature death caused by diseases; computed by subtracting the actual age of death of an individual from the average age of death in a population (arriving at the YPLL for the individual), and then summing the YPLL for each individual in the population (i.e., the United States) being studied for a specific cause of mortality.

Index

Note: Italicized page locators indicate a figure; tables are noted with a *t*.

A

AADR. *See* Age-adjusted death rate
AAP. *See* American Academy of Pediatrics
Absenteeism data, 214*t*, 233
Absolute effects, 362–365, 381
   population risk difference, 364–365
   risk difference, 362–364
Abstracts, online databases and, 207
Academic workers, 617
Accidents
   personal behavior and, 591
   seasonal variations in, 188
Acculturation hypothesis, 164
ACE. *See* American College of
   Epidemiology
Acquired immune deficiency syndrome, 56,
   63, 178, 339, *440*, 464, 480, 482
   death certificate data, stigmatization and,
   215
   geographic variation, within U.S., 180
   high case fatality rates with, 455 (exhibit)
   incompleteness in reporting of, 222
   objectives of descriptive epidemiology
   and, 143
   percentage of reported cases, by
   race/ethnicity, in U.S., 2005, *160*
Active immunity, 444
Active prevention, 86
Acton, G. S., 604
Acute myeloid leukemia, 562, 563
Acute myocardial infarction, case-control
   study on passive smoking and, 274
AD. *See* Alzheimer's disease
Adaptive randomization, 340
Adenomatous polyps, screening for
   colorectal cancer and, 566
Adjusted rates, 108, 123–124, 130–133
   methods for, 124, 128, 130
Adjustment, person-environment fit model
   and, 584

Adolescents
   cancer survivors among, 299
   smoking prevalence among, in U.S., by
   survey, 1974–1991, *261*
Adults, health issues and, 147
Adventist Health Study 1 and 2, 170
Adventist Mortality Study, 170
Adverse effects, human experimentation
   and, 341
Adverse environmental events, stress and,
   583
Advertising, for alcoholic beverages, 595
Advocacy, by epidemiologists, 632
   (exhibit)
Africa
   HIV/AIDS epidemic in, 465
   infant mortality rates in, 178
African-American females
   age-adjusted breast cancer death rates
   among, 161
   obesity and, 154
   secular decreases in breast cancer among,
   190
African-American males
   calculation of proportion of deaths,
   among African-American and white
   boys, aged 5 to 15 years, 95*t*
   prostate cancer among, 161
   secular time trends in heart disease and,
   189
African Americans, 155, 160–162
   AIDS cases among, 160, *160*, 180, 464
   blood lead levels for percentage of
   children aged 1–5 years of age, *502*
   cancer rates among, 161
   definition of, in Census 2000, 158
   (exhibit)
   hypertension among, 162
   infant mortality rates and, 63, 112, *113*,
   160, 174

life expectancy among, 161, *161*
mortality rates and, 160
sickle cell anemia among, 61
survival rates for cancer and, 82
in urban areas, coronary heart disease and, 183
Age
  characteristics of persons and, 146–150
    adults, 147
    childhood, 146–147
    older adults, 147
    teenage years, 147
  community health and, 59
  family history for disease and, 541
  rate adjustment and
    formula for, 131, 124
Age-adjusted death rates, group comparison of crude death rates and, 127*t*
Agents
  in epidemiologic triangle, 438, 439, *439*
  partial list of, food-borne illness and, 458*t*
Age-specific death rates, calculating, 121*t*
Age-specific rates, 120, 122*t*
  sample calculation, 121 (exhibit)
Age standardization (age adjustment), 129 (exhibit)
Age stratum, 400
Aging population
  cancer rate increases in, 177
  future predictions about, 58
  leading causes of death and, 54
  reduced immune function and, 444
Ahlquist, D. A., 566
AI/AN. *See* Alaska Natives; American Indians
AIDS. *See* Acquired immune deficiency syndrome
Air bags in vehicles, 63
Airline flight attendants, red spots on, 9, 10, 18
Air pollution, 39, 509, 513–516, 522
  indoor, 513
  positive association between bronchitis and, 395
  studying health effects of, 494
Air quality, indoor, 510 (exhibit), 513
Alamade County Study, 310*t*
Alaska Natives, 155, 162–163

chronic diseases among, 162
definition of, in Census 2000, 159 (exhibit)
disparities in health care for, 163
Alcohol consumption, 590
  excessive
    disease and, 594–595
    selected number of deaths and years of potential life lost related to, 595*t*
Alcoholism
  community health and, 61
  death certificate data, stigmatization and, 215
  genetics and, 43
Alleles, 535 (exhibit)
  modes of inheritance and, 546
Allergens and molds, 497*t*, 504–505
Altitude, inverse relation between coronary heart disease mortality and, 395
Aluminum, 499
Aluminum workers, lung cancer, pulmonary emphysema and, 508
Alzheimer's disease
  molecular and genetic epidemiology of, 563–564
  in older women, combination hormone therapy and, 306
Ambispective cohort study, 302
  on physical activity and CHD, 315
Amebiasis, *440*, 441, 458, 464
American Academy of Pediatrics, 621*t*
  Section on Epidemiology, 620
American Association for Cancer Research, 624
American Cancer Society, 351, 411 (exhibit)
  Cancer Prevention Study, 310*t*
  Cancer Prevention Study II, 555 (exhibit)
American College of Epidemiology, 621*t*, 622
American Indians, 155, 162–163
  chronic diseases among, 162
  death rates among, 162–163
  definition of, in Census 2000, 159 (exhibit)
  disparities in health care for, 163
  infant mortality rates among, 160
American Journal of Epidemiology, 620, 622, *623*

American Journal of Public Health, 622–623, 635

American Medical Association, 299

American Public Health Association, 622, 626

Epidemiology Section, 621*t*

American Statistical Association, Section on Statistics on Epidemiology, 621*t*

Amino acids, coding of, in human body, 532–533 (exhibit)

AML. *See* Acute myeloid leukemia

Analogy, 376

causality and, 79

Analysis, bias in, 403–404

Analysis strategies, to control confounding, 399, 401–403

Analytic epidemiology

basic premise of, 262

descriptive epidemiology *vs.,* 143

Analytic studies, 246

Anaphylactic shock, 504

Anesthesia (general), case-control study on neural tube defects and maternal exposure to, 274–275

Angell, Marcia, 72

Animal fats, consumption of and disease, 596

Animal testing

clinical trials and, 332 (exhibit)–333

problem of iatrogenic reactions and, 341

Anopheles mosquito, malaria and, 450

Anthrax, 6–7, 13

Antibiotic-resistant infections

case-control studies and research on, 275

staphylococcus, 438

Anticancer drugs, testing phases for, 338, 339*t*

Antigenicity, 442

Antimony, 499

Anxiety, cohort study data for coffee use and, 384*t*

APC gene, 567

familial adenomatous polyposis and, 565

APHA Public Health Career Mart, Web site for, 626

APIs. *See* Asians; Pacific Islanders

Apolipoprotein E (Apo E), 563, 564

Appendicitis, 591

AR. *See* Attack rate

Arboviral diseases, 477

Armed forces, morbidity statistics for, 234–235, 241*t*

Arms, of Project Respect, 350 (exhibit)

Armstrong, B., 170

Arsenic, exposure to, 499–500

Arteriosclerosis, 596

Arthritis, psychosocial epidemiology and, 578

Arthropod-borne diseases, *440,* 441, 477, 479

Arthropod vectors, control of, 451

Artificial, passive immunity, 445

Artificial immunity, 444

Asbestos, 499

Asbestosis, 18, 491

Asbestos-related lung diseases, clustering and, 192

Ascariasis, 441

Aseptic meningitis, *440*

Asia, HIV/AIDS epidemic in, 465

Asians, 155, 163–165

definition of, in Census 2000, 159 (exhibit)

infant mortality rates among, 160

Aspergillosis, 441

Assault death rates, South Atlantic states (U.S.), 2003, *62*

Association for Professionals in Infection Control and Epidemiology, 621*t*

Association of Public Health Epidemiologists in Ontario, 621*t*

Association of Schools of Public Health, 624

Associations

epidemiologic, chance and, 374

measure of, in case-control studies, 269–270

Asthma, 504

clustering and, 192

Athlete's foot, 441

Atomic Bomb Casualty Commission (Hiroshima and Nagasaki), 598

Attack rate, 103, 122*t,* 451–452

data to illustrate calculation of, for given food, 452*t*

formula for calculating, 452

Attitudinal surveys, 638

Attributable fraction in the population, 368
Attributable risk, 362
Australia, infant mortality rates in, 178
Australian Epidemiological Association, 621*t*
Autosomal dominant diseases, 546–547
Autosomal recessive diseases, 547
Autosomes, 533 (exhibit), 546
Availability of the data criterion, 205–206, 236
Avian flocks, pathogenic avian influenza in, 40–41, *41*
Avian influenza (H5N1), 39, 40–41
  web of causation for, *378*

B

Baby Boom generation, maturation of, and demand for epidemiologists, 632
Bacillus anthracis, 6
Bacteria, 439, 441
Bar graph, 17*t*
Behavioral-epidemiologists, 531
Behavioral epidemiology, 576, 605
  research designs used in, 580–581
Behavioral medicine, 576–577
Behavioral Risk Factor Survey (2001), 393
Benzene, 508
  leukemia and, 491
Berkman, L.F., 171
Beryllium, 499
Beta-carotene, 596
Biafran war refugees, weight and height measurement team and assessment of nutritional status of, *616*
Bias, 404
  in analysis and publication, 403–404
  defined, 391
  ecologic fallacy, 254
  epidemiologic associations and, 374
  family recall, 540
  information, 393–394
  lead time, 428–429
  length, 429
  linkage analysis and, 550
  measurement, 421–422
  nonreporting, 224
  reducing, techniques for, 396–399

selection, 392, 429
sources of, in epidemiologic studies, *397*
Bibliographic databases, computerized, 206–207
Bicycle helmet use, 63
Bimodal distributions, of disease, 150
Biologic gradient, causality and, 78
Biologic hazards, in workplace, 507
Biologic plausibility, 376
Biomarkers, 538, 561, 562
Biomphalaria glabrata, 458
Biostatisticians, 617
Biostatistics, 13, 14
  Graunt's contributions to, 22–23
Biotech industry researchers, 617
Bioterrorism, 632
Bipolar disorder, 564
Birth certificates, 216
Birth defects
  across maternal age: California, 1983–1986, *259,* 259–260
  infant mortality rates due to, 160
Birth rates, 133
  by age of mother, 1990–2004, U.S., *110*
Birth records, medical data from, 212 *t*
Births, 58
Birth weight, low
  alcohol intake during pregnancy and, 595
  environmental hazards and, 491
  smoking and, 594
Bisgard, K. M., 392
Black Adventists, health profiles of, 170
Black Death, 20, 22
Black lung disease, 507
Blacks. *See* African-American females; African-American males ; African Americans
Bladder cancer
  arsenic exposure and, 500
  in dye workers, 491
Blanc, D. S., 561
Blinding, 337, 398
BLLs. *See* Blood lead levels
Blood chemistry, 638
Blood lead levels, 501
  percentage of children aged 1–5 years with, by race/ethnicity and survey period, *502*

Blood pressure levels, stroke mortality rates and, 251, 253
Boddeker, I. R., 558
Bogalusa Heart Study, 390, 391
Bortner, R. W., 589
Botulism, *440*, *458t*
  infant, 13
Bovine spongiform encephalopathy, 178
  case study, 180–181
Bowel cancer, 591
Boys, relative risk calculation for sexual abuse history and suicide attempts by, 308 (exhibit)
BPAD. *See* Bipolar disorder
BRCA1 gene, 551 (exhibit), 552, 554 (exhibit)
BRCA2 gene, 551 (exhibit), 554 (exhibit)
Breast cancer, 43
  age-adjusted total U.S. mortality rates for, all ages, females for 1995–2004, *191*
  early-onset
    genetic epidemiology of, in CASH Study, 549 (exhibit)
    linkage analysis of, 551 (exhibit)
  ecologic correlation of dietary fat intake and, 251, *252*
  genome-wide association studies of, 554–556 (exhibit)
  Iowa Women's Health Study, incidence density and, 105 (exhibit)
  male, electromagnetic field exposure and, 502
  marital status, mortality rates and, 155
  postmenopausal, calculating incidence rate of, in Iowa Women's Health Study, 102 (exhibit), 104, 108
  retrospective cohort studies on, 302–303
  secular decreases in, 190
Breast Cancer Detection Demonstration Project, 411 (exhibit)
Breast cancer screening, 393–394, 410
  for women aged 40–49 years, 411–412 (exhibit)
"Breeder hypothesis," 173
Breslow, L., 590
Brigham and Women's Hospital (Boston), 313 (exhibit)
Brinton, L. A., 272

British physicians, dose-response relationships between smoking and lung cancer mortality among, *78*
British Registrar General, 171
Broad Street pump (London), visit to, cholera epidemic and, 34, *35*
Bromodichloromethane, spontaneous abortions and, 521 (exhibit)
Bronchitis, positive association between air pollution and, 395
Bronchus, malignant neoplasms of, by age group, U.S. 2003, 138t
Brown lung disease, 18
BSE. *See* Bovine spongiform encephalopathy
Buboes, 22
Bubonic plague, 22
  untreated, high case fatality rates with, 455 (exhibit)
Buechley, R., 395
Buffering model, social network tie and, 590
Buffler, P. A., 508
Buka, S. L., 308 (exhibit)
Bureau of the Census, 171
  publications of, 235
  racial categories in Census 2000, 155–156
Burkitt, D. P., 187, 591, 596
Byssinosis, occupational environment and, 491

C

Cadmium, 499
Calcium, colon cancer risk and, 568
California, Smokefree Bars Law in, 65–67 (exhibit)
California Birth Defects Monitoring Program, 259
California Health Interview Survey, 229, 584
California State Legislature, 65 (exhibit)
California Tumor Registry, 223
Cambodian Americans, smoking rates among, 164
Campylobacter enteritis, *458t*
Canada
  infant mortality rates in, 178
  mad cow disease in, 180, 181

Canadian Mormons, mortality rates among, 170

Canadian Society for Epidemiology and Biostatistics, The, 621*t*

Cancer, 82, 339
among African Americans, 161
applications of molecular epidemiology to, 562–563
arsenic exposure and, 500
asbestos exposure and, 499
childhood survivors of, 299
clustering and, 192
diet and, 596
disease registries and information on, 223, 224, 224 (exhibit)
environmental hazards and, 491
family aggregation of, 540–541
increasing rates of, worldwide, 177
infectious agents and, 438
Iowa Women's Health Study and, 98 (exhibit)
localized concentrations of ionizing radiation and, 183
Mormons
place variation and, 185
rates of, 170
older adults and, 147
premorbid psychologic factors and, 602–603
psychosocial epidemiology and, 578
rural areas and rates of, 183
smoking and, 593, 594
urban areas and rates of, 182

Cancer death rates
age-adjusted: females, by site, U.S., 1930–2003, *153*
age-adjusted: males, by site, U.S., 1930–2003, *152*

Cancer Epidemiology, Biomarkers & Prevention, 624

Cancer etiology, case-control methodology and, 272

Cancer incidence rates, 15-year trends: age-specific, 125–126*t*

Cancer screening, 63
secondary prevention and, 87

Cancer sites, age-specific incidence rate for, by race and sex, 1986–1990, U.S., *149*

Cancer Surveillance Program, 401

Cancer survival rates, socioeconomic status and, 174–175

Candidate genes, 557

Candidiasis, *440,* 441

Canon, Walter, 582

Carbon monoxide, 513, 514

CARDIA. *See* Coronary Artery Risk Development in Young Adults

Cardiovascular disease, 63
smoking and, 76 (exhibit)
Stanford Five-City Project and lowering risk of, 346–347 (exhibit)

Cardiovascular health, vigorous exercise and, 597

Cardiovascular Health Study, 311*t*

Career opportunities, in epidemiology, 614

Career roles, for epidemiologists, 617–618, 620

Cartoons, educating about infectious disease with use of, 32, *33*

Casarett and Doull's Essentials of Toxicology, 495

Case clustering, 191–192

Case-control design, 81

Case-control family studies
ascertainment considerations for, 543
design of, 542–545
on lung cancer risk in southern Louisiana, 544–545 (exhibit)

Case-control studies, 246, 247, 262–276, 284, 580
comparisons of, 320–321*t*
distribution of exposures in, *269*
in environmental epidemiology, 494
examples of research conducted with, 272*t*
family histories, disease traits and, 540
illustration of selection in, *263*
limitations with, 276
nested, 316–318
objective of, 269
retrospective cohort studies *vs.,* 303
selection of cases, 264
selection of controls, 265–266
smaller sample size in, 276
sources of cases, 264–265
sources of controls, 266–275

Case-control studies (*Continued*)
  hospital controls, 268
  measure of association, 269–275
  population-based controls, 266–268
  relatives or associates of cases, 268–269
  summary of, 275–276
  with three different sample sizes, odds
    ratio, *P* value, and 95% confidence
    intervals for, 372*t*
Case fatality rate, 122*t*, 455–456, 455
    (exhibit)
  virulence and, 442
Case finding, 414
Case identification, investigation of
    infectious disease outbreaks and, 456
Case reports, 145, 246
Cases
  guide for selection of comparable controls
    and, 267*t*
  selection of, in case-control design, 264
  sources of, in case-control design,
    264–265
Case series, 145, 146, 246
CASH Study, genetic epidemiology of early-
    onset breast cancer in, 549 (exhibit)
Casmalia Waste Disposal Facility
    (California), 512
Cassel, J., 73, 74
Caucasians. *See* Whites
Causal associations, 376, *376,* 377
Causal criteria, for classification of illness,
    432
Causal inference, statistical inference and, 79
Causality, 88
  criminality and, 80 (exhibit)
  in epidemiologic research, 71–74
  in epidemiology, 362–363
  Henle-Koch concept of, 72
  modern concepts of, 74, 76–79
  multiple, 377
  nine issues related to epidemiologic
    research and, 77–79
Causal relationships, models of, 376–381
Causal Thinking in the Health Sciences
    (Susser), 73
Cause, defined, 362
Cause-and-effect relationship, epidemiologic
    associations and, 375–376

Cause-specific rate, 118, 122*t*
CDC. *See* Centers for Disease Control and
    Prevention
Cellular telephone use, health effects related
    to, 503
Census data, 214*t*
Census reports, Farr's use of, 31
Census tracts, 236
Census 2000, overview of race and Hispanic
    origin, 157–159 (exhibit)
Census (U.S.), 235
Center for Epidemiologic Studies depression
    (CES-D) scale, 601
Centers for Disease Control and Prevention,
    19, 260, 414, 463
  anthrax cases investigated by, in wake of
    2001 terrorist attacks, 6–7
  Cancer and Steroid Hormone (CASH)
    study, 549 (exhibit)
  E. coli 2006 outbreak and, 4
  employment Web site, 626
  epidemiologists employed by, 618, *618*
  establishment of epidemiology section of,
    36
  information cycle, *219*
  intestinal parasite surveillance programs,
    179
  SARS cases, 14
  surveillance systems of, 219
    influenza and, *220*
Centers for Medicare and Medicaid Services,
    267
Central Africa, infant mortality rates in, 178
Central nervous system tumors, 273
Centre d'Etude du Polymorphisme Humain
    (CEPH), 557
CEPH. *See* Council on Education for Public
    Health
Cervical cancer
  case-control study on, 272–273
  human papilloma virus and, 37*t,* 39
CFR. *See* Case fatality rate
Chagas disease, 178
Chain of infection, 446, *447*
Challenge, hardiness and, 588
Chance, familial aggregation and, 540–541
Changes in disease markers, 300, 300*t*
Charts, pie, 17*t*

Cheerfulness, 604, 605
Chemical agents, 497–499, 497*t*
  asbestos, 499
  pesticides, 498–499
  sources of exposure to, 498
Chernick, M. R., 266, 290, 294
Chernobyl nuclear power plant accident,
  516
Chickenpox, *440*
  vaccinations and, 466
Chikungunya virus (CHKV), spread of,
  478
Childhood, health issues in, 146–147
Childhood Cancer Survivor Study, 299
Childhood lead poisoning, wheel model for,
  379–380
Childhood lead poisoning study
  (Massachusetts), 251
Childhood leukemia
  magnetic field exposure and, 501–502
  spatial clustering and, 192, 193
Children
  lead exposure and, 501
  passive smoking and cardiorespiratory
    health in, 515
Chili pepper consumption, gastric cancer
  cases and, 270 (exhibit)
China, air pollution in, 513
CHIS. *See* California Health Interview
  Survey
Chi square, 638
Chlordane, 498
Chlorination, water and, 519
Cholera, 19, 178, 219, *440, 445, 458t*
  Broad Street pump (London) and
    outbreak of, 34, *35*
  clustering of, 191
  Snow's investigation of, 25–31
  Snow's mapping of cases, in Broad Street
    district, London, 457
  spread of, in Latin America, *463,
    463*–464
Cholesterol levels, exercise and, 597
Cholinesterase inhibitors, Gulf War
  Syndrome and, 511 (exhibit)
Choropleth map, 185
Chromium, 499
Chromosomes, 533 (exhibit)

homologous pairs of, recombination and,
  549
Chronbach's α coefficient, 419
Chronic conditions, as major causes of
  morbidity and mortality, 53
Chronic disease, lifestyle, health promotion
  and, 42
Chronic fatigue syndrome, 510 (exhibit)
Chronic obstructive pulmonary disease
  air pollution and, 514
  rubber dust exposure and, 507
CI. *See* Confidence interval
Cigarette consumption, cancer and, 273
Cigarette smoking
  changes in prevalence of, among
    successive birth cohorts of U.S. men,
    1900–1987, *288*
  community interventions and, 351
  indoor air pollution and, 513
Cirelli, Dorothy, 332 (exhibit)
Clark, E. G., 84
Classification, defined, 431
Claus, E. B., 548
Cleaning of data files, 305
Clinical end points, 335
Clinical medicine, 13
Clinical observation, investigation of
  infectious disease outbreaks and, 456
Clinical picture, of chronic diseases,
  completing, 52 (exhibit)
Clinical significance, statistical significance
  vs., 373–374
Clinical trials, 244, 328, 330, 331–344, 356
  blinding (masking) in, 337
  for cancer drug, description of, 339*t*
  community trials *vs.*, 350–351, 355–356*t*
  crossover designs and, 340
  defined, 331, 333
  ethical aspects of experimentation with
    human subjects, 340–342
  examples of, 335–336
  external validity and, 389
  history behind, 331
  limitations with, 343–344
  outcomes of, 335
  phases of, 337–339
  prophylactic and therapeutic trials,
    333–334

Clinical trials (*Continued*)
  randomization and, 339–340
  reporting results of, 342
  schematic diagram of, *334*
  strengths of, 342
  summary of, 342–344
  why, what, when, and where of, 332–333
    (exhibit)
Clustering, 191–193
  case, 191–192
  spatial, 192–193
  temporal, 192
CNVs. *See* Copy number variations
Coal workers' pneumoconiosis, 491, 507
Cobb, S., 583, 589
Coccidioides immitis, 476
Coccidioidomycosis, 476, 477, *478*
Codominance, 547
Codons, 532 (exhibit)
Coffee drinking, 596
Coffee use and anxiety, cohort study data
    for, 384*t*
Coherence, 376
Coherence of explanation, causality and, 79
Cohort, 319
  cohort studies and size and cost of, 304
  defined, 284
Cohort analysis, 285, 319
Cohort designs
  temporal differences in, 301–303
    prospective cohort studies, 301–302
    retrospective cohort studies, 302–303
Cohort effects, 190
Cohort studies, 81, 246, 276, 283–321, 580
  availability of exposure data, 303–304
  data collection and data management,
    304–305
  defined, 284–285
  design of, 247
  examples of, 309, 314–316
  exposure-based, 297, 319
  follow-up issues, 305–306 ·
  limitations with, 318–319
  major, examples of, 310–312*t*
  outcome measures in, 300–301
  practical considerations with, 303–307
  size and cost of cohort, 304
  strengths of, 318

  sufficiency of scientific justification,
    306–307
  summary of, 318–319
  types of outcomes for, 300*t*
Colds, 443, 446
  seasonal variations in, 188
College graduates, as cohorts in studies, 300
Collins, F. S., 537, 558
Colon cancer, 567
  diet and, 596
Colonization and infestation, 449
Colonoscopies, 375, 566
Colon polyps, 375
Colorado Plateau Uranium Miners Study,
    310*t*
Colorectal cancer, 565
  colonoscopic screening study and,
    273–274
  interventions for high-risk populations,
    566–567
  precursors to, 375
  screening for, 87, 566
  tailored interventions with, 567–568
Commitment, hardiness and, 588
Communicable diseases
  international variation in, 178
  social and cultural factors related to, 599
Communities
  diagnosing health of, 51 (exhibit)
  enrolling in community trials, 344
  infectious diseases in, 39
    epidemiologically significant, 457–458,
    462–471, 475–480
Community Clinical Oncology Program,
    349
Community environmental health hazards,
    509, 512–519
  air pollution, 513–516
  drinking water, 518–519
  hazardous waste sites, 509, 512–513
  nuclear facilities, 516–517
Community health
  descriptive variables for, 60 (exhibit)
  impact of population dynamics on,
    58–59, 61–64
Community interventions, 244–245
  evaluation of, 351
    posttest, 351, 352*t*, 353

pretest/posttest, 352*t*, 353
pretest/posttest/control, 352*t*, 353
Solomon four-group assignment, 352*t*, 353–354
stages of, 352 (exhibit)
Community Intervention Trial for Smoking Cessation, 349
Community obligations, epidemiologists and, 631 (exhibit)
Community trials, 330–331, 344–356
clinical trials *vs.*, 355–356*t*
examples of, 344–345
schematic diagram of, *345*
Stanford Five-City Project, 346–347 (exhibit)
summary of, 350–351
Comparison (nonexposed) group, cohort studies and, 298–300
Competencies, for epidemiologists, 624–625
Completeness of the data criterion, 236
Computerized bibliographic databases, 206–207
Computers, epidemiologic research studies and, 37
Conclusions, drawing, in investigating infectious disease outbreaks, 457
Concurrent validity, 420
Condom use clinical trial, preventing spread of STDs and, 336
Conduct, unacceptable, confronting, 631 (exhibit)
Confidence intervals
for case-control study with three different sample sizes, 372–373, 372*t*
interpreting, 372–373
Confidentiality
data from physicians' practices and, 232
data sharing, record linkage and, 207, 210, 211
disease registries and, 224
protecting, 629 (exhibit)
Conflict situations, stress and, 583
Conflicts of interest, avoiding, 631 (exhibit)
Confounders, criteria for, 394
Confounding, 394–396
control of, 399–403
analysis strategies, 401–403
prevention strategies, 399–401

Confounding variables, epidemiologic associations and, 374
Congenital malformations
across maternal age: California, 1983–1986, 259, *259*
environmental hazards and, 491
Connecticut Tumor Registry, 223
Consistency, 376
CONSORT statement, 342
Construct validity, 420–421
Contamination, 450
Content validity, 420
Continuing education degree programs, 625–626
Continuous variables, 297
Control, hardiness and, 588
Controls
demographic variables, 638
guide for selection of comparable cases and, 267*t*
hospital, 268
number of, in case-control design, 266
population-based, 266–268
ratio of, 266
selection of, in case-control design, 265–266
sources of, in case-control design, 266
Cook, D. J., 403
Cooperative Cardiovascular Project, 153
COPD. *See* Chronic obstructive pulmonary disease
Copy number variations, 535 (exhibit)
Core values, in epidemiology, 627 (exhibit)
Coronary Artery Risk Development in Young Adults, 311*t*
Coronary bypass surgery, risks to individual and prognosis of survival from, 82–83
Coronary heart disease, 144
cohort study of, 295–296
cultural mobility and, 584
epidemiology of, 615*t*, 616
etiologic models developed for, 579–580
Japanese population and, 163–164
life dissatisfaction and, 600
low rate of, in Japan, 598, 599
Mexican Americans, Puerto Ricans and rates of, 166

Coronary heart disease (*Continued*)
mortality due to, 177
inverse relation between altitude and, 395
occupational environment and, 491
physical activity and, examples of cohort studies built upon theme of, 309, 314–316
psychosocial epidemiology and, 578
risk difference and, 363
sedentary lifestyle and, 597
Seventh-Day Adventists and
place variation in, 185
rates of among, 170
sex differences in mortality from, 152
type A behavior pattern and, 588–589
Coroners, 215
Council of State and Territorial Epidemiologists, 621*t*
Employment Listings Web site, 626
Council on Education for Public Health, 626
Count, 133
definition of, 94
County and City Data Book, 235
Coxiella burnetti, 475
CRC. *See* Colorectal cancer
Creutzfeldt-Jakob disease, 178
variant in, 180
Crider, A., 583
Criminality, causality and, 80 (exhibit)
Criterion-referenced validity, 420
Crossover designs, 340, 356
Cross-sectional studies, 145, 146, 247, 256–262, 580
applications of, 258–262
comparisons of, 320–321*t*
disadvantages with, 284
ecologic, 250
examples of, 258–260, 262
illustration of subject selection in, *256*
limitations with, 262
Cross-sectional surveys, 246
Crowther, M. A., 403
Crude birth rate, 108, 122*t*
defined, 109 (exhibit)
Crude death rate, 96 (exhibit), 97, 122*t*, 124, 129 (exhibit)

group comparison of age-adjusted death rates and, 127*t*
Crude mortality rate, 96, 97, 124, 133
Crude rate, 108–117, 124, 133
birth rate, 108
examples of, 109 (exhibit)
fertility rate, 110
fetal mortality, 112, 114
infant mortality rate, 112
maternal mortality rate, 117
neonatal mortality rate, 115
perinatal mortality, 117
postneonatal mortality rate, 115–117
Cruickshank, Robert, 622
Cryptococcosis, 441
Cryptosporidiosis, 441
Cryptosporidium, 481*t*
Cubans, 165
mortality rates and, 167
Cultural diversity, respecting, 632 (exhibit)
Cultural identification, race and, 156
Cultural mobility, increased coronary heart disease risk and, 584
Culture, defined, 598
Cumulative incidence, 104
absolute effects and, 362, 363
Cutaneous leishmaniasis, 178
Cut points, establishing, relationship between sensitivity, specificity and, 426–428
CVD. *See* Cardiovascular disease
Cyclic fluctuations, 187–188

D

DALYs. *See* Disability-adjusted life years
Danish Epidemiologic Society, 621*t*
Data
on absenteeism, 214*t,* 233
on armed forces personnel and veterans, 234–235
birth statistics, 216
census, 214*t*
confidentiality, record linkage and sharing of, 207, 210, 211
criteria for quality and utility of, 205–206
different presentations of, 17*t*
in disease registries, 223–224

on diseases treated in special clinics and hospitals, 213*t*, 231–232
from employment records, 493
exposure, 250
HIPAA privacy rule and, 210–211 (exhibit)
hospital, 230
insurance, 229–230
on morbidity in armed forces, 214*t*
morbidity surveys, 225–229
   California Health Interview Survey, 229
   Health Examination Survey, 226–228
   National Health Interview Survey, 225–226
mortality statistics, 215–216
other sources of, relevant to epidemiologic studies, 235–236
overview of sources, 212–214*t*
from physicians' practices, 232–233
on populations, 204–205
reportable disease statistics, 216, 219–220, 222
from school health programs, 214*t*, 233–234
screening surveys, 223
SEER Program, 224 (exhibit)
for serologic testing, 436*t*
sources of, for use in epidemiology, 203–236
Data analysis, in empirical research reports, 638
Data and safety monitoring board, 341, 342
Data appraisal, investigation of infectious disease outbreaks and, 456
Databases, computerized bibliographic, 206–207
Data collection
   cohort design options for timing of, *301*
   cohort studies and, 304–305
   study designs and methods of, 242
   study designs and timing of, 242
Data interpretation issues, 385–404
   bias in analysis and publication, 403–404
   methods to control confounding, 399–403
   sources of error in epidemiologic research, 390–396

   techniques for reducing bias, 396–399
   validity of study designs, 386, 388–389
      external validity, 389
      internal validity, 386, 388
Data management, cohort studies and, 304–305
Day care centers, infectious disease outbreaks in, 438
DDT. *See* Dichlorodiphenyltricloroethane
Dearden, K. A., 317
Death
   age and causes of, 146
   leading causes of, and rates for those causes, 1900 and 2003 in U.S., 92*t*
   10 leading causes of
      among non-Hispanic blacks, 161
      25–34 years, all races, both sexes, U.S., 2003, 119*t*
Death certificates
   data from, 215
   sample, 217–218 (exhibit)
Death rates
   for African Americans, 160
   age-adjusted (U.S.), for selected causes of death, 1958–2003, 55
   direct method for adjustment of, 128*t*
   National Center for Health Statistics adopts new standard population for age standardization of, 129 (exhibit)
Decennial Census of Population and Housing, 235
De-identified health information (HIPAA), 211 (exhibit)
Dementia rates, hormone replacement therapy and, 307
Demographic characteristics, systematic case-control differences in, 265–266
Demographic transition, 58
Demographic variables, community health and, 60 (exhibit)
Dengue fever, 178
Deoxyribonucleic acid. *See* DNA
Department of Veterans Affairs Medical Center (Minneapolis), 232
Dependent variables, 578
Depression, 578, 606
   measures of, 601–602
   socioeconomic status and, 173

Dermatitis, 504

DES. *See* Diethylstilbestrol

Descriptive epidemiology, 141–193, 530
  analytic epidemiology *vs.*, 143
  characteristics of persons in, 146–175
  characteristics of place in, 175, 177–180, 182–187
  characteristics of time in, 187–193
  hypotheses and use of, 143–144
  objectives of, 143
  of selected health problem, 201–202
  three approaches to, 145–146
  of unintentional injury, 505

Descriptive studies, 246
  in environmental epidemiology, 491
  epidemiologic hypotheses and, 143–144

Descriptive variables, for community health, 60 (exhibit)

Determinants, 6

Developmentally disabled children, coordination of health services project for, 68–69

Deykin, E. Y., 308 (exhibit)

Diabetes/diabetes mellitus, 56, 63, 591
  among American Indians, 162
  among Mexican-American population, 166
  diet and, 596
  mortality rates and, 175
  psychosocial epidemiology and, 578

Diagnostic and Statistical Manual of Mental Disorders, 432, 602

DIALOG, 206

Dialogues, The (Socrates), 309

Dichlorodiphenyltricloroethane, 498–499

Die Aetiologie der Tuberkulose (Koch), 32

Diet, 590
  health and, 596–597
  Seventh-Day Adventist church members, 169

Dietary fat intake, ecologic correlation of breast cancer and, 251

Dietary intake patterns, familial nature of, 541–542

Diet-heart hypothesis, 596

Diethylstilbestrol, vaginal adenocarcinoma in young women and maternal exposure to, 191–192, 272

Difference measure of association, 362

Dight Institute of Genetics (University of Minnesota), 302

Diphtheria, *440*
  vaccinations for, 465

Direct method
  for adjustment of death rates, 128*t*
  of rate adjustment, 124, 128, 130

Direct rate adjustment, weighted method for, 130*t*

Direct relationship, 251

Direct transmission of disease, 446, *447*, 448–450
  colonization and infestation, 449
  generation time, 449
  herd immunity, 448–449
  iceberg concept of infection, 449, *450*
  inapparent/apparent case ratio, 450
  inapparent infection, 446, 448
  incubation period, 448

Dirty bombs, 503

Disability, stress and risk of, 587

Disability-adjusted life years, 290, 292, 581, 582

Disappearing disorders, 54

Discrete events, 300, 300*t*

Disease. *See also* Infectious disease
  association between exposure and, 388
  classification systems for, 431–432
  within country geographic variation in rates of, 178–180
  cyclic fluctuations in, 187–188
  diet and, 541–542
  effects of personality on, 603
  effects of prevalence of, on screening test results, 424–426
  enlargement of clinical picture of, 84
  environmental factors and global burden of, 490
  environment and causes of, 20–22
  germ theory of, 32
  identifying specific agents of, 32
  localized place comparisons of, 183–184
  methods for ascertainment of epidemic frequency of, 19–20
  natural history of, 84
    in relation to time of diagnosis, 428, *429*

pie model for three sufficient causes of, *380*
prevention of, 84–87
primary prevention, 85–86, 88
secondary prevention, 87, 88
tertiary prevention, 87, 88
reasons for place variation in, 185–187
reportable, statistics on, 216, 219–220, 222
screening for, 410, 413–414
mass health examinations, 414
mass screening and selective screening, 413–414
multiphasic screening, 413
secular time trends in, 189–190
temporal aspects in occurrence of, 187–193
urban/rural differences in rates of, 182–183
Disease-causing factors and outcomes, map of possible associations between, *376*
Disease etiology, epidemiologic applications relevant to, 71–74, 76–79, 81–87
Disease frequency
calculating absolute difference in, 362
international comparisons of, 175, 177–178
measures of, community health and, 61
Disease markers, levels of and changes in, 300, 300*t*
Disease prevalence, effects of, on predictive value of screening tests, 425*t*
Disease registries, 212*t*, 223–224
Disease-specific defense mechanisms, 443, 444–445
Disease status
cross-classification of exposure and, *248*
2 by 2 table classifying exposure and, 246, 247*t*
Disinfection byproducts, drinking water and, 519
Disorders
disappearing, 54
new epidemic, 56
persisting, 56
residual, 54, 56
trends in, 54, 56

Distribution, 11
Diverticular disease, 591, 596
Division of Microbiology and Infectious Diseases, 342
Divorce, gender, adverse health outcomes and, 154
Dizygotic twin pairs, military data on, 235
DMID. *See* Division of Microbiology and Infectious Diseases
DNA, 549
genetic code and, 532–533 (exhibit)
model of helix, *531*
physical arrangement of, 533 (exhibit)
protein and, 533–534 (exhibit)
DNC. *See* Do Not Call Registry
Doll, R., 37
Donora, Pennsylvania, lethal air pollution episode in (1948), 513
Do Not Call Registry, 267
Dorland's Illustrated Medical Dictionary, 16
Dose-response, 376
Dose-response curve, *495,* 495–496
Double-blind design, 337
"Downward drift hypothesis," 173
Drinking water, 518–519
Drop-out rates, 637
Drug testing, clinical trials and, 332 (exhibit)
DSMB. *See* Data and safety monitoring board
Duncan, O. D., 172
Dunham, H. W., 173
Dust
diseases related to, 41
work environment exposure to, 507–508
Dynamic populations, 58

E

E. coli O157:H7, 3, 480
Early Developmental Stages of Psychopathology study, 580
Eastern Airlines, 9, 10
Eastern Europe
HIV/AIDS epidemic in, 465
reduced life expectancy in, 581
Eastern European Jewish population, Tay-Sachs disease among, 61
East India Shipping Company, 331

Easton, D. F., 554, 555 (exhibit)
Ebola virus, 481*t*
Ecologic comparison studies, 249–250
Ecologic fallacy, 253
  defined, 254
  example of, 253, *254*
Ecologic studies, 246, 249–255
  advantages with, 250
  applications and merits of, 251, 253
  comparisons of, 320–321*t*
  defined, 248
  disadvantages with, 253–255
  examples of questions investigated by, 249*t*
  illustration of sample selection for, *250*
Ecologic study designs, in environmental epidemiology, 494
Ecologic trend studies, 251
Ectoparasites, 187
EDSP. *See* Early Developmental Stages of Psychopathology study
Education
  community health and, 59
  health status and, 173
  life expectancy and level of, 174
  occupational prestige and, 172
  resources for, in epidemiology, 625–626
Education Index, 206
Effects
  absolute, 362–365, 381
  measures of, 361–381
  relative, 365–370, 381
  statistical measures of, 371–374
EIS. *See* Epidemic Intelligence Service
Electromagnetic fields, 497*t*, 501–503
  suicide and, nested case-control study of, 317
Electronic health records, defined, 230
Emerging infections, 479–480
  examples of, 481*t*
Empirical research reports
  conclusions in, 639
  discussion in, 639
  introduction in, 636
  methods in, 636–637
    data analysis, 638
    measures (instruments), 637–638
    study sample, 636–637

reading, 635
results in, 639
Empirical validity, 420
Employers, of epidemiologists, 617
Employment
  psychosocial aspects of health and, 509
  resources for, in epidemiology, 626
Employment records, data collected from, 493
Encephalitis, *440*, 477
Endemic, 18
Engel, G., 576
England, cancer survival rates among socioeconomic groups in, 174
Entamoeba histolytica, 464
Environment
  bad, familial aggregation and, 541–542
  disease causation and, 20–22
  in epidemiologic triangle, 438, 439, *439*
  epidemiology of infectious diseases and, 445
  health and, 39, 41–42
Environmental disease agents, 497*t*
  allergens and molds, 497*t*, 504–505
  chemical agents, 497–499, 497*t*
    asbestos, 499
    pesticides, 498–499
  electromagnetic fields, 497*t*, 501–503
  ionizing radiation, 497*t*, 503–504
  metallic compounds, 497*t*, 499–501
    arsenic, 499–500
    lead, 500–501
    mercury, 500
  physical and mechanical energy, 497*t*, 505–506
Environmental epidemiological research, applications of molecular epidemiology in, 561–562
Environmental epidemiology, 490–491, 519
  study designs used in, 491–494
    case-control studies, 494
    ecologic study designs, 494
    healthy worker effect, 493–494
    methods for selection of research population and collection of exposure data, 493
    retrospective cohort studies, 492–493
    toxicologic concepts related to, 495–497

dose-response curve, 495–496
latency, 496
synergism, 496–497
threshold, 496
water quality and, 518–519
Environmental factors, community health and, 61
Environmental hazards, 18
health effects associated with, 491
notable human exposures to, 490
in workplace, 506–509
biologic hazards, 507
industrial chemicals, 508–509
mineral and organic dusts, 507–508
Environmental health risks, Geographic Information Systems and, 185*t*
Environmental Protection Agency
environmental tobacco smoke report by, 515
water standards and, 518
Environmental reservoir, 445
Environmental variables, community health and, 60 (exhibit)
Enzootic diseases, 476
EPA. *See* Environmental Protection Agency
EPIC, 516
Epidemic Intelligence Service (CDC), 36, 618
graduating class of 2004, *619*
role of, in investigating disease outbreaks, 39
Epidemics
defined, 18
early beliefs about, 20
point, 188–189
Epidemiologic approach
interdisciplinary, 43
quantification with, 14, 16, 43
special vocabulary for, 16, 18, 43
Epidemiologic associations, evaluating, 374–376
Epidemiologic data. *See* Data
Epidemiologic designs, application of genes in, 558–565
Epidemiologic/public health research article
guide to critical appraisal of, 635–639
conclusions, 639
discussion, 639
introduction, 636
methods, 636–638
results, 639
Epidemiologic research
causality in, 71–74
large data sets needed for, 205
media and controversies about, 2
nine issues related to causality and, 77–79
skepticism about, 71–72
sources of error in, 390–396
factors contributing to random error, 390–391
factors contributing to systematic errors, 391–396
typology of, 244*t*
Epidemiologic Reviews, 276
Epidemiologic studies
proliferation of, 50
sources of error and bias in, *397*
Epidemiologic transition, 58
Epidemiologic triangle, 377, 438–439, *439*
Epidemiologists
career roles for, 617–618, 620
competencies required of, 624–625
ethics guidelines for, 627–632 (exhibit)
professional role of, 628 (exhibit)
public health policymaking and, 64
societal trends and demand for, 632–633
Epidemiology
aims and levels of, 12
attack rate in, 103
causality in, 362–363
clinical applications of, 84
components of, 6, 11–12
count in, 94
data sources used in, 203–236
defined, 5, 6
descriptive, 141–193
domestic and international organizations in, 621*t*
foundations of, 13–14, 16–20
historical antecedents of, 20–36
historical use of: study of past and future trends in health and illness, 52–58
history and scope of, 1–46
incidence rate in, 101–102
of infectious disease, 39, 437–482
journals related to, 622–624

Epidemiology (*Continued*)
methods and procedures, 5, 14, 16
molecular and genetic, 43
morbidity and mortality measures used
in, 93–133
observational *vs.* experimental approaches
in, 243
operations research, program evaluation,
and application of, 67–71
population dynamics and, 58
positive states of health and, 12
practical applications of, 49–88
prevalence in, 97–98, 100–101
as a profession, 613–633
professional associations related to, 620,
622
professional ethics in, 627–632 (exhibit)
proportion in, 95
rate in, 95–96, 97
ratio in, 94
recent applications of, 37, 39, 41–43
resources for education and employment,
625–626
seven uses of, 51–52 (exhibit)
specializations within, 615–617, 615*t*
triumphs in, 37–38*t*
vocabulary in, 16, 18–19
Epidemiology, 623
Epidemiology and Infection, 623
Epidemiology Monitor, The, 614, *614*
Epidemiology surveillance workers, 617,
618
Epi Info, 638
Epimonitor.net Job Bank, 626
"Epi-speak," 362
Epizootic diseases, 476
Epstein-Barr virus, 450
Error
random, factors contributing to, 390–391
poor precision, 390
sampling error, 390–391
variability in measurement, 391
sources of
in epidemiologic research, 390–396
in epidemiologic studies, *397*
systematic, factors contributing to,
391–396
confounding, 394–396

information bias, 393–394
selection bias, 392
Escherichia coli (E. coli), 480, 560
2006 outbreak of, 2
distribution of cases across United
States, *4*
number of confirmed cases, *3*
Ethical requirements, communication of,
631 (exhibit)
Ethical review, submitting proposed studies
for, 630 (exhibit)
Ethical situations for screening, 415
(exhibit), 416–417
Ethics, experimentation with human
subjects and, 340–342
Ethics guidelines, for epidemiologists,
627–632 (exhibit)
Ethics review boards, 630 (exhibit)
Ethnic composition, community health and,
61
Ethnic diversity, *156*
Ethnicity
percentage of children aged 1–5 years
with blood lead levels by, *502*
psychologic and social processes in disease
and, 579
tuberculosis incidence by, U.S.,
1995–2005, *165*
Ethnicity. *See also* African Americans; Alaska
Natives; American Indians; Asians;
Hispanics; Mexican Americans;
Minorities
health disparities, rural areas and, 183
infant mortality rates by, *113*
race and, 155–167
smokeless tobacco study in Minnesota
and, 258
social class and, 171
tuberculosis and, 470
Etiologic agents, linking of, in investigating
infectious disease outbreaks, 457
Etiologic fraction, 366–368, 381
formula for, 367
Etiologic studies, in environmental
epidemiology, 492
EUROCAT epidemiologic surveillance of
congenital anomalies, 517
European Epidemiology Federation, 621*t*

Evaluation
formative, 352 (exhibit)
impact, 352 (exhibit)
outcome, 352 (exhibit)
process, 352 (exhibit)
Evans, A. S., 79
Evidence, rules of: criminality and causality,
80 (exhibit)
Evidence-based decisions, 63
Exercise, 590
Exons, 534 (exhibit)
Experimental approach, observational
approach vs., in epidemiology, 243
Experimental studies, 244–245
Experimental study designs, 327–356, 580
Experimentation with human subjects,
ethical aspects with, 340–342
Experiments
miscellaneous issues related to design of,
354–355
of opportunity, 52 (exhibit)
Exposure
association between disease and, 388
case-control studies and, 263
to chemical agents, 497–499
cross-classification of 2 by 2 table and, 248
determining in cohort studies, 296–297
disease status and, in 2 by 2 table, 246,
247t
distribution of, in case-control study, 269
dose-response curve and, 495–496
etiologic fraction and, 366–368
internal validity and, 388
latency and, 496
monitoring and surveillance of, with
occupational hazards, 506–509
odds ratio and approximation of risk with
given level of, 271
population etiologic fraction and,
368–370
population risk difference and, 364–365
risk difference and, 362, 363
study designs and directionality of, 242
synergism and, 496–497
threshold and, 496
Exposure-based cohorts, examples of,
298–300
Exposure-based cohort studies, 297, 319

Exposure data
cohort studies and availability of,
303–304
collection of, 493
examples of, 250
Exposure-disease connection, case-control
design and, 265
Exposure status, cohort studies and, 295
Exposure variables, 638
Expressed sequences, 534 (exhibit)
Extensively drug-resistant tuberculosis, 470,
471 (exhibit)
actions to protect public health and case
of, 472–473
External environment, epidemiology of
infectious disease and, 445
External validity, 206, 236, 354, 389
Extrinsic motivation, 600

F

Falls, 505
Familial adenomatous polyposis, 565
Familial aggregation
causes of, 540–542
bad environment, 541–542
bad luck, 540–541
of psychiatric disorders, 564
Familial factors
disease traits and, 539
psychologic and social processes in disease
and, 579
Family Educational Rights and Privacy Act,
210 (exhibit)
Family environment, familial aggregation
and design of case-control family
studies, 542–545
Family recall bias, 393, 540
Family studies, defined, 542
FAP. See Familial adenomatous polyposis
Farm workers, pesticides and, 508
Farr, William, 20, 491
classification scheme of, 31
FAS. See Fetal alcohol syndrome
FDA. See Food and Drug Administration
Federal Trade Commission, 267
Female paradox, 151
Females, age-adjusted cancer death rates for,
U.S., 1930–2003, 153

Fertility rates, 133
  defined, 109 (exhibit)
  general, 110
  in United States, 1950–1992, *111*
Fetal alcohol syndrome, 595
Fetal death, certificates of, 216
Fetal death rate, 112, 122*t*
  calculation of, 115
  defined, 109 (exhibit)
Fetal death ratio, 114, 122*t*
  calculation of, 115
  defined, 109 (exhibit)
Fetal mortality, 112, 114
FGFR2 gene, 555 (exhibit)
Fibrositis, 510 (exhibit)
Filoviridae, 481*t*
Firearm-related death rates
  community health and, 61
  South Atlantic states (U.S.), 2003, *62*
Fixed populations, 58
Fixed randomization, 340
Fleming, Alexander, 36
Flies, disease transmission and, 441
Fluoridation of water, 63
Fluorosis, 183
Flu pandemics, 18
Folic acid, neural tube defects and study of, 335–336
Follow-up, to cohort studies, 305–306
Follow-up rates, 637
Fomites, indirect transmission of disease via, 450
Food and Drug Administration, 4–5, 332, 333 (exhibit)
Food-borne disease, 39, 216, *440*
  calculating attack rates for outbreak of, 452, 452*t*
  in the community, 457–458
  Escherichia coli and, 480
  textbook case of, *459–460*
Food poisoning, 458*t*
Formaldehyde, indoor air pollution and, 513
Formative evaluation, 352 (exhibit)
Fourfold table, relative risk calculation with, 308 (exhibit)
Fox, B. H., 602
Frameshift mutations, 534 (exhibit)

Framingham Heart Study, 37, 295–296, 310*t*
France
  infant mortality rates in, 178
  mad cow disease in, 180, 181
Frazier, T. M., 507
Freedman, Larry, 387 (exhibit)
Freedom of Information Act, 207
Freeman, H. E., 344, 351
French, J. R. P., Jr., 584
Friend, S. H., 558
Friis, R. H., 64, 68, 168, 222, 266, 290, 294, 504
Frost, Wade Hampton, tabular data by, on tuberculosis, 36, 285, 319
Fruits, health and consumption of, 596, 597
Fumes, occupational exposure to, 508
Functional cloning, 537, *538*
Functional mapping, 537
Fungal disease, *440,* 441
  agents of, 445
Future predictions, population dynamics and, 56, 58

G

Gable, C. B., 228
Gabriel, S. B., 556
Galen, 567
Gallbladder disease, 591
Gardisil, 39
Garrod, A. E., 567
GASP, 553
Gas stoves, indoor air pollution and, 513
Gastric cancer cases, chili pepper consumption and, 270 (exhibit)
Gastric juices, nonspecific defense mechanisms and, 444
Gender, characteristics of persons and, 151–154. *See also* Females; Males; Men; Women
Gene/environment interaction, place variations in disease and, 186
Gene mapping
  segregation and linkage analysis, 545–550, 552–553
    determining mode of inheritance, 548
    LOD score linkage analysis, 548–550, 552

modes of inheritance, 546–548
nonparametric linkage analysis,
552–553
General adaptation syndrome, stages in,
582, 583
General fertility rate, 110, 122*t*
sample calculation, 111
Generalizability, 389
Generation time, 449
Genes, 533 (exhibit), 535 (exhibit)
application of, in epidemiologic designs,
558–565
candidate, 557
human, strategies in identification of,
538
Genetic Analysis Workshop (GAW10),
564
Genetic code, 532–533 (exhibit)
Genetic-epidemiologists, 536
Genetic epidemiology, 43, 530
of Alzheimer's disease, 563–564
description of, 536–537
of early-onset breast cancer in CASH
Study, 549 (exhibit)
molecular epidemiology *vs.*, 531, 536,
539
of psychiatric disorders, 564–565
Genetic factors, epidemiologic evidence for,
539–540
Genetics, 13
human, basic principles of, 532–536
(exhibit)
nonspecific defense mechanisms and, 444
public health and, 565–568
interventions for high-risk populations,
566–567
screening for colorectal cancer, 566
tailored interventions, 567–568
Genetic terminology, review of, 535–536
(exhibit)
Genetic variation, 534–535 (exhibit)
Genome-wide association studies, 531, 553
Genotypes, 535 (exhibit)
modes of inheritance and, 546
Geographic Information Systems, 184–185
map of infant mortality rates in Idaho,
186
representative applications of, 185*t*

Geographic mobility, risk *vs.* rate and, 104
Geographic variation, within country, in
rates of disease, 178–180
Germ theory of disease, 32
Giardia lamblia protozoan, geographic
variation in, within U.S., 179
Giardiasis, *440,* 441, 458
Gila River Indian community, death rate for
Pima Indians at, 162–163
GIS. *See* Geographic Information Systems
Glaucoma, referral criteria set for screening
of, 426–427
Global burden of disease, environmental
factors and, 490
Global Burden of Disease Study, 581
Global warming, 505
demand for epidemiologic researchers
and, 633
movement of disease vectors and, 187
Goiter, 183
Goldberger, Joseph, 36
Golden Square district (London), 1849
cholera outbreak in, 25–31, *30*
Gonorrhea, *440*
Google, 207
Government agencies, epidemiologists
employed by, 618
Grab-bag sample, 636
Graphs
bar, 17*t*
line, 17*t*
Graunt, John, 22, 43, 374
Great Britain, infant mortality rates in,
178
Greenland, S., 73, 380
Green tea, lung cancer study and, 272
Grief, 576, 578
as disease?, 577 (exhibit)
Grizzly bear meat, trichinosis and, 461
(exhibit)
Groopman, J. D., 561
Group A streptococci, 481*t*
Group Health Incorporated, 413
Group Health of Puget Sound, 298
Gulf War Syndrome, 509, 511 (exhibit)
GWAS. *See* Genome-wide association
studies
GWS. *See* Gulf War Syndrome

H

Haemophilus influenzae type b infections, 465

Haldane, J. B. S., 567

Halo effect, 422

HANES. *See* Health and Nutrition Examination Survey

Hanford, Washington, nuclear weapons production in, 516, 517

Hansen's disease (leprosy), 168, *169*, 187

Hantaviral pulmonary syndrome, 479, 480

Hantaviruses, 481*t*

Haplotype blocks, 556

Haplotypes, 556–558

HapMap Project, 556–558

Hardiness, 588

Hartmann, L. C., 303

Harvard University, School of Public Health, Summer Session for Public Health Studies at, 626

Hatch, M., 517

Hats, hypothetical ecologic relationship between sunburn and, 254–255, 255*t*

HAV. *See* Hepatitis A virus

Hawaiian Japanese, coronary heart disease rates among, 599

Hawthorne effect, 354

Hazardous waste exposure, reported adverse effects of, 512–513

Hazardous waste sites, 509, 512–513

Hazard surveillance, 507

HBV. *See* Hepatitis B virus

HCV. *See* Hepatitis C virus

Health. *See also* Community health
dietary practices and, 596–597
environment and, 39, 41–42
habitual mental outlook and, 604–605
personal behaviors, lifestyle and, 590–598, 606
psychological and social factors in, 42
religion and, 168–170
smoking and, 593–594
social context of, 581–582
sociocultural influences on, 598–599
socioeconomic status and, 170–171

Health, United States, 2006, 108

Healthcare planners, 617

Health disparities
adult Latinas and, 71
eliminating, 62

Health Examination Survey, 225, 226–228

Health fairs, 223

Health Insurance Plan of New York, 229

Health Insurance Portability and Accountability Act, protected health information and de-identified health information under, 210–211 (exhibit)

Health insurance statistics, 212*t*, 229

Health maintenance organizations, insurance data and, 229

Health phenomena, 11–12

Health policy/planning, Geographic Information Systems and, 185*t*

Health professionals, as focus of cohort studies, 299

Health promotion, chronic disease, lifestyle and, 42

Health-related outcome variables, community health and, 60 (exhibit)

Health Sciences Library System (University of Pittsburgh), 207

Health services, studying working of, 51 (exhibit)

Health services research epidemiology, 615*t*, 616

Healthy migrant effects, 168

Healthy People 2000, 592

Healthy People 2010, 501, 592
goals and focus areas of, 592–593 (exhibit)

Healthy worker effects, 493–494

Heart attack victims, wives of, 603

Heart disease, 147. *See also* Coronary heart disease
air pollution and, 514
case-control study on passive smoking and, 274
personality factors and, 42
seasonal variations in, 188
secular time trends in, 189
urban areas and rates of, 182
water hardness and, 184

Heart disease research project, person-years of observation for hypothetical study subjects in, 106t
Heart health, diet and, 596
Helminths, 441
Hemolytic-uremic syndrome, 480
 E. coli 0157:H7 and, 3
Hemophilia, 534 (exhibit)
Henderson, B. E., 513
Henle-Koch postulates, 72
Hepatitis, *440*
 viral, forms of, 471
Hepatitis A virus, 441, 446, 450, 471
 modes of transmission for, 471
 vaccinations against, 465
Hepatitis B virus, 471
 modes of transmission for, 471
 vaccinations against, 465
Hepatitis C virus, 471, 480, 481t
 fact sheet on, 474–475 (exhibit)
Hepatoblastoma, in childhood, parental smoking and, 273
Herbicides, 498
Herd immunity, 448–449
Herpes simplex, *440*
H5N1 virus (avian influenza), 40–41
HHANES. *See* Hispanic Health and Nutrition Examination Survey
Hidden homeless population, 101
High blood pressure, biobehavioral approaches to, 577
High-density lipoproteins, 596
High-risk populations, interventions for, 566–567
High School Seniors Survey, 260
High throughput genotyping, 536
Hill, Sir Austin Bradford, 74, 77, 78, 79
Hinkle, L. E., Jr., 586
HIPAA. *See* Health Insurance Portability and Accountability Act
Hip fractures, risk difference and, 363–364
Hippocrates, 43
 hypothesis of, 21
Hispanic Health and Nutrition Examination Survey, 71, 166, 226, 227 (exhibit), 260, 602

Hispanic mortality paradox, 166–167 (exhibit)
Hispanic origin
 overview of race and, census 2000, 157–159 (exhibit)
 population by, for U.S., 2000, 159t
Hispanics, 165–166. *See also* Latinas; Latinos; Mexican Americans
 AIDS and, 464
 prevalence surveys on health needs of, 260
Historical prospective cohort design, *301*
Historical prospective cohort study, 302
Historical Statistics of the United States, Colonial Time to 1970, 235
History of health of populations, studying, 51 (exhibit)
HIV. *See* Human immunodeficiency syndrome
Hlady, W. G., 560
Hodgkin's disease, spatial clustering and, 192
Holistic medical concept, coordination of services and, 68
Hollingshead, A., 171, 173
Holmes, T., 586
Homelessness, point and period prevalence and, 100–101
Homeless persons, tuberculosis among, 469 (exhibit)
Homicide rates, community health and, 61
Hong Kong Epidemiological Association, The, 621t
Honolulu Heart Program, 310t
Honolulu Heart Study, 163
Hooker Chemicals & Plastics Corporation, 18
Hookworm, geographic variation of, within U.S., 179
Hormesis, 496
Hormone replacement therapy, 306, 307
Hospital controls, advantages and disadvantages with, 268
Hospital data, 230
Hospital employees, biologic hazards and, 507
Hospital inpatient statistics, 213t

Hospitalization rates, for American Indians/Alaska Natives, 162
Hospital outpatient statistics, 213*t*
Hospitals, infectious disease outbreaks in, 438
Host
in epidemiologic triangle, 438, 439, *439*
incubation period and, 448
House, J., 600
Household Interview Survey, 226
Household products, exposure to chemical agents in, 498
HRT. *See* Hormone replacement therapy
Human biologic clock, age and, 147, 150
Human genetics, basic principles of, 532–536 (exhibit)
Human genome, mapping of, 530, 558–559
Human Genome Project, 558
influence of, *559*
Human immunodeficiency virus, 178, 465
accidental needle sticks and possible transmission of, 507
community-based interventions and prevention of, 349, 350 (exhibit)
early treatments for, 332 (exhibit)
world estimates of adults and children living with, 465, *465*
Human papilloma virus, cervical cancer and, 37*t*, 39
Human Population Laboratory (California), 590
Human subjects
clinical trials and, 332–333 (exhibit)
ethical aspects of experimentation with, 340–342
Hunter, D. J., 555 (exhibit)
Hurricane Katrina, post-traumatic stress disorder in wake of, 601
Hurricane Rita, 505, 601
Hurricanes, mold growth in aftermath of, 505
HUS. *See* Hemolytic-uremic syndrome
Hutt, M.S.R., 187
Hydrocarbons, 513
Hypercholesterolemia, 370, 410
Hypertension
among African Americans, 162
psychosocial epidemiology and, 578

Hyperthermia, mortality and, in U.S., 506 (exhibit)
Hypertrophic pyloric stenosis, 103
Hypotheses
epidemiologic, descriptive studies and, 143–144
formulating, in investigating infectious disease outbreaks, 457
stating, 144

I

Iatrogenic reactions, human experimentation and, 341
IBD. *See* Identical by descent
Ibrahim, M. A., 63
Iceberg concept of infection, 449, *450*
Idaho, GIS map of infant mortality rates in, *186*
Identical by descent, 552–553
Identical by state, 553
Illness. *See also* Disease; Infectious disease
cultural backgrounds and perception of, 599
severity of, variations in, *443*
Immigrants, morbidity, mortality and culture of, 164
Immune status, social support and, 590
Immune system, nonspecific defense mechanisms and, 444
Immunity
herd, 448–449
types of, 444–445
Immunization histories, school health programs and, 233
Immunizations, 63, 86, 168
Immunogenicity, 442
Impact evaluation, 352 (exhibit)
Implicit question, 144
Inapparent/apparent case ratio, 450
examples of, for viral infections, 451*t*
Inapparent infection, 446, 448
Incidence
analogy of prevalence and, *99*
interrelationship between prevalence and, 106–108
Incidence data, applications of, 108
Incidence density, 105 (exhibit), 122*t*
absolute effects and, 362, 363

Incidence rate (cumulative incidence),
101–103, 102 (exhibit), 122*t*, 133
number of new cases, 101
population at risk, 102–103
specification of time period, 103
Incident cases
advantages with, 264–265
cohort studies and, 295
Income level
life expectancy and, 174
measurement of, 172
mortality and, 171
Incubation period, 448
Incubation term, generation time *vs.*, 449
IND. *See* Investigational New Drug
Application
Independent variables, 578
in psychosocial epidemiologic research,
582–588
general concepts of stress, 582–583
person-environment fit model,
584–585
social incongruity theory, 583–584
stressful life events, 585–587
stress process model, 587–588
Index case
for measles, 454
secondary attack rate and, 453–454
Index Medicus, 206
India, infant mortality rates in, 178
Indiana, import-associated measles outbreak
in, 467–468 (exhibit)
Indiana State Department of Health, 467
(exhibit)
Indirect age adjustment, illustration of:
mortality rate calculation, 132*t*
Indirect causal associations, 377
Indirect method of rate adjustment, 124,
131–132
Indirect noncausal associations, 377
Indirect transmission of disease, 450
Individual matching, 400
Indoor air pollution, 513
Indoor air quality, 510 (exhibit)
Industrial chemicals, occupational exposure
to, 508–509
Industrialized nations, sex-age structure of
population in, 56, *57*

Infant botulism, 13
Infant mortality rates, 123*t*, 133
among African Americans, 174
community health and, 63
defined, 109 (exhibit)
GIS map of, in Idaho, *186*
international, comparison of, 2000, *114*
international variations in, 178
by race, 112, *113,* 160
sample calculation, 112
soceioeconomic status and, 174
in United States, 1940–2003, *116*
Infection
chain of, 446, *447*
iceberg concept of, 449, *450*
inapparent, 446, 448
Infectious disease
agents of, 439, 441
characteristics, 441–442
applications of molecular epidemiology to
study of, 560–561
case-control studies and research on, 275
clustering of, 191
in the community, 39
controlling, 438
designation of, as notifiable at the
national level, 2005, 221–222
(exhibit)
direct transmission of, 446, 448–450
colonization and infestation, 449
generation time, 449
herd immunity, 448–449
iceberg concept of infection, 449
inapparent/apparent case ratio, 450
inapparent infection, 446, 448
incubation period, 448
emergence/re-emergence of, and demand
for epidemiologists, 632
emerging, 479–480, 481*t*
environment, 445
epidemiologically significant, in
community, *440,* 457–458,
462–471, 475–480
arthropod-borne diseases, *440,* 477,
479
mycoses, 476–477
sexually transmitted diseases, *440,*
464–465, 482

Infectious disease (*Continued*)
 tuberculosis, 468–470, 482
 vaccine-preventable diseases, *440,*
  465–467, 482
 viral hepatitis, 471, 475
 water- and food-borne diseases, *440,*
  458, *459–460,* 462–464, 482
 zoonotic diseases, *440,* 475–476
 epidemiology of, 437–482
 familial clustering and, 542
 Geographic Information Systems and,
  185*t*
 host and, 442–445
  disease-specific defense mechanisms,
   444–445
  nonspecific defense mechanisms, 444
 indirect transmission of, 450–451
 international variations in, 177
 life expectancy and, 581
 measures of outbreaks, 451–456
  attack rate, 451–452, 482
  case fatality rate, 455–456, 482
  secondary attack rates, 453–455, 482
 migration and, 168
 procedures used in investigation of
  outbreaks, 456–457
 social class standing and, 173
 transmission of, 446–451, 482
Infectivity, 442
Infertility, environmental hazards and, 491
Infestation and colonization, 449
Influenza, 82, 438, 441, 446
 avian, 40–41
 CDC surveillance system for, 219
 geographic variations in morbidity and
  mortality rates due to, U.S.,
  179–180
 mortality from, for U.S. cities
  (2003–2007), *19, 20*
 1918 epidemic, 32, 36
 seasonal variations in, 188
 surveillance systems for, *220*
 vaccinations, 466
Informational brochures, 334
Information bias, 393–394
 reducing, 398
Informed consent
 clinical trials and, 337

 document signing, 342
 from human subjects, 340, 342
 obtaining, epidemiologists and, 629
  (exhibit)
Infrastructure variables, community health
 and, 60 (exhibit)
Inheritance, 536 (exhibit)
 modes of, 546–548
 determining, 548
Injection drug users, AIDS and, 465
Injury control epidemiology, 42
Injury epidemiology, 615*t,* 616
Insecticides, classes of, 498
Insects, disease and, 441
Institutional review boards, 630 (exhibit)
Institutional settings, infectious disease
 outbreaks in, 438
Insurance data, 229–230
Intelligence tests, minority community and,
 599
Interior cell totals, 2 by 2 table, 247, 248
Interjudge reliability, 419
Internal consistency reliability, 419
Internal validity, 386, 388
International Classification of Diseases, 216
 Farr's contribution to, 31
International comparisons, of disease
 frequency, 175, 177–178
International Corresponding Club, 622
International Epidemiological Association,
 621*t,* 622
International Genetic Epidemiology Society,
 621*t*
International HapMap Project, 553,
 556–557
 application and implications of,
  557–558
International Journal of Epidemiology, 623
International Society for Environmental
 Epidemiology, 621*t*
International Society for
 Pharmacoepidemiology, 621*t*
*International Statistical Classification of
 Diseases and Related Health Problems,*
 216, 432
Internet, 207
Internet addresses, selected, of interest to
 epidemiologists, 208–209 (exhibit)

Intervening sequences, 534 (exhibit)
Intervention designs
   clinical trials, 330
   community trials, 330–331
Intervention studies, 330–331
   oversight and monitoring of, 341
   summary of: clinical trials *vs.* community
      trials, 355–356*t*
Interviewer/abstractor bias, 393
Intestinal parasites, geographic variation of,
   within U.S., 179
Intrinsic motivation, 600
Introns, 534 (exhibit)
   mutations within, 535 (exhibit)
Invalidity, sources of, 421–422
Inverse relationship, 251
Investigational New Drug Application, 333
   (exhibit)
Ionizing radiation, 497*t*, 503–504, 522
   Chernobyl nuclear power plant accident
      and, 516
   emissions of, from nuclear power
      facilities, 509
   localized concentrations of, 183
   nuclear testing and health effects of
      exposure to, 187
Iowa Women's Health Study, 97, 98
   (exhibit), 306, 311*t*, 314 (exhibit),
   401, 568
   calculating incidence of postmenopausal
      breast cancer in, 102 (exhibit), 104,
      108
   cohorts in, 296
   incidence density, breast cancer and, 105
      (exhibit)
   information bias and, 393
   lifetime history question in, 100
   selection bias and, 392
   smoking question response in, 99
Iraq war veterans, post-traumatic stress
      disorder among, 601
Ireland, mad cow disease in, 180, 181
Ischemic heart disease, 591
Italy, mad cow disease in, 180
IWHS. *See* Iowa Women's Health Study

J

Jacobsen, S. J., 431 (exhibit)

JAMA. *See Journal of the American Medical
   Association*
Japan
   infant mortality rates in, 178
   low rate of coronary heart disease in, 598,
      599
   low rates of coronary heart disease
      mortality and degree of
      acculturation to, 163
   mad cow disease in, 181
   stomach cancer death rates in, 177
Japan Collaborative Cohort Study, 154
Japanese population, mortality rate for, 163
Jarvis, G. K., 170
Jenkins, C. D., 589, 600
Jenkins Activity Scale, 589
Jenner, Edward, 20, *24,* 331
   smallpox vaccination and, 23–25
Job dissatisfaction, 600, 606
Job environment, psychosocial aspects of,
   509
Job listings, 626
"Jogging female heart," 152
Johns Hopkins Bloomberg School of Public
   health, Graduate Summer Institute
   of Epidemiology and Biostatistics at,
   626
John Snow Pub, *35*
Journal of the American Medical Association,
   307
Journals
   epidemiology-related, 620, 622
   online databases and, 207
Judjmental samples, 258

K

Kaiser Medical Plan, 229
Kaiser Permanente, 298, 413
Kassirer, Jerome, 72
Khoury, M. J., 565
King, L. S., 32
King, Mary-Claire, 551 (exhibit)
Klebsiella pneumoniae, 560
Knowler, W. C., 162
Kobasa, S. C. O., 588
Koch, Robert
   criteria for concept of causality by, 72–73
   postulates of, 32, 43

Korean War, data on twin pairs in, 234
Korte, R., 178
Kuder-Richardson reliability coefficient, 419

L

Labor statistics, 214*t*
Lambeth Company (London), 26
Langmuir, Alexander, 36
Langner, T. S., 586
    22-item Index of Psychophysiologic Disorder by, 601
Lassa virus, 481*t*
Last, J. M., 389
Late fetal death rate, 114, 123*t*
    calculation of, 115
Latency, 495, 496
Latency effects, age and, 147
Latency period, of disease, 77
Latin America
    air pollution in, 513
    HIV/AIDS epidemic in, 465
    spread of cholera in, *463,* 463–464
Latinas
    adult, health disparities and, 71
    obesity and, 154
Latino mortality paradox, 166–167 (exhibit)
Latinos, 165–166. *See also* Hispanics
    population by, for U.S., 2000, 159*t*
Laws, public health and, 63, 64*t*
LD. *See* Linkage disequilibrium
Lead
    air pollution and, 513
    exposure to, 500–501
Lead poisoning
    childhood, 501
        wheel model for, 379–380
    in inner cities, 182
    Massachusetts study on, 251
Lead time bias, 428–429
Leavell, H. R., 84
Lee, J., 64
Lee, N. L., 63
Leggette, Carlisle, 9
Leggette, Gilbert, 9
Leggette, Joseph, 9
Legionella, 560

Legionella pneumophilia culture specimen, laboratory technician and viewing of, *625*
Legionellosis, 458
Legionnaires' disease, 13, 84, 145, 560
    clustering of, 191
    New York City outbreak (1978), 8–9
Leishmaniasis, 441
Length bias, 429
Leprosy, 168, *169,* 187, *440*
Less developed nations, sex-age structure of population in, 56, *57*
Leukemia, 273, 562
    childhood, spatial clustering and, 192
    clustering and, 192
    electromagnetic fields and, 501–502
    in upper Middle West, death rates due to, 179
Levels of disease markers, 300, 300*t*
Licensing of drugs, clinical trial phases and, 337–339
Life cycle phenomena, age-associated problems and, 150
Life dissatisfaction, 600, 606
Life expectancy
    at birth, by race and sex: 1970–2003, 161, *161*
    period life tables and, 290
    in selected countries, 2001, 175, *176*
    social context of health and, 581
    socioeconomic status and, 174
Life insurance statistics, 213*t,* 229
Life span, age and validity of diagnoses across, 147
Lifestyle
    chronic disease, health promotion and, 42
    personal behaviors, health and, 590–598, 606
        alcohol consumption, 594–595
        dietary practices, 596–597
        sedentary lifestyle, 597–598
        smoking, 593–594
Life tables, 319
    illustration for total population, U.S., 2000, 291–292 (exhibit)
    methods for, 290, 292
Lilienfeld, A. M., 26
Lilienfeld, D. E., 11, 26

Liljefors, I., 600
Lind, James, 331
Lindane, 498
Line graph, 17*t*
Link, B. G., 101, 170
Linkage analysis
  of early-onset breast cancer, 551 (exhibit)
  LOD score, 548–550, 552
  nonparametric, 552–553
Linkage disequilibrium, 555 (exhibit)
  haplotypes and, 556–558
Lloyd, D. A., 588
Localized place comparisons, of disease, 183–184
Locus, 535 (exhibit)
LOD (logarithm of the odds) score, 550
LOD score linkage analysis, 548–550, 552
Logical validity, 420
London, England, lethal air pollution episode in (1952), 513
London, S. J., 501
Long Beach City Council, 66 (exhibit)
Long Beach Smoking Ordinance (California), 66 (exhibit)
Longevity
  health habits related to, 591
  mental outlook and, 604–605
Lopez, A. D., 581
López-Carrillo, L., 270 (exhibit)
Los Angeles Times, 387 (exhibit)
Love Canal (New York), 18, 512
Low birth weight
  alcohol intake during pregnancy and, 595
  environmental hazards and, 491
  smoking and, 594
Low-density lipoproteins, 596
Lung cancer, 56
  asbestos insulation workers and, 496–497
  case study: smoking and, 75–76 (exhibit)
  causal mechanisms and etiology of, 380–381
  dose-response relationships between smoking and, among British physicians, *78*
  environmental tobacco smoke and, 515
  family study of risk of, in southern Louisiana, 544–545 (exhibit)

green tea study and, 272
international variations in, 177
obesity and, 395–396
secular increase in, 190
smoking and, 37, 74, 286
Lung cancer death rates, in United Kingdom and United States, 288, 289*t*
Lung cancer mortality, women and increase in, 193
Lung diseases, occupational environment and, 491
Lungs, malignant neoplasms of, by age group, U.S. 2003, 138*t*
Lyme disease, 371, *440,* 477, 479, 480
  reported cases of, by county in U.S., *479*
Lymphomas, 273
Lynch syndrome I and II, 565

M

MacMahon, B., 54, 78, 145, 147
Mad cow disease (bovine spongiform encephalopathy), 178
  case study, 180–181
Magnetic fields, 501–503
Magnitude of health problems, social screening and, 415–416
Malaria, 18, 177, 178, *440,* 441
  Anopheles mosquito and, 450
  environmental hazards and, 491
  seasonal variations in, 188
  sickle-cell trait and, 186
Males
  age-adjusted cancer death rates for, U. S., 1930–2003, *152*
  electromagnetic field exposure and breast cancer in, 502
Malignant neoplasms, of trachea, bronchus, and lung, deaths by age group, U.S., 2003, 138*t*
Mammographies, 393, 410
  for women aged 40–49 years, 411–412 (exhibit)
"Mandatory Reporting of Infectious Diseases by Clinicians, and Mandatory Reporting of Occupational Diseases by Clinicians" (CDC), 220

Man-environment interactions, wheel model of, *379*
Manic-depression, 564
Manifestational criteria, for classification of illness, 432
Manipulation of the study factor (M), 243, 244*t*
Mantel-Haenszel procedure, 402
MAPMAKER/SIBS, 553
Maps and mapping
   choropleth, 185
   functional, 537
   of human genome, 530, 558–559
   investigation of infectious disease outbreaks and, 456
   by John Snow, of cholera deaths in Broad Street neighborhood (England), 1849, *29*
   physical, 537
Marginal totals, 247
Marital selection model, 155
Marital status
   characteristics of person and, 154–155
   social support process and, 590
Marmot, M. G., 163, 598
Marriage, protective hypothesis and, 155
Masking, in clinical trials and, 337
Maslow, J. N., 560
Massachusetts
   childhood lead poisoning study in, 251
   tuberculosis death rates in, all forms, 1880–1930, 285, 286*t*
Mass diagnostic and screening surveys, 212*t*
Mass health examinations, 414
Mass screening, 413
Master of Public Health, 624
Masuda, M., 586
Matanoski, G. M., 64
Matching, controlling confounding and, 400–401
Maternal mortality rate, 109 (exhibit), 123*t*
   factors related to, 117
   formula for, 117
Matsumoto, Y. S., 598
Mayo Clinic (Minnesota), 231, 303
   Alzheimer's Disease Patient Registry, 563
   hip fracture investigation at, 363–364

MBG. *See* Molecular biology and genetics
McCauley, L. A., 508
McCunney, R. J., 424
MCI. *See* Mild Cognitive Impairment
Measles, 39, 61, 216, *440, 443*
   import-associated outbreak of, Indiana, 2005, 467–468 (exhibit)
   incidence of, by year, U.S., 1970–2005, *466*
   incubation period for, 448
   index case for, 454
   outbreaks of, 466–467
   vaccinations against, 466
Measurement bias, 421–422
Measures and measurements
   of disease outbreaks, 451–456
      attack rate, 451–452
      case fatality rate, 455–456
      secondary attack rate, 453–455
   of interpretation and examples, 307–309, 314–316
   of type A (coronary prone) behavior pattern, 588–589
   of validity of screening tests, 422, 424
   variability in, 390, 391, 404
Measures (instruments), in empirical research reports, 637–638
Mechanic, D., 599
Medicaid, health care access and, 69, *70*
Medical insurance, private, health care access and, 69, *70*
Medical Research Council Vitamin Study, 335
Medical tests, radiation doses and, 504
Medicare, health care access and, 69, *70*
MEDLINE, 206
Meiosis, 533 (exhibit), 549
Men
   AIDS and, 464
   ailments common among, 151
   coronary heart disease and, 152
   marital status, mortality, morbidity and, 154
   successive birth cohorts of (U.S.), changes in prevalence of cigarette smoking among, *288*
Mendel, Gregor, 536 (exhibit), *547*
Mendelian inheritance, 536 (exhibit), 546

Mendel's law of independent assortment of traits, 548
Men having sex with men, 464, 465
Meningococcal disease
  incidence of, by age group, in selected U.S. areas during 1989–1991, *148*
  seasonal variations in, 188, *189*
Meningococcal infections, outbreak of, in summer school class, *107*, 107–108
Meningococcal meningitis, vaccinations against, 466
Mental health
  life stresses and, 586
  social class and findings for, 173
  stressors and, 601–602
Mental illness, social factors related to, 42
Mental illness survey, in New Haven, Connecticut, 172 (exhibit), 173
Mental outlook, health and, 604–605
Mental retardation
  mild, frequency of by social class, 175
  sociocultural factors in, 599
Mercer, J. R., 599
Mercury, exposure to, 500
Mesothelioma, latency period for, 496
Metallic compounds, 497*t*, 499–501
  arsenic, 499–500
  lead, 500–501
  mercury, 500
Methionine, 532 (exhibit)
Method of agreement, 144–145
Method of analogy, 145
Method of concomitant variation, 145
Method of difference, 144
Method of residues, 145
Metropolitan Atlanta Congenital Defects Program, 274
Metropolitan statistical areas, 235
Meuse Valley, Western Europe, lethal air pollution episode in (1930), 513
Mexican Americans, 165. *See also* Hispanics
  blood lead levels among, in percentage of children aged 1–5 years, *502*
  coronary heart disease and, 166
  medical services preferences of, 599
  mortality rates and, 167
Mexican-origin women, health disparities and, 71

Mexico City, air pollution in, 513
MI. *See* Myocardial infarction
Michael, S. T., 586
Microbial agents, 439, 441
Microbiology, 13
Middle East
  air pollution in, 513
  infant mortality rates in, 178
MIDSPAN Study on passive smoking, 514–515
Migrant farm workers, tuberculosis among, 468–469 (exhibit)
Migration, 58
  nativity and, 167–168
Miké, V., 340
Mild Cognitive Impairment, hormone replacement therapy and, 307
Mild mental retardation, frequency of, by social class, 175
Milham, S., 508
Mill, John Stuart
  canons of inductive reasoning
    method of agreement, 144–145
    method of concomitant variation, 145
    method of difference, 144
    method of residues, 145
Minamata disease, 500
Mineral dusts, work environment exposure to, 507–508
Minnesota Breast Cancer Family Study, 305
Minnesota Heart Health Program, 345
Minnesota Multiphasic Personality Inventory, 602
Minorities. *See also* Ethnicity; Race
  AIDS and, 464
  evaluation of access by, health insurance coverage and, 70–71
  health of, in rural areas, 183
  intelligence tests and, 599
  prevalence surveys on health needs of, 260
  social class and, 171
Minority women
  chronic diseases and, 154
  smoking and secular increase in lung cancer among, 190
Miracidia, 462

Miscarriages, drinking tap water and (Los Angeles area), 520–521 (exhibit)

Misclassification errors, linkage analysis and, 550

Moderating (intervening) variables, 578
examples of, 588
in psychosocial epidemiologic research, 606

Modes of inheritance, 546–548
determining, 548

Molds, 497t, 504–505

Molecular biology, advances in, 530

Molecular biology and genetics, 532 (exhibit)

Molecular-epidemiologists, 531

Molecular epidemiology, 43, 530
of Alzheimer's disease, 563–564
applications of
in cancer studies, 562–563
in occupational and environmental epidemiologic research, 561–562
in study of infectious disease, 560–561
description of, 537–539
genetic epidemiology vs., 531, 536, 539
of psychiatric disorders, 564–565

Monoclonal antibody subtyping, 560

Monozygotic twins
military data on, 234–235
psychiatric disorders among, 564

Monson, R. R., 493

Morbidity, 12
from accidents, 591
environmental hazards and, 491
infectious diseases and, 482
issues in classification of, 429, 431–432
marital status and, 154
physical/mechanical energy effects and, 505–506
predictions about the future and, 56, 58
rates of, 97
smoking and, 593
summary of undadjusted measures of, 122–123t

Morbidity rates, gender and differences in, 151

Morbidity surveys, 225–229

California Health Interview Survey, 229
of general population, 212 t
Health Examination Survey, 226–228
National Health Interview Survey, 225–226

Mormons
mortality rates among, 170
place variation in disease and, 185

Morris, J. N., 52, 309, 597, 598

Morrison, A. S., 418

Mortality, 12
absolute effects and, 362, 363
from accidents, 591
age effects on, 150
environmental hazards and, 491
healthy worker effect and, 493–494
high temperature and, in U.S., 505, 506 (exhibit)
infectious disease and, 482
issues in classification of, 429, 431–432
leading causes of, 53, 54
marital status and, 154
physical/mechanical energy effects and, 505–506
predictions about the future and, 56, 58
rates of, 97
reduced, healthful habits and, 591
retrospective cohort studies and, 492
by selected age groups, males and females, U.S., 2003, 138t
sex differences in, 151
smoking and, 593
summary of undadjusted measures of, 122–123t
10 leading causes of, in Graunt's time, 23
total, from selected causes, males and females, U.S., 2003, 139t

Mortality count, use of, 22–23

Mortality difference, 363

Mortality rates
for African Americans, 160
air pollution and, 514
for American Indians, 163
Hispanic mortality paradox and, 166–167 (exhibit)

social class and, 170–171
for tuberculosis in Massachusetts, all
forms, 1880–1930, 285, 286*t*
Mortality statistics, 212*t*, 215
Mosquitoes
arthropod-borne disease and, 477
disease transmission and, 441
spread of chikungunya virus and, 478
West Nile virus and, 482
Motivation, job-related, 600
Motorcycle fatalities, sex ratio for, 94
Motor vehicle death rates, South Atlantic
states (U.S.), 2003, *62*
Motor vehicle-traffic injuries, 505
MPH. *See* Master of Public Health
MSAs. *See* Metropolitan statistical areas
MSM. *See* Men having sex with men
Multicenter AIDS Cohort Study, 311*t*
Multicenter trials, 331
Multifactorial etiology, 377
Multimodal age-specific incidence curves,
150
Multimodality, age and, 147
Multiphasic screening, 223, 413
Multiple causality, 377
pie model, 380–381
web of causation, 378
wheel model, 378–380
Multiple chemical sensitivity, 510 (exhibit)
Multiple regression analysis, 638
Multiple sclerosis, latitude in U.S. and,
179
Multiracial category, 156
Multisample, illustration of sample selection
in, *299*
Multivariate modeling, 402–403, 404
Mumps, *440*
vaccinations against, 466
Munoz, A., 319
Murphy, J. M., 173
Murray, C. J., 581
Murray, D. M., 258
Mutations, 534–535 (exhibit)
Mycoplasma pneumoniae, 189
cases of, among clients and staff members
of a sheltered workshop, *190*
Mycoses, 476–477

Mymin, D., 597
Myocardial infarction, 11

N

National Academy of Sciences, National
Research Council of, 234
National Ambulatory Medical Care Survey,
69, *70,* 227
National Cancer Act of 1971, 224 (exhibit)
National Cancer Institute, 224, 349, 387
(exhibit), 393, 411 (exhibit)
Surveillance, Epidemiology, and End
Results Program of, 98 (exhibit)
National Cancer Program, 224
National Center for Biotechnology
Information, 557
National Center for Health Statistics, 116,
160, 166, 207, 210, 290, 306
examples of data products from, *228*
new standard population for age
standardization of death rates
adopted by, 129 (exhibit)
National Change of Address Service, 106
National Child Development Study, 317
National Death Index, 106, 306
National Fetal Mortality Survey, 227
National Health and Nutrition Examination
Survey, 162, 226
portable units used by, for data collection,
228
National Health and Nutrition Examination
Survey I, purpose of, 226
National Health and Nutrition Examination
Survey II, 226, 260
National Health Interview Survey, 70,
225–226, 260
National Health Survey, 225
surveys conducted by, 227
National Health Survey Act of 1956, 225
National Heart Failure Project, 153
National Hospital Discharge Survey, 227
National Household Surveys on Drug
Abuse, 260
National Institute for Occupational Safety
and Health, 10
National Institute of Environmental Health
Sciences, 562

National Institute of Mental Health
Epidemiological Catchment Area
Program, 602
National Institute of Occupational Safety
and Health, epidemiologists
employed by, 618, 620
National Institutes of Health, 206, 332, 333
(exhibit)
intervention studies policy of, 341
jobs Web site of, 626
National Library of Medicine, 206
National Longitudinal Mortality Study, 174
National Mortality Followback Survey, 227
National Natality Survey, 227
National Nursing Home Survey, 227
National Nutrition Surveillance Survey, 226
National Occupational Mortality
Surveillance Program, 174
Native Americans. *See* American Indians
Native Hawaiians, 155
definition of, in Census 2000, 159
(exhibit)
Nativity, migration and, 167–168
Natural, active immunity, 444
Natural, passive immunity, 445
*Natural and Political Observations Mentioned
in a Following Index, and Made
Upon the Bills of Mortality* (Graunt),
22
Natural disasters, post-traumatic stress
disorder in wake of, 601
Natural experiments
causality and, 79
use of, 25–28
Natural history of disease, 84
levels of application of preventive
measures in, *86*
Natural immunity, 444
Natural radiation, sources of, 503
Natural Selection Foods (California), 2, 5
Nature of the data criterion, 205, 236
NCBI. *See* National Center for
Biotechnology Information
NCHS. *See* National Center for Health
Statistics
NCI. *See* National Cancer Institute
NDI. *See* National Death Index
Negative declaration (null hypothesis), 144

Nelmes, Sarah, 24
arm of, with lesions of cowpox, *25*
Nelson, D. E., 260
Neonatal mortality rates, 123*t*
defined, 109 (exhibit)
formula for, 115
in United States, 1940–2003, *116*
Nephritis, 443
Nerve gas exposure, Gulf War Syndrome
and, 511 (exhibit)
Nested case-control studies, 316–318, 319
advantages of, 316–317
defined, 316
examples of, 317–318
illustration of cohort studies and, *317*
Netherlands, mad cow disease in, 181
Neural tube defects
case-control studies on, 274–275
Medical Research Council Vitamin Study
and, 335–336
Neuro-epidemiologists, 531
Neuroepidemiology, 615*t*, 616
Neurotoxicity and lead exposure example,
cohort studies and, 297, 298
New cases, number of, incidence rate and,
101
New England Journal of Medicine, 50,
71–72, 82
New epidemic disorders, 56
New Haven, Connecticut, socioeconomic
status and mental illness survey in,
172 (exhibit), 173
New York City, mortality and air pollution
in, 514
New York State Cancer Registry, 223
New York University Women's Health Study,
311*t*
NHANES I. *See* National Health and
Nutrition Examination Survey I
NHANES II. *See* National Health and
Nutrition Examination Survey II
NHS. *See* National Health Survey
Nickel, 499
Nile River, transmission of schistosomiasis
along, 458, 462
1918 influenza pandemic, 32, 36
NIOSH. *See* National Institute for
Occupational Safety and Health

Nitrogen oxides, 513
Nomenclature, defined, 431
Noncausal associations, 376, *376*
Noncompliance, 354, 355
Non-ionizing radiation, 501
Nonparametric linkage analysis, 552–553
Nonprobability samples, 257
  defined, 257
  examples of, 258
Nonreporting bias, 224
Nonspecific defense mechanisms, 443, 444
Nonsteroidal anti-inflammatory drugs,
    peptic ulcer disease and, 365, 367,
    369–370, 377
North Africa, infant mortality rates in,
    178
North Karelia Project, 345
Northridge earthquake, 1994 (California),
    post-traumatic stress disorder in
    wake of, 601
Nosocomial infections, 39
  in hospitals, 438
Nosologists, death certificates and, 215
Notifiable diseases, 216
Notifiable disease statistics, surveillance
    systems for, 219
NSAIDs. *See* Nonsteroidal anti-
    inflammatory drugs
NTDs. *See* Neural tube defects
Nuclear power facilities, 516–518
  emissions of ionizing radiation from, 509,
    522
  health effects of ionizing radiation from,
    503
Nuclear weapons, adverse health effects and
    above-ground atmospheric testing
    of, 518
Nucleic acids, in DNA, 532 (exhibit)
Null hypothesis (negative declaration),
    144
Nurses, as focus of cohort studies, 299
Nurses' Health Study, 310*t*, 313 (exhibit),
    555 (exhibit)
Nutrition epidemiology, 615, 615*t*

O

Oak Ridge, Tennessee, nuclear weapons
    production in, 516

Obesity, 56
  among Mexican-American population,
    166
  built environment and, 42
  diet and, 596, 597
  lung cancer and, 395–396
  minority women and, 154
Objectivity, of clinical trials, 337
Observational approach, experimental
    approach *vs.*, 243
Observational studies, 245–246
  analytic studies, 246
  descriptive studies, 246
  Women's Health Initiative, 313 (exhibit)
Observational study designs, comparisons
    of, 319, 320–321*t*
Observations
  study designs and number of, 242
  study designs and unit of, 243
Occupational classification, education,
    disease mortality and, 174
Occupational dermatoses, 41
Occupational epidemiologic research,
    applications of molecular
    epidemiology in, 561–562
Occupational hazards, monitoring and
    surveillance of exposure to, 506–509
Occupational prestige, 171, 172
Occupational status, extrinsic-intrinsic
    motivation, coronary heart disease
    and, 600
Occupations, within epidemiology,
    617–618, 620
Odds ratio, 270, 276, 362
  for case-control study with three different
    sample sizes, 372–373, 372*t*
  cautionary note on interpretations of, 271
  sample calculation of, 270 (exhibit)
O'Donnell, L. N., 336
Office visits, percent distribution of, by
    primary expected source of payment
    according to patient's age, U.S.,
    2000, *70*
Older adults, health issues for, 147, 154
Olmsted Community Hospital (Minnesota),
    232
Olmsted Medical Group (Minnesota), 231,
    232

Omnibus Budget Reconciliation Act (1987), 245
On Airs, Waters, and Places (Hippocrates), 21
One-sample, illustration of sample selection in, *296*
Online databases, 206–207
On women's health, 313–314 (exhibit)
Oocytes, 533 (exhibit)
Ooi, W. L., 544
Operationalization, 580–581, 637
Operations research, 88
epidemiology applied to, 67–71
examples of questions asked in, 68
Opportunistic screening, 414
Optimism, 604
OR. *See* Odds ratio
Oral cancers, smoking and, 273
Oral Contraception Study of the Royal College of General Practitioners, 310*t*
Oral contraceptives, Nurses' Health Study and examining long-term consequences of use of, 313 (exhibit)
Oral/dental epidemiology, 615*t, 617*
Ordinances, public health and, 63, 64*t*
Organic dusts, work environment exposure to, 507–508
Organocarbamates, 498
Organochlorides, 498
Organophosphates, 498
OS. *See* Observational studies
Osteoporosis, risk difference and, 363–364
Osteoporotic fractures, cohort studies on, in women, 314 (exhibit)
Outbreak investigations, case-control design and, 263
Outcome evaluation, 352 (exhibit)
Outcome measures, 638
in cohort studies, 300–301
Outcomes
of clinical trials, 335
internal validity and, 388
types of, for cohort studies, 300*t*
Outcome variables
examples of, 606
physical health, mental health, affective states and, 600–605
Ovarian cancer, 43

Oxidants, air pollution and, 513
Ozone, 513

P

Pacific Islanders, 156, 159 (exhibit), 163–165
infant mortality rates among, 160
Paffenbarger, R. S., Jr., 233, 315, 597, 598
Paisley, 514
Pandemics, 18
Black Death, 22
influenza, 1918, 32, 36
PAP, 548
Paré, Ambroise, 331
Partiality, avoiding, 631 (exhibit)
Participation rates
validity and generalizability of studies and, 398
validity of epidemiologic findings and, 375
Passive follow-up, 305–306
Passive immunity, 444
Passive prevention, 86
Passive smoking
case-control studies on, 274
MIDSPAN Study on, 514–515
by parents, and wheezing respiratory illness in children, 371
Pathogenesis period, 84, *85*
Pathogenicity, 442
Pathognomonic, meaning of, 75 (exhibit)
Pathology, 13
Patients, withdrawal of, from studies, 340
Pawtucket Heart Health Program, 345, 347, 349
Payment sources, operations research on, 69, *70*
Pearlin, L. I., 587
Pellagra, discovering cure for, 36
Pemberton, John, 622
Penicillin, development of, 36
Penicillium notatum, 36
Peptic ulcer disease, nonsteroidal anti-inflammatory drugs and, 365, 367, 369–370, 377
Perera, F. P., 537
Perinatal mortality rate, 109 (exhibit), 123*t*, 133

formula for, 117
Perinatal mortality ratio, 123*t*
    formula for, 117
Periodic life tables, 290
Periodontal health status, work-related stress
    and, 509
Period prevalence, 100
Persisting disorders, 56
Person, characteristics of, 193
Personal behaviors, lifestyle, health and,
    590–598, 606
Personality
    effects of major diseases on, 603
    smoking and, 603–604
    variables in, health outcomes and, 588
Personal risk taking, 590
Person-environment fit model, 584–585,
    605
Persons, characteristics of, 142, 146–175
    age, 146–150
    findings, 173–175
    marital status, 154–155
    measurement, 171–172, 173
    nativity and migration, 167–168
    race and ethnicity, 155–157, 160–166
    religion, 168–170
    sex, 151–154
    socioeconomic status, 170–171
Person-to-person transmission of disease,
    440, 446, 468–471, 475
Persson, V., 168
Pertussis vaccinations, 465
Pesticides, 41, 498–499
    farm workers and exposure to, 508
Peters, R. K., 315
Peto, R., 37
p53 gene, 554 (exhibit), 562
Pharmaceutical industry researchers,
    617
Pharmaco-epidemiologists, 531
Pharmacoepidemiology, 615*t*, 616
Pharmacogenetics, 567
Phenotypes, 535 (exhibit)
Phillips, R. L., 170
Phipps, James, 24–25
Physical activity, coronary heart disease and,
    examples of cohort studies built
    upon theme of, 309, 314–316

Physical environment, epidemiology of
    infectious disease and, 445
Physical mapping, 537
Physical/mechanical energy, 497*t*, 505–506
Physicians, as focus of cohort studies, 299
Physicians' practices, data from records of,
    213*t*, 232–233
Physiological measures, 638
Pie chart, 17*t*
Pie model, 377, 380–381
    for three sufficient causes of disease, *380*
Pima Tribe, diabetes mellitus among
    members of, 162
Pinworm, 441
Place, characteristics of, 142, 193
    within country geographic variation in
    rates of disease, 178–180
    geographic information systems, 184–185
    international comparisons of disease
    frequency, 175–178
    localized place comparisons, 183–184
    reasons for place variation in disease,
    185–187
    types of comparisons, 175
    urban/rural differences in disease rates,
    182–183
Placebo, 334, 337
Placebo control, Hawthorne effect and, 354
Place variation, in disease, reasons for,
    185–187
Plague, 20, 22, 216, 219, *440*, 445
Planned crossovers, 340
Planned experiments, 52 (exhibit)
Planning interventions, prevalence surveys
    and, 260
Plasmodium vivax, 450
Plausibility, causality and, 78
PMR. *See* Proportional mortality ratio
Pneumococcal disease, vaccinations against,
    466
Pneumonia, 438
    geographic variations in morbidity and
    mortality rates due to, U.S., 179
    mortality from, for U.S. cities
    (2003–2007), *19*, 20
    seasonal variations in, 188
Point epidemics, 188–189
POINTER, 548

Point prevalence, 98, 99
Poisonings, 505
Policy cycle, phases of, 64, *65*
Policy evaluation, epidemiology and, 63
Poliomyelitis, 39, *440*
  disappearing disorders and, 56
Polio vaccines, 466
Pollution
  air, 513–516
  water, 518–519, 520–521 (exhibit), 522
Polychlorinated biphenyls and dioxins, 498
Polymorphic traits, 550
Polyps, colon, 375
Polyunsaturated fats, 596
Poor precision, 390
Population, 11
Population at risk, incidence rate and,
  102–103
Population-based cohort studies, 295–297,
  319
Population-based controls, 266–268
Population-based samples, epidemiologic
  associations and, 375
Population dynamics
  epidemiology and, 58
  future predictions about, 56, 58
Population etiologic fraction, 368–370,
  381
  formula for, 369
Population research, 14
Population risk difference, 364–365, 381
Populations, epidemiology and, 204–205
Population screening, 413
Portal of entry, 446, *447*
  portal of exit, mode of transmission and,
  448*t*
Portal of exit, 446
  portal of entry, mode of transmission and,
  448*t*
Port Pirie Cohort Study, 311*t*
Portugal, mad cow disease in, 181
Positional cloning, 537, *538*
Positive declaration (research hypothesis),
  144
Postneonatal mortality rates, 109 (exhibit),
  115, 123*t*
  formula for, 116
  in United States, 1940–2003, *116*

Postpartum depression, temporal clustering
  and, 192
Posttest design, 351, 352*t*, 353
Posttraumatic stress disorder, 601
Postvaccination reactions, temporal
  clustering and, 192
Pott, Percival, 77
Poverty
  life expectancy and, 581
  stress, depression and, 173
  urban areas, disease and, 182
Precision, poor, 390
Predictive validity, 420
Predictive value (+)
  falling prevalence of disease and, 426
  screening tests and, 424
Predictive value (–)
  falling prevalence of disease and, 426
  screening tests and, 424
Predictive values, 432
  sample calculation of, 425 (exhibit)
Pregnancy outcomes, drinking tap water
  and, Los Angeles area, 520–521
  (exhibit)
Premorbid psychologic factors, cancer and,
  602–603
Prempro™, dementia risk and, 307
Prepathogenesis period, 84, *85*
Presidential Advisory Committee on Gulf
  War Veterans' Illnesses, 511 (exhibit)
Press coverage: leaving out the big picture,
  387 (exhibit)
Prestige, occupational, 171, 172
Presymptomatic stage, 84
Pretest/posttest/control, 352*t*, 353
Pretest/posttest design, 352*t*, 353
Prevalence, 133
  absolute effects and, 362, 363
  analogy of incidence and, *99*
  definition of, 97–98, 100–101
  interrelationship between incidence and,
  106–108
  period, 100
  point, 98, 99
Prevalence difference, 363
Prevalence study, 256
Prevalence surveys
  planning interventions and, 260

on vasectomies, 259
Prevarication bias, 393
Prevention of disease, 84–87
primary, 85–86, 88
secondary, 87, 88
tertiary, 87, 88
Prevention strategies, to control
confounding, 399–401
Preventive measures, levels of application of,
in natural history of disease, *86*
Primary prevention, 85–86, 88
Primordial prevention, 85
Principles of Epidemiology (CDC), 219
Prions, 180
Privacy
of data, 207, 210, 211
data from physicians' practices and, 232
protecting, 629 (exhibit)
Privacy Act of 1974, 207
Probability-based sample, in empirical
research reports, 636
Probability samples, definition and examples
of, 257
Probands, 542, 543, 546
Problem definition, investigation of
infectious disease outbreaks and, 456
Process evaluation, 352 (exhibit)
Professional associations, epidemiology-
related, 620, 622
Program evaluation, 88
epidemiology applied to, 67–71
Project RESPECT, 350 (exhibit)
Prophylactic trials, 333
Proportion, definition of, 95
Proportional mortality ratio, 118–120, 123*t*
sample calculation, 119
Prospective cohort design, *301*
Prospective cohort studies, 301–302
Prostate cancer, 430–431 (exhibit)
among African-American males, 161
Protected health information (HIPAA), 210
(exhibit)
Protective hypothesis, marriage and, 155
Protein, DNA and, 533–534 (exhibit)
Protozoan diseases, 441
PSA screening rates, 430–431 (exhibit)
Pseudomonas aeruginosa, 561
Psittacosis, *440*

Psychiatric disorders, molecular and genetic
epidemiology of, 564–565
Psychiatric genetic epidemiology, 564
Psychological Abstracts, 206
Psychological factors, in health, 42
Psychological therapy interventions,
developing rigorous evaluations of,
341
Psychologic epidemiology, research designs
used in, 580–581
Psychology, 13
Psychosocial aspects of health and
employment, 509
Psychosocial epidemiologic research, 600
Psychosocial epidemiology, 576, 577–580,
605
psychologic, behavioral, and social
examples of variables, *579*
PTSD. *See* Posttraumatic stress disorder
Publication, bias in, 403–404
Public health
competencies in epidemiology by MPH
degree candidates in, 624–625
genetics and, 565–568
laws and ordinances and, 63, 64*t*
risk and, 82
Public health advocacy, by epidemiologists,
632 (exhibit)
Public health clinics, data from, 213*t*
Public health nurse epidemiologists, 617
Public Health Service Act, 207
Public health surveillance, 219
Public trust, maintaining, 630 (exhibit)
Puerto Ricans, 165
coronary heart disease and, 166
mortality rates and, 167
Pugh, T. F., 54, 78, 145, 147
Pulmonary embolism, 591
Pulsed-field gel electrophoresis, 4, 560
Pure determinism, 72
P values, 371–372, 373
for case-control study with three different
sample sizes, 372*t*
Pyrethroids, 498

Q

Q fever, *440,* 441, 475–476
reported cases of, in U.S., *476*

Qualitative traits, codominance for, 547–548
Quantification, 14, 16, 43
language of, SARS cases in United States and, 14, 16
Quantitative traits, codominance for, 547
Quarantinable diseases, CDC reports on, 219
Quasi-experimental designs, 351
overview of, 352*t*
posttest, 351, 352*t*, 353
pretest/posttest, 352*t*, 353
pretest/posttest/control, 352*t*, 353
Solomon Four-Group assignment, 352*t*, 353–354
Quasi-experimental studies, 245
Quasi-experiments, 328, 329, 356
Quota samples, 258

R

Rabies, *440, 443*, 445, 450
high case fatality rates with, 455 (exhibit)
Race, 155–167. *See also* African Americans; Alaska Natives; American Indians; Asians; Hispanics; Mexican Americans; Minorities; Whites
African Americans, 160–162
age-adjusted total U.S. mortality rates for breast cancer by, all ages, females for 1995–2004, *191*
age-specific incidence rate for cancer sites by, 1986–1990, U.S., *149*
AIDS and, 160, *160, 464*
American Indians/Alaska Natives, 162–163
Asians/Pacific Islanders, 163–165
blood lead levels and, 501
categories of, 155–156
defining categories of, in Census 2000, 158–159 (exhibit)
five-year survival rates by year of diagnosis and, in U.S. 1996–2002, *83*
health disparities, rural areas and, 183
Hispanics/Latinos, 165–166
infant mortality rates by, 112, *113,* 160
life expectancy, at birth by sex and: 1970–2003, 161, *161*

overview of, and Hispanic origin, Census 2000, 157–159 (exhibit)
percentage of children aged 1–5 years with blood lead levels by, *502*
population by, for U.S., 2000, 159*t*
social class and, 171
tuberculosis and, 470
tuberculosis incidence by, U.S., 1995–2005, *165*
Racial composition, community health and, 61
Racial diversity, *156*
Radiation
ionizing, 503–504
non-ionizing, 501
Radon gas
cancer rates and, 183
health effects and exposure to, 504
Rahe, R. H., 586, 600
Railroad Retirement Fund, 309
Railroad workers, retrospective cohort study of, on physical activity and CHD, 309, 314
Random-digit dialing, 267
Random errors, 390, 404
Randomization, 356
in clinical trials, 339–340
of study subjects, 243, 244*t*, 330
controlling confounding and, 399–400
Randomized controlled trials, 329, 331, 428
Randomized trials, flow diagram of progress through, *343*
ras family of proto-oncogenes, 562–563
Rate difference, 362
Rate ratio, 308
Rates, 95–97, 133
adjusted, 123–124, 128, 130–133
attack, 103
calculation of, 96 (exhibit)
categories of, 108
crude, 108–117
elements within, 96 (exhibit)
incidence, 101–103
risk *vs.,* 104–106
specific, 118–121
summary of, 122–123*t*
Ratio, 133
definition of, 94

Rational validity, 420
Ratio of controls, 266
RDD. *See* Random-digit dialing
Reading frame, 534 (exhibit)
Recall bias, 393
  reducing, 398
Recombination, of homologous pairs of
    chromosomes, 549
Recombination fraction, 550
Record linkage, 211
  confidentiality, data sharing and, 207,
    210, 211
Redlich, F., 171, 173
Red spots on airline flight attendants case, 9,
    10, 18
Reference groups, 364
Reference population, 96
Refusal rates, 637
Relative effects, 365–370, 381
  etiologic fraction, 366–368
  population etiologic fraction, 368–370
Relative risk, 319, 362
  defined, 307
  etiologic fraction and, 367
  sample problem, 308 (exhibit)
  statistical significance testing and,
    373
Relative risk ratio, smoking, lung cancer
    and, 75 (exhibit)
Relatives or associates of cases controls,
    268–269
Reliability
  graphic representation of, *421*
  interrelationships between validity and,
    421
  of screening tests, 418–419
Reliability coefficient, 419
Reliability types, 419
Religion
  health and, 168–170
  psychologic and social processes in disease
    and, 579
Religious composition, community health
    and, 61
Renal epidemiology, 615*t*, *617*
Renfrew, 514
Reportable disease statistics, 212*t*, 216,
    219–220, 222

Reportable infectious diseases, 221–222
    (exhibit)
Representativeness criterion, 206, 236
Reproductive and perinatal epidemiology,
    42
Reproductive epidemiology, 615, 615*t*
Research designs
  facets of, 243
  use of, in psychologic, behavioral and
    social epidemiology, 580–581
Research hypothesis (positive declaration),
    144
Research participants, minimizing risks and
    protecting welfare of, 628 (exhibit)
Research workers, 617
Residential water supplies, pollution levels
    and, 520–521 (exhibit)
Residual disorders, 54, 56
Resistance, 442
Respiratory illnesses, indoor air pollution
    and, 513
Respiratory infections, 446
Restriction of admission criteria, 404
  controlling confounding and, 400
Results, reporting, 342, 632 (exhibit)
"Retirement syndrome," 150
Retrospective cohort design, *301*
Retrospective cohort studies, 302–303
  advantages to, 302–303
  case-control studies *vs.*, 303
  in environmental epidemiology, 492–493
  of railroad workers, physical activity and
    CHD, 309, 314
Rheumatic fever, 443
Ribonucleic acid. *See* RNA
Rice, D. P., 228
Rickettsia, 441
Rickettsia bacteria, Rocky Mountain spotted
    fever and, 188
Ringworm, 441
Risk
  rate *vs.*, 104–106
  study of, to individuals, 81–83
Risk assessment, epidemiologists and, 64
Risk difference, 362, 377
  defined, 363
Risk factors, criteria for, 74
Risk taking, 591

RNA, 534 (exhibit)

Robison, Leslie, 192

Rochester Epidemiology Project (Minnesota), 231–232

Rochette, H. E., 507

Rocky Flats, Colorado, nuclear weapons production in, 516

Rocky Mountain spotted fever, *440*, 441
seasonal variations in, 188

Rodenticides, 498

Rorschach test, 602

Rosenman, R. H., 589

Ross, Julie, 192

Ross, R. K., 401

Rossi, P. H., 344, 351

Rotaviral enteritis, vaccinations against, 466

Rothman, K. J., 74, 362, 363, 374, 380

Rubella, 216
thalidomide and, 79
vaccinations against, 466

Rural areas
cancer rates in, 183
disease rates and, 182–183

Russia, life expectancy in, 175, *176*

Rutstein, D. D., 507

S

Safe sex practices, clinical trials and impact on, 336

SAGE, 548

Sales, S. M., 600

Saliva, nonspecific defense mechanisms and, 444

"Salmon bias effect," 167 (exhibit)

Salmonella infection, attack rate formula and, 103

Salmonellosis, 439, *440,* 458*t*
CDC surveillance system for, 219

Samet, J. M., 63, 319

Sample size, clinical *vs.* statistical significance and, 373, 381

Sampling, cohort formation options and, 295–301

Sampling error, 390–391, 404

Sampling frame, 257
for case-control family study, 543

Sampling unit, 257

San Antonio Heart Study, 166

Sand flies, arthropod-borne disease and, 477

San Joaquin Valley fever, 441, 445, 476–477

San Onofre nuclear power plant (California), 517

Sarin, Gulf War Syndrome and, 511 (exhibit)

SARS. *See* Severe acute respiratory syndrome

SAS, 638

Saturated fats, 596

Saudi Arabia, mad cow disease in, 181

SBS. *See* Sick building syndrome

Scandinavia, infant mortality rates in, 178

Schistosoma mansoni, 441, 462
life cycle of, *462*

Schistosomiasis, 177
transmission of, along Nile River, 458, 462

Schizophrenia, social class and, 172 (exhibit), 173

Schlesselman, J. J., 276

Schoenborn, C. A., 154

School health programs data, 214*t,* 233–234

Schottenfeld, D., 155, 340

Science, 71

Scientific justification, cohort studies and sufficiency of, 306–307

Scientific situations for screening, 415 (exhibit), 416

Screening surveys, 223

Screening tests and programs
appropriate situations for, 414–417
ethical, 415 (exhibit), 416–417
scientific, 415 (exhibit), 416
social, 415–416, 415 (exhibit)
case-control design and, 263
for colorectal cancer, 566
controversies about, 430–431 (exhibit)
effects of disease prevalence on predictive value of, 425*t*
evaluation of, 418–421, 428–429
interrelationships between reliability and validity, 421
reliability, 418–419
validity, 419–421
good, characteristics of, 417–418
importance of, 410
mass, 413
measures of validity of, 422, 424

multiphasic, 413
opportunistic, 414
results of
effects of prevalence of disease on,
424–426
fourfold table for classification of, *423*
selective, 414
Scurvy, 331
Search engines, 207
Seasonality
disease and, 187–188
hip fracture rates and, 364
Seat belt laws, 245
Seat belt use, 63
Secondary attack rate, 453–455, 453
(exhibit)
calculating, 454
hypothetical data for military cadets, 453,
454*t*
Secondary prevention, 87, 88
Secondhand smoke, 515
adverse effects related to, 65–66 (exhibit)
Secular time trends, 189–190
Secular trends, 52, 193
Sedentary lifestyle, 597–598
SEER program. *See* Surveillance,
Epidemiology, and End Results
Program
Segregation analysis, 546, 548, 552
Selection bias, 392, 429, 637
exposure data and, 493
preventing, 396
Selective screening, 414
Self-pay, health care access and, 69, *70*
Self-reports, 492
Seligman, P. J., 507
Selikoff, I. J., 496, 499
Sellers, T. A., 302, 568
Selye, Hans, 582, 583
Semenza, J. C., 506
Semmelweis, Ignaz, 26
Sensitivity, 432
relationship between specificity and,
426–428, *427*
sample calculation of, 425 (exhibit)
screening tests and, 422, 424
Sentinel health event, 507
Sequential design, clinical trials and, 341

SER. *See* Society for Epidemiologic Research
Serologic testing, data for, 436*t*
SES. *See* Socioeconomic status
Seven Countries Study, 251, 253
Seventh-Day Adventist church, lifestyle and
health status of members in,
169–170
Seventh-Day Adventists
place variation in disease and, 185
studies on dietary practices by, 596
Severe acute respiratory syndrome, 39
exposure category, clinical features, and
demographics of reported cases of,
15*t*
language of quantification: cases in
United States, 14, 16
Sewage workers, biologic hazards and, 507
Sex
age-specific incidence rate for cancer sites
by, 1986–1990, U.S., *149*
characteristics of persons and, 151–154
life expectancy, at birth by race and:
1970–2003, 161, *161*
Sex composition, community health and, 59
Sex ratio, 133
for motorcycle fatalities, 94
Sex-specific rates, 120
Sexual abuse, of boys, relative risk
calculation of suicide attempts and,
308 (exhibit)
Sexually transmitted diseases, 61, 216, *440*,
446, 464–465
clinical trial evaluating effectiveness of
education about, 336
community-based interventions and
prevention of, 350 (exhibit)
SFB Law. *See* Smokefree Bars Law
Shanghai Cancer Registry, 272
Shanghai Women's Cohort Study, 304
Shekelle, R. B., 583
Shigellosis, CDC surveillance system for,
219
Sibling pairs, nonparametric linkage analysis
and, 552–553
SIBLINK, 553
Sick building syndrome, 509, 510 (exhibit),
513
Sickle-cell anemia, 61, 535 (exhibit)

Sickle-cell gene, gene/environment interaction and, 186
Side effects, monitoring human subjects for, 340
Sigmoidoscopies, 375, 566
Significance tests, 371
Silicosis, 507
Simple random samples, 257
Simpson's paradox, 394–395, 395*t*
Single agent causal model, 73
Single-blind design, 337
Single nucleotide polymorphisms, 553, *554*, 555 (exhibit)
Size, of risk, 81–82
Skin cancer, Sunbelt areas and, 179
Sleeping sickness, African, 186–187
Smalley, W. E., 365
Smallpox, 20, 39, 443, 445
  disappearing disorders and, 56
Smallpox vaccine, 23–25, 331
Smokefree Bars Law (California), evaluating responses to, 65–67 (exhibit)
Smokeless tobacco study (Minnesota), 258, 262
Smoking, 590
  among Asians, 164
  case study: lung cancer and, 75–76 (exhibit)
  changes in prevalence of, among successive birth cohorts of U.S. men, 1900–1987, *288*
  cohort effect example and, 285–288
  confounding of body weight–lung cancer association, 395–396, *396*
  cross-sectional surveys on, 260, *261,* 262
  health and, 593–594
  lung cancer and, 37, 74
  lung cancer mortality among British physicians and, *78*
  oral cancers and, 273
  passive, 514–515
  personality and, 603–604
  side-stream, case-control studies on, 274
Smoking and Health, Report of the Advisory Committee to the Surgeon General of the Public Health Service, 74
Smoking cessation, community trials on, 349

Smoking habits, clustering of, within families, 541
Smoking prevalence, among adolescents in U.S., by survey, 1974–1991, *261*
SMR. *See* Standardized mortality ratio
SMSAs. *See* Standard metropolitan statistical areas
Snail fever, 441
Snow, John, 20, *34,* 43, 184, 191, 456
  cholera epidemic investigated by, 25–31
  Pub named in honor of, *35*
Snow on Cholera, 20
  cholera deaths in neighborhood on Broad Street, 1849, *29*
  excerpt, 27–28
SNP. *See* Single nucleotide polymorphism
Social class
  coronary disease and, 583–584
  measures of, 171–172, 173
  mental health findings and, 173
Social context of health, 581–582
Social desirability effects, 422
Social environment
  epidemiology of infectious disease and, 445
  psychosocial factors and, 581
Social epidemiology, 576, 605
  research designs used in, 580–581
Social factors, in health, 42
Social incongruity theory (status discrepancy models), 583–584
Social mobility, morbidity and, 583
Social networks, 590
Social network ties, 590
Social Readjustment Rating Scale, 586
Social Security numbers, linking to National Death Index with, 306
Social Security statistics, 214*t,* 229
Social situations for screening, 415–416, 415 (exhibit)
Social support, 589–590
Social variables, community health and, 60 (exhibit)
Society for Clinical Trials, The, 621*t*
Society for Epidemiologic Research, The, 620, 621*t,* 622, 626
Society for Healthcare Epidemiology in America, The, 621*t*

Society for Pediatric and Perinatal
  Epidemiologic Research, 621*t*
Sociocultural influences on health, 598–599
Socioeconomic indices, epidemiologic
  evaluations of utilization of surgical
  operations, 70
Socioeconomic status
  community health and, 59
  health and, 42, 170–171
  psychologic and social processes in disease
    and, 579
  stress process model and, 587, 588
  survey of, in New Haven, Connecticut,
    172 (exhibit), 173
Sociological Abstracts, 206
Sociology, 13, 171, 578
Socrates, 309
SOLAR, 553
Solomon Four-Group assignment, 352*t*,
  353–354
South Asia, air pollution in, 513
South Atlantic states (U.S.), motor vehicle,
  assault, and firearm injury death
  rates, *62*
Southwark and Vauxhall Company
  (London), 26
Soviet Union (former), reduced life
  expectancy in, 581
Space and time clustering, 192
Spain, mad cow disease in, 181
Spanish Flu, 32. *See also* 1918 influenza
  pandemic
Spatial clustering, 192–193
Special clinics, data on diseases treated in,
  213*t*
Specializations, within epidemiology,
  615–617, 615*t*
Specificity, 376, 432
  causality and, 77
  relationship between sensitivity and,
    426–428, *427*
  sample calculation of, 425 (exhibit)
  screening tests and, 424
Specificity hypothesis, interpersonal
  relationships and, 590
Specific rates, 108, 118–121, 133
  age-specific rate, 120
  cause-specific rate, 118

  limitations with, 123–124
  proportional mortality ratio, 118–120
Speizer, Frank, 313 (exhibit)
Sperm, 533 (exhibit)
Spinach, *E. coli* 2006 outbreak and, 2, 3–5
SPLAT, 553
Spontaneous abortions,
  bromodichloromethane and, 521
    (exhibit)
Spot maps, investigation of infectious
  disease outbreaks and, 456–457
SPSS, 638
Stacey, S. N., 555 (exhibit)
Standard error of measurement, 419
Standardized mortality ratio
  disadvantages with use of, 133
  sample calculation for, 131, 132
Standard metropolitan statistical areas, 183
Stanford Five-City Project, 345, 346–347
  (exhibit)
  design, methods, and results of, 346–347
    (exhibit)
  design of, *348*
Staphylococcal disease, *440*
Staphylococcus aureus, food-borne illness and,
  458, 458*t*
Staphylococcus epidermidis, 560
State Health Registry of Iowa, 98 (exhibit)
Statistical Abstract of the United States, 235
Statistical inference, causal inference and, 79
Statistical measures of effect, 371–374
  clinical *vs.* statistical significance,
    373–374
  confidence interval, 372–373
  P value, 371–372
  significance tests, 371
Statistical power, 354–355, 373
Statistical significance, clinical significance
  vs., 373–374
Statistical software, epidemiologic research
  studies and, 37
Statistical validity, 420
Statistics. *See also* Data
  birth, 215
  in empirical research reports, 638
  mortality, 215
  on reportable diseases, 216, 219–220,
    222

Status incongruity, morbidity and, 583
STDs. *See* Sexually transmitted diseases
Stomach cancer, worldwide prevalence of, 177
"Stop" codons, 535 (exhibit)
Strata/stratum, 257–258, 400
Stratification, 402, 404
Stratified samples, 257
Streissguth, A. P., 595
Streja, D., 597
Strengths *versus* limitations criterion, 206, 236
Streptococcal infections, 439
Stress, 605
    general concepts of, 582–583
    health and, 42
    mental health and, 601–602
    occupational, 509
    person-environment fit model and, 585
    poverty and, 173
    psychosocial epidemiology and, 579
    social supports and buffers against, 590
    work-related, 491
Stressful life events, 585–587, 605
Stress-illness relationship
    moderating factors in, 588–599
        personal behavior, lifestyle, and health, 590–598
        social support, 589–590
        sociocultural influences on health, 598–599
        type A (coronary-prone) behavior pattern, 588–589
Stress process model, 587–588
Stringfellow acid pits (California), 512
Stroke mortality rates, blood pressure levels and, 251, 253
Study designs
    case-control, 262–276
    choice of, 242
    cross-sectional, 256–262, 276
    differences among, 242–243, 276
    ecologic, 249–255, 276
    in environmental epidemiology, 491–494
    hierarchy of, 328–329
    overview of those used in epidemiology, 244–248
        experimental studies, 244–245, 276

        observational studies, 245–246, 276
        quasi-experimental studies, 245
        2 by 2 table, 246–248
        temporality of, 284
        validity for etiologic inference according to, 329 (exhibit)
Study of Osteoporotic Fractures, 311*t*, 314 (exhibit)
Study sample, in empirical research reports, 636–637
Study subjects, randomization of, 330
Subclinical infection, 446, 448
Subject attrition, 637
Subjects
    randomization of, 339–340
    study designs and availability of, 243
Subject selection
    illustration of, in case-control studies, *263*
    illustration of, in cross-sectional study, *256*
Substance abuse, community health and, 61
Suchman, E. A., 142, 591
Sudden infant death syndrome, 42
Sufficient cause, 362, 380
Suffocation, 505
Suicide
    among electric utility workers, nested case-control study of, 317
    clustering and, 192
    rates of
        among widowed persons, 154–155
        community health and, 61
        international variations in, 178
    relative risk calculation of sexual abuse of boys and attempts of, 308 (exhibit)
Sulfur oxides, air pollution and, 513
Sulindac, 567
Sunburn, hypothetical ecologic relationship between hats and, 254–255, 255*t*
Surgical utilization, socioeconomic indices and, 70
Surrogate end points, 335
Surveillance, 19
Surveillance, Epidemiology, and End Results Program, 224, 224 (exhibit)
Surveillance programs, preventing occupational illness and, 506–509

Survival curves, 293–294, *294,* 319
Susser, M. W., 73, 74, 79, 394, 598
Susto (folk illness), 599
Swan, S. H., 520 (exhibit)
Swedish Cancer Registry, 501
Syme, S. L., 171, 576, 584
Syndromes, identifying, 51 (exhibit)
Synergism, 495, 496–497
Synthetic radiation, sources of, 503
Syphillis, *440*
Systematic errors, 390, 404
Systematic samples, 257

T

Tabulations, investigation of infectious
    disease outbreaks and, 456–457
Taco Bell restaurants, 5
Tagging, of haplotypes, 556, 557
Tailored interventions, 567–568
Tamoxifen and Finasteride Prevention Trials,
    349
Tanzania, HIV/AIDS prevention programs
    in, 349
Targeted screening, 414
Taylor, J. A., 562, 563
Tay-Sachs disease, 61
    place variations in rates of, 186
TB. *See* Tuberculosis
Tea drinking, 596
Tecumseh, Michigan, cohort study in,
    296
Teenage pregnancy, 61
    decline in, 260
    prevalence study on, 259–260
Teenagers, smoking by, and secular increase
    in lung cancer, 190
Teenage years, health issues during, 147
Teen fatherhood, nested case-control study
    on, 317–318
Telemarketers, 267
Temperature, high, mortality and, in U.S.,
    505, 506 (exhibit)
Temporal clustering, 192
Temporal differences in cohort designs,
    301–303
    prospective cohort studies, 301–302
    retrospective cohort studies, 302–303
Temporality, 284, 376

Terris, M., 13
Terrorism, dirty bombs and, 503–504
Terrorist attacks of September 11, 2001
    anthrax cases in wake of, 6–7
    post-traumatic stress disorder in wake of,
        601
Tertiary prevention, 87, 88
Tetanus, 216, *440*
    vaccinations against, 465
Thalidomide, 79
Therapeutic trials, 334
Thomas, Lewis, 71
Thoroughness criterion, 206
Three Mile Island nuclear accident, 516
Threshold, 495, 496
Thucydides, 20
"Thucydides' plague," 20
Thyroid cancer, Chernobyl nuclear power
    plant accident and, 517
Ticks, disease transmission and, 441, 477
Time, characteristics of, 142, 193
    clustering, 191–193
        case, 191–192
        spatial, 192–193
        temporal, 192
    cohort effects, 190
    cyclic fluctuations, 187–188
    point epidemics, 188–189
    secular time trends, 189–190
Time period, specification of, incidence rate
    and, 103
Times Beach (Missouri), 512
Time sequence, causality and, 77
Tin, 499
Tinea pedis, 441
Tobacco
    cohort effect and use of, 285–288
    consumption of, by adults aged 18 and
        older, U.S., 1900–1990, *287*
Tobacco control policy, Smokefree Bars Law
    and, 65–67 (exhibit)
Toxicity, monitoring human subjects for,
    340
Toxicology, 13
Toxic shock syndrome, 11, 13, 18
Toxic waste disposal, 18
Toxic waste sites, 509, 512, 522
Toxigenicity, 442

TOXLINE, 206
Trachea, malignant neoplasms of, by age group, U.S. 2003, 138*t*
"Trailing skirt" cartoon, *33*
Transcribing, 533 (exhibit)
Trans fats, 597
Translation, 534 (exhibit)
Transmission of infectious disease, 446–451
  direct transmission, 446, *447,* 448–450
  colonization and infestation, 449
  generation time, 449
  herd immunity, 448–449
  iceberg concept of infection, 449, *450*
  inapparent infection, 446, 448
  incubation period, 448
  indirect transmission, 450
Treatment efficacy, case-control design and, 263
Trichinella spiralis, 441
Trichinosis, 441, 458
  meat from Alaskan grizzly bear and, 461 (exhibit)
Trihalomethanes, 520 (exhibit)
Tropical diseases, 177
Trypanosomiasis (African sleeping sickness), 186–187, 441
Tryptophan, 532 (exhibit)
Tsai, M-S., 563
TSS. *See* Toxic shock syndrome
t-test, 638
TTHM. *See* Trihalomethanes
Tuberculosis, 61, 150, *440,* 443, *443*
  among homeless persons, 469 (exhibit)
  among migrant farm workers, 468–469 (exhibit)
  bacteria and, 439
  culturally related delay in treatment of, among Mexicans, 599
  death rates from, all forms, for Massachusetts, 1880–1930, 285, 286*t*
  expected and observed number of cases, in U.S., during 1980–1992, *470*
  incidence of, by race/ethnicity: U.S., 1995–2005, *165*
  mortality from, Frost's tabular data on, 285, 286*t,* 319
  rates of, among Asians/Pacific Islanders, 164–165
  resurgence of, 468
Tucson Epidemiological Study of Airways Obstructive Diseases, 514
Turner, R. J., 588
Twin panel, military data and, 234
Twins, life dissatisfactions and heart disease in, 600
2 by 2 table, 246–248
  association between exposure and disease status in, 247*t*
  disease status and exposure cross-classification, *248*
Type A (coronary prone) behavior pattern, 588–589, 606
  interview measure of, 589
  self-administered measure of, 589
Type A personality, 42
Type B behavior pattern, 589
Type 2 diabetes, 56
Typhoid fever, 445
Typhoid Mary, 445

U
Unintentional injuries, deaths from, 505
United Kingdom
  lung cancer death rates in, 288, 289*t*
  mad cow disease in, 180, 181
United Kingdom Childhood Cancer Study, 273
United Nations, 216, 236
United States
  age-adjusted death rates for selected causes of death in, 1958–2003, *55*
  birth rates by age of mother, 1990–2004, *110*
  coccidioidomycosis cases in, *478*
  coronary heart disease mortality in, 177
  crude birth rate in, during 2004, 109
  fertility rates, 1950–1992, *111*
  infant, neonatal, and postneonatal mortality rates, U.S., 1940–2003, *116*
  infant mortality rates in, 178
  leading causes of death and rates for those causes, 1900 and 2003 in, 92*t*
  life table for total population in, 2000, 291–292 (exhibit)

lung cancer death rates in, 288, 289*t*
Lyme disease cases, by county in, *479*
mad cow disease in, 180, 181
per capita tobacco consumption for adults aged 18 and older, 1900–1990, *287*
population by race and Hispanic origin for, 2000, 159*t*
Q fever cases in, *476*
rising obesity rates in, 597
tuberculosis cases in, 1980–1992, *470*
viral hepatitis incidence in, 1975–2005, *475*
within-county rates of disease in, 179
years of potential life lost, before age 65, 2004, all races, both sexes, all deaths, *293*
University of Michigan, School of Public Health, Graduate Summer Session in Epidemiology at, 625
University of Michigan Tecumseh Study, 600
University of Minnesota hospitals, 232
Unplanned crossovers, 340
Unreliability, sources of, 421–422
Urbanization
    American Indians, Alaska Natives and, 163
    disease rates and, 182–183
    environmental pollutants and, 520 (exhibit), 522
U.S. National Center for Chronic Disease Prevention and Health Promotion, behavioral risk factor surveillance program of, 591

V

Vaccine effectiveness, 338
    case-control design and, 263
Vaccine-preventable diseases, *440,* 465–467
Vaccines/vaccinations
    cervical cancer, 39
    hepatitis, 465
    licensing of, 337, 338 (exhibit)
    measles, 466
    mumps, 466
    smallpox, 20, 23–25, 331
    steps in development of, 338 (exhibit)
    tetanus, 465

Vaginal adenocarcinoma, in young women, maternal exposure to diethylstilbestrol and, 191–192, 272
Validity, 419–421
    construct, 420–421
    content, 420
    criterion-referenced, 420
    empirical, 420
    graphic representation of, *421*
    interrelationships between reliability and, 421
    predictive, 420
Validity of diagnoses across life span, age and, 147
Validity of study, defined, 386
Validity of study designs
    external validity, 389
    internal validity, 386, 388
Validity types, 419
Valley of the Drums (Kentucky), 512
Vampire bat rabies, 178
Vapors, occupational exposure to, 508
Variability in measurement, 390, 391, 404
Variant Creutzfeldt-Jakob disease, 180
Variolation, 23–24
Vasectomy study, 258–259, 262
vCJD. *See* Variant Creutzfeldt-Jakob disease
Vector-borne disease, 477, 479
Vectors, indirect transmission of disease via, 450
Vegetables, health and consumption of, 596, 597
Vehicle transmission of disease, 450
Veterans
    as cohorts, 299
    data on, 234–235
    statistics on, 214*t*
Veterans Administration Cooperative Study, 82–83
Veterinary epidemiology, 615*t, 617*
Vibrio cholerae, 463, 481*t*
Vinyl chloride, cancers and occupational exposure to, 508
Viral hepatitis
    forms of, 471
    incidence of, by year in United States, 1975–2005, *475*
    vaccinations against, 471

Viral infections, examples of
    subclinical/clinical ratio for, 451*t*
Viral meningitis, 441
Virology, 13
Virulence, 442
Viruses, diseases caused by, 441
Vital registration system statistics, 215–216
    birth statistics, 216
    mortality statistics, 215–216
Vital Statistics Bureau, 264
Vital Statistics of the United States, 215
Vocabulary, in epidemiology, 16, 18–19, 43
Volunteers
    in clinical trials, 337
    for health studies, 389

W
Waldron, I., 151
Wales, cancer survival rates among
    socioeconomic groups in, 174
War veterans, post-traumatic stress disorder
    among, 601
Waste, hazardous, 509, 512–513
Water-borne disease, *440*
    food-borne disease and, 458, 462–464
    outbreaks of, 519
Water hardness, heart disease and, 184
Water pollution, 522
Water quality, degradation of, 509
Water supplies
    environmental contaminants and,
        518–519
    toxic waste sites and, 512
Weapons testing, 522
Web of causation, 377, 378
    for avian influenza, *378*
Wegman, D. H., 491
Weighted method, for direct rate
    adjustment, 130*t*
Weinstein, 537
Weiss, Noel, 387 (exhibit)
Western Collaborative Group Study, 589
West Nile virus, 480, 482
Wheel model, 377, 378–380
    of man-environment interactions, *379*
WHI. *See* Women's Health Initiative
WHIMS. *See* Women's Health Initiative
    Memory Study

White, definition of, in Census 2000, 158
    (exhibit)
White men, secular time trends in heart
    disease and, 189
Whites, 155
    blood lead levels, in percentage of
        children aged 1–5 years, *502*
    infant mortality rates among, 63, 112,
        113, 160
    life expectancy for, 161, *161*
    secular decreases in breast cancer in, 190
    survival rates for cancer and, 82
WHO. *See* World Health Organization
Widowed persons
    gender, adverse health outcomes and, 154
    suicide rates and, 154–155
Willard, Harold N., 622
Willett, Walter, 313 (exhibit)
Williams, P. L., 477
WNV. *See* West Nile virus
Wolf, S., 582
Women. *See also* Minority women
    AIDS and, 464
    ailments common among, 151
    coronary heart disease and, 152–153
    lung cancer mortality rate increase in, 193
    marital status, mortality, morbidity and,
        154
    smoking and secular increase in lung
        cancer in, 190
Women's health, cohort studies on, 313–314
    (exhibit)
Women's Health Initiative, 307, 313–314
    (exhibit)
    Extension Study, 314 (exhibit)
    Memory Study, 307
    Observational Study, 312*t*
Work absenteeism, 491
Workers, healthy worker effect and,
    493–494
Workplace Safety Law (1995), 65 (exhibit)
Work setting
    environmental hazards found in, 506–509
        biologic hazards, 507
        industrial chemicals, 508–509
        mineral and organic dusts, 507–508
        psychosocial aspects of employment
            and health, 509

World Health Organization, 175, 216, 219,
    432, 490, 510 (exhibit), 594
  employment Web site for, 626
World War I, 286
World War II
  data on twin pairs in, 234
  development of penicillin near end of, 36
World Wide Web, 207

X

X chromosomes, 533 (exhibit)
XDR-TB. *See* Extensively drug-resistant
    tuberculosis

Y

Yaws, 177, 187
Y chromosomes, 533 (exhibit)

Years of potential life lost, 290, 594
  before age 65, 2004, U.S., all races, both
    sexes, all deaths, *293*
Yellow fever, 219
Yersinia pestis, 22
Yngve, A., 168
YPLL. *See* Years of potential life lost

Z

Zaire, ebola and outbreak of fear in, 7–8
Zhao, L. P., 540
Zheng, W., 304
Ziegler, A., 558
Zoonoses, 445
Zoonosis, example of, 475
Zoonotic disease, 178, *440,* 475–476

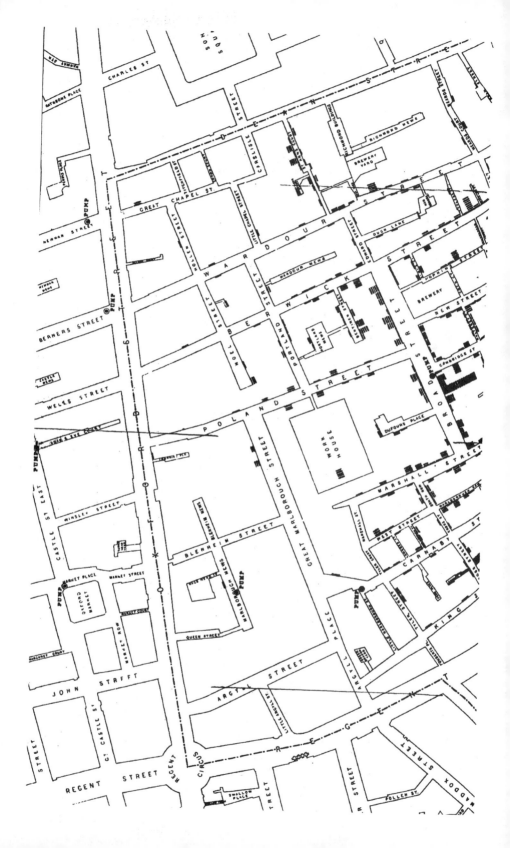